Church and State
in England in the 18th century

Church and State

IN ENGLAND IN THE XVIIITH CENTURY

by

the Rev. NORMAN SYKES, M.A., D.PHIL.

Professor of History in the University of London (Westfield College);
sometime Hastings Senior Scholar of The Queen's College, Oxford;
Examining chaplain to the Bishop of Chichester, and to
the Bishop of Exeter; and Birkbeck Lecturer,
Trinity College, Cambridge,
1931–33

*The Birkbeck Lectures
in Ecclesiastical History delivered
at Trinity College, Cambridge, 1931–3*

OCTAGON BOOKS

A DIVISION OF FARRAR, STRAUS AND GIROUX

New York   1975

First published 1935

Reprinted 1975
by permission of Cambridge University Press

OCTAGON BOOKS
A DIVISION OF FARRAR, STRAUS & GIROUX, INC.
19 Union Square West
New York, N.Y. 10003

Library of Congress Cataloging in Publication Data

Sykes, Norman, 1897-1961.
    Church and state in England in the XVIIIth century.

    (The Birkbeck lectures, 1931-3)
    Reprint of the 1934 ed. published by the University Press,
Cambridge, Eng.

    Bibliography: p.
    Includes index.
    1. Church and state in England. 2. Church of England—History. I. Title. II. Series.
BR758.S9   1975   261.7'0941   75-29470
ISBN 0-374-97690-2

Manufactured by Braun-Brumfield, Inc.
Ann Arbor, Michigan
Printed in the United States of America

To

G. K. A. BELL
BISHOP OF CHICHESTER

CONTENTS

PREFACE

The present volume takes its origin from the invitation conveyed by the Master of Trinity College, Cambridge, on behalf of the Council to accept the office of Birkbeck Lecturer in Ecclesiastical History in the College for the academical years 1931–2 and 1932–3. To the Council and to the Society I am indebted for the honour done me by their invitation, and for the cordial hospitality which made my visits to deliver the lectures so pleasant and enjoyable an episode of the two sessions of my office.

When the invitation reached me in February 1931 I had been engaged for some time upon a study of the MSS. of Archbishop Wake with a view to a biography of their subject, of which one chapter is actually written. I had therefore to consider whether the occasion thus presented should be utilised for the fulfilment of this intention, or whether it would be more appropriate to the Birkbeck foundation to select a more comprehensive theme in an endeavour to portray the salient characteristics of the English Church during the century dividing the domestic revolution of 1689 from the French cataclysm of 1789. After taking the counsel of friends I decided upon the latter alternative, of which the following pages represent the result. It has been my purpose to concentrate attention upon aspects of the eighteenth-century Church which have been comparatively little examined hitherto, though in my judgment of vital importance for the understanding of its history. To this end the bulk of the volume, from chapters II to VIII, consists of a series of sketches in which an endeavour is made to portray the episcopate in its political and ecclesiastical character, the higher and lower clergy in their several states and conditions, the parochial standards of the age, the predominant theories of the relations of church and state, and the true significance of the careers of Bishops Hoadly and Watson. The first lecture suggests an introductory approach by a survey of the heritage of the Caroline epoch, and the last indicates briefly the effect upon the church of the religious and social changes operative during the last quarter of the century. In the delivery of the lectures I included a detailed account of the methods of episcopal appointment employed during the several reigns of Anne, George I and II, including the long period of office as church minister of the duke of Newcastle, and of George III. Owing to the inability of the publishers to entertain a book of such proportions as would have resulted from the inclusion of the full text of all the twelve lectures, I have omitted the three dealing with these questions, save for summary references in the first and last chapters. I hope to have opportunity to publish the detailed evidence in some other place.

The adoption of this interpretation of my subject has involved necessarily the omission of certain aspects of eighteenth-century Church life which would find a place in any complete history of that epoch. Thus I have said nothing of the Church of Ireland, nor of the Episcopal Church of Scotland, nor even of the Anglican Church in the American colonies. I have refrained also from a detailed discussion of the theological controversies of the age, save in so far as was necessary for the illustration of its religious temper and practice of churchmanship, since this aspect of its record has been the subject of frequent study. Such omissions are deliberate; and occasioned in part by considerations of space and in part by the desire to preserve an unity of theme. Upon some of the topics here omitted, I may have opportunity to write separately. What is here written may serve, I hope, as a contribution towards the complete history of the English Church in the eighteenth century, which is still unwritten.

In expressing my thanks to the persons who have assisted me in divers ways in the execution of this task, I would mention first the Bishop of Chichester, to whom I am indebted for many good offices and not least for the honour of permission to mention his name in the dedication of this volume. To the Dean of Christ Church[1] and his colleagues of the Wake Trustees I am grateful for the grant of very liberal conditions of access to the Wake MSS., without which this study could not have been attempted. To the Bishop of Gloucester and to the Bishop of Worcester I am indebted for placing at my disposal the episcopal records and manuscripts in their custody and for a generous hospitality whilst engaged in their perusal. To the Bishop of Exeter I am likewise indebted for permission to consult the registers of his see, and to the Bishop of Llandaff for giving me ready access to the subscription books and other papers of Bishop Richard Watson. Canon F. J. Meyrick, vicar of Hove, kindly allowed me to read and to reproduce extracts from the four manuscript sermons of Parson James Woodforde in his possession, a privilege which I greatly prized.

From Professor G. M. Trevelyan I have received a host of kindnesses too numerous to mention and bestowed with prodigal generosity from the time of my acceptance of the office of Birkbeck Lecturer until now.

[1] Since this preface was written, Dr H. J. White has died in July 1934.

I am especially grateful for his criticism of the lectures upon delivery, for his reading of part of my manuscript, and for his help in negotiation with the Syndics of the Cambridge University Press. Sir Charles Firth has continued to me the privilege of access to his counsel and library, and has helped me much by his advice and comments. If Canon E. W. Watson should recognise in the ensuing pages frequent echoes of his words spoken both in lectures and private discussion, I hope he will receive them as tokens of gratitude and perhaps also as evidence that his pains bestowed upon a former student have not been wholly in vain. To Professor L. B. Namier I am indebted for occasions of discussion of the labyrinthine policies and exhaustive correspondence of the duke of Newcastle, and for the avidity of appetite which has enabled him to sustain even the ecclesiastical divagations of his grace's career.

Upon Mr S. J. Bruton of Sion College Library I have descended for some years as a recurrent plague, pressing requests for the discovery of sundry dusty and forgotten eighteenth-century tomes, scarcely to be found elsewhere than among the shelves of his treasure-house; and to his unfailing courtesy and help I owe a great debt of gratitude. To Mr S. C. Roberts of the Cambridge University Press I am indebted for his kindness in allowing me to see the proof-sheets of his edition of *A Frenchman in England* before publication, and for his interest and assistance in seeing this book through the press. To my friend the Rev. J. C. Hardwick I am grateful for his laborious pains in proof-reading of the entire volume.

The most especial obligation is owing to my wife, who, in addition to continuous reading and criticism of these lectures at every stage of their composition, has discharged the formidable task of converting my manuscript into type. Without her unremitting help the completion of the task would have tarried long. The composition and revision of the lectures have occupied the whole of my leisure during the space of three years; the greater part of the work having been undertaken of necessity in vacations, since the preparation and delivery of the course proceeded concurrently with the duties of teaching and lecturing in Exeter and London. I hope that the volume may contribute somewhat to a juster and more equitable verdict upon the English Church and state in the eighteenth century, and may provide a foundation upon which other and wiser heads may build a comprehensive survey of all aspects of the history of that epoch.

N. S.

London
February, 1934

CHAPTER I

FROM RESTORATION TO REVOLUTION:
SEED TIME AND HARVEST

In an essay contributed to *The Spectator* of 6 August 1711 and based upon a letter received from "one of the greatest liars this island has produced", Steele projects the formation of a society of liars.

"If you think fit," he adds modestly, "we might be called 'The Historians'; for liar is become a very harsh word. And that a member of the society may not hereafter be ill received by the rest of the world, I desire you would explain a little this sort of men, and not let us historians be ranked, as we are in the imaginations of ordinary people, among common liars, makebates, impostors, and incendiaries. For your instruction herein, you are to know that a historian in conversation is only a person of so pregnant a fancy that he cannot be contented with ordinary occurrences."

More prosaic in conception, though scarcely more complimentary in intention, is the verdict of Dr Johnson upon the mean talents requisite for the profession of history.

"Great abilities are not requisite for an historian," he pronounced, "for in historical composition all the greatest powers of the human mind are quiescent. He has facts ready to his hand, so there is no exercise of invention. Imagination is not required in any high degree; only about as much as is used in the lower kinds of poetry. Some penetration, accuracy, and colouring will fit a man for the task, if he can give the application which is necessary."[1]

It is proper that a student of eighteenth-century history should present thus contemporary credentials of his capacity to that office, the more especially if he be a student of the ecclesiastical history of that epoch. For if the modest requirements of Johnson may peradventure excuse his assumption of the status of historical lecturer, only the constant and grateful remembrance of the generous recognition accorded by Steele to leasing may embolden him to select, as the subject of his discourse, *The Relations of Church and State in Eighteenth-century England.*

The study of the history of Church and State in the Age of Enlightenment is not commonly recommended as an exercise "for example of life and instruction of manners", much less "to establish any doctrine". It has suffered indeed the singular misfortune to incur the censure of

[1] Boswell, *Life of Johnson,* 6 July 1763.

almost all schools of ecclesiastical historians. Even students of widely separated centuries turn aside from the exposition of their proper theme to fling a congenial barb at the baseness of the Hanoverian age. Dr B. J. Kidd, in a pungent *obiter dictum* of his *History of the Church to A.D.* 461, observes in relation to the Licinian persecutions that "Licinius forbade the bishops to have intercourse with each other, and to hold synods, knowing as he did, like other tyrants, Maximin, the Vandal king Gaiseric, Henry VIII, and the minister Walpole, the powerlessness of the church when deprived of synodical action".[1] It matters little to his purpose, and weighs lightly upon his conscience, that the offence, duly specified in a footnote, for which Walpole is scourged by his inclusion in such incongruous company, namely the suspension of the sessions of the Canterbury Convocation on 17 May 1717, was the act of an administration from which he had resigned already on 10 April previous; nor that Walpole himself in 1741, at the instance of Gibson and other bishops, allowed the Convocation again to sit for debate until a revival of the contumacy of the lower house towards the upper compelled its prorogation; nor that the Church of England had been deprived similarly of synodical action for a quarter of a century during the primacies of Sheldon and Sancroft, by the royal disuse of sitting convocations from 1664 to 1689. Such considerations are as irrelevant as irrefutable from the standpoint of his polemic, the intent of which is plainly to discredit the Church for its gross subordination to whiggism, which, in the picturesque if prejudiced phrase of Johnson, "as a mere party distinction under Walpole and the Pelhams was no better than the politics of stock-jobbers and the religion of infidels".

It is indeed in the alliance with whiggery that the gravamen of the charge against the Georgian Church consists. Notwithstanding the staunch toryism of George III and Pitt, whose granitic conservatism during the last quarter of the century left the Church of England at the commencement of the reform age as a booth in a vineyard, as a lodge in a garden of cucumbers, and as a besieged city, the character of apostacy and decline is affixed upon its record by reason of its acceptance in 1689 and 1714 of the Protestant successions of William of Orange and George of Hanover with their attendant whig administrations, in preference to the Popish rule of James II and his son. The conventional representation of the Hanoverian Church, dilating duly upon its alleged torpor and corruption, ascribes these qualities to the malevolent influence of whig politicians, with their licentious German princes and their allies of free livers and free thinkers. Accordingly, the attitude and policy of

[1] B. J. Kidd, *op. cit.* ii, 4.

the new dynasty and its political advisers towards the national establishment of religion are presented generally in terms reminiscent of Gibbon's account of the imperial patronage of religion in the age of the Antonines:

The policy of the emperors and the senate, as far as it concerned religion, was happily seconded by the reflections of the enlightened, and by the habits of the superstitious, part of their subjects. The various modes of worship which prevailed in the Roman world were all considered by the people as equally true, by the philosopher as equally false, and by the magistrate as equally useful. And thus toleration produced not only mutual indulgence but religious concord.[1]

Unhappily the eighteenth-century Church has won no greater measure of approval in its more specifically religious character, largely in consequence of the spell cast upon different minds by the two secessions of its epoch, the Non-juror and the Methodist. To admirers of the Caroline school of high-church divines the departure of the non-juring clergy at the outset of the century marked the removal of the candlestick of the apostate Church whose communion they forsook; and to disciples of the later Methodist revival the success of John Wesley and his associates compromised fatally the reputation of the contemporary episcopate which rejected his apostolate. Situate in a strait betwixt two such contradictory currents of depreciation, the character and achievement of the conformist remnant of Latitudinarian bishops and clergy who clung to the fleshpots of the establishment have received double for their sins from critics and historians. Portrayed in the mordant comments of Lord Hervey and Horace Walpole, and embellished by pertinent (if usually inaccurate) reference to Bishops Hoadly and Watson, the typical prelate of the Hanoverian age has been paraded as an exact if unedifying parallel to the polite and eloquent Synesius, bishop of Ptolemais, who "loved profane studies and profane sports, was incapable of supporting a life of celibacy, disbelieved the resurrection, and refused to preach fables to the people unless he were permitted to philosophise at home".[2] The reaction against the traditions of the Age of Commonsense set in swiftly after the completion of its course, reinforced by the new intellectual and political temper of the early nineteenth-century. The *epigoni* of the Georgian epoch disavowed its theological shibboleths under the persuasion of the Tractarian movement, and blushed at the uncovering of its shame by the radicals of the reform spirit, who satirised the abuses of its administrative system.

[1] E. Gibbon, *Decline and Fall of the Roman Empire* (ed. Bury), i, 28.
[2] *Ibid.* ii, 325, n. 118.

Of the vigour of the ecclesiastical revulsion, an apt, if inconsiderable, illustration may be drawn from the curious and amusing comments which Mr Cassan felt himself conscientiously bound to append to his account of the career of Bishop Kidder of Bath and Wells. Editing in 1829 the fragment of Kidder's autobiography preserved at Wells, he found the lax sentiments of a prelate of the Revolution Church almost intolerably improper and offensive to the clerical conscience. Although Kidder had received episcopal ordination during the difficult times of the Commonwealth, not even this loyalty could palliate his charitable sentiments towards presbyterians. Before all his references to the presbyterian ordinations of that period, his editor was careful to prefix the epithet "Mock" to "ordinations"; and, lest the meaning of this rebuke should be lost upon the reader, to append the observation that "to call by the venerable name of 'Orders' the self-appointed office of a presbyterian teacher, is an unaccountable misnomer, and I cannot but wonder how Kidder could have let the word drop from his pen".[1] But despite his reception of episcopal orders, Kidder could not subscribe to the revised Prayer Book of 1662 before its publication enabled the perusal of its contents, and accordingly was deprived in that year of his benefice; yet this scrupulous regard for the sanctity of subscription seemed to Cassan as "contumacious rather than conscientious"; whilst to his author's avowal that he "was entirely satisfied with episcopacy", there is added the severe censure: "this is but cold approbation of episcopacy: he should have said: 'I was convinced that there alone could be the church where a divine commission transmitted from the apostles to their successors, the bishops, was to be found'". Even the term "dissenters" as used by Kidder was too gentle for so redoubtable an editor, who wished they had been called "schismatics, whereby their sin would be intimated". At a later date also it was Kidder's misfortune to find many parishioners of his church in the city of London unwilling to receive the Communion in a kneeling posture, whereupon he administered the Sacrament to them without their compliance with the Canon, having secured first the approbation of the bishop of London. Upon such scandalous laxity the unrestrained wrath of Cassan was launched, in his comment that "Bishop Henchman should have been brought before the Convocation for such uncanonical advice", since "the canons of the church should not be relaxed to please schismatics". Not the mildest acts of Kidder pass without censure; as when he preached a sermon against papists in the reign of James II on "the necessity of allowing the judgment of private discretion", an

[1] S. H. Cassan, *Lives of the Bishops of Bath and Wells*, pp. 102–63 (London, 1829).

editorial footnote admonishes the reader that "private judgment in religion is a point full of danger; the less of it the better; it is the never-failing source of schism". Finally, when the choice of the crown fell upon Kidder to succeed the deprived Bishop Ken at Bath and Wells, he continued to show a charitable tenderness towards presbyterians and a desire to reconcile both pastors and their congregations to the Established Church. In this capacity his actions earned the reproof of some members of his cathedral chapter no less than of his later editor; especially in regard to his ordination in 1693 of a former dissenter without requiring him to preach a recantation sermon; which leniency Cassan reprobated, since "public recantation should ever be insisted upon previously to ordaining a dissenting minister: in such recantation the chief point to be exacted being: the utter inefficacy of his former assumed administration of the sacraments, and the sinfulness of such assumption without episcopal ordination—the only visible medium of a divine commission to administer in holy things". To avoid misunderstanding, he even added, "I do not design any pun on the word *cant*".

Between the intellectual outlook of the Latitudinarian bishop of the Revolution epoch and that of the zealous assertor of episcopacy on the eve of the Oxford Movement, there existed hardly the relation of contradiction. Accordingly, the history of the Hanoverian Church has suffered especial severities at the hands of disciples of the High Church revival, whose zeal (though not according to knowledge) has led "under the influence of inferior spirits" (to quote the piquant phrase of Dr Brilioth) to the production of "a vulgate in High Anglican writing of history as regards the representation of the time before 1833".[1] Furthermore, the radical reforms in the ecclesiastical administration effected during the whig domination of the third decade of the nineteenth century left the memory of the pre-reform Georgian era as a distant chimera, whose survival in its medieval constitution seemed a discreditable corruption of the times of ignorance. Thus the Establishment, which to the eye of Bishop Warburton seemed so perfect that it might have been derived "solely from the contemplation of nature and the unvariable reason of things", appeared to the author of *The Extraordinary Black Book of* 1831 in its temporal estate "an immense waste, which wanted surveying and enclosing, if not by act of parliament, then by act of the people", so that "although the Church of England was ostentatiously styled the *reformed* church it was in truth the most unreformed of all the churches".

Amid the volume of contumely and denunciation there have been

[1] Y. Brilioth, *The Anglican Revival*, p. 8.

heard a few voices of appreciation and understanding—*apparent rari nantes in gurgite vasto*. The student of the eighteenth century in England may never be unmindful of nor ungrateful for the work of Abbey and Overton, to which he stands deeply indebted and to which he must have recourse at every stage of his quest. But the majority of writers have borrowed their censures whilst forgetful of their praises. During the half-century which has elapsed since the publication of their *History of the English Church in the Eighteenth Century*, moreover, a number of new sources of information, both printed and manuscript, have been made available for the investigation of students. The five volumes of *The Diary of a Country Parson* have won for James Woodforde, and by implication for his times, an unexpected sympathy from a wide circle of readers; whilst the recent publication of other clerical diaries, *The Diary and Letter Book of Thomas Brockbank* by the Chetham Society, *The Journal of a Somerset Rector*, John Skinner of Camerton, *The Diary of William Jones* of Broxbourne, and *The Blecheley Diary of William Cole*, have revealed a variety of aspects of parish life and religion during the early, middle, and later years of the century. In the sphere of ecclesiastical administration *The Visitation Returns of Archbishop Herring*, 1743, edited by Canon Ollard and Mr Walker, justify fully their conclusion concerning the clergy of the York diocese that "the strong impression left by these Returns is that of a body of dutiful and conscientious men, trying to do their work according to the standards of their day",[1] although in several aspects, and notably in regard to the problems of pluralism and non-residence, Canon Ollard cannot escape the tendency to determine his judgment in accordance with anachronistic nineteenth-century standards. The survey of *The Diocese of Bangor during three centuries* by the Registrar of that diocese has resulted in an unexpectedly favourable delineation of the religious tradition of the Church in North Wales upon the eve of the Methodist revival. Amongst unprinted materials the large and numerous volumes of Archbishop Wake's manuscripts and the recovered papers of Bishop Gibson afford invaluable insight into the religious and political principles of two leading prelates of the early Hanoverian period; whilst to students of the ecclesiastical equally with other aspects of eighteenth-century history, the inexhaustible correspondence of the duke of Newcastle presents a mine of detailed information, illustrating the distribution of ecclesiastical patronage. From the perusal of these, and other contemporary sources, too numerous to admit of detailed specification, evidence may be found to justify a more sympathetic and impartial

[1] S. L. Ollard and P. C. Walker, *op. cit.* i, p. xviii.

survey of the religious tradition and standards of the Hanoverian Church; whilst the exploration of the not inconsiderable field of the interaction of political and ecclesiastical events, which lay generally without the scope of Abbey and Overton, may illustrate afresh an aspect of church history insufficiently studied, that of the social position and recruitment of the several grades of the clerical order; and thus the reader may be emboldened to offer his essay towards a reinterpretation of *The Relations of Church and State in Eighteenth-century England.*

The approach to this subject lies naturally through consideration of the position of the episcopate, not only as the keystone of the ecclesiastical constitution, but as representative also in peculiar degree of the intimate association of Church and State in England; and more particularly attention may be directed to the subtle changes in its situation produced by the assertion of the claim of the rival political leaders, both whig and tory, to influence the disposal of the ecclesiastical patronage of the crown in the interest of their respective parties. The situation of the episcopate will be considered therefore in its dual capacity, politically through the influence of the bench in parliament and the country, and ecclesiastically in the discharge of the spiritual duties of its diocesan administration. By a natural and easy transition the status of the superior clergy, the cathedral dignitaries and pluralists, may be described next, with illustrations of the social classes from which they were recruited and of the way to high preferment; whilst, in sharp contrast thereto, the following lecture depicts the poverty and obscurity of the depressed clergy, possessed only of the poorer benefices or relegated to the condition of unbeneficed curates serving the cures of non-resident incumbents. From the consideration of the administrative system of the Church, attention may be turned to the salient characteristics of the religious services and traditions of the parochial clergy of Georgian England, for the interpretation of which an understanding of the theological and intellectual temper of the age is necessary. Complementary to this may be reckoned the review of contemporary speculation concerning the nature of the alliance between Church and State, in which the chief writers on this subject are briefly considered. Forasmuch also as no record of the achievement of the eighteenth-century Church may evade the challenge of the names of Hoadly and Watson, it will be profitable to devote more particular attention to their episcopates. Finally, an endeavour must be made to indicate briefly the importance of the long reign of George III, and of the impact of new forces, religious and economic, which transformed the environment of pre-reform England, and contributed thereby to the growing realisation towards the end of the century of the need of drastic reform in the constitution of the Established Church. But the study of the Church of the eighteenth century must seek its commencement in the history of the Restoration epoch, of which the Hanoverian age was the descendant by affiliation and reaction. It is necessary therefore to look backward first to the *Ecclesia Anglicana* of the Caroline days.

The ecclesiastical patrimony to which the exiled fathers of Anglicanism returned in 1660 presented, like the vineyard of Israel, a distressing spectacle of confusion and disorder. The careful planting of the Royal Martyr had been uprooted by the revolution of the Commonwealth, which had broken down both the hedge of sound doctrine and the wall of episcopal regimen in order to admit godly ministers of whatever persuasion to the fruits of its husbandry. Nor, despite the enthusiasm of the nation for the restoration of crown and church, did the initial concomitants of that Restoration itself assure satisfaction to the zealots of the episcopal allegiance. The Convention parliament which had invited Charles II's return was predominantly presbyterian in sympathy, and the royal declaration issued on 25 October 1660 concerning ecclesiastical affairs was inspired by the same sentiment of cautious compromise. His majesty referred to his desire "to determine many things now in difference", reinforced both in wish and ability by "the experience we have had in most of the reformed churches abroad, in France, in the Low Countries, and in Germany, where we have had frequent conferences with the most learned men, who have unanimously lamented the great reproach the protestant religion undergoes from the distempers and too notorious schisms in matters of religion in England".[1] Accordingly, Charles seemed to draw chief satisfaction from the moderation of "the most able and principal assertors of the presbyterian opinions", whom he had found full of affection to himself, "of zeal for the peace of church and state, and neither enemies. . . to episcopacy or liturgy, but modestly to desire such alterations in either, as without shaking foundations, might best allay the present distempers". So persuaded was the king of the justice of this opinion as to assert that, having found that "they all approve episcopacy, they all approve a set form of liturgy, and they all disapprove and dislike the sin of sacrilege and the alienation of the revenue of the church", he made no doubt but that by the concessions to be adumbrated the peace of the Church might be wholly restored. Among the concessions suitable to heal the dis-

[1] King Charles' Declaration Concerning Ecclesiastical Affairs, 1660. E. Cardwell, *Documentary Annals of the Reformed Church of England*, ii, 285–301.

temper of the times were specified: the nomination to the episcopate of "men of learning, virtue, and piety", who should "be frequent preachers,...and preach very often in some church of their diocese"; the appointment of suffragan bishops to assist the diocesan prelates in their episcopal administration; the compulsory association of presbyters with the bishops in the offices of ordination and jurisdiction, such presbyters being drawn in equal proportion from the cathedral chapters and by election of the priests of the diocese; the performance of confirmation "rightly and solemnly, by the information and with the consent of the minister of the place"; the constitution of a commission, composed of "an equal number of learned divines of both persuasions", to revise the Book of Common Prayer; and finally concerning cere-monies, the allowance, until this task of revision should be completed, of liberty to receive the Sacrament in a sitting instead of a kneeling posture, to disuse such ceremonies as the sign of the cross in baptism, the bowing at the name of Jesus, the wearing of the surplice, and the temporary dispensation from taking the oath of canonical obedience and making the canonical form of subscription before institution to a living.

Against so comprehensive a list of concessions to tender (that is non-episcopal) consciences the fervent Anglicans might count it small comfort that their royal sovereign should have affirmed his personal conviction that the English Liturgy was "the best he had seen", after having "seen all that are extant and used in this part of the world and well knowing what reverence most of the reformed churches, or at least the most learned men in those churches, had for it"; or that in regard to its ceremonies, he should pronounce his "more esteem of all, and reverence for many of them, by having been present in many of those churches where they are most abolished or discountenanced", and should insist in his own chapel upon the kneeling posture for reception of the Holy Communion and the use of the surplice. Indeed the significance of the offer of the bishoprics of Hereford, Lichfield, and Norwich to Baxter, Calamy, and Reynolds respectively (the last named accepting the see of Norwich upon the terms of the declaration), as interpretative of the policy of Charles in religion, with the impression that other notable presbyterian divines would be so elevated after the settlement of outstanding differences, was far from reassuring to members of the episcopal party. The possibility was present to their mind of a religious establishment which would be as tender towards the scruples of the Church's enemies, as it would be offensive to the principles of its confessors. Not until the problem of the relations of episcopacy and presbyterianism had been resolved could the Caroline

Church settlement assume definite shape; and accordingly, the primary object of interest was the Savoy Conference, assembled on 15 April 1661, between the respective divines of both sides to determine the matters referred to their deliberation by the royal declaration.

In the abstract there seemed much probability of an eirenical compromise, for the acceptance by the presbyterian leaders of the principle of episcopacy and a fixed liturgy, together with their strong belief in the necessity of a National Established Church, offered a substantial ground of agreement with their episcopal brethren, the more especially along the lines of Usher's famous "Reduction". At the actual conference the presbyterian representatives were misled by the latitude of the concessions adumbrated in the royal declaration, and outwitted by the strategy of Sheldon, who invited them to put forward all their demands at once, thereby provoking "a mighty outcry against them as people that could never be satisfied" by reason of the number of alterations proposed. In the comprehensive documents wherein the exceptions and additions to the Liturgy desiderated by the presbyterians were set forth, so many points were touched upon as to justify in appearance the bishops' attitude of stiffness and non-compliance, and to suggest that their opponents sought, not the permissive disuse of a few nocent ceremonies, but the re-ordering of much of the doctrine, worship, and discipline of the Church of England. Notwithstanding the unfortunate tactics adopted by the presbyterians in thus presenting the full statement of their objections, it is probable that they could have been won to conformity by concessions upon major matters, relatively few in number. But the circumstances of the conference were no longer those of the royal declaration of October 1660. Meantime the Cavalier parliament had replaced the Convention, resolved that the ecclesiastical settlement should not err on the side of moderation as the political had done; and with the new parliament had been convoked a new Convocation in both provinces of the Church, which in turn was ready to embark upon the task of liturgical revision in a direction less favourable towards presbyterian sympathies.

"A meeting at the Savoy", observes the historian of Nonconformity, "between divines of the two schools in the spring of 1660, would have been different from such a meeting in the spring of 1661. Something at least like equal terms might have been secured at the former date, but it is plain that afterwards the men of Geneva stood no chance with those of Canterbury. Episcopacy and the Liturgy were in possession."[1]

[1] J. Stoughton, *The Church of the Restoration*, p. 160 (ch. v) ; vol. iii of *A History of Religion in England*.

The break-up of the Savoy Conference, due largely to the defensive attitude adopted by the Anglican representatives in their refusal to alter the Book of Common Prayer save in such respects as the presbyterians could convince them of the wisdom and need of change, was of far-reaching importance for the religious development of England, alike in the Established Church and in the churches dissenting from its communion. From the episcopal side the result seemed to presage the complete triumph of the Laudian tradition within its borders. Not only had the prospect of a liturgical revision acceptable to non-episcopalians been frustrated, but the actual revision made by the churchmen, approved by convocation, and accepted by the Cavalier parliament, comprised a variety of changes, some six hundred in number, enriching, expanding, and emphasising the Anglican tradition as "the mean between the two extremes". The terms of subscription were couched in stricter phrase, episcopal ordination was required as an indispensable qualification for ministering in the Church, and the preface to the Ordinal defined the position of the Church of England in relation to episcopal government and ordination. In the political sphere, the enactment of the several measures of the mis-called Clarendon Code inaugurated a severe persecution of dissenters, designed to enforce conformity to the Established Church and to suppress all schismatics. Despite these evidences of the Anglican victory, however, the restoration of the Laudian *régime* was by no means complete nor unqualified. The authority of the Canons of 1640, which had been a bone of contention between the Convocation and the Long Parliament, was formally disavowed by an act of parliament of 13 Charles II, cap. 12, prohibiting any archbishop, bishop, or any other ecclesiastical judge or officer from the attempt "to confirm the Canons made in the year 1640, or any of them, or any other ecclesiastical laws or canons not formerly confirmed, allowed, or enacted by parliament, or by the established laws of the land as they stood in the year of our Lord 1639". The constitution of the Court of High Commission was branded as illegal; and even the faithful commons of the Cavalier parliament, in accepting on 16 April 1662 all the changes in the Prayer Book proposed by convocation without discussion, did so only by the narrow majority of ninety-six votes to ninety and with a carefully recorded reservation of their right to debate them if they so desired. Not least of the limitations of the Anglican restoration was the surrender, based upon a false sense of security and protection, by a private agreement between Archbishop Sheldon and Clarendon, of the right of the clerical order to tax itself in convocation in favour of the inclusion of the clergy in the financial subsidies voted by parliament. The immediate consequence of which misplaced confidence was the suspension of sitting convocations for a quarter of a century, until in 1689 they were allowed again to embark upon the discussion of business. These tokens of the Restoration Church settlement indicated the victory of parliament in its struggle to extinguish a distinct and co-equal right of legislation in the convocations; and though the fervent loyalty of the Cavalier commons might evoke the spontaneous desire of Charles II to continue their assembly till they were all bearded, yet they remained mortal alike individually and corporately, and their successors might pull down the ecclesiastical fence which they had erected against dissenter or papist to ensure the safety of the Anglican Church as by law established.

From the political standpoint also the failure of the comprehension project, which had inspired the assembly of the Savoy Conference, was productive of more difficulties than were suspected at the time. If terms of union and conciliation had been agreed upon, such as would have fulfilled Calamy's expectation of bringing in the great majority of presbyterians, England would have witnessed the creation of a strong National Church, commanding an overwhelming proportion of the population, and zealous for the suppression of dissenters, whether protestant or papist. In such circumstances the fate of the sects which still remained nonconformist would have been hard and rude, for the full weight of the persecuting authority of Church and State would have been invoked against them. The exclusion of the influential body of presbyterian opinion from the restored Anglican Church created a problem of dissent, of far greater magnitude than would have been presented by the minority of dissentients from a wide comprehension, and to the solution of which the policy of the Clarendon Code was wholly inadequate. The attempt to enforce by proscription the ideal of a National Church unfringed by dissenters, which the Savoy Conference had failed to realise by concession, was foredoomed to frustration by reason of the solid presbyterian withdrawal from the episcopal organisation after the operation of the Act of Uniformity on St Bartholomew's Day, 1662. For a time the rigours of the persecuting code might drive the expression of this dissent underground; but the abiding legacy of the Commonwealth to the religious development of England lay in its nourishing of the seeds of Protestant nonconformity with such vigour as to defeat all future attempts towards their uprooting. Nor was this prospect unwelcome to Charles II himself, who found in the situation arising therefrom a pretext for the exercise of his royal clemency in the attempted Declarations of Indulgence, which would have enabled him to favour papists under the appearance of helping the Protestants. The endeavour indeed to encompass by royal prerogative what had been forbidden by parliament involved the king in discredit; yet not even this mistake could prevent the final triumph of the principle of toleration. The Toleration Act of 1689 was the necessary outcome of the failure of the Savoy Conference of 1661; but to the victorious churchmen of the earlier date the approach of such a contingency seemed remote and fantastic. Not until the crisis of James II's further Declaration of Indulgence, combined with his resolute intrusion of papists into ecclesiastical dignities, had revealed the lineaments of a new and dangerous situation did the conscience of high churchmen ponder seriously the problems of toleration, and of the relation of the Established Church to Protestant dissenters from its communion.

Meanwhile the nomination to the many vacant sees of divines from the ranks of the dominant Anglican party completed the external framework of the ecclesiastical settlement, and set the *Ecclesia Anglicana*, protected by the professed favour of Charles II and the real zeal of Clarendon, upon the way to establishing its system in the affections of the nation. Upon the Caroline episcopate Gwatkin, albeit no partial apologist for its high-church traditions, has bestowed the rare compliment of a superlative:

The episcopate never stood higher than in the time of Charles II. The nine survivors of Laudian times include Juxon, Wren, and Duppa; but their successors are a brilliant group. Learning was represented by Cosin and Sanderson, Morley, Pearson, Gunning, and Jeremy Taylor in Ireland. Sheldon also had a name for learning in his younger days, in Falkland's circle at Great Tew. To these we must add the future Nonjurors, Sancroft, Ken, and Frampton. For secular learning stood the astronomer Seth Ward, who nearly anticipated Newton's discovery of gravitation, and was further an accomplished lawyer. Then there was the universal scholar John Wilkins, who was not refused preferment for having married Cromwell's sister, and, with Sprat of Rochester, was no purely honorary member of the Royal Society. If Isaac Barrow never reached a bishopric, he may have been more in his place as Master of Trinity, where his eccentricities were better understood. The nominations of Charles II were as generally good as his successor's were generally bad. The two worst were Wood of Lichfield and Crewe of Durham; and these were creatures of the duchess of Cleveland and the duke of York. To James we owe Trelawny, but also Cartright, Parker, and Timothy Hall, and Watson of St David's, the only English bishop deprived since the Restoration for gross misconduct, though Wood and Jones of St Asaph (William's nominee) narrowly escaped. The dignitaries were men of varied experience. Dolben and Lake and Mews and Compton had fought in the wars, Archdeacon Basire had travelled the Levant as a missionary for fifteen years. Frampton had been chaplain at Aleppo, and many another had followed strange trades to get a living in a land of exile.... Many of them had gone out in the civil wars to poverty and exile, and others went out as Nonjurors at the Revolution. The bench has never been more fully adorned with splendid examples of learning, of courage, of princely munificence, of true devotion.[1]

The eminent piety and learning of these glories of the Caroline age were in no wise diminished by the continued custom and practice of pluralism which were unreformed and unchanged by the Restoration settlement. Indeed one unexpected consequence of the sterility of the Savoy Conference was the failure to implement the royal promises in the declaration concerning ecclesiastical affairs of October 1660 in relation to reforms in the administration and constitution of the Church. Even the modest contribution there suggested of the revival of suffragan bishops perished in the disavowal of all schemes tainted with the presbyterian advocacy; and, save for the provision of the Act of Uniformity (13, 14 Charles II, cap. 4), which extended to holders of cathedral dignities the requirement of the possession of priest's orders (an interesting modification of medieval usage), the administrative system continued unchanged until the whig reforms of the nineteenth century.

The standards of pluralism and of rapid promotion accepted by the Restoration divines may be illustrated not inaptly from the series of preferments enjoyed by Sancroft. Upon the enthronement of Bishop Cosin at Durham, Sancroft was appointed by his episcopal friend to the rectory of Houghton-le-Spring and to a prebend of Durham Cathedral, the latter of which he held from 1661 until 1675. During this period he was preferred successively to the mastership of Emmanuel College, Cambridge, in 1662, and to the deanery of York in January 1664, which he resigned the following November on his appointment to the more lucrative deanery of St Paul's. In that cathedral he held also till 1667 the prebend of Oxgate, though he resigned his mastership of Emmanuel in 1665. In the opinion of his biographer, "a stronger proof can scarcely be afforded of the general estimation in which his character was held, than by the fact of so many preferments flowing upon him, in this short space of time, from so many various quarters".[2] To the deanery of St Paul's he added in 1668 the archdeaconry of Canterbury, which he held until 1670; and his biographer again accounts it a matter of

[1] H. M. Gwatkin, *Church and State in England to the Death of Anne*, pp. 380–1.
[2] D'Oyly, *Life of Sancroft*, i, 133.

particular praise that "he was probably induced to resign it by finding that he was precluded by the other demands on his time from properly attending to its duties".[1] In 1677, upon his elevation to the see of Canterbury, he resigned all his other preferments at St Paul's, as he had already done in 1675 his prebend at Durham.

Nor were examples lacking among the episcopal preferments of Charles II of nominations which might be pronounced by the uninstructed to have been made by Sir Robert Walpole or the duke of Newcastle, in their blend of mundane with other merits and motives. Dr Peter Mews, bishop successively of Bath and Wells and of Winchester, had borne arms on behalf of Charles I in the Civil War, had been sent to command the Scottish highland insurrection in favour of Charles II in 1653, and had spent some years in exile before the Restoration enabled him to reap the rewards of his efforts by receiving high office in the Church Militant. Nor were his preferments inadequately proportioned to his services: for he became archdeacon successively of Huntingdon, and of Berkshire, President of St John's College, Oxford, and dean of Rochester, holding concurrently with these preferments a canonry of Windsor, before being raised to the episcopate. His assumption of the crozier did not prevent his exercise of the temporal sword again, when during Monmouth's rebellion he directed the royal train of artillery at Sedgmoor, receiving a serious wound in the discharge of that honourable office. In assessing the claims of Hanoverian prelates to censure for non-residence it should be remembered also that the Caroline episcopate included Thomas Barlow, Provost of Queen's College, Oxford, raised to the see of Lincoln in 1675, who during his long tenure of that see till 1691, "diocesin quidem amplissimam ita administravit, ut per sedecim annos nunquam praesens visitationem celebraret, aut Ecclesiam Lincolniensem umquam conspiceret; unde Episcopi Buckdeniensis potius quam Lincolniensis nomine decantabatur".[2] How great indeed would have been his fame, had he been a third to the names of Hoadly and Watson in the eighteenth century!

Even more remarkable were the circumstances of William Beaw, nominated bishop of Llandaff in 1679, whose story may be recorded best in the graphic words of his own relation.

"I was in the beginning of the late rebellion", he wrote to archbishop Tenison in 1699, "a fellow of a college in Oxford, when, out of zeal to my

---

[1] D'Oyly, *op. cit.* i, 147.

[2] J. R. Magrath, *The Queen's College*, ii, 34–5, n. 1, quoting Richardson's edition (1743) of Godwin, *De Praesulibus Angliae.*

religion, and my king, (animated by his presence), I took up arms in the cause of both; in the exercise of which I became by degrees to be a major of horse; under which character, after having first been wounded, I was taken prisoner, sent up to London guarded by a troop of the rebels' horse, brought before a committee (a little portion of the Great Rump idol), examined and committed to a prison, and that one of the vilest too. After a long while of sufferance and patience, by the help of some friends, I obtained my liberty; but a very naked one; for not long after I was stripped of all that I possessed in this world and constrained to seek my bread in another, I mean but beyond the sea, where I continued not long, but I procured for myself a commission for a lieutenant-colonelship of horse under the Czar of Mosco. But upon a representation made me of the king's necessity of having an agent in Denmark, and of my being that one, or else to the great prejudice of his affairs, he must have continued without one, I suffered myself to be prevailed upon to quit my commission, and to go and negotiate the king's business in that kingdom....In this place I resided so long, spending all the while out of mine own little stock, (bills of exchange on the king's part failing me), that I was forced to quit this my civil employment, and return to my old trade of soldiering again; which to exercise I went into the service of the king of Sweden in his wars in Poland. I was one of the first that under that king's banner entered that kingdom and one of the last that thence marched out. Upon hearing afterward of some likelihood of a turn of affairs here in England, I returned hither and the revolution happened as I expected; and then there was no preferment in the Church which I could reasonably have demanded, but upon asking I might have obtained. But I was not then in Orders, nor was as then resolved ever to be in them. That afterwards I took them, 'twas upon the long and earnest solicitations of a bishop, now long since (I hope) with God; upon the assurance of a good living then in his hands, void and reserved for me; which upon my ordination I instantly received; but upon the receipt from mine own college soon after of a better, I quickly resigned; contenting myself, as then but a single man, with a single benefice."[1]

Accordingly, in 1661 Beaw settled down upon the vicarage of Adderbury to which he had been presented by New College, of which he had been fellow from 1637 to his expulsion in 1648, enjoying the income of £330; and (as his relation continued)

happy in my privacy, and as I judged, a competency. But so it was that I could not for ever lie hid. I was found out by some who thought it an indignity (otherwise than I thought myself) that my past services should continue unrewarded; whereupon I was sent to pitch upon any preferment

[1] Beaw to Tenison, 21 Aug. 1699. Lambeth MSS. 930, f. 49.

in the church, (I know not whether a bishopric was intended in the message: it was not excepted), and it should be secured unto me. The answer that I returned was that I would pitch upon nothing, lest I should be tempted to wish the death of somebody. Then his majesty caused it to be entered in with the Secretary's offices that I should have the first dignity that fell; but this order I neglected. At last there came a letter to me from a person of honour, that a little bishopric was fallen, and that I was thought of, but it was not thought good enough; yet he had assured them that I should not refuse the king's favour. Within two days after, comes another letter from a person of quality yet living, to whom I am the more obliged than any in the world, the first words of which were these: "A little bishoprick is fallen, but we thought not to let it pass because it puts you in order to a better". Upon these two letters I went up to London, yet with a doubtful mind; having no inclination to a bishoprick, much less to a poor one; yet upon the persuasion of all my friends, and in expectation of a sudden remove, I was at last moved to accept of it.

The rest of Beaw's story belongs by chronology no less than temper to the following century, where in due course it will recur. But the naïve confession of the exterior circumstances and inner motives which compassed his elevation to the little bishopric of Llandaff may refute any suggestion of discontinuity of form or spirit between the Caroline Church and its successor of the eighteenth century.

The churchmanship of the restored Laudian school was characterised by its wealth of patristic scholarship and learning, and by its interest in the Eastern Orthodox Church. This latter connection was due in part to the experiences of some of its members who had wandered in the East during the Commonwealth period, but in greater measure to the extensive British trade with the Levant, which had flourished during the former half of the century, and was to attain such proportions as to form an important element in the War of the Spanish Succession, when English naval operations were directed towards the extinction of French commercial competition in the Mediterranean basin. The development of this commerce carried many British merchants to reside in the Levant, and with the establishment of trading centres went the appointment of chaplains to provide for their spiritual needs, amongst whom were numbered not a few of the distinguished clergy of the later seventeenth and early eighteenth centuries, such as Frampton of Gloucester. From this contact with the Eastern Orthodox Church there resulted a careful study of its history and traditions, a revived zeal for Greek patristic literature, and a natural resolve to cultivate closer and friendly relations with so venerable and apostolic a communion, which rejected uncompromisingly the papal supremacy claimed by the Latin Church. As a corollary of this interest there ensued a re-emphasis upon the episcopal character of the English Church and upon the points of difference which separated it from the Protestant dissenters in England. Nor was this sentiment of *rapprochement* confined to the Greek Church. Occasional correspondence was established with leading churchmen and prelates of the Gallican Church of the Latin obedience. Dr George Bull, one of the glories of Anglican scholarship and as yet discharging the humble office of parish priest in the Gloucestershire villages of Suddington and Avening, received the thanks of the clergy of the Gallican Church for his exposition of their common Christian profession in his *Defensio Fidei Nicaenae*, conveyed in a letter from Bossuet to a correspondent in London: which letter, Burnet observed, "I read and so can deliver it for a certain truth, how uncommon soever it may seem to be".[1]

The incident was neither so surprising nor improbable as Burnet supposed, for Bossuet conducted a correspondence with Leibnitz lasting for a decade upon the differences between papists and Lutherans and the possibility of reunion. Nor was the notion of an *entente* between the English and Gallican Churches so inconceivable as some writers have imagined; for the Romanism to which Charles II would have fain reconverted his realm was assuredly of the character patronised by the *régime* of Louis XIV rather than of the ultramontane pattern beloved of the Jesuits. Indeed the adulation paid by Bossuet himself to *le Grand Monarque*, whom he compared to a second Constantine, indicated the tendency of contemporary Gallicanism to exalt the authority of the sovereign in matters ecclesiastical to the depression of that of the Pope. The issue in 1682 of the famous Gallican Articles, affirming the superiority of a General Council to the Pope and the necessity for the *consensus Ecclesiae* to the irreformability of dogmatic decrees, gave classic expression to the nationalism of the French Church, and provoked a conflict between Louis XIV and Innocent XI, which had the indirect result upon British history of enabling William of Orange in 1689 to embark upon his expedition to England with the papal approbation. From this rekindling of sympathy between the English and French Churches there sprang the correspondence of Archbishop Wake with the theologians of the Sorbonne which, though belonging chronologically to the eighteenth century, was in spirit allied to the Caroline age, of which indeed Wake was the heir in this regard.

[1] Burnet, *History of His Own Time* (edn. 1833, Oxford, with Notes by the Earls of Dartmouth and Hardwicke, and Speaker Onslow), v, 185.

Furthermore, the close interest of the Caroline divines in the Gallican and Eastern Churches rested upon a genuine spiritual kinship, expressed in their affinity with catholic methods of piety and devotion, no less than upon the common tradition of episcopacy. The patristic learning of Bull was typical of the strength of Caroline erudition, appealing constantly to the practice of the primitive undivided Church, compiling impressive *catenae* of patristic opinions, and relying implicitly upon the inerrancy of Holy Scripture and interpreting its tenor by the traditions of the oecumenical decrees. The same catholic tradition governed the devotional life of its leaders, which was marked by disciplined austerity, and their modes of public worship (as illustrated in minute detail by Mr Wickham Legg's studies of *English Church Life from the Restoration to the Tractarian Movement*), which rejoiced in the use of symbol and ceremony. In particular many of its champions esteemed highly the estate of celibacy, as did Sancroft, who even as primate "put on a monastic strictness and lived abstracted from company".[1] The eclectic theological taste of Ken was remarked by his biographer Dean Plumptre, from the evidence of the bishop's library, which included a very considerable number of works on the Roman Liturgy and of Roman Catholic books of ascetic and mystical character, to the complete exclusion of the Reformers, English and Continental, and even of some of the standard Anglo-Catholic divines. "The German Reformers, Luther, Melancthon, and their fellows; the English Reformers, Tyndale, Cranmer, Ridley, Latimer, Parker and the others...these are simply conspicuous by their absence. So also are the Puritan divines, Baxter, Manton, Howe, Calamy, and Owen, and even most of those of the Anglo-Catholic school, Bramhall and Bancroft, and Bull and Andrewes' sermons, and Pearson". On the contrary, the prominence of volumes of Roman Catholic theology "is perhaps the most striking feature" of Ken's library.[2] In like manner Peter Gunning, with his "special subtlety of arguing", avowed his desire "for our conforming in all things to the rules of the primitive church, particularly in praying for the dead, in the use of oil, with many other rituals. He formed", added Burnet prophetically, "many in Cambridge upon his own notions, who have carried them perhaps farther than he intended".[3]

The ecclesiastical heritage, alike in spiritual and material circumstance, into which the revived school of Laudian churchmanship entered upon its restoration in 1660 differed considerably and importantly from that which its predecessors had enjoyed during the reign

[1] Burnet, *op. cit.* ii, 89–90. [2] E. H. Plumptre, *Life of Ken*, ii, 295–7.
[3] Burnet, *op. cit.* i, 311.

of Charles I prior to the outbreak of the Civil War. The influence of
the Commonwealth religious experiments remained after the collapse
of the exterior structure which had made possible their execution. In
the sphere of material possessions the chief destruction had fallen upon
the cathedrals, which had been the especial objects of Oliverian violence.
In St Paul's the Commonwealth troopers had been quartered in the
choir, at St Asaph the postmaster stabled his horses in the nave,
Lichfield had served both parties in the war as a military post so that
Bishop Hacket found it sorely dilapidated and battered. Such were
pre-eminent instances of abuse, but of the majority of cathedrals, save
Salisbury, some damage could be reported.[1] In great part the worst
ravages of the conflict were repaired during the generation which
divided the Restoration from the Revolution, Hacket superintending
the virtual rebuilding of Lichfield, Ward collecting £25,000 for the
repair of Exeter and continuing the good work when translated to
Sarum, whilst before St Paul's could recover from the plunder of the
republican period, the great fire necessitated an entirely new cathedral
in the city of London, undertaken according to the design of Wren.
Despite much activity in building and repairing, however, it would
scarcely be an exaggeration to say that the cathedrals of England and
Wales suffered so grievously in fabric and tradition during the
Commonwealth that their restoration to full glory awaited not the
eighteenth, but the nineteenth-century Church revival. In lesser degree
many parish churches had deteriorated from neglect, and evidences
could be gathered from so wide a range as Northumberland, Carlisle,
Suffolk, Sussex, and East Anglia of the dilapidated and neglected
condition of churches which would parallel those brought in accusation
against the succeeding century. Nor was this exterior decay the sum
of the problem. During the interregnum, Puritanism had penetrated far
more widely and deeply than in the days of Charles I and Laud, in such
manner as to affect profoundly, if unostentatiously, the national
religious traditions. Not all the puritan clergy who had become
possessed of benefices under the Commonwealth departed from the
communion of the restored episcopal Church in 1662 when the Act
of Uniformity came into operation on St Bartholomew's Day. The
circumstance which presented difficulty to scrupulous consciences such
as Richard Kidder, that of inability to secure a copy of the Revised
Prayer Book, to which assent must be made, before the appointed
24 August, made easier the path of conformists of less exacting standards.

[1] J. H. Overton, *Life in the English Church*, 1660–1714, ch. IV: to which this
survey of the Restoration Church is much indebted.

Others remained, having seen and disliked the new Liturgy but believing that so long as conformity was not sinful the better part lay in continuing in possession of their benefices, and striving, as their predecessors of Elizabeth's days had done, for such modification at some future date as would the more satisfy their consciences and reopen the way for the comprehension of their separated brethren. The presence of a considerable volume of puritan opinion in the Church constituted a manifest obstacle to the indoctrination of clergy and laity with the principles of the high churchmen of the Caroline school. For not only did the conformist puritans retain the adherence of many laymen to the Established Church, binding together the congregations to which they had ministered during the Commonwealth and which would otherwise have scattered, but they maintained a tradition of sympathy and friendliness towards their non-conforming brethren which was itself strengthened and reinforced by influential tendencies of the age of secular rather than ecclesiastical provenance.

In the face of such conditions the Laudian divines were but one element in the heterogeneity of the *Ecclesia Anglicana*, distinguished indeed by piety, learning, and zeal, but no longer possessed of the peculiar favour and prestige which had belonged to their tradition in the reign of the royal martyr. The rise of a new theological temper, associated with the names of the Cambridge Platonists and later of the men of Latitude, indicated the changing intellectual atmosphere of the age. The school of Cambridge divines thus denominated were indeed the antithesis alike of the Calvinist and Laudian teachers.[1] Their elevation of reason as the divinely implanted governor of the life of man, and the arbiter also in the interpretation of Holy Scripture, cut at the root of the predestinarian doctrines of the former and the reliance upon ecclesiastical tradition of the latter. "To proceed to the study of their works after struggling with the Calvinistic and Roman controversies", observes a disciple of the Tractarian school, "is to enter into a calmer and, it can hardly be denied, a saner world."[2] Their sermons were constructed rather with a view to encourage men to the practice of virtue and piety than to direct their attention to abstruse points of divinity. Whichcote defined the best Christian as he "whose heart beats with the truest pulse towards heaven, not he whose head spinneth out the finest cobwebs"; and the tendency of this school was to emphasise the ethical and philosophical elements in the Christian

[1] F. J. Powicke, *The Cambridge Platonists* (1926, London).
[2] F. L. Cross, *The Oxford Movement and the Seventeenth Century*, p. 22 (Oxford Movement Centenary Series).

tradition in accordance with the principles of the Platonists of Alexandria in whose steps their feet were directed. This emphasis upon the moral duties of religion had a direct relevance to the contemporary situation, and was designed to stem the torrent of antinomianism which characterised the society of Restoration England in reaction against the censorship of manners during the Commonwealth. In the sphere of ecclesiastical politics the natural inclination of this school was towards measures directed to the assuagement of differences and bitterness between the various Christian Churches. They regarded matters of Church polity as at most of secondary importance; and the points upon which all Christians agreed in the cultivation of virtue and the inner life of the Spirit were to them of greater weight than the episcopal government or ceremonies of a church. "Why should not consent in the main be more available to concord and union than difference in less principal matters prevail to distance and separation?" asked Whichcote; to whom it seemed indeed "the greatest folly and madness in the world" that men should be "constituted and denominated Christians" by their opinions upon things indifferent. Accordingly the Cambridge Platonists, though contented themselves with episcopacy and the prescribed Liturgy, desired reasonable concessions to the dissenters; and, when these were refused in 1661, they endeavoured by personal kindness to diminish the ill-effects of separation and expulsion. "They continued to keep a good correspondence with those who had differed from them in opinion", observed Burnet, "and allowed a great freedom both in philosophy and divinity. From whence they were called men of Latitude; and upon this, men of narrower thoughts and fiercer tempers fastened upon them the name of Latitudinarians".[1]

Between the Laudian and the Latitude men of the Restoration age the balance was unevenly weighed by reason of a variety of circumstances which told against the predominance of the former tradition. The influence of the Commonwealth religious experiments was felt especially in relation to the two Evangelical Sacraments of Baptism and the Eucharist. In regard to the former, the custom of private baptism in houses was exceedingly prevalent (in like wise as its irregularity was the theme of many episcopal charges), but proved often the only means of ensuring the performance of the rite, as a compromise between its total omission and the reluctance of parents to bring their children to the parish church. A similar neglect had prevailed in respect of the Holy Communion, and the minimum allowed by George Herbert of five or six times a year had been too frequent for many parishes during

[1] Burnet, *op. cit.* i, 324.

the republican interregnum. Nor could the Caroline high churchmen achieve success in their endeavours to bring parishioners to a more frequent reception, since even Bull at Suddington "could only bring the Holy Communion to seven times in the year", a condition of affairs which could be paralleled easily in many other dioceses and churches of the kingdom.[1] Against such customs the Laudian divines contended earnestly, but with very partial success. Other forces added to their difficulties. During the generation which divided the restoration of the Stuart line from its final expulsion, the first stirrings were felt of the reaction against the ecclesiastical controversies and wars of the seventeenth century, and of the theological implications of the incipient study of natural science. The incorporation of the Royal Society by Charles II marked the beginning of a new influence upon religion no less than upon philosophy, characterised by an especial devotion to mathematics and astronomy, typical of which were the surrender by Isaac Barrow of his chair of Greek for that of mathematics and the publication in 1699 by John Craig, afterwards a prebendary of Salisbury, of his *Theologiae Christianae Principia Mathematica*. Into such *schemata* of theology the patristic erudition and the chief dogmatic tenets of the Caroline school found no entrance, for the new temper in religion did not so much bend itself to refute as resolve to ignore many of their characteristic doctrines. In such a *milieu* the Laudian tradition withered and died of inanition; and for the space of a century from the Restoration the men of Latitude enjoyed a popularity and vogue of astonishing proportions.

The Achilles heel of the loyal high churchman of the days of Charles II lay, however, not in the rigidity of his theological dogmas, but in the exuberance of his political principles; and it was this circumstance which wrought the discomfiture of his brethren of that allegiance within a brief generation of their triumph in 1660. As a natural concomitant of the political restoration the pulpits rang with the revived tenets of divine indefeasible hereditary right, of passive obedience, and of the sinfulness of rebellion. Only by a fervid subscription to this political creed indeed did it seem possible to find a sure barrier against the repetition of the horror of a regicide republic. The Prayer Book revision of 1662 provided for the special annual remembrance on 30 January of the decollation of King Charles I, and on 29 May of the birthday and restoration of Charles II; and around these two new state holy days there developed a fervour of political loyalty to the royal martyr and to the reigning monarchy, illustrated further by the revival of the practice of the royal touch for the healing of scrofula. Nor were

[1] J. H. Overton, *op. cit.* pp. 163–8.

such sentiments of allegiance to the lawful dynasty and of abhorrence of that spirit of revolt which had led to the establishment of the Oliverian military dictatorship confined to the adherents of the high-church party. No churchman could have been more insistent upon the sin of rebellion than Tillotson in his ministrations to Lord Russell before his execution in 1683. Upon the eve of that tragic event indeed, Tillotson wrote a letter setting forth his persuasion on the matter, based upon the three grounds:

first that the Christian religion doth plainly forbid the resistance of authority; secondly, that though our religion be established by law (which his lordship argued as a difference between their case and that of the primitive Christians), yet in the same law which established our religion, it is declared *that it is not lawful upon any pretence whatsoever to take up arms* etc. Besides that, there is a particular law declaring the power of the militia to be solely in the king. And this ties the hands of subjects, though the law of nature and the general rules of Scripture had left us at liberty, which he believed they did not, because the government and peace of human society could not well subsist upon these terms; thirdly, his lordship's opinion was contrary to the declared doctrine of all Protestant churches.

Upon this argument the dean urged the whig lord to repentance, since being

in a very great and dangerous mistake, and being so convinced, that which before was a sin of ignorance, would appear of a much more heinous nature, as in truth it was, and call for a very particular and deep repentance; which if his lordship sincerely exercised upon the sight of his error, by a penitent acknowledgement of it to God and men, he would not only obtain forgiveness of God, but prevent a mighty scandal to the reformed religion.

In his intercession with his lordship on the scaffold, Tillotson prayed that "all we who survive, by this and other instances, of Thy providence, may learn our duty to God and the King".[1] No stronger words were used by Ken in his attendance upon the duke of Monmouth upon a like melancholy occasion, and the harmony of sentiment testified to the widespread disavowal of the doctrine of the lawfulness of resistance among low churchmen no less than in the ranks of the high-church party.

It was evident that provocation of no small importance and character would be necessary to overthrow so staunch a loyalty and so convinced an allegiance; yet this challenge was destined to be forthcoming from the very side of royal adherence to the established religion itself. The

[1] T. Birch, *Life of John Tillotson*, pp. 102–4 (London, 2nd edn. 1753).

shadow cast over the rejoicing and enthusiasm of churchmen in the restoration of the Stuart line lay in the personal ecclesiastical allegiance of the sovereigns. Whereas the royal martyr had been a devoted champion of the *Ecclesia Anglicana*, his son was a secret papist, and the heir apparent, James, duke of York, an avowed papist. During the reign of Charles II the pressure of the inconsistency whereby the Supreme Governor of the Church was an apostate from its communion was eased by the circumstance that the restored monarch was by nature a *politique* who would not hazard his crown for any adventure of politics or religion. It was indeed theoretically conceivable that a popish sovereign, whilst unable to participate personally in the rites of the Church, might fulfil nevertheless the constitutional functions of Supreme Governor. Charles II towards the end of his reign had set a valuable precedent in regard to one branch of the ecclesiastical supremacy of the crown by his commission issued in 1681 to certain bishops and laymen for the recommendation of persons to be appointed to ecclesiastical preferments.[1] By virtue of this warrant the archbishop of Canterbury, and the bishop of London, together with the earls of Radnor and Halifax, Viscount Hyde, and Edward Seymour, were to recommend to all Church promotions, and without their approbation no nomination was to be made by the sovereign. It remained for the accession of a zealous proselyte in the person of James, duke of York, to determine the question whether this theoretical possibility could be translated into practical security.

The brief reign of the last of the Stuarts made actual the danger which had been hitherto potential in relation to the position of the Church under a popish monarch. It is agreed generally that the presage of trouble which in the days of Charles II had borne no greater proportions than a cloud of the size of a man's hand, became under his brother a tempest which shook speedily the foundations of Church and State, and that the responsibility for this rapid change lay at the door of the king personally. Nor is it doubted that the merry monarch had bequeathed to his successor a situation of greater promise in regard to the absolutism of the monarchy than had been the lot of any sovereign during the seventeenth century in England. The fatal mistake and madness of the whigs in their campaign to exclude James from succession to the throne, by the adoption of James, duke of Monmouth, as their puppet-candidate instead of William of Orange and Mary, had discredited the opposition to the royal house and frustrated temporarily the enactment of constitutional safeguards against the possible extremes

[1] E. Cardwell, *op. cit.* ii, 350–1.

of a papist sovereign. In the political reaction which followed the defeat of the whig exclusionist programme, Charles II had seized skilfully the opportunities presented of ruling without a parliament, and of revising the charter of the city of London (and of other boroughs) in such wise as to prevent whig domination and to instal good tories in municipal office. Such was the heritage of James II. Nor was there any sign of opposition to his personal profession of the Roman Catholic faith and its exercise within the royal household. His coronation oath to defend the Established Church was accepted without cavil or suggestion of safeguards. The most recent historian of the Jacobite movement allows that "all that James had to do was to follow his brother's example, prove that the Catholics did not constitute a national menace, and he could almost certainly have secured a measure of toleration for his co-religionists".[1] Thus far most historians are agreed. But there has developed a fashion of apologising for James on the ground that what he desired was not the destruction of the *Ecclesia Anglicana* and the substitution of popery as the established religion, nor any persecution of heretics and dissenters from his own faith such as Louis XIV was undertaking by the revocation of the Edict of Nantes, but simply the granting of toleration to all religious societies and the admission of papists to office in the state on the same terms as other citizens.

"So tactless were his methods", the apologist for his *régime* allows indeed, "that it is hardly surprising that both contemporaries and posterity should have come to the conclusion that his real aim was not toleration for, but the supremacy of, his co-religionists; yet it is impossible to believe that such was really the case. James was shortsighted to a degree, but he was not blind. What he desired was that Catholics should have their share of appointments at once and that in future there should be no discrimination in matters of religion."[2]

It is upon the point of James' intentions that criticism must be directed, in so far indeed as they were set forth by his policy and actions. It may be granted that the king desired to admit papists to his service in the state and that he had a genuine desire for religious toleration; but sundry of his actions, not the least important in provoking the Revolution, were scarcely patient of so restricted an interpretation. It was one matter to appoint papists to commissions in the army, but quite another to suggest to the compliant treasurer, Laurence Hyde, earl of Rochester (who had consented even to serve in the High Commission

[1] Sir C. A. Petrie, *The Jacobite Movement*, p. 54 (London, 1932).
[2] *Ibid.* p. 59.

Court), that he should receive instruction concerning the Roman Catholic faith, and finally to dismiss him when he refused to apostatise from Anglicanism. The implication of this episode, the more influential because of Rochester's position at the head of the treasury, was rather that no minister was sure of the royal favour unless he became a convert to popery. In like manner the readiness of Sancroft at the king's coronation not to proceed to the service of the Communion, though a sign of the tolerance extended to his majesty's personal adherence to the popish church, was surely ill-repaid when James appointed to the deanery of Christ Church, Oxford, a papist layman, Massey, with a dispensation from all the religious obligations of his office, including that of receiving the Sacrament in his own cathedral church. Nor did the royal dispensation to the Master of University College and other fellows to absent themselves from all Anglican rites in the college chapel, as well as from taking the oaths of supremacy and allegiance, suggest a policy strictly confined to religious toleration; the more especially when the Roman Mass was said in that chapel in consequence of this act.[1] Further, if full liberty were to be given for popish priests to preach and endeavour to make proselytes in England, the terms of religious toleration implied surely an equal freedom of the clergy of the English Church to protect their congregations against such efforts by instructing them in the principles of Anglican churchmanship and upon the points wherein Canterbury differed from Rome. Yet the fidelity of Dr John Sharp in discharging this fundamental pastoral responsibility towards his parish of St Giles in the Fields, London, led to a royal order to Bishop Compton of London to suspend him from the exercise of his ministerial duties. The resuscitation of the High Commission Court was itself an illegal act, though Sancroft grounded his refusal to serve as a member not upon this legal principle but upon the evasive issue of his age and infirmities; and the credit of the court was not improved by the presidency of Judge Jeffreys and its episcopal membership consisting of Sprat of Rochester, Crewe of Durham, and Cartwright of Chester. The decision of the court to suspend Compton from the exercise of the duties of his episcopal charge, because of his refusal to proceed to a suspension of Sharp on account of his sermon against

---

[1] The 3rd Article of the address presented to the king by Sancroft and several bishops on 3 October 1686 required the cessation of dispensations: "by virtue whereof any person, not duly qualified by law, hath been or may be put into any place, office, or preferment in Church or State, or in the Universities; or continued in the same; *especially such as have cure of souls annexed to them*" (D'Oyly, *op. cit.* i, 339–42).

popery, indicated further something more serious than a desire to give religious toleration to papists, namely the suppression of freedom of speech on the part of their adversaries. The issue of the Declaration of Indulgence raised no point of principle not brought forward already by the creation of the High Commission Court, though it provoked the crisis of the protest of the seven bishops which contributed so dramatic an element to the fall of James. These episodes, together with the violation of the freedom of election at Magdalen College, Oxford, and the temporary appointment by James of a papist to the presidency there, agreed rather with a design for the supremacy of the king's co-religionists than for their simple toleration; nor in such circumstances may the persuasion of contemporaries be esteemed of little weight in adjudging the purpose of the royal policy. When the true Israelites were prepared to become martyrs, albeit nothing could induce them to commit the sin of rebellion, for their church and religion, James had provoked a situation from the responsibility for which not even a sympathy with the principles of religious toleration could absolve him and his counsellors.

Others of the fellow-countrymen of the true Israelites, who would advance not a step beyond the challenge of passive resistance, shrank not from sending an invitation to William of Orange to save the liberties of the kingdom, nor from active support of rebellion when he had responded to the appeal. The event of the Revolution of 1689 penetrated the confusion of domestic politics with the sharpness of a two-edged sword, piercing to the dividing asunder of precept and practice. The exigency of practical circumstances compelled the enthronement of William, neither as regent for the absent king, nor as consort of Mary, but as king *de facto*; and the true revolution was effected whereby a dynasty ruling by divine hereditary right was replaced by an elective monarchy, created by a Convention parliament lacking legal authority. Apart from the unpleasing phraseology (doubly revolting to tory stomachs) of the resolution of the lords and commons, which smacked of the contractual theory of the relations of sovereign and subjects, the fact of the requirement of oaths of allegiance to William and Mary during the lifetime of James II, to whom his subjects had taken identical oaths but a few years previously, created a situation of extreme difficulty to many churchmen. Doctrines of divine, indefeasible, hereditary succession, which had been preached so boldly during the reign of Charles II, and of the sinfulness of resistance to divinely constituted authority, such as Tillotson had expounded so cogently to Russell upon the eve of his execution, were difficult of reconciliation with the new position. The pious fiction of an abdication by James II and of the consequent vacancy of the throne, even when supported by the further imagination of the suppositious character of the young Prince of Wales, was too transparent to carry conviction. Some moderate tories, like Sharp of St Giles shortly to be made archbishop of York, accepted the Revolution settlement on the ground that the law was supreme over the sovereign; justifying their assent by the argument "that the laws of the land are the only rule of our conscience in this matter, and we are no further bound to pay obedience to governors, nor to any other governors, than the laws enjoin. If therefore King William in the eye of the law be our king, we must in conscience pay obedience to him as such". This conclusion could only be allowed if the premiss, upon which Sharp avowedly based it, were valid, namely that "as the law makes the king, so the same law extends, or transfers, or limits our obedience and allegiance".[1] The hands were the hands of tories, but the voice was the authentic voice of whigs; for the theory of the supremacy of the law to the king was of the essence of whig doctrine. To tory churchmen who identified allegiance to the divinely constituted authority of government with personal loyalty to the monarch ruling by divine appointment as the sovereign by hereditary descent, no theory which separated loyalty to the constitution from that to the person of the king was acceptable. Filmer and Locke were to them not complementary but contradictory prophets; and allegiance to the Revolution monarchy justified a similar acceptance of the great rebellion, the Commonwealth, and the Oliverian republic. Accordingly Sancroft, together with five of his suffragans, and followed by about four hundred of the inferior clergy, suffered deprivation of their benefices rather than perjure their conscience by taking oaths of allegiance to the usurpation in Church and State effected by the expulsion of James II.

Amongst the problems demanding resolution from the authors of the Revolution settlement, not least urgent were those of the relations of the sovereign to the Established Church, and of that Church towards the Protestant dissenters. The occasion of the Revolution itself had lain chiefly in the attack of James II upon the Church, and, although disavowed by the non-juring secession, the terms of its settlement contributed signally to the protection of the Church from possibility of future assault. Statutory provision was made that future kings should receive the Sacrament according to its rite and remain in communion with it, whilst papists or persons marrying papists were disqualified

[1] T. Sharp, *Life of Archbishop John Sharp*, i, 263–4.

from succession to the throne. More difficult was the problem of the situation of Protestant dissenters and their legal relationship towards the establishment. During the severe trial to which the episcopalians had been subjected by the policy of James II, a marked *rapprochement* had taken place between the bishops and the leading Protestant nonconformists. Indeed the episcopate were vitally concerned lest the dissenters should accept the toleration offered them by the illegal dispensing power of James in his Declarations of Indulgence, and should thereby break the unity of front of the Reformed Churches towards their common enemy, Rome. On the other hand, much suspicion had existed in nonconformist circles concerning the alleged popish leanings of Sancroft and others of the Laudian school, albeit quite unjustly, for there had been no tinge of popery in their outlook or practice. So early as 1678 Sancroft and Morley of Winchester had approached James, duke of York, in an attempt to recover his allegiance for the Church of his baptism, and in their interview with his highness had not scrupled to denominate the communion of his conversion as "the proudest, the cruellest, and the most uncharitable church in the world", and one which "teacheth and practiseth doctrines destructive of salvation".[1] Again, in a letter to the Princess Mary in 1687 the primate had declared that "the greatest calamity that ever befell us, was that it pleased God, in His wise and just providence, to permit wicked and ungodly men, after they had barbarously murdered the father, to drive out the sons from abiding in the inheritance of the Lord, as if they had said to them, Go and serve other gods".[2] Under the imminent danger of the triumph of popery during James II's reign, therefore, Sancroft made more definite overtures towards the Protestant dissenters by the issue on 27 July 1688 of a series of articles to the bishops of his province, for communication by them to the clergy of their dioceses; in the eleventh of which articles the entire clergy were exhorted

more especially that they have a very tender regard to our brethren, the Protestant dissenters, that upon occasion offered they visit them at their houses, and receive them kindly at their own, and treat them fairly whenever they meet them, discoursing calmly and civilly with them, persuading them (if it may be) to a full compliance with our church; or at least that "whereto we have already attained, we may all walk by the same rule and mind the same thing". And in order hereunto, that they take all opportunities of assuring and convincing them, that the bishops of this church are really and sincerely irreconcilable enemies to the errors, superstitions, idolatries, and

---

[1] D'Oyly, *op. cit.* i, 165–76.   [2] *Ibid.* p. 245

tyrannies of the church of Rome, and that the very unkind jealousies which some have had of us to the contrary were altogether groundless; and in the last place that they warmly and most affectionately exhort them to join with us in daily fervent prayer to the God of peace for an universal blessed union of all Reformed churches, both at home and abroad; that all they who do confess the holy name of our dear Lord and do agree in the truth of His holy Word, may also meet in one holy communion, and live in unity and godly love.[1]

In order still more to further this hope of unity and concord the primate pondered afresh the question of comprehension, "considering how utterly unprepared they had been at the Restoration of king Charles II to settle many things to the advantage of the church, and what a happy opportunity had been lost, for want of such previous care, for its more perfect establishment". With the assistance privately rendered of divers eminent prelates and clergy of the Church, Sancroft advanced to the consideration of details, adumbrating such a scheme of liturgical revision as might effect the desired end of reconciling the majority of Protestant dissenters, then well disposed towards the establishment because of the stout defence of its bishops and divines against popery.

"The design was in short this", testified Wake in a speech delivered upon the Sacheverell trial, "to improve, and, if possible, amend our discipline; to review and enlarge our Liturgy by correcting some things, by adding others, and if it should be thought advisable by authority, when this matter should be legally considered, first in Convocation, then in Parliament, by omitting some few ceremonies which are allowed to be indifferent in their nature, also indifferent in their usage, so as not to make them of necessity binding on those who had conscientious scruples respecting them, till they should be able to overcome either their weaknesses or their prejudices respecting them, and be willing to comply."[2]

Upon the determination of the ecclesiastical aspect of the Revolution settlement, it was natural that this scheme of comprehension should be revived, though upon this occasion the hand of the archbishop was necessarily withheld upon the ground of his inability to take the oath of allegiance to the new monarchy. Other hands took up the work, moved alike by the general desire to improve the existing cordiality into an organic union and by the example set by Sancroft himself. On 11 March 1689 the earl of Nottingham introduced into the house of lords a bill "for uniting their majesties' Protestant subjects", and on

[1] E. Cardwell, *op. cit.* ii, 375–6. [2] D'Oyly, *op. cit.* i, 327–30.

the 14th another bill "for exempting their majesties' Protestant subjects dissenting from the Church of England from the penalties of certain laws". Similar bills were introduced into the house of commons; but whilst the Toleration Bill proceeded rapidly through all its stages and received the royal assent on 24 May, the comprehension project suffered a far different fate. In the lords a proposal was made for the issuing of a royal commission to a mixed body of clergy and laity to consider revision of the Liturgy, but was not carried; and in the commons an address was carried requesting the king to summon a Convocation for the deliberation of ecclesiastical matters, in which address the lords joined. Accordingly the Convocations were summoned to meet, and preparatory thereto on 13 September 1689 a commission was issued to ten bishops and twenty of the inferior clergy to consider business to be laid before them. From the outset the work of the commission was hindered by the withdrawal of some of its nominated members who were opposed to the policy of revision to conciliate dissenters, but the majority continued their labours until a comprehensive project was prepared, making many concessions to scrupulous consciences in regard to nocent ceremonies, and effecting a variety of changes in the Liturgy. The temper of the commissioners of 1689 indeed was as disposed to concession as that of the Anglican leaders at the Savoy Conference had been towards maintaining the traditional position of the Church upon disputed points. Notwithstanding, the project was entirely abortive; for upon the assembly of the Canterbury Convocation the temper of the lower house was indicated decisively by the election as Prolocutor of Dr Jane, dean of Gloucester, who had been a dissentient member of the commission, against Tillotson, dean of St Paul's, who had been equally enthusiastic in support of eirenic measures.[1] In view of this testimony of the attitude of the clergy, the commissioners' recommendations were never laid before the house, and the opportunity of comprehension passed finally into the limbo of causes lost.

The Protestant dissenters had to be contented therefore with the meagre provisions of the Toleration Act, which though allowing legal recognition to corporate dissent from the Established Church and granting freedom of public worship to orthodox Protestant dissenters, provided their meeting-houses were registered in the archdeacons' courts and their assemblies were held with unlocked doors, did not repeal in any wise the restrictive clauses of the Test and Corporation Acts, which excluded all persons unwilling to receive the Sacrament according to the rite of the Established Church from municipal office

[1] T. Birch, *op. cit.* pp. 167–84.

and from the service of the crown. Toleration, not equality, was the keynote of the measure; but though its intrinsic concessions to dissenters appeared slight, the situation of the Church of England was vitally affected by the legal protection of nonconformist public worship, of which an immediate consequence was the growth of meeting-houses and the number of applications for their registration. From the episcopal side also strong advocates of comprehension, such as Burnet, came upon reflection to the opinion that "there was a very happy direction of the Providence of God observed in this matter", since the rejection of their scheme had prevented a schism within the Anglican Church which might have outweighed the access of strength from the reconciliation of presbyterians. The non-juror party indeed, which was challenging in a vigorous controversy the fundamental position of the Established Church as apostate from the true principles of the catholic and apostolic Church of England, would have secured a great augmentation of force if its champions had been able further to point to changes made in the Liturgy in order to placate dissenters. Lacking this aid, its polemic was concentrated upon the proper occasion of schism, namely the lawfulness of the Revolution and the authority of the new monarchy to deprive ecclesiastics refusing the oath of allegiance to its rulers. To this attack the conformist clergy had of necessity to make reply.

From the circumstances of this controversy proceeded many of the outstanding characteristics of the ecclesiastical history of the reign of William and Mary. It was evident that little defence of the new *régime* could be anticipated from the majority of tory clergy, whose hearts were still moved towards the exiled Stuart king though their lips had framed the words of allegiance to the usurping dynasty. Further, their attempts towards a more cordial acceptance of the *de facto* monarchy were frustrated constantly by the accusing spectacle of their non-juring brethren, whose fidelity to conscience, unsullied by considerations of expediency, had brought them to affliction and deprivation. At best the Revolution settlement seemed but a makeshift compromise; and even its authors defended it as a delicate balance of conflicting interests. Upon the whigs therefore devolved the uncongenial rôle of defending the Established Church as part of the constitutional settlement, and moreover as a corporation of vast political influence, which must be enlisted in their service if the new *régime* in State and Church were to prosper. "The distinguishing characters of a whig", as delineated by Bishop Gibson to Walpole in 1733, "for thirty years together" were constituted by "the settled principle of maintaining the Protestant succession, the church establishment, and the Toleration."

The conversion of the whig party into the situation of supporters of the position of the Established Church was undoubtedly the most important factor of the ecclesiastical development of the first half of the eighteenth century. By the lay politicians the duty was undertaken involuntarily and with a very imperfect appreciation of the obligations of its assumption. To the church-whigs however this aspect of whig policy was vital; since their apologia for the Church against non-juror assaults rested upon their ability to affirm with conviction and assurance that its situation was as secure under the patronage of their allies as it had been under the tutelage of "the church-party" of the tories. Furthermore, the clerical whigs had to undertake the insistent task of asserting the continuity of the Church of the Revolution era with its Caroline predecessor and of rebutting charges of apostasy and schism. For this end there was need to create a strong school of church-whigs; and by a singular irony of fortune the non-juror schism itself offered the opportunity for this creation in the large number of bishoprics vacant by death or deprivation. By the nomination to the episcopate of divines of pronounced zeal for the new dynasty and its administration a dual objective was attained; the provision of adequate clerical support for the Revolution settlement and also of safeguards against the possibility of further concessions to dissenters prejudicial to the position of the Established Church.

The Revolution of 1689 opened therefore a century of acute party contention for the control of the ecclesiastical preferment of the crown in the interest of the rival political allegiances of whig and tory. During the reign of William III circumstances were unusually favourable for the impressing upon the bench of a definite political and ecclesiastical complexion, since no fewer than twenty presbyters were elevated to the episcopate. The result of the prudent management of so considerable a volume of preferment was writ large in the division list of the house of lords after the debate on the Occasional Conformity Bill on 14 December 1703; when in the critical vote which separated sharply whig from tory, no fewer than thirteen bishops of William's nomination voted with the majority for the rejection of the bill, whilst only two were numbered with the minority in its favour. To such a persuasive pattern Queen Anne could pay no other compliment than a devout imitation, though in a reverse political direction; and the degree of her well-doing in the disposition of episcopal promotions was testified with equal clarity and force by the division list of the upper parliamentary house on 19 December 1718 upon Stanhope's Bill for the repeal of the Occasional Conformity and Schism Acts. Upon this latter occasion ten prelates owing their nomination to her majesty cast their suffrages against the proposed relief for the dissenters, and only three in its support.[1] From such examples the lesson to be learned was plain; nor were tories any less eager than their rivals to turn so potent an agent of political influence to the service of party as well as of the Church. Fortune however resolved to give its bounty to the whigs; and from the accession of George I to the death of George II toryism suffered a protracted and severe ostracism. After an initial phase of confusion and

[1] In the following lists of episcopal votes, the reign in which the bishop was first raised to the bench is given, together with the see occupied at the date of the division. The name of the see is given first, followed by that of the bishop.

Division in the Lords on 14 December 1703 on the Occasional Conformity Bill.

For the Bill.
York—Sharp (William III).
London—Compton (Charles II).
Winchester—Mew (Charles II).
Rochester—Spratt (Charles II).
Chester—Stratford (William III).
St Asaph—Hooper (Anne).

Proxies.
Durham—Crewe (Charles II).
Exeter—Trelawny (James II).
Llandaff—Beaw (Charles II).

Against.
Canterbury—Tenison (William III).
Worcester—Lloyd (Charles II).
Salisbury—Burnet (William III).
Ely—Patrick (William III).
Lichfield—Hough (William III).
Norwich—Moore (William III).
Peterborough—Cumberland
(William III).
Lincoln—Gardiner (William III).
Chichester—Williams (William III).
Oxford—Talbot (William III).
Bangor—Evans (William III).

Proxies.
Hereford—Humphreys (William III).
Gloucester—Fowler (William III).
Bristol—Hall (William III).

Division in the Lords on 19 December 1718 on Stanhope's Bill for the repeal of the Occasional Conformity and Schism Acts.

For the repeal.
Worcester—Hough (William III).
Salisbury—Talbot (William III).
Llandaff—Tyler (Anne).
Norwich—Trimnell (Anne).
Ely—Fleetwood (Anne).
Gloucester—Willis (George I).
Lincoln—Gibson (George I).
Bangor—Hoadly (George I).
Exeter—Blackburne (George I).
Carlisle—Bradford (George I).
Peterborough—White Kennett
(George I).

Against.
Canterbury—Wake (Anne).
York—Dawes (Anne).
London—Robinson (Anne).
Durham—Crewe (Charles II).
Winchester—Trelawny (James II).
Bath and Wells—Hooper (Anne).
Chichester—Manningham (Anne).
Hereford—Bisse (Anne).
St David's—Ottley (Anne).
Rochester—Atterbury (Anne).
Bristol—Smalridge (Anne).
Chester—Gastrell (Anne).
St Asaph—Wynne (George I).
Oxford—Potter (George I).
Lichfield and Coventry—Chandler
(George I).

internal schism during the early years of the new dynasty, the alliance of Gibson and Walpole settled itself to the exploitation of the land of promise and to the establishment of a virtual whig monopoly of episcopal preferment.

Apart from the intrusion of Sherlock upon the bench in 1727 as bishop of Bangor, at the insistence of Queen Caroline, and his translation to Sarum in 1734, no tory divine broke through the fence of prohibition raised up by Gibson against their kind; so that the bishop of London could express to his political ally towards the end of their association his gratification that whereas "the body of tory priests had stood entire for fourteen years' last past", on the other hand "the number of whig presbyters was much narrowed by frequent removes to the bench". Upon the dissolution of their partnership in 1736 the golden age of the Church-whig alliance was ended; and with the defeat a decade later of the final Jacobite rebellion the period of whig monopoly likewise came to an end. During the twenty years which followed from 1746 to 1766, in which the duke of Newcastle was almost continually in office as "ecclesiastical minister", the episcopate reverted gradually to its former motley complexion; and stout whigs like Archbishop Herring, who had been bred in the straitest school of Gibson, shook their heads over the spectacle of their patron's lapses from orthodoxy, lamenting especially such aberrations as the translation of Sherlock to London in 1748, and the elevation of James Johnson, a reputed Jacobite, to Gloucester in 1752 and his translation to Worcester in 1759. Yet the duke's policy was dictated by circumstances, which were changing rapidly from the clear-cut distinctions in which Gibson had deemed it a patriotic duty for the whig prelates to have no "concern with the tory bishops beyond common civility". "In truth", commented Horace Walpole, "this was the era of faction; though it did not immediately predominate. Hitherto it might be said that the two parties of whig and tory still subsisted; though Jacobitism, the concealed mother of the latter, was extinct."[1] In the new *milieu* in which "the contests were rather a struggle for power than the settled animosity of two parties", the path of the duke of Newcastle was necessarily tortuous and uncertain, in his attempt to conciliate as many interests as possible and to prepare for the inevitable day when his old master George II should be gathered to his fathers and the young men who had stood around his grandson George III should direct the counsels of the nation and enjoy the favour of the new sovereign.

The intense party contests for the control of the ecclesiastical pro-

[1] H. Walpole, *Memoirs of the Reign of George III* (edn. 1848), ii, 93–4.

motions of the crown did not necessarily imply, as has been commonly supposed, the extinction of the personal influence of the monarch in Church matters. William III indeed was notoriously indifferent towards ecclesiastical issues and unsympathetic towards clerical controversies. Burnet admitted that "his indifference to forms of church government and his being zealous for toleration together with his cold behaviour towards the clergy, gave them generally very ill impressions of him".[1] Accordingly, apart from occasional interventions such as the nominations of Burnet to Sarum and of Tillotson to succeed the deprived Sancroft at Canterbury, he was content to rely upon the advice of his consort Mary, "to whom he wholly left the matters of the church, consulting chiefly with his grace, whom she favoured and supported in a most particular manner".[2] After the queen's death, his majesty reverted to the precedent set by Charles II, by his issue on 9 May 1700 of a warrant to Archbishops Tenison of Canterbury and Sharp of York, and Bishops Burnet of Sarum, Lloyd of Worcester, Patrick of Ely, and Moore of Norwich (a purely clerical commission), empowering them to present recommendations through the secretaries of state of persons for preferment to bishoprics and to all other promotions in the gift of the crown above the value of £20 in the king's books.[3]

Such a self-denying ordinance was speedily removed by Anne upon her accession to the throne, for her majesty valued no branch of her royal prerogative more highly than that of replenishing the bench with sound tories. In profession of impartiality to the factions of whig and tory and of desire to be the queen of all her subjects she proclaimed an ideal of regal policy to which she could scarcely hope to attain, least of all in her ecclesiastical interests. Her ineradicable partisanship was displayed not only in her private remonstrance with the duchess of Marlborough in the first year of her reign—"I know the principles of the church of England and I know those of the whigs; and it is that and no other reason which makes me think as I do of the last"[4]—but even more emphatically in her injunction to Archbishop Sharp upon the nomination of Bull to the see of St David's in 1705 "that she would always desire that the bishops she put in should vote on the side that they who call themselves the church party do vote on".[5] In the matter of Church preferments she confided fully in Sharp, whose influence was such "that the queen would rarely give her promise without his advice,

---

[1] Burnet, *op. cit.* iv, 550.   [2] T. Birch, *op. cit.* p. 312.
[3] E. Cardwell, *op. cit.* ii, 403–8.
[4] *Memoirs of Sarah Duchess of Marlborough* (ed. King), pp. 90–1.
[5] *Life of Sharp*, i, 323.

and generally speaking, consent first obtained".[1] The outstanding example of her assertion of the personal prerogative of the sovereign occurred in relation to the sees of Exeter and Chester in 1707; wherein upon the translation of Trelawny from Exeter to Winchester, her majesty received in her closet Dr Offspring Blackhall and Sir William Dawes, who kissed hands respectively for Exeter and Chester, without any intimation of her intention to the ministers of state. The royal action was deliberate; for the queen desired to forestall the possibility of unwelcome recommendations on the part of the whig administration by her initiative. But the anticipated conflict was postponed, not averted, thereby; and upon the publication of the secret the full force of whig fury was unloosed. Even the duke of Marlborough, sufficiently engaged in the military embarrassments of the unfortunate campaign of 1707, was embroiled in the political crisis engendered by the ecclesiastical appointments; and Godolphin and Sunderland plied him with gloomy forecasts of the ill-effect of her majesty's action upon the whig members of the house of commons on whose support the war policy of the government depended for its continuance. Despite the most solemn objurgations of the duke, Anne stood her ground:

"I cannot think", she replied, "that my having nominated Sir William Dawes and Dr Blackhall to be bishops is any breach, they being worthy men, and all the clamour that is raised against them proceeds only from the malice of the whigs...I do assure you that these men were my own choice. They are certainly very fit for the station I design them; and indeed I think myself obliged to fill the bishops' bench with those that will be a credit to it and to the church".[2]

Ultimately, after a protracted vacancy of the sees, the matter was settled by a compromise; Dawes and Blackhall being consecrated to Exeter and Chester, the vacant see of Norwich bestowed upon Dr Charles Trimnell, chaplain to Sunderland, and the duke of Marlborough being gratified by the appointment of his *protégé* Dr John Potter to the regius professorship of Divinity at Oxford. A further assurance was given to the cabinet council, and communicated to the whig leaders in the commons' house, of her majesty's intention in future vacancies to consult the wishes of her ministers.[3] In this episode the queen's obstinacy had been increased by the natural antipathy which she cherished towards the whigs; but upon occasion she could show equal

[1] *Life of Sharp*, i, 335.
[2] W. Coxe, *Memoirs of the Duke of Marlborough*, ii, 158: and chapters LVIII and LXII *passim*.
[3] Burnet, *op. cit.* iv, 208.

determination in opposing the recommendations of the leaders of the Church party. It was to her firmness that the Church owed its fortunate escape from the indignity of the elevation of Sacheverell to the bench, pressed upon Anne by Lord Harcourt after the tory triumph in 1710; and in yielding with the utmost reluctance to the suggestion of the nomination of Atterbury to a bishopric in 1713, her majesty did so in the belief that she was accepting the less discreditable alternative alike to herself and the Church to which she was devoted.[1]

With the arrival of the first monarch of the Hanoverian dynasty, the warm personal interest of the sovereign in ecclesiastical preferment suffered an evident chill. George I indeed was most solicitous for the advancement of his Hanover chaplains, and upon occasion Archbishop Wake deemed it a proper sign of respect to his majesty to draw up for his consideration a statement in French of recommendations and opinions. But after the consolidation of the alliance of Gibson and Walpole, the king readily allowed the care of the Church to pass into such zealous and competent hands. Tradition has done more than justice to the commerce of Caroline, wife of George II, in this branch of the royal prerogative; but her husband also, especially after the death of his consort, exercised a real interest and influence in episcopal promotions. It would be too flattering to that monarch to pretend that his participation was well-informed or intelligent; for it showed itself chiefly in a desire to thwart the wishes of the duke of Newcastle in particular and in general to tease his ministers; yet occasionally George II could be as stubborn in prejudice as Anne had been. In 1750 he insisted upon the translation of Butler from Bristol to Durham, having allowed himself to be overpersuaded by Newcastle in 1748 into offering the see of London to Sherlock instead of Butler; and again in 1752 when Durham was vacant by the early death of Butler and the duke pressed the claims of Trevor of St David's, he returned a peremptory refusal, denominating Trevor "a high-church fellow, a stiff, formal, fellow, and nothing else". In this case his majesty gave way to ministerial importunity, as indeed he usually did; but in 1757 he seized avidly the opportunity afforded by the vacancy of the see of Canterbury during the brief interval of the Devonshire-Fox administration to determine by his personal predilection a series of important episcopal removes. Having decreed the translation of Hutton from York to Canterbury, he proceeded to bring Gilbert from Sarum to York, Thomas from Peterborough to Sarum, and to nominate Richard Terrick to the vacant see, much to the chagrin of Newcastle, who in this anticipated contingency

[1] Burnet, *op. cit.* vi, 176 (Lord Dartmouth's note).

had designed the advancement of Thomas to York and the promotion of Philip Yonge, his chief Cambridge friend, to Peterborough. Such examples preserved certainly the tradition of the personal authority of the sovereign in ecclesiastical preferments, and afforded precedents to George III which he in turn was not slow to act upon and improve to his own advantage.

The sowing of the Church of the Restoration epoch was brought thus to harvest amid the unfamiliar *milieu* of the foreign dynasties imported in 1689 and 1714 in consequence of the Revolution settlement and the strife of the rival political factions of whig and tory. Of the reality of the influence of these factors upon ecclesiastical affairs in Hanoverian England no doubt may be entertained; and to the exploration of the nature and extent of this influence the following lectures are directed. In surveying the political and ecclesiastical situation of the episcopate, and the several grades of the inferior clergy, no less than in a delineation of the theological and religious traditions of the age, evidence may be adduced upon which to form a considered judgment of the effect of new forces upon the heritage of the Caroline Church. From one standpoint indeed judgment may be pronounced at once and adversely, as the generality of historians have testified, upon Church and State in eighteenth-century England, in accordance with the prejudice which Queen Anne naïvely confessed to the duchess of Marlborough in retrospect of the rule of her predecessor upon the throne. "As to my saying the church was in danger in the late reign, I cannot alter my opinion. For though there was no violent thing done, everybody that will speak impartially must own that everything was tending towards the whigs. And whenever that is, I shall think the church beginning to be in danger."

CHAPTER II

THE BENCH IN PARLIAMENT AND POLITICS

"No man can now be made a bishop for his learning and piety", observed Dr Johnson in his discourse on the state of the nation on Good Friday, 1775, "his only chance for promotion is his being connected with somebody who has parliamentary interest."[1] To this unhappy circumstance the doctor ascribed the decline of learning in England. "There are other ways of getting preferment. Few bishops are made now for their learning. To be a bishop, a man must be learned in a learned age, factious in a factious age, but always of eminence. Warburton is an exception, though his learning alone did not raise him."[2] Some grain of comfort may perchance be drawn from the admission of so stout a tory that eminence was requisite for promotion to the bench, even though displayed in the sphere of faction. In the year also which saw the elevation of Richard Hurd to the episcopate it may be inferred that regard was still paid to scholarship. But the close connection between parliamentary interest and ecclesiastical preferment, noted by Johnson, was of particular importance in his age, being in fact the peculiar expression in the conditions of eighteenth-century society of the secular association of the episcopate with affairs of state which was characteristic of English Christianity.

If it were desired to trace this association to its source, attention would have to be directed to the beginning of that history wherein "the holy Church of England was founded in the estate of Prelacy within the realm". The Roman missionaries who laboured for the conversion of Anglo-Saxon England received their first establishment as royal chaplains of the several ruling princes, whose territorial authority conditioned the limits of their dioceses, and when the heptarchy resolved gradually into an united kingdom, the ecclesiastical jurisdictions retained the memory of former sub-divisions whilst their prelates became counsellors of the English monarchy. The intimate connection of Church and State typified in the charter of Canute, where ealdormen and shire-bishops were charged together to maintain "God's right, my royal authority and the behoof of all the people", was not broken by the episode of the Norman Conquest. The bishops retained their position as tenants *in capite* of the crown, holders of ecclesiastical baronies, and members of the royal council, whilst their learning drew

[1] Boswell, *Life of Johnson*, 14 April 1775.   [2] *Ibid.* 21 Aug. 1773.

them into the service of the sovereign as treasurer or chancellor. With the development of the administrative system of the Angevin kings, opportunities of office in the royal civil service multiplied greatly, and the road to high ecclesiastical preferment lay through apprenticeship in the royal household. Though a lay chancellor was appointed first in 1340, during the greater part of the fourteenth century the chancellorship was held by clergy, and the crown still depended upon the clerical order in large part for its trained officials. Typical prelates of the middle age, William of Wykeham and Stapledon of Exeter, illustrated the importance of service in the royal administration as the path to high office in Church and State; whilst the Statute of Provisors in justification of its endeavour to prevent the intrusion of aliens into English benefices, recited the custom of sovereigns "to have the greatest part of their council for the safeguard of the realm when they had need, of such prelates and clergy so advanced". Upon the eve of the Reformation the medieval tradition was personified in the massive pluralism of ecclesiastical and civil offices concentrated in the hands of Cardinal Wolsey, who stood in fact at the parting of the ways.

In many aspects the Reformation movement bore the appearance of an irruption of the hungry laity into the patrimony of the Church.

"In an age", observed Macaulay, "which produced such laymen as William Cecil and Nicholas Bacon, Roger Ascham and Thomas Smith, Walter Mildmay and Francis Walsingham, there was no reason for calling away prelates from their dioceses to negotiate treaties, to superintend the finances, or to administer justice. The spiritual character not only ceased to be a qualification for high civil office, but began to be regarded as a disqualification."[1]

Yet despite the substantial accuracy of this verdict, the Reformation in effect changed the form rather than the principle of the commerce of ecclesiastics in affairs of state. Upon occasion divines still fulfilled offices of civil administration. The principle of this connection received explicit approbation from the authority of Hooker, not only in his eulogy of episcopacy as "the temperature of excess in all estates, the glue and soder of the public weal, the ligament which tieth and connecteth the limbs of this body politic to each other",[2] but emphatically in his judgment of the propriety of divines sustaining offices of state.

Wherefore, if it please God to bless some principal attendants on His own sanctuary and to endue them with extraordinary parts of excellency, some

[1] Macaulay, *History of England* (ed. C. H. Firth), vol. i, ch. III, p. 314.
[2] Hooker, *Ecclesiastical Polity*, VIII, vi, 8.

in one kind, some in another, surely a great derogation it were to the honour of Him who bestowed so precious graces, except they on whom He hath bestowed them, should accordingly be employed that the fruit of these heavenly gifts might extend itself into the body of the Commonwealth wherein they live; which, being of purpose instituted (for so all commonwealths are) to the end that all might enjoy whatsoever it pleaseth the Almighty to endow each one man with, must needs suffer loss when it hath not the gain which eminent civil ability in ecclesiastical persons is now and then found apt to afford.[1]

Although the Elizabethan age was prone, as in the case of Sir Thomas Smith's nomination to the deanery of Carlisle, to reward the services of its eminent laity with provision of ecclesiastical revenues, the piety of the early Stuart kings redressed the balance by the appointment of Bishop Williams of Lincoln as lord keeper in 1621, and by that of Bishop Juxon of London as treasurer in 1636, whilst the influence of Laud through his friendship with Strafford and that of both with Charles I was exercised on political no less than ecclesiastical affairs, albeit indirectly. The close association of episcopacy with monarchy brought about the fall of both during the Commonwealth, which proceeded logically to the abolition of crown, peerage, and prelacy.

Not even the severe purgation of this republican experiment could break the tradition of the concern of the episcopate with statecraft, and the revival in the eighteenth century of the practice of the appointment of a bishop to the office of lord privy seal testified to the conservative character of English political development. The promotion by Harley of Dr John Robinson, bishop of Bristol, to be lord privy seal in the tory administration on the death of the duke of Newcastle in 1711, and thereafter to be plenipotentiary with the earl of Strafford at the peace conferences at Utrecht, was hailed by contemporaries as bearing the character of a portent. The clergy received it as a particularly graceful compliment to their order.

"The only doubt is, whether it be not too great an instance of respect and kindness to us," commented Canon Stratford of Christ Church to Edward Harley, "The laity, ever since the Reformation, in days better disposed to us than these are, have been very uneasy when any of our gown, how great soever their abilities were, have been admitted to any share of secular honours...I expect the run in the pamphlets will be that the clergy are grasping at power again. That will not signify much, but the several pretenders will be uneasy to see themselves disappointed by one they never suspected."[2]

[1] Hooker, *op. cit.* VII, xv, 6.   [2] Portland MSS. VII, 51–2.

The honour done to Robinson was not of a merely formal character, for Harley had formed the highest opinion of his abilities and talents, which had indeed received no easy training as chaplain and then ambassador at the court of Charles XII of Sweden, where he had spent a full quarter of a century and in which he had rendered particular service during the negotiations of Marlborough with that sovereign in 1707. In accordance with typical medieval tradition also, the re-compense for his diplomatic attendance at Utrecht took the form of his promotion in 1714 to the wealthy see of London. But if the admission of Robinson to civil office had been a recognition of such eminent political ability in ecclesiastical persons as Hooker believed might upon occasion be found, the intention of Bolingbroke to nominate Francis Atterbury to the same office of lord privy seal in his projected adminis-tration upon the fall of his rival was regarded even by his friends as a comedy of statecraft. The advancement of the bishop of Rochester was frustrated by the death of Anne, and its memory was preserved chiefly in the form of "the famous coach shewn in Drury Lane for a shilling to anyone, bound with purple velvet and trimmed with gold, that was designed for the new ecclesiastical privy seal".[1] Such appointments, whether actual or potential, were at that date an unusual exception rather than the rule, for the evocation of Robinson from his diocese to negotiate treaties was the last incident of its kind. Nor could even the eighteenth century furnish many instances of the reward of notable parts in a divine by such happy means as the bestowal of the office of usher of the exchequer upon Dean Francis Hare in 1722 by the influence of Walpole, with the intimation that "in case he should have a mind to execute it by a deputy he might have £800 or £1000 a year to himself".[2] The laity were sufficiently numerous and clamant to extrude their clerical brethren from the enjoyment of such sinecures.

The influence of churchmen upon affairs of state suffered a change of form rather than of substance by their exclusion from formal offices of civil administration, and their concern in matters of political strategy was no less potent because exercised indirectly. Traditionally the episcopate was closely attached to the sovereign as counsellors, and the eighteenth century witnessed an important development in the political situation and interest of the bench, which submitted in a manner characteristic of its own history and that of English institutions to the adoption of new forms correspondent with the changes consequent

[1] Portland MSS. vii, 203.
[2] H. Pelham to Dean Hare, 22 Sept. 1722. Hist. MSS. Comm. 14th Report, Appendix, Pt. ix, p. 234.

upon the Revolution settlement of 1689. The conditions upon which the crown was offered to and accepted by William and Mary, whilst leaving still a wide sphere of authority to the sovereign, had excluded the possibility of an absolute monarchy ruling without the counsel of parliament. The tendency thus expressed by the constitutional settlement was implemented by the long series of military campaigns which engaged the attention and ennobled the annals of William III and of Anne. In the debates in the house of lords on the Triennial Bill in 1692 Archbishop Sharp of York protested against the danger that "the king be obliged to hold parliaments every year, in time of peace as well as in time of war, whether he needs them or needs them not", and had expressed the pious hope that "a time may come when we can live a year without them".[1] In similar vein Burnet in the conclusion of his *History of His Own Time* echoed the hope that "when the wars were ended, parliaments would not give the necessary supplies from year to year, as in the time of war, but would settle methods for paying the public debt and for the support of the government for two, if not for three, years", since "the ill effects of an annual meeting of parliament were so visible and so great that he hoped nothing but invincible necessity would ever keep men under the continuance of so great an inconvenience".[2] But the parliament was loth to abandon the control of royal policy secured by the exigencies of war, and preferred the burden of annual sessions in time of peace to the surrender of the advantage gained thereby over the crown. A parallel tendency, working towards the same end of strengthening the power and position of parliament relative to the sovereign, underlay the rapid development of the organised parties of whig and tory. The leaders of these parties, in addition to their relationship to the crown as its nominated servants, were dependent in some measure upon the support of a majority in the houses of parliament, the members of which in turn realised the opportunities of power thus accorded to them. The corporate prestige of the parliament combined with the increased importance of its individual members to give to the eighteenth century a peculiar character in the development of the political institutions of the nation.

The episcopal bench was affected inevitably by the constitutional changes in the position of the parliament of which it formed an element. By tradition the bishops attended for the greater part of the year upon the residence of the court in London, fulfilling thereby their office as

---

[1] T. Sharp, *Life of Archbishop John Sharp*, i, 288, 293.

[2] Burnet, *History of His Own Time*, Conclusion: of Shorter Sessions of Parliament, vi, 215.

spiritual counsellors of the royal family, as Lancelot Andrewes had done in the golden age of Jacobean churchmanship. With the establishment of the custom of annual parliamentary sessions, extending over the winter half of the year, the attendance of the lords spiritual in the upper house became a duty of increasing importance, the more particularly in consequence of the rivalry of whig and tory parties in the state. The contest waged throughout the quarter of a century between the Revolution settlement and the Hanoverian succession by the leaders of the rival parties for the enjoyment of the royal favour and the control of royal policy involved necessarily the demand for the disposition of crown patronage in Church and State. Inevitably and imperceptibly the bench became divided by the same ties of party loyalty as the temporal lords and the faithful commons, and the prize of nomination to the archiepiscopal and episcopal sees was contended for eagerly by the chiefs of whig and tory ministries. Nor was there any element of inherent impropriety in the new situation of the episcopate as allies and champions of whig and tory principles in politics. The security of the Established Church was bound up vitally with the maintenance of the Revolution settlement and of its essential corollary the Protestant succession; and apart from this controlling factor in domestic politics from the expulsion of James II to the defeat of the Young Pretender in 1746, other problems, of the relations of the Church to the dissenters and of the high- and low-church parties within the establishment to each other, furnished grounds of difference of opinion which enrolled their respective defenders amongst the ranks of whig and tory parties in the nation. From the standpoint of the party leaders also the support of the clergy was as essential as that of country squires or merchants, and towards its confirmation the possession of the means of ecclesiastical preferment provided an invaluable agent. The conversion of the whigs, the traditional party of the dissenters, albeit involuntarily, into the position of defenders of the Church establishment as part of the Revolution settlement, testified to the importance of the clerical order in political matters.

The situation of the episcopate divided thus by the names and allegiance of whig and tory embraced an element of delicacy in relation to its position towards the crown. The protracted contest between the whig administration and Queen Anne in 1707 for the control of nominations to the bench illustrated the difficulties latent in the new development. For whereas the ministers of state insisted necessarily that the ecclesiastical patronage of the crown should not be employed to raise to the dignity of lords spiritual divines who would oppose the measures of their party in the house of lords, the sovereigns were faced with the problem of the maintenance of cordial and intimate relations with prelates whose tenure of their office, unlike that of their political associates, did not terminate with the fall of the ministry of their alliance. The sharpness of conflict alike between crown and ministers and between the monarch and the bench was averted generally by the circumstance that the rulers of eighteenth-century England were in fact, if not in name, themselves partisans of the rival factions, for Anne and George III were essentially tories, as George I and II were fundamentally whig. Notwithstanding, occasions of friction arose when the episcopal nominees of a party outlived the *régime* of their appointment, and Archbishop Secker in particular experienced much difficulty in his primatial station when the advisers of the new sovereign George III ostentatiously omitted to consult him in their recommendations for ecclesiastical preferment. "I go sometimes to court, but I am not wanted there", he confessed to his old ally Newcastle, in 1767: "No questions are asked me about the disposal of anything or the character of any person." [1] Not the least afflicting or anomalous consequence of the political character of the Hanoverian episcopate was the delicate situation of an archbishop in opposition, although Secker had striven to the utmost to avoid this difficulty by insisting to Newcastle that "it would be very inconvenient to the public that he should offend those with whom he must from time to time transact business of an ecclesiastical nature". [2]

In consequence of the increased authority of parliament, one of the most important duties of the Hanoverian prelate, according to contemporary estimation, was his attendance upon the sessions of the house of lords. In the eyes of the political administration, the fidelity of a bishop to his senatorial obligations was a matter of especial weight, and in expectation of a difficult session or upon warning of a series of crucial divisions, urgent monitions were despatched to the spiritual peers to attend in person if possible (for when the upper house was in committee proxies were not permitted), or if that were impossible, to place their proxies in the hands of such of their brethren as were of approved fidelity and parliamentary diligence. The possibilities of paying a personal attendance through the whole, or part, of a parliamentary session from November to May varied with the particular circumstances of individual bishops and of their dioceses. Prelates of the remote northern province, or of the more distant sees of the southern province, could

[1] Secker to Newcastle, 9 Nov. 1767. Add. MSS. 32986, f. 323.
[2] Same to Same, 26 May 1767. Add. MSS. 32982, f. 138.

not undertake easily the long journey to London, more especially in response to a summons in mid-session. For in addition to the constant difficulty of distance, other uncertain factors supervened, weather, health, and the condition of roads, to hinder the fulfilment of projected travel. Nor was the expense of journeying to and residing in the capital an item to be forgotten in determining the episcopal itinerary.

"I am very sensible that my attendance on the next session of parliament would be of some service to me," confided Nicolson of Carlisle to Wake in October 1717, when fifteen years in that border see had made a translation urgently to be desired; "but permit me, my lord, to make you my confessor. I have seven children; my two sons, by your grace's good help, are in a fair way of subsisting; the eldest of my five daughters is comfortably enough settled, but the other four expect, and deserve, far more than my circumstances will allow me to do for them. I have attended my duty in parliament for fifteen years as constantly as any of my brethren. I have not one senior on the bench (the Bishop of Peterborough only excepted) who has not been translated, and very few juniors who do not hold commendams. I live at the greatest distance, and, considering the forementioned charge, am the least able to continue the service."[1]

The bishop indeed estimated the cost of residence in London to attend the parliamentary session to be £100 per year; and in view of such accumulation of difficulties, it is little surprising that in the following autumn instead of saddling horse to ride to Westminster, he preferred to take ship with his household effects to enjoy a lucrative translation to the Irish see of Londonderry.

Even when resolution had led prelates to embark upon the road, the accidents of nature might interfere to frustrate their good purpose. In November 1722 Tyler of Llandaff, though he "set out in September when he thought the ways and the weather fair", realised that he "could not hold the journey and turned back" owing to ill-health;[2] whilst in January 1746 Maddox of Worcester, having delayed his setting out until the winter had begun, found the vale of Evesham so very bad that he must go round by the Chester road, which he would fain avoid unless parliamentary business were very pressing.[3] Few more convincing evidences of determination of will unhappily impeded by infirmity of body could be adduced than the letter, breathing assurance of political

[1] Nicolson to Wake, 21 Oct. 1717. Arch. W. Epist. 20, item cccxvi, f. 416.
[2] Tyler to Wake, 28 Nov. 1722. Arch. W. Epist. 22, item clxi, f. 238.
[3] Maddox to Hardwicke, Jan. 1746. Add. MSS. 35589, f. 166.

fidelity, addressed to Newcastle by Peploe of Chester in the autumn of 1739.

"Your grace knows my distance from London," he observed; "and I being in the seventy-second year of my life, cannot bear long and cold journeys as I have done formerly. But if there be any necessity for personal attendance, I will venture all, and be at the house in time, though I travel but ten miles in the day. If it may not be interpreted as a backwardness in me to serve my king and country, I could choose to appear by proxy, which I shall send to the bishop of Ely; and lest he should be unable, as he was last session, to attend, I can send another to any bishop your grace shall approve of, to be in readiness in case the bishop of Ely should happen to be kept from the house when my proxy may be of service."[1]

In such cases the delivery of a proxy was accepted by ministers, who understood better than modern critics of episcopal activity the difficulties of travel in an age lacking the invention of railways, motor transport, or even good roads, which evoked such a list of necessary absentees from parliamentary duty as that presented by Archbishop Potter in July 1746, when the important business of the trial of the rebel lords implicated in the recent Jacobite rebellion was to be transacted.[2]

The justification of an urgent ministerial summons to prelates to pay due attendance in the house of lords may be perceived from a consideration of the influence of the bench both in number and personnel in that chamber. In 1714, after the addition of sixteen Scottish peers by the Act of Union and of the tory creations necessary to carry the peace settlement of Utrecht, the upper parliamentary house comprised 213 members, a total which remained so steady until the accession to office of the younger Pitt that in 1780 it had risen only to 224. Of this average aggregate of 220 members, a very varying number were present at important divisions, but rarely did the attendance exceed 120 to 145 persons.[3] Accordingly the twenty-six archiepiscopal and episcopal votes represented a not inconsiderable proportion even of the numerical

[1] Peploe to Newcastle, 22 Oct. 1739. Add. MSS. 32692, f. 409.
[2] Potter to Newcastle, 26 July 1746. Add. MSS. 32707, f. 480. "1. The Bishop of Peterborough hath lately been very ill, and was scarce able to write. 2. Chester hath sent a certificate from his physician and apothecary that he is under a course of medicines for the stone, and not able to take a journey to London without hazard of his life. 3. Carlisle is four-score and last winter contracted such an illness during the rebellion as hath ever since adhered to him. 4. Ely is very infirm at Ely. 5. St David's is in his remote diocese, where he is wanted, and cannot return thither, the season being so far advanced."
[3] A. S. Turberville, *The House of Lords in the Eighteenth Century*, pp. 44–6.

strength of the house; and in contending for the control of royal nominations to the bench, the political ministers were seeking the manipulation of a solid phalanx of votes which constituted a prize of tangible and practical character. Indeed the personnel of the episcopate was alone open to direct alteration by the party leaders, and episcopal promotions, both translations and creations, afforded valuable occasions to any administration of increasing its hold upon the house of lords. During the protracted whig dominance under Walpole and the Pelhams the effect of a long series of episcopal appointments upon the position of the ministry in the upper house was fully displayed, and neither ministers nor their opponents were in danger of underrating the importance of such a ready means of influence. To Sir Robert Walpole there fell the most gratifying experience of the worth and solidity of episcopal support witnessed during the century, when by the suffrages of the lords spiritual he was delivered from defeat at a juncture in his career when a reverse in the chamber of peers would have shaken his position to the ground. In 1733, shortly after the success of the opposition in the commons in thwarting his favoured excise scheme, the dissentient peers resolved to challenge his majority in their house, with a view to the coming general election in the following year, by a resuscitation of the malodorous question of the South Sea Company. Upon the first division on 17 May, the government motion for an adjournment of the debate was defeated by thirty-five votes to thirty-one and the original proposal for an enquiry into the disposition of the money arising from the forfeited estates of the directors was carried without a division. Upon this occasion only seven bishops had voted, six for the administration, and one against; and during the interval of a week which elapsed before the renewal of the matter, desperate efforts were made to secure the position of the government, and "many lords were closeted, schooled, and tampered with, some by ministers, some by the king and more by the queen". Notwithstanding, on 24 May the opposition were confident of success, for during the debate itself "the court were overmatched in good speakers"; and upon a division the number of votes cast in person and by proxy were found to yield an exact equality of seventy-five on each side, so that the motion was lost according to the rules of the house. At this crisis the ministers had been saved solely by the steadiness of the bench, "for out of the 26, 25 were present or voted by proxy, of which 24 were for the court, and the Bishop of Lincoln [Reynolds] was left alone on the bench of bishops". Only Archbishop Wake, being ill, was absent without proxy. Once more, in the final repercussion of the subject on 2 June when the government defeated the assault by seventy-five votes to seventy, "the bishops to a man voted as they had done on the 24th of last month".[1]

The occurrence of so spectacular an episode provoked naturally the zeal of poetasters who enforced in better politics than verse its dual moral; by denouncing on the one hand the subservience of the bench to its paymaster, Walpole,

> His creatures they're 'tis plain to see
> by voting stiff that no South Sea
> inquiry should be made; for why?
> if they did once with that comply
> egregious faults they would descry.

and by fulminating on the other hand against the dangerous power of a prelacy raised to a situation of dictation towards Sir Robert by the evident warning of the incident to

> consider the Ch[ur]ch is your rock of defence
> your South Sea escape in your memory cherish,
> when sinking you cry'd, "Help, L[or]ds or I perish".

The unanimity with which twenty-four episcopal suffrages were cast for the government marked indeed the high-water mark of whig control of the bench, and as such needed no emphasis in its witness to the potential value of a wise distribution of ecclesiastical preferment. But in lesser degree throughout the century successive ministers relied upon the support of prelates of their elevation. Even in opposition during the lean years following the accession of George III, the duke of Newcastle enjoyed the gratification upon several occasions of the fidelity of those whom he denominated his "firm friends on the bench" in matters of purely political relevance. In 1763 upon the debate in the lords on the proposed excise on cider, which formed part of Dashwood's budget, the cider lords were joined in their opposition by the whigs, and in a division, although the motion to commit was carried by eighty-three votes to forty-four, nine bishops supported Newcastle in the minority, against eleven with the majority.[2] Still greater pleasure was accorded to the duke four years later when on 23 May 1767 the government majority in the upper chamber upon the subject of the

---

[1] A. S. Turberville, *op. cit.* pp. 202–6; N. Sykes, *Edmund Gibson*, pp. 146–8; Lord Hervey, *Memoirs of the Reign of George II*, i, 222–33; Carlisle MSS. 118–19; H.M.C. 15th Report, Appendix, Pt. VI.

[2] Newcastle Papers. Add. MSS. 32947, f. 339.

Massachusetts free pardon fell to six, the voting being sixty-two to fifty-six, and seven bishops were numbered with the minority. The comment of Horace Walpole, that such was "the consequence of the crown permitting great lords to nominate to bishopricks, the reverend fathers sometimes having at least gratitude, or farther expectations, if they have no patriotism", was sufficient evidence of the success of Newcastle's diligent canvassing and justification of his pleasure in the result.[1] Encouraged by this division the opposition continued to harass the administration in relation to the affairs of the East India Company, but the government carried the day on 3 July 1767 by the comfortable majority of fifty-nine to forty-four, thirteen bishops voting, six with the majority and seven with the opposition, "a thing that does not often happen in divisions where the court is concerned", as his lordship of Ely commented to Newcastle.[2]

It would appear indeed that a wide gulf separated the twenty-four votes given to the whig administration in office in 1733, and the handful of seven or nine episcopal supporters upon which the duke could rely in opposition thirty years' later; but in his grace's opinion "nine such bishops joining with disgraced ministers was a new circumstance in the country and did them great honour".[3] The expectation of support from the bishops of his creation entertained by Newcastle was shared by other ministers of different political complexion, though for the establishment of a weighty and numerous following on the bench a protracted period of office was necessary. The series of short administrations which characterised the reign of George III before the succession to power of Lord North was evidently unfavourable to the creation of a strong episcopal interest, and two of the bishops nominated during the ministry of Grafton, Shipley of St Asaph and Hinchcliffe of Peterborough, distinguished themselves as opponents of the royal policy in the American War. But apart from such exceptions "the bishops during the ascendancy of Lord North were usually as staunch in their support of the government as their predecessors had been in the days of Newcastle".[4] Upon one point ministers and opposition, whig and tory, agreed, namely in their recognition of the value of the control of ecclesiastical preferment and of the influence of the bench in the house of lords. An incidental illustration of the latter fact was

---

[1] H. Walpole, *Memoirs of the Reign of George III*, iii, 45–6; A. S. Turberville, *op. cit.* p. 335.

[2] Bp. of Ely to Newcastle, 3 July 1767. Add. MSS. 32983, f. 39.

[3] Newcastle to Rockingham, 5 Feb. 1768. Add. MSS. 32988, f. 188.

[4] A. S. Turberville, *op. cit.* p. 426.

accorded by the action of the upper chamber on 9 June 1767 in adjourning its consideration of the East India Company affairs until Wednesday of the week following, 17 June, in deference to the convenience of the episcopate.

For the duke of Bedford, with his usual sincerity and frankness, owned that the reason he hoped the house would adjourn to the Wednesday, and not to the Monday or Tuesday, which was much contended for, was that as Trinity Sunday was the general Ordination day, it would be difficult for the bishops to return to parliament before Wednesday, and his grace wished to have all the bishops. This reason prevailed so strongly with the house that Wednesday was immediately ordered.[1]

The result was that seventeen prelates were present, though the opposition were not saved from defeat by their attendance, in a division which left them in a minority of fifty-two to seventy-three.

The relations of the duke of Newcastle with his episcopal friends during the period in which his grace was in opposition to the policy of the administration of George III revealed the delicate situation of the bench in its political allegiance and the difficulty of maintaining cordial correspondence both with the sovereign and the fallen statesman. The position was aggravated indeed by the personal affronts heaped upon the duke by the vengeful attitude of his rivals in encompassing his dismissal even from the most insignificant of his offices. Upon this ground his grace was justified in appealing to his clerical allies to protest against the ungenerosity of private malice, and it was natural that he should denounce their reluctance to quarrel with the new monarch and his advisers. "Can Christian bishops, made and promoted to the highest stations in the Church by me, see such repeated acts of cruelty, uncharitableness and revenge to one who has been their benefactor, and sit still without publicly declaring against and resenting such measures."[2] His reproach was levelled particularly against Archbishop Drummond of York—"whom I *singly* carried from the duke of Leeds' house to be archbishop of York"—who had ventured the incautious dictum that "he regarded things and not persons".[3] But the issue was neither so simple nor so private as the duke would have pretended. Expressions of personal sympathy were not sufficient in his mind, but should be implemented by public protest in parliament and at court. Yet the personal conduct of prelates in parliament could not be divorced

[1] Newcastle to Bp. of Worcester, 9 June 1767. Add. MSS. 32982, f. 266.
[2] Newcastle to Hardwicke, 5 Jan. 1763. Add. MSS. 32946, f. 68.
[3] Newcastle to Devonshire, 16 Nov. 1762. Add. MSS. 32945, f. 53.

from their attitude to matters of public policy then impending, such as the important question of peace or war.

"The present state of public affairs is far from being in that situation that every true friend to his king and country must wish it," his grace wrote himself to Archbishop Secker. "The uncertainty of peace or war, the conditions of that peace, or the nature of the war, if it is to be continued, are far from being known or agreed. In these circumstances therefore it is the duty of every member of parliament in either house to attend, and give his assistance in promoting what may appear to him to be most for the honour and permanent interests of this country. I therefore submit it to your grace whether you would think proper to let such bishops as you may meet and can talk to in confidence, know that their attendance in parliament the beginning of this session would be particularly proper in the present circumstances of the kingdom and the doubtful state of peace or war."[1]

The prime offence of Drummond of York in the mind of Newcastle was his announcement of his intention to retire to Yorkshire for a twelvemonth until the political situation had cleared sufficiently to enable him to form a considered judgment as to the proper course to pursue.

This expedient represented no mere desire for avoidance of personal controversy, but a real necessity for pondering the problem of episcopal conduct in parliamentary matters. For if contemporary standards made difficult the position of a political minister in opposition, still weightier arguments could be adduced against the participation of the bench in a "formed opposition" to the king's administration and the policy of his servants.[2] Nor was the situation eased by the blunder of Newcastle in the debate in the lords on 29 November 1765 upon Wilkes and No. 45 of the *North Briton*, when his grace after defending the secretaries' warrant and voting against concurrence with the commons' resolutions, saw the greater part of his episcopal allies carried into the number of the majority by the speech of Lord Mansfield.[3] The archbishop of York indeed had given him a fortnight's warning of the unwisdom of the attempt to cast the mantle of the whig opposition over the indiscretions of Wilkes, in a letter declaring his unflinching hostility to any such

---

[1] Newcastle to Abp. Secker, 16 Oct. 1762. Add. MSS. 32943, f. 242.

[2] For the constitutional situation see L. B. Namier, *England in the Age of the American Revolution*, Book 1, Government and Parliament under the Duke of Newcastle: I. Prolegomena to 1760.

[3] A. S. Turberville, *op. cit.* p. 318.

action and expounding incidentally that primate's conception of the limits of an opposition.

I can very shortly give my opinion, that in this infamous affair of Mr Wilkes, I will never concur in obstructing or parrying the blow which he so justly deserved. I neither think it for the honour of any person, nor the good of the cause of the whigs to espouse such a man and put yourselves so totally in the wrong in the eyes of all the world. I would wish to look up always to the support of the king's person and family, and the essentials of the constitution. I can never approve the system that seems to me to be established at present, and began by driving from the king's countenance the best persons that have supported his family upon Revolution principles. But in my endeavours to alter that system, or to undeceive my sovereign, I would neither make a random or ineffectual opposition, nor vindicate points or persons which would disgrace the integrity of my intentions.

In accordance with these principles he wished to restrict opposition in the upper house to acts definitely unconstitutional.

If anything anti-constitutional occurs, let it not go unnoticed. But to oppose at all times does not seem to me to answer to that credit and dignity which I wish the whigs to maintain in the opinion of the world. This is my general opinion, and the same which I have always embraced; and I desire to be understood so, that nothing different from this may be expected from me.[1]

From this standpoint Drummond's abstention from parliamentary attendance was alike intelligible and justifiable, and demonstrated the delicacy of the episcopal situation.

Despite this warning, and the previous debate in the lords on 15 November upon Wilkes' blasphemous poems *An Essay on Woman* and a parody of the *Veni Creator*, which had discredited the writer and his defenders, Newcastle was deeply chagrined by the votes of the bishops on 29 November, and reproached the bishop of Norwich with his own desertion in leaving the house before the division, and that of his brethren who had voted with the majority. Against Bishop Yonge of all members of the bench such rebuke was unfair, for as chief of the Cambridge bishops his support had been unvarying to his patron in a myriad circumstances. He replied accordingly in an apologia, reluctantly written, but the more valuable as expressing, with greater weight than that of Drummond because of his long and faithful service, the limits of private gratitude when opposed to public obligation. On the morrow of the episode he had written to assure the duke that his

[1] Abp. Drummond to Newcastle, 16 Nov. 1763. Add. MSS. 32952, f. 370.

abstention "was wholly owing to the most full conviction of conscience, and not to the least particle of disrespect for his grace";[1] but this assurance being insufficient, he embarked upon a fuller statement of his reasons.

I said to your grace the next morning that I had slept well after that division, and that I never should have slept well again, had I staid in my place under so full a conviction. I have not altered my mind, nor can I, upon the most serious recollection of what passed that day, judge otherwise than that the question was a question strictly referring itself to conscience. I may indeed have a bad head and so be mistaken; but by the grace of God, I will not have a bad heart. Had your grace's resentment at that time rose higher than it did (and I thank your grace that it did not) my resolution was then made and determined; and nothing which your grace could have said or done, would have driven me into the arms of others, or prevented my taking that part which I shall think dutiful to my king and country, agreeable to you, and honourable to myself.

I hate tyranny, and will oppose tyrannical ministers. If I hate anything in a higher degree, it is ingratitude. And I hope your grace knows it. Yet I shall be very sorry to see those times when private gratitude shall be the *only* guide of publick conduct. It is a principle which seems to me teeming with the worst of consequences, and inconsistent with that religion, honour, and invariable love of liberty which have always actuated your grace's breast; and it is a principle which I am far, very far from supposing to be entertained by your grace...In public conduct questions of friendship and attachment, of prudence and of mere policy, are, I think, easily distinguishable from those which call upon every man to think for himself, and to consult his own heart.[2]

Servility in political action could not be imputed to Yonge, albeit one of the closest of Newcastle's dependants; and the duke was well advised to accept this apologia, though retaining his persuasion that any means was lawful which might unsettle the position of ministers whose course was "to govern, oppress, and at last, as would be found, to ruin this country".

The circumstances of the Peace of Paris proved disastrous to another episcopal friendship, that of Warburton and Pitt, for the bishop of Gloucester, moved to indignation by the attack of Wilkes on George III in No. 45 of the *North Briton*, promoted the presentation of a loyal address from the clergy of his diocese, written by his own hand. In

[1] Bp. of Norwich to Newcastle, 30 Nov. 1763. Add. MSS. 32953, f. 129.
[2] Same to Same, 22 Dec. 1763. Add. MSS. 32954, f. 152.

the course of this innocent expression of loyalty his lordship ventured to declare the thanks of his brethren for the restoration of peace, an action which gave umbrage to his patron, Pitt, who had disavowed its conditions as dishonourable. Many of Warburton's colleagues, like Yonge of Norwich, were "astonished beyond measure" at the address, being unable to conjecture "what inducements he could have, from principle or connection, to such a piece of singularity".[1] To the offended statesman, his episcopal *protégé* offered the defence that the clergy

did not venture, as it was a matter foreign to their profession, even to hint their sentiments on the political question of an adequate or inadequate peace. They confined their thanks to his majesty for procuring them peace, as the greatest blessing in the estimation of ministers of the Gospel, war and bloodshed being the opprobrium of Christianity.[2]

The Great Commoner was by no means appeased by such lukewarm gratitude, but replied curtly that

the high station and still higher consideration which his lordship so deservedly held in the world, together with the peculiar delicacy of the subject, must draw upon himself the charge of temerity, if he presumed to exercise his own judgment on the propriety of that step. He would only venture to observe, that it was singular, insomuch that the cathedral of Gloucester, which certainly did not stand alone in true duty and wise zeal towards his majesty, had however the fate not to be imitated by any other episcopal see in the kingdom in that unaccustomed effusion of fervent gratulations on the peace.[3]

The consequence of the incident was the rupture of intercourse between the statesman and the prelate, and Warburton was left to reflect upon the narrow path which constituted the way of political rectitude betwixt the claims of patriotism, conscience, and private obligation. "Singularity in civil matters wears a more ambiguous aspect than it does in religious," he commented; "because in the first we should for peace sake generally go with the many, in the latter we are obliged for truth's sake as generally to go with the few."[4]

In addition to the service of a silent vote, ministers of state desired their brethren of the bench upon occasion to render the more redoubtable assistance of speech in the house of lords, though while all could respond to the summons for vote or proxy, the maintenance of

---

[1] Bp. of Norwich to Newcastle, 11 July 1763. Add. MSS. 32949, f. 322.
[2] Warburton to Pitt, 4 Sept. 1763. *Chatham Correspondence*, ii, 253.
[3] Pitt to Warburton, 10 Sept. 1763. *Ibid.* p. 256.
[4] Warburton to Pitt, 14 Sept. 1763. *Ibid.* p. 257.

a worthy part in debate was reserved for prelates of oratorical gifts and fervent sentiment. Lord Shelburne expatiated indeed with contempt to Chatham upon the general silence of the episcopate, "the bishops waking, as your lordship knows, just before they vote, and staring in finding something the matter".[1] Individual members however were prominent in debate, Burnet speaking frequently and exhaustively, Hoadly considerably, Sherlock and Secker effectively, whilst Hinchcliffe and Watson emphasised their singularity of opinion by interventions generally unacceptable to the administration of the day. In view of the usual reticence of the bench, individuals possessing the gift of tongues received a welcome hearing, and George III in nominating Beilby Porteus to the see of Chester in 1776 paid an unwilling compliment to the abilities of Hinchcliffe by expressing his hope that Porteus "would be an ample match in any debate in the house of lords in answering the Bishop of Peterborough".[2] The extreme of silence was preserved by Newton of Bristol, who "never attempted to speak in parliament, for he, as well as most other bishops, entered into the house of lords at a time of life too late to begin such exercises", a difficulty ascribed to the suppression of the convocation, which, "while it was allowed to sit, was a kind of school of oratory for the clergy".[3] Upon the elevation of Warburton to the episcopate rumour pretended to see a second Atterbury in his lordship, but in point of fact his intervention was infrequent. He defended his abstention on the ground that "haranguing is a trade, like other trades, and generally the bishops came to the bench so advanced in years as to be too old to learn".[4] In the discussion of measures of an ecclesiastical character, affecting directly the interest of the Church or indirectly as in projects for the repeal of the Test and Corporation Acts, the bishops spoke fully and freely; but upon matters of purely political import their general record was one of abstention.

The service of vote and voice did not exhaust the possibilities of political action open to the bench and to divines aspiring to its eminence. There remained another field of argument in which clergy were equally expert with the laity and to which increasing attention was devoted by the eighteenth century. Not the least remarkable characteristic of the Georgian episcopate was its apprenticeship and participation in the

---

[1] Shelburne to Chatham, 27 Feb. 1774. *Chatham Correspondence*, iv, 328.
[2] George III to North, 13 Dec. 1776. *Correspondence of George III* (ed. J. Fortescue), iii, 407, No. 1939.
[3] *Life of Dr Thomas Newton*, by himself, in *Lives of E. Pocock, Z. Pearce, T. Newton, and P. Skelton* (2 vols.), ii, 186.
[4] A. W. Evans, *Warburton and the Warburtonians*, p. 240.

vogue of pamphleteering. The potentialities of the pamphlet as a means of public education in statecraft were realised and fulfilled by the genius of Dean Swift, than whom no age has witnessed a more skilful writer. In the brilliantly destructive criticism of *The Barrier Treaty* and the satirical version of *The Conduct of the Allies*, the mysteries of foreign policy were revealed before the forum of public opinion. The mordancy of Swift's satire indeed overshot his mark and deprived him of the coveted rewards of service; for the natural stolidity of Queen Anne's unimaginative mind disenabled her to perceive beneath the sallies of the political partisan the authentic lineaments of the divine, and refused the dignity of a mitre, even in Ireland or the Plantations. To the palate adjusted to the graces of Swift's style, the laboured productions of imitators might seem tedious indeed, but in an age avid of political controversy they were useful and even convincing propaganda; and the lesser breed of scribblers succeeded in the object of their ambition largely because of their inferior talents. Assuredly there was no lack of clerical pamphleteers, of varying degrees of literary and ecclesiastical eminence, once the writing of a scrub defence of some item of domestic or foreign policy of an administration had been recognised as an agency to preferment or pension. Among the superior order were numbered many divines who attained to the episcopate. Francis Hare, chaplain to the duke of Marlborough during the campaigns of the Spanish Succession War, entered the lists in defence of his noble patron against the venom of Swift, and wrote an apologia for whig policy in regard to the Netherlands, the perusal of which during the War of the Austrian Succession convinced the duke of Newcastle of the wisdom of Great Britain's concern to preserve the independence of the Dutch. Benjamin Hoadly after his elevation to the bench contributed under the pseudonym of *Britannicus* a series of articles to *The London Journal* in justification of the foreign policy of Walpole after 1723; whilst Gibson of Lincoln published in 1721 a small tract in extenuation of the precautions taken by the administration to prevent the outbreak in England of a plague raging at Marseilles, which provoked the comment of his enemies that "this is a very mean work that he submits to for his hopes of London", to which see he was translated in 1723.

The vogue of pamphleteering prevailed amongst tory no less than whig divines, though the clerical adherents of the former party bore the heat and burden of the day without expectation of that speedy reward which attended the ventures of supporters of the faction in office. Of the disproportion between services rendered and rewards received by the tory clergy the career of Dr John Douglas furnished abundant if melancholy evidence. Attracted into the household of William Pulteney, earl of Bath, in 1748, his pen was devoted to the championship of the cause of the opposition to the whig *régime*; particularly by the publication in 1759 of a *Letter to Two Great Men on the Approach of Peace*, "which was written in the name of lord Bath who adopted it as his own", and in 1761 of *Seasonable Hints from an Honest Man on the Present Crisis of a new Reign and a new Parliament*, "written by him to represent lord Bath's sentiments", in which he voiced the impatience of the tory exiles to see the dismissal from the royal service of their whig rivals.[1] The latter tract called openly for a declaration of the new king's resolve not "to content himself with the shadow of royalty, while a set of undertakers for his business intercepted his immediate communication with his people and made use of the legal prerogatives of their master to establish the illegal claims of a factious oligarchy". The returns made for such stout doctrine were a canonry of Windsor in 1762, tardily exchanged for a residentiaryship of St Paul's in 1776 by favour of Lord North, in whose support Douglas had written a series of papers in the *Public Advertiser* in 1770–1 under the pseudonyms of *Tacitus* and *Manlius*; but not until 1787 did the fruit of a bishopric come, after the service of a generation in political controversy. The critical years of Lord North's administration and of the American War of Independence afforded many opportunities for clerical politicians, and John Butler, having published under the pseudonym of *Vindex* a series of pamphlets in support of the ministerial policy, was brought upon the bench at the express desire of North in 1777 as bishop of Oxford.[2] The tradition of episcopal pamphleteering had established itself so well by 1782 that Lord Shelburne in nominating Richard Watson to the see of Llandaff "expressed to the duke of Grafton his expectation that Watson would occasionally write a pamphlet for their administration", in recompense and loyalty to the party of his advancement. The fortunes of the new prelate indeed illustrated aptly the uncertainty of such a means of recommendation to the bench, for his promotion was due to Shelburne's opinion "that he was a warm, and might become a useful, partisan".

"I had opposed the supporters of the American war," testified Watson, "because I thought that war not only to be inexpedient but unjust. But all this was done from my own sense of things, and without the least view of pleasing a party. I did however happen to please a party and they made me

---

[1] *Autobiography of Bishop Douglas*, p. 23. B.M. Eg. 2181.
[2] J. Fortescue, *Correspondence of George III*, iii, 438, Nos. 1984–5.

a bishop. I have hitherto followed, and shall continue to follow, my own judgment in all public transactions; all parties now understand this, and it is probable that I may continue to be Bishop of Llandaff as long as I live."[1]

The alliance between the episcopate and ministers of state and the consequent political pressure upon the bench were powerfully reinforced by the circumstance of the wide disparity in revenue of the several ecclesiastical sees. According to a valuation of the church preferments in the gift of the crown drawn up for George III during the early years of his reign, the primatial sees of Canterbury and York possessed revenues of £7000 and £4500 respectively, followed by the rich bishoprics of London with £4000, Durham with £6000, Winchester with £5000, Ely with £3400, and Salisbury and Worcester with £3000. In the intermediate stage were several sees, such as Chichester, Exeter, Lincoln, Hereford, and Lichfield, with between £1400 and £1000 per annum, whilst at the foot of the scale stood Bristol with £450, Oxford with £500, Rochester with £600, and Llandaff with £550.[2] The contrast between these small bishoprics and those heading the list of episcopal promotions was indeed overwhelming. Yet the expenses of the occupants of the poorer sees were little less than those of their wealthier brethren, since upon the shoulders of all there fell the costs of residence in London during the parliamentary session and of the ministration of hospitality in their dioceses when resident therein. Among sees in England the penury of Bristol became proverbial. When in 1734 Thomas Secker was nominated to that diocese, he explained to Viscount Percival the necessity he lay under of retaining his prebend of Durham and the rectory of St James', Westminster *in commendam*, "the revenue of Bristol being no more than £360 a year, out of which he was to pay £27 a year tenths and maintain a steward, so that the true profits were but £300 a year, and there was £900 to be paid in first-fruits".[3] A quarter of a century later Thomas Newton, on accepting that same bishopric, found that its certain income was little more than £300, which he improved to £400 by a judicious management of its rents and leases.[4] Without some provision of benefices to be held *in commendam* it would have been impossible to induce divines of ability and position to accept the onerous obligations of the episcopal office, the discharge of which would have spelt simple bankruptcy in the case of the "little bishopricks".

[1] R. Watson, *Anecdotes of the Life of*, i, 153–4.
[2] J. Fortescue, *Correspondence of George III*, i, 33–44, No. 26.
[3] *Diary of Viscount Percival*, 25 Dec. 1734. Egmont MSS. ii, 137, H.M.C.
[4] *Life of Dr Thomas Newton*, in *op. cit.* ii, 200–1.

Upon occasion indeed it was difficult to persuade clergy of repute to come upon the bench, especially when their elevation involved the resignation of valuable preferments, as Newton's surrender of a prebend of Westminster, the precentorship of York, and the lectureship of St George's Hanover Square for the embarrassing parsimony of Bristol. In 1699, upon the vacancy of the see of Oxford by the translation of Hough to Lichfield and Coventry, William Wake, then chaplain to archbishop Tenison, canon of Christ Church, and rector of St James', Westminster, strove hard to avert the intended offer of that dignity to himself.

"I have done what I could to prevent it," he confided to Dr Charlett, Master of University College, "but should my lord of Canterbury insist upon it, ... the construction I must make of it, is that he wants to get rid of me and that I am to be kicked upstairs for the convenience of another person for whom he has a great kindness.... If I would alter my condition, Oxford is the bishopric of all England I should least desire to fix upon. To say nothing of the revenue, which is but mean, other reasons there are enough to make a man unwilling to come to it, and I have too much approved the bishop's desire and grounds of leaving it to be ever easy in coming myself to it. In short 'tis a post fit only for a Dean of Christ Church or President of Magdalen."[1]

Accordingly Wake did decline the offer of nomination when made to him; and in like manner, three-quarters of a century later, in 1775 John Moore, dean of Canterbury and prebendary of the fifth stall at Durham, who was destined afterwards to succeed to the primacy in 1783, intimated to his kinsman, Sir William Eden, first Lord Auckland, his reluctance to entertain the prospect of a poor bishopric which would involve him in pecuniary difficulties.

If my turn comes next, which now seems likely, I must depend greatly on you to take care they don't strip me and send me to a bishopric that won't find me clothes. It ought to be, I suppose, my deanery and a small bishopric; or Durham and a middling one; or if both preferments are to be given up, a pretty good one. The last is not likely to happen, and my wish is to keep my deanery. But lord North must understand that I will not be a bishop without he contrives that I may live with some degree of comfort. I mean without such income as may enable me to support my station.[2]

In such circumstances the provision of *commendams* was a plain necessity, and the practice by which the deanery of Westminster was

---

[1] Ballard MSS. iii, f. 17.
[2] Moore to Eden, n.d. Add. MSS. 34412, f. 281.

attached to the see of Rochester, or that of St Paul's to the see of Bristol, or the deanery of Christ Church to the bishopric of Oxford, was an attempt to ease the situation of the prelates, especially when as at Bristol and Oxford the deaneries of the cathedral churches were of superior emolument to the bishoprics. But even the bestowal of such *pourboires* was an uncertain and impermanent expedient to meet the pressing necessities of the moment, and the desire of occupants of the "little bishopricks" was for translation to a rich see which would maintain the dignity of their station without the burden of *commendams*.

Herein lay the most powerful motive for the party loyalty of the junior members of the bench and the strongest weapon of discipline possessed by the political ministers towards the bishops of their creation. The inevitable result of the wide inequalities in episcopal revenues was the continued dependence of the poorer prelates upon their political allies and the temptation to surrender their independence of judgment and action to the urgent need of translation. The ministers of state established the custom of advancing ambitious divines of their allegiance by preferment first to a little see, their tenure of which was of long or short duration according to the character of their public conduct and the approved consistency of their political fidelity. The aptest illustration of the fulsome reward accorded to party services was seen in the rapid progress of Hoadly through a series of episcopal promotions from Bangor to Hereford in 1721, thence to Sarum in 1723, and finally to Winchester in 1734; but though few prelates passed through four sees during their public career, the bestowal of lucrative translations bore a marked correspondence with political action. Robert Hay Drummond, one of Newcastle's clerical *protégés*, was elevated to the episcopate in 1748 at St Asaph, translated to Sarum in June 1761, and thence in the October following to York, having volunteered during his brief and nominal tenure of Sarum to accept a further removal to London *en attendant* a vacancy at York, if this would assist the ministerial shuffling of episcopal personnel! Next to the authority of nomination to the episcopate, the control of translations was probably the most valued weapon in the armoury of party leaders, and a failure to secure a further preferment beyond the initial step which brought a divine upon the bench was accounted clear evidence of lapse from the expected rectitude of political conduct. The protracted tenure by Secker of the poor sees of Bristol and Oxford, which he held for sixteen years without other *commendam* than the onerous parish of St James', Westminster, was the deliberate punishment for an early display of parliamentary independence. On 1 March 1738–9, after the debate in the lords on the

Convention of El Pardo, he together with Benson of Gloucester (known as "the two brothers") and the bishops of Lincoln and Lichfield had voted against the government; and again on 28 January 1741, in that difficult session of Walpole's administration, Benson and himself had voted with the "formed opposition" in their house in favour of the appointment of a Secret Committee to enquire into the conduct of the war, especially in relation to the alleged insufficiency of reinforcements to Admiral Vernon's expedition to the West Indies. For the enormity of his joining with a "formed opposition" the court could not forgive him;[1] and when in 1750 Herring and Hardwicke approached George II to ask that Secker might have the deanery of St Paul's *in commendam* with his poor bishopric, they brought the assurance that "he had long since declared himself entirely convinced of the mischievous tendency of formed oppositions, and had expressed his resolution in the rightest manner on that subject".[2] The king therefore was persuaded after so long an interval to pardon the indiscretion and provide an easier *commendam* than St James' parish.

"When I told him", related the duke of Newcastle concerning his interview on the subject with George II, "how the bishop of Oxford had renounced opposition, the king answered: 'I know: Benson has. He has acted like a gentleman, and I know has declared it to the opposition themselves. He has told lord Limerick that he would never be for a secret committee again as long as he lived'."[3]

It was particularly remarkable that the only occasions during the century of a long episcopate at Llandaff were the result of the disfavour at court of William Beaw, bishop from 1679 to 1706, and of the stubborn political independence of Richard Watson, left to rusticate in that obscure station from 1782 to 1819. The contrast between the rapid translation of Jonathan Shipley from Llandaff, to which he was consecrated in February 1769, to St Asaph in the July following, and his long continuance there till his death in 1788 was explained likewise by royal and ministerial disapproval of his opposition to the policy of the crown in relation to the rebellion of the American colonists.

The literal penury of the "little bishoprics", combined with the association of translation with political loyalty, provided a potent spur to the juniors of the bench in regard to their parliamentary attendance,

[1] Parliamentary History (Notes from Secker MSS.), XI. 1015; Hare MSS. p. 224 (H.M.C. 14th Report Appendix, Pt. IX). For evidence of court opinion of "formed oppositions" see L. B. Namier, *op. cit.* pp. 55–8.
[2] Hardwicke to Newcastle, 20 July 1750. Add. MSS. 32721, f. 418.
[3] Newcastle to H. Pelham, 23 Aug./3 Sept. 1750. Add. MSS. 32722, f. 223.

no less than an inducement to rectitude of party conduct. Only by these means could they establish impeccably their claim to further preferment, and in general the painful discipline of repeated failure to recognise their merit by translation was necessary to provoke the retaliation of continued absence from the sessions of parliament. Richard Watson's retirement from London to his house at Windermere was justly interpreted as the abandonment of hopes of preferment, and his reply to the reproach of friends who lamented his dereliction of duty confirmed the contemporary estimate that ministerial neglect implied disapprobation of the political conduct of a bishop.

"To you, my friend, I will say, that my church-preferment will not afford a journey to London every year," he wrote in 1803, "and I do not feel myself bound by any principle of prudence, of honour, or of duty, to waste my little private fortune, which by incessant exertions of my own and the kindness of my friends I have provided for my children, in the public service. For eighteen years I attended parliament; my children during that period wanted education; that want being over, I gave up three years ago my house in Town with a determination that till I was better provided for, I would not go to London excepting every other year."[1]

The belief that translation followed party allegiance contributed not a little to the difficulties of the situation of Newcastle's bishops when their patron was dismissed from office by George III, and influenced their desire to withdraw to their dioceses and abstain from parliamentary duty, since their political conduct in the house of lords must expose them either to the rebuke of the duke by supporting the court, or to the hostility of the sovereign by voting with the opposition, which latter course would extinguish hopes of further promotion. The retirement to Yorkshire of Archbishop Drummond, who had been a notable debater during the *régime* of Newcastle, upon the supersession of the whigs by George III was a testimony at once to the strength of his disapprobation of the new men and their measures and to his sense of the delicacy of his parliamentary position, whilst the vigorous attempts of Newcastle to dissuade other bishops from following his example illustrated the importance attached by contemporary opinion to the parliamentary attendance of the episcopate.

The manipulation of episcopal translations thus delineated brought inevitably upon the bench charges of servility and time-serving towards their political allies. These accusations were an easy handle of attack upon which the party oppositions were not slow to seize, and demands

[1] R. Watson, *Anecdotes*, ii, 165–6.

5

for the abolition of so potent and corrupt an engine of influence were part of the accepted stock-in-trade of critics of the whig administrations. Upon occasion the righteous zeal of soi-disant friends of the Church found expression in formal attempts to prohibit the offending practice, and in 1731 the house of commons debated a motion for permission to introduce a bill to prevent the translation of bishops. The promoters of the measure alleged edifying reasons for their desire; arguing from the scriptural injunction that

a bishop should be the husband of one wife, meaning that he should stick to one bishopric; and this bill would oblige him to be chaste and give his wife due benevolence, that is reside in his diocese; whereas the bishops are now universally guilty of spiritual adultery, looking after other men's wives, that is their bishoprics.

Other motives indeed were ranged in ancillary subordination to zeal for the incorruptibility of the prelacy, for the movers observed that the whig ministries had so abused their power in this regard as to bring the bench "all together to advance any proposition that had a court air", and to unite them "in all measures that were destructive to their country".[1] Most of the political opposition might be discounted as the conventional polemic of the party out of office, whose true concern was not for the elimination of means of influence, but their transference from whig to tory hands. Notwithstanding, it may be remembered that so conservative a reformer as Gibson of London had wished for legislation to decree "that no bishop should be allowed more than one translation, nor that till he had continued full seven years in his first bishopric"; and that amongst his list of "things fit to be done for the church", he embraced the items "poorer bishoprics to be augmented by assignments out of the rich ones" and "a more equal division of dioceses".[2] Half a century later Richard Watson, a dauntless episcopal reformer, complained of the spectacle of "the generality of the bishops bartering their independence and the dignity of their order for the chance of a translation, and polluting gospel-humility by the pride of prelacy". Accordingly he urged upon Lord Rockingham "that the rendering the bishops independent in the house of lords by taking away translations would be a measure exceedingly useful in a political light, and this might be done without injuring any individual by annexing as the sees became vacant part of the property of the rich bishoprics to the poorer ones so as to bring the whole as near as possible

[1] *Diary of Viscount Percival*, 4 March 1730/1. Egmont MSS. i, 153.
[2] N. Sykes, *Edmund Gibson*, pp. 214–15.

to equality". To Lord Shelburne also, upon that minister's intimating a desire to consult Watson upon ecclesiastical matters, he adumbrated a similar scheme of reform by the introduction of "a bill to render the bishoprics more equal to each other both with respect to income and patronage, by annexing as the richer bishoprics became vacant a part of their revenues and their patronage to the poorer". From such a project he hoped for good results; "for the two great inducements to wish for translations, and consequently to reside in London, namely superiority of income and excellency of patronage, would in a great measure be removed".[1] It was hardly to be expected that ministers of state would be so indifferent to the possibilities of influence latent in the weapon of translation as to accept such advice; and neither whig nor tory showed any desire to sponsor such a radical programme of change.

The social and political interest of the bench was not confined to the activity of its members in parliament and at court, but extended to their influence in the dioceses of their jurisdiction. No estimate of the position of the bishop of Hanoverian England would be adequate which failed to take account of the authority which he exercised in his diocese, where he occupied the station of a territorial magnate, enjoying a considerable estate and temporal dignity, no less than the responsibility of an ecclesiastical administration. Amidst the many examples of declension from the pattern of primitive episcopacy laid to the charge of the Georgian prelacy, it may afford some consolation to observe its fidelity to the apostolic precept that a bishop should be given to hospitality. Tradition indeed counted it a prime duty of the bishop when resident on his see to maintain a magnificent hospitality towards both laity and clergy of his jurisdiction. Archbishop Sharp, though by nature averse from the distraction caused by the presence of a multitude of company, schooled himself to excel in this branch of episcopal responsibility at Bishopthorpe.

Nor did he refuse to converse with any who were admitted to him with great cheerfulness and condescension; in large and mixed companies he had something to say to everybody....His conversation was contrived and adapted for the entertainment of all that heard him; and it may be added for their edification too; because he frequently and as often as decently he could, introduced into his discourse serious and religious topics, and such things as might make his company either wiser or better....Yet there was no topic so trifling and so much out of his own way but that he would pleasantly enter into it for the sake of making himself agreeable to such as were addicted to

[1] R. Watson, *op. cit.* i, 116, 145, 156–8.

that sort of conversation and pleased with it. A noted fox-hunter in Yorkshire that dined with him, was surprised at his entertaining him so suitably with a discourse about horses, and said after he came away, that surely the archbishop had been reading the *Gentleman's Jockey*.[1]

Archbishop Herring during his primacy at York likewise paid a round of visits "upon the catholic scheme" to the nobility and gentry of Yorkshire and Nottinghamshire, visiting such notable houses as Castle Howard, Temple Newsam, Thoresby, and Worksop, and receiving from his hosts pleasing tokens of their respect in the form of such presents as that sent to Bishopthorpe by his grace of Norfolk of "a three-dozen hamper of very fine claret, champagne, and burgundy". The archbishop indeed found such convivialities more exhausting than the ecclesiastical oversight of his large diocese. "I had much rather confirm three thousand people after a visitation", he confessed to Hardwicke, "than bear the fatigue of the chat and bottle among forty or fifty strangers"; though he accepted this duty as necessary to the "knowing many of the gentry, and people of note in the great towns".[2] The see of York was fortunate in its succession of primates, for Drummond who ruled from 1761 to 1776 was enabled by his private fortune to maintain the most magnificent traditions of episcopal entertainment and by his territorial connections with the county to establish the most cordial relations with its chief laity.

The main burden of hospitality fell of necessity upon the archbishops of Canterbury, who maintained open table at the houses of their residence at Lambeth or Croydon, attended personally to receive guests on their public days and made provision of doles for the beggars at their gates. Of the entertainment at Lambeth during the primacy of Secker, a friend of Beilby Porteus (then chaplain in the household) drew a typical picture.

The society of the archbishop is usually made up of the domestic chaplains and the resident and visiting clergy; and in no place in the world is the reception more hospitable, and according to clerical decorum more magnificent than in the archiepiscopal palace. The greater part of the year there are public days in every week, upon which whatever clergyman chooses to present himself is hospitably entertained. To say all in a word, everything at Lambeth usually bears that air of hospitable magnificence which becomes the wealth and dignity of a British archbishop.[3]

[1] *Life of Sharp*, ii, 51.
[2] Abp. Herring to Hardwicke, 1 July 1743. Add. MSS. 35598, f. 20.
[3] *Life of Bishop Beilby Porteus*, by a Lay Member of Merton College, p. 173 (London, 1810).

Archbishop Tillotson after his elevation to the primacy understood the purport of Nehemiah's recital amongst the meritorious services which he had rendered to his people of the entertainment at his table of "an hundred and fifty of the Jews and rulers, beside those that came unto them from the heathen that were round about them", and the huge provision daily of one ox, six choice sheep, and fowls.[1] For he found that in the archiepiscopal hospitality

besides the bounty and sometimes charity of a great table...there may be exercised two very considerable virtues: one is temperance and the other self-denial, in a man's being contented for the sake of the public to deny himself so much as to sit down every day to a feast and to eat continually in a crowd, and almost never to be alone, especially when, as often happens, a great part of the company that a man must have is the company that a man would not have.[2]

The dread of the expense and further demands of such entertainment was a powerful motive in Herring's desire to decline translation to Canterbury, since he feared the possibility that he might die in debt; whilst Cornwallis earned much commendation for his discharge of this duty, since "his board upon public days was in general as noble as his own moderation in the enjoyment of it was exemplary. The courtesy with which he received those who had occasion to approach him was not the affected politeness of a court; it was the courtesy of religion and morality".[3] The city of Canterbury felt itself aggrieved that the ruinous condition of the palace there should deprive it of the dignity and profit of archiepiscopal entertainment;[4] and to compensate in some measure for this lack of habitable residence, it became customary for one of the archbishop's relatives to receive from the king nomination to some dignity in the cathedral, so that his grace might have a roof whereunder to receive guests upon his visits. Archbishop Secker laid before the duke of Newcastle in 1761 the precedents for his request that a prebend of that church might be conferred upon his nephew.

I have no house or lodging of my own in or near Canterbury, and yet am expected to entertain so much company in a very expensive manner when I am there. For these reasons, I presume, it hath been usual for the crown

[1] Nehemiah v. 17–19.
[2] T. Birch, *Life of John Tillotson*, pp. 259–60.
[3] A. W. Rowden, *The Primates of the Four Georges*, p. 344.
[4] Cf. the poetic lament of the City:
   "I scarcely know my Masters but by name,
   Triennial visits and the voice of fame,
   For ah! my palaces in ruins lie".

to indulge the archbishop with leave to recommend to a vacant place in the church. Archbishop Wake obtained the deanery for his son-in-law, and Archbishop Potter a prebend for his son.[1]

Accordingly George Secker was preferred on 21 April 1761 to the eighth prebend of that cathedral, and his uncle enabled thereby to administer seemly hospitality in his see-city.

The hospitality characteristic of Canterbury and York was imitated in due measure by the suffragans of their provinces, who held their public days in course when resident in their dioceses. Burnet indeed avowed that "it was one of the great burdens of his life to see so much time lost, to hear so much idle talk, and to be living in a luxurious waste of that which might have been much better bestowed"; and advocated therefore that "the pomp of living and the keeping of high tables be quite taken away", since it was "a great charge and no very decent one, and a great devourer of time". But he confessed significantly that he himself "had not strength enough to break through that which custom had imposed on those provided with plentiful bishoprics".[2] So strait a compliance with the custom was expected of bishops that surprise and criticism were evoked in England by the report that Bishop Robinson at Utrecht, despite his dual dignity as prelate and pleni-potentiary, "kept no open table, nor was it understood that any were to dine with him but such as were particularly invited";[3] whilst it was accounted a sign of the penury of the see of Bristol that there was a custom there "for the neighbouring gentry to let the bishop be as retired as possible", since without expensive entertainment his revenues were insufficient for the maintenance of his *ménage* of "nineteen very habitable bedrooms for himself, friends, and servants, besides offices".[4]

The exact point at which social intercourse with friends passed into the cultivation of political interest with the leading whig or tory magnates of the diocese was perhaps difficult of definition, but the obligation of the bishop to confer in a serious manner with the nobility and gentry of his particular persuasion, with a view to advancing the influence of their party, was unquestioned. The political authority of the episcopate was exercised no less powerfully in the country than in the house of lords itself. Upon the translation of Bishop Johnson from

[1] Abp. Secker to Newcastle, 31 March 1761. Add. MSS. 32921, f. 236. Dr Lynch (Wake's son-in-law) was dean of Canterbury 1734–60; John Potter, prebendary of the 12th prebend 1745–67, and dean 1766–70.

[2] Burnet, *op. cit.* vi, 185.

[3] Gibson to Nicolson, 18 April 1712. Add. MSS. A. 269, f. 9, Bodley.

[4] Bp. Yonge to Newcastle, 12 July 1759. Add. MSS. 32893, f. 16.

Gloucester to Worcester in 1759, the duke of Newcastle was at pains, in view of former suspicions of the bishop's political allegiance, to assure the earl of Coventry and through him the other whig lords of the county, of his protégé's fidelity to their party and of his readiness to co-operate in its cause. His grace promised on behalf of the new bishop that "if it should be thought proper, he was sure he would be ready to acquaint anybody of the other side that his grace had laid an injunction upon him before he had the bishopric" not to assist any persons opposed to the whigs.[1] An amusing illustration of the strict rectitude of public behaviour expected of prelates in this regard was furnished by the request made to Archbishop Wake in 1720 by Trelawny of Winchester, before paying a visit to his old friends in Devon and Cornwall, that "to prevent jealousies and unjust reflections, if his grace heard that he visited some known or suspected tories, he would not fear their converting him, but believe he was endeavouring to convert them!"[2] During their residence in their dioceses and especially in the course of their triennial visitations, the episcopate found opportunities of testing the political sentiments of the country, and of reporting to the ministers of state any alarming signs of discontent. In the spring of 1718 Bishop Hough of Worcester, lately translated from Lichfield and Coventry, reported to Wake that

in the diocese he had left and even in that where he now was, the disaffection of the people to the royal family appeared greater than ever, and their declarations were more open; what ground they had for their confidence time must shew, but they were certainly big with an expectation they could not conceal of some enterprise that was almost ripe for execution, and, as they flattered themselves, not likely to miscarry.[3]

During the same period of acute difficulty for the whig administration arising from financial crises and Jacobite intrigues, Archbishop Dawes of York reported from the north an "angry spirit which had gone out amongst them and had taken possession of all sorts of good people", urging upon the ministers measures of healing lest "by what he saw there, in one of the most dutiful parts of his majesty's dominions, they might be in danger of being involved in very great and lasting troubles".[4] On the other hand it fell to the lot of succeeding primates of York to reassure the government in later times of crisis of the prevalence in their jurisdiction of cordial sentiments of loyalty towards the Hanoverian

[1] Newcastle to Coventry, 3 Oct. 1759. Add. MSS. 32896, f. 246.
[2] Trelawny to Wake, 9 Sept. 1720. Arch. W. Epist. 21, item cclxiii, f. 373.
[3] Hough to Wake, 28 May 1718. Arch. W. Epist. 20, item ccclxvi, f. 486.
[4] Dawes to Wake, 19 April 1721. Arch. W. Epist. 22, item xii, f. 14.

dynasty and its public servants. In 1744, upon the eve of the second Jacobite rebellion, Herring informed Newcastle of his pleasure "to find it the general sense of the king's friends in that great county that his majesty's and the public affairs could not be in better hands than Pelham and the duke of Newcastle, an opinion he was extremely zealous to cultivate";[1] and in 1750, after the conclusion of the Peace of Aachen and the end of the Austrian Succession War, Hutton likewise reported that his itinerary in Yorkshire convinced him that "everything was well. The gentlemen seemed to be in great harmony with one another, and the flourishing state of the woollen trade would, he hoped, make all sensible of the wisdom and care of his majesty's measures for the wealth and prosperity of the public".[2]

Upon occasion during the first half of the eighteenth century the sees of the northern province had need of prelates whose militancy could be exercised in civil no less than ecclesiastical warfare, and who would not scruple in time of national peril to cast off the cassock for the regimental coat. In the border diocese of Carlisle in 1702 the memory of troubles with Scottish neighbours was sufficiently recent to inspire the conviction that "considering upon what terms we were with Scotland, it seemed to be very necessary at that juncture to place some person of wisdom, interest, and authority upon that frontier, who might have a constant eye upon the counsels of the borders, and power enough within his diocese to assist in an opposition if incursions should be made".[3] The nomination in that year of Archdeacon William Nicolson, a native of the diocese, to the bishopric was well calculated to supply this need, for he proved as militant as watchful in that outpost of English dominion. During the preliminary negotiations of the Act of Union with Scotland in 1707 he was consulted informally by the commissioners, and sent reports to his friends in London of the attitude of local opinion towards the project. Even with the stilling of border feuds which followed the act, the need of vigilance was not ended, for in 1715 the Jacobite rebels passed into England by the western route, consisting mainly of Scottish clansmen who had rallied to the Old Pretender's standard. Nicolson on this occasion did what he could, by the issue of a letter to his clergy exhorting them to loyalty and active resistance, and by his personal presence at the skirmish between the insurgents and the *posse comitatus* above Penrith, being "an eye-witness of the posse's flight and the rebels' marching into Penrith". His situation at Rose Castle, in expectation

---

[1] Herring to Newcastle, 23 Sept. 1744. Add. MSS. 32703, f. 319.
[2] Hutton to Newcastle, 11 July 1750. Add. MSS. 32721, f. 303.
[3] Gibson to Charlett, 8 April 1702. Ballard MSS. vi, f. 40.

of the fulfilment of Mar's threat to plunder his beef and mutton to feed the invading host, involved the possibility of danger no less than discomfort; yet, as he observed humorously to Wake, the bishop, unlike lay peers, having "but one house, must be forced to abide in that whatever perils surround him".[1] After the collapse of the insurrection, Nicolson was absorbed in a variety of business relating to the confinement of the rebel prisoners in Carlisle and the conduct of their trial by a special judicial commission, in which he rendered divers useful services to the administration in his locality.

Second only to Carlisle as a strategic episcopal centre was Chester, surrounded by a county traditionally Jacobite in sentiment and containing many papists, and like the border diocese also, twice harassed by the progress of the Jacobite rebels through its regions in 1715 and 1745. This see needed a prelate of approved whig and Hanoverian politics, albeit during the reign of Anne it was occupied by a triumvirate of tories, Stratford, Dawes, and Gastrell. In 1725 therefore, upon Gastrell's death, Gibson, as ecclesiastical adviser of the administration, resolved to place there an unequivocal whig.

"The diocese of Chester", he insisted to Townshend, "is full of papists, and the late bishop has given great strength to the tories' interest there, especially among the clergy; which will require a person not only of zeal for his majesty's service, but also of experience and authority, such as may awe the clergy and preserve the bishop from errors of administration among a people who will not fail to improve upon and expose them if any be committed."[2]

After a severe contest, he carried his candidate, Samuel Peploe, Warden of the Collegiate Church of Manchester, already a figure obnoxious to the tories as the victor in a suit which established the legal validity of Lambeth degrees as a qualification for office, who strove hard to discharge the duty laid upon him by his elevation. Some small measure of success attended his zeal, for in 1739 he related to Newcastle that

"he had of late secured a majority in the chapter in favour of the whig interest, by which the opposite party were much displeased. The clergy of the honest side of the question," he added, "increased in the city, which was a great eyesore, they having eight or nine of that sort in the quire and in the town; and not one, excepting the then dean, that he could depend on when he was first concerned at Chester".

[1] Nicolson to Wake, n.d. Arch. W. Epist. 20, item clxv, f. 241.
[2] N. Sykes, *Edmund Gibson*, pp. 124–6.

Notwithstanding this partial victory, progress was slow; and the strength of the opposition was shown by the visit in the previous August of the lord-lieutenant of Cheshire, Lord Cholmondley, to the city of Chester, when not one single person connected with the government of the city appeared to receive him. The bishop therefore still found himself "in a place which did not encourage persons of his inclination", nor would it do so until the apparently distant time when the influence of Mr Watkin Williams was removed by his being unseated as knight of the shire for Denbigh.[1] A last ebullition of Jacobite sentiment was evinced in 1745 when the Collegiate Church of Manchester received with the utmost fervour of enthusiasm the attendance at divine service of the rebel host; but at the age of seventy-eight Peploe was too infirm to make a personal appearance against the insurgents, though after the suppression of the rising he wrote several letters to the ministers demanding the infliction of condign punishment at Manchester, "where some particular persons were as insolent as ever in their behaviour towards the friends of the government".[2]

In Chester also the anti-whig majority in the corporation intruded into the cathedral foundation as bedesmen certain of their creatures who, in the estimation of the dean, were "neither well-behaved nor well-affected towards the present happy establishment". The purpose of this strategy was revealed by the circumstances that the persons intruded "were all voters in the city or freemen, and their annuity from the church gave them voices in the county elections, and in the late contest they all resolutely opposed the king's friends". Their presence further introduced an element of disharmony into the cathedral body, "since there was hardly a man in that church then, the bedesmen excepted, who would ever refuse to vote as the dean and prebendaries directed him".[3] In view of these conditions, the demand of Archbishop Herring of York in 1747 that a stout whig should succeed when Peploe should vacate the see was couched in no less vigorous terms than the insistence of Gibson in 1725.

"Give me leave to suggest my lord", he observed to Hardwicke, "that when the old bishop drops, it will be of great moment to the state to fill up that see well. It should not be a bishop of the women's making, or an election, or a family bishop; but a good scholar, a good Christian, and a stout Protestant; of strong spirits and constitution, who knows how to fix his post and how to maintain it. Such a man might do good and make a

[1] Bp. Peploe to Newcastle, 7 Nov. 1739. Add. MSS. 32692, f. 448.
[2] Same to Same, 14 July 1745. Add. MSS. 32707, f. 411.
[3] Dean of Chester to Newcastle, 10 Oct. 1747. Add. MSS. 32713, f. 234.

lasting impression on that Jacobite and Popish county. I speak the plainer on this point, as it is an affair within my province, and for which I am in some sort accountable".[1]

Before the venerable Peploe dropped at the ripe age of eighty-five, Herring had been translated to Canterbury, but in 1752 the see was filled by the nomination of the Master of Peterhouse, Edmund Keene, who had distinguished himself as vice-chancellor at Cambridge by carrying a series of new orders and regulations for the better discipline of the university, and whose skill as an academic governor had marked him out for the task of subduing the unruly fellows of the Manchester Collegiate Church and the Jacobite citizens of the counties of Chester and Lancaster.

The experiences of Archbishop Herring himself during the Jacobite rebellion of 1745 demonstrated the practical relevance of his demand that prelates of the northern province should be capable of temporal no less than spiritual militancy. During the alarums raised by the incursion of the Young Pretender, Herring emulated the examples of his medieval predecessors, Thurstan, Greenfield, or Melton; and from his friend Hardwicke, his conduct evoked a recollection of the description in Shakespeare's *Henry IV* that

> the gentle Archbishop of York is up
> with well-appointed powers; he is a man
> who with a double surety binds his followers:

albeit Herring's influence was happily cast in support of the reigning king against the endeavours of a pretender.[2] The extensive correspondence between the primate of York and the lord chancellor during the course of the episode illustrated the variety of Herring's exertions no less than his zeal for the preservation of the religion and liberties of the kingdom.[3] So early as 31 August 1745, only twelve days after the planting of the Pretender's standard at Glenfinnan, Hardwicke counselled his grace to remember that "archbishops of York had before then drawn the secular as well as the spiritual sword, and he hoped his grace would stand between them and danger"; and from that date to the retreat of the rebels into Scotland again, the two friends continued in regular communication. Herring arranged a private meeting with the chief temporal aristocracy of Yorkshire to consider the position,

---

[1] Herring to Hardwicke, 29 Aug. 1747. Add. MSS. 35598, f. 277.
[2] *Second Part of Henry IV*, Act 1, Scene 1, l. 189.
[3] The Correspondence is printed in the *English Historical Review*, 1904, xix, 528–50, 719–42, by Dr R. Garnett.

and it was agreed to call a general meeting of the gentry and clergy at York at which the formation of a loyal association for the defence of the dynasty might be proposed. If that were carried unanimously, the next step was the raising of money by which volunteers might be equipped with arms and provided with food during the time of their service against the rebels. On 21 September the insurgents' victory at Prestonpans emphasised the reality and urgency of the danger and assisted materially the archbishop's endeavours to arouse the patriotism of the north. On 22 September he preached in York Minster a sermon couched in the strongest terms of loyalty and zeal, copies of which were duly printed and dispersed, and two days later he addressed the meeting of persons of quality of the shire to such effect that before separating they not only formed a loyal association but also pledged themselves to raise the sum of £40,000 for the equipment of troops. "The spirit of the country is prodigious", he reported to the chancellor, "and we are all in motion from one corner to the other."

The towns were of equal ardour with the nobility of the countryside, and Ripon in particular, where the archbishops of York had a temporal estate, offered a voluntary donation of nearly £400. With such ubiquitous activity on the part of the primate, it seemed eminently desirable to the ministers in London that he should in no wise leave York for attendance upon the parliamentary session, since "his presence in Yorkshire would be of infinitely greater service that it could be at Westminster". Similar sentiments were entertained in York itself, where Herring's martial ardour was believed to have so inspiring an effect that he rode with General Oglethorpe upon the Knavesmire to review the troops. Accordingly, since the county subscriptions amounted "to more than £40,000 and the forces to 4000 horse and foot", the archbishop's chief efforts were directed towards stimulating the administration to rise to the occasion by sending adequate supplies of arms to equip the volunteers in view of the increasing menace of the rebels' advance in Scotland. To Herring and his countrymen indeed the over-confidence of the capital appeared astounding, when the question debated at Bishopthorpe was whether the insurgents would march into South Britain by the west or east coast route; and when the primate, convinced of the impossibility of an effective resistance, had counselled the magistrates of York to open the gates to the rebels without hesitation.

"As to my own safety for the present," he observed to Hardwicke on 22 November, "I will stay till the last moment, and if any scheme of defence of any likelihood can be formed, I will share in the common danger. If not,

I know of no duty that obliges me to run the hazard of being knocked on the head, or taken prisoner. I stand ready to escape at half an hour's warning, and shall endeavour to do so. This upon supposition that these ruffians take the York road. If they take the other, I am determined to fix my abode and wait the fate of, and as I may, serve my country here."

Thus far the northern counties had been the chief scene of activities, though, with the resolve of the invaders to follow the western route through Lancashire, the situation in Yorkshire changed instantly and pleasantly. "Our apprehensions here are gone," the archbishop wrote only two days later, "and for aught I know York may for the ensuing month be one of the quietest towns in England which, after a few sleepless nights, will be a great consolation." Henceforth his grace needed only to fix his abode at Bishopthorpe and become a quiescent spectator of events in the midlands. His immediate interest was revived when the rebel host was in retreat to Scotland, but their condition on that march inspired no dread in Yorkshire. The accident of their choice of route into England had prevented Herring from the uncertain hazard of appearing in arms actually to engage in military conflict, but his conduct and presence had been none the less valuable and important to the dynasty. In a time of crisis an archbishop of York could still, as he reflected, "with a little self-conceit fancy himself a kind of Lord President of the North", even in the middle of the eighteenth century. Only two generations indeed divided the incidents of 1745 from the battle of Sedgmoor at which Bishop Mews of Winchester had commanded the royal artillery train, and from the episode of 1689 in which Compton of London had ridden forth in martial garb. But, although Herring's resolve to exchange his cassock for a regimental coat and his pastoral staff for a musket was the last occasion on which a primate prepared to lead military activities, the circumstances of his influential action may serve as a timely reminder that during the first half of the Hanoverian century vital issues concerning the religious and civil liberties of the kingdom were still at stake, and that the defence of the Revolution settlement and the Protestant succession was a cause requiring active aid no less than tacit sympathy.

The political service usually required of Georgian prelates was not that of the sword but of the persuasion and influence of their authority at parliamentary elections. The expectation of their assistance in forwarding the interest of their party in the election of members of parliament for constituencies situated within their territorial jurisdiction was a corollary of their political character in the house of lords, and in this respect the party chiefs accounted the bench amongst their most valuable allies. In an age when political education was imparted mainly through the pulpit, the ecclesiastical organisation of which the bishop was head together with his widespread influence with the clergy of his diocese furnished the most practicable means of party organisation then available throughout the country. Accordingly, few political ministers faced the fortunes of a general election without previous consultation and negotiation with their episcopal friends, nor were the majority of the episcopate unwilling to become partners in the enterprise. Even Archbishop Sharp of York, whose rule not to meddle in parliamentary elections caused him in 1695 and 1698 to refuse to "appear as a party in the election of city members" at York and in 1702 not to take any part in assisting the candidature of Lord Hartington for the county, found it impossible to make practice conform wholly to principle. At Ripon in virtue of his temporal jurisdiction "he made no scruple to recommend such candidates as he approved of", establishing as a member his eldest son, John Sharp, who thereby held "an interest that preserved him in parliament so long as the archbishop lived". Further, his grace's vaunted neutrality was not personal but only official in York itself. "He was not always wary enough to carry the matter so equally between the contesting candidates as never to discover his own inclination as to the issue of the dispute.... But what is meant by his adherence to this rule, is that he never interested himself by requests or by his agents or by his letters."[1]

Such a degree of abstention was unusual amongst bishops of the eighteenth century, who in general accepted the responsibility of participation in parliamentary elections. During the heated contests of the reign of Anne two prelates fell under the displeasure of the house of commons for their zeal in local elections. In 1702 Lloyd of Worcester incurred the censure of that house for his canvass of his clergy against Sir John Packington, knight of that shire, and the queen was requested to dismiss him from the office of Almoner, which her majesty did despite a protest of the lords;[2] and in 1710 the conduct of Nicolson of Carlisle likewise provoked the formal censure of the lower house. Few more striking illustrations of the close relation of political and ecclesiastical questions could be adduced than the combined parliamentary and proctorial elections in the south-western counties in 1705, the issue of which set two divines, Wake and Blackburne, upon the road to archiepiscopal eminence.[3] From Exeter also in the less turbulent

---

[1] *Life of Sharp*, i, 122–32.   [2] Parliamentary History, vi, 50–8.
[3] N. Sykes, "The Cathedral Chapter of Exeter and the General Election of 1705", *E.H.R.* April 1930, xlv. 260–72.

Hanoverian days there came in 1747 the generous offer of Dean Holmes to Newcastle of a valuable quota of suffrages, tendered in gratitude for his grace's promotion to a situation which in fact "entitled him to twelve votes in four different counties, which should be most faithfully employed in promoting the honour and peace of his majesty's good government".[1] That the most conscientious bishops had no scruple in exerting their influence in support of party causes in elections was demonstrated by the endeavours of Wake during his episcopate at Lincoln, especially in relation to the candidature of Lord Edward Russell for the county of Bedford. In 1707 the duke of Bedford having approached his lordship concerning the intended attempt of his son at the next general election, the bishop in turn sounded his archdeacon of Bedford on the sentiments of the clergy. Mr Archdeacon Frank replied expressing his apprehension of the clergy "coming off with scratched faces" from interference in politics, explaining his own practice generally "to vote on both sides or in effect to sit still", but promising notwithstanding to serve Lord Edward "if he would accept of what he could do without noise".[2] In response to further pressure from his diocesan, Mr Frank entered more cordially into the projected measures.

"I have the honour of yours of the 23rd inst. in relation to the election for knights of this county to serve in the ensuing parliament," he replied on 29th December 1707. "Your lordship may assuredly believe that I do most heartily concur with your measures in securing the interest of both church and state, as believing them the wisest and most proper to preserve and continue our most happy establishment. Your lordship will believe me also whilst I declare that I think it my own interest so to do, since I may thereby also have the honour and satisfaction of obliging two such great and good men as the duke of Bedford and my lord chamberlain. Their lordships need not doubt of my sincere endeavours; . . . and if they will be pleased to dispense with me as to the means, I do sincerely promise that I will fully pursue the end. What determined the last election in favour of Sir Pyncent Chernocke was the multitude of single votes; and if that game can be prevented now, my lord must in all probability obtain in this. On this principle I have already, I think, secured a great part of my own parish for lord Edward who before voted singly for Sir Pyncent, and shall make it my endeavour to confirm them. To take them off wholly is impossible, Sir Pyncent being a justice of the peace, living in the next parish, and having an estate in this. The like method I shall observe with such of my friends amongst the clergy

[1] Dean Holmes to the duke of Newcastle, 5 May 1747. Add. MSS. 32711, f. 13.
[2] Archdeacon T. Frank to Bp. Wake, 22 Dec. 1707. Arch. W. Epist. 1, Lincoln, f. cxxx.

as I can trust, so far as I can do it without noise and public controversy; and I do verily think that I shall be hereby enabled to serve lord Edward more effectually than if I made a public work of it."[1]

The bishop continued to exhort his archdeacon to zeal in the matter, and further correspondence passed between them concerning the practical organisation of victory, so that on 19 May 1708 Lord Edward Russell and Sir William Gastwick were elected for the county of Bedford to the exclusion of Chernocke. Even more remarkable was the success attending the archidiaconal efforts in the following election of 1710, when the tories generally swept away the triumphs of their whig rivals but in Bedfordshire the representation remained unchanged.

"On Thursday last," reported the archdeacon to his diocesan on 6 October 1710, "the election was made for the county of Bedford, and Mr Harvey lost it by only 39 voices. I pursued your lordship's commands to Mr Leith, who notwithstanding voted singly for Mr Harvey, as did about twenty more of my brethren in a body, headed by Mr Dean of Gloucester. But notwithstanding this show, which was over before I got to Bedford, by the best information I can get, near 40 of our brethren voted for my lord or Sir William or both; which must be a terrible mortification to Mr St John who sometime ago, by way of advertisement in the *Post Boy*, told the world with equal truth and modesty that 'Mr Harvey would offer himself for the service of his county at the request of the whole body of the clergy of Bedfordshire'....Some men have a strange knack of fibbing for the truth."[2]

The example of Wake in the diocese of Lincoln was paralleled by the action of Herring at York in 1747, when his interest was exerted to secure the return of at least one whig member instead of the two tories previously elected for the city; who, upon applying for his grace's countenance were informed that, although "speaking personally he had nothing to do with elections, whatever influence his authority could be supposed to carry with it, in a sort of secret operation, that would be directed to the service of his majesty and the present administration".[3] The archbishop indeed deemed it prudent not to appear in York in person on behalf of any candidate (preferring as he observed humorously

---

[1] Archdeacon Frank to Bp. Wake, 29 Dec. 1707. Arch. W. Epist. 1, Lincoln, f. cxxxi.
[2] Same to Same, 6 Oct. 1710. *Ibid.* f. cclv. Mr Leith was rector of St Catherine and St Paul, Bedford, and prebendary of Bedford Minor in Lincoln Cathedral. The dean of Gloucester, Dr Knightly Chetwood, had a temporal estate at Tampsford in Bedfordshire.
[3] Herring to Hardwicke, 15 April 1747. Add. MSS. 35598, f. 238.

"to trundle his bowls" at Bishopthorpe), but employed his influence indirectly, though with such effect as to provoke a complaint from one of the tory aspirants of the activity of his grace's secretary in canvassing the clergy against him.[1] In the issue Herring entirely approved the compromise by which one whig and one tory were returned without contest, contending that "all things considered that was a great point gained, and though not complete, was an improvable victory".[2] Nor had he been inactive in other parts of his vast diocese: writing to the clergy at Hull on behalf of Sir William Milner for that city, giving his "assurances" to Lord Robert Sutton and Mr John Thornagh, the successful candidates for Nottinghamshire, ordering his agent at South-well "to attend and countenance" the whig meeting at Mansfield, and authorising his son Dr William Herring to communicate his desires to the archdeacon of Nottingham and the clergy of that jurisdiction.[3] The loyalty in elections expected of prelates by their party allies was illustrated at Canterbury in 1761, when, despite the waning fortunes of the duke of Newcastle, one of the opposition candidates for that city called upon Archbishop Secker, not indeed to ask his vote, "which he appeared sensible ought to be given to the other side", but to request his grace to assure the duke that if successful "he would not enter into opposition or put himself on a party footing, but concur with the administration in everything as far as he honestly could".[4]

The election which illustrated the church-whig alliance of the eighteenth century in its most cordial relations was staged appropriately in Sussex, where Newcastle's interest was especially concerned, and where in 1734 a determined assault was planned upon the whig party in the favourable year following the defeat of the excise project in the house of commons. The intriguing character of that contest, as revealed in the correspondence between the duke and his henchmen, captured the imagination of Professor Basil Williams more than a generation ago;[5] but its details are worthy of renewed attention from the standpoint of the ecclesiastical participators. The political canvassers were not indeed exclusively clerical, but the commerce in the campaign of the clergy of the cathedral church at Chichester was astonishingly intimate and extensive. Four candidates offering themselves for election for the

[1] Herring to Hardwicke, 22 June 1747. Add. MSS. 35598, f. 252.
[2] Same to Same, 27 June 1747. *Ibid.* f. 258.
[3] Same to Same, 17 and 20 June 1747. *Ibid.* ff. 246, 250.
[4] Secker to Newcastle, 16 March 1761. Add. MSS. 32920, f. 253.
[5] B. Williams, "The Duke of Newcastle and the Election of 1734", *E.H.R.* 1897, xii, 448–523, to which this Summary is much indebted.

county, Henry Pelham and James Butler the sitting members, and their challengers, Sir Charles Bishop and John Fuller, the contest was stimulating; and "in estimating the resources employed by the duke in his campaign hardly too much weight can be attached to the influence of the clergy".

Although the strategy was directed by Newcastle with the active co-operation of the bishop of Chichester, attention may be directed first towards the parts played by the inferior clergy of the diocese. Foremost was Mr Thomas Ball, vicar of Boxgrove and Eartham and a residentiary of the cathedral, who assured his grace not only that "he could not give up or oppose the whig interest in Sussex (of which he took his grace and his family to be the main supports)", but that he had engaged already, six months before the time of the elections, "a tolerable posse of freeholders" in his parishes to vote for the sitting members. His efforts, nourished by a hospitable visit to Bishopstone, did not falter; and in reward he was preferred to the archdeaconry of Chichester in 1736, offered the deanery of that church in 1741, which he declined in the hope of the more lucrative one of Worcester, but which he accepted in 1754 after the disappointment of his other ambition. Next in the cohort of canvassers came Mr James Barker, archdeacon of Chichester, prebendary of Rugmere in St Paul's Cathedral, vicar of Cocking and rector of Nuthurst, who risked a rough handling at Steyning races in order to support the Pelham interest there, and in addition visited the freeholders of his own parish and that of his father, being allowed by the duke a discretionary commission in regard to the treating of doubtful voters. Other diocesan clergy whose services were enlisted were Prebendary John Penfold, Prebendary James Hargreaves, rector of East Hoathly, rector of St Margaret's, Westminster, prebendary of Chichester and of Westminster, whose zeal was rewarded by the deanery of Chichester in 1739; and Prebendary George Jordan, vicar of Burwash and of Heathfield, who made a bonfire and entertainment at Burwash on the king's birthday with the hope of bringing many votes in return for a "pretty large" expenditure. The activities of these several canvassers were directed by Dr Thomas Hurdis, domestic chaplain and secretary to his grace of Newcastle, who as virtual election agent of the whig cause was ubiquitous and indefatigable in his efforts. At the Steyning races, at the cricket match at Lewes, again at the races at Bourne and Brighthelmstone, no less than in the visitation of his father's parish of Ringmer, he laboured continuously to secure the promise of votes; and when the death of his father in October 1733 vacated the vicarage of Ringmer, of which the archbishop of Canterbury was patron, no endeavour was omitted to procure the appointment of a successor equally zealous on the whig behalf. Hurdis indeed was the faithful servant of the duke alike in temporal and spiritual affairs throughout his parliamentary adventures, and though his utility was so great as to delay long the expected preferment commensurate with his services, in due course he received a prebend of York in 1750, of Chichester in 1755, and a canonry of Windsor in 1766, all which he held until his death in 1784.[1]

Behind the intervention of the lesser clergy, the greater ecclesiastical dignitaries of the church of Chichester and without stood in equal readiness to lend their aid in the stirring contest. Sir Thomas Gooch, Master of Gonville and Caius College, Cambridge, and residentiary of Chichester, assured Newcastle that "he had already, and would again declare his firm resolution of supporting Mr Pelham and Mr Butler's interest at the next election", adding that "he had lived to see and observe many oppositions to the ministry but he never yet knew an opposition put on so pitiful a foot".[2] He consented to use his influence with Mr John Parke, the single tory of the chapter at Chichester, but counselled that Bishop Sherlock of Bangor also should be approached in that regard; and accordingly his lordship, who before his nomination to that see in 1727 had been dean of Chichester from 1715, likewise was drawn into the fray. Bishop Gibson of London, a former residentiary of the cathedral, allowed Mr Ball to use his name in canvassing a voter at Midhurst, and Dr John Newey, the dean, "spoke and sent to all persons whom he could hope to have any influence on". Even Archbishop Wake, in assuring Newcastle of the political fidelity of the new vicar of Ringmer, offered his help in laying his commands upon any clergy presented by him to the archiepiscopal peculiars in Sussex of whose attitude the duke might be uncertain. One of these protégés, Mr William Clark, rector of Buxted and prebendary of Chichester, so exerted himself that he could report that "Buxted would be an entire parish" for the whigs, fulfilling therein the primate's monition upon his presentation to the rectory that "he might make the duke of Newcastle his friend by voting for him as occasion should serve", to which the grateful clerk had replied succinctly, "Ay, sure".[3] There remained

[1] A mural tablet in the cloister of Chichester Cathedral testifies that "the solemn discharge of his ministerial office reflected dignity on his sacred function and in the respective connections of private life displayed each social and moral virtue in its native lustre". Cf. Add. MSS. 32969, f. 431.

[2] Gooch to Newcastle, 6 Sept. 1733. Add. MSS. 32688, f. 281.

[3] Dr W. Wootton to Abp. Wake, 16 July 1724. Arch. W. Epist. 22, item ccxciv, f. 444.

finally the interest of the diocesan, Francis Hare, whose declaration of his support left nothing to be desired.

"What little influence I have", he informed Newcastle, "will always be invariably employed to support the interest your grace is engaged in. The gentlemen of the opposition want not to be informed what side I am of.... I am in all views and upon all counts entirely in the interest of the present government and the present ministry; and wish nothing so much as that they would steadily pursue those measures that will tend most surely to support themselves....As to the clergy, they have their relations, friendships, interests, and opinions as others have; and therefore it can't be expected that they should all act alike, or as one could wish in affairs of this nature; but if any, not content to be of a different side, act a rude, violent, or factious part, as I shall know it, I shall be sure to remember it on occasion."

With the approach of the election, the bishop showed a very practical zeal. His palace at Chichester was placed entirely at the duke's service, with good beds well aired (for his grace had a dread of catching cold in strange beds), with stabling for twenty horses, and supplies of liquor laid in; and all was crowned by the earnest greeting: "I wish you good success, most heartily, in the modern style: Pelham and Butler for ever". The final issue of the poll justified the activity of the clerical host, who had indeed forecast with surprising accuracy the details of the votes; for whereas their prediction read: Pelham 2262, Butler 2046, Bishop 1698, and Fuller 1570, the official figures were Pelham 2271, Butler 2053, Bishop 1704, and Fuller 1581. Naturally the excellent organisation thus created by the clergy was not suffered to fall into desuetude; and though by the date of the next election in 1741 several of the prominent actors were deceased, others of the duke's old friends rallied again to his call, and few counties and dioceses could produce tangible evidence of so complete an accord of the representatives of Church and State as Sussex and Chichester, where thanks to the beneficence of his grace of Newcastle politics and religion were wedded in harmony and peace.

The cordial support accorded to the duke by Bishop Hare was quite compatible with the frankest criticism of the minister's political policy which the bishop did not scruple to give when occasion demanded. The penetrating, and not very palatable, advice proffered by his lordship of Chichester to his friend in 1739, when the relations between Walpole and Newcastle were very strained, afforded the strongest illustration of the fact that intimacy by no means implied dependency or servility. After receiving the confidences of both ministers upon the difficulties of their co-operation for three years past, Hare delivered himself of a weighty remonstrance to Newcastle in a letter of 8 November 1739.

"As those misunderstandings, so far as I can judge," he observed, "seem all to have arisen from your grace's uneasiness that he should have the lead and be first in the king's favour, give me leave, my lord, since this is the rock great men oftener split upon than any other, to say two things to your grace which I take to be most certain truths; one is that while Sir Robert is in the king's service, you can be but second; the other, that whenever his death or any other incident shall make it be thought necessary to take in any of the Patriots, they will never suffer you to be the first. If you would conjure the friends you most confide in to tell you their real sentiments, I'm persuaded your grace will find them of the same opinion. If this be so, the consequence from these premises is plainly this, that your grace should unite again heartily with Sir Robert and with the same intimacy as formerly in the common cause, and live on a good footing with his friends, and to be upon your guard against the Patriots who will never be true friends to you. If I was not fully persuaded of these two points myself and did not find it to be the sense of everybody I ever talked with of these matters, I should think it inexcusable in me to say these things; but if I am in the right, I hope your grace will give a due attention to them. As nothing but a very sincere concern for your grace's interest can excuse the liberty I have taken, so nothing in the world besides could tempt me to it. Nobody living is directly or indirectly privy to my writing this; and I desire your grace would not give yourself the trouble of any answer to it."[1]

The delicacy of pointing out to Newcastle the circumstance which always escaped his grasp of the essentially second-rate character of his talents and abilities and the necessity of his co-operation with some person of superior gifts in the public administration, was a task difficult of undertaking even by tried friends and assuredly not to be essayed by sycophants. In 1742, upon the fall of Walpole, the contingency foreseen by Hare was realised, and Bishop Sherlock, always characterised by an independence and freedom of opinion, reinforced the counsel of the late bishop of Chichester by insisting upon the necessity of the new ministry of Carteret and Newcastle conciliating as great a volume of support in the house of commons as possible. Again, during the following year, when Newcastle was jealous of the secrecy of Carteret and his apparent monopoly of the king's confidence, Sherlock, whilst admitting that such conduct "would naturally produce a jealousy, the thing most to be guarded against with new friends", argued that the

[1] Bp. Hare to Newcastle, 8 Nov. 1739. Add. MSS. 32692, f. 450.

succession of Henry Pelham to the treasury in August 1743 was a token of the king's goodwill towards the Newcastle family so that his grace should seize upon the occasion "of piecing up matters to go on as they were".[1] Similar freedom of speech was used to the duke upon the far greater crisis of 1757 in relation to the forming of a coalition with William Pitt for the prosecution of the Seven Years' War by the Irish primate, Archbishop Stone of Armagh; who urged the minister to cease the endless round of requests for advice, in which "one conversation destroyed another and his grace was forced to leave off where he began", and to remember that "the people were all looking towards his grace for their deliverance, and circumstanced as things were, though he alone was not sufficient to effect it, yet it could not be effected without him". After surveying the alternative courses of action, the primate counselled an alliance with Pitt, affirming that "in such cases true greatness of mind is shewn in condescension, and his grace never had, never could have, an opportunity of exerting it in so striking an instance as that would be".[2]

The public station of the archbishop of Canterbury inevitably involved the occupants of that see in matters of state, even of purely political import, as Herring found in the perplexing days which followed the death of Henry Pelham on 6 March 1754 when the reconstruction of the whig administration was a task of equal delicacy and difficulty. The moment seemed to have arrived for the assertion of Newcastle's claim to pre-eminence, but the awkward problem remained of finding a leader in the commons who combined ability and dependence in proper proportion in order to enable his grace to direct policy from the upper house.

"It is a great difficulty", observed Herring to Hardwicke on 10 March, "to find such another man as Mr Pelham; but a greater difficulty than that is to create an union of intention and action in so disjointed times...I am only a spectator, but I have seen so much of men, know a little of the interior of the court, and am so sensible of what I could call the complexion of the times, that I can't help thinking we were in less danger though more alarm in 1745."[3]

The archbishop was not suffered long to remain a spectator of political events, for on the following day the chancellor addressed an urgent

[1] Bp. Sherlock to Newcastle, 25 April 1742; 4 Sept. 1743. Add. MSS. 32699, f. 191; 32701, f. 95.
[2] Abp. Stone to Newcastle, 12 May 1757. Add. MSS. 32871, f. 61.
[3] Herring to Hardwicke, 10 March 1754. Add. MSS. 35599, f. 163.

appeal for his co-operation, since the king had committed to the lords of the cabinet council the duty of advising him as to the disposition of offices. The whigs were in a strait betwixt two courses, that of giving power and office to Fox and that of leaving the leadership of the ministerial forces in the commons to an inferior person.

"The opinion therefore which I with my friends in the cabinet have formed", reported Hardwicke to Herring, "is that there is at present no person in the house of commons fit to place entirely in Mr Pelham's situation with safety to this administration and the whig party. Upon this they have proceeded to think of advising his majesty to place some peer at the head of the treasury, with a chancellor of the exchequer in the house of commons under him; that peer must be somebody of great figure and credit in the nation, in whom the whigs will have an entire confidence. He must be one who will carry on the election of the next parliament upon the same plan on which Mr Pelham had settled it without deviation. This is at present the immediate and fundamental point; that once well settled and effected the rest will follow with time."

In this contingency what was desired of the primate was the despatch of a letter to the lords of the cabinet to be read at their meeting; and declaring

that in his view of the present circumstances his grace apprehended that it would be most for his majesty's service to divide the two offices of first commissioner of the treasury and chancellor of the exchequer, and to put some peer of great rank and weight at the head of the treasury and to fill the chancellor of the exchequer's place out of the house of commons, as had been done in many instances; that if his majesty would be pleased to direct the duke of Newcastle, who had served him long with great ability and integrity, to change his office of secretary of state for that of first commissioner of the treasury, his grace thought that it would be the best measure for his majesty's service in that critical juncture, and maintain the system of things upon the same footing upon which they had been for several years past carried on with great success.[1]

The faithful archbishop duly complied with the request of his friend verbatim, though he was of too timorous a nature to give effective aid in a time of crisis; for having in a private letter expressed his approbation of the entire scheme and especially of the proposed offer to Fox of the secretaryship of state for the southern province, as a provision which "would be much to his advantage and leave him as much insignificancy

[1] Hardwicke to Herring, 11 March 1754. Add. MSS. 35599, f. 165.

as would be consistent with a state of proper dependency",[1] he repented of this indiscreet utterance and besought the chancellor on the morrow to "let his letter and name remain a secret". For, whilst rejoicing indeed, "if the signing his name to a plan of the duke of Newcastle and his lordship had happily made the machine move easier", he thought his private missive because of its particulars capable of invidious and disgusting turns, adding that "he was an ecclesiastic and would not willingly aim at anything *ultra crepidam*, or be thought to do so".[2] A similar solicitude for archiepiscopal opinion was shown by Newcastle during his period of office as lord privy seal in the Rockingham administration, when he was most anxious to secure the approbation of Secker, and therewith the support of the bench, for the repeal of the Stamp Act projected by the ministry. Any bishop of strong and consistent political convictions might possess a very considerable influence upon public affairs during the Hanoverian century, as the repeated attempts to attach Bishop Watson to the service of a party indicated. Indeed if that prelate's vigour of mind and speech had been allied to a steady allegiance either to whig or tory ministers, he might probably have attained to the primatial dignity, for his abilities were recognised and his suffrage widely canvassed.

The political commerce and party alignment of the eighteenth-century episcopate were natural concomitants of the increased importance of parliament itself consequent upon the Revolution of 1689 and of the consolidation of the rival parties of whig and tory. Even critics of the conduct of the bench did not contemplate the only means of extinguishing episcopal intervention in politics by advocating the drastic surgery of their exclusion from the house of lords. When Sir Adam Ferguson·hinted to Dr Johnson a doubt of the propriety of bishops having seats in parliament, the doctor, despite his denunciation of the political influence necessary to obtain ecclesiastical promotion, retorted sharply: "How so, sir? Who is more proper for having the dignity of a peer than a bishop, provided a bishop be what he ought to be; and if improper bishops be made, that is not the fault of the bishops but of those who make them".[3]

Not the least interesting consequence of the political character of the bench and the alliance of its members with the party ministers lay in the considerable degree of influence exercised by the temporal aristocracy in pressing for the nomination to sees in their counties of divines of

---

[1] Herring to Hardwicke, 12 March 1754. Add. MSS. 35599, f. 173.
[2] Same to Same, 13 March 1754. *Ibid.* f. 175.
[3] Boswell, *Life of Johnson*, April 1772.

approved loyalty, with whom they might work easily and certainly in the negotiation of general elections. Apart from the many instances in which the chaplains and relatives of the nobility were nominated to bishoprics, their authority was felt in the exclusion of clergy of doubtful loyalty. In 1749 upon the vacancy of the see of Lichfield and Coventry, Archbishop Herring endeavoured to secure the translation of Secker of Oxford; "but upon the mention of it to lord G[ower] and earl P[owis], they both flew into prodigious violence", so that his grace of Newcastle did not dare to press the point with George II.[1] Even where the duke's private feelings were most strongly engaged, as in the translation of James Johnson from Gloucester to Worcester in 1759, the most definite assurances were given that the bishop had laid aside his former doubtful political associations. In announcing the event to Johnson, Newcastle intimated that he had assured the earl of Coventry on his behalf that "in everything that concerned the whig interest in the county or town of Worcester, he would support it and take his lordship's advice upon all occasions relative thereto, and particularly support his interest everywhere".[2] To Lord Coventry himself even more specific was the guarantee given of the prelate's loyalty; "in such manner", added the duke, "that if you will only tell me what you would have him to do, and what public and private declarations he should make, I am sure of his compliance".[3]

So great was the influence of the territorial nobility upon episcopal preferment in the eighteenth century as to register an apparent approach towards the system of mediate bishoprics from which the English Church had so happily escaped during the middle ages. Indeed the temporal peers of the Hanoverian age achieved a greater measure of success than the marcher lords of the medieval epoch in controlling nominations to the Welsh and border bishoprics. It was fortunate for the Church that the right of nomination remained always in the crown, and that though the sovereigns generally acted upon the prompting of their ministers, there remained a sufficient number of cases of personal appointment to prevent the usurpation of royal prerogative in this regard by party leaders. Notwithstanding, the English Church by virtue of the widespread influence of ministers of state and the territorial nobility in ecclesiastical promotions offered a marked contrast during this epoch to its neighbour the Gallican Church, in which the last traces of mediate bishoprics, albeit dignified by long tradition, were swept

[1] Herring to Hardwicke, 30 Dec. 1749. Add. MSS. 35598, f. 440.
[2] Newcastle to Johnson, 2 Oct. 1759. Add. MSS. 32896, f. 214.
[3] Newcastle to Coventry, 3 Oct. 1759. *Ibid.* f. 246.

away by the acquisitive monopoly of the crown, when in 1714 Louis XIV deprived the duke of Nevers of his right of patronage of the small see of Clamecy.

The eighteenth century maintained, with characteristic variation and development congenial to its particular genius, the secular tradition of the English episcopate that its members should be *verum etiam regi fideles et regno utiles, necnon ad auxilium et consilium efficaces*. The most outstanding aspect of the political character of the bench lay in the increased importance attached to parliamentary attendance, in an age which saw so great an advance in the prestige and authority of both houses and in which the house of peers played no insignificant part in debate and legislation. With this emphasis there went inevitably and naturally the division of its interest between the rival allegiances of whig and tory, though the sharpness of such division was softened by the party predilections of the successive sovereigns, a circumstance enabling the episcopate to maintain generally a proper relationship with the crown despite the party association of their individual profession. It was therefore an occasion of congratulation that neither party espoused a policy of hostility to the church which might have added to the political differences the pernicious labels of clerical and anti-clerical. The tories rejoiced indeed in the name of "the Church party"; but their whig supplanters from 1714 to 1760 were sufficiently wise in their generation as children of this world to support the external lineaments of the Church establishment and the restrictive test law. During their administration the cry of "the Church in danger", when sporadically raised, was ineffective because untrue. In consequence of this felicitous circumstance the worst evils of party differences amongst bishops and clergy were avoided; and if many of the Hanoverian prelacy were warm partisans in parliament and in the exercise of their election interest, no gulf was fixed thereby between themselves and their brethren of opposite persuasion in the discharge of their common ecclesiastical administration. The good estate of Church and State suffered little from the new condition of party differences amongst the bench. In few centuries of English history was the association of these two powers more intimate and harmonious; an allegory and symbol of which was furnished by the experience which befell Archbishop Herring and John White, whig candidate and member for Retford, during their joint sojourn in that town in the course of the general election of 1747.

"I am just returned from church," related his grace to Lord Hardwicke, "where Protestant John and myself have given an evidence that religion and the king's government go hand-in-hand; for while the writs for the greater solemnity according to ancient custom were reading in one part of the church, Confirmation was going on in the other."[1]

Such customs ministering perhaps rather to unity than to edification were typical of the alliance of Church and State in eighteenth-century England.

[1] Herring to Hardwicke, 27 June 1747. Add. MSS. 35598, f. 258.

CHAPTER III

THE OFFICE AND WORK OF A BISHOP

"As for this holy function into which I enter," wrote Burnet in his meditation upon the eve of his consecration to the episcopate, "as Thou hast given me high and sublime notions concerning it, so I will, by Thy grace, put all these in practice. I will preach in season, both in public and from house to house; I will not spare myself, much less will I lose that time which now in a more particular manner [is] thine, in following a court or any other impertinent cares, for I will give my[self] wholly to this great work. I will go round and be frequent in inspecting my clergy and will apply reproofs and censures as well as encouragements without passion or partiality. I will be careful not to lay hands suddenly on any, nor become partaker of other men's sins, for Thou knowest that I have but too many of my own to answer for. I will harden myself to all entreaties and recommendations in the conferring either of Orders or benefices, and I will study to form as many as I can to a high sense of the care of souls, and employ such in Thy vineyard. I will lay aside the prejudices of party, and as I will not rule over any by force or cruelty, so I will shew all kindness not only to such as may differ from me, but even to gainsayers: for I will love all men. I will live with my brethren of the clergy in all brotherly love and humility. I will not act by my own single advice, but by the concurrence of the best of my clergy, and will do what in me lies to carry on the reformation of this church to a full perfection, by cutting off the corruptions that do still remain among us, and by adding such things as are wanting. Nor will I ever suffer myself to be biassed by the base considerations of interest, and I will set myself to do the work of a bishop in my diocese without ever designing to remove to aspire higher; for I hope to fall here, unless Thou for the exercise of my faith and patience call me to suffer for Thy name. These are my desires, and these are the vows which I now offer up to Thee in the sincerity of my heart."[1]

The high conception of the office and work of a bishop which inspired the resolutions of Gilbert Burnet upon Easter Eve, 1690, when he was about to assume the responsibility of the episcopal charge, would have reflected credit upon any age of the Church. The careful preparation made by him for the solemnity of his consecration, paralleled by the reluctance of Tillotson to accept the office of primate and his spending

---

[1] *A Supplement to Burnet's History* (ed. H. C. Foxcroft), p. 538.

the day before his consecration likewise in fasting and prayer, indicated further that a proper esteem of the pastoral duties of the episcopate was no monopoly of any school of churchmanship within the *Ecclesia Anglicana*. No words could express more strongly that those of Burnet, a whig and Latitudinarian divine, the gravity and dignity of the pastoral oversight nor the spiritual importance of the ecclesiastical administration. In the course of the rude experience of a protracted episcopate, indeed, even his zealous and unresting spirit was schooled to accept a certain degree of compromise between the ideal and the practicable. In particular he found that his purpose to cease following a court in order to devote the whole of his time to the government of his diocese could not be realised without a violent breach with the secular English episcopal tradition. At the heart of the problem of episcopal administration lay the distraction from the proper business of diocesan oversight involved in the residence of bishops in London during the greater part of each year; and it is in the light of this circumstance that all estimate of the diligence of their pastoral care must be made. "The attendance on parliaments", complained Burnet in the conclusion of his *History of His Own Time*, "is a great distraction, and puts us to a great charge, besides calling us off half the year from doing our duty." In substance there was nothing novel nor peculiar to the Hanoverian episcopate in this absence from their dioceses for protracted periods to attend upon the affairs of state; for the medieval bishop whose apprenticeship had been served in the royal household, and who continued after his consecration to hold office of state, was of necessity but an infrequent visitor of his diocese. The Caroline bishops, the immediate predecessors of Burnet's generation, had recognised fully the obligation of attendance upon the Stuart kings and their court, and had contented themselves with repairing to their sees generally for a quarter of each year.

Residence in London for the greater part of the year was indeed essential if the episcopate was to maintain an interest and concern in public affairs. In an age of slow travel and slower circulation of news, propinquity to the capital was indispensable for bishops desiring to participate in the business of state. "Out of Town is so far out of the world", observed White Kennett to Wake during his residence in the country, "and all reports come down hither like the river itself, with windings and turnings, and tides high and low";[1] whilst Wake himself, in apologising to Tenison for a neglect of correspondence in July 1709,

[1] White Kennett to Wake, 26 April 1712. Arch. W. Epist. 17, item cclxxxii, f. 361.

explained that he had "but just come off from his visitation for several weeks abroad, when oftentimes for many days together he neither received any news by letter nor saw a public paper".[1] In the more remote dioceses of the north and west, and especially in Wales, the bishop during his withdrawal to his see was virtually cut off from knowledge of the affairs of the kingdom. Bishop John Moore during his episcopate at Bangor remarked humorously that "the truth was, the Post Office, taking the warm temper of the Welsh into consideration, had thought it prudent not to give them an opportunity of answering their letters but upon mature deliberation, and after three nights' sleep".[2] Difficulties reminiscent of the middle ages even beset Herring at Bangor through an unexpected prolongation of his residence there in 1742, when the available supply of provisions threatened to become exhausted. "I stayed at Bangor by an accident to a relation a month longer than usual", he related to Hardwicke when safely back in Town; "and forage, to speak in the language of the time, began to fail me; and though I love Wales very much, I would not choose to be reduced to butter, milk, and lean mutton."[3] A general consequence of such disadvantages was that many members of the bench regarded retirement to their sees as having somewhat of the nature of an exile, from which they desired speedily to escape; as Willis of Gloucester announced to Wake that, after fulfilling the duties of his Advent ordination and the Christmas holy days, "the curiosity of knowing something more of public affairs would incline him to come pretty quickly" to London.[4] So zealous a prelate as Samuel Horsley confessed upon his translation to Rochester from St David's in 1793 that "having made that place his residence for the greater part of six summers", he would welcome a change accompanied by "the circumstances of having a house in Town and saving himself the annual expense and fatigue of that long journey".[5]

The tradition was established accordingly among Georgian bishops to set out in October upon their annual journey to London, returning to the country at the end of the parliamentary session in May or June. Custom required of them residence upon their sees during the summer recess of parliament, and on other emergent occasions, and with this standard contemporary opinion was well satisfied. Bishop Newton of

[1] Wake to Tenison, 7 July 1709. Arch. W. Epist. 17, item cxcv, f. 233.
[2] Moore to Eden, n.d. Add. MSS. 34413, f. 80.
[3] Herring to Hardwicke, 18 Sept. 1742. Add. MSS. 35598, f. 14.
[4] Willis to Wake, n.d. Arch. W. Epist. 20, item lxxx, f. 116.
[5] Bp. Horsley to Bp. Hurd, 27 Sept. 1793. Hurd MSS. vol. iii, Section 4.

Bristol, who held *in commendam* with that see first a canonry and then the deanery of St Paul's, recorded with pride that

from the time that he was first made bishop, he constantly went to Bristol every summer, and usually stayed there the three months intervening between his last residence at St Paul's and the next following, and when he was no longer able to go to St Paul's, he continued at Bristol four or five months, and went to church as often as his health and the weather would permit.[1]

The biographer of Secker likewise related of him that during his episcopate at Bristol he kept an annual residence there in the summer, living during the greater part of the year at his rectory of St James', Westminster; whilst after his translation to Oxford, "in the summer months he resided constantly in his episcopal house at Cuddesdon".[2] Viscount Percival indeed, a sympathetic and well-informed churchman, was but expressing the contemporary standpoint in his tribute to Bishop Willcocks of Gloucester in 1730 that

he resides as much as any bishop in his diocese, at least four months in the year, and keeps a very generous and hospitable table, which makes amends for the learning he is deficient in. However, though no great scholar nor a deep man, he is a very frequent preacher; and this, with his zeal for the government, good humour, and regular life, makes him very well liked by the government and all that know him.[3]

The continuance of this practice throughout the century is illustrated by the autobiographical fragment of Bishop John Douglas, which depicts him in 1788, 1789, and 1790 setting out for his remote see of Carlisle in July and returning to the capital in October, while after his translation to Sarum in the years 1792 to 1795 he left London towards the end of July and spent the time until the end of October or mid-November in the ecclesiastical administration of his diocese.[4] The tradition of summer retirement to their sees on the part of the episcopate was acknowledged by the terms in which George III invited Hurd to accept translation from Lichfield to Worcester in 1781, expressing the "hope that he would allow Hartlebury to be a better summer residence than Eccleshall".[5] Even so zealous a reformer as Gibson ventured only in his scheme of necessary reforms to suggest that the bishops should

[1] *Life of Dr Thomas Newton*, in *Lives of E. Pocock, Z. Pearce, T. Newton, and P. Skelton* (2 vols.), ii, 170.
[2] B. Porteus, *Life of Secker*, i, p. xxv.
[3] *Diary of Viscount Percival, Earl of Egmont*, i, 100. H.M.C. Egmont MSS.
[4] *Autobiography of Bishop John Douglas*, B.M. Egerton MSS. 2181.
[5] George III to Hurd, 2 May 1781. *Hurd Papers*, vol. i, No. 3.

exercise care "not to be in Town longer than their parliamentary attendance requires", giving no hint of disapprobation of the duty and propriety of their discharge of that senatorial responsibility.

Notwithstanding, the circumstance of protracted residence in the capital militated inevitably against the efficient execution of episcopal administration, since, apart from the varying degrees of strictness in individual bishops, the thorough oversight of their dioceses was impossible to prelates absent of necessity so long from their sees. In respect of the difficulties of diocesan supervision the Hanoverian bishop was removed but a short step from his medieval predecessors; for the Reformation had contributed comparatively little towards the solution of this problem. Albeit five new dioceses had been permanently established, the huge territorial extent of York (or even of Chester which had been separated from it) or of Lincoln (despite the creation of Oxford and Peterborough) was sufficient alone to prevent close oversight; whilst the newly founded see of Bristol suffered the misfortune to have its see-city severed from the diocese which comprised the county of Dorset. Further, to offset the advantage of a greater number of dioceses, the provision made by the statute of 26 Henry VIII, cap. 14, for the consecration of English suffragan bishops had never been consistently acted upon, so that the post-Reformation diocesan episcopate were handicapped by comparison with their medieval predecessors in lacking such assistance as might have been afforded by suffragans in the discharge of their administration. In face of such difficulties and the continued obstacles of distance and bad roads, in which regard the eighteenth century was much nearer to the medieval age than to the railway and motor-car epochs which have followed it with so great rapidity, it is perhaps a matter of surprise and gratification that the prelates of Georgian England achieved so considerable an approximation to the ideal of the office and work of a bishop.

Of the three essential branches of the episcopal office, ordination, visitation of the clergy, and confirmation of the laity, the first-named was least hindered by these adverse conditions. To a prelate resident in London from October to June indeed, the fulfilment of the canonical rule that Holy Orders should be conferred "only upon the Sundays immediately following *Jejunia quatuor temporum*, commonly called Ember weeks", and "that this be done in the cathedral or parish church where the bishop resideth", presented difficulties especially in relation to the Advent and Lenten embertides. The problem might be solved by the retirement of the bishop to his diocese for a brief space (if sufficiently near to the capital to permit of an easy journey), by the summons of candidates to attend upon his lordship in town, by the issue of Letters Dimissory to other bishops ordaining in neighbouring dioceses, or by reserving all save urgent cases to ordinations held by the diocesan in person *extra quatuor tempora*. The last custom was contrary to the express injunction of the 31st Canon, but in this, as in other regulations relating to the admission of persons to sacred orders, precept was more honoured in the breach than the observance. The practice of Hanoverian prelates in the conferment of Holy Orders differed so considerably according to individual predilection and local circumstance as to defy an attempt at generalisation; but instead of deducing rules of general observance, attention may be directed to examples of varying customs prevalent amongst the episcopate. It may be doubted perhaps whether even the most exhaustive survey of available evidence would afford ground for sure and confident generalisation, in view of the wide latitude within which bishops did what seemed right in their own eyes. Nor are the uncertainties attendant upon episcopal practice a problem only for subsequent historians, since to contemporaries they were often a source of considerable confusion; as when on the one hand White Kennett reported to Wake in September 1709 that "there was no one bishop in Town and tomorrow no ordination on that side Chelmsford",[1] the parliament not being in session, whereas on the other hand Dr Tanner in September 1719 related from Norwich that, since their lordships of Norwich, Ely, and Lincoln were all out of their dioceses, "all their young men that were candidates for orders were trooped away to Peterborough".[2]

Many bishops desiring to remain in London throughout the winter session adopted the solution of requiring candidates from their dioceses to receive the sacred character at their hands in some church within the cities of London or Westminster. Amongst prelates favouring this practice were Wake and Gibson during their episcopate at Lincoln; for of forty ordinations undertaken by Wake in person as bishop of Lincoln from 1705 to 1716, twenty-two were held in London against sixteen at the episcopal residence at Buckden, and two in Lincoln Cathedral; and of sixty ordinations held by Gibson from 1716 to 1723, fifty were held in London, only seven at Buckden, two in his cathedral church, and one at Stamford. The predominance of ordinations held in town is the more remarkable by reason of the fact that both bishops enjoyed a deserved reputation for diligence and care in the conduct of all matters relating to the admission of candidates to Holy Orders. Equally note-

[1] White Kennett to Wake, 24 Sept. 1709. Arch. W. Epist. 17, item ccvi, f. 246.
[2] Tanner to Charlett, 16 Sept. 1719. Ballard MSS. iv, f. 72.

worthy are the figures revealed by the episcopal registers of the smaller diocese of Chichester, in which during the century from 1689 to 1792 (at which latter date the register of Bishop Ashburnham breaks off abruptly), of a gross total of 294 ordinations held by the several bishops, no fewer than 123 were held outside its boundaries (114 actually in London), and 167 within, the high proportion of ordinations in town being especially notable because of the comparative nearness of Chichester to the capital.

In the more remote dioceses the alternatives lay generally between the issue of Letters Dimissory to neighbouring bishops or the holding of ordinations by the diocesan during the periods of residence upon his see, since evident objections of a serious character could be made to the summons of persons from Carlisle, Exeter, Durham, or Wales to make the expensive and tedious journey to London. The diaries and correspondence of Bishop Nicolson of Carlisle illustrate the ingenious expedient adopted in the province of York during his episcopate from 1702 to 1718 to circumvent the difficulty, by which the bishops attendant on the parliamentary session bore there the proxies of their absent brethren, who in turn undertook the task of ordaining for the dioceses deprived of their pastors. Nicolson held in person thirty-eight ordinations for his diocese, at eighteen of which there were candidates from Durham, at eight from York, and at seven from Chester. Two of these occasions were particularly interesting, since they coincided with important political crises. On 9 June 1712 the bishop of Carlisle reported to Wake his prospect of a heavy Trinity ordination undertaken on behalf of his brethren engaged in the house of lords. "I am like to have a throng day of it at Carlisle", he wrote, "my two great fellow-suffragans (of Durham and Chester) giving me the honour of their proxies on this occasion, whilst they are personally ratifying the safe and honourable peace at Westminster".[1] Even more striking was the second instance of Advent 1718 when Nicolson, although he had been translated to the Irish see of Derry in the previous spring, ordained at Carlisle not only for his successor in that diocese, Bishop Bradford, but for other prelates of the province whose attention was absorbed in the debates on the repeal of the Occasional Conformity and Schism Acts. "I am now, my lord", reported Nicolson to Wake on 20 December, "on my last Ember duty for the whole province of York, surrounded with candidates in great plenty, chiefly from the diocese of Durham."[2] His ordination was the only one within the boundary of the northern

---

[1] Nicolson to Wake, 9 June 1712. Arch. W. Epist. 17, item cclxxx, f. 365.
[2] Same to Same, 20 Dec. 1718. Arch. W. Epist. 21, item lxix, f. 110.

province, for on 19 December when the house of lords divided on the question of repeal, the archbishop of York and the bishops of Chester and Carlisle recorded their votes in person.

Upon occasion indeed the practice of the issue of Letters Dimissory suffered a wider and somewhat illegitimate extension, as during the primacy at York of Lancelot Blackburne, who from 1733 to his death in 1743 held no ordinations in person; "and candidates for Holy Orders in his large diocese were given letters dimissory 'to any catholic bishop', and betook themselves to Carlisle, Chester, and Lincoln for the most part, and sometimes to London and even further afield".[1] Candidates from the Welsh dioceses often found themselves required to wander in search of a bishop ordaining near the marches to whom they might present their Letters Dimissory, as Warburton described in picturesque phrase to Hurd in 1769. "I am now to give you an account of my Michaelmas ordination. Though I gave notice of it, according to your direction, in the *Gloucester Journal*; yet, had it not been for a little Welsh deacon, who flew hither from his native mountains by accident, like a woodcock in a mist, it had been a maiden ordination, and I must, like the judges, have given gloves to my officers; for an examination is a kind of execution."[2] The practice of Warburton himself was characterised by a similar freedom in the issue of Letters Dimissory. Although in October 1769 he assured Hurd that "he had stopped his Letters Dimissory, on his first admonition, some time ago" in order to subject candidates to the formidable ordeal of examination by himself, the terror of such an experience led to a "great demand of Letters Dimissory and the scarcity of candidates in person";[3] and the surviving fragment of his Act Book contains the record on several occasions of the issue of Letters Dimissory commending their bearer "to be ordained Deacon [or Priest] by any bishop of this realm of England who should be willing to ordain him".[4] During the period of his episcopate covered by the Act Book from February 1768 to April 1774, his lordship of Gloucester ordained in person only five times in his cathedral church. The diversity of ordinands foregathering to receive the grace of orders by Letters Dimissory is illustrated not inaptly by an ordination held by Bishop Hallifax of Gloucester in

[1] S. L. Ollard and P. C. Walker, *Archbishop Herring's Visitation Returns*, i, p. xxii.

[2] *Letters of a Late Eminent Prelate*, Warburton to Hurd, 23 Sept. 1769, Letter ccxix, p. 440.

[3] *Ibid.* 17 Oct. 1769, Letter ccxx, pp. 441–2.

[4] Act Book for the Diocese of Gloucester, 20 Feb. 1768–23 March 1789 (Gloucester City Library, 304 (10)).

December 1781, in St James' Chapel, London, at which no fewer than ten dioceses were represented; since five deacons were ordered for his lordship of Lichfield, two for his grace of York, four for the bishop of London, and one each for the bishops of Sarum and Chester; whilst two priests were ordained for Norwich, three for Bristol, four for Canterbury and London, two for Sarum, and one each for Oxford, Exeter, Chester, and Lichfield.

Some bishops adopted the expedient of holding ordinations during their summer residence upon their sees, irrespective of the canonical embertides. Archbishop Blackburne at York during the years 1725 to 1732 held ten ordinations, all "in the months of July, August, and September, when he was in residence at Bishopsthorpe", for which he is censured by Canon Ollard,[1] albeit somewhat undeservedly, since the alternatives of summoning candidates to London or granting Letters Dimissory were certainly less satisfactory. Bishop Hurd upon his nomination to the see of Lichfield and Coventry invited William Arnald of St John's College, Cambridge, to serve him as chaplain, promising to "consult his time and ease as much as possible", and asking only that he might "oblige him with his company at Eccleshall for some part of the summer, and particularly for a fortnight or three weeks about Michaelmas, when his principal ordination would be".[2] After his translation to Worcester, Hurd held forty-seven ordinations between 1781 and 1804 (after which ill-health compelled him to relinquish the office), of which forty-four were held at Hartlebury, and thirty-three of which fell during the period of his summer residence at Hartlebury Castle between the months of June and October.[3] The practice of different bishops was influenced largely by individual convenience and the situation of their dioceses which forbade any approximation to uniformity of action. In the extensive diocese of Exeter during the century from the translation of Trelawny in 1689 to the death of Ross in 1792, of a total of 388 ordinations, no fewer than 347 were held within the counties of Devon and Cornwall, 252 being held within the chapel of the palace at Exeter, and only twenty-six in London, of which number Claggett was responsible for fifteen. The remoteness and scattered character of the diocese made any concentration of ordinations in London impracticable, and its bishops ordained at Exeter, finding that a sufficient journey for the candidates from the south-western counties.

[1] S. L. Ollard and P. C. Walker, *op. cit.* i, p. xxii.
[2] Hurd to Arnald, 21 Dec. 1774. Hurd MSS. iv, Section 11.
[3] Act Book of Bishop Hurd (Worcester).

The register of an eighteenth-century prelate had been shorn by long desuetude of the intimate and personal items recorded in medieval registers; but upon occasion the reader may penetrate beneath the conventional lists of names, degrees, and licences to discern the lineaments of individual personalities and the dramatic properties of human interests. At Chichester on 10 August 1705 Bishop Williams admitted to the diaconate two Waldensian refugees, whose destiny it is impossible unfortunately to trace further in the pages of his register: "Cyprianus Appia et Paulus Appia Fratres Pedomontani religionis gratia suis sedibus pulsi Oxonii studiis incubuere per multos annos, redditumque ad suos jam meditantes ad rem Christianam promovendam...ad sacrum diaconatus ordinem...admissi sunt". Occasional glimpses of the unhappy state of the Plantations may be gathered from incidental records of the ordination of young men from the new world who had braved the perils of the Atlantic ocean in their desire to receive the episcopal commission; as when Bishop Keppel of Exeter, ordaining in St James' Chapel Royal for the bishop of London on 13 November 1763, admitted to the order of deacon two graduates of Yale and one of Harvard, and again on 25 April 1774, in St George's Chapel, Windsor, a graduate of King's College, New York. Even more challenging to the imagination of the sympathetic student is the record of Keppel's ordination to the diaconate on 25 April 1765, again for his lordship of London in St James' Chapel, and for the service of the Plantations, of Philip Quaque, a West African negro and the first non-European to receive Anglican Orders since the Reformation, who was supported by the missionary enterprise of the S.P.G. Notable pages in the domestic religious history of the century were written likewise when Bishop Martin Benson of Gloucester admitted to the diaconate in his cathedral church on 19 June 1736, George Whitefield, B.A. of Pembroke College, Oxford, to whom "Mr John Phillip allowed £30 a year to officiate at the Castle in Oxford"; and when the registrar of Bishop Egerton of Bangor entered under the date of 15 March 1767 the admission to the priesthood in St James' Chapel of "John William Fletcher, University of Geneva, at request of the bishop of Hereford", afterwards famous as Fletcher of Madeley.

Amongst the several members of the Hanoverian episcopate there existed, as in all centuries of ecclesiastical history, examples of great care and of laxity in the execution of their episcopal administration. The recently published survey of the diocese of Bangor indicates the varying standards which characterised the bishops of that period.[1] The

[1] A. I. Pryce, *The Diocese of Bangor during Three Centuries.*

episcopal registers contain no record of any ordination between Advent 1713 and September 1723, a decade embracing the last years of the episcopate of Bishop Evans, translated to Meath in 1715, the entire rule of Hoadly from 1715 to 1721, and the brief tenure of the see by Reynolds, translated to Lincoln in 1723. Such an indictment of neglect against Hoadly is difficult of extenuation; though it is impossible to be certain that the omission may not be due to the registrar rather than to the bishop. In regard to a later prelate, Bishop Zachary Pearce, it is observed that he "was an absentee, and his register of ordinations shows a record scarcely better than that of Bishop Hoadly. During the eight to nine years of his episcopate there is no entry of ordination services in Bangor diocese in the years 1750, 1753 to 1756 inclusive, but several entries are given of ordination services held by the bishop in London on behalf of English bishops".[1] Against this accusation of absenteeism there must be set the affirmation of his biographer that "he was not hindered by the distance of Bangor from annually resorting to that diocese (one year only excepted), and discharging his episcopal duties there, to 1753; after which having suffered greatly from the fatigue of his last journey, he was advised by his physician...and prevailed on, not to attempt another". Further, during the last seven years of the life of Sherlock of London, who died in 1761, Pearce "ordained all candidates for holy orders in his diocese",[2] from which it may be presumed that the candidates for ordination in his own see of Bangor either attended upon his ordinations in London or sought Letters Dimissory to other bishops ordaining nearer the Welsh border.

Even Richard Watson of Llandaff, the *bête noire* of the eighteenth-century episcopate, has suffered in reputation from the sins of his registrar, for the surviving records of his episcopate, three Subscription Books, bear more evident testimonies of the neglect of the registrar than of the bishop. Although they relate the holding in Llandaff Cathedral in the summer months of an annual ordination by the bishop personally in each of the years 1784, 1785, 1787, 1788, 1790, 1791, and 1795, and again in 1804, 1805, 1809, 1811 and 1813, the entries of subscriptions during the intervening years are so imperfectly made as to render impossible a sure conclusion that the bishop ordained once every year at Llandaff.[3] A partial confirmation of such a conjecture is

---

[1] A. I. Pryce, *op. cit.* p. lxiii.

[2] *Life of Zachary Pearce*, in *op. cit.* i, 402, 420.

[3] Subscription Books of Richard Watson, Nos. 8, 9, 10, in the Diocesan Registry at Cardiff.

afforded by the evidence of a private list of ordinations compiled by Watson himself,[1] which establishes the circumstance of his conferring Holy Orders in his cathedral in the years 1802, 1807, 1808, 1810, and 1812, in addition to those recorded in the Subscription Books; from which it would appear probable that the bishop paid an annual visit to his see-city in June to ordain for his diocese, though it must be admitted that the available evidence falls short of proof. In addition, Watson held several ordinations upon his residence in the Lake District though the journey there was formidable, as Mr Thomas Morgan, B.A. of Jesus College, Oxford, experienced in September 1792, when he travelled to Windermere to receive ordination to the diaconate in that parish church and a licence to serve the curacy of Llanover at £20 per annum.

Against one disabling circumstance, that of old age, the eighteenth century had no remedy, and many bishops felt the need of the assistance of suffragans in consequence of ill-health and infirmity. Nor did the traditions of the epoch admit of episcopal resignation, as Zachary Pearce discovered in his repeated endeavours at the age of seventy-three to relinquish the see of Rochester. Even Lancelot Blackburne at York, who desisted from ordaining in person during the last decade of his primacy from 1733 to 1743, had fulfilled seventy-four years in 1733, and doubtless found the journey from London to Bishopsthorpe too formidable for his strength. Such circumstances, though extenuatory of the personal culpability of the individual bishop, afforded no safeguard against the ill-consequences which often followed the failure of bishops to ordain in person for their dioceses. During the long episcopate of Cumberland at Peterborough from 1691 to 1718 sundry irregularities crept into the episcopal administration with the increasing age of his lordship. From the outset of his rule he had found the burden of "the public affairs and the necessity of spending the great part of the year in London" to draw him "very much off the active part that was needful in a bishop", so that his chaplain affirmed to Wake, upon the death of the bishop, that he could "without arrogance say that the great part of the business of the see had been of late years done by him", more particularly the care of ordinations.[2] In the last year of Cumberland's life, White Kennett, dean of Peterborough, doubted

[1] MSS. of Watson preserved in the Chapter Archives at Llandaff. It is worthy of note that Bishop George Bull at St David's held a public Ordination only in September, whilst at "the other Ember Seasons he ordained but a small number, more or less, as occasion required" (R. Nelson, *Life of George Bull*, p. 423).

[2] S. Payne to Wake, 14 Oct. 1718. Arch. W. Epist. 21, item xli, f. 66.

whether his lordship's conferring of Orders might not be open to suspicion of invalidity by reason of his infirmities.

"He was pleased to think himself sufficient to perform the chief part of the Communion Service", observed the dean to the archbishop; "though his frequent mistakes in it were a matter of pity and even offence to many people. On the last Trinity Sunday he had a large ordination of 13 or 14 persons, though it was not possible for his lordship to distinguish their characters or titles, or to perform the very office but in such a way as would create doubts (in that age) of the validity of ordination."[1]

When White Kennett himself succeeded to the see of Peterborough, he found a crop of difficulties arising from such incidents as the admission by his predecessor to the priesthood of a person who had never been ordained deacon and the ordination to the diaconate of candidates under the canonical age.

In like manner the aged Bishop Lloyd of Worcester applied to Wake in 1716 for the renewal of the "general discretionary leave" which he had enjoyed from successive primates ever since his consecration to ordain *extra quatuor tempora*. "As I am now too old to undertake the fatigue of ordaining myself", he added, "and must therefore be glad to make use of any opportunity that may be offered for having it done by such of my brethren as shall be so kind as to call upon me here at Hartlebury, I must desire your grace to give me a general leave, as your predecessors did, of which no ill use shall be made, to have ordinations *extra quatuor tempora* as occasion shall require."[2] Bishop Hurd of Worcester was incapacitated from ordaining in person by age and infirmity from July 1804 to his death in 1808, during which period he issued Letters Dimissory on twelve occasions to the bishop of Lichfield and Coventry, and on four each to his lordship of Hereford and to the bishop of Gloucester, to ordain candidates for his diocese. The dangers of the practice of candidates for Holy Orders armed with general Letters Dimissory wandering often from diocese to diocese in search of a bishop ordaining in his see were evident; and the most careful scrutiny and examination of such documents was essential, as in the case of a candidate for priests' orders whom Bishop Chandler of Lichfield in 1720 found to have been ordained at the age of nineteen. "I chid him for imposing upon the bishop that ordained him", observed his lordship, "but he denied that he had imposed upon him; for being of this diocese in 1715, and going to London for Orders, the bishop

[1] White Kennett to Wake, 24 June 1718. Arch. W. Epist. 20, item ccclxxxi, f. 505.
[2] Bp. Lloyd to Wake, 3 Sept. 1718. Arch. W. Epist. 7, Canterbury 11.

having no one beside to ordain, transmitted him to the bishop of Gloucester, who, supposing the bishop of the diocese to be satisfied about every particular required by the canons except his abilities (as is the common practice), ordained him without enquiry into his age".[1] In order to guard against such possibility of fraud, Bishop Benson of Gloucester was careful to record opposite the names of candidates ordained by him on the authority of Letters Dimissory that they had been "examined, and approved and recommended" by the bishop whose authorisation they bore.[2]

Within the limits of the prevalent tradition which withdrew the episcopate from diocesan business for the greater part of the year, individual bishops strove often with diligence and perseverance to administer the rite of ordination with the solemnity and dignity appertaining to so high a transaction. Archbishop Sharp of York set a signal example of personal care and devotion to public duty in this, as in other branches of the episcopal character. He held ordinations

regularly at all the stated times, when he was in his diocese. And as it was a business of the greatest weight and consequence that appertained to his office, he used the properest means to qualify himself for the discharge of it. He usually repaired privately to his chapel to beg God's presence with him and blessing upon him, or, to use his own expression, "to implore the guidance of His spirit in that work". He measured candidates for Orders more by their modesty and good sense and the testimonials of their virtue than by their learning. To have a right notion of the main doctrines of religion, to understand thoroughly the terms of the new covenant, both on God's part and man's; and to know the reasons and to apprehend the force of those distinctions upon which the Church of England explained and stated those terms differently from the Church of Rome and other communions separating from her, were with him the chief qualifications for the ministry in regard to learning.[3]

In his charge to candidates concerning the pastoral office, he emphasised the gravity of their vocation "to be made stewards of the mysteries of Christ, the ministers of reconciliation between God and man", laying especial stress upon the study of the Scriptures and of divinity, upon the character of their preaching, their private life and conduct, and upon the necessity of personal residence upon their cure in order to fulfil the ends of parochial administration. At the opposite

[1] Bp. Chandler to Wake, 28 May 1720. Arch. W. Epist. 8, Canterbury III.
[2] *Ordinations*, 1736–41, in the Gloucester City Library (284 c).
[3] T. Sharp, *Life of Archbishop John Sharp*, i, 145–54.

pole of ecclesiastical and political allegiance stood the bishop of Sarum; yet no prelate exceeded Burnet in eager solicitude for the proper conduct of all matters relating to the admission of candidates to Holy Orders.

"I looked on ordinations", he testified, "as the most important part of a bishop's care, and that on which the law had laid no restraints, for it was absolutely in the bishop's power to ordain or not, as he judged a person qualified for it, and so I resolved to take that matter to heart. I never turned over the examining of those who came to me for Orders to a chaplain or an archdeacon, I examined them very carefully myself. I began always to examine them concerning the proof of the Christian religion and the nature of the Gospel Covenant in Christ; if they understood not these aright, I dismissed them, but upon a competent understanding of these, I went through the other parts of divinity, and soon saw into the measure of their knowledge. . . . When I was satisfied that they had a competent measure of knowledge, I directed the rest of my discourse to their consciences, and went through all the parts of the Pastoral Care to give them good directions and to awaken in them a right sense of things. I pressed them to employ their time in prayer, fasting, and meditation, and in reading carefully the Epistles to Timothy and Titus, I spoke copiously to them every day for four days together upon these subjects, sometimes to them altogether and sometimes singly. I referred the examining them in Greek and Latin to the archdeacon, and brought them to a public examination in the Chapter House before the dean and prebendaries. . . . I must confess the ordination weeks were much dreaded by me and were the most afflicting parts of the whole year and of the whole episcopal duty."[1]

Into the private, and peradventure painful, mystery of the nature of the examinations required of candidates for Holy Orders in the Hanoverian Church it is not possible generally to penetrate. Upon occasion, however, the veil of privity is lifted, and the ordinand may be seen wrestling with the tests imposed by bishops and their chaplains, and sometimes discomfited upon points of divinity or language. One such revelation was vouchsafed by the re-examination of a candidate in the diocese of Lincoln, who had been once rejected for deacons' orders, in September 1712, by Bishop Wake, his chaplain, and the archdeacon. To Sir Thomas Alston, brother of the unhappy youth, the bishop sent a faithful account of the ordeal.

After having made a short experiment of him in the Greek Testament, I proceeded to examine him in English, and only in the articles of the Apostles' Creed in order as they lie there. I asked no questions out of the way, but

[1] Burnet's *Autobiography*, in H. C. Foxcroft, *A Supplement to Burnet's History*, pp. 502–3.

only the plain sense and meaning of each article, without entering into any further particulars concerning them. Some few proofs of Scripture I put him upon when the passages were notorious to anybody who knew anything at all of the subject, but not otherwise. I am sorry to say that upon the whole he appeared to all of us by no means qualified for Holy Orders. My archdeacon professed that he could not present him according to the solemn form our church requires; nor indeed could I think myself at liberty to ordain him if he would.[1]

Nor was this adverse verdict the sum of the tragedy. The paper on which this report is roughly drafted bears upon the obverse a more pathetic evidence of trial in the form of a Latin exercise, signed "Alston", headed *De Sacra Scriptura sufficienter ad Salutem*, and representing the candidate's endeavour to turn into that tongue Article VI. A striking parallel to this examination is afforded by the tests to which Archdeacon Frank of Bedford subjected a wandering curate who had appeared within his jurisdiction without satisfactory evidence of his ordination.

"After some pert behaviour by way of demur to my authority of examining him and requiring his letters of orders and testimonials," related the archdeacon to the bishop; "he did unwillingly submit to an examination, and endeavoured to turn the Article of Original Sin into Latin, as I send it under his own hand; I referred him to the beginning of the first chapter of the Epistle to the Hebrews in Greek, whereof he could make no tolerable construction. The enclosed questions he answered readily and tolerably well in English, and defended the true doctrine by Scripture; and in the close told me 'A man might be a good divine without your Latin and Greek'."

Confirmatory evidence of the general character of examinations for Orders is furnished by the practice of Richard Kidder, bishop of Bath and Wells from 1690 to 1703, whose autobiographical memoirs refer to his "custom when he gave any of the candidates a collect or an article to turn into Latin to cause them to set their names at the bottom", and to his careful examination of them "in the Greek and Latin tongues", and "also in theological matters". Like Burnet and Sharp, Kidder undertook the examination personally, attended by his chaplains and the canons of his cathedral church.[2] Similar tests were applied by Bishop Reynolds of Lincoln in 1724 to a candidate for the priesthood, who during a twelve years' diaconate had "forgotten most of his Greek

---

[1] See N. Sykes, "Episcopal Administration in England in the Eighteenth Century", in *E.H.R.* vol. xlvii, No. 187, July 1932, pp. 414–46.

[2] *Life of Richard Kidder, Bishop of Bath and Wells*, by Himself, ed. by Mrs A. E. Robinson, pp. 75, 183–4 (Somerset Historical Society, vol. xxxvii (1922)).

and Latin". "He can just read a verse or two in the Greek Testament", reported his lordship to Wake, "and turn an article out of Latin into English, but seems to do it *memoriter* rather than upon any strength he hath in the Latin language or the rules of Syntax. But what is still worse, he is utterly ignorant of everything that relates to the doctrines of the Articles and of every branch of Divinity".[1]

The acquisition of the gift of divers languages seems indeed a perennial difficulty in the Church, requiring in every age the exercise of episcopal discretion and mercy. Archbishop Wake in 1716 expressed to Dr Charlett, Master of University College, Oxford, his anxiety that colleges should provide better instruction in sacred learning. "Surely you may bring tutors to read some system or body of divinity to their pupils, and engage them to make them at least masters of the Greek of the New Testament, which I am sorry to tell you so few who come to us for Holy Orders, or even for faculties, are."[2] In reply Charlett admitted it "a very grievous complaint to hear that their candidates should be so scandalously deficient in so low a part of learning as the Greek Testament, which yet every freshman from Westminster, Eton, or Winchester pretended to....As to systems of divinity, he wished his grace would be so good as to recommend any".[3] In the latter regard the primate confessed himself in a difficulty.

As to your question about systems of divinity to be read to pupils, I know of none that I could recommend. Our church stands upon a different bottom from most of those in which the system-writers have been bred. Expositions of our Church Catechism and of the Articles there are several. And some very good. I wish such as those (though in English) were duly read, and the young men examined in them. And that every tutor should exact of his pupils the constant reading of the Greek Testament, so as at least to make them well acquainted with the text and language of it. This would be a good beginning, and I believe, lay the foundation of much good to our church. For indeed you cannot believe how great the defects of our clergy in all respects are, especially when they first apply to us for Holy Orders.[4]

The persuasion of the importance of proficiency in the Greek Testament would appear to have been shared by the examiner of Parson Woodforde, the totality of whose examination for deacons' orders

---

[1] Bp. Reynolds to Wake, 12 Aug. 1724. Arch. W. Epist. 22, item cccv, f. 459.
[2] Wake to Charlett, 19 June 1716. Ballard MSS. iii, f. 63.
[3] Charlett to Wake, 23 June 1716. Arch. W. Epist. 20, item lxvii, f. 98.
[4] Wake to Charlett, 27 June 1716. Ballard MSS. iii, f. 64.

consisted in an exercise from the Epistle to the Romans. His diary contains under the date 23 May 1763 the following entry:

I went this afternoon at five o'clock to Mr Hewish, the bishop of Oxford's chaplain, before whom I was examined for deacons' orders, and I came off very well. I was set over in the middle of the fifth chapter of St Paul to the Romans and construed that chapter quite to the end. I was quite half an hour examining. He asked a good many hard and deep questions. I had not one question that Yes or No would answer.... Mr Hewish is a very fair examiner and will see whether a man be read or not soon.[1]

Woodforde might have reckoned himself fortunate alike in the brevity of his examination and in the circumstance of his being tested by only one chaplain; for when Thomas Tanner presented himself as a candidate for ordination in the diocese of London during Compton's episcopate in 1694, he had a more exacting ordeal in the chapter house of St Paul's.

"I was examined", he reported to Dr Charlett, "above two hours by the bishop himself, and Dr Beveridge, Dr Stanley, Dr Isham, Dr Alston, and Dr Lancaster. I had a note writ by the bishop himself on the back of my testimonials signifying that I had passed their examination, and accordingly I delivered them in the evening to the Registrar at London House, and subscribed to the Articles and did the other business this afternoon, so that nothing remains but the ordination itself, which will be to-morrow at St Peter's, Cornhill."

It is little surprising in such circumstances that Tanner should have recorded his sentiments of gratitude towards Dr Lancaster, the future Provost of Queen's College, Oxford, of which society he was himself a member, because "when it came to his turn to examine him, he only asked what divinity books he had read, and then was so kind as to tell him that he would trouble him with no more questions".[2] Such careful scrutiny prevented the possibility of fraud and impersonation such as Trelawny of Winchester remembered in a case of one person being "ordained for another who could not undergo the examination for the order of priest".[3] Doubtless the custom of vicarious examination (and ordination) would have been welcomed by many aspirants to the priesthood, more particularly by the candidate who in reply to the question of Bishop Kidder as to "how many there were of the Articles", answered "Two and twenty".[4]

---

[1] *The Diary of a Country Parson* (ed. J. Beresford), i, 25 (cf. p. 19).
[2] Tanner to Charlett, 22 Dec. 1694. Ballard MSS. iv, f. 12.
[3] Trelawny to Wake, 28 Oct. 1716. Arch. W. Epist. 7, Canterbury 11.
[4] *Life of Kidder*, p. 87.

The difficulty of examinations varied naturally according to the zeal of individual bishops; and in the diocese of Gloucester during the episcopate of Warburton, the formidable character of that prelate's learning produced a veritable dearth of ordinands, occasioned, as the bishop pleasantly observed to Hurd, "by their fear of an examination which carried greater terror along with it at Gloucester than elsewhere. Hence the great demand for Letters Dimissory and the scarcity of candidates in person".[1] A perusal indeed of the *Directions for the Study of Theology* written in 1769, though not published until after Warburton's death, affords abundant justification for his lordship's humorous quip that "an examination is a kind of execution".[2] In the eighteenth century, as in all generations of men, it is comforting to reflect that the severity of examinations for Holy Orders was tempered generally by the clemency of the episcopate which mingled mercy with justice in unequal proportions; and there is a note of oecumenical charity in the report of Bishop Gibson in 1718 to Dr Charlett upon the young man whom he had just ordained to the diaconate to serve the cure of the Master's church of Hambledon.

> I admitted Mr Page to deacons' orders on Sunday last, but think myself obliged to acquaint you that his answers upon the examination were not so ready and pertinent as I could have wished....I mention this as the ground of a request to you that he may be made sensible that a like performance will not procure his admission to the order of a priest, and that therefore he must apply himself to the study of divinity.[3]

Of such is the calibre of examinees, and of such the forbearance of bishops, in all ages of the Church Militant.

Around the administration of the rite of ordination there gathered a further crop of difficulties, associated particularly with the grant of testimonials and the bestowal of titles, which increased the embarrassment of the episcopate. A general agreement existed that the aggregate of ordinations was too great, and considerably in excess of the practical possibilities of regular employment, but the establishment of a due and proportionate relation between the number of persons admitted to Holy Orders and the benefices available for their preferment was a task entirely beyond the execution of the bench. Bishop Stillingfleet in the Caroline age had wished to discover some means by which "the multitude of ordinations could be prevented, which had long been a

[1] *Letters of a Late Eminent Prelate*, Warburton to Hurd, 17 Oct. 1769, Letter ccxx, p. 442.
[2] *Ibid.* Letter ccxix, p. 440.
[3] Gibson to Charlett, 23 Sept. 1718. Ballard MSS. vi, f. 78.

great injury to the church", since he was persuaded that "there were at least double the number of clergymen to the benefices and preferments in the kingdom". In particular the episcopate desired to stop the frequent perfunctory grant of letters testimonial to candidates for Orders by which unfit men often secured ordination. Nor were either individual clergy or corporate societies, as colleges in the universities, without blame in respect of the utterance of testimonials often containing unwitting misstatement if not deliberate inveracity. A series of royal and archiepiscopal injunctions had been issued, charging upon the conscience of all persons granting testimonials the duty of strict investigation and rectitude in this regard; and William III's injunctions of 1694, reinforced by Tenison's letter to the bishops of his province in 1695, and the letter of Wake in 1716, laid particular emphasis upon the necessity of personal knowledge of the character of the person recommended on the part of the signatory, and of the proper signing and sealing of college testimonials.[1] Notwithstanding this multitude of exhortation, irregularities and abuses continued.

The enforcement of archiepiscopal regulations in the universities depended evidently upon the bishops particularly connected therewith. Bishop Potter of Oxford reported to Wake in 1723 that

his grace might easily imagine that the obliging all the colleges to conform themselves to those rules had given him some trouble.... The country clergy usually followed the universities, and therefore had the same rules been introduced at Cambridge, they would, of course, in some time come to be observed in all the dioceses of England; and he could not doubt that the bishops of Ely and Lincoln agreeing together, might do in one university what he had done in the other.

He added, however, that a candidate for Orders from Cambridge had presented to him at his last ordination a testimonial so imperfect "that not only the college seal was wanting, but the date", together with other minor irregularities, such as omission to specify the occasion of granting the testimonial.[2] Further, during the compass of one year, he had twice received testimonials from Trinity and Caius Colleges, "both expressly said to be for holy orders, yet in neither of them was there any seal, nor anything spoken of personal knowledge, nor any time specified for which they were certified".[3] Such carelessness in the authentication of testimonials opened an easy and wide door to for-

---

[1] E. Cardwell, *Documentary Annals of the Reformed Church of England*, ii, 380–88, 418–21.
[2] Bp. Potter to Wake, 8 Oct. 1723. Arch. W. Epist. 23, item ccxxxii, f. 352.
[3] Same to Same, 20 Oct. 1723. *Ibid.* item ccxxxiii. f. 354.

geries; and, as Potter observed, the practice of colleges was followed only too faithfully by the parochial clergy. Bishop Burnet confessed that in regard to clerical testimonials "he had found such an easiness in signing these, that unless he knew the men, he grew to regard them very little";[1] whilst Bishop Chandler of Lichfield and Coventry reported to Wake in 1718 that during his primary visitation of his diocese, he had found a candidate for Orders who

"carried with him a college testimonial, and had procured another from clergymen in whose neighbourhood he had not lived of late, no more than he had resided at the university. There is need", added his lordship, "of putting a speedy stop, if the law can do it, to this way of certifying untruths. Within the short time I have been bishop, two testimonials have been offered me for the sobriety of a drunken person upon three years' knowledge, while he was known to the certifiers not above one".[2]

The gravity and persistence of the evil are illustrated by the frequency and iteration of episcopal references to the prevalent laxity in visitation charges throughout the century. Archbishop Secker, in his first charge at Canterbury in 1758, laid particular stress upon the necessity of

"regular testimonials; every part of which ought to be considered before it is given, and no consideration given to neighbourhood, acquaintance, friendship, compassion, importunity when they stand in competition with truth. It may be sometimes hard", he allowed, "to refuse your hand to improper persons; but it is only one of the many hardships which conscience bids men undergo resolutely when they are called to them. It would be much harder that your bishop should be misled, the church of God injured, and the poor wretch himself assisted to invade sacrilegiously an office, at the thought of which he hath cause to tremble".[3]

Similar injunctions were given by Bishop Porteus, who was raised to the see of Chester in 1777, and translated to London in 1787, in his visitation charges, since he found that

it hath become a very mischievous custom among the clergy to consider the holy office of the priesthood in a very mistaken point of view, i.e. as furnishing a ready provision for those who, being in trouble and distressed circumstances, but of a condition removed from the vulgar, were unfit for anything else. Under these notions several very worthy but mistaken clergymen acted very imprudently in giving testimonials of character and ability to very improper

[1] H. C. Foxcroft, *Supplement to Burnet*, p. 503.
[2] Bp. Chandler to Wake, 24 Oct. 1718. Arch. W. Epist. 7, Canterbury II.
[3] Secker, First Charge to the Diocese of Canterbury, *Works*, v, 436.

objects; to those who had nothing but their unprovided nakedness to recommend them. Dr Porteus, like Dr Secker, always warmly condemned this mischievous practice. He was compelled, in many cases, to receive these testimonials on credit; but he never discovered any deception, whether arising from intentional deception or weak compassion, without visiting it with exemplary reproof. In nothing, indeed, should the clergy be more cautious than in these testimonials.[1]

The general condonation afforded by the standards of the age to irregularity in the recommendation of candidates for Orders may be illustrated by the attempted deception practised upon Wake, when bishop of Lincoln, by Mr John Evans, rector of Uffington in Lincolnshire, and prebendary of Peterborough. In 1711 Evans recommended to Wake for admission to Holy Orders a youth of only twenty-two years of age, and "after a repulse at Buckden", he renewed the presentation at Peterborough, where Bishop Cumberland's carelessness allowed the stratagem to succeed. In reply to a severe reproof from Wake that a clergyman of such standing should be a party to a breach of the Canons, the culprit could only plead "the pregnancy of parts by his own examination", shown by the candidate, which "he thought would answer for the design of the canon and make him pass for twenty-six, though but twenty-two years old, and little more by the register", together with "his poor and discouraging circumstances, the present advantageous offers that were made to him, and the pressing solicitations of his relations and other neighbours". The significance of the incident was augmented by the circumstance that in the previous year, being present at the Trinity ordination at Peterborough, Evans had contrasted the laxity there with the strict and careful administration at Lincoln, where Wake "took the nicest care imaginable to prevent all sham and complimental titles and testimonials, and to stop up those scandalous gaps which let ill men so easily into the sacred offices of the church".[2]

The episcopate exercised indeed a certain discretion in interpreting the rule concerning the age of candidates to be admitted to the diaconate.

"I will own to your grace", wrote Bishop Chandler to Wake in 1720, "I have sometimes ordained deacons before they had fulfilled the twenty-third year; and it seems to me the preface to the form of ordination does allow it. The words are: 'None shall be admitted a Deacon, except he be twenty-three years of age, unless he have a faculty; and every man to be admitted a Priest

---

[1] *Life of Porteus*, by a Lay Member of Merton College, p. 219.
[2] N. Sykes, in *E.H.R.* vol. xlvii, No. 187, July 1932, pp. 414–46.

shall be full twenty-four years old'. This I understand of twenty-three years current as opposed to full twenty-four years old. But if he was not entered upon his twenty-third year, then a faculty must be sought for."[1]

A further example of this elasticity was afforded by the circumstances of the recommendation to Richard Hurd at Thurcaston in November 1762, by Dr S. Ogden of St John's College, Cambridge, of a curate to assist him in the duties of that parish.

"I should flatter myself that I had executed your orders most luckily," he wrote of the favoured candidate, "but for one capital objection, which I know not whether you will be able to get over. The young man, I fear, is too young, not to do your duty as he should, but to be put into Orders. But this depends upon the bishop's sentiments, and those probably upon the chaplain's."[2]

Three months later he reported the circumvention of the obstacle.

The little difficulties that were in our way, I believe, are most of them removed. My lord of Lincoln's secretary wrote us a very grave letter about the age of the young man intended for your curate, who wanted some days of twenty-two and a half, and put us in a great fright; but his lordship happening to pass this way shortly after, I waited upon him, and left him, as it seemed to me, in a disposition more gentle.[3]

Accordingly the young man assumed office in March 1763.

The same problems of fraud and falsity connected with testimonials were associated with the grant of fictitious titles. The laxity was not due indeed to any lack of sufficient theoretic instructions, for Canons 31–35 of the Canons of 1604 had laid down precise and careful rules for the conferring of orders, and their precepts had been reinforced by a series of subsequent injunctions, comprising the prohibitions of Laud in 1633 against ordaining *sine titulo,* the detailed orders issued by Sancroft in 1685 concerning the age, academic status, titles, and testimonials of candidates, the similar injunctions issued by William III through Tenison in 1694, and those drawn up by Wake on his accession to the primacy in 1716. Despite this armoury of prohibition and definition, false titles continued to be presented, and on their authority candidates were admitted to Holy Orders. In 1748 Archbishop Herring was exceedingly alarmed at the probable effects of the proposed bill to

[1] Bp. Chandler to Wake, 23 May 1720. Arch. W. Epist. 8, Canterbury III.
[2] Dr S. Ogden to Hurd, 24 Nov. 1762. Hurd MSS. IV, Section 2.
[3] Same to Same, 19 Jan. 1763. *Ibid.* Section 3.

legalise in Scotland only Orders conferred by English and Irish bishops, which he foresaw would lay the English episcopate under the necessity of ordaining Scottish candidates without any guarantee as to their titles, thereby increasing the confusion of the ecclesiastical administration.

Contrary to all common rules of prudence, in ordaining these people in this vagrant way, we shall use the least caution where all we can use will be extremely necessary, and our own people, whom we know and see every day, will be the only subjects of our care and reserve. The restraint of a title is so necessary in the administration of our dioceses, that if the rule was once dropped, we should all be in confusion very soon.[1]

It is perhaps worthy of note that Bishop Richard Watson appears to have maintained an unblemished record in this regard; for in May 1812, in refusing to ordain a candidate who had no title in his diocese, he declared that "he did not consider a title as a mere ecclesiastical formality, but as an ancient and an useful institution, from which he had never deviated, except in one instance, when he ordained Mr Brown, who was going in 1765 to superintend the Orphan School, then established in Bengal by the British officers".[2]

For the solution of the complex of difficulties surrounding the conditions and circumstances of the admission of candidates to Holy Orders no single measure of reform could be adequate. Nor could effective reform be undertaken until the episcopate, liberated from extraneous duties, could devote more time to their ecclesiastical administration and maintain a less intermittent and more continuous contact with their extensive dioceses.

The difficulties which beset the bishops in their endeavours to regulate wisely the admission of candidates to Holy Orders were multiplied greatly in the other branches of their administration, especially in relation to the confirmation of the laity. For whereas persons desirous of receiving ordination and institution to a benefice might attend upon their diocesan in London, their lordships must needs proceed in person to their dioceses to confer the grace of confirmation upon the children and adult members of their flock. The 60th Canon of the Canons of 1604, entitled *Confirmation to be performed once in three Years*, reciting the tradition whereby "this holy action hath been accustomed in the church in former ages to be performed in the bishop's visitation every third year", decreed "that every bishop or his suffragan, in his accustomed visitation, do in his own person carefully observe the said

---

[1] Herring to Hardwicke, 7 May 1748. Add. MSS. 35598, f. 325.
[2] Watson MSS. in the Chapter Archives at Llandaff.

custom. And if, in that year, by reason of some infirmity, he be not able personally to visit, then he shall not omit the execution of that duty of confirmation the next year after, as he may conveniently". Accordingly the association of the two offices of visitation and confirmation was accepted generally as the only practicable arrangement, and the rite was administered triennially by the episcopate in the course of their visitation, supplemented upon occasion by shorter circuits during the summer parliamentary recess. Even to the most diligent prelate the execution of this aspect of his office was encompassed by almost insuperable obstacles. In this, as in no other branch of his pastoral charge, the difficulties of the unwieldy extent of some dioceses and of the problems of travel pressed with intolerable gravity. On the part of the bishops themselves, the mode of travel was restricted to the alternatives of horseback or coach; and a glance at the territorial extent of such sees as Chester and York in the north, Lincoln in the midlands, Winchester in the south, Exeter in the west, and St David's in the remoteness of South Wales indicates sufficiently the difficulty of covering such vast distances. Further, when the details of episcopal itineraries were being projected, consideration must be had to a variety of local factors: such as the distances to be travelled between the several centres of visitation and confirmation, the condition of the connecting roads, the exigencies of the summer harvesting operations from the labours of which the country people could not easily be withdrawn, the incidence of the grand market days of the county, and the determination of the day and hour at which the laity could with least inconvenience attend; so that the bishop's route might be ordered with the maximum of profit to his people and the minimum of fatigue to himself. It was not only political necessity which restricted the season of confirmation to the summer months, but natural circumstances also; for the majority of roads were wellnigh impassable in winter, and the maximum of daylight was requisite for the episcopal itinerary; and therefore when the offices of visitation and confirmation were combined, the former was generally held in the morning and the latter in the afternoon, enduring not infrequently so long as the summer light allowed. Under such difficulties even the most conscientious prelates were unable to satisfy the demands of all their critics, or even of themselves, since many gaps remained and many regions of their dioceses were unvisited for long years. The extreme of uncertainty in regard to the opportunities for receiving the grace of confirmation may be illustrated not inaptly from the *Diary* of Bishop Cartwright of Chester, which records two occasions in December 1686 and September

1687 on which his lordship, on the eve of their ordination, administered the rite to three and four candidates for the diaconate, who had lacked occasion for its reception previously although they had been born and bred up in the Restoration Church after the return of the Anglican episcopate and discipline in 1660.[1]

Many examples might be adduced of the zeal and endeavours of bishops of the eighteenth century to surmount the obstacles to the discharge of this branch of their duty; and indeed it is from the practical testimony of contemporary accounts that an understanding may best be reached alike of the shortcomings and of the real achievement of the Hanoverian prelacy. Burnet excelled in care for this, as for all functions of the episcopal office.

"I resolved", he wrote in retrospect of his work in 1710, "to go round my diocese about three weeks or a month once a year, preaching and confirming every day from church to church,...I continued still to go about preaching and confirming, so that I have preached and confirmed in 275 churches of my diocese, and ten or twelve times in all the market towns and considerable places. I look upon confirmation, if rightly managed, as the most effectual means possible for reviving Christianity, but I could never prevail with the greater part of my clergy to think of any other way of preparing their youth to it but to hear them repeat their catechism; they did not study to make them consider it as the becoming a Christian by an act of their own. I have now settled upon a method in which I intend to continue as long as God continues my strength to execute it. I stay a week in a place where every morning I go and preach and confirm in some church within six or seven miles of the place; and then at 5 o'clock after evening prayer I catechise some children and explain the whole catechism to them, so that I go through it all in six days and confirm there the next Lord's day; and make presents to the value of about a crown a child to all whom I catechised, and I have them all to dine with me on the Lord's day".[2]

In like manner Archbishop Sharp held confirmations in his diocese with greater frequency than his triennial visitations, embarking upon these circuits with a grave sense of the responsibility of his office; and particularly

upon one time, while he confirmed with the gout upon him that he could not stand, but sat in his chair at the communion rails, and the catechumens were brought to him, one after another, he first recovered so much strength as by resting one knee upon a chair, which was gently moved along, he could

[1] *Diary of Bishop Cartwright*, pp. 19, 81. Camden Society, 1843.
[2] H. C. Foxcroft, *Supplement to Burnet*, pp. 499–500.

proceed as usual along the rails, and soon after he quitted that support, and confirmed some thousands of persons, and after profuse sweating lost his distemper entirely.[1]

In fidelity to the highest standards of pastoral duty bishops of high- and low-church traditions were equally pre-eminent; for diligence transcended all distinctions of party. Kidder of Bath and Wells embarked in 1693 upon a confirmation tour in several market towns of his diocese, finding at Bridgwater especially "a vast appearance" of candidates.

"I did indeed give notice," he related, "I also appointed a worthy divine to preach upon that occasion, and I likewise did it myself. I had sent about to the ministers thereabouts a printed paper containing directions to the ministers not only to give notice of the confirmation, but what method to take the better to prepare their youth for it, together with a printed exhortation to be read two Sundays in the church to the parishioners to awaken them to a sense of their duty. I also ordered the ministers to draw up all the names of those persons whom they had examined and thought fit to be confirmed, and to deliver me these lists signed with their own hands, that these persons might be called over, and that I might not be imposed upon by others, who might thrust themselves upon me and perhaps had neither been instructed nor baptised before. The ministers did their duty exactly, and many were prepared and thus confirmed, and I make no doubt to their great advantage. And the people were made sensible that confirmation was not a mere ceremony to be trifled with, or done perfunctorily....I thought I had never done in my whole life a better day's work; I am sure a more painful and wearisome day I never spent."[2]

In the diocese of Peterborough the results of many years' incapacity on the part of Bishop Cumberland were reflected in the paucity of confirmations held during his long episcopate, so that his successor White Kennett set to work at once to recover the arrears and to offer as many opportunities as possible for the reception of that grace. In his primary visitation of his clergy in 1720 he invited their earnest co-operation in this task.

"I do intend", he declared, "if God permits, to have frequent confirmations, not only at the times and places where I visit, but at other seasons, and in other populous towns and parishes, (especially upon your requests), of which due notice shall be given. And in the meantime, if in any of your congregations there be a number of adult persons who shall be ready and desirous to be confirmed, and are unwilling to wait for an uncertain oppor-

[1] *Life of Sharp*, ii, 82.   [2] *Life of Kidder*, pp. 81–2.

tunity, they shall be admitted to the benefit thereof in the mother cathedral church at any stated hours of morning or evening prayer while I am in residence there, upon their being presented by their respective ministers or bringing commendations from them. And in the seats of noblemen who have domestic chapels, and desire the confirmation of their children and family in them, I shall be ready to attend and perform the office there, upon signifying such desire, that there may be no let or impediment on my part of dispensing that excellent ordinance throughout every district and if possible to all and singular persons in this diocese who are baptised and bred and will live in our communion."[1]

Even before his visitation he had begun the urgent work by holding "solemn confirmations at the neighbouring towns, with very great appearance, there having been none (no, not in the cathedral church) for many years". Nor did his practice fall below the precept and promise made to his clergy. In 1720, during the course of his visitation, he "stayed to confirm three several days at Northampton, where his predecessor had not been able to perform that duty for about thirteen years' last past";[2] and in 1722 he went further afield into Rutland.

"I have entered on my stages of confirmation", he wrote to Wake in July of that year, "and began at Uppingham in Rutland, within which county they have had no confirmation these forty years. The numbers as taken by one of my attendants were 1700 and odd. I appoint it on Sundays after noon, because the good folks have their best clothes and horses to spare; otherwise we should have very few upon these dripping days when they must wait upon their hay and corn. I intend constantly to preach myself in the morning and to have evening prayer over before 3, and to spend the remainder of the day in that office. I had not done at Uppingham till after ten at night."[3]

In view of these evidences of the pastoral zeal of White Kennett, it is worthy of recollection that in the famous altar-piece of the Last Supper set up in the parish church of Whitechapel by Dr Welton, the rector, the features of the bishop were represented in the person of Judas Iscariot, because of the unpopularity of his political whiggism amongst high churchmen. So great was the power of political rancour to intrude upon the sacred offices of religion; yet it is from such biased sources that most of the denunciations of whig and Latitudinarian bishops have descended into the common form of historical writers, to whom the instance of White Kennett may serve alike as caution and rebuke. In 1722 likewise Bishop Chandler of Lichfield found at Wolverhampton

[1] White Kennett, *Primary Visitation Charge* (1720), p. 19.
[2] White Kennett to Charlett, 4 Sept. 1720. Ballard MSS. vii, f. 82.
[3] White Kennett to Wake, 18 July 1722. Arch. W. Epist. 22, item cxxxviii, f. 216.

similar conditions to those prevailing at Northampton, since that town, as he reported to Wake, "being very populous and without confirmation these twenty-seven years, will afford business for two or three days".[1] It was at this same town of Wolverhampton also that Bishop John Douglas halted on his northward journey to his diocese of Carlisle in 1788, and "as dean there with an exempt jurisdiction, held a confirmation of above 3000 persons on Saturday July 19th".[2]

Archbishop Wake writing in 1718 to Charlett concerning the recent holding of a confirmation in his parish of Hambledon by Gibson of Lincoln, declared that he "believed the confirmations had never been so regular throughout the kingdom as within the last thirty years, nor the episcopal visitations and that by the bishops in person, so constant".[3] Nor did the standard suffer evident decline during the half-century following, for examples may be quoted from different dioceses and bishops, often unexpected in their provenance, to illustrate the diligent endeavour of the episcopate to grapple with the formidable obstacles to the execution of confirmation tours. In a letter of 1761 to Hurd, Bishop Warburton, who is generally reported to have carried lightly the administrative duties of his office, adumbrated his proposal to render edifying his forthcoming visitation and confirmation.

I am taking care to have the principal work done with all the decency I can. God knows whether my clergy will be benefited by my visitation. But I am sure I benefit the young in a proper administration of the very important rite of Confirmation. To administer it properly, I have thoughts of confining it (by the leave of my clergy, for there it will rest at last) to females of fourteen and upwards, and males of sixteen and upwards. Pray tell me what you think of this particular. Then as to the decent administration, as there are intermediate days in the visitation, I intend to use those days in *other* more commodious places for confirmation. So that this celebration being distributed between the days of confirmation and days of visitation, it may be done without hurry or confusion. And for a further security against this scandal, I propose to have blank certificates printed, to be distributed amongst the clergy, to fill up and give to those they have examined and judged fit.[4]

In his charge at Oxford in 1741 Secker assured his clergy that "so long as it pleased God to continue his health and strength, confirmations should be frequent in every part of the diocese", adding that "for this

[1] Chandler to Wake, 30 June 1722. Arch. W. Epist. 9, Canterbury IV.
[2] *Autobiography of Bishop John Douglas*, p. 56. B.M. Eg. 2181.
[3] Wake to Charlett, 23 May 1718. Ballard MS. iii, f. 74.
[4] Warburton to Hurd, 24 Mch. 1761. *Letters of a Late Eminent Prelate*, Letter cli, pp. 326–7.

purpose, when confirmations were on a Sunday, which was the time he would usually pitch upon for the convenience of the people excepting at the places of his visitation, they might omit for that day the morning or the evening prayers as they saw occasion". In regard to the age of candidates to be presented, Secker mentioned "the age of fourteen, not with a design of absolutely tying them down to it, but as being for the most part early enough", and as a rule to be opposed by the clergy "to the indiscreet forwardness of parents".[1] In like manner Wake, before embarking upon a confirmation tour in the diocese of Canterbury in 1724, sent out notice of his intention to admit to that ordinance only "such as should be certified to him in a list under the hands [of the clergy] to have been examined and approved as duly qualified for it, and being boys were of the age of 14, and being girls were 12 years old or more".[2] Gibson, in deference to the authority of Lyndwood, who had laid down that no person should be allowed to be adult till he was above fourteen years of age, accepted this as a satisfactory minimum for confirmation, though preferring the age stated in the 112th Canon of the Canons of 1604, namely sixteen years, as that before which no person could be required to receive the Holy Communion.[3]

In consideration of the problems attending the administration of confirmation and of the efforts of the episcopate to overcome them, attention may be directed to a variety of examples taken from dioceses of diverse extent and character and from episcopates covering different generations of the eighteenth century. In the compact, albeit remote, border diocese of Carlisle, Nicolson, who succeeded to the bishopric in 1702, was faced by a considerable volume of arrears, since his predecessor Thomas Smith, who held the see from 1684 to 1702, had omitted to hold any visitation in person during the entire eighteen years of his office. In his primary visitation therefore the new bishop reported that "he confirmed (in that small unpeopled diocese) 5449 persons, very few of which were under 16 years of age".[4] Throughout his episcopate he combined the work of confirmation with that of visitation, and without great difficulty, since the smallness of his territory, comprising only four deaneries and little more than a hundred parishes, "seldom kept him above two nights from his own bed". The only other figures available are for the year 1707, when he confirmed at

---

[1] Secker, Charge II, *Works*, v, 337–9.
[2] Wake MSS. Arch. W. Epist. 9, Canterbury IV.
[3] N. Sykes, *Edmund Gibson*, p. 220.
[4] Nicolson to Charlett, 24 Sept. 1702. Ballard MSS. iv, f. 7.

the four usual visitation centres of Carlisle, Wigton, Penrith, and Appleby a total of 1153 candidates.[1] At Appleby in 1702 his lordship had laid hands upon 800 persons "without pause and singly". Notwithstanding the advantages of so small a diocese, Nicolson's successor in the see, Bishop Samuel Bradford, resolved to separate the work of confirmation from that of visitation in order to the more edifying discharge of the former.

"I made my visitation", he related to Wake, in 1719, "at the four usual places...that I might as soon as possible acquaint myself with the state of my diocese....I have hitherto met with all due respect from the clergy, which I hope to preserve by a faithful discharge of my duty amongst them. I did not confirm during my visitation, as believing it could not be done in so orderly and decent a manner as I desired; but have promised to go through the diocese again, as far as I am able, to confirm a few parishes at a time, such as can most easily be got together."[2]

This project he executed in 1721, "appointing one or two days in a week for that purpose, that it might be done more regularly and with greater ease both to himself and the people".[3]

During the episcopate of Wake and Gibson at Lincoln the conditions of episcopal itineraries for the work of confirmation in the largest diocese of England and Wales, embracing over 1300 parishes, were fully indicated in the schemes and arrangements made by these prelates. It is fortunate that the details of Wake's confirmations in the visitations of 1709 and 1712 have survived, for they shed a clear light on the magnitude of the task to which he had set his hand. During the course of the former circuit, he confirmed at twenty-four different centres of his diocese, at twenty-one of which he halted only for one day, staying two days at Leicester, three at Lincoln, and two at Huntingdon, embarking upon his itinerary on 31 May and concluding on 18 September. The number of persons upon whom he laid hands was approximately 12,800; of whom 5200 were from the county of Lincoln, 3100 from that of Leicester, and 1250 from that of Buckingham. The heaviest figures for single places were 1200 at Grantham, 1000 at Boston, 800 each at Harborough, Melton Mowbray, Banbury, and Lincoln, each batch being dealt with in one day, save at Lincoln, where the bishop sojourned to hold his visitation of the cathedral and his ordination on Trinity Sunday. Three years later, in 1712, he set out on 22 May and

---

[1] I am indebted for these figures to Mr P. J. Dunn's M.A. thesis (London).
[2] Bradford to Wake, 22 June 1719. Arch. W. Epist. 21, item cxx, f. 182.
[3] Same to Same, 6 July 1721. Arch. W. Epist. 9. Canterbury IV.

concluded on 24 July, halting at twenty-eight different centres, and confirming approximately 18,330 persons, exclusive of a further small company of 160 at Buckden in the autumn before his return to London. Upon this visitation he lodged at Leicester three days to admit 960 candidates, confirmed at Lincoln on four separate days a total of about 1900 persons, whilst at Caistor there were over 1000, and at Spalding "fere 2000".[1]

Despite the large numbers thus confirmed during the last two visitations of Wake, his successor in the see, Gibson, found no less overwhelming crowds attending upon his appearance. At his primary visitation he announced his intention, owing to ill-health, of dividing the task of visitation from that of confirmation; but upon setting out in 1718 for the sole purpose of confirming he found himself unable to sustain the fatigue of that duty.

"I had laid out my course of confirmations", he wrote to Wake, "for seven places in Buckinghamshire and four in Bedfordshire, in hopes that my repairing to so many places might reduce the numbers to 300 or 400 at each place; which I knew was as far as my broken constitution would carry me, especially for eleven days together. But to my great surprise I found 700 at Beaconsfield, and the same numbers at Wendover and Wiccomb respectively, within a very few over or under; which I went through on Tuesday, Wednesday, and Thursday with a good deal of difficulty and fatigue. And having good reason to apprehend that the numbers would increase upon me as I went forward into the more open and populous parts of the country, and that it would be impossible for me to go on in that way without the greatest hazard of health and indeed of life, I found it necessary to give it over for the present till I can bring it into a method that may be more practicable for me."[2]

This experience convinced Gibson that the only means

"for doing the work on the one hand regularly and effectively and on the other hand consistently with the lives and safety of the bishops", was "to send to each minister six weeks or two months beforehand, to know how many they have who desire confirmation and are fitted for it; and then to summon as many neighbouring parishes as will furnish out 400 or thereabouts to some certain place to be confirmed there, exclusive of all other parishes, and so to go on from district to district at the rate of 400 a day".[3]

[1] See Appendix A for lists of Confirmation Tours of the dioceses of Lincoln, Worcester, and Exeter, pp. 429–36.
[2] Gibson to Wake, 24 May 1718. Arch. W. Epist. 20, item ccclxiv, f. 483.
[3] Gibson to Charlett, 31 May 1718. Ballard MSS. vi, f. 76; Sykes, *Edmund Gibson*, p. 75.

Modern estimates of the efficiency of the administration of the rite of confirmation during the eighteenth century need frequent qualification by reference to contemporary difficulties such as were experienced by Gibson in the vast diocese of Lincoln.

Parallel problems of territorial extent and arduous itineraries were present in the archdiocese of York, as the figures collected by Canon Ollard in his survey of confirmations, especially those of Archbishop Drummond, abundantly testify.[1] During the archiepiscopate of Blackburne indeed confirmations appear to have been virtually discontinued, save for the magnificent endeavour of Bishop Martin Benson of Gloucester in 1737, who laid hands at Halifax and Ripponden upon approximately 8922 persons and also consecrated a new church, being in church "from about 9 in the morning till near 7 at night on the 10 and 11 of September". The next primate in succession, Herring, remained at York only four years, confirming in the years 1743–4 and 1747, whilst Archbishop Hutton confirmed in 1748–9 in person, and Bishop Keene of Chester on his behalf in 1755. In like manner Archbishop Gilbert used the services of Drummond of St Asaph and of Bishop Hotham of Clogher in 1758 (each of whom laid hands upon about 15,000 candidates), and of the bishops of Chester and Durham in 1760, in addition to his personal circuits in 1759–60. This insight into the vast territory of the see was of particular value to Drummond, who succeeded Gilbert in 1761, and of whose confirmation tours fuller details have survived. In 1763 he confirmed in the Nottinghamshire part of his diocese 3957 persons, and in 1769 in the same area 8423; whilst in the former year he confirmed also in the chief towns of the west riding 15,827, and in the year 1768, again, 17,777 persons; and in 1763 in the scattered area of the north and east ridings he confirmed 5896 candidates, and in 1770, 13,300. Amidst the conditions of travel and the distances to be covered, Drummond laboured zealously in laying hands upon 41,600 persons during the short period from 1768 to 1771; and it is interesting to observe that in 1768 his confirmations in the populous towns of the west riding were undertaken in the course of his journey northwards from the capital. Together with Lincoln, York indeed presented the greatest difficulties, by reason not only of vast extent but scattered deaneries.

Within the more compact territory of the see of Worcester, the episcopate of Bishop Hurd from 1781 to 1808 established a pattern of

[1] S. L. Ollard, "Confirmation in the Anglican Communion", pp. 199–201, and Appendix II, pp. 225–31; in *Confirmation*, vol. i (S.P.C.K. 1926). The essay is valuable throughout.

orderly and regular confirmation tours.[1] In 1782 the bishop embarked upon his primary visitation, combining with it the work of confirmation, halting at nine places between 20 July and 4 August, and laying hands upon a total of 6490 persons. The greatest numbers were 2000 at Shipston and 1200 at Alcester. Three years later, in 1785, between 21 August and 18 September, Hurd confirmed at nine centres again, with a total of 5260 candidates, of which the largest companies were 1200 at Old Swinford and 1000 at Bromsgrove. After this dual experience of the combination of confirmation with visitation his lordship resolved henceforth to separate the functions, and to make special circuits for the confirming of the laity. Accordingly in 1788 he held confirmations at ten places, commencing on 10 June and terminating on the 27th, confirming 8200 persons, 1200 at Alcester, 1100 at Warwick, 1000 each at Kineton and in Worcester Cathedral, and 900 each at Shipston and Hales Owen. The visitation was postponed until 1790, and in 1792 the bishop resumed his confirmation itinerary, staying at eleven centres between 31 May and 17 June, and administering the rite to 3945 people, of whom 1850 were gathered at Bromsgrove, 1248 at Old Swinford, and 1022 at Stratford. In 1793 Hurd visited his diocese, and in 1795 undertook a further confirmation circuit, setting out on 27 May and finishing on 14 June, during which period he had confirmed at ten places a total of 5794 candidates, no single locality rising higher on this occasion than 883 at Bromsgrove. In the following year he held a visitation, and in 1799 confirmed in his diocese for the last time in person, commencing at Hartlebury on 26 May and concluding at Pershore on 13 June, halting at eleven places, and laying hands upon 7464 people, the greatest numbers being 1152 in the cathedral church and 1069 at Bromsgrove. "It pleased God", ran an entry in his diary, "that I was able this summer to confirm over all parts of my diocese", and in the following summer "to visit my diocese in person once more." Owing to old age and infirmities—for with the end of the century Hurd attained his eightieth year—the bishop held his visitation of 1803 by commissaries, and likewise in 1806, whilst in 1805 Bishop Majendie of Chester confirmed on 27–29 March at Stratford, Bromsgrove, and Hales Owen, and Bishop Cornwall of Hereford on 14–17 June at Worcester, Pershore, and Kidderminster, a total of 7184 people on behalf of the diocesan. The restriction of the number of centres in 1805 led to the lowest figures being 826 and 830 at Hales Owen and Pershore respectively, whilst 1019 were confirmed at Kidderminster, 1283 at

[1] Act Book of Bishop Hurd, in the Diocesan Registry at Worcester. See Appendix A, pp. 431–2.

Stratford, 1441 at Worcester, and 1785 at Bromsgrove. The record of the fidelity of Hurd in discharging the duty of confirmation during the last quarter of the eighteenth century indicates no declension from the pastoral standards of Queen Anne's episcopate so far as his diocese of Worcester was concerned.

Of equal value and interest are the details of confirmation circuits undertaken in the large see of Exeter by Bishops Keppel in 1764–5 and Ross in 1779, 1782, 1785, and 1786. In view of the political circumstances which influenced the elevation of Keppel to the bench and his character as a scion of the aristocracy, it is the more interesting to observe that he is reputed to have been "the first of the Exeter bishops to hold systematically visitations of his diocese", visiting four times during his episcopate and "making it his practice to go through his diocese every three or four years".[1] In regard to his primary visitation indeed Keppel earned the approbation of Archbishop Secker, who was "highly pleased with his conduct, behaviour, and attention in the long visitation he made that summer" of 1765.[2] In the previous year the bishop had confirmed throughout the county of Devon, between 17 May and 6 July, no fewer than 23,946 persons, the figures in some centres being astonishing in their magnitude.[3] At Honiton on two successive days he laid hands upon 1785 candidates, at Tiverton 1762 were confirmed, 1172 in one day and the rest on the morrow, at Barnstaple in three days 2496 persons presented themselves, at Torrington likewise in three days 2079, at Okehampton 1362, at Plymouth 1482, both needing two days' halt, and at Totnes 4396 people were assembled to receive the grace of this rite; whilst for the parishes neighbouring Exeter itself the bishop confirmed on nine days a total of 3616 persons. During the course of the following year he extended his visitation and confirmation tour to Cornwall, and there in like manner laid hands upon 17,696 people, making a grand total of 41,642 for the entire diocese.[4]

Fuller details survive of the itineraries of his successor in the see, Bishop Ross, who in 1779, between 9 June and 30 July, confirmed throughout the extent of his diocese 25,548 candidates; at Barnstaple in the course of one day there being no fewer than 4016 people who received confirmation, whilst at Torrington there were 1640 on two days,

---

[1] R. J. E. Boggis, *History of the Diocese of Exeter*, pp. 458–9.

[2] Newcastle to Albemarle, 24 Sept. 1765. Add. MSS. 32970, f. 39.

[3] Confirmation Records, item 543, in the Exeter Diocesan Registry. See Appendix A, pp. 433–6.

[4] R. J. E. Boggis, *op. cit.* p. 465. I have not found details of the 1765 confirmation in the Diocesan Registry.

at Okehampton 1354 on two days, and likewise 1048 at Launceston, 901 at Truro, 928 at Helston, 947 at Redruth, 1399 at Liskeard, and 2024 at Plymouth, with 1464 at Totnes on the bishop's return journey to Exeter.[1] Three years later, in 1782, Ross embarked again upon the tour of his scattered diocese, confirming 14,939 people between 19 June and 6 August, travelling to the extreme west at Penzance, but finding at Totnes only a company of over 1000; whilst upon his next triennial circuit in 1785 he laid hands upon 13,156 persons in Devonshire, and in 1786 upon 9133 in Cornwall. During the former year totals of over one thousand were registered again at Barnstaple with 1101, Totnes with 1380, and Plymouth with 1700; whilst in Cornwall at Launceston there were 1012, Truro 1051, 985 at Penzance, and 1333 at Liskeard.

"The journeys were in many cases long," observes the historian of the diocese, "they would be long to us with our railways and good roads; and we are filled with wonderment as we try to picture the arrangements for such undertakings as would be necessary, when many candidates had to be conveyed fifteen or twenty miles, as from Lynton to Barnstaple, or from Hartland to Bideford, or from Holsworthy to Okehampton, or from Kilkhampton to Launceston, or Torrington."[2]

Nor may the tribute of admiration be withheld from the prelates who made sustained and protracted journeys throughout the counties of Devon and Cornwall in diligence for the fulfilment of the office and work of a bishop. No little fatigue was the result of such arduous travelling, and of the long days' work of laying hands upon so great companies of laity assembled to receive the episcopal grace. Certainly it ill becomes critics of the railroad and motor-car ages to disparage the endeavours of bishops of previous centuries, even the eighteenth, until before casting their stones they have made trial of the task under like conditions of difficulty and distance.

Of the shortcomings and disadvantages of the methods of administering confirmation in the Hanoverian epoch no doubt may exist. Nor were contemporaries blind to such circumstances, the severest critics of the episcopate being in general their inferior clergy. Bishop Manningham of Chichester, who was very much of a valetudinarian— in 1715 he had sent to Wake a formidable catalogue of his afflictions, "continual colds, frequent cholics and languishing sweats, . . . besides a cluster of smaller infirmities, headaches, toothaches, sore throats,

---

[1] Confirmation Records, item 544, in the Exeter Diocesan Registry. See Appendix A, pp. 433–6.
[2] R. J. E. Boggis, *op. cit.* p. 464.

etc."—ventured in 1718 upon a short confirmation tour, staying at Horsham a week and at Lewes four days.

"I thank God", he related to the primate, "that under all my weaknesses, I have been enabled to do my duty and to undergo rough journeys, and bad lodgings better than I thought I could; besides this, 'tis very bad for one who is subject to frequent strangenesses and gripings to be confined so long together in the church, with one's episcopal habit on. The expense one is at in doing this duty (which I look upon as the least of the burthens that attend it), would be considerable to some, for it cost me nearly £20 in executing this little part of my office; a constant table to be kept for the clergy and some others; paying for ringing, when there are hardly any bells; giving to the poor who are ready to devour one; besides other items which make a good sum when put together; but all this I count dross for the sake of serving our great Master."[1]

From the standpoint of the archdeacon of Lewes, Mr Richard Bowchier, however, these gratifying features of the episcopal itinerary presented a very different aspect.

"The Bishop of Chichester", ran his report in September, also to Wake, "about the latter end of June confirmed at Lewes, and it is much to be wished that he would have given himself the trouble, and the county the satisfaction, in proceeding into the eastern parts of the diocese, and there have confirmed at Hastings, Winchelsea, Rye, and other places where there hath not been a confirmation these many years, and of which the clergy of the archdeaconry of Lewes do very much complain."[2]

Even in the area covered, his lordship was subject to severe criticism as having stayed at Lewes only two full days, an insufficient time, and having arrived there suddenly without notice, "and sent the apparitor about after his arrival to Lewes, so that very few could be brought in to be confirmed".

Similar complaints were vented against Bishop Green of Lincoln in 1766 by the diarist William Cole, in no small spleen and temper.

When I receive a citation from a Right Reverend John, Lord Bishop, on this day by the Apparitor (August 5), to attend his visitation at Newport-Pagnell, on the 27th, where I am to pay my procurations, exhibit my letters of Orders and institution, and he is to confirm the children of my parish, when there is barely three weeks' notice to prepare them for that ordinance;

---

[1] Manningham to Wake, 26 June 1718. Arch. W. Epist. 20, item ccclxxvii, f. 501.
[2] R. Bowchier to Wake, 27 Sept. 1718. Arch. W. Epist. 21, item xxxv, f. 60.

and when he comes, it is done in such hurry, with such noise and confusion, as to seem more like a bear-baiting than any religious institution and so must haste to have it over, that it evidently appears it is no small burthen to attend at all, I then say that such farces make one ashamed and confused.[1]

Considerable injustice was done to the bishop in this tirade; for on the day of the confirmation Cole fell foul of his diocesan because of the latter's requirement that "everyone should have a written certificate" before being presented, a rule which the diarist had failed to observe, although designed precisely to prevent such confusion and disorder as had provoked his denunciation.[2] Further, if Cole had been diligent in catechising according to the canonical rule, he would not have been caught unawares by the three weeks' notice, but would have needed only to use that interval for the revision of previous preparation.

The attempt of a bishop moreover to take precautions for order and solemnity in the administration of confirmation did not always meet with a sympathetic response from his clergy. When Gibson at Lincoln announced at his primary visitation his resolve to separate the work of confirmation from that of visitation, this breach of traditional custom was displeasing to his auditors. Archdeacon Trimnell of Leicester reported to Wake that "the whole country was dissatisfied"; so that it was stated "that the reason given by the Corporation of Boston why they did not receive his lordship with the usual ceremony...was because he did not confirm; but the expectation his lordship had put them under of coming round again on purpose for that work, had made that matter more easy". The archdeacon added further that he did not hear that "the bishop preached himself anywhere;...and yet his healthy looks would not convince people that his infirmities were as great as his complaints".[3] When Gibson was compelled later to abandon in mid-course even his confirmation circuit, much comment was evoked by the difficulty of sending round an apparitor to the various parishes already summoned, to announce the change of plans. In this regard it must be allowed that more justice resided in a criticism made of Willis of Salisbury in 1723 by one of his clergy.

My diocesan, Willis, was to have held his primary visitation this week. The days were fixed, and public notice given to all the clergy to bring their children to be confirmed. Upon the death of Winchester, his lordship appears not, but sends his chancellor. Many poor clergy, who can have no notice,

---

[1] *The Blecheley Diary of William Cole*, pp. 22–3.   [2] *Ibid.* p. 99.
[3] Archdeacon Trimnell to Wake, 3 July 1718. Arch. W. Epist. 20, item ccclxxxiv, f. 508.

may bring their children with them and find no bishop to confirm them. No doubt his lordship is employed on that which will be of more use to the church of God, the getting a better bishopric for himself.[1]

This pungent censure would have been even more barbed if its author, Canon Stratford of Christ Church, had been resident personally upon his benefice in the diocese of Sarum, instead of delegating the preparation of children for confirmation to his curate, whilst he enjoyed the society of Oxford; but, allowing for the animus of a pluralist tory presbyter against a whig bishop, the fact remained that Willis, having been appointed to Salisbury only in 1721, forsook that see for Winchester in September 1723.

The criticisms voiced thus by contemporaries have been repeated with emphasis by later writers, not uninspired by a desire to discredit the episcopate of the pre-Tractarian epoch. Canon Ollard, after quoting the large numbers confirmed by Archbishop Drummond in 1768, observes that "the conditions under which confirmation was administered to such enormous numbers, in churches which could accommodate but a small part of the candidates at one time, can be realised from the account of confirmations in the diocese of Ely in 1829 and 1833 below",[2] the example being chosen for its peculiar character of chaos and disorderliness. The dissatisfaction of the critic was happily not shared by the archbishop, who wrote to the duke of Newcastle, in relation to the very confirmation tour thus aspersed, that "the numbers were greater than five years ago in my last tour, and the order and regularity increased, which was very happy".[3] Ten years earlier Drummond, confirming for Archbishop Gilbert in 1758, had found in the towns of the west riding everything to pass "with great ease and order", since "the persons concerned in the different towns kept great order, the constables and churchwardens all attended and everything was well conducted".[4] Notwithstanding the satisfaction of Drummond with the decorum of his confirmations, there is real point in the criticism concerning the difficulty of managing so great crowds and numbers. But the problem and the confusion were not unique to the whig prelates of the eighteenth century. One of the chief complaints of the seventeenth-century Puritans against the Anglican episcopate of their generation was in regard to the noise, hurry, and chaos attendant upon the administration of confirmation; and upon this ground of its

[1] Portland MSS. vii, 365.   [2] S. L. Ollard, in *Confirmation*, i, 200.
[3] Abp. Drummond to Newcastle, 30 Sept. 1768. Add. MSS. 32991, A. f. 154.
[4] S. L. Ollard, in *Confirmation*, i, 226–7.

unedifying performance they built much of their objection to the ordinance itself.

"Indeed", observed Richard Baxter, "it is here made impossible to be done any otherwise ordinarily than as a ceremony. For the dioceses are so vast that the bishop cannot do this and other his offices for the hundredth part of his flock. Suppose this diocese [London] have but five or six hundred thousand souls...do you think that the bishop is able (did he work as hard as any nonconformist) to confirm six hundred thousand persons, or the twentieth part of them, or the hundredth, in that serious manner as belongs to the binding of a soul to Christ in so solemn a covenant? It becometh not me to enquire whether bishops be men that are for so much seriousness in Christianity themselves, and so much labour to attain it. Some are far better than others....But I must say, that as far as I can learn, there is not one of an hundred confirmed at all. All the thousands that are unconfirmed live in the parishes as reputed Christians, and may come to the Sacrament when they will....What a mere running ceremony it is usually made, I need not tell you. I have formerly said that I was at 15 years of age confirmed myself by Bishop Morton (one of the learnedest and best bishops that I ever knew), and we ran thither from school, without the minister's knowledge, or one word from our master to tell us what confirmation is; and in a church-yard in the pathway, as the bishop passed by, we kneeled down, and, laying his hands on every boy's head, he said a few words, I knew not what; nor did any one of my schoolfellows, as far as I could perceive, know what he said; nor know what confirmation is, any more than to have a bishop's blessing; nor were we asked by him, or any, whether we stood to our baptismal covenant, save only by saying by rote the catechism to our master; nor did I see any one make any more than a ceremony of it."[1]

In consequence of the Puritan objections, the declaration of Charles II concerning ecclesiastical affairs promised the appointment of suffragan bishops in order to facilitate the due performance of the episcopal functions, though no step was taken to implement the promise. The criticism of Baxter, though relating to Thomas Morton, bishop successively of Chester 1616–19, Lichfield 1619–32, and Durham 1632–59, was not directed against any one individual but against the entire method of administering confirmation traditional in the English Church from the Norman Conquest to the railroad age of the nineteenth century. So long as dioceses remained so few and their territory so large, roads

[1] R. Baxter, *The English Nonconformity, as under Charles II and James II, Truly Stated and Argued* (London, 1689), chap. XIX, Point XVI, pp. 100–1. [I do not observe any notice to be taken of this criticism by Canon Ollard in his article.]

so bad and means of conveyance so restricted, infrequent episcopal confirmation tours were inevitable with the consequent pressure of numbers and confusion. In one respect the medieval bishops enjoyed an advantage denied to their post-Reformation successors, in their possession of the assistance of bishops consecrated to titular sees *in partibus infidelium* and anxious to perform episcopal offices for diocesan prelates engaged in business of state. Moreover the critics of the eighteenth century cannot with equity ask to have the argument both ways; for if they account it a sign of peculiar piety in medieval bishops to be ready always to confirm by the wayside, and in Caroline prelates such as Morton to confirm in churchyards, they cannot disparage the Georgian episcopate by observations concerning the confusion due to the attempt to lay hands in small churches upon large hosts of people, the very crowds of which when recorded by medieval writers are accounted for a particular evidence of devotion and zeal. In respect of numbers confirmed and the frequency of confirmation circuits, the Hanoverian Church may challenge comparison with any century of its predecessors; but it may not rightly be judged by standards based upon the improved roads, and the construction of railways, much less upon the smaller dioceses and motor-car travel, of later centuries.

If the difficulties attendant upon the actual administration of confirmation be thus cleared of supposititious criticism, it is possible to estimate fairly the gravity and importance of their operation, and the endeavours made to circumvent them. Of the reality of the pressure of crowds no doubt may be entertained. Bishop Nicolson of Carlisle found so great a number at Appleby in 1702 that one girl was nearly crushed to death. In the scattered parishes of the diocese of Exeter the problem was present in unusual proportions.

The churches at Honiton and Liskeard are not very spacious, and much good management must have been needed to enable the bishop to lay hands on 1386 candidates at one service in the former, and on 1399 in the latter; and the same might be said concerning the 1314 confirmed at one time at Bideford, and the 1414 at South Molton. . . . There was always a huge throng at Totnes, and in 1764 the difficulty was partly met by holding a confirmation on each of three successive days, the numbers being 1509, 889, and 1998 (from 21 parishes)—a total of 4396. How busy the town must have been; and what scenes of excitement and confusion in connection with the supply of food and drink for such a multitude; and the conveying of them to their homes, some having to journey very far, as 79 to Stokenham, and 110 to Widecombe-in-the Moor![1]

[1] R. J. E. Boggis, *op. cit.* pp. 465–6.

Bishop Ross had practical experience, which can hardly be supposed to have been unique, of the difficulty of coping with numbers when at Kingsbridge on 27 July 1779 he laid hands upon 706 candidates, "besides the number that must have been confirmed by means of the chancellor's altering the scheme of confirming at Kingsbridge to Lodderswell after the church at Kingsbridge was filled with candidates and tickets delivered in".[1] Such last-minute changes, due there to the inadequacy of Kingsbridge Church to receive all the persons present, were productive of further uncertainty, since it was impossible to keep out stray individuals who had no ticket in such circumstances. In a notice of Bishop Keppel's confirmation in Exeter Cathedral on 2 October 1766 it may be observed that 212 candidates were confirmed at 11 o'clock and a further batch of 195 at half-an-hour after eleven, an expedient evidently designed to reduce the danger of overcrowding and confusion. A further ill-consequence of the large number of candidates usually gathered to receive the grace of confirmation was the custom of persons to present themselves for the episcopal laying-on of hands upon more than one occasion; often indeed upon each time of the bishop's visit. Samuel Wesley confessed to Wake after his lordship had held a confirmation at Epworth in 1712 that the administration would have been more edifying "if according to his lordship's directions, a way could have been found for every parish to have come by themselves and none to have been confirmed but those whose names had been given in by the minister; for want of which great numbers were confirmed who ought not to have been; . . . and many who had been confirmed before, some of them twice and thrice over".[2]

Episcopal charges and confirmation injunctions referred frequently to the necessity of vigilance on the part of parish clergy to prevent their people from coming repeatedly to be confirmed. Wake in 1724 enjoined his clergy "to take care not to present any to be confirmed who have been already confirmed"; and Secker exhorted his presbyters carefully "to instruct those whom they brought, in the whole nature of the institution, and particularly in this, amongst other more important points, that they are never to be confirmed any more than baptised a second time".[3] Notwithstanding a multitude of precept, custom was

[1] Confirmation Records 544 in Exeter Diocesan Registry.
[2] S. Wesley to Wake, 4 Aug. 1712. Arch. W. Lincoln i, item ccc.
[3] Secker, Charge II, *Works*, v, 338. In the seventeenth century Nicholas Ferrar, confirmed at the age of six, was actually confirmed twice during the same ceremony. 'I did it because it is a good thing to have the bishop's prayers and blessing twice and I have got it." H. M. Smith, *The Early Life and Education of John Evelyn*, pp. 110–12 (Oxford, 1920).

not easily uprooted; and the Marquis de la Rochefoucauld during his visit to England in 1784 was struck particularly by the prominence accorded to confirmation in the Anglican system and herein by the practice of frequent reception of that grace.

"Confirmation", he noted in his diary, "is regarded as much more necessary [than confession]—in fact according to the Protestant religion, it is practically indispensable. The view is that a baptised child of himself cannot participate in anything and therefore, as soon as he has reached an age when he can think for himself, he must take on the part of a good Christian, and by confirmation fulfil within himself the benefits received at baptism. Such is the account given to me by all those with whom I have discussed the subject. They do not feel that this sacrament necessarily stamps an indelible character, for there are some who are confirmed more than once. I was told yesterday that at Bury [St Edmunds] there are three or four old women who are confirmed every time the bishop comes into the town. Their plea is that you cannot have too much of a good thing." [1]

To prevent such repeated confirmation, the episcopate adopted the expedient of requiring tickets from the parish clergy for all the candidates presented; and the detailed figures of confirmations in the diocese of Exeter by Keppel and Ross indicate the general success of this means, though exceptions evidently occurred. At South Molton on 26 May 1764 Keppel's record notes the discovery, among the 1414 candidates, of one admitted "by a forged ticket"; at Barnstaple on 25 June 1779 Ross confirmed, amongst the vast number of 4016 persons, "400 without tickets, supposed to be", and at Plymouth on 25–6 July, amongst the 2024 candidates there were "without tickets, supposed at least 400". Perhaps the paucity of such exceptions is more remarkable than their occurrence, for the problems with which bishops and clergy alike had to grapple were difficult and complex. The ideal solution was that advocated to Archbishop Gilbert of York by Drummond in 1758; "fewer numbers in a place and frequent confirmations will bring only the proper persons before you; and bring all into a further sense of this reasonable institution".[2] A practical fulfilment of which counsel was furnished by Bishop Manners Sutton of Norwich when he held a confirmation at Reepham on 7 October 1794, at which Parson Woodforde presented candidates. The confirmation began about a quarter before eleven, only 200 persons were confirmed, three clergy

[1] *A Frenchman in England*, 1784 (tr. S. C. Roberts), p. 86 (Cambridge, 1933).
[2] Quoted by S. L. Ollard, in *Confirmation*, i, 227.

"were with the bishop in the church, arranging the people in order as they came, and the chaplain received the tickets at the church gates", the rite being completed by 2 o'clock.[1]

Archbishop Gilbert of York is remembered particularly by an experiment which he essayed in the actual laying-on of hands, as a means of discharging the office more effectually in the presence of great companies of persons. Whereas many notable bishops continued the practice of laying hands upon one or not more than two candidates at a time, as did Sharp of York, Nicolson of Carlisle, Benson of Gloucester at Halifax in 1737, and Secker also, Gilbert adopted a novel method. According to the testimony of Dr Thomas Newton, who attended him as chaplain, his grace proposed it

to the clergy of Nottingham at his primary visitation, and upon their unanimous approval, he put it into practice. This was instead of going round the rail of the Communion Table and laying his hands upon the heads of two or four persons held close together and in a low voice repeating the form of prayer over them; he went round the whole rail at once, laid his hand upon the head of every person severally, and when he had gone through the whole then he drew back to the Communion Table and in as audible and solemn a manner as he could, pronounced the prayer over them all. This had a wonderful effect. The clergy and people were struck with the decency as much as with the novelty of the ceremony. The confirmations were performed in less time and with less trouble, with more silence and solemnity, and with more regularity and order. It commanded attention, it raised devotion, in so much that several bishops have since adopted the same method.[2]

Peradventure the testimony of Newton was unduly favourable and partial to the method of his archiepiscopal patron, and it is probable that the standards of later ages would pronounce it less edifying than he confidently affirmed. But in view of the very practical difficulties of confirmation circuits, alike in distances to be covered and numbers to be confirmed, other justification need not be sought for its adoption if it facilitated the order and regularity of the administration of the rite.

It is impossible to pass from the subject of confirmation without mention of the record in that regard of Bishop Hoadly, admittedly the best known of Hanoverian prelates. Nor may it be denied that his episcopate, not only in one but all the sees of his incumbency, presents a scandal in this regard. But it is more important to understand the

---

[1] *The Diary of a Country Parson* (ed. J. Beresford), iv, 140.
[2] *Life of Dr Thomas Newton,* in *op. cit.* ii, 105.

reason for this circumstance than to indulge in indiscriminate denuncia-tion. The fundamental disqualification which should have prevented Hoadly from nomination to any bishopric lay in his lameness of body; since a prelate unable to ride upon horseback, to ride abroad save in a carriage, and to walk without the aid of a stick, was manifestly unfitted for the discharge of the duties of his office. In all cases therefore he was unable to administer the rite of confirmation to the laity of his dioceses and had to rely upon the occasional assistance of his brethren. At Bangor the duty was undertaken on his behalf in 1720 by Bishop Wynne of St Asaph, at the request of Archbishop Wake.

"I shall very readily comply with your grace's desire as far as conveniently I can," he assured the primate. "I am afraid I shall not be able to go this year into the remoter parts of the diocese of Bangor, but shall be willing to go into such places as are not very far distant from me. And if the same occasion should require it another year, I shall be ready to go, God willing, and do the same office in the remoter parts of that diocese."[1]

In like manner at Winchester, Bishop Mawson of Chichester confirmed for Hoadly in 1749, breaking in thereby upon his entertainment in Sussex of Archbishop Herring, who related that his host went off "to confirm in the Isle of Wight in aid of the decrepit bishop of Winchester, who has this felicity however, that his spirits make ample amends for his want of legs".[2] The consolation of good spirits being unavailing to discharge the duty of confirmation, once again in 1753 Hoadly's chaplain, Edmund Pyle, found his summer travels curtailed by the necessity "to go through all the diocese of Winchester with Bishop Pearce, who confirmed in all the great towns for his lordship in part of the months of June and July".[3] Of the impropriety of nominating a cripple to any see the example of Hoadly is sufficient proof; and Queen Anne was well advised to reject in 1709 the suggestion of the preferment of Dean Hayley to the bishopric of Chichester, on the ground of his being "a cripple and without hopes of remedy".

Her majesty would have been wiser also if she had refrained from her intention to raise Dr George Bull to the episcopate in 1705 when he had attained three score and ten years; much less to nominate him to St David's, the remotest and one of the largest dioceses of the kingdom. The natural consequence of this step was the regretted inability of the aged prelate to encompass the territory of his jurisdiction; and it gave

[1] Bp. St Asaph to Wake, 6 Aug. 1720. Arch. W. Epist. 21, item cclv, f. 364.
[2] Herring to Hardwicke, 28 Aug. 1749. Add. MSS. 35598, f. 421.
[3] E. Pyle, *Memoirs of a Royal Chaplain*, p. 191.

him especial grief that "he was prevented from travelling over his diocese, in order to administer in all parts of it that holy apostolical rite...known...in the church by the name of Confirmation". Instead of which he had to content himself with "affording opportunities of receiving it to all such as were disposed to embrace them" in the place of his residence and the immediate neighbourhood, and "therefore he confirmed at Brecknock, Caermarthen, Landeilo, Abermarless as often as there was occasion".[1] It may be remembered to the credit of Richard Watson of Llandaff that in his visitation of 1809, when he likewise was over seventy years of age, he

went over the mountains from Neath to a place where no bishop had ever held a confirmation before, Merthyr Tydvil. In his time this place had become, from a small village, a great town containing ten or twelve thousand inhabitants, occupied in the fabrication of iron; and he thought it his duty not only to go to confirm the young people there, but to preach to those that were grown up.[2]

Nor should the zeal of Zachary Pearce be forgotten, who on 1 October 1773, albeit in his eighty-third year, confirmed at Greenwich 700 persons, and having overtaxed his strength "found himself next day unable to speak, and never regained his former readiness of utterance", dying in the June following.[3] Such examples give timely warning against the attempt to draw an indictment against the eighteenth-century episcopate upon the evidence of isolated incidents of unrepresentative individuals.

In the allied work of visitation the episcopate was hindered likewise by the same obstacles of distance and extent from maintaining such a regular and intimate knowledge of and communication with the inferior clergy as were necessary for the fulfilment of the ideal of the pastoral office.

"It is well known", observed White Kennett to his clergy at his primary visitation of the diocese of Peterborough, "that an episcopal visitation was from the beginning, and is still in effect, a diocesan synod, prorogued by the bishop from place and time to other place and time, wherein the bishop is to preside and his clergy to appear and assist; and so jointly to enquire, to inform, to examine, to reprove, correct, and amend all persons, manners, and things within the proper cognisance of the bishop."

But when executed triennially and confined to the summer months of the year, such a comprehensive enquiry was evidently not possible. More particularly when the offices of visitation and confirmation were

[1] R. Nelson, *Life of George Bull*, pp. 422–3. (London, 1713.)
[2] R. Watson, *Anecdotes*, ii, 367–8.
[3] *Life of Zachary Pearce*, in *op. cit.* i, 411.

joined, the general custom was for the bishop to meet and address his clergy in the morning, and to proceed to the confirmation of the laity in the afternoon. The character of visitation charges varied enormously in accordance with the individual predilections of the bishop. Secker's charges have become a recognised mine from which to dig evidences of the pastoral ideals of the eighteenth-century episcopate; those of White Kennett, Wake, and Gibson likewise were full of sound practical advice. Hoadly discoursed chiefly upon theological matters, and Warburton at his primary visitation delivered a charge which would have profited his clergy indeed if they had all possessed the learning for its interpretation. Among eighteenth-century episcopal utterances Butler's primary charge at Durham is remembered as one of the noblest defences of the external rites and practices of religion of all ages; whilst Richard Watson in his regular triennial appearances at Llandaff discoursed of a great variety of theological and political issues. But how greatly soever the clergy might be edified by the episcopal charge, their infrequent contact with their bishop made the occasion of visitation rather a social than an ecclesiastical event. Bishop Simon Patrick of Ely confessed to Wake in 1701 that, having had to miss one of his visitation days at Cambridge owing to a chill, "he appeared at dinner with his clergy, which he believed they liked as well as appearing at church".[1] Archbishop Herring likewise during his primary visitation at Canterbury in 1749 related that "the *coenae pontificum* and the repetition of a pitiful charge began to tire him, but he blessed God he was well".[2]

Of the incidental and infrequent nature of the relations between bishops and their clergy, the *Diary* of James Woodforde offers apt illustration. In April 1775 the diarist journeyed to London to present his credentials to, and to ask institution from, Bishop Yonge to the benefice of Weston Longeville in the diocese of Norwich. Twice on 10 and 11 April he called at the bishop's lodging without success; but upon the third occasion, on the 12th, he was fortunate to find him at home; "and was instituted very soon, his lordship behaving exceedingly handsome and free".[3] The next mention of Yonge occurs on 10 June 1777, when Woodforde went to Norwich to attend the bishop's primary visitation, at which however the chancellor acted for his lordship.

I dressed myself in a gown and cassock after breakfast and at 11 o'clock went to the cathedral, and heard prayers and a sermon preached there by

[1] Bp. Patrick to Wake, 26 July 1701. Arch. W. Epist. 17, item cxv, f. 139.
[2] Herring to Hardwicke, 7 June 1749. Add. MSS. 35598, f. 417.
[3] *The Diary of a Country Parson* (ed. J. Beresford), i, 149–50.

Mr Whitmell, rector of Wood Norton, and a good discourse he gave us. The Chancellor Dr Sandly who represented the bishop was there, and the dean, and a great many of the clergy of the deaneries of Blofield, Sparham, and Taverham. After divine service we all went into the consistory court in the cathedral and there the names of the clergy were called over and each delivered the bishop's letter with answers to his lordship's questions. We then attended the chancellor to the Maid's Head Inn not far from the cathedral, where we dined and spent the afternoon and the chancellor with us.... We had a very elegant dinner and 28 sat down to dinner together.[1]

No further news of his diocesan is recorded until on 26 April 1783 there comes the melancholy tidings of his death, with the pious epitaph, "he was a man much beloved by his clergy";[2] though the affection would not seem to have rested upon very frequent contact.

With Bishop Lewis Bagot, Parson Woodforde had closer connections and more frequent intercourse. On 4 September 1783 he was taken by the Custance family to dine with his lordship at Norwich, at which, in addition to the "very elegant dinner" served, the diarist noted that "the bishop behaved with great affability towards him,...and was also very affable and polite to all the clergy present".[3] In the month following Woodforde visited the palace at Norwich upon a less pleasing errand, in an endeavour to persuade the bishop to dispense him from the command to preach in the cathedral in the ensuing February, which his lordship refused to do, assuring his visitor "that it was rather a compliment conferred by him on those that he so appointed".[4] On 7 November Bagot was entertained to dinner by the Custances at Weston House, at which the rector was present of course.[5] The favour of the bishop being an undesired notoriety Woodforde was under the difficulty again in December 1785 of waiting upon his lordship to beg that he might be excused from the command to preach a sermon on behalf of the Charity Schools since he had so preached five years earlier in 1780, upon which ground his plea was allowed.[6] The next visit of the diarist to Norwich was in relation to the bishop's notice of intention to hold a confirmation on 6 June 1787 at Foulsham, whereupon on 1 June Woodforde "spent half an hour with him, talking with him about Confirmation at Foulsham on Wednesday, being near 10 miles from Weston", for which reason apparently he was excused from presenting candidates from his parish.[7] On 25 August of the same year

---

[1] *The Diary of a Country Parson* (ed. J. Beresford), i, 205.
[2] *Ibid.* ii, 70.   [3] *Ibid.* ii, 91–2.   [4] *Ibid.* ii, 100.
[5] *Ibid.* ii, 103.   [6] *Ibid.* ii, 221.   [7] *Ibid.* ii, 325.

the bishop again dined at Weston house, the rector being of the company;[1] and the diarist concludes on 4 April 1790 with a record of the bishop's translation to St Asaph,[2] having mentioned only one visitation, on 28 May 1784, when forty clergy attended his lordship in person at his cathedral, heard "a very long but very good charge", and adjourned duly to the Maid's Head Inn, where his lordship dined with them, treating his clergy with wine, and staying at the convivialities of the table from 4 to 6 p.m.[3]

The successor of Bagot in the see of Norwich, Bishop Horne, was unfortunately much of a valetudinarian, who was unable to attend his primary visitation on 15 June 1791, being at Bath and "having been very ill lately"; but his chancellor represented him, and administered the episcopal hospitality at dinner in the shape of one bottle of wine between two clergymen at his lordship's expense.[4] After a very brief episcopate Horne died at Bath in January 1792, being succeeded by Charles Manners Sutton, of whom Woodforde recorded that he was "a young man for bishop, only 36, but married and had 11 children, Mr Custance says that he is a little man, but well-spoken of in London and elsewhere".[5]

The clergy did not wait long to confirm these impressions of their new ruler, for on 1 August 1792 he summoned them to meet him at the cathedral, in order to secure their subscription to an address to the king in relation to his recent proclamation respecting seditious publications and meetings. On the following day also. his lordship preached at a musical meeting in Norwich for the benefit of the public hospital.[6] His primary visitation took place on 30 June 1794, at which he delivered "a very excellent charge", and continued the traditions of episcopal hospitality at the Maid's Head Inn afterwards.[7] On 7 October of the same year also Woodforde presented candidates from his parish at the bishop's confirmation held in Reepham Church, where everything was a model of orderly arrangement.[8] Save for the mention of the receipt of an episcopal brief calling for parochial collections for the French refugee clergy on 31 May 1793,[9] and of a pastoral letter in August 1801 containing directions for action in case of a hostile invasion,[10] the activities of the bishop find no further record in the diarist's volumes, albeit Woodforde lived until New Year's Day, 1803. From the paucity and brevity of his references to his episcopal superiors, and especially

[1] *The Diary of a Country Parson* (ed. J. Beresford), ii, 341.
[2] *Ibid.* iii, 181.		[3] *Ibid.* ii, 136.		[4] *Ibid.* iii, 276–7.
[5] *Ibid.* iii, 339.		[6] *Ibid.* iii, 365–7.		[7] *Ibid.* iv, 118.
[8] *Ibid.* iv, 140.		[9] *Ibid.* iv, 32.		[10] *Ibid.* v, 329.

from the infrequency of his contact with their lordships of Norwich upon ecclesiastical business, the small degree of oversight achieved by an eighteenth-century bishop may be well deduced. The country clergy were left to discharge the duties of their office with little interference from the episcopate, and much justification existed for the humorous address of Warburton to his clergy at his primary visitation concerning the aloofness which separated prelates from their presbyters.

"In the simplicity of the good old times," observed his lordship of Gloucester, "when the clergy first met their bishop, who might be then said in every sense to do the honours of the assembly, he held it incumbent upon him to inform them by what means this relation had sprung up between them; that it was neither clerical intrigue on his part, nor court intrigue on the part of his patrons which drew him from his beloved obscurity; but a mere sense of the church's want of good governors, that had induced the state to force out his reluctant merit into so eminent but hazardous a station. This was an ancient custom and a good. The acquaintance between the bishop and his clergy could not commence more happily than in the information he gave them of the confessed importance of his character. In course of time this friendly confidence was found to have its inconvenience, which by degrees brought on the disuse; and this without much violence on the communicative disposition of the diocesan. For now the clergy were become little curious to know how or from whence their bishop had dropped down amongst them; and he as little disposed to tell them a ridiculous or unedifying story. It was enough that they met, and that their meeting was to their mutual consent."[1]

The most cursory survey of the administration of the Hanoverian episcopate serves to emphasise the necessity, felt and voiced by several of its members, for the consecration of suffragan bishops to assist the diocesan prelates. It is difficult indeed to account for the disappearance of the suffragan bishops, for which provision had been made by the statute of 26 Henry VIII, cap. 14, in abundant measure. According to the provisions of this act twenty-six sees had been named for the consecration of bishops suffragan, of which two towns, Gloucester and Bristol, became subsequently the seats of diocesan bishoprics. During the reign of Henry VIII thirteen suffragan bishops were consecrated, and during that of Elizabeth a further three were added; but after the consecration in 1592 of John Sterne to the see of Colchester the series dried up, not to be resumed until 1870.[2] Yet the purposes for which the Henrician statute had decreed the appointment of bishops suffragan,

[1] Warburton, Charge (1761), *Works* (ed. Hurd), v, 585.
[2] W. Stubbs, *Registrum Sacrum Anglicanum.*

"for the more speedy administration of the sacraments, and other good, wholesome, and devout things, and laudable ceremonies, to the increase of God's honour, and for the commodity of good and devout people", continued operative during the seventeenth and eighteenth centuries. At the Restoration indeed the possibility of the revival of this useful office seemed strong, for Charles II's declaration concerning ecclesiastical affairs specified it as a necessary reform. It may have been that the provenance of the demand for suffragan bishops, with the attendant Puritan criticism of the neglect by diocesans of their spiritual administration, conspired to frustrate its fulfilment together with other suggestions from the same source which perished after the failure of the Savoy Conference; but the loss of this item of the presbyterian programme was grievous to the episcopal church. Many of the most conscientious bishops were foremost in voicing the desire for such assistance. The experience of Gibson during his first confirmation circuit at Lincoln convinced him of the need "to obtain suffragan bishops, to assist the diocesan bishop in large dioceses, as there should be occasion, and particularly in the work of confirmation, which undoubtedly would be a great service to religion, were it thoroughly and constantly performed in all dioceses". This item of reform was included in his list of "things fit to be done for the church", but no result came of his advocacy.[1] In like manner Lloyd of Worcester expressed to Wake in 1716 in regard to his chancellor the wish "that he could prevail to have him consecrated as a coadjutor or suffragan", adding however that such a step "might be liable to several objections, and was a greater favour than they could pretend to have merited or hope to obtain of their most gracious king".[2] Wake himself projected a revival of the suffragan see of Leicester in his large diocese, but all such schemes failed to fructify. In part the failure may not improbably be ascribed in the eighteenth century to the fear of an extension of the practice, if allowed in England, to the Plantations, where the antipathy to prelacy was extremely violent amongst the dissenting sort of colonists, and in part to the *vis inertiae* characteristic of the age. But the omission of Charles II to implement his promise in this regard inflicted a severe loss upon the Church of England, and upon the efficiency of the spiritual administration of the episcopate.

If any man desired the office of a bishop in the Georgian Church, he desired indeed a good work, but also a very arduous and exacting. The comment penned by Torcy upon receipt of the news that the Abbé

[1] N. Sykes, *Edmund Gibson*, p. 76.
[2] Bp. Lloyd to Wake, 8 Nov. 1716. Arch. W. Epist. 7, Canterbury II.

Gaultier wished, as the reward of his diplomatic services, nomination to a bishopric of the Gallican Church may be applied with equal aptitude to the state of prelates of the contemporary English Church.

> J'écrivis, il y a quelques jours, à l'Abbé, ce que je pensais sur la fantaisie qui lui est venu d'être évêque. Les hommes demandent souvent à Dieu ce qui serait leur perte, et il rejette les vœux de ceux qu'il aime. Il ne faut pas que celui qui a tant travaillé au repos public, soit mis dans une place où il serait tourmenté toute sa vie. Et en vérité, my lord, ce que les amis de l'Abbé Gaultier doivent souhaiter et demander pour lui, est une bonne abbaye dont il puisse à son aise toucher et manger les revenus, sans être obligé de s'embarrasser des soins d'un diocèse, tel principalement que celui de Tournay, où il aurait à ménager différentes puissances, et être toujours exposé à des embarrass sans nombre et sans fin.[1]

Rich deaneries or residentiaryships offered the *otium cum dignitate* to Anglican divines, which was lacking in the many duties, political and ecclesiastical, required of the episcopate. Many were the laments of the fatigue and labour encountered by bishops in the visitation and confirmation of their dioceses.

"Very glad should I be to see you as able to engage in, and go through with, these fatigues as our robust brother of Chester", wrote Nicolson to Wake in 1709 in relation to his visitation of Lincoln and that undertaken by Dawes at Chester, "who has undoubtedly the largest diocese in England next to your own, but is so far from being wearied with any such slender circuit as it can afford him. He came hither last week from Whitehaven, and went hence to Newcastle-on-Tyne. He is now at Durham, from whence he comes back to the remaining parts of his visitation at Richmond and Boroughbridge about the middle of this week. When his own necessary duties are over, he goes on to Bishopthorpe; and thence returning by Nottingham to Chester, will have visited every county in this whole Province."[2]

In similar vein Gibson of Lincoln declared to Nicolson in respect of his visitation of 1721, his rejoicing that, though it "would be a great labour, when it was over he would be at rest for two years from that kind of work. As to all other kinds, a bishop of Lincoln had no vacation, which might remind his lordship of the happiness he enjoyed in having his work within so narrow a compass" as the small diocese of Carlisle.[3]

---

[1] Torcy to Bolingbroke, 10 Dec. 1712. *Letters and Correspondence of Bolingbroke* (ed. G. Parke), iii, 218 (4 vols.), 1798.
[2] Nicolson to Wake, 18 July 1709. Arch. W. Epist. 17, item clxxxviii, f. 224.
[3] Gibson to Nicolson, 15 Aug. 1721. MSS. Add. A. 269, f. 98. (Bodley.)

Or again Chandler of Lichfield and Coventry confessed in 1722 that he had been compelled to halt in the mid-course of his itinerary, and "to put off his visitation of Derbyshire for a month in order to give his body some refreshment, for what with bad ways, travelling to so many different places, and the ordinary duties at each place, he was sufficiently wearied".[1] Verily a trustworthy horse and a pair of stout legs were the chief requisites of the Hanoverian prelacy, without which they might count all other things as but vain to save them in their protracted journeys.

In their endeavours to grapple with the many obstacles to pastoral oversight and to discharge the spiritual administration of their office, the eighteenth-century episcopate merit a juster measure of appreciation than has been their lot at the hands of subsequent historians. The Georgian bench indeed has been pilloried as a byword of sloth, inefficiency, and neglect. Apologists have shown a marked capacity for differentiation between the same characteristics when present in bishops of the Caroline age and in those of its successor. The biographer of Lancelot Andrewes allows that "we know little of his distinctively episcopal work, his few extant letters make no special mention of pastoral duties"; but he is careful to add that "the standard by which a bishop's work was measured in those days was not that of our own time".[2] The nicest degree of discrimination between prelates of the high- and low-church traditions is shown by Canon Ollard in his survey of confirmations. Although referring to the enquiries of Barlow of Lincoln concerning confirmation, he makes no mention of that bishop's complete and protracted neglect of his diocese; whereas he is at pains to note of Hoadly that "he never visited his diocese of Bangor, nor apparently Hereford".[3] In recalling the instances in Cartwright's *Diary* of the confirmation of ordinands upon the eve of their ordination, instead of a suggestion of censure upon the episcopate for infrequent administration of the rite, he observes with satisfaction that "it may be presumed fairly that Bishop Cartwright was only doing what was usually done by bishops of the time, and that before ordaining they were careful to see that candidates had been confirmed".[4] The admittedly scandalous episode of Wood of Lichfield is covered by the fact that he "was a Puritan" albeit "a bad one".[5] The restriction by Bishop Bull of confirmations to the places near his residence, owing to

---

[1] Chandler to Wake, 30 June 1722. Arch. W. Epist. 9, Canterbury IV.
[2] R. L. Ottley, *Lancelot Andrewes*, p. 108.
[3] S. L. Ollard, in *Confirmation*, i, pp. 173, 187.
[4] *Ibid.* p. 176.   [5] *Ibid.* p. 175.

his inability to visit his diocese in person and to travel throughout its territory to confirm, is applauded as "an advance upon the practice which confined confirmation to the bishop's visitation";[1] whilst of Gilbert Burnet it is stated that in his *Discourse of the Pastoral Care* "confirmation is not mentioned under a bishop's duties", although that prelate is allowed the credit of having been "active in administering confirmation and in twenty years had confirmed in 265 churches in the diocese".[2] Finally, following a summary of the confirmation tours of Archbishop Drummond of York, who died in 1771, and without any later evidence save a reference to confirmations in the diocese of Ely in 1829 and 1833, Ollard affirms that "the evidence for the later years of the eighteenth century and for the earlier years of the nineteenth, points to the conclusion that carelessness and infrequency in administering confirmation were reaching their lowest level, comparable only to the period of neglect when Calvinism was at its height two hundred years before".[3]

Before such a tribunal the eighteenth-century episcopate may well decline to plead its defence. For the appreciation of its achievement regard must be had to the difficulties of its situation, and comparison be made with previous centuries without regard to differences of high and low church. In face of the many obstacles of unwieldy dioceses, limited means of travel, pressure of other avocations, and the infirmities of body incident to mortal flesh, the bishops of Hanoverian England and Wales strove with diligence and not without due measure of success to discharge the spiritual administration attached to their office. No better epilogue to a survey of their itineraries could be offered than that written by Pearce of Bangor, successor in the see to the intrepid traveller Herring, of his adventures in visitation of his jurisdiction.

"Since my arrival here", he wrote from his see-city to Hardwicke in July 1749, "I have been upon a visitation through the largest and worst part for journeying of my whole diocese. I set out on the 15th from Bangor, and on the following day I reached and confirmed at Conway; on the 17th I went through Denbigh to Ruthin, where on the 18th I visited and confirmed; and from thence I went to Dolgelle in Merionethshire (a long day's journey of full 40 miles), and there I visited and confirmed; and after that I returned home through Carnarvonshire, where I met with worse roads, [and] higher mountains than I could possibly have conceived.... As my horse, who was a native of Merionethshire, had never been used to any but such rough and

---

[1] S. L. Ollard, in *Confirmation*, p. 183.
[2] *Ibid.* pp. 183–4. The number should be 275, not 265.
[3] *Ibid.* p. 201.

stony ways, he carried me very safe, and had (as I found) a peculiar skill to step from one stone to another without once stumbling upon the whole journey. This gave me leisure and courage to look much about me; and it is an amazing thing to an English traveller to find himself in such a situation as I often found myself. In those parts the ridge of mountains called Snowdon hills runs along for many miles. Our road lay generally in the valley beneath rocky mountains on each side, a rapid river running at the bottom, by the edge of which we travelled, and the water of which running so violently through numberless large stones fallen from the mountains, occasioned such a noise as made us unable to hear ourselves speak.... I saw several very deep falls of water, which as they made natural cascades, they were much more agreeable than any that I ever saw made by art. Our road for several miles was rather a pair of stone stairs than a path; and wherever we might have gone off from this rough pavement, we should have run the hazard of being set foot in a bog. I thought within myself as I passed there that if Milton's description (in his Paradise Lost) of the battle of the angels had been true, it might have seemed as if the rocks and mountains which the one army threw at the heads of the other, had fallen down upon the earth in this place, and had continued in that fallen situation."[1]

[1] Pearce to Hardwicke, 27 July 1749. Add. MSS. 35590, f. 342.

CHAPTER IV

THE LADDER OF PREFERMENT

"We may divide the clergy into generals, field officers, and subalterns", wrote Addison in *The Spectator* of 24 March 1710–11. "Among the first we may reckon bishops, deans, and archdeacons. Among the second are doctors of divinity, prebendaries, and all that wear scarfs. The rest are comprehended under the subalterns. As for the first class, our constitution prevents it from any redundancy of incumbents, notwithstanding competitors are numberless. Upon a strict calculation, it is found that there has been a great exceeding of late years in the second division, several brevets having been granted for the converting of subalterns into scarf officers; insomuch that within my memory the price of lute string is raised above twopence in a yard. As for the subalterns, they are not to be numbered."

The traditional comparison of the church to an army, accepted generally as a compliment, was especially congenial to the genius of the eighteenth century, which interpreted it as lending an august authority to the contemporary practice whereby circumstances of birth and seniority determined the prospects of promotion in both national institutions. "The Church is, in some respects, like the army", observed his grace of Newcastle to Lord Albemarle in 1765; "though it is necessary to break through it at times, yet some sort of regard ought to be had in a proper manner, to seniority." In each corporation the higher grades of preferment were generally the preserve of the aristocracy, whilst the common soldiers, recruited largely from a lower social order, contended fiercely for the minor occasions of advancement presented with infrequency. Within the Church the division between the privileged minority and the depressed majority was deep; and the gulf was widened by the agglomeration of pluralities upon the fortunate favourites whose feet were set securely upon the ladder of preferment.

From the Reformation to the whig reforms of the third decade of the nineteenth century, the practice of pluralism in the Church was regulated by the statute of 21 Henry VIII, cap. 13, entitled Spiritual Persons abridged from having Pluralities of Livings, supplemented by the later 41st Canon of the Canons of 1604. The Henrician statute, after laying down the general rule that any person possessing a benefice with cure of souls of the value of £8 a year or more should forfeit it upon institution to any other benefice with cure, proceeded to enact a comprehensive list of exceptions. All spiritual persons being members of the king's council might purchase dispensations to hold three such benefices, whilst chaplains of the king, queen, and members of the royal family were eligible to possess two incompatible benefices. The privilege allowed to royal chaplains was extended to chaplains of the several degrees of the nobility, temporal and spiritual; thus archbishops and dukes might have six chaplains each, marquesses and earls five, viscounts and bishops four, the lord chancellor, barons, and knights of the garter three, noblewomen being widows two, the treasurer and comptroller of the king's household, the king's secretary, the dean of his chapel, the almoner, and the master of the rolls, each two chaplains; and the lord chief justice and the warden of the cinque ports, one chaplain each. In addition to this army of retainers, the right to hold two incompatible benefices in plurality was granted to brothers and sons of temporal lords, and to all doctors and bachelors of divinity, doctors of law and bachelors of canon law of the British universities whose degrees were not of grace; whilst final provision was made for the allowance to archbishops, because they must occupy eight chaplains at the consecration of bishops, and to all bishops, because they must occupy six chaplains at the giving of orders and consecration of churches, of two additional chaplains, one of which could hold two benefices with cure of souls, and for the exception of chaplains of the king from all the restrictions of the act, so that they might enjoy as many benefices as their sovereign should bestow upon them. To all persons legally qualified the archbishop of Canterbury was required to issue a licence for dispensation to hold two incompatible benefices in plurality, after due examination of their learning. To this comprehensive provision Canon 41 added the conditions that every person so licensed should be at least of the degree of Master of Arts, a public and sufficient preacher duly licensed, that he should reside personally in each of his benefices "for some reasonable time in every year", that his benefices should be not more than thirty miles apart, and that he should employ in the benefice in which he did not reside a preacher lawfully allowed.

The distinction recognised by the canon law between compatible benefices, that is benefices *sine cura animarum*, and incompatible benefices, that is *cum cura animarum*, was specifically allowed by the statute of 1529 in its provision that "no deanery, archdeaconry, chancellorship, treasurership, chantership, or prebend in any cathedral or collegiate church, nor parsonage that had a vicar endowed, nor any benefice perpetually appropriate [was] to be taken or comprehended under the name of benefice having cure of soul". The operation of this law permitted therefore the accumulation of a series of benefices, with and without cure of souls, in the hands of clerks whose good fortune enabled them to acquire the necessary qualification. The means of translating theory into practice was furnished by the multitude of prebends in the several cathedral and collegiate churches of the realm, to which the hungry host of chaplains looked for the satisfaction of their needs. For, whilst the possession of benefices with cure of souls was a prize not to be despised, far more pleasant was the enjoyment of cathedral dignities unencumbered generally by the obligation of residence. According to the indictment presented by the *Extraordinary Black Book* in 1831, the cathedral and collegiate foundations embraced 514 simple prebends, in addition to the dignitary prebends to which a jurisdiction was annexed, and which numbered sixty-one archdeaconries and twenty-six chancellorships. The crown itself was a considerable fount of honours, since it commanded the patronage of the prebends of Westminster, Windsor, and Worcester, of nine of the twelve prebends of Canterbury, of three residentiaryships of St Paul's, and of the canonries of Christ Church, Oxford; so that, exclusive of the Oxford canonries attached to the regius professorships of Divinity and Hebrew, and of one prebend of Worcester annexed to the Lady Margaret professorship of Divinity at Oxford, the king presented in his own person to nearly fifty cathedral dignities. In addition the lord chancellor, by virtue of his office, nominated to six prebends of the cathedral church of Bristol, and to five each of Gloucester, Norwich, and Rochester. The attractiveness of the royal prebends lay primarily in their revenues, for according to the valuation compiled for George III about 1762, those of Windsor were worth £450 per annum, of Oxford £400, of Canterbury £350, of Westminster £300, and of Worcester £220, whilst the residentiaryships of St Paul's were estimated at £800 per year.

It is little surprising that the duke of Newcastle considered these dignities the most precious source of patronage. Indeed he described a canonry of St Paul's as "the ecclesiastical preferment in the king's disposal next to bishoprics and the deanery of Durham", and the Westminster and Windsor prebends as "the first and most eligible next to deaneries and bishoprics, and sometimes more difficult to be had than a deanery".[1] In particular his majesty laid such especial store by the prebends of Windsor, that the collegiate church "was always called the King's free chapel and, as such, distinguished from the other cathedrals".[2] In the scramble for these desirable preferments the episcopate even

---

[1] Newcastle to the Marquis of Huntingdon, 17 Sept. 1749; to the Earl of Bristol, 22 Aug. 1754. Add. MSS. 32719, f. 180; 32873, f. 208.

[2] Newcastle to Secker, 10 Feb. 1766. Add. MSS. 32973, f. 397.

became an occasional competitor with the inferior clergy. The heavy initial costs of entry into possession of a see necessitated often the grant of a temporary dispensation to hold *in commendam* other benefices, until the bishop was in enjoyment of the revenues of his diocese; whilst the poor endowment of the little bishoprics converted the *commendam* into a perpetual endowment during the prelate's tenure of the particular see. Bishop Nicolson computed the fees for his confirmation, consecration, homage, and the restitution of temporalties, upon his elevation to Carlisle in 1702, at not less than £500 in addition to the £115 consumed by his journey to and sojourn in London, a disproportionate charge in relation to the revenues of his see, which he accounted to be not more than £775 per annum. A generation later Bishop Secker lamented in 1734 that his nomination to the poor bishopric of Bristol, worth £360 per year, entailed the payment in firstfruits of £900. Even the rich see of Lincoln sustained such onerous costs that Gibson insisted, on his acceptance of that episcopal charge in 1716, upon a dispensation to hold *in commendam* until November 1717 the rectory of Lambeth, the precentorship and residentiaryship of Chichester, and the mastership of St Mary's hospital there, in order to reimburse himself for the expenses of the promotion. In like manner, when Richard Hurd was preferred to the bishopric of Lichfield and Coventry in 1774, despite its rich emolument of £1800 a year, his finances were severely strained by the necessary costs of £502. 16s. 6d. attendant upon the promotion. Further, in the choice of dignities to hold *in commendam* prelates of the poor or remote sees and those lacking an episcopal house in London had a strong predilection for prebends of Westminster and Windsor and the residentiaryships of St Paul's, because of their convenience for attendance upon the court and parliament. The demands of residence in the capital during parliamentary sessions led Lancelot Blackburne of Exeter to prefer in 1716 a typical request that his *commendam* might include "a prebend of Westminster when one should fall vacant, that he might have an house also to put his head in for the parliamentary attendance".[1]

A natural consequence of the episcopal competition for *commendams* was the interest of the crown and its ministers in selecting for promotion to the bench divines who might vacate thereby suitable preferments for the reward of royal and other chaplains. Among the many papal prerogatives annexed to the crown at the Reformation was that of presentation to all the benefices and dignities held by clerks nominated to bishoprics, from which ensued the inevitable tendency so to contrive

[1] Bp. Blackburne to Wake, 8 Dec. 1716. Arch. W. Epist. 20, item clx, f. 234.

episcopal appointments as to discharge a series of other obligations by the one promotion. The generality of elevations to the bench were followed by a number of minor shuffles of prebends and other dignities. Thus in 1774 when the death of Bishop Pearce of Rochester was imminent, Bishop Markham of Chester canvassed strongly the claims of Dr John Moore, dean of Canterbury and prebendary of the fifth stall in Durham Cathedral, largely on the ground of the valuable offices which his advancement would bring into the gift of the sovereign. Moore reported to Sir William Eden that his lordship of Chester thought even "the smallness of the income an improvement of his chances. His reasoning is", continued the dean, "it is an object to me to get on the bench and I can give up Durham for it. It is not likely that any competitor can give up anything for it, because few are possessed of two considerable preferments, and a man who has but one and gives up that, must starve upon the bishopric".[1] The argument, though unavailing at the particular moment, proved valid in the following year when Moore was nominated to the see of Bangor and surrendered both his dignities to the crown. By this means the Cornwallis family was gratified by the appointment of James Cornwallis to the deanery of the cathedral in which his brother was enthroned as primate; and such possibilities of recompensing multiple obligations could not be foregone by harassed kings and ministers of state.

Next to the consideration of the provision of episcopal *commendams* the primary claim upon the preferments in the gift of the crown was allowed to the persons of royal chaplains. The king's chaplains constituted indeed a class apart in the contest for promotion, for nomination to their office was accounted traditionally "a sure and certain way to greater preferments".[2] Within their privileged corporation the accidental concomitants of the accession of the Hanoverian dynasty introduced a novel method of qualification for advancement, the selection of one person to accompany George I and George II as chaplain on their frequent visits to Hanover. The faithful discharge of this duty bestowed upon the traveller a particular primacy in expectation of reward. The precedent was created in the person of Lancelot Blackburne, who was chosen by Archbishop Wake on the first journey of George I abroad in the summer of 1716, and accordingly, upon the vacancy of the see of Exeter in the November of that year, his claims were canvassed strongly by the primate. George I, tarrying still in Hanover, caused an assurance to be sent to his chaplain "that upon his

[1] J. Moore to Eden. Auckland MSS. B.M. Add. MSS. 34412, f. 295.
[2] White Kennett to Charlett, 11 May 1700. Ballard MSS. vii, f. 32.

arrival in England he intended the bishopric for him", which promise was fulfilled in due season.[1] In 1721 Dr Joseph Wilcocks was similarly rewarded for his services to the royal household, his majesty "being very desirous to do something" for him, as Sunderland explained to Wake, "not only upon his having been abroad with him last year, but upon account of his attendance upon the young princess".[2] Upon occasion this pleasing reward could be secured without even the trouble of attendance overseas; for in 1723 Dr William Baker, Warden of Wadham College, received the see of Bangor in compensation for his disappointment in having missed a Hanover journey, being nominated thereto by the king personally because "he was to have attended his majesty to Hanover, if he had gone last year".[3] Evidently the dignity of an episcopal promotion could not be anticipated by every divine who performed a single continental journey, but the principle had become well established before the death of George I of the prior claim of the Hanover chaplain to some important ecclesiastical preferment.

The tradition was continued gladly by George II, who found in it a welcome means of ensuring the advancement of favourite clergy, since the right of the sovereign to nominate personally the Hanover chaplain could scarcely be challenged even by ministers devoted to the interest of their own clerical friends. An important illustration of the credit attaching to this position was furnished by the case of Dr John Thomas, English chaplain at Hamburg, whose thorough knowledge of German gave him an especial merit in the eyes of George II. The king expressed his desire to bestow on him some preferment in England, but when Thomas asked for a royal prebend, his majesty declared that to be a matter of great difficulty.

"It is not in my power to get you any such thing," he observed, according to the account of Dr Thomas Newton, bishop of Bristol, "my ministers lay their hands upon them all, as necessary for my service; but I will tell you what I will do for you. They do not much mind livings, and I will give you the first living that falls, and then I will make you one of my chaplains, and then the next time I come to Hanover you shall come over with me as my chaplain; and then if a prebend or deanery should happen to fall, you would have a good chance of succeeding to it; and this is the only way wherein I can procure any such thing for you."

The royal word was a faithful bond. Thomas was appointed to the rectory of St Vedast, Foster Lane, in the city of London, made a royal

---

[1] Blackburne to Wake, 31 Dec. 1716. Arch. W. Epist. 20, item cxciii, f. 287.
[2] Sunderland to Wake, 21 Sept. 1721. Arch. W. Epist. 9, Canterbury iv.
[3] Townshend to Wake, 14 April 1723. Arch. W. Epist. 22, item clxxxviii, f. 287.

chaplain, and in the spring of 1740 commanded to make ready for a Hanover journey. Despite the strong desire of Bishop Gibson to secure that office for Dr Nicholas Claggett, bishop of St David's, the king insisted upon being accompanied by Thomas.

"It happened in the course of the summer", related Newton, "that the deanery of Peterborough became vacant, and Dr Thomas had the honour to kiss his majesty's hand for it. At the same time the duke of Newcastle wrote to him from England that he had in a manner engaged that deanery to Dr Newcombe, the Master of St John's College in Cambridge, and should be greatly obliged to Dr Thomas if he would be so good as to waive his turn; the duke would certainly procure for him a better deanery, or the first residentiaryship of St Paul's that should become vacant. Dr Thomas wrote in answer that as the king had been graciously pleased to give him the deanery, he could not with any decency or good manners decline his Majesty's favour; but his grace might vacate the deanery by giving him a better thing as soon as ever he pleased."[1]

The suggestion that Thomas might forgo his present claim on promise of future recompense had been actually made to Newcastle by Bishop Mawson of Llandaff, who was anxious to favour the cause of Newcombe, and argued in relation to Peterborough that, "as it was... the smallest deanery in the gift of the crown, in case it should be intended for Dr Thomas, who was then with his majesty, he would think Dr Thomas would run no hazard of being a sufferer, were he to stay till something else fell which might be in all respects as convenient for him and perhaps of better value".[2] Thomas prudently refused to waive his claim to this present earnest of favours to come, and Newcombe had to wait until his rival's elevation to the see of St Asaph in 1743 opened the way for his succession to the little deanery. This case became the invaluable precedent quoted by Newcastle that "the king's chaplain at Hanover has always set aside at all times all other promises".[3]

Such a precedent was indeed of the utmost service to Newcastle in his strenuous efforts to provide suitably for his clerical friend Dr James Johnson. In 1748 he took Johnson to Hanover in his own company and that of George II as chaplain, when fortune favoured him by the vacancy of two good preferments, a residentiaryship of St Paul's and a canonry of Christ Church, Oxford. Gleefully quoting the case of

[1] *Life of Dr Thomas Newton,* by himself, in *Lives of E. Pocock, Z. Pearce, T. Newton and P. Skelton* (2 vols.), ii, 83.

[2] Bp. Mawson to Newcastle, 17 July 1740. Add. MSS. 32694, f. 169.

[3] Newcastle to H. Pelham, 19/30 Oct. 1748 (Hanover). Add. MSS. 32717, f. 153; Newcastle to Carteret, 13 May 1743. Add. MSS. 32700, f. 122.

Dr Thomas, the duke affirmed to his brother Henry Pelham that "sure the king's chaplain there should have one, and naturally and according to all custom, the best", since "to be sure it would not be decent for two such preferments to fall during his majesty's being there and the chaplain attending him to have neither".[1] Accordingly, Johnson was appointed to St Paul's, to which dignity the lord chancellor Hardwicke added the compliment of the small prebend of Consumpta per mare in that cathedral in his gift, as a token of his approbation of the principle that the chaplain attending his majesty abroad should "have one of the best preferments vacant during his attendance upon that service".[2] After so propitious an initial visit, it was not surprising that Newcastle's choice fell twice further upon his friend for the congenial foreign journey, and in 1752 their attendance witnessed a series of episcopal vacancies in England. The duke could not allow so fair an opportunity to escape; and though expressing in private to Andrew Stone the fear lest "the king would suspect that this was the view of Johnson's coming thither",[3] he insisted publicly to Archbishop Herring and his other correspondents that "it was generally thought, that considering Dr Johnson's merit, situation and present attendance upon the king his promotion to the vacant bishopric would not only be very natural, but perhaps thought the most proper just at this time".[4] Despite considerable opposition and the obvious delicacy of the situation, Newcastle continued to emphasise the importance of three Hanover journeys combined with the providential coincidence of the vacancies, until he carried successfully the nomination of his friend to the see of Gloucester. This instance established beyond possibility of dispute both the claims of the Hanover chaplain and the importance of so valuable a surety of high preferment, so that the succession to the crown after George II of a sovereign who preferred the pleasures of Windsor to those of Germany dealt a severe blow to the hopes of clerics and ministers who had welcomed the addition of so recognised a means of rapid ecclesiastical preferment.

To the majority of royal chaplains the occasions of Hanover visits were too infrequent to encourage hopes of the circulation of the honour of attendance, and, whilst envying the favoured divines their good fortune, the rest of their brethren had to moderate their ambitions and extend their patience. Their prospects of good preferment depended wholly upon the fidelity of the sovereign to his clerical servants, for, as

[1] Newcastle to H. Pelham, 19/30 Oct. 1748 (Hanover), *ut supra.*
[2] Hardwicke to Newcastle, 8 Nov. 1748. Add. MSS. 32717, f. 294.
[3] Newcastle to Stone, 26 June/7 July 1752. Add. MSS. 32728, f. 107.
[4] Newcastle to Herring, 8/19 July. *Ibid.* f. 216.

one of George I's chaplains observed to Archbishop Wake, their service being unremunerated implied a greater obligation upon their master not "to suffer even his nearest ministers to crowd their own chaplains upon him and let his own labour for nothing".[1] This circumstance gave a peculiarly doleful and melancholy significance to the action of George III upon his accession in nominating above a score new chaplains, thereby sealing the fate of those friends of his predecessor whose services were still unrequited. Not indeed that any accusation could be entertained against George II of forgetfulness of the interests of his servants. On the contrary, his determination to regard the royal prebends as the province of royal chaplains added greatly to the embarrassment of his ecclesiastical minister, the duke of Newcastle. In 1748, his majesty refused unequivocally to bestow a prebend upon Dr Jonathan Shipley in return for his service as chaplain to the army of the duke of Cumberland, with the positive affirmation: "I will not prefer my son's servants to my own";[2] and again in the following year, when Newcastle solicited a prebend of Durham for his kinsman, the dean of Chichester, he found "the king was so strongly inclined to give the preference to his own chaplains that he was pleased absolutely to refuse a preferment for Dr Ashburnham".[3] Repeated experience convinced the duke that he would meet with "difficulties and disagreeable incidents" whenever "he mentioned anybody that was not one of his majesty's chaplains";[4] and solicitors for preferment were admonished accordingly that "ecclesiastical preferments were more difficult to get than any other as the king generally insisted upon his own chaplains".[5] Not even this resolute restriction could ensure satisfaction to every member of the royal household; for the number of royal prebends totalled only forty-nine and the rota of chaplains embraced forty-eight divines.

Many aspirants therefore had to wait a long space of years before receiving satisfaction. Dr Balthasar Regis complained to Newcastle in 1738 of the extreme disproportion between the services he had rendered and the reward received.

"I have had the honour", he wrote, "to be one of his majesty's chaplains above eleven years. Neither the consideration of my health nor of my affairs ever hindered me from waiting in my turn. I have waited not only for myself,

---

[1] F. Hutchinson to Wake, Arch. W. Epist. 22, item ccvii, f. 299.
[2] Newcastle to H. Pelham, 29 Oct./9 Nov. 1748. Add. MSS. 32717, f. 222.
[3] Newcastle to Lord Bateman, 13 Oct. 1749. Add. MSS. 32719, f. 239.
[4] Newcastle to Hardwicke, 27 July/7 Aug. 1750. Add. MSS. 32721, f. 473.
[5] Newcastle to Lord Brooke, 26 June 1759. Add. MSS. 32892, f. 239; cf. 32725, f. 229.

but also often for my brother chaplains. No duty has ever been omitted in our month. The last time of my waiting, had it not been for my cautiousness, there had been no preacher in St James' Chapel on the Sunday just before the king's birthday. I preached then, though I had preached before and I am the senior. Many prebends of Canterbury in our neighbourhood have been disposed of since I have been appointed chaplain, and within a twelvemonth four have been vacant, and no notice has been taken of me who have been a long time one of his Majesty's faithful servants."[1]

A full decade later Regis was still without preferment, though in the meantime he had added further services to the royal house, notably in 1745 when

at the time they were threatened with an invasion, whilst some were frightened out of their wits and did fright all them they conversed with, and had packed up their best effects, he went up and down to encourage everybody, and to induce them, if there was an invasion, to defend themselves bravely and to beat back their inveterate enemies; and he assured them he would share the dangers with them.[2]

Not until 1751 did the deferred reward come in the shape of a prebend of Windsor, after serving George II as chaplain ever since his accession. Archbishop Potter was struck so forcibly by the difficulties and disappointments attending the office of royal chaplain, that in 1742 he suggested that instead of divines without any considerable preferment being appointed, care should be taken to select clergy already possessed of some dignity, to the profit both of king and chaplains. "It seemed to be for the king's service", he argued, "that he should be attended by those who have the dignities of the church", whilst "this method would prevent much solicitation and discontent. For as they who had been preferred might reasonably attend some time without further expectation, so it could scarce be hoped that such as had attended for ten and perhaps almost twenty years, and this at more expense than they could well bear, as some of the present chaplains had done, should remain easy and contented."[3] Indeed the king might account himself fortunate who did not carry out of this world the reproach that some of his clerical servants still lacked due provision of bread.

The best complementary qualification to the office of royal chaplain as an agent of preferment was the advantage of noble birth. Relationship to some noble family was indeed a recognised passport to ecclesiastical

---

[1] Dr B. Regis to Newcastle, 15 Dec. 1738. Add. MSS. 32690, f. 515.
[2] Same to Same, 13 April 1748. Add. MSS. 32714, f. 478.
[3] Potter to Newcastle, 19 July 1742. Add. MSS. 32699, f. 311.

promotion, and the Hanoverian Church was characterised by the number of scions of the nobility who sought sanctuary and aliment in its establishment. The influx of the aristocracy into the profession of Orders provoked a typically mordant comment from Warburton to Hurd upon the occasion of the vacancy of the see of Durham in 1752. "Reckon upon it", he observed, "that Durham goes to some noble ecclesiastic. 'Tis a morsel only for them. Our grandees have at last found their way back into the church. I only wonder they have been so long about it. But be assured that nothing but a new religious revolution, to sweep away the fragments that Harry the VIIIth left, after banqueting his courtiers will drive them out again. The church has been of old the cradle and the throne of the younger nobility. And this nursing mother will, I hope, once more vie with old imperious Berecynthia:

> Laeta Deum partu, centum complexa Nepotes,
> Omnes Caelicolas, omnes super alta tenentes."[1]

The sentiments of Warburton were reduced to a fixed maxim of policy by the affirmation of George Grenville to Bishop Newton of Bristol that "he considered bishoprics as of two kinds: bishoprics of business for men of abilities and learning, and bishoprics of ease for men of family and fashion. Of the former sort he reckoned Canterbury and York, and London, and Ely on account of its connection with Cambridge; of the latter sort Durham, and Winchester, and Salisbury, and Worcester".[2]

The younger sons of the temporal nobility turned to the Church as a natural means of providing for their necessities the appanage denied to them by juniority of birth, the cadets of the peerage in expectation of a deanery or bishopric and those of the lesser knights and baronets prepared to be contented with a prebend or living. A cursory glance at the personnel of the eighteenth-century episcopate illustrates the strength of the aristocratic element in its composition. Of its number three prelates were baronets in their own right, Sir William Dawes, successively bishop of Chester and archbishop of York, Sir Thomas Gooch, bishop of Norwich and Ely, and Sir William Ashburnham, bishop and dean of Chichester. For the space of two generations, from 1724 to 1788, the see of Hereford enjoyed the distinction of occupation in turn by three noble prelates, the Honourable Henry Egerton, Lord James Beauclerk, and the Honourable John Harley; two members of the family of Cornwallis ruled over the diocese of Lichfield, the elder,

---

[1] *Letters of a Late Eminent Prelate*, Warburton to Hurd, Letter xlvii, p. 118.
[2] *Life of Dr Thomas Newton*, in *op. cit.* ii, 154.

Frederick, passing thence to the primacy of Canterbury; Frederick Keppel, son of the second earl of Albemarle, was nominated by George III to the see of Exeter; James Yorke, son of the lord chancellor Hardwicke occupied successively the sees of St David's, Gloucester and Ely, whilst Thomas Thurlow, brother of a later chancellor, was elevated to Lincoln and Durham; Brownlow North, brother of George III's minister, was preferred to the bishoprics of Lichfield, Worcester, and Winchester, John Egerton, grandson of the earl of Bridgwater, to the sees of Lichfield and Durham, Shute Barrington to those of Llandaff, Sarum, and Durham; and Robert Hay Drummond, son of the earl of Kinnoul, presided over the sees of St Asaph and Sarum before his elevation to the archbishopric of York. If the ministerial conventions of the century, as expounded by Grenville, recognised certain "bishoprics of ease for men of family and fashion", its social traditions furnished a supply of candidates to adorn these dignities.

The return of the nobility to the profession of Orders afforded indeed a recruitment chiefly of the generals and field officers of the Church Militant. The scions of the aristocracy cast themselves for the part of commanders and rulers in its service, not of servants or subalterns. Nor did they so undervalue their talents as to wait long or patiently for the firstfruits of rewards, as the careers of Frederick Keppel and Shute Barrington well indicated. The family of Barrington illustrated with peculiar aptness the possibilities of emolument in Church and State open to cadets of the nobility. The eldest son of the first Viscount Barrington, William, became secretary at war, 1760–1 and 1765–78, and chancellor of the exchequer, 1761–2; the third son, John, adopted the profession of arms, and rose to the rank of major-general, the fifth, Samuel, became an admiral of the navy, and the sixth, Shute, entered into Holy Orders. In 1759, when Shute Barrington had been only two years in priests' orders, his brother Lord Barrington solicited Newcastle for his preferment.

"I have but one anxiety in this world," he assured the minister, "my youngest brother remains still without any provision, which is the more distressful to me because every other brother I have is most happily provided for; and I seem to have singled out for neglect a most amiable and accomplished young man, who is loved and esteemed by all who know him; and who has never in his whole life done anything which I have not approved. He has been two years in priests' orders, and will be one of the first king's chaplains that are made. Anything in the church not under £300 would make both him and me completely happy. As we belong to Berkshire a stall at Windsor would be peculiarly acceptable."[1]

[1] Lord Barrington to Newcastle, 26 Dec. 1759. Add. MSS. 32896, f. 333.

With such private virtues united to his public station, the promotion of the young divine was naturally rapid. In 1760 he was made chaplain to George III, encouraged by which qualification, his brother on 11 April again applied to the duke, upon this occasion for the deanery of Bristol. Lord Barrington admitted that the deanery "would not naturally occur to his grace as a first preferment for a person under thirty", but urged their strong family connections with that city; "their grandfather having served in parliament for that city many years, and his memory being still loved and honoured there, he himself had been thought of for their representative, his brother the lawyer would be unanimously chosen their Recorder when Judge Foster died, and they would be very pleased to see his parson brother their dean"![1] Other claims pushed aside this plea for the deanery of Bristol, but in October 1761 Shute Barrington, who had added to his merits that of his marriage with the sister of the duke of St Albans (albeit his brother thought "rather imprudently"), was nominated to the fifth stall of Christ Church, Oxford, at the early age of twenty-seven, to which were added two prebends of Hereford in 1761–2, and the prebend of Consumpta per mare in St Paul's in 1768. But for the unhappy political circumstances which brought about the downfall of George Grenville's administration in May 1765, the aspiring divine might have been installed in the deanery of Windsor upon its vacation in the following September, for Lord Barrington assured Archbishop Secker that "Mr Grenville near two years since had asked that preferment for him of his majesty, who was graciously pleased to authorise him to acquaint him with his promise of granting it to him, whenever it should become vacant".[2] Notwithstanding this disappointment, due to other plans of the duke of Newcastle, who was then lord privy seal, the promotion of Dr Barrington was little hindered, for he was raised to the see of Llandaff in 1769, translated to Sarum in 1782, and thence to Durham in 1791.

Even more remarkable was the rise of Frederick Keppel, who was chaplain to both George II and George III, and received at the hands of the former a prebend of Windsor in 1754 when he was only twenty-five years of age. Two years later he was offered a canonry of Christ Church in exchange for Windsor, which he refused with the explanation to Newcastle that "he flattered himself his grace would not expect him to do anything to his disadvantage, which that certainly would be, for

[1] Barrington to Newcastle, 11 April 1761. Add. MSS. 32918, f. 408.
[2] Barrington to Secker, 25 Sept. 1765. Add. MSS. 32970, f. 60. *Grenville Correspondence*, ii, 486.

by the exchange he would lose £50 a year besides the expenses of removing and the chance of livings falling in his own gift".[1]

Despite such a sufficiency of reward, the earl of Albemarle continued to press for his further advancement, to which the duke replied that Keppel "must rise by degrees and not go all at once", observing that his years did not justify his further promotion, to which the earl could only rejoin that if his grace made his brother a bishop "for him before he went, he would lay him under an everlasting obligation".[2] The dismissal of Newcastle from office in February 1762 prevented his discharge of so great a favour, but in the following October Keppel was nominated to the see of Exeter, thanks to his brother's influence with George III and Bute. Nor was his ambition contented even with this elevation, for his eyes and those of his brother were set covetously upon the see of Sarum, the bishop of which, John Thomas, had over-passed three score years and ten. The bishop of Exeter described it as "his great object and preferable to any other on the Bench, Durham and Winchester excepted", and urged his brother "to press the duke of Newcastle in the strongest terms and procure him a promise of the bishopric".[3] Indeed both suppliants asserted that they could have secured a promise of the preferment from George III through Lord Bute, if they had pressed their suit at an earlier date. To appease them, the duke of Newcastle undertook to secure for Bishop Keppel the deanery of Windsor to hold *in commendam* with his see, "a very fine preferment for a man of quality who has a bishopric at a distance", being worth £950 per annum, and bestowing no less influence than affluence upon the youngest prelate on the Bench,[4] whose years still fell short of thirty-seven when in 1765 he received this lucrative deanery.

The tacit recognition of the claims of the temporal nobility to provide for their brothers in Orders, more especially in the cathedrals of their county, received convincing illustration in relation to the vacancy of the deanery of Norwich in 1760. The entire interest of the Townshend family was concentrated on behalf of Mr Edward Townshend, pre-bendary of Westminster, so that, although Newcastle felt the method of application, with its reflections upon his past neglect, to be somewhat indelicate, he admitted that "he thought Neddy Townshend (and had always thought so), must have the deanery, when thus pressed by all

[1] F. Keppel to Newcastle, 9 April 1756. Add. MSS. 32864, f. 202.
[2] Newcastle to Albemarle, 21 July 1761; Albemarle to Newcastle, 17 Jan. 1762. Add. MSS. 32925, f. 241; 32933, f. 346.
[3] Albemarle to Newcastle, 29 July 1765. Add. MSS. 32968, f. 333.
[4] Newcastle to Albemarle, 7 Oct. 1765. Add. MSS. 32970, f. 213.

the Townshend and Walpole families".[1] To Mr Frederick Hervey, whose brother, Lord Bristol, had solicited since 1756 for some preferment for him, especially because "an imprudent marriage attended with several children had made him importunate", his grace replied that for Norwich there could be only one claimant to his support. He declared that

he had received such strong applications from the Townshend family, the Walpoles, and all the nobility and first gentlemen in the county of Norfolk, in favour of Mr Edward Townshend, son to the late lord Townshend;...and his near relation to the Townshend family and the regard which must be paid to the gentlemen of Norfolk, in which county the preferment was, were such that it would be impossible for him to avoid recommending Mr Townshend to the king, and employing any credit he might have in support of it.[2]

For the king himself the duke drew up an imposing series of memoranda, "Dean of Norwich: Mr Edward Townshend: The Townshends, the Walpoles, the nobility and gentry; Lord Buckingham; Mr Bacon"; and again, "All the nobility and M.P.'s of Norfolk";[3] and although George II's stubbornness protracted the vacancy until his death, George III could not withstand so great a cloud of witnesses testifying to the necessity of making this appointment.

The accession of a new sovereign and the admission of new favourites to the royal confidence involved no breach in the traditions of aristocratic influence upon ecclesiastical promotions and the bestowal of rich preferments upon divines of noble birth and connection. Brownlow North equalled the distinction of Barrington, whom he succeeded in the fourth prebendal stall at Christ Church, by securing that dignity at the age of twenty-seven, but proceeded to outstrip all rivals by his nomination to the deanery of Canterbury in 1770 whilst under thirty, and his elevation to the episcopate as bishop of Lichfield, within a month of the completion of his thirtieth year. Nor were the noble prelates satisfied without the addition of valuable *commendams* to sees which in the earlier part of the century had been deemed sufficient without further revenues. The bestowal *in commendam* of the deanery of Windsor in 1765 on Bishop Keppel of Exeter, and that of St Paul's in 1766 upon Cornwallis of Lichfield, justified the mordant comment of the high churchman William Cole of Blecheley that the nobility were "doing all they can to heap preferment upon preferment upon

---

[1] Newcastle to Hardwicke, 7 June 1760. Add. MSS. 32907, f. 60.
[2] Newcastle to F. Hervey, 9 June 1760. *Ibid.* f. 90.
[3] *Ibid.* ff. 88, 182.

their relations".[1] Indeed the practice of *commendams* received under the new king so wide and liberal an extension that the record of the administration of the younger Pitt in this regard exceeds considerably the custom of the duke of Newcastle. The rich deanery of St Paul's, after being held by Bishop Cornwallis of Lichfield from 1766 to 1768, reverted until 1782 to the poor see of Bristol in the person of Newton, but upon his death it was held *in commendam* for thirty-eight years by Bishops Thurlow and Pretyman of Lincoln successively until the translation of the latter to Winchester in 1820. The addition of so affluent a deanery to so valuable a see provoked much criticism; for as Dr John Douglas, afterwards bishop of Carlisle, observed in 1787, Lincoln, "being worth £2000 per annum, required no *commendam* at all", whilst St Paul's, with "a noble income, at least £2000", involved the obligation of "more residence and hospitality at the deanery than a bishop could possibly comply with, unless he neglected his episcopal function"[2]. Equally noteworthy was the appropriation of the deanery of Windsor as an appanage to various sees, to that of Carlisle under Douglas himself from 1788 to 1791, to the richer see of Lichfield under James Cornwallis from 1791 to 1794, and then to Norwich during the episcopate of Manners Sutton until his translation to Canterbury in 1805. Even the distant deanery of Durham could not escape because of its great wealth, but was held *in commendam* by Bishop Hinchcliffe of Peterborough from 1788 to 1794, and then by Cornwallis at Lichfield in exchange for Windsor for more than a generation, until 1827. The cadets of noble families whose abilities were devoted to the culture of the ecclesiastical vineyard showed themselves indeed expert husbandmen if judged by the spectacle of their progress with joy, bringing their sheaves with them.

It was fortunate for the efficiency of the Hanoverian episcopate that the same aristocratic tradition which denominated certain sees as "bishoprics of ease for men of family and fashion", recognised also others as "bishoprics of business for men of abilities and learning". Clerical subalterns who began their career without the accidental advantage of nobility of birth might aspire therefore to eminence by virtue of their outstanding capacities. But in such circumstances their chances of securing recognition depended largely upon their attracting the notice of some peer, temporal or spiritual, into whose corps of retainers they might become incorporated as chaplains or tutors. The life of Archbishop John Sharp afforded an outstanding example of this method of progress; and the fact that the foundations of his success were laid

[1] *The Blecheley Diary of William Cole*, p. 53.
[2] *Autobiography of Bishop John Douglas*, p. 52. B.M. Eg. 2181.

during the golden age of Caroline high churchmanship testifies not only to the essential continuity between that epoch and its Latitudinarian successor, but also to the wisdom by which the children of light deigned to make use of the same human agents of promotion as their brethren of this world. Upon Sharp's coming down from Christ's College, Cambridge, he was admitted forthwith into the household of Sir Heneage Finch, then solicitor-general, in 1667 as tutor to his family and domestic chaplain. Upon this title he received both the orders of deacon and priest on the same day, and settled down to await his inevitable reward. The promotion of his patron to be attorney-general seemed to require some mark of distinction for the chaplain, and at the age of twenty-eight Sharp became archdeacon of Berkshire, despite his protest, quickly brushed aside by Finch, that he was too young and too ignorant of the law to assume such office. Thenceforth, as his biographer piously recorded, "it was observable that he never had any preferment afterwards but what he had under the seals".[1] In 1673 Finch was appointed lord keeper, and delegated to his chaplain the charge of recommending clergy for preferment to the patronage of his office, in the disposal of which he bestowed duly upon his *protégé* three promotions in the course of the one year, 1675: a prebend of Norwich, the living of St Bartholomew's Exchange, and the rectory of St Giles in the Fields. With such a basis securely laid Sharp made in 1676 a prudent marriage, which, though it involved his leaving the household of his friend, did not place him out of reach of further advancement. The final service rendered by his grateful patron, himself now raised to the peerage as earl of Nottingham, was the offer of the deanery of Norwich in 1681; and this generous provision was recompensed by the future archbishop in a manner eminently characteristic of the times by his own promotion of the younger sons of the lord chancellor to dignities in York Minster, in which Henry Finch was made prebendary of Wetwang in 1695 and dean in 1702, whereupon his brother Edward succeeded to the prebend.

In the universities the office of tutor to a nobleman was an accepted avenue to preferment, and, as such, much coveted by fellows of colleges; for the sentiments of gratitude for pedagogical pains were as strong in the breast of an incorruptible minister like the younger Pitt in relation to George Pretyman as in that of the legendary father of corruption, Walpole, in respect of Francis Hare. The latter divine indeed made assurance doubly sure by adding to the relationship of tutor to the future political manager that of chaplain to the duke of Marlborough

[1] T. Sharp, *Life of Archbishop John Sharp*, i, 21.

during the extensive campaigns of the war of the Spanish Succession. At the height of his grace's military fame and political influence in 1707 his chaplain was preferred to a canonry of St Paul's, from which safe vantage point he defended his patron in the time of the tory triumph against the mordant satire of Swift; for which the grateful whigs on their return with George I advanced him to the deanery of Worcester in 1715 and to that of St Paul's in 1726. From this station his elevation to the bench in 1727 as bishop of St Asaph was a natural step, whence he was translated to Chichester in 1731, holding his deanery *in commendam* with both sees. In 1737 indeed, upon the death of Wake, his friendship with Walpole made him a formidable candidate for succession to the primacy, especially in view of his support of the minister against the apostasy of Gibson, but he died as bishop of Chichester in 1740. Later in the century John Moore whilst at Pembroke College, Oxford, enjoyed the good fortune of being tutor to Lord Blandford, son of the second duke of Marlborough, by whose influence his rise in the church through the deanery of Canterbury and the see of Bangor to the archbishopric of Canterbury was largely accomplished. Nor should the fidelity of the duke of Newcastle to John Hume, the tutor to his nephew Lord Lincoln, be forgotten in estimating the importance of the office of academic and domestic tutor in opening to divines of ability the golden road to ecclesiastical dignity.

Domestic tutorships suffered from the unhappy disadvantage of paucity in number, for even the greatest of families scarcely required the services of more than one tutor for each successive generation of cadets. But whereas tutors were few, chaplains were legion; and the extensive plurality of spiritual retainers accorded by the statute of Henry VIII to the several grades of nobility presented another potential means of promotion, albeit thronged by a multitude of competitors. Young divines whose worldly prospects hung upon a prudent exploitation of their natural talents contended bravely for the honour of appointment as chaplain; for that office conveyed not only the legal title to plurality of benefices but also the introduction to a patron whose influence might be expected to convert possibility into fact. Nor was the patronage of an eighteenth-century peer restricted to the narrow sphere of political services. Tradition decreed the fashionable vogue by which noblemen deemed it a proper evidence of the dignity of their station to accord some measure of encouragement to literary talent; and contemporary divines were not lacking distinction of scholarship, whether sacred or profane, for the fruits of which some patron must be found. John Potter, son of a linendraper of Wakefield, dedicated the first volume of his *Archaeologia Graeca* in 1697 to Robert Harley, then speaker of the commons and destined to become a fecund foster-father of clerical dignitaries; but being appointed chaplain in the family of Archbishop Tenison in 1704 he was drawn into the circle of whig politics, and, fashioning his further fortunes upon that basis, became in 1708 regius professor of Divinity at Oxford upon the nomination of Marlborough to the discomfiture of Harley's candidate, Smalridge. In like manner Edmund Gibson sought eminent patronage for the early scholastic exercises of his career by the dedication of his edition of Camden's *Britannia* to Lord Somers, and of his *Reliquiae Spelmannianae* to Archbishop Tenison, into whose household he in turn had the honour to be received, and laid thereby the foundation of his progress upon a church-whig basis. Zachary Pearce also dedicated his first literary enterprise, an edition of Cicero, *De Oratore*, to Lord Chief Justice Parker, to whom he became chaplain when his patron was elevated to the office of lord chancellor; and thus was drawn into the royal entourage of Queen Caroline which assured his advancement. Even the prolific literary genius of Warburton could not raise its possessor to the episcopal dignity without the reinforcement of secular patronage, for though the eighteenth century appreciated learning, it preferred it spiced with politics. Dr Johnson lamented that, although Warburton appeared to be an exception to his dictum that "few bishops were now made for their learning", even in his case "his learning alone did not raise him", since the interest of Allen and Pitt was necessary to bring him upon the bench. From the eminence thus attained he in turn employed his influence, in conjunction with that of Mansfield and Charles Yorke, to secure the advancement of his literary friend and satellite, Richard Hurd.

Of the importance and reality of this avenue to preferment opened to poor scholars by the patronage of the nobility, no doubt may be entertained. By its means such students of ability and talent as Potter, Gibson, and Hurd, despite the humble circumstances of their parentage, not only attained to the eminence of the episcopate, but each had the honour of being offered the primacy of Canterbury. It was a notable feature of the Hanoverian bench that sandwiched amidst the Corn-wallis', the Egertons, and other prelates of noble family and extraction, there sat bishops such as Secker, educated first at a dissenting academy and nurtured in the household of Bishop Talbot and his son Lord Chancellor Talbot, Warburton, who was a graduate of no university until Cambridge conferred upon him an honorary degree, and Maddox, whom Gibson fostered as an orphan in a London charity school, and who was elevated to the see of St Asaph. To a system of promotion which mingled merit and ability with nobility of estate and pedigree in such measure there must be allowed the virtue, at least within limits, of opening a career to talent notwithstanding the *res angusta domi*. Proof was required indeed of the genius and industry of the aspiring divine, which entailed a period of hard work and often of extreme penury and frugality of living, before recognition was awarded in the shape of admission to some powerful family. Courage and perseverance no less than talent of no mean order were requisite to the poor scholar who left the university to try his fortunes in London and in the world of letters; and the tension of the protracted probationary period might undermine the physical health of some or the nervous vigour of other apprentices to this uncertain profession. But to those possessing ability and diligence, a way of advancement was opened which might not fall short of the highest dignity of the Church; nor was it in any wise to the discredit of peers and bishops that they deemed it an honourable association to themselves that divines of parts should become attached to their retinue and by their appreciation attain to eminence.

It might be contended indeed that men of genius have attained promotion in every age and through every method of patronage, which, notwithstanding, may have frustrated rather than encouraged learning and integrity upon a general survey of its operation. Nor may it be denied that the strong and ubiquitous primacy accorded in the eighteenth century to political services tended to determine preferment in accordance with the degree of their fulfilment. No little prescience and political acumen were needed in a young cleric to discern the rising and falling of ministerial fortunes; for nothing could be more fatal to his chance of success than to follow a statesman doomed to protracted exile from office and influence. Of this circumstance a singular example was afforded in the long neglect by the duke of Newcastle of Dr Thomas Newton. Newton's attachment to and intimacy with the family of William Pulteney seemed to promise his rapid promotion in the Church, and on the fall of Walpole the opportunity of both the political minister and his clerical *protégé* appeared to have arrived. Instead, the ineptitude of Pulteney allowed the reins of authority to pass to other hands, and Newton had to be contented to receive the rectory of St Mary-le-Bow, Cheapside, as the measure of his reward. For other preferment he must rely upon the petitions of his patron to Newcastle. These requests were made indeed continually.

Lord Bath had long solicited the duke of Newcastle for a prebend for him, particularly of Westminster, and the duke often promised and as often failed. So long ago as in the year 1749 were these words in a letter from the duke to the noble lord. "Dr Newton from the regard you have for him and from his own merit, is entitled to any favour I can do for him, and you may be assured I will be as good as my word"; but he was not so good as his word for more than seven years afterwards; and in the meantime there passed some shuffling excuses on one side and some smart remonstrances on the other.[1]

The memory of Newton is corroborated by the correspondence of Newcastle and Bath. On 16 October 1749 Bath informed Newcastle that "he had made Dr Newton extremely happy in transcribing and sending him a paragraph of his grace's letter concerning himself; and he desired him to press his grace no further than for the second or third opportunity he had of disposing of one of the prebends of Westminster or Windsor".[2] In the following July the earl renewed his request, with an apology for being "a most importunate dun in ecclesiastical affairs", and a reminder that the duke had promised the third vacancy, whereas he had now seen "a third given away, a fourth and a fifth" before writing.[3] This importunity was but the beginning of solicitation, to which Newcastle replied in his customary tone of embarrassment and humility. Observing that Newton had already a considerable living from the crown, he urged that

"it might be thought that amongst the many that were daily soliciting, he might be the better able to stay. I very well remember your lordship's recommendation of him", his grace added, "and that was and always will be a reason for me to assist him whenever it is in my power. But I took the liberty to tell your lordship then, that it was always difficult when the person recommended was not chaplain to the king. I must have explained myself very ill and been carried by my inclination to serve your lordship further than I can hope to succeed, if I gave any encouragement to Dr Newton to expect within the compass of this time a prebend of Westminster. I feared when I talked to him upon that subject that I had rather discouraged him too much.... There is nothing so hard to obtain as ecclesiastical preferments of this kind. A Westminster scholar, a Cambridge man, a man of learning and merit, will always be recommendations to me upon a proper occasion.... But indeed my lord I am but one among many; and therefore I the more wish that the necessary qualifications, or those which may be alleged to be such (as is that of being the king's chaplain) should be previously had. I will heartily join with your lordship in speaking to the duke of Grafton that Dr Newton may be made King's chaplain".[4]

[1] *Life of Dr Thomas Newton*, in *op. cit.* ii, 100.
[2] Lord Bath to Newcastle, 16 Oct. 1749 (N.S.). Add. MSS. 32719, f. 214.
[3] Same to Same, 20 July 1750. Add. MSS. 32721, f. 291.
[4] Newcastle to Lord Bath, 15 Oct. 1751. Add. MSS. 32725, f. 289.

To soften the series of disappointments which were the lot of Newton, Andrew Stone undertook to explain "his grace's goodness to him", so that he might talk "in a very right way" to his noble patron; until on 25 April 1756 the expected letter actually arrived from Newcastle announcing the offer of a Westminster prebend, only to be followed by an urgent message the same day by the mouth of Bishop Johnson that his grace had made a mistake in thinking that two prebends of that church were vacant, whereas only one was vacated and that already promised! On the morrow therefore the rejected candidate interviewed the minister.

The duke perhaps never looked more simple and confounded; he made the doctor come and sit by him; he held and pressed his hand all the time he was talking to him; he begged a thousand and a thousand pardons; the house of Commons was a sad, unruly place; he was often forced to make sacrifices to it contrary to his own inclinations;...he hoped that the doctor would have the goodness to forgive him; he should ever esteem it a very great obligation; he would make him ample amends for his disappointment; and concluded with the warmest professions of the highest regard for him and with the strongest assurances of the most determined resolution to serve him.[1]

These resolutions issued in the offer of a royal chaplaincy in 1756, and this opened the way for the desired prebend of Westminster on 22 March 1757. Such a delay justified the quip of Archbishop Herring to the ecclesiastical minister that "he could not help smiling to see with how much more ease his grace filled up a bishopric than a prebend".[2] The reward of a bishopric indeed did not come to Newton until George III insisted upon overruling the opinion of Newcastle, and advancing him to the see of Bristol in 1761.

From Bristol there proceeded also another instance of the superior merit of political services to pure learning in the person of Dr Josiah Tucker, whose original writings upon economic themes contributed less to his preferment than a practical intervention in the arena of politics by his support of Robert Nugent in the election in that city in 1754. In gratitude Nugent immediately solicited Newcastle for the recompense of a prebend for the cleric "who had so eminently distinguished himself upon various occasions in the whig cause, and recommended himself beyond any other person whatever by his merits and sufferings to his majesty's best friends in Bristol".[3] Accordingly in

[1] *Life of Dr Thomas Newton*, in *op. cit.* ii, 102.
[2] Herring to Newcastle, 15 Feb. 1755. Add. MSS. 32852, f. 473.
[3] R. Nugent to Newcastle, 1 Aug. 1754. Add. MSS. 32726, f. 136. R. L. Schuyler, *Josiah Tucker*, pp. 21-5.

1756 Lord Chancellor Hardwicke bestowed upon Tucker a prebend of Bristol, an action commended warmly by Newcastle with the comment that there could not have been "a more acceptable thing to the king's friends, nor a righter thing in itself than the giving the prebend" to such a zealot.[1] Even George II was moved to "express of himself a great desire to reward" Dr Tucker, and in 1758 the deanery of Gloucester was offered to him and accepted.[2] With this preferment Tucker's ecclesiastical career reached its culmination, for his publications upon political and economic matters were too original and independent in judgment to command the protracted allegiance of any party administration.

The degree of political loyalty required of divines by the ministry which preferred them was illustrated by the episode of the nomination of Zachary Pearce to the deanery of Winchester by Walpole in 1739, which, although the transaction of a whig minister, was typical of the standard of conduct expected by both parties throughout the century. Pearce had already won the friendship of Queen Caroline and her confidante Lady Sundon, so that the only barrier to his advancement seemed to lie in his association with William Pulteney, the chief antagonist of Walpole's administration. Upon the vacancy of the deanery of Wells in 1739 Pearce resolved to attend the minister's levee "to put himself in the way and in the thoughts" of Sir Robert, who sounded him as to his political persuasion, intimating to him "that the members of parliament for Wells and several others of the town had been with him, that nothing but election work ran in their heads, and that they had pressed him not to give the deanery except to one who would assist them at elections". To this observation Pearce could make no reply until assured of the attitude of Pulteney towards such a demand; who in turn waited upon Walpole to request that Pearce's relationship to himself might not prejudice his chances of preferment. The deanery of Winchester having become vacant meanwhile, Pearce was recommended to his majesty for appointment; whereupon Pulteney released his clerical friend from all political obligations to himself in the handsomest possible manner.

"Dr Pearce," he observed, "though you may think that others besides Sir Robert have contributed to get you this dignity, yet you may depend upon it that he is all in all, and that you owe it entirely to his good will towards you. And therefore as I am now so engaged in opposition to him,

[1] Newcastle to Hardwicke, 23 Sept. 1756. Add. MSS. 32867, f. 400.
[2] Newcastle to Lord Ducie, 22 Oct. 1757. Add. MSS. 32875, f. 214.

it may happen that some who are of our party may, if there should be any opposition for members of parliament at Winchester, prevail upon me to desire you to act there in assistance of some friend of ours, and Sir Robert at the same time may ask your assistance in the election for a friend of his own against the one whom we recommend. I tell you therefore beforehand, that if you comply with any request other than with Sir Robert's to whom you are so very much obliged, I shall have the worse opinion of you."[1]

If the appointment to bishoprics and deaneries presented problems of the delicate balance of learning and loyalty, little doubt may be entertained of the pernicious effect of the association of politics with preferment in relation to the simple prebends and to the office of chaplain in the various grades of the temporal nobility. Indeed the number of chaplains allowed by the statute of 1529 was a direct incentive to abuse, since not even the most devout members of the aristocracy could provide adequate spiritual duties for four or six clerical retainers. Accordingly, the nomination to a chaplaincy became often a formality granted merely to furnish the legal qualification for plurality and without spiritual duties. This creation of titular chaplains in no wise added to the efficiency or credit of the Church; and it was accounted therefore a mark of peculiar strictness in Archbishop Sharp that he would not "make any titular chaplains to qualify them for holding more benefices than one". His reason for this refusal was the odium attaching to pluralism, and his realisation "how much the bishops had been blamed upon that account with respect to their chaplains"; and his biographer was at pains to counteract the impression that such stiffness in his grace showed "too great a strictness and disregard for the inferior clergy in refusing them favours which the lay lords were willing to bestow upon them as far as they had opportunity".[2] The extreme of negligence and abuse arising from the creation by the temporal nobility of titular retainers was illustrated by an episode related to the duke of Newcastle by Lord Poulett in 1760.

"Having given a scarf to Mr Pelham many years ago for a friend of his," the earl wrote on 30 August, "your grace would oblige me by directing one of your secretaries to enquire whether the person be living or dead, for I have never seen or heard of him since. I find Charles Dixon and John Davies on the register as my chaplains, who are both strangers to me, but one of 'em I suppose to have been the person recommended by Mr Pelham on a particular occasion, and known perhaps to the late Mr Pelham's people; but who the other should be I can't guess, since I don't remember ever having given a

---

[1] *Life of Zachary Pearce*, in *op. cit.* i, 390–2.   [2] *Life of Sharp*, i, 201–2.

scarf to a stranger, except so many years ago to a friend of Mr Pelham. The favour I would ask of your grace on this occasion, when I am much distressed for a scarf to qualify a friend of mine to hold two livings which are now vacant...is to be informed whether the person be still living who was recommended to me by the late Mr Pelham, and if either of the gentlemen on the register be the person. The office is certainly ill-kept, for they still place one to my account that I know nothing of."[1]

In reply Newcastle was able to identify Dixon, whom he remembered as needing a qualification to hold two livings in Sussex and who was probably the person recommended by Pelham, but had been dead some years.

The incident, albeit isolated, emphasised strongly the necessity of revision of the law of pluralities and the abolition of the office of chaplain in the majority of cases in which it had become merely titular. Equally pernicious was the practice of some nobles in the latter part of the century to bring within the ambit of chaplains the Swiss tutors who attained great popularity as domestic pedagogues. Archbishop Moore in 1789 protested to his kinsman Sir William Eden, Baron Auckland, that he could not present to an English benefice a native of Languedoc whose "broken English would be discovered in the moment of his beginning to read the service in his church in order to take possession". The next day both priest and patron would be pilloried in the press; which, added the primate, "I can't stand after the efforts I have lately made to keep out some of the Swiss governors who have lately been rewarded in this way in order to exonerate rich men from pensions which they were bound to pay them". The archbishop returned to the point in a later letter, in which he refused to entertain the idea of presenting a Frenchman to any benefice except in the Channel Islands, in view of the outcry against other foreigners. "People who have employed Swiss tutors for their children have found it a cheap way of discharging their obligations by getting them into Orders and procuring them livings. The public prints have been filled, sometimes with wit, sometimes with indignation, on the subject; and in fact it bears hard on our inferior clergy."[2] Against such an extension of the acquisitive instinct of the nobility, which regarded the Church as a private patrimony even for foreign tutors in addition to younger sons and chaplains, the archbishop indeed contended justly, for their zeal had clearly outrun both discretion and decency.

[1] Poulett to Newcastle, 30 Aug. 1760; Newcastle to Poulett, 1 Sept. 1760. Add. MSS. 32910, f. 443; 32911, f. 19.
[2] Abp. Moore to Eden, n.d. and 23 Nov. 1789. Auckland Papers, Add. MSS. 34461, ff. 36, 45.

Reform however would need to be directed primarily to the simple prebends of the cathedral and collegiate churches, which constituted the chief field of solicitation and reward of the chaplains of the nobility. It was evident that the half-hundred royal prebends, eked out by the twenty-six in the gift of the lord chancellor, were wholly insufficient to meet the demands pressed insistently upon the ministers of state; and the unhappy consequence of this inadequacy was the labyrinthine complexity of promises and engagements into which statesmen betrayed themselves in the attempt to satisfy friends and supporters. Leaders of political parties could not afford to be indifferent to the goodwill of the territorial aristocracy, who thought it eminently suitable that their spiritual retainers should be encouraged by the gift of prebends in the cathedrals of their locality; but the combination of personal friendship and political obligation produced an embarrassing plethora of recommendations for each vacancy, extending upon occasion to requests for the second or third dignity to be vacant in a particular church. The temptation in such circumstances being strong to multiply promises without present prospect of fulfilment, the duke of Newcastle found himself not uncommonly faced by the nemesis of promiscuous prodigality, as in 1750 in a particularly complex situation relative to a prebend of Worcester.

On 7 October 1748 Lord Gower had recommended Mr Thomas Hinton, chaplain to Lord Anson, for some dignity, though it was not clear that any particular cathedral was specified. His lordship urged that Hinton "at the late elections did more to support the friends of his majesty than anyone in his station"; so that "if he had had the good fortune to have known him sooner", he would have recommended him for the recent vacancy of the deanery of Lichfield, since it was essential that Anson and himself should be able to procure preferment for those that were honest enough "to stand firm to the true interest in spite of all the difficulties and disadvantages they laboured under in that city".[1] Since Newcastle was then away in Hanover and much preoccupied by the episcopal promotions occasioned by the death of Gibson of London, the request does not appear to have made any strong impression on his memory. In the following year, he promised Lord Bateman to use his good offices in relation to the next prebend of Worcester for Mr Crusius, his lordship's former tutor, and Master of the Charterhouse.[2] This engagement he reaffirmed in 1750 to Lord Deerhurst, who had applied to him in behalf of the chaplain of the earl of Coventry, whereupon

[1] Gower to Newcastle, 7 Oct. 1748. Add. MSS. 32717, f. 42.
[2] Newcastle to Bateman, 13 Oct. 1749. Add. MSS. 32719, f. 239.

Gower thought it expedient to renew his request for Hinton. Lord Deerhurst indeed was so considerate as to express himself satisfied if he could have the promise of the second prebend, since his sole aim was "to promote the whig interest in that county which had been recovered at a vast expense to his family".[1] The expectation of a vacancy proceeded from the illness of Mr Meadowcourt, whose life was prolonged actually until 1760; but this uncertainty could not defer the prosecution of the various candidatures. The duke of Newcastle, who always answered even the most delicate letters, pointed out therefore to Lord Gower the priority of Lord Bateman's claims, adding that he had also received requests from Lord Deerhurst, and from Mr Harrison, M.P. for Hertford, in behalf of his nephew, though insisting of course that he did not mention these "as what should stand in competition with his lordship's recommendation of Mr Hinton", whom he did not design to put off but "really to serve as soon as he could". He suggested, however, that the matter should be talked over with Archbishop Herring and Henry Pelham, with a view to contenting all parties by the promise to Hinton of the second prebend at Worcester or possibly one at Canterbury.[2]

Unfortunately the mediators were unable to pacify Gower. The primate reported that both Gower and Anson regarded it "as of the last consequence that Hinton should be immediately taken care of, and more especially at such a juncture, when so bad a spirit was stirring in that county";[3] whilst Henry Pelham, though himself supporting the contention of Lord Bateman's priority, found the lord chancellor Hardwicke convinced that the application of the two lords had been "as long ago as when the king was at Hanover last".[4] His advice to his brother therefore was that since Gower "deserved better of the king than all of them put together", it would be politic to oblige him, and that an enquiry into the dates should be made. Out of this slight contretemps the duke created a crisis of great importance, increased in magnitude by his absence from England and by the series of verbose letters which must be written to all parties to the negotiation. In regard to dates he was convinced that Lord Bateman's application had been made whilst he was under an engagement to the duke of Somerset for Mr John Dalton for the first Worcester prebend, on which account he

---

[1] Deerhurst to Newcastle, 30 June 1750. Add. MSS. 32721, f. 204.
[2] Newcastle to Gower, 4/15 July 1750. *Ibid.* f. 221.
[3] Herring to Newcastle, 12 July 1750. *Ibid.* f. 347.
[4] H. Pelham to Newcastle, 13 July 1750; Hardwicke to Newcastle, 20 July 1750. *Ibid.* ff. 359, 410.

had given his promise for the second. This had occurred during his former visit to Hanover in 1748, since Dalton had been nominated on 11 January 1748–9. On both these points he refreshed his memory by consulting the office books, which substantiated his story and afforded "almost a proof that his promise to Lord Bateman for the first prebend of Worcester after Mr Dalton had one, must have been some time before the application made by Lord Gower and Lord Anson, since the king returned to England on 25 November and the warrant for Mr Dalton's prebend was signed in the January following". Despite this proof presumptive, and the fact that their lordships' original letter of 1748 in behalf of Hinton did "shew that there was no mention made of a prebend of Worcester", so that his grace "thought they desired a prebend of Westminster or Windsor", his anxiety not to offend two such powerful persons (for Gower had great local influence and Henry Pelham had testified that Bateman "behaved as well and as zealously as any man in the house of commons") was such that he offered a compromise. He besought Lord Hardwicke as "a common friend to all parties" to become his plenipotentiary and to present the following offer.

If his lordship and Mr Pelham could persuade the duke of Marlborough to prevail upon his nephew Lord Bateman to discharge him from his promise of recommending Mr Crusius to the first vacancy, he would then most readily recommend Mr Hinton to it. But otherwise he could not.... The application of Mr Harrison (which, he very well remembered, at the time Mr Pelham thought deserved attention), and the new strong application of Lord Deerhurst (a young nobleman of great consequence in the county of Worcester), he was very ready to postpone, and to give the preference infinitely to Lord Gower and Lord Anson's recommendation.... The second prebend of Worcester might not be worth Mr Hinton's while to wait for; but if all the king's servants agreed...he was very ready in their name and his own to recommend Mr Hinton for the first prebend of Westminster, Windsor, or Canterbury.... So, if his lordship and Mr Pelham would write him a letter, representing the case of Mr Hinton and the great service he had been of at Lichfield, and the great stress that Lord Gower and Lord Anson laid upon his having some immediate mark of his Majesty's favour, and therefore recommending him for the first vacancy at Westminster or Windsor or Canterbury, he would lay it before the king, and back it in that manner he was persuaded it would succeed; and he believed Mr Hinton would think such a promise of so much a more valuable preferment in three churches a much better thing than a promise of the first prebend of Worcester.[1]

[1] Newcastle to Hardwicke, 27 July/7 Aug. 1750. Add. MSS. 32721, f. 473.

To this recital of the official embarrassments of his situation, Newcastle added a characteristic private and despairing postscript: "Get me out of the scrape with Gower and Anson; or at least let others share it with me". The chancellor therefore exerted himself to secure the acceptance of the compromise; and the providential death of a canon of Windsor enabled the smooth accomplishment of this task. Hinton was duly nominated to the prebend at Windsor on 22 January 1751, whilst Crusius succeeded in due season to the first stall at Worcester on the 20 December following.

The promiscuous and complicated game of barter to which the procedure of appointment to the royal prebends had been reduced by the middle of the eighteenth century was further illustrated by the apologia of Newcastle to the earl of Halifax in 1754, excusing his neglect of his lordship's solicitation for a Canterbury prebend for his chaplain.

"I honour and esteem you for your public qualities," he affirmed; "I love you (if you will give me leave to say and to do so) for your private ones. But this honour and that love can't make me force the king to do what he may be disinclined to.... Your lordship is mistaken if you think I can do what I please. The king has his own way of thinking and acting in the disposal of preferments, especially ecclesiastical ones. It was from this cause that a great number of ecclesiastical preferments were undisposed of for near two years. It was from his majesty's own determination that my lord chancellor could not obtain to this day an exchange only for his friend and neighbour, Dr Barnard of the city, (a most valuable and eminent clergyman) from a prebend of Norwich to one of Windsor. This is the case, with other reasons, why Dr Carter, a most zealous whig clergyman and magistrate in Suffolk, espoused by the duke of Grafton and father-in-law to the earl of Rochford, brother-in-law to Mr Drake of the East India Company and zealously insisted upon by both, has not in upwards of seven years' solicitation obtained a prebend in the king's gift. My Lord Bath has in vain solicited also for a very meritorious and able man, Dr Newton of the city. Had it been in my power, I assure your lordship that above half, if not all, of the persons abovementioned would have been provided for long before now.... When I was last at Hanover there was a vacancy of a prebend of Canterbury. The duke of Dorset [for Mr Thomas Curteis], my Lord Abergavenny for his uncle Dr Tatton, and Dr Head, deputy clerk of the closet, were solicitors. The king was pleased of himself to give it after a year and a half to my Lord Abergavenny's uncle. The duke of Dorset was extremely mortified at it; that in his own county (where there was then a contested election, in which his grace had a great, meritorious, and expensive share) his recommendation of

Mr Curteis (an active and zealous man in the cause) should be set aside. His grace was not well pleased with me. For indeed he had a right to my assistance, as he had given a bishopric in Ireland to a Cambridge friend of mine in expectation of this preferment for Mr Curteis. This being the case, I must assist Mr Curteis preferably to everybody. Dr Head has pretensions of his own, as having long served the king as clerk of the closet. These pretensions are strongly backed by the archbishop of Canterbury, and are such in themselves as I have long given Dr Head reason to think I should not oppose."[1]

The pressing obligation to his grace of Dorset was satisfied the year following by the nomination of Curteis to the eleventh prebend at Canterbury, but the complete discharge of so comprehensive a list of obligations was a labour of Sisyphus, impossible of achievement.

The wide disproportion between the number of dignities in the royal gift and of the aspirants thereto, which provoked Newcastle to declare that "he was more plagued about the prebends than about all the rest", led naturally also to his attempt to encroach upon episcopal patronage by pressing the divines whose elevation to the bench he had accomplished, to ease his difficulties by liberating an occasional prebend in their cathedrals for his instant necessities. Bishop Newton found consolation in being made prelate of a see of which the prebends were in the gift of the lord chancellor, by the freedom from importunity which his poverty brought. Relating the confession of his friend Bishop Green of Lincoln, that "he stood engaged eleven deep to the duke of Newcastle, lord Hardwicke and their friends", his lordship of Bristol "less regretted his want of patronage, having nothing in his gift worthy of a minister to lay his paw upon".[2] Dr Edmund Pyle, whose situation enabled him to collect a good deal of court gossip on ecclesiastical affairs, presented a sinister picture of the arch-dispenser of patronage preying upon all his episcopal *protégés*.

He torments the poor archbishop of Canterbury for everything that falls in his gift. . . . He is as great a plague to the other bishops, asking even for their small livings. Ely gives him everything (they say by bargain): Chichester, Peterborough, Durham, Gloucester, Salisbury, are slaves to him in this respect. Only London and Winchester give him flat denials, unless we are to add York, which is a point problematical.[3]

The mordancy of Pyle's wit sharpened his pen invariably against his grace of Newcastle, yet his record bears the face of verisimilitude, since

---

[1] Newcastle to Halifax, 8 Aug. 1754. Add. MSS. 32733, f. 182.
[2] *Life of Dr Thomas Newton*, in *op. cit.* ii, 205–6.
[3] E. Pyle, *Memoirs of a Royal Chaplain*, p. 218.

all the prelates enumerated as complaisant, Mawson, Ashburnham, Thomas, Trevor, Johnson, and Gilbert, owed their promotion to the duke's efforts. Archbishop Hutton of York returned indeed a peremptory refusal to a request in 1748 for a prebend of his cathedral to meet the minister's political obligations.

"How can it be expected", he urged, "that I should lay myself under a promise to give one of the best prebends in my church to an entire stranger, unconnected with me or my diocese?...Can it be thought reasonable that I should give the preferment to this gentleman before every one of my own chaplains, dependents, and relatives, and baulk the expectation of some of the principal gentlemen and friends of the government in Yorkshire with whom I have lived in esteem from my infancy, after being above five years upon the bench, without a possibility of gratifying anyone with above £50 a year? It will be impossible for me to preserve the confidence of my own dependents or maintain the share of esteem and affection I have met with among my countrymen and clergy, if they find themselves slighted in the first instances of favour I have it in my power to dispense."[1]

The firmness of this denial did not imply an absolute prohibition for the future; and not the least piquant item of Newcastle's correspondence, in view of the animus displayed by Dr Pyle in his references to the duke, is the letter from the same archbishop in 1751 acknowledging the recommendation by his grace of that divine for promotion to the archdeaconry of York. The northern primate accepted gladly the nomination, assuring Newcastle that although Pyle "was a stranger to himself and to the diocese, he doubted not his good character would give him the same weight with the clergy of his district that his grace's recommendation had with himself to collate him to it"![2]

The precise point at which the anticipation of returns from grateful prelates by their patron passed into simony would be difficult of definition, though Butler of Durham refused upon his translation in 1750 to that see to be a party to a transaction which bore even the appearance of illegality. His intended removal from Bristol would vacate the deanery of St Paul's which he had held *in commendam*, the nomination to which of Bishop Secker in turn would liberate a prebend of Durham; and this last preferment the administration designed for Dr Thomas Chapman, Master of Magdalene College, Cambridge. Accordingly the duke of Newcastle, in congratulating Butler upon his

---

[1] Hutton to Newcastle, 23 June 1748; M. Bateson, "Clerical Preferment under the Duke of Newcastle", in *E.H.R.* 1892, vii, 685–96.
[2] Hutton to Newcastle, 7 Sept. 1751. Add. MSS. 32725, f. 146.

translation, observed that "his majesty had ordered him to put his lordship in mind of his request of the first prebend for Dr Chapman".[1] To this Butler returned a disquieting answer.

"When I came to the postscript", he replied, "and found a command accompanying that nomination, it gave me greater disturbance of mind than I think I ever felt. Your grace will please to remember that when you mentioned this to me near three-quarters of a year ago, I made not a word of answer, but went on talking of other things; and upon your repeating the mention of it at the same time, just as I was going out of your dressing room, I told your grace it did not admit of an answer. This my silence and this my reply were owing to my being in so great a surprise at such a thing being asked of me *beforehand*, that I did not trust myself to talk upon the subject. But upon settling within myself what I ought to say, I proposed to wait upon your grace and let you know that I could not take any church promotion upon the condition of any such promise or intimation as your grace seemed to expect. But before I had time to do this I met the archbishop who began, as from you, to talk of the affair; upon which I desired him to let your grace know what I had purposed, as I now said, to tell you myself. My words, so far as I can remember, were that my principles would not permit me to accept of any promotion upon the condition of making any promise or raising any expectation *beforehand* of giving away preferment. After this, my lord, I had not the most distant suspicion but that if his majesty would nominate me to Durham, your grace would have permitted the nomination to come free. My lord, the bishops as well as the inferior clergy take the oaths against simony; and as I should think an express promise of preferment to a patron *beforehand* an express breach of that oath and would deny institution upon it, so I should think a tacit promise a tacit breach of it. I am afraid your grace may think I have already said too much; but as this affair, that I am to give Dr Chapman the first prebend of Durham is common talk at Cambridge, and consequently will be so, if it be not already, wherever I am known, I think myself bound, whatever be the consequence of my simplicity and openness, to add that it will be impossible for me to do it consistently with my honour and character, since if I should it would be understood (though your grace and I know the contrary) to be done in consequence of some previous promise either express or tacit."[2]

The prospect of so promising a scheme going awry perturbed the duke exceedingly, nor was it easy to find an expedient which would encompass the end designed and satisfy the probity of the bishop. Archbishop Herring had at the outset been "apprehensive of scruples" and fearful that it would be "a matter of great delicacy", and had

[1] Newcastle to Butler, 27 July/7 Aug. 1750. Add. MSS. 32721, f. 487.
[2] Butler to Newcastle, 5 Aug.; quoted by M. Bateson in *E.H.R.* vii, 685–96.

accordingly only mentioned it to Butler "gently and obiter and then dropped it instantly". Even Newcastle himself had represented the affair only "as a point of gratitude and honour that by being hinted might be naturally expected to be fulfilled, but was by no means understood as a condition annexed to the grant of the bishopric". Lord Hardwicke, whilst wishing that the question had been left until the actual translation had been perfected, could suggest only as a compromise "that the affair were suffered to rest as it was, upon the bishop's refusal in writing, which might satisfy the point of conscience, and after he was completely made bishop of Durham, he should think it right to satisfy the point of honour and equity...by doing it voluntarily".[1] An alternative solution was hinted fortunately by Butler himself to Dr James Johnson for transmission to Newcastle; that Secker's prebend would devolve in equity to the crown, and that he himself would thereupon "be extremely glad to have Dr Chapman as one of the prebendaries".[2] This expedient he further pressed upon Herring, and Hardwicke ascertained that Chapman would accept it; so that the letter of the law was preserved whilst discharging also the point of honour. It must be admitted that Butler had fulfilled the appearance of rectitude rather than its substance; for neither primate nor chancellor could accept the legal fiction of a devolution to the crown, since Secker could not become dean of St Paul's until Butler was fully bishop of Durham, and by consequence his resignation of his prebend in Durham would not occur *sede vacante* but after the full installation of Butler. Herring indeed confessed that in conversation with Butler, he "said nothing to discountenance his expedient, but laughed at it inwardly"; whilst Hardwicke though not understanding "the law of this", consented to "make no objection against it", since he was glad to see the bishop disposed to give way to expedients.[3]

Bishop Trevor, the successor of Butler at Durham, knew better how to respond to a gentleman's agreement; for when in 1758 Newcastle solicited for Dr Markham, headmaster of Westminster School, the richest prebend of Durham worth £700 per year, pleading in extenuation that the request "was the first of the kind since his lordship's removal to Durham", the bishop not only assured his grace that his desires had the force of commands, but added the delicate compliment of thanks "for so worthy a recommendation, so agreeable to himself

[1] Hardwicke to Newcastle, 23 Aug. 1750. Add. MSS. 32722, f. 235; cf. 35599, f. 17.
[2] Butler to Johnson, 8 Aug. 1750. Add. MSS. 32722, f. 74.
[3] Herring to Hardwicke, 8 Sept. 1750. Add. MSS. 35599, f. 25; Hardwicke to Newcastle, 20 Sept. 1750. Add. MSS. 32722, f. 448.

and so honourable to both".[1] Even more generous was his action in
1767 when, the duke being deprived of the possibility of rewarding his
friends by his banishment from ministerial office, Trevor bestowed upon
Dr Edmund Law, Master of Peterhouse, a divine whose theological
unorthodoxy had drawn upon him the opposition of Archbishop Secker,
a prebend of Durham of the value of £500 per annum. "Such a valuable
preferment in the church", wrote his grace, "at a time when I have not
the opportunity of procuring them elsewhere, is not only the greatest
mark of your goodness and affection to me, but must be the most
agreeable favour conferred on a chancellor of the university who has at
present no other way of rewarding men of merit than by the goodness
of his friends."[2]

In the case of prelates whose promotion had cost the minister so great
travail as the translation of Trevor, the return of favours might be
expected. But the generality of the episcopate found the friendship of
Newcastle as embarrassing to sustain as delicate to decline. Archbishop
Herring, torn between the timorousness of nature which drew him to
compliance and the fear of leaving his own servants desolate, confessed
to Hardwicke that "he wished he knew how to parry his grace, for his
friends were somewhat disposed to murmur if not to clamour" against
the surrender of their interest to the importunity of the ecclesiastical
minister.

Inevitably also the duke's importunity was intensified after his final
dismissal from office in 1766, when the bishops of his creation could not
escape his iterated requests. From Hume of Sarum he solicited even a
small prebend of £16 per annum for a Cambridge divine.

"You must not be surprised that I am so pressing", he explained, "but
at a time when my nearest relations have deserted me; when some of those
I vainly thought were my best friends, have done the same; and when the
Townshends, Ashburnhams, bishops of Lichfield and Chichester have done
so also; I say you must not be surprised that I should press those of my
friends, the bishops who have it in their power, to reward my deserving
friends in the universities, when I have no other way but through them of
doing it. The bishops of Durham and Worcester have done it amply; the
archbishop of York and bishop of Lincoln as far as has been in their power;
and my good friend the bishop of Norwich, who is a very small patron, has
destined one of his best preferments that way if it falls."[3]

[1] Newcastle to Trevor, 12 June 1758; Trevor to Newcastle, 14 June 1758.
Add. MSS. 32892, ff. 32, 70.
[2] Newcastle to Trevor, 25 Aug. 1767. Add. MSS. 32984, f. 285.
[3] Newcastle to Hume, 9 Nov. 1766. Add. MSS. 32986, f. 325.

Such a confession was the best testimony to episcopal gratitude, amongst the instances of which it would be invidious to particularise; for as Bishop Hume replied to his grace, "I did not want to be put in mind of my promise or to be told what other bishops have done: *Ista commemoratio est quasi exprobratio*".[1]

The effect of this labyrinthine method of ecclesiastical preferment upon the cathedral churches was the creation of a singular and often bizarre mosaic of capitular dignitaries. The cathedrals whose prebends were in the gift of the crown and the chancellor were furnished with a supply of dignitaries of the most varied character and provenance. Royal chaplains, chaplains to the nobility, friends of the peerage, dependents of the ministers of state, and odd individuals whose presence could hardly be accounted for even by contemporary ways of promotion, adorned especially the churches of Windsor, Westminster, and Canterbury. The tradition was well established by the testimony of Mr Speaker Arthur Onslow of the house of commons in 1742, that "the chaplains of the house of commons had always been provided for in the churches of Westminster or Windsor"; and that energetic president of debate improved the good custom with such diplomatic skill that within twenty years from 1742 to 1762 he planted five chaplains in these coveted offices. Richard Terrick was nominated to a prebend of Windsor in June 1742 and his successor Mr John Fulham in April 1750, whereas the next three chaplains of the house were settled at Westminster, Richard Cope in 1754, Reeve Ballard in 1758 (reinforced by the magniloquent request of Pitt that "since he had not had one word to say concerning hierarchies and powers, he might be indulged an humble prebend in the name of the commons of England"), and Charles Burdett in 1761. In accordance with this usage George III assured Sir John Cust, Speaker of the House in 1763, that his brother, who held the chaplain's office, "must be confined to one of the three churches of Windsor, Westminster, and Canterbury, but that he might fix his choice upon the first vacancy in any one of them".[2] Whereupon Mr Richard Cust, having chosen Windsor, had the disappointment to see vacancies occurring successively in Westminster and Canterbury rather than in the church of his preference, and in 1765, in despair, accepted the fifth prebend of Christ Church. Even so zealous a churchman as Archbishop Secker agreed in this circumstance to lay aside the claims to reward of Dr Thomas Bray whom he was anxious to serve, with the reflection that "even though the preferment in itself were ever

[1] Hume to Newcastle, 11 Nov. 1766. *Ibid.* f. 372.
[2] Sir J. Cust to Newcastle, 27 July 1765. Add. MSS. 32968, f. 291.

so suitable, he could not be opposed to the speaker's brother and chaplain".[1] In like manner when Henry Fox, after having been member of parliament for Windsor fifteen years, was appointed to office in the administration in 1755, his promotion needed for its authentication the preferment of Mr John Bostock, the minister of Windsor, since it would disgrace him to confess "that, as secretary of state, he could not procure one prebendary in the church of a place he had served for so many years".

In cathedrals whose dignities were in the patronage of the bishop, the personnel of the chapter depended upon his fidelity to the responsibility committed to him. The pressure of political ministers upon their episcopal *protégés* for the surrender of prebends was accepted or resisted according to the independence of position and character of the several prelates. The value of the prebends of Durham Cathedral brought upon the prelates of that see repeated solicitations from their political allies, for, as Bishop Trevor explained to Newcastle in 1764 concerning "the state of his church, he had but one prebend of so little value as £350 per annum, and that is no small thing; all the rest are £500 per annum and upwards".[2] Archbishop Sharp at York made it his rule "to bestow the prebends in his gift upon such only as were either beneficed in his diocese or retained in his family", to which the only exception was his preferment of two sons of the earl of Nottingham his patron. Accordingly in York Minster and the collegiate church of Southwell, "of the forty-six stalls which he filled...in less than half that number of years, all were filled agreeably to the foregoing resolution", those of Southwell for the clergy of Nottinghamshire and of York for the Yorkshire clergy. In this disposal of his patronage he paid particular attention to the clergy of York city, and of the large market towns of his diocese, such as Hull, Beverley, Leeds, Sheffield, Wakefield, Doncaster, Nottingham, and Newark, the dignity of which was recognised by the bestowal of prebends upon their incumbents.[3] This laudable practice was followed in the neighbouring diocese of Chester, where, as Mr Browne Willis, the historian of cathedrals, related to Wake in 1724, "in Chester cathedral there had not been for many years any prebendary but what had been beneficed in Cheshire or Lancashire".[4] Similarly Zachary Pearce, upon his nomination to the see of Bangor, "established in himself a resolution of conferring Welsh preferments or benefices only on Welshmen; and to this resolution he adhered in

---

[1] Secker to Newcastle, 29 Sept. 1765. Add. MSS. 32969, f. 443.
[2] Newcastle to Dr L. Caryl, 6 Dec. 1764. Add. MSS. 32964, f. 226.
[3] *Life of Sharp*, i, 117–19.
[4] Willis to Wake, 28 Sept. 1724. Arch. W. Epist. 22, item cccxxii, f. 483.

defiance of influence or importunity. He twice gave away the deanery and bestowed many benefices, but always chose for his patronage the natives of the country, whatever might be the murmurs of his relations or the disappointment of his chaplains".[1]

No small measure of the attractiveness of prebends lay in the circumstance that their duties were often nominal. In most cathedrals the simple prebendaries were not required to keep residence, but only to preach in their turn, a condition which facilitated the conversion of the office into a sinecure. When Gibson was nominated by Archbishop Tenison to his option of the precentorship of Chichester, he consoled himself with the reflection that, if a residentiaryship were not attached to it (since that dignity lay in the election of the chapter), he would enjoy £70 a year and "a very good sinecure attended by no duty but three sermons per year *per se aut per alium*".[2] The biographer of Sharp of York likewise allowed that the prebends of his churches were "acceptable promotions...on account of the credit that attends them without any burden or inconvenience".[3] The natural consequence of the political provenance of much cathedral preferment was the spectacle in some churches of an extensive non-residence. Bishop Newton at Bristol, where all the prebends were in the chancellor's gift, lamented the absence of its dignitaries from public service.

"The deanery is worth at least £500 a year," he noted, "and each prebend is worth about half that sum, and their estates are capable of much improvement; and for these preferments the residence usually required is three months for the dean, and half that time for each prebendary. But alas! never was church more shamefully neglected. The bishop has been several times there for months together without seeing the face of dean or prebendary, or anything better than a minor canon. The care and management of the church was left to Mr Camplin, precentor or senior minor canon, and to the sexton. His example having no kind of effect, he remonstrated several times that their preferments deserved a little better attendance, as they would well bear the expense of it; their neglect was the more conspicuous and culpable, being in the second city in the kingdom; that their want of residence was the general complaint not only of the city but likewise of all the country; that great numbers resorted every year to the wells and generally came, at least on a Sunday, to see the cathedral; that they were astonished at finding only one minor canon both to read and preach, and perhaps administer the sacrament; that this was not a time for such relaxation and neglect of all order and

---

[1] *Life of Zachary Pearce*, in *op. cit.* i, 420.
[2] Gibson to Nicolson, 2 June 1702. Bodley Add. MSS. A. 269, f. 5.
[3] *Life of Sharp*, i, 117.

discipline; that the church had too many enemies, and deans and chapters in particular; that they furnished their adversaries with the strongest arguments against themselves; that there were those who contended for the worthlessness and uselessness of deans and chapters; and they could not point out a more flagrant instance of good pay received and little duty done than in the church of Bristol."[1]

One flagrant instance of negligence does not constitute evidence for a general censure of cathedrals. Indeed Newton envied the happy estate of Gloucester, Norwich, and Peterborough. In the first church in particular, Dean Tucker was most diligent in residence. Despite the witticism of Warburton concerning deans Squire and Tucker that "the one made religion his trade, and the other trade his religion", the dean of Gloucester in no wise neglected his spiritual duties. Not only did he earn the approbation of Newton as "an excellent parish priest and an exemplary dean, keeping residence and performing his duty, in managing the chapter estates, in repairing and improving his house, and in adorning and beautifying the church and the churchyard"; but he also justified himself as having attended alike to the duties of his parish and cathedral and "written near three hundred sermons and preached them all, again and again"!

Amongst the prebendaries in enjoyment of the six hundred cathedral dignities, simple and carrying jurisdiction, perhaps none illustrated the lighter side of Georgian churchcraft better than Edmund Pyle, preferred to the archdeaconry of York by Archbishop Hutton at the instance of his grace of Newcastle. Announcing to his friend, Dr Samuel Kerrich, his transformation "into a joint (almost the last in the tail) of the body ecclesiastico-political, called an archdeacon", he recited an astonishing story of his adventures in the cathedral at his installation. "I had like to have lost my heart at York", he declared. "It is a terrible thing to have such a place in the church as I have; nothing but ladies by dozens (and very pretty ones) on the right hand, or the left, or in front of my stall. But, through mercy, having the service to read, I was forced to look at least as much upon the rubrick of the book as upon that of their cheeks. So I am returned safe and sound."[2]

Since the only restriction upon the plurality of prebends was that no person should hold more than one prebend of the same church, the most pleasing circumstance was the combination of a series of prebends in cathedrals situated in different parts of the country, thereby affording profitable change of climate and environment. When Pyle by favour of

---

[1] *Life of Dr Thomas Newton*, in *op. cit.* ii, 172.   [2] E. Pyle, *op. cit.* p. 168.

his patron, Bishop Hoadly of Winchester, was presented in 1756 to the first prebendal stall in that church, he outlined his intended scheme of life: "May, June, July and August at York and his livings; thence to the end of January at Winton, the other three months in London";[1] which would ensure an enjoyable variety of society and surroundings. Through the pages also of the *Diary* of Parson Woodforde there passes the courtly figure of Mr DuQuesne, cousin to Charles Townshend, and distantly connected with the household of Archbishop Cornwallis, who mingled freely on terms of equality with these notables on their visits to Norfolk. DuQuesne had been made prebendary of Ruiton in Lichfield Cathedral during the episcopate of Cornwallis there in 1765, and though in 1781 he professed to Woodforde, during the stay of the primate and his wife at Rainham, to be "fretting himself about being so tied by the leg, in dancing backward and forward to Townshend's with his great company", he was sufficiently worldly-wise to accept shortly afterwards an invitation to Lambeth. In addition to his benefices with cure of souls, at Honingham, East Tuddenham, and Osmondeston, he secured in 1776 the chancellorship of St David's, and in 1783 the prebend of the fifth stall at Ely, which gave him "the occasion for pleasant holidays" from Honingham.[2] Such a genial pluralist might hope surely to escape without censure, for so long as prebends continued in such plenty, prebendaries might accept them without twinge of conscience. White Kennett, when archdeacon of Huntingdon and prebendary of Combe and Harnham in Sarum, confessed to Wake in 1706 his coveting a residentiaryship of Salisbury because "he would be very glad of such retirement for three months in a year"; affirming that in addition thereto he desired "nothing more in the world than a prebend of about £20 per annum in his lordship's church at Lincoln, which he would value more for the gift and giver than for the value of it".[3] Disappointed at Sarum, he received from Wake the prebend of Marston St Lawrence at Lincoln, together with the deanery of Peterborough in 1708. To diverse temperaments the enjoyments of such dignities were likewise of different character. Scholars like Thomas Tanner found the residence of fifty days at Ely exceedingly delectable, "having nothing to do but to mind one's prayers, and studies, a state of living very acceptable";[4] whilst more worldly clerics like Pyle expressed the prevalent opinion of cathedral duty in his naïve confession that "the life

[1] *Ibid.* p. 268.
[2] J. Beresford, *Mr DuQuesne and Other Essays*, pp. 3–97.
[3] White Kennett to Wake, 23 July 1706. Arch. W. Epist. 17, item cxxix, f. 152.
[4] Tanner to Charlett, 5 Dec. 1713. Ballard MSS. iv, f. 60.

of a prebendary is a pretty easy way of dawdling away one's time: praying, walking, visiting;—and as little study as the heart could wish".[1] The seduction of cathedral society was such that the chief difficulty lay in contriving vacancies to reward the multitude of competitors. For as Dr Robert Freind, formerly headmaster of Westminster School and prebendary of the churches of Westminster and Windsor, observed to Newcastle in 1740, "we who hold good preferments are careful enough in observing that rule left us by an old monk: *In omnibus tuis cogitationibus, mi filii, cave de resignationibus"*.[2]

Contemporary recognition of the influence of aristocratic connections upon ecclesiastical preferment was testified particularly in the sermon preached at the consecration to the episcopate of William Warburton by Dr Thomas Newton on 20 January 1760; in which the preacher, remarking the wide difference between the ministry of the apostolic church, whereunto not many wise, nor noble, nor mighty after the flesh were called, and that of the Georgian English Church, strove to establish the congruity of each tradition to the circumstances of its times.

"Though the apostles for wise reasons", he observed, "were chosen from among men of low birth and parentage; yet times and circumstances are so changed that persons of noble extraction by coming into the church, may add strength and ornament to it; especially as long as we can boast of *some*, who are honourable in themselves as well as in their families; and whose personal merits and virtues, if they had not been nobly descended, would have entitled them justly to the rank and pre-eminence that they enjoy. God forbid that the Church of England should ever be reduced to the state and condition of the Gallican church, incumbered with the weight of prelates of quality without learning or virtue."[3]

It may be doubted whether this apologia for the English Church as standing in an imagined *via media* between the apostolic and Gallican Churches was strengthened by the discourteous reference to the French episcopate as representing the extreme of mediocrity divorced from talent. It might have seemed indeed to some of Newton's auditors that the difference between the English and Gallican Churches in respect of aristocratic influence was one of degree rather than of kind; and even this distinction due rather to accidental circumstances than to superior merit. Geographical conditions made the English episcopate much less numerous than the French, totalling twenty-six sees against 136 in

[1] E. Pyle, *op. cit.* p. 266.
[2] R. Freind to Newcastle, 26 Nov. 1740. Add. MSS. 32695, f. 441.
[3] T. Newton, *On Our Saviour's Choice of His Apostles*: a Sermon preached at the consecration of William Warburton to the see of Gloucester on 20 January 1760.

France including Corsica; and historical tradition had fashioned the English dioceses of wide territory and extent, so that they could afford no parallel to the twenty dioceses of the Gallican Church containing less than fifty parishes each, a condition which might tend more easily to the creation of an ornamental rather than a distinguished episcopate. But in principle the aristocratic recruitment of the episcopate allied the English and French Churches more closely to each other than to their common prototype in the apostolic college. In England this influence operated least adversely upon the prelacy, because of the complementary custom by which lords spiritual and temporal accounted it a duty and distinction to set forward the fortunes of divines of ability but of humble birth; so that the bench was adorned not unequally with bishops of family and talent. In respect of the episcopate the eighteenth-century Church may claim a greater proportion of credit than of censure.

It was evidently in regard to the cathedral prebends that the graver problems existed and the strongest case for reform could be urged. The presence amongst the Georgian prebendaries of Durham of Secker, Warburton, and Lowth may constitute a sufficient triumvirate of distinction to establish the claims of learning; but it may not be doubted that the hazard of political canvassing was an unsatisfactory means of replenishing the cathedral and collegiate churches of the realm with divines apt for erudition and piety to the discharge of the duties of their office. The multitude of prebends and the attendant prevalence of pluralism were indeed no novel features of the eighteenth century. Not to speak of medieval precedents, the worst examples of which had been reformed by the Tudor legislation, it may suffice to recall that Lancelot Andrewes, the saintly Jacobean prelate and high churchman, was an abundant pluralist; being Master of Pembroke College, Cambridge, from 1589 to 1605; prebendary of St Pancras in St Paul's Cathedral 1589–1609; prebendary of North Muskham in Southwell collegiate church 1589–1609; prebendary of the fifth stall in Westminster Abbey 1598–1601, and dean of that church 1601–5; in addition to holding the vicarage of St Giles-without-Cripplegate from 1588 to 1605. Upon his elevation to the see of Chichester in 1605 he continued to hold *in commendam* his prebends of Southwell and St Paul's, which he resigned only upon his translation in 1609 to the rich see of Ely. If the centuries which are without sin in the matter of pluralism were alone allowed to cast stones at the Georgian Church, its reputation would not have suffered such severe dilapidation.

Notwithstanding, it may not be denied that the entire system of cathedral administration stood in need of extensive reform, and during the latter half of the eighteenth century new circumstances lent additional support to this plea. The accumulation of great wealth by the capitular bodies of Durham by reason of the mining of coal, and of St Paul's by virtue of the value of land for building (two cathedrals which illustrated most markedly the appreciation of prebendal estates), established a strong case for a redistribution of revenues. Without some drastic financial reform it was impossible to arrest the increasing decline of the parochial system, produced in turn by the extension of non-residence and pluralism; and apart from the restoration of the efficient operation of the parochial organisation the good estate of the entire Church could not be compassed. It was to the credit of Bishop Richard Watson that he seized upon this point as the crux of the problem of ecclesiastical administration; so that his voice and pen were engaged in season and out of season to urge the appropriation of prebendal revenues for the rescue of the parish clergy. His scheme "for appropriating as they became vacant, a half or a third part of the income of every deanery, prebend, or canonry of the churches of Westminster, Windsor, Canterbury, Christ Church, Worcester, Durham, Ely, Norwich etc., to the same purpose *mutatis mutandis* as the first fruits and tenths were appropriated by Queen Anne", was designed to enable the enforcement of clerical residence by making proper provision for the parochial ministry. It was set aside both by ministers of state and primates of the Church as unsuited to the conservative temper of the age; albeit posterity proved its relevance to its needs. With the delay to attempt even moderate reforms the scandal became progressively greater; and the Georgian Church, through the timorousness of statesmen during the last quarter of its century, bore the reproach of all the centuries in respect of pluralism and the unreformed cathedrals. But although the Hanoverian clergy may not justly be saddled with blame for the evils of the system, nor with responsibility for the enjoyment of its prebends after the pattern of Andrewes and his contemporaries, the ill-consequences of the continued existence of so many dignities with nominal duties and considerable revenues combined with the method of preferment to such sinecures may not be ignored in assessing the religious tradition of the cathedral foundations. Albeit individuals of unusual piety and sanctity might hold plurality of prebends, the multitude of lesser men found in them rather occasions of worldliness and stumbling than avenues to a disciplined austerity of life. It is little surprising if many of the prebendaries fortuitously established in the comfortable dignities of the cathedrals, demonstrated that with the bestowal of their hearts' desire there had entered withal leanness into their soul.

CHAPTER V

THE CLERICAL SUBALTERNS

In a letter of William Mason, poet and residentiary of York Minster, to his friend Bishop Hurd of Worcester in 1791, in which the writer solicits some preferment for a poor curate of his acquaintance, there is an arresting comparison of the ecclesiastical system to a lottery. "Observe me, my dear lord, I make no personal request," explained Mason. "I only throw a letter, like a lottery ticket, into a wheel, where it may possibly turn up a *small* prize; or from a possibility you may transfer it into some other ecclesiastical wheel, where small prizes may bear a greater proportion to blanks than in your own."[1] The metaphor was current in eighteenth-century correspondence, as the letters of War-burton and Pyle illustrate, and moreover it was exceedingly apt. To the majority of clerical subalterns, whose temporal fortunes were committed to its vagaries, the operation of the unreformed ecclesiastical administration presented the appearance of a game of chance, in which the dice were biased heavily against their condition. Denied the advantages of birth and influence which opened to the privileged minority an easy way to promotion, their entrance into the profession of Orders partook in truth of the nature of a lottery; and of a lottery in which the number of blanks was alarmingly high, and the proportion of small prizes still higher. From this circumstance proceeded the oft-quoted contrast between the position of the higher and lower clergy, between the wealth of the pluralist and the misery of the curate or incumbent of a poor benefice. The majority of candidates admitted each year into the diaconate cast their various talents and abilities into the ecclesiastical wheel, and passed forthwith to the protracted obscurity of a country curacy or benefice, whence they might scarcely hope to emerge into public view, unless some fortuitous turn of the lottery called them to an unexpected dignity or preferment.

The source of this admitted disproportion between the number of persons entering into Holy Orders and the benefices available for their incumbency was to be found largely in the host of poor scholars discharged year by year from the universities, needy and improvident, and seeking with urgency some provision of bread. In his essay in *The*

[1] Mason to Hurd, 26 Nov. 1791, *Correspondence of Hurd and Mason* (ed. E. H Pearce and L. Whibley), p. 102.

Spectator of 24 March 1710–11, Addison voiced a widespread concern at the constant spectacle of the overcrowding of the learned professions.

"I am sometimes very much troubled", he confessed, "when I reflect upon the three great professions of divinity, law, and physic: how they are each of them overburdened with practitioners, and filled with multitudes of ingenious gentlemen that starve one another.... How many men are country curates that might have made themselves aldermen of London by a right improvement of a smaller sum of money than what is usually laid out upon a learned education."

In the majority of cases the ill success of these country curates could have been predicted from the moment of their admission to Holy Orders; indeed it might be contended with some measure of truth that obscurity was predestined as their lot from the circumstance of their entry into the university of their graduation. Oxford and Cambridge, the seminaries of their education, had prepared them by the rigid social distinctions of academic life for the later gulf which divided the dignitaries from the inferior clergy of the Church. There were indeed outstanding examples of the rise of poor students to positions of the highest eminence in church and state, but these were occasional and exceptional cases. To the majority of servitors and *pauperes pueri* who maintained a precarious foothold in the colleges of their adoption, rendering menial services in return for the rudiments of letters, the entry into the ministry of the Church perpetuated the sense of inferiority and uncertainty, and opened the door to a career ungarnished by wealth or comfort. Not the least illuminating method of approach to the understanding of the lot of the poorer parish clergy, both beneficed and unbeneficed, may be sought through the consideration of the academic circumstances of the class of needy students from which they were largely recruited.

To a lecturer who has not the privilege of membership of this university, there may be indulged the limitation of concentrating attention upon the condition of the university of Oxford in the eighteenth century; and within that university it may likewise be pardoned to filial piety to pay more particular regard to Queen's College, a royal and religious foundation designed to be an especial nursery of clerks. The close territorial connection of Queen's College with the northern counties from which it drew much of its personnel, traditional from its foundation and strengthened during the Hanoverian age by the pious munificence of the Lady Elizabeth Hastings—to which a scholar upon her foundation may be permitted a humble tribute of gratitude—brought each year to its society a considerable company of rustic youths whose worldly prospects depended upon the academic distinction achieved during their residence in its fellowship. Indeed the periodic emigration of the sons of yeoman households of Cumberland and Westmorland to pursue alike letters and manners in the polite circle of Queen's College afforded a congenial theme for the wit of satirists. The sparse talent of poetasters was exercised upon the supposed ambition of illiterate farmers to convert their dunces into pedagogues.

> Our farmer being something proud
> T' advance his youthful heir thought good;
> Sent him to pedagogue to hammer
> Tough nouns and pronouns, and learn grammar.
> Here the dull dolt with aching head
> And small improvement, nine years read.
> At last grown man, though child in knowledge,
> They send the bumpkin to Queen's College.

There his course was naturally lacking in scholastic distinction; and

> so our blade,
> Though son of Alma Mater made,
> The more he plodded after sense,
> The deeper sunk in ignorance.
> 'Tis fully known by parts confest,
> He's every sneering freshman's jest;
> Let's leave him there to College ale,

and to the inevitable consequence of his going down without degree.[1]

Against this unflattering picture of the north-country student, debauched by ale and unenlightened by intelligence, though notwithstanding received into the ministry of the Church according to the scribbler's libel, there may be some compensation to be found in the mean opinion entertained by the wit likewise of the clergy

> when first turned out of B[alliol] College
> with little merit and less knowledge.

But the fortunes of the poor scholars of Queen's College during the first half of the eighteenth century may be delineated with more authentic record from the contemporary letters and diaries, fortunately preserved for posterity, of a company embracing Edmund Gibson of High Knipe, Thomas Brockbank, son of John Brockbank vicar of

---

[1] *The Farmer's Daughter, or the Art of getting Preferment,* n.d. Bishop Gibson Pamphlets, 45, B 19, No. 4, Sion College.

Witherslack, George Fothergill of Ravenstonedale and his brothers, Henry and Thomas, and Robert Robson, son of a yeoman farmer of Sebergham in Cumberland, all destined for the profession of Orders. Nor was this company unrepresentative of the clergy of the age, and of the variety of position achieved by poor students, since Edmund Gibson rose to the dignity of the episcopate, George and Thomas Fothergill attained academic eminence in the university, and Henry Fothergill, Thomas Brockbank, and Robert Robson fulfilled the lifelong vocation of parish clergy.

The two north-western counties of Cumberland and Westmorland were no mean seed plot for the recruitment of scholars of Queen's College. Bishop Watson indeed affirmed that they possessed good grammar schools "almost under every crag", typical of which were those of Ravenstonedale, where the Rev. Dr Robinson unaided educated for the sacred ministry no fewer than twenty pupils, and of Sebergham, where Josiah Relph, poet and parish priest no less than master, sent an equal number of students to Queen's College. There the greater part of the poor northern boys assumed the humble academic status of batteler, poor boy, and servitor. At the head of the undergraduate hierarchy of the college stood the Commoners and Upper Commoners, the latter of which were usually sons of baronets, knights, or gentlemen of greater fortune. In Queen's as in other colleges this privileged class had little inclination for serious study, and even the less affluent were freed from the pressing necessities which governed the conduct of their less fortunate fellows. There was an element of truth no less than the spice of satire in the famous differentiation of rich and poor undergraduates by Dr Johnson: "The difference, Sir, between us Servitors and Gentlemen Commoners is this, that we are men of wit and no fortune, and they are men of fortune and no wit". Within the humble ranks of this academic society Edmund Gibson was batteler, larder man, and poor boy, whilst George Fothergill was servitor and poor child. Across the High at University College, John Potter, son of a Wakefield linendraper, commenced servitor in 1688. The duties of such offices were the recognised badge of poverty and the condition of the officiants' education.

"I cannot tell well", George Fothergill wrote to his parents, "how to give you a notion of what we servitors do. We are seven of us, and we wait upon the Batchelors, Gentlemen Commoners, and Commoners at meals. We carry in their Commons out of the Kitchen into the Hall, and their bread and beer out of the Buttery; I call up one Gentleman Commoner, which is ten shillings a quarter when he's in town, and three Commoners which are five shillings each on the same conditions. My servitor's place saves me, I believe, about thirty shillings a quarter in battels, one quarter with another."

He congratulated himself, however, on his good fortune in having escaped the position of junior servitor, "a slavery which he had always dreaded, and which he could not well have undergone".[1]

Thomas Brockbank, having been entered as batteler, attained the position of larder-man in December 1689, his duty being "to set down each man's Commons, for which he was equal with the Poor Children at table".[2] This situation he endured for three years in the hope of being elected Taberdar, but failing in that ambition in 1692, when four Taberdars were chosen leaving himself as senior Poor Child, he was "not willing to stay any longer under that slavery", and proceeded to the degree of bachelor of arts.[3]

Only the pressure of severe financial necessity induced students to accept such offices, and of this poverty the correspondence of Fothergill and Brockbank afforded abundant evidence. Both scholars insisted in letters to their parents on the frugality of their living, and the parsimony of their economy, notwithstanding which they could not avoid the burden of debt. "Continual running into debt, and sometimes upon urgent occasions being obliged to apply to my friends without being able punctually to return their obligations," reported George Fothergill in 1729; "these and the like are difficulties which I find, let me live as frugally as I can, I cannot avoid."[4] In similar tones Thomas Brockbank lamented his impecuniosity to his father in 1693.

I know my expenses are great and such as in the country may seem very extravagant; and justly, because you do not rightly apprehend the many ways that money goes, neither indeed can you. You know little, I suppose, of our exercises here, which we do perform for our degrees; every month almost now I have something to do in the Schools which costs money, sometimes a noble a time, sometimes ten shillings....Everything is extraordinary dear, winter comes on very sharp, the snow lies thick about our doors, and we must have fire. In a word, 'tis altogether impossible for me to live here at any cheaper rate than I do.[5]

Justification of this confidence in his integrity was furnished by the convincing circumstance that the total cost which John Brockbank

---

[1] *The Fothergills of Ravenstonedale*, C. Thornton and F. McLaughlin, pp. 79, 88.
[2] *The Diary and Letter Book of the Rev. Thomas Brockbank* (ed. R. Trappes-Lomax), Chetham Society, p. 16.
[3] *Brockbank*, p. 42.   [4] *Fothergill*, 14 April 1729, p. 124.
[5] *Brockbank*, p. 68.

estimated for his son's eight years' residence in Oxford from 1687 to 1695 amounted to £273, an average of little more than £34 per year, and a figure which compares instructively with the sum of £446 expended by Bishop Nicolson of Carlisle upon the residence of his son Joseph for the shorter period from February 1707 to the summer of 1712, and with the general estimate of the expenses of a Gentleman Commoner as £120 per annum, and of an ordinary Commoner at £60. Other testimony could be called in support of the essential frugality of these north-country students. George Fothergill, even after taking his degree, confessed that "his clothes were getting somewhat bare considering his standing, but he was very well content to fall short of others in matters which concerned the outside, if he could make shift honestly to get through the Foundation"; to which he added the later reassurance that "his coat was a little taken notice of at first, but was now grown by use unheeded".[1] Similar frequent reference to the pressing problem of the cost of repairing the necessary wastage of clothes occupied much space in the correspondence of Brockbank with his parents; in reply to which the carrier brought regular parcels, whether of warm outer leather garments with vests of best Kendal keasar, or of underwear of serge and heavy shoes "to keep both wet and cold" out, accompanied by the maternal injunction to "put on two pairs of stockings to keep you from cold, for fuel with you is dear". During the period when Brockbank had a chamber-fellow, his bed-linen was always carefully marked, again with the counsel to "take care of his linen when put forth to wash, for fear of changing and altering his name". A not unnatural concomitant of these outward signs of penury was a certain lack of the gentler social graces, which led George Fothergill to implore his parents to "send any of his brothers which they intended should ever stir from home to a dancing school", for he "daily found the want of it", and though "these might seem little things, they may be of much consequence in life".[2]

To such students, compassed about with so many evidences of their poverty and inferiority, the collegiate life was one of severe effort and discipline. Marked by the outward badge of threadbare garments no less than by the academic sign of their servitorship, and compelled by poverty to avoid expensive recreations, they became deeply conscious of the gulf separating them from the Gentlemen Commoners and accepted the imprint of social inferiority. Not infrequently they sought compensation in a devotion to study which impaired their physical health. George Fothergill continued throughout his life of a weak

[1] *Fothergill*, pp. 95, 103.   [2] *Ibid.* p. 128.

physique, bearing signs of the strain and struggle of his early undergraduate years. At the outset of his residence in Oxford Thomas
Brockbank was warned by his father to take due care of the body.

Have a care of your bodily health that it be not wronged either through
want of meat, drink, clothes, physic, or any other thing convenient thereunto,
or overcharged with too much study....If God be pleased to preserve you
in life and health, doubt not but learning will come in time. Suppose a man
had as much learning and as great parts as our late bishop of Chester [Pearson],
and yet want either health of body or soundness of mind, what would either
learning or parts signify? Therefore take recreation when occasion serves
that your body may be better able to endure study....You now want your
mother to drive you from your book, ergo be a mother to yourself, and be
moderate.[1]

Notwithstanding such wise counsel, young Brockbank earned the
repute of being a most diligent student; and report travelled to remote
Witherslack that "he was a noted student all the college over, and
studied much by candlelight, and that his careful tutor had come to
him to forbid him of it".[2] Much space was given in George Fothergill's
letters home to accounts of his studies in classics, philosophy, Hebrew,
and especially his devotion to the best English writers in order to
achieve "a good way of talking and writing English which might be
more serviceable to him if ever it should please almighty God to call
him to the work of the ministry". His estimate of his academic progress
was unduly modest when he "could not express his thoughts of it
better than likening it to the hand of a clock, for if one looked never
so earnestly for a quarter of an hour together, one could not discern
the hand go forward".[3] Piety no less than a zeal for learning characterised his conduct, for he attended regularly upon the College prayers
twice daily in the new chapel at 6 a.m. and 5 p.m., upon two sermons
each Sunday in the university church, and upon the quarterly administration of the Holy Communion. In view of such labours to
attain academic distinction it was natural that the parents should
respond, as did Brockbank's father, to advice that their sons "should
be continued there without interrupting their studies that the college
might take the more notice of them for their preferment".[4]

The way to such preferment was long as well as costly. When by
plainness of living and persistence in study the poor scholar graduated
bachelor of arts, fresh problems, both academic and financial, pressed

---

[1] *Brockbank*, p. 4.   [2] *Ibid.* p. 23.
[3] *Fothergill*, p. 86.   [4] *Brockbank*, p. 29.

upon him. If he desired to remain in the university he must discover some means of maintenance until he secured the emolument of a fellowship, and if he wished to embark upon a profession, entrance to each of the learned callings was beset by obstacles. In that of divinity a further period of waiting was necessitated for most students by the canonical rule that deacons' orders should not be conferred until the age of twenty-three. George Fothergill matriculated at sixteen and took his degree at nineteen; Thomas Brockbank entered college at the same age and proceeded bachelor at twenty-one, and Edmund Gibson, entering towards the end of his sixteenth year, graduated also at twenty-one. Though the average age of matriculation had risen somewhat since the preceding century, there remained still a difficult interval before a title and ordination could be secured. Richard Watson, during his tenure of the office of fellow and tutor at Trinity College, Cambridge, "frequently observed the great difficulty with which clergymen with small incomes, farmers, tradesmen, and others in slender circumstances, sustained the expense of their sons' education, and was sensible that it was from such sort of families that the church was principally supplied with parochial ministers".[1] For the relief of the problem he counselled the admission of university graduates to the diaconate at the age of twenty-two, thereby shortening the period of expense. Lacking such a concession, the poor scholar found many obstacles to his continuance in the university. Brockbank was compelled to transfer to St Mary Hall, since the bursar of Queen's had stopped his name for non-payment of battels; yet even so he "ran deep in his creditor's books", and began reluctantly "to wean his thoughts from an university life and to submit himself wholly to the direction and commands of parents and friends" as to the practical ordering of his profession.[2] George Fothergill reflected, as the time approached of taking his degree, that "if he could possibly make a shift to stay three years longer, which...was as soon as he could take Orders, he could come on Taberdar, and then, after a year's longer expenses, which he could upon his own credit borrow in the college, or of some friend or other, he could, he believed, get leave to go out on a curacy and keep on the foundation too".[3]

Edmund Gibson's hesitation between the rival professions of law and divinity illustrated the practical problems which faced the poor scholar. His immediate financial straits were relieved by his reception into the house of Dr Thomas Gibson, his uncle, a noted physician in

[1] R. Watson, *Anecdotes*, ii, 201–2.   [2] *Brockbank*, pp. 74–5.
[3] *Fothergill*, p. 92.

London, on such generous terms that "diet, lodging, and washing did not cost him a farthing", and the rest of his expenses he intended to "hammer out of booksellers for little odd jobs". In such circumstances his mind was poised very uncertainly between law and church, albeit the latter profession "he had had all along in his eye". Friends assured him that he could master the law by the age of thirty, "that the greatest men never come to the bar before that time, that the more experience and knowledge a man set out withal, his journey was like to be so much the more successful; and that no settlement in the church of any consequence could be reasonably expected before that time".[1] Accordingly he resolved upon the venture. "For industry," he wrote to Dr Charlett, "I fancy I could secure myself of that, and methinks when a man comes to the bar, 'tis a cold business if he cannot get himself meat and clothes. And if a man can have but that prospect, 'tis inducement enough so long as nothing more can reasonably be expected in the church either before that time or then either".[2]

Apart from any doubtful division of allegiance, the fulfilment of the vocation to Orders was difficult to students lacking the magic key of influence. In 1693 John Brockbank had exhorted his son to make choice of a profession.

Son, I think it is convenient that you should resolve what is best for God's glory, and yours and your country's good, wherein to employ your learning, and to that end consider what is that which God most of all suggests into your mind, whether divinity or physic. If divinity, then in time there will be some place found where you may be serviceable for God's glory and the country's good, though places are hard to get at present. If physic, then you are like to have a good place of residence where you may by God's goodness be instrumental for God's glory and your country's good.[3]

Thomas Brockbank, like George Fothergill, had resolved firmly to seek Holy Orders, if the way should prove possible to his resources. Two alternatives lay before the student lacking friends to ensure his success: he must either secure nomination to some curacy, a problem of difficulty whilst he remained in the university; or strive to encompass his election to a fellowship, which in addition to relieving his present pecuniary necessity, was the recognised means of ensuring ultimate possession of a benefice. The latter choice was more pleasing, and serious students were reluctant to abandon hopes of its realisation in

[1] Gibson to Tanner, 20 April 1694. Tanner MSS. xxv, f. 138.
[2] Gibson to Charlett, 7 May 1694. Ballard MSS. v, f. 19.
[3] *Brockbank*, p. 64.

favour of the rustication and obscurity of a country curacy. Both Brockbank and Fothergill coveted a fellowship, and were loth to leave Oxford for their native county, an action tantamount to the abandonment of academic aspirations, until fortune finally flouted or finance constrained them. After graduation George Fothergill declined a suggestion that he should become a candidate for the perpetual curacy of Ravenstonedale, arguing that "to quit something of certainty as those advantages he then enjoyed in college, he hoped, were, for such an uncertainty would by all that knew him, be reckoned very great imprudence"; and adding that "so far as he could perceive, most people desired to have preferment in the south who had the opportunity of procuring it".[1] During the period of Brockbank's waiting there came a proposition singularly expressive alike of the needs of poor students and of the position of the colonial Church.

"Here has been a proposal", he related to his parents in December 1693, "to me and the rest of my brethren in college, of going over into Maryland next spring, to supply some vacant places there, to which indeed I was not very unwilling, neither shall be, if you think convenient. The places will not be despicable, and transportation would cost nothing; besides the bishop of London will give each man that goes £20 in hand."

The invitation was declined by Brockbank, as a similar offer had been by Thomas Hearne, upon receipt of a peremptory command from his father to think no more of it.

I advise you to steer your course any way where it may be for God's glory and the good of souls, but sea-wards. And I earnestly desire you to banish out of your heart what thoughts, intents, and purposes you have to pass over the sea. This kingdom is large enough, and places many in it, and though at present good places are hard to come by, yet for anyone that truly fears God and lives in sincerity and truth, need not fear but in time to obtain a place sufficient.

To the poorest students the offer, as Brockbank admitted, was "both very profitable and honourable"; but the calibre of person thus accepting recruitment for the service of the Church in the Plantations may be judged from the parental counsel given to Brockbank, by his father's exhortation to "let those go who are not so well provided for as you are", and by his mother's postscript, "son, I hope you have done nothing you need depart the land for".[2]

In the prevalent chaos of ecclesiastical administration even the procuring of a *bona fide* title was a problem of real difficulty, as Brockbank

[1] *Fothergill*, p. 117.   [2] *Brockbank*, pp. 68, 70.

found to his bitter disappointment. By the 33rd canon of the Canons of 1604 the candidate for Orders was required to exhibit to the bishop at whose hands he sought the rite

a presentation of himself to some ecclesiastical preferment then void in that diocese; or a true and undoubted certificate that either he is provided of some church within the said diocese where he may attend the cure of souls, or of some minister's place vacant, either in the cathedral church of that diocese, or in some other collegiate church therein also situate wherein he may execute his ministry; or that he is a fellow, or in right as a fellow, or to be a conduct or chaplain in some college in Cambridge or Oxford; or except he be a Master of Arts of five years' standing that liveth of his own charge in either of the universities.

At the time of Brockbank's search for a title a series of royal injunctions of recent issue on 14 February 1694 had required the bishops, amongst other matters, to secure full satisfaction "that all persons that are to be ordained have a real title, with sufficient maintenance, according to the 33rd canon"; and accordingly when he designed to receive ordination at Oxford at the Trinity season his lack of sufficient title proved an insuperable barrier.

"I was disappointed", he related to his parent, "through I do not know what order lately made at Lambeth, that no man must be ordained who has not a real title....So that now I find myself in a sort of dilemma, out of which it will be difficult to get, for since I have no preferment I cannot be ordained, and because I am not ordained I can have no preferment."[1]

At the succeeding Embertides of September and Advent 1694 the bishop of Oxford was away in London so that "it was not so easy at that place to be ordained as might be supposed", during which time Brockbank had the refusal of both a curacy and a vicarage from which he was barred by lack of Orders; and finding finally at Trinity 1695 that no success attended his application, since "how to get a title he was almost at a loss, for now none but real ones would be taken", he resolved to return to his own county and there seek a curacy amongst his father's friends.[2] The irony of his situation was heightened by a report from his parent that irregularities disallowed in Oxford were no barrier in remote country parishes, where academic distinction was meanly esteemed.

"Here is little hopes", wrote John Brockbank in March 1695, "in the country to obtain any place; they mind not your degrees, nor your long

---

[1] *Ibid.* p. 74. [2] *Ibid.* pp. 79, 81.

continuance in the university. A man that never saw any college, or an undergraduate, if he can but talk at a great rate and get interest, will be preferred before a Master of Arts.... Here was Burton lately vacant, and it had abundance of competitors; but one never thought on, a young man born in Furness, and coming accidentally from the college at Dublin, undergraduate, under age, got...letters to the donor and the bishop, and got the presentation, ordination, institution and induction all at once."[1]

The truth of this prophecy was proved when Brockbank was driven to petition the bishop of Chester in April 1696 for admission to the diaconate upon the nominal title of curate to his father, and after his ordination to set out again in quest of a more substantial provision. In his letter to the diocesan he set forth the unhappiness of his condition; that

he had ever esteemed it to be the greatest honour he could possibly attain to, to be numbered amongst the sons of the clergy, yet so long as he remained at Oxon, that honour was denied him, for not being either fellow or chaplain of his college, or master of arts of so long standing as was required, he could find nothing in the canon favourable to his desires. But now he hoped an advantageous construction might be put upon it in reference to him, since his father was an aged man, and had been incumbent at Witherslack a long time, and was both able and willing to afford him a competent allowance to assist him as his curate.[2]

In no sphere was the contrast between the fortunate possessors of influence and their less happy brethren more striking than in the circumstances of their admission to Holy Orders. In the case of candidates nominated forthwith to a benefice or to an academic office, ordination to the diaconate and priesthood was achieved with great rapidity. "The dates of the ordinations shed a light on the system of the day", observes Canon Ollard in relation to the Visitation Returns of Archbishop Herring at York in 1743; "it will be seen how often the better-born or more highly-placed clergy were ordained deacon and priest within a few days or a few weeks, and then admitted to a benefice which they held for life".[3] In cases of urgency, despite the express prohibition of the 32nd canon that "no bishop shall make any person, of whatever qualities or gifts soever, a deacon and minister both together upon one day", episcopal registers may be found to record the issue of an archiepiscopal dispensation: *habita prius licentia cum*

---

[1] *Brockbank*, p. 86.   [2] *Ibid.* p. 103.
[3] *Archbishop Herring's Visitation Returns* (ed. S. L. Ollard and P. C. Walker), i, p. xx.

dispensatione canonum ad utrosque tam diaconatus quam presbyteratus ordines uno die conferendos. The requirement by the Act of Uniformity of 1662 of the possession of priests' orders as a necessary qualification for institution to a benefice led to an increased prevalence of this practice of conferring both orders upon the same day, or within a very short period. Nor was the irregularity offensive to the most scrupulous divines. John Sharp, archbishop of York, received both deacons' and priests' orders on the same day, 12 August 1667, by archiepiscopal dispensation, though his title was not to a cure of souls, but to the office of tutor and chaplain in the household of Sir Heneage Finch. His biographer, commenting on the violation of canonical rule, quoted the precedent of George Bull, who "had likewise received both orders in one day, and was then but twenty-one years of age when he was thus ordained by bishop Skinner"; and added that whereas the latter irregularity was excused "by the necessity of the times", in the case of Sharp more justification existed in the shape of a dispensation from Archbishop Sheldon.[1] In like manner Dr Johnson's ideal clergyman, Prebendary Zachariah Mudge, had received both orders at the hands of Bishop Weston of Exeter on 21 September 1729. Far different was the lot of the portionless aspirant. Having procured a sufficient title whereby to obtain admission to the diaconate, too often he languished for many years in his remote country curacy escaping both archidiaconal and episcopal oversight. Not infrequently also he might continue in deacons' orders for a protracted period, until the happy accident of presentation to a benefice afforded occasion and necessity for seeking ordination to the priesthood. To the stipendary curate indeed, appointed to serve the cure of a non-resident pluralist or of a sequestered living, little inducement existed to proceed to that order in view of the legal expenses involved in the step, provided the services of a priest could be secured for the quarterly celebration of the Sacrament. In the old age of Parson Woodforde at Weston, provision had to be made for the celebration of the Holy Communion on the Sunday after Christmas Day in 1799 by Mr Stoughton of Sparham, since Woodforde's curate, Mr Dade, was only in deacons' orders.[2]

A characteristic feature of the ecclesiastical administration was the prolonged diaconate of many curates of this class. During the course of his primary visitation at Lincoln in 1706, Wake found three curates who had become almost perpetual deacons. Mr C. Avery of Cosby, who had continued in deacons' orders fourteen years since his ordination

[1] T. Sharp, *Life of Archbishop John Sharp*, i, 16.
[2] *The Diary of a Country Parson* (ed. J. Beresford), v, 229–30, 232.

in 1692; Mr W. Bower curate of Bag-Enderby, who had fulfilled a score years since receiving ordination as deacon in 1686; and Mr I. Taylor, curate of Barleston, who had been seventeen years a deacon, having been admitted to that order in 1689. Nor could the bishop ensure prompt obedience in these and other cases to his admonition to the defaulters to present themselves for priests' orders. Mr Taylor, after neglecting a first injunction in 1706 and a second at the following episcopal visitation in 1709, presented himself finally in 1710 after a diaconate of more than twenty years. Mr J. Lloyd, curate of Ashby Magna, received three exhortations at the visitations of 1706, 1709, and 1712 respectively to enter into the priesthood, but failed to comply until the Trinity season of 1715, after securing presentation to the vicarage which he had served as curate so long. From the same diocese there came a request to Wake, now archbishop, in 1724 from Bishop Reynolds for advice concerning a deacon whose protracted diaconate had resulted in the total disappearance of his original scanty portion of learning.

"Mr Lodington, eldest son of Dr Lodington near Horncastle, brings a presentation from his mother to the rectory of Fleet void by his father's death", reported the diocesan on 17 August. "He hath served the cure of that place about ten years, all this time in deacons' orders only. Upon examination I find that in these ten years since his being made deacon, he hath forgot most of his Greek and Latin. He can just read a verse or two in the Greek Testament, and turn an article out of Latin into English, but he seems to do it memoriter rather than upon any strength he hath in the Latin language or in the rules of syntax. But what is still worse, he is utterly ignorant of everything that relates to the doctrines of the Articles and of every branch of divinity. It is now about three months since I advised him to sit close to the study of divinity, and I expect that at this next ordination he will present himself again to me for priests' orders and for admission to this good living. But I have very little hope that he can come so qualified as in strictness he ought to be. Your grace now knows his case. He is a deacon, the son of a clergyman. He hath been idle, is woefully illiterate, but he is modest, sober, and well-behaved. I humbly beg your grace's advice upon the matter, and how I shall behave in a case beset, as this is, with difficulties and inconveniences on all hands. I mean how shall I deal with him if I find him as illiterate as I fear I shall find him?"[1]

The reply of Wake to this delicate enquiry does not appear to have survived in the volumes of archiepiscopal correspondence, but that mercy most probably triumphed over justice may be inferred from the

[1] Reynolds to Wake, 12 Aug. 1724. Arch. W. Epist. 22, item cccv, f. 459.

circumstance that Lodington, who had received deacons' orders at the hands of Wake on 25 June 1712, was admitted to the priesthood by Reynolds on 20 December 1724, and received institution to the rectory of Fleet which he held until his early death in 1729.

In many cases, as has been observed, lack of money and of prospect of preferment led to neglect on the part of curates to ask admission to priests' orders. When Thomas Brockbank in 1697 accepted the curacy of Coulton, the parishioners subscribed a special petition to the bishop of Chester "to ordain him priest that they might not have to seek to another parish as formerly for one to administer the Sacrament";[1] but in the following year, upon his transference to the curacy of Garstang, there appeared an itinerant deacon, Mr Thomas Taylor, to plead for his commendation to the parish and the bishop as successor to the curacy. His lordship desiring to know "where Mr Taylor formerly officiated, by whom he was ordained, and information concerning his carriage and behaviour", it was revealed that he had received deacons' orders at the hand of the same bishop some four or five years before, the exact date being uncertain since he had not his letters of Orders with him, and that he had served as curate at Winwick, Wood Plumpton, and temporarily at Garstang. His reputation was that "of a civil, good-natured man, and a pretty preacher", and he had proceeded so far towards seeking priests' orders as to cause his *Si quis* to be read at Wood Plumpton, "but want of money or some such thing, not any crime objected against him, made him give over that design".[2] Accordingly, Taylor received a licence to the curacy, and established himself at Coulton, but did not hurry to procure full Orders until 1709 when Brockbank, in the autumn of that year, recommended him to the new bishop of Chester, Sir William Dawes, affirming that "he never saw or knew any evil in him, but by such information as had been given him, thought him qualified to be ordained priest".[3]

Possession of the qualification of full Orders did not ensure of itself rapid preferment to a benefice, as the circumstances of Robert Robson of Sebergham and of Queen's College, Oxford, clearly testified. After graduation Robson was ordained deacon by Bishop Mawson of Chichester in 1745, licensed to serve the cures of East Dean and Woollavington, and admitted to the priesthood by the same bishop in 1748. Having married in 1751, he removed in 1753 to act as curate at Cocking and Selham in place of the rector, Dr Thomas Hutchinson, who was also vicar of Horsham. Thus he continued for a full quarter of a century, much to the distress of his relatives and friends, who

---

[1] *Brockbank*, p. 119.   [2] *Ibid*. p. 161.   [3] *Ibid*. p. 386.

feared that he would never escape the inferiority of a curate's position. One of his brothers, John, being steward to the bishop of Durham, vainly sought to obtain for him some preferment in that diocese. "You may excuse what I have heretofore hinted with regard to your advancement", wrote John to Robert on 12 October 1758, "and for the present only accept of the will for the deed. I sincerely wish that anything could be obtained in your favour in the north, yet as that may be at the greatest distance, I shall trouble you no further on that head."[1] Similar approaches had been made to a friend of the family, Isaac Denton of Sebergham, secretary to the bishop of Carlisle, in the hope of procuring a benefice in his own county, but Carlisle proved as unpromising as Durham.

"I wish with all my soul", replied Denton on 3 October 1755, "that I could be anyhow instrumental in removing you and your family to our neighbourhood; there's nothing would please me better than being allowed to act bishop for one year, on purpose to have it in my power to make you a present of a living worth your acceptance. But if I should be indulged so far, it is a hundred to one whether any vacancy would happen, for the parsons in our country live intolerably long. I cannot help thinking they live out of spite for their successors."[2]

Robert was advised therefore on all sides to cultivate an interest with the nobility of Sussex. His brother, James, the prosperous London bookseller in New Bond Street, urged him to secure the friendship of Viscount Cowdray, and "over a bottle with the viscount make him set his hand to a letter in your favour"; whilst when in 1766 the duke of Richmond was appointed secretary of state for the southern department, James again exhorted Robert to remember that "now is your time for advancement, so sit not down with indifference", since the ducal seat at Goodwood was so near to Cocking.[3] Unhappily none of these injunctions was fruitful; and meanwhile a fellow-countryman, Thomas Denton, who had proceeded as bachelor of arts at Queen's College in the year after Robert Robson's ordination as deacon, had shown him markedly the way to advancement. For being appointed curate of Ashtead for Dr Graham of Netherby, he became chaplain to Lady Widdrington, "was in Town all week and went to his curacy in Surrey every Saturday", added to his qualifications by a prescient

[1] G. Smith and F. Bengor, *The Oldest London Bookshop*, Appendix, The Robson Family Correspondence: John Robson to Robert Robson, 12 Oct. 1758, p. 54 (London: Ellis, 1928).

[2] *Ibid.* p. 80. Isaac Denton to Robert Robson, 3 Oct. 1755.

[3] *Ibid.* pp. 87, 90. James Robson to Robert Robson, 28 Feb. 1764, 6 June 1766.

marriage with her ladyship's companion, Mrs Clubbe, and thereby induced his patroness in 1754 to persuade Graham to resign the benefice in his favour.[1] Thirteen years after Denton's prudent contrivance of this settlement, John Robson wrote from Durham to his brother, on 21 May 1767, that "it would give him inexpressible satisfaction to hear of his better success at that time of life after the toil of so many years in the curatical state; nothing but drudgery and patience for many in his situation, while many a worthless rector was as hard put to it to live upon 5 or £600 per annum as his honest worthy curate upon £50". He added also the practical counsel that "if you expect preferment, you must bustle and try to peep after it, as most of the profession do in these days; a friend and application may yet advance you to something better".[2] Four years later he wrote again that "prospects of any further advancement here [Durham] are quite out of sight, as those who don't want them are quite ready to hold of every vacancy for themselves".[3] Not until 1778 did the influence of James Robson with Sir James Peachey secure for his brother the presentation to the benefice of Stedham with Heyshot, where, after some reluctance to reside in the vicarage house at Stedham, he settled his family until his death in 1783.

The moral of Robert Robson's twenty-five years in the curatical state was emphasised by the spectacle of promotion attendant upon influence in the careers of Isaac Denton, son of the secretary to the bishop of Carlisle, and George, son of James Robson himself. Isaac Denton matriculated at Queen's College in the year of Robert Robson's preferment to Stedham with the confident anticipation that there would be no tarrying in his promotion when his academic courses were completed. The fact of his father's standing well with Bishop Edmund Law of Carlisle and his son, Bishop John Law of Clonfert, afforded just ground for hoping that he himself "would be served in good time by one or both".[4] In April 1785 he married, and received from his lordship of Carlisle presentation to the vicarage of Bromfield, some four miles from Wigton, but before entering into possession returned to Oxford to keep the final term necessary to his taking the degree of bachelor of civil law. In the following October Isaac Robson reported to his brother James that "the two cousin Dentons by the young Bishop Law's mediation with his father, the bishop of Carlisle, had exchanged their livings of Crosthwaite, Keswick, and Bromfield, so that our

[1] *Ibid.* pp. 22, 80.
[2] *Ibid.* p. 91. John Robson to Robert Robson, 21 May 1767.
[3] *Ibid.* p. 92. 19 May 1771.
[4] *Ibid.* p. 108. Isaac Robson to James Robson, 30 May 1783.

Denton's residence would be Crosthwaite, amongst the Lakes, one of the most desirable in the diocese".[1] There indeed the young incumbent and his bride settled their habitation in the "good and commodious" parsonage, from which proceeded in due time a further generation of the family whose names appeared on the books of Queen's College. In that society likewise was entered George Robson, son of James, and destined at first to follow his father's profession, until his inclinations "declined the bookseller and became and meant to continue the book-reader". Having been ordained deacon in 1796, and priest in the following year, and elected to a Michel Fellowship of his college in 1797, he reaped the fruits of his father's friendship with Bishop Samuel Horsley, whose first visitation charge as bishop of St David's in 1791 had been published by James Robson and whose financial necessities on his translation to Rochester in 1793 had been eased from the same source. These good offices were repaid on his lordship's final translation to St Asaph in 1802 by his preferment of George Robson successively to the prebend of Llanvain (first portion) in St Asaph Cathedral in 1803, to the vicarage of Chirk in 1804, and the rectory of Erbistock in Denbighshire in 1805.

Of the conditions of service in the country curacies in which the majority of clerical subalterns passed no small period of their career, it is difficult to paint an optimistic picture in view of the general evidence of the deprivation and hardship of their lot. Two features in particular received much notoriety and comment; the insufficiency of salary and the insecurity of tenure. By an act of 13 Anne, cap. 11, the bishops were empowered before granting licence to curates and after enquiry into the value of the living and other emoluments of the rector or vicar, to appoint "a sufficient certain stipend or allowance not exceeding £50 and not less than £20 per annum" for the curate. During the first half of the eighteenth century these figures represented the general extremes between which the salaries of the curates varied, with a marked tendency towards an average of £30–£40 per year. The most prosperous curates were those of the wealthy churches of London and Westminster, where remuneration might rise to £60 per annum, whilst the extreme of poverty was reached amongst the dales of Carlisle and the Welsh dioceses. At the beginning of the century Bishop Nicolson of Carlisle found several chapels in his diocese served by Readers in deacons' orders, approximating closely to the status of perpetual deacon, with salaries of £3 to £4 per year; upon which he commented that "mean as those salaries looked, the readers in the

[1] G. Smith and F. Bengor, *op. cit.* p. 127. 7 Oct. 1785.

dales were commonly more rich than the curates (much better provided for in appearance) in other parts of the diocese, having the advantage of drawing bills, bonds, conveyances, wills etc., which the attornies elsewhere claimed as their property".[1] In the contemporary *History of Warton Parish* compiled by Mr John Lucas, schoolmaster of Leeds, in 1740, the writer recorded the information furnished to him by Mr James Atkinson, the pious curate of the Chapel of Ease at Silverdale, that "he had then, April 1720, officiated at that chapel thirty-eight years, in all which time he never received more than £5 a year, which was allowed him by the vicars of Warton, who were obliged, when no curate was at Silverdale, to perform Divine Service there once a month". Even this small pittance was subject to such uncertainty that for one period of four years the curate received only £2. 10s. for that entire time.[2] In relation to the payment of curates, lay impropriators were agreed to be the worst offenders.

"The cheapest curates", complained Archbishop Tenison in 1713, "are notwithstanding the care of bishops, too often chosen, especially by lay impropriators, some of whom have sometimes allowed but £5–6 per annum for the service of the church; and such curates, having no fixed place of abode, and but a poor and precarious maintenance, are powerfully tempted to a kind of vagrant and dishonourable life, wandering for better subsistence from parish to parish, even from north to south."[3]

Similar conditions prevailed in the diocese of St David's upon the nomination in 1788 to that see of Bishop Horsley, who in his primary visitation found many curacies of the value of £10, and some still of £5 per annum, for the improvement of which he laboured to fix a minimum stipend of £15.[4]

Compared with such exiguous emolument, the curate might well count himself "passing rich on £40 per year", and tolerably prosperous with an average stipend of between £30 and £35 per annum. When Thomas Brockbank served the curacy of Coulton, by adding to that duty the office of schoolmaster he received between £30 and £40 per year; but when he transferred to Garstang he could not secure more than "an equivalent of £30".[5] After a short period the vicar found

[1] W. Nicolson, *Miscellany Accounts of the Diocese of Carlisle*, 1703 (ed. R. E. Ferguson, 1877), p. 96.
[2] J. Lucas, *History of Warton Parish* (ed. J. R. Ford and J. A. F. Maitland, Kendal, 1931), p. 50.
[3] Abp. Tenison to Queen Anne, 31 Jan. 1712/13. Arch. W. Epist. 6, Canterbury I.
[4] H. H. Jebb, *Life of Bishop Samuel Horsley*, p. 68 (London, 1909).
[5] *Brockbank*, pp. 137, 141.

even this sum beyond his resources, and the hapless Brockbank migrated to Sefton, Liverpool, where he received "£35 per annum, besides weddings, churchings, buryings, and funeral sermons", together with a room in the parsonage to be furnished by himself.[1] In 1730 John Wesley was offered a curacy "to continue a quarter or half a year, which he accepted with all his heart. The salary was £30 a year, the church eight miles from Oxford, seven of which were, winter or summer, the best road in the country". More than thirty years later Parson Woodforde had the option of two curacies worth £28 plus surplice fees and £40 respectively at Newton Purcell in Oxon, and Thurloxton in Somerset, the latter of which he accepted.[2] Having left Oxford for Somerset, he transferred shortly from Thurloxton to Babcary for £20 a year plus "the surplice fees, Easter offerings, and free use of parsonage, gardens, and stables"; but since he refused for this sum to perform divine service more than once per Sunday, it was agreed that he should have £30 for two services, an agreement which was renewed upon the arrival of a new rector in July 1764.[3] In the following September Woodforde was ordained to the priesthood, and became thereby a more desirable curate for non-resident rectors. In April 1765 he resolved to take also the curacy of Castle Cary to his father, receiving £20 a year, but officiating once each Sunday there and at Babcary, which curacy he relinquished in the following October. Finally, in 1771, the death of his father necessitated fresh arrangements for the curacy, which he continued to hold at the former sum of £30 plus surplice fees, combining with it a temporary curacy at Ansford.[4] Ten years later the diarist in 1782 recorded the payment of the curate of Dr Bathurst at the rate of £50 per annum; whilst in 1798 and 1799, when age and infirmity compelled the assistance of a curate at Weston, his own standard of remuneration was still £30 per year, which was paid in half-yearly instalments to Cotman and Dade, the latter receiving no increase after his ordination to the priesthood at Advent 1800.

The salaries of curates indeed rose slowly, notwithstanding the steady increase of the practice of non-residence and the general tendency towards an augmentation of the value of benefices. In the later years of the century the standard of emolument rose to an average of £70, stimulated by the act of parliament of 1796 empowering the bishop to appoint a maximum stipend of £75 for curates serving the parishes of non-resident pluralists, though the minimum was not raised from the £20 of 1714. But in the diocese of Worcester during the quarter of a

[1] *Brockbank*, p. 219.　　　　　　[2] *The Diary of a Country Parson*, i, 24.
[3] *Ibid.* pp. 33–7.　　　　　　　[4] *Ibid.* pp. 47, 114.

century of Hurd's episcopate from 1781 to 1807, whilst forty cases were recorded of curates receiving £50 and over, 113 received between £30 and £50; and in Llandaff during the first decade of the nineteenth century the average salary of curates was still between £25 and £30. In a parliamentary paper of 1830 containing returns from the several dioceses relative to the numbers and stipends of curates, out of 4254 members of that class, 1631 were still in receipt of salaries not exceeding £60; whilst in 1835 the Report of the Commissioners appointed to enquire into ecclesiastical revenues of England and Wales returned the total number of curates as 5230 with an average salary of £81 per annum. Generalisation concerning the salaries of curates is rendered more difficult, however, by the widespread prevalence of the practice of serving two curacies, and even of combining the cure of a small benefice with that of a neighbouring curacy. The combination of two curacies, made possible by the custom of alternating divine service with sermon in the morning and afternoon, was characteristic of all dioceses; whilst the spread of non-residence enabled incumbents of poor livings to eke out their scanty endowment by undertaking services in other churches. Such customs added a further element of confusion to the crazy patchwork of parochial administration, which defied regularisation and generalisation concerning the conditions of curates and incumbents.

Next to inadequate remuneration, the curatical state was characterised chiefly by inferiority of status and uncertainty of tenure. Of the conscious inferiority of the curate's position no apter illustration could be afforded than the letter of recommendation to Richard Hurd, rector of Thurcaston, by Dr Samuel Ogden of St John's College, Cambridge, of Mr David Ball to act as his assistant. The aspiring curate was described as "one who has a good voice, a decent behaviour, somewhat rustic, a reasonable share of understanding, and of learning a quantity rather less, but not nothing; one who will not be shocked at the table of a farmer, and may think your curacy a preferment. I have promised him no civilities from you", added Ogden, "on purpose, not that you may lessen them, but that he may think himself the more obliged to you".[1] With such an introduction it was little surprising that Ball should declare "that he had never been treated with such distance or rather disdain", as by Hurd. The hazards of the curate's state were exemplified by the many changes suffered by Brockbank during his search for a settlement, typical of which was the intimation made to him in 1701 by Mr Richmond, vicar of Garstang, whom he had served as curate since 1699, that he "found Garstang not sufficient to maintain

[1] S. Ogden to R. Hurd, 24 Nov. 1762. *Hurd Papers*, IV, Section 2.

two, and therefore all on a sudden told him they must part, but... that he would serve him in seeking out a place".[1] In like manner on 19 July 1773 Frank Woodforde, having been instituted that day to the living of Ansford, intimated to his kinsman and curate, James Woodforde, that "he intended serving Ansford next Sunday himself"; which notice, commented the diarist, "of my leaving the curacy is, I think, not only unkind but very ungentlemanlike".[2] Contracts were entered into and dissolved upon the shortest notice, and from the curate's standpoint with entirely insufficient security. A characteristic cause and also a consequence of this circumstance was the widespread neglect among curates to obtain an episcopal licence. Archbishop Secker indeed allowed that "the expence of a licence, by means of the stamps, might be to some rather inconvenient; at least if they were likely to remove and so repeat that expence in a short time; and such curates he would excuse; only desiring them to consider what security of continuing in their station and receiving their salary a licence brought them".[3]

Their condition was made even more undesirable by the lack of suitable lodging in many villages, which often compelled them also to non-residence, and induced them to seek speedy removal. In most villages there was no house save the parsonage which offered proper accommodation, and in the case of protracted non-residence on the part of incumbents, this might have fallen into a ruinous and dilapidated state. When James Woodforde wished to take up residence at Thurloxton, he found no lodging available, and was fortunate indeed when Squire Cross admitted him to his house, "a noble house, good enough for any nobleman", on terms recorded gratefully by the diarist. "That I should live as he does, (which is very well, I am sure), that I should have my linen washed by him, and that he should keep my horse, (corn excepted), £21: and that for every day that I was absent I should be allowed for each day 1s. 1½d., which per year is £21".[4] Similar cause for congratulation existed in the settlement of Henry Fothergill, who, on accepting the office of curate to Archdeacon Huddlestone of Bath at his living of Kelston, was lodged in the house of his brother-in-law, Henry Harrington, lord of the manor, to whose children he acted as tutor.[5] Such instances of comfortable establishment were not general, and the lot of the majority of curates predisposed them to frequent changes of place and a quasi-itinerant course of life. Archbishop Secker acknowledged the uncertainty of the curate's position by his admission

---

[1] *Brockbank*, p. 217.   [2] *The Diary of a Country Parson*, i, 118.
[3] Secker, Charge VI, *Works*, v, 433.
[4] *The Diary of a Country Parson*, i, 32.   [5] *Fothergill*, p. 140.

that "he would consider himself as being with the parishioners only for an uncertain, and he may hope, a short time; which will tempt him to neglect them".[1] "What is £40 per annum for the support of a good man with comfort?" observed Sir Basil Dixwell to Archbishop Wake in relation to the chapel of ease at Barham, which experienced the common fate of "changing in every little space of time", and having to rest content with "the unhappy shift to be supplied with some raw, volatile, university young man till he can be otherwise provided for".[2] From the standpoint of the raw academic graduate the prospect, though different, was little more certain. "At present I am a poor curate without a patron, and have enough to do every day in the week from morning to night", commented Brockbank from Coulton to his friends in Oxford; an apt description of the curate's position, supplemented by the philosophic reflection which made tolerable such a situation, that "£30 per annum, though but a small salary, yet I think will keep me and my horse, and then 'twill be enough".[3]

In weighing the disadvantages of small curacies regard should be paid to the comparative poverty also of many benefices and of the lesser offices of academic societies. College fellowships were valued chiefly as a means whereby to ensure a settlement later in life by the succession to a good benefice, whilst in many cases the remuneration of academic labours was exiguous. Brockbank, though frustrated during his residence in Oxford in his ambition to live an university life, received the offer whilst serving the curacy of Coulton of the vice-principalship of St Mary Hall, Oxford, a house which had only eight undergraduates and three bachelors resident. The primary duty of the vice-principal would be to endeavour to turn to the profit of his hall the circumstance that "the university in general was very full", by attracting to his care a greater number of its members. Brockbank believed that he might "by a diligent care increase the number of scholars in the house", but reflected that, enjoying at Coulton both "the love of his parishioners" and also "a known salary well paid, to leave that for an uncertainty would not be prudence". Whilst assuring his Oxford friends that "he still retained a very good will to an university life, and had he but the assurance of £40...for his own part he would be as willing to begin a journey for Oxon as ever he was", he yet declined the invitation to return on such terms.

[1] Charge VI, *Works*, v, 426.
[2] Sir B. Dixwell to Abp. Wake, 28 Dec. 1721 and 4 Jan. 1721/2. Arch. W. Epist. 22, items xc, xciii, ff. 132, 136.
[3] *Brockbank*, pp. 129, 141.

To a friend of Queen's College he acknowledged the motive of his decision: "I remembered the old proverb, one bird—I doubt not that house is almost desolate, and I had as good preach twice every Sunday and teach school for £30 or £40 per annum as to come thither to starve with honour".[1] Nor were the emoluments of a great proportion of benefices superior to those of many curacies, and often upon acceptance of a small living the incumbent had to continue to serve his curacy in order to secure a sufficient maintenance. In the Representation of the Governors of Queen Anne's Bounty to her majesty on 19 January 1709–10 in relation to the discharge of livings not exceeding £50 from the payment of firstfruits and tenths, it was stated "that out of near 10,000 benefices in England and Wales near 4000 were now discharged". More detailed computation indicated that at the establishment of that bounty there were 5597 benefices the revenues of which did not exceed £50 per annum, whilst Ecton estimated that of these no fewer than 2122 were under £30 per annum and 1200 under £20.[2] After the lapse of a century, with its changes in the value of money and the general rise in the revenues of benefices, the Diocesan Returns of 1809 reckoned that 3998 livings were still under £150 per annum, whilst the Report of the Commissioners appointed to enquire into the ecclesiastical revenues of England and Wales demonstrated that in 1835 of a total of 10,480 benefices (exclusive of sinecure rectories and benefices annexed to other preferments) 3528 enjoyed an income of not more than £150 per year. Promotion to a small benefice of £40 or under, according to the values of the earlier part of the century, brought little advantage to a curate, as Brockbank realised when preferring to remain in his curacy of Sefton rather than accept the benefice of Clitheroe where "he found the income of the church but £20 per annum".[3] The poverty of many livings added another to the manifold causes of non-residence and compelled the incumbents to aspire either towards a plurality of small benefices or to the addition of a neighbouring curacy. Bishop Reynolds of Lincoln lamented to Archbishop Wake in 1724 the particular poverty of benefices in the county of Lincoln, which abounded in very small parishes,

the number of houses in many of them not above eight or ten, a great number of them not affording £20 per annum to the minister, very few more than £40, some not £5. Hence it came to pass that the clergy thereabout were

[1] *Brockbank*, pp. 128–9.
[2] J. Ecton, *A State of the Corporation of Queen Anne's Bounty*, 2nd edn. pp. 109, 249.
[3] *Brockbank*, p. 217.

obliged to undertake three, or four, or five churches a man to piece out a scanty subsistence, under the uneasy reflection all along that neither the public worship, nor any other part of the pastoral charge could in these parishes have a due attendance.[1]

Yet preferment to one of the poorer livings was all that the generality of journeyman curates, without influence, could expect. The richer prizes, even amongst benefices with cure of souls, in addition to the sinecure cathedral dignities, were reserved for clergy possessing the requisite interest. Tradition assumed without comment or criticism that bishops must provide first for their relatives and chaplains before weighing the claims of the inferior clergy of their dioceses, and even the strictest prelates conformed to this standard. "I don't presume to find fault with the bishop of Worcester for preferring his nephew", observed Mr Nathaniel Collier, curate of Harfield, whom Archbishop Wake had recommended without success to his lordship of Worcester in this regard. "I only wish it were my good fortune to be a bishop's nephew too".[2] Lacking this powerful engine of promotion he announced to the primate his resolve to close with an offer of the vicarage of Ilfracombe made by Archdeacon Martin Benson in virtue of his prebend of that place in Salisbury Cathedral, for "though the real value of it was but £47", he accepted because it was "something certain and better than a precarious curacy of £30 per annum". The nature of reward enjoyed by episcopal relatives was illustrated by Archbishop Wake's continued promotion of his kinsman, Robert Wake, whom as bishop of Lincoln he had preferred to the rectory of Farthington worth £92 per annum, in the diocese of Peterborough, where the presentee developed doubtful political sentiments. In 1719 the archbishop admonished him "to live quietly and peacably under the present government" and to be "well-affected to his majesty", whereupon the culprit returned the assurance of having taken "a firm oath to King George and daily and heartily prayed for him in his public and private prayers". His loyalty was rewarded in the following year by presentation to the rectory of Buxted with the chapel of Uckfield, an archiepiscopal peculiar in the diocese of Chichester, which he found "with the hop gardens, was worth communibus annis at least £300 per year, with a most excellent house, garden, stables, and fishponds".[3]

[1] Bp. Reynolds to Wake, 27 July 1724. Arch. W. Epist. 9, Canterbury IV, f. 314.
[2] N. Collier to Wake, 19 Sept. 1724. Arch. W. Epist. 22, item cccxix, f. 479.
[3] R. Wake to Abp. Wake, 12 July 1720. Arch. W. Epist. 21, item ccxlvii, p. 353. The value of Farthington is given as £140 per annum in 1788 (Lloyd's Edition of Ecton's *Thesaurus Ecclesiasticus*).

Out of these profits he allowed the liberal stipend of £40 a year to his curate at Uckfield, whilst the rectory of Farthington vacated by his promotion was bestowed by Bishop Gibson of Lincoln upon his step-brother, Dr John Gibson, Provost of Queen's College, Oxford.

Even more illustrative of the importance of influence was the request preferred to Wake in 1719 by Thomas Tanner, chancellor of Norwich (and afterwards archdeacon of Norfolk and bishop of St Asaph), on behalf of his youngest brother William. This brother, having been ordained deacon by Wake at Trinity 1712, had been presented in 1713 by Bishop Moore of Ely to the living of Griston in Norfolk, "a little vicarage of £30 per annum", to which Bishop Fleetwood of Ely had added in 1718 "another of about the same value", that of Stanford. Thus provided William Tanner had "lived in a single state contentedly and had been so good a manager as to save £30 or £40 which he was obliged to lay out on one of his vicarage houses" in 1718. Therefore, upon the vacancy of a contiguous rectory worth about £80, he desired his brother to procure an interest for him to hold this also in plurality since the churches were but half a mile apart. When Thomas Tanner applied to the patron the church had been already promised, but he received an assurance that if an equivalent could be found within the statutory six months, his brother should have his wish. To this end he applied to the primate, and to Bishops Gibson of Lincoln and Fleetwood of Ely, to request that if "any such living of £80, £90, or £100 per annum happened within a few months to fall in their gift, they would be pleased to consider him and enable him with the disposal of it to make as good provision for his brother as he should desire".[1] This immediate purpose was not secured, but William Tanner was presented by the bishop of Norwich in 1723 to the rectory of Topcroft and in 1725 to that of Redenhall in Norfolk.[2] The significance of the incident lay in Chancellor Tanner's estimate of "what would make a very complete subsistence" for his brother, and his excuse for his request to the archbishop that he was "sensible that such kind of living as he now desired was below the acceptance of his chaplains or other men of merit that depended on his grace".

In like manner Lawrence Echard, the historian, having incurred great expenses by his historical studies, received recompense by a modest quota of pluralities, holding two compatible benefices without cure of souls, the archdeaconry of Stow and the prebend of Louth in Lincoln

[1] T. Tanner to Abp. Wake, 10 Feb. 1719. Arch. W. Epist. 21, item cxcix, f. 290.
[2] The value of Topcroft is given as £110 and that of Redenhall as £250 per annum in Lloyd's edition of Ecton, 1788.

Cathedral, and being presented in 1722 to two benefices with cure in the diocese of Norwich, the rectories of Rendlesham and Sudburn cum Orford. For these preferments he expressed grateful thanks to Archbishop Wake, as for the constant patronage of the primate "ever since he was first his chaplain". In regard to his livings,

"that on which I am to live, Rendlesham", he reported, "is pleasantly and warmly situated in a clean soil and a good air, about five miles from Orford, which is a sort of port town near the sea, where I design and desire to go once a month and to take particular pains in a place where the air will not permit me constantly to reside. Rendlesham has less than 20, and Orford has near 100 families. As to the real revenue, I find that Rendlesham is £110;...the other may with certainty be said to be £160 a year. If, after paying my curate (which is at least to be £40 a year), with taxes and other charges, I can make in all near £200 a year, I shall be fully contented with a grateful remembrance of my benefactors; and I shall not so much as think of any other preferment, unless it should be such as is consistent with and will no ways interrupt the duty belonging to these two livings".[1]

The problem of plurality was the factor which made havoc of all attempts towards an orderly administration of the parochial system of the Hanoverian Church. The wide exemptions allowed by the statute of 1529 and the Canons of 1604 perpetuated, though in greatly modified degree, the abuses of the middle ages, of which indeed they were a survival no less in the spirit than in the letter. The unreformed Georgian Church did not question the inherited medieval tradition that ecclesiastical revenues existed for the support of ecclesiastical persons, irrespective of their residence in the locality from which their revenues were drawn. The act of 21 Henry VIII, cap. 13, regulating the possession of pluralities, provided necessarily a dispensation from residence of pluralists upon one of their benefices, though requiring residence at one of them, except in the cases specified of chaplains attending their duty upon the nobility and students abiding in the universities. By a later statute of 28 Henry VIII, cap. 13, the exception relating to students in the universities was changed so as to exclude all clergy of the age of forty years and over (save clerks actually engaged in teaching or holding academic office in the universities) from its benefits, and to require clergy under that age to fulfil all the statutable requirements for proceeding to their degrees. The wide allowance of non-residence thus recognised was extended by the interpretation of the phrase of the act imposing penalties upon any clerk who should "absent himself

[1] Echard to Wake, 23 March 1723. Arch. W. Epist. 22, item clxxxii, f. 278.

wilfully" from his benefice. According to the comment of Gibson in his *Codex* this was construed to mean: "that if he hath no parsonage house, or remove by the advice of his physician for better air, in order to the recovery of his health, or be detained and removed by imprisonment, or the like: he is not punishable within this statute, which supposeth the absence to be voluntary".[1] Further qualifications were imposed by the 41st canon of the canons of 1604, which forbade the issue of a licence for holding plurality of benefices with cure of souls except to persons "very well worthy for learning", that is of the degree of master of arts at least, and except personal residence were made on each benefice "for some reasonable time in every year", the benefices were not more than thirty miles apart, and a licensed curate was maintained in the benefice where the incumbent did not reside.

Through the gate so widely opened, non-residence entered into all parts of the ecclesiastical patrimony, spreading alike from above and below, from the cathedral dignitaries enjoying both sinecures and benefices with cure of souls, and from the inferior clergy possessed of small livings insufficient singly for their sustenance. In the Commissioners' Report of 1835 it was computed that no fewer than 2878 benefices lacked a parsonage house, whilst in 1728 others the parsonage house was uninhabitable, affording an additional legal reason for non-residence. Ill-health being recognised likewise as a ground for non-residence, the onus of maintaining the divine service in unhealthy parishes was placed without qualm on the shoulders of the luckless curates. Characteristic of such conditions was the hesitation expressed to Archbishop Wake in 1722 by Mr Richard Meadowcourt as to the prudence of quitting a college fellowship for the rectory of Passenham in the diocese of Peterborough, worth £200 per year but "with respect to health, as bad as could be conceived". Since "it stood upon a river, in the midst of a large meadow which lay under water the whole winter, upon that account he would be obliged to keep a curate, who would expect, what others had constantly been paid, the yearly salary of £40".[2] Against similar arguments Archbishop Secker could direct only the reply that the allegation of health should not be urged too far, nor too much regarded. "For places, called unwholesome, prove upon trial very wholesome to many persons; and those which are least so must have some ministers in or near them; and whom rather, generally

[1] Gibson's *Codex*, ii, 887.

[2] R. Meadowcourt to Abp. Wake, 18 May 1722. Arch. W. Epist. 22, item cxxvii, f. 182. Meadowcourt resolved to retain his fellowship at Merton College, Oxford.

speaking, than such as enjoy the whole profits?"[1] The extent of non-residence as estimated in the Diocesan Returns for 1827, published by order of parliament in 1830, amounted to 6120 non-resident incumbents out of 10,583 total returns, a proportion representing a considerable decrease from the 7358 non-residents of the total of 11,194 benefices returned in 1809. In the Commissioners' Report of 1835 it was further reckoned that of the 5230 curates in England and Wales, 1006 were employed by resident incumbents and 4224 by non-residents.

Against the many loopholes, both legal and incidental, for pluralism and non-residence, archiepiscopal vigilance could avail little, either by exhortation or by exercise of metropolitan authority. Indeed the archbishops' function was restricted to enquiry whether the legal qualifications had been secured, the limit of thirty miles' distance had not been transgressed, and the learning of the candidate was sufficient to meet the needs of the canon. Archbishop Tenison at the outset of the century struggled continually to restrain the issue of dispensations for plurality within the legal bounds, and protested strongly in 1713 to Queen Anne against a proposed royal dispensation in the case of benefices outside the canonical distance. His own procedure in cases of application for a dispensation bore every evidence of careful scrutiny, according to the account preserved for the direction of his successor.

When the late archbishop was applied to for a dispensation, he proceeded in the following manner. The person who desired it, first acquainted the secretary with his desire and delivered into his hands the necessary instructions; viz., his Orders, both priest and deacon (his grace having found in one instance a person really ordained priest who had never been deacon); his Testimonials from the neighbouring clergy or college; a qualification from some nobleman registered in the Faculty office and attested to be so registered; or else a certificate from one of the universities of his being Bachelor of Divinity or Law; a certificate of his being Master of Arts complete; the presentation to the second living; and the bishop's certificate concerning the value and distance of the benefices....

The instruments being all in due form, his grace directed the person praying the dispensation to be examined by his chaplain; if an Oxford man by the Oxford chaplain; and if a Cambridge man by the Cambridge chaplain. His method of examination was the writing on a sheet of paper seven or eight questions, or as many as were judged requisite, (sometimes by himself, but generally by the chaplain), and, spaces for the answers being left, to put the person examined in a room by himself, with pen, ink, and paper, and

---

[1] Secker, Charge VI, *Works*, V, 428.

a Bible and Concordance; that he might set down his particular answers to every question.

His grace was very frequently importuned to grant dispensations to persons without coming up to London themselves; but very seldom yielded in that particular.... The answers being approved, the secretary prepared a petition which was signed by his grace and directed to the Faculty office.[1]

The standard of learning required of postulants for pluralities by Tenison is illustrated by sundry papers of questions and answers preserved amongst his correspondence at Lambeth, which embraced divers points of divinity written in Latin.[2] But the degree of proficiency in learned tongues and in knowledge of the Scriptures necessary to fulfil the canonical condition of "being very well worthy for learning" was

[1] Dispensations: a paper in the hand of Edmund Gibson, chaplain to Tenison. Arch. W. Epist. 6, Canterbury 1.

[2] The character of examinations for plurality may be judged from the following exercises performed by the Rev. Charles Ley, M.A., of Sidney Sussex College, Cambridge, chaplain to Lord Charles Baron Fitzwalter (from which appointment he secured the qualification for plurality), who was possessed of the Rectory of Sutton Magna, in the diocese of London and the county of Essex, and who desired to receive from the bishop of London collation to the Rectory of Bishops' Wickham in the same diocese and county, distant about 12 miles from Sutton Magna. The dispensation was granted by fiat, after examination, on 14 December 1706. (Act Book, Archbishop Tenison, v, 235.)

Q. Quinam sunt praecipue Socinianorum errores?

A. Sociniani negant Divinitatem Jesu Christi et omnes etiam doctrinas ab ea deductas.

Q. Quomodo probas necessitatem paedobaptismi?

A. Baptisma ordinabatur loco circumcisionis et pueri circumcidebantur; ergo nisi homo renascatur, i.e., baptizetur aquâ et Spiritu Sancto, non potest intrare in regnum caelorum.

Q. Unde constat jus divinum ministerii evangelici?

A. Christus elegit duodecim apostolos et dedit eis potestatem admittendi ministros in ecclesiam manuum impositione, et successoribus etiam in aeternum ut patet ex vicesimo octavo capite evangelii secundum Matt: ver: 19° et 20°.

Q. Quomodo probas Sacram Scripturam esse perfectam regulam Fidei?

A. Scriptura vel evangelium est potestas Dei ad salvationem omnium qui credunt, Judaeis etiam et Graecis; Rom: 1°, 15° et ver: 16° sequitur. In ea Sacra Scriptura, justitia Dei revelatur a fide ad fidem. Omnis Scriptura datur per inspirationem Dei et utilis est ad doctrinam, reprehensionem, correctionem, instructionem in justitia; ut servus Dei perfectus fiat et ad omnia opera bona aptus. 3° Cap: Secundo Lib: Tim: ver: 16°, 17°.

6 December 1706.   Carolus Ley.
Tenison MSS. 982, f. 44. Lambeth Library.

I should like to take occasion to acknowledge my indebtedness to His Grace the Lord Archbishop of Canterbury for permission to publish this item.

capable of diversity of interpretation, and in examinations for plurality as in others of their kind promise must have been accepted upon occasion instead of performance. Such was certainly the case of a clerk of the diocese of York, Mr Henry Woods, B.A., of Christ's College, Cambridge, rector of Lambley, Nottinghamshire, who, having been presented by Archbishop Dawes to the rectory of Stanford-on-Soar in 1722, applied to Archbishop Wake for a dispensation for plurality. Upon examination the candidate was found sadly deficient in erudition, notwithstanding which the dispensation was issued on 21 July 1722. "I am sorry that your grace found Mr Woods so meanly qualified in respect of learning", wrote his grace of York in acknowledging the kindness of his brother of Canterbury in granting his request for the dispensation; "he having been ordained by my predecessor (whom I knew to have been a careful man in his ordinations) and having been some time a curate in the diocese, I did not examine him when I instituted him to his living. But I will do the best I can to quicken him in making good his promise of future improvement to your grace".[1] The duty of executing this supervision was committed to Archdeacon Marsden, of Nottingham, who likewise apologised for the deficiency of Woods "in the Latin as well as the Greek tongue", adding that "he had seen some of his letters and heard him preach, and thought him passable", and promising diligence in oversight of his studies.[2] The archdeacon therefore required of the rector that by the following Christmas he should have construed St Luke's Gospel in Greek and a work of Terence, but towards the end of the February after, he had received no visit nor report of progress in the task![3] In like manner in the November again following Marsden reported that the second exercise, due at Michaelmas, had not been presented;[4] and finally in February 1724, though still aspiring towards a learned clergy, the archdeacon had to content himself with relating to Wake in regard to Woods that "'tis true indeed that the knowledge of the English tongue only would make a good divine, in the country especially"; and thereafter the rector's studies seem to have evoked no further supervision.[5] In the Visitation Returns of Archbishop Herring in 1743 there is a note appended to

---

[1] Dawes to Wake, 23 July 1722. Arch. W. Epist. 22, item cxxvii, f. 196. Woods was ordained deacon by the bishop of London on 21 Sept. 1711; and priest by Archbishop Sharp of York, 20 Sept. 1713. He was instituted to Lambley on 2 June 1719.
[2] R. Marsden to Wake, 11 Aug. 1722. Arch. W. Epist. 22, item cxxxvi, f. 212.
[3] Same to Same, 23 Feb. 1722/3. *Ibid.* item clxxiv, f. 265.
[4] Same to Same, 16 Nov. 1723. *Ibid.* item ccxli, f. 366.
[5] Same to Same, 1 Feb. 1723/4. *Ibid.* item cclvi, f. 390.

the entry concerning Stanford-on-Soar that Mr Woods, the minister, "can't reside because his curate who lives in the vicarage has filled it with children".[1]

Upon occasions when bishops caused candidates for institution to benefices to submit to examination, albeit such rigour was rare, the results might not be reassuring; as the statement signed by Mr William Newton, who received institution to the vicarage of West Hythe in Kent and in the diocese of Canterbury from Archbishop Wake on 14 March 1719, upon the presentation of the archdeacon of Canterbury, well testified.

Whereas upon my very small progress in the Latin tongue, his grace my lord Archbishop of Canterbury has been pleased to indulge me the institution to the vicarage of West Hythe in his grace's diocese: I hereby solemnly promise that I will diligently cultivate the Latin tongue, and as far as in me lies, make myself a master of it; that in case of future preferment in the church I might be better qualified for institution, and answer the designs of the canon and of his grace's orders the better; and that in case I do not perform this my promise, the present indulgence of institution shall be of no advantage to me for the obtaining of any other.[2]

Sterner measures and wider powers of prohibition were requisite indeed before archbishops could check the extension of the practices of pluralism and non-residence. Generally they had to rest content with exhortations to their clergy to remember the responsibilities of the pastoral office, as Secker frequently reminded his auditors at visitations.

It must not be pleaded that however necessary the residence of some minister may be, that of a curate may suffice. For your engagement is, not merely that the several duties of your parish shall be done, but that you personally will do them; and if it were enough to substitute another to do them, a layman would be in point of conscience and reason, as capable of holding a benefice as a man in holy orders. . . . There are indeed cases in which the law dispenses with holding two livings and by consequence allows absence from one. But persons ought to consider well, supposing they can with innocence take the benefit of that law, whether they can do it on other terms than their dispensation and their bond expresses, of preaching yearly thirteen sermons, and keeping two months' hospitality in the parish where they reside least. For the leave given them on these conditions is not intended to be given them, however legally valid, if the conditions are neglected.[3]

[1] *Archbishop Herring's Visitation Returns*, iv, 131–2 (ed. Ollard and Walker).
[2] W. Newton, Lambeth House, 12 March 1719/20. Arch. W. Epist. 8, Canterbury iii.
[3] Secker, Charge vi, *Works*, v, 427.

If the pluralist was a scandal to the orderly administration of the Church, the class of vagrant, strolling clergy were a menace and danger to the regularity and validity of its spiritual ministrations. To some degree the unsatisfactory conditions of the majority of curates gave an element of migration to their life, tempting them, as Tenison had observed, "to a kind of vagrant and dishonourable life, wandering for better subsistence from parish to parish, even from north to south". Complaints of their vagrancy came from diverse parts of the country, as Bishop White Kennett from Peterborough reported the trouble caused by "a sort of itinerant curates or preachers that ramble without licence or settled employ to spread faction and disorder";[1] whilst from Wales Dr Wootton lamented that they were infested by "a parcel of strolling curates in south Wales, and some such there were also in north Wales, who for a crown or at most for a guinea, would marry anybody under a hedge".[2] Episcopal correspondence abounded indeed in incidents of the discovery of curates whose rapid transference from diocese to diocese had eluded the eye of archdeacons and bishops alike until some accident or scandal revealed their presence. Inevitably these vagrants concentrated upon the capital city, where, until Lord Hardwicke's Marriage Act of 1754, they secured a lucrative if illicit reward by Fleet marriages. There also they offered their services for occasional sermons and reading of prayers, and some at least of their number sank to the position of hack writers of Grub street.

> At Coffee house that's nigh St Paul's
> The meaner parsons have their calls,
> On Saturdays the papers ply
> Like watermen at clearest sky.
> Men ply to preach and read the prayer
> From half a crown to guinea fair.[3]

It was at Will's Coffee House that Eugenio, the hapless divine of Swift's *Essay on the Fates of Clergymen*, fell into the company of several men of wit, "where in some time he had the bad luck to be distinguished. His scanty salary compelled him to run deep into debt for a new gown and cassock, and now and then forced him to write some paper of wit or humour, or preach a sermon for ten shillings, to supply his necessities".[4] Amongst this company of nomadic clerks there intruded a number of

[1] Bp. Kennett to Abp. Wake, 26 Sept. 1726. Arch. W. Epist. 9, Canterbury IV.

[2] W. Wootton to Abp. Wake, 23 Feb. 1720/1. Arch. W. Epist. 21, item ccxcviii, f. 419.

[3] N. Sykes, *Edmund Gibson*, p. 231.

[4] Swift, "An Essay on the Fates of Clergymen", *Works* (ed. T. Scott), iii, 298.

persons performing ecclesiastical functions without having ever received ordination. The detection of such impostors was often secured by happy accident rather than by design, for the neglect of curates to seek licences from the bishop combined with the accepted itinerancy of their careers, opened many gaps for the admission of pretenders bearing forged Letters of Orders. No better illustration of the facility with which such deception could be practised and of the protracted period of success before its detection, could be adduced than the case of Mr William Bannester in the diocese of Lincoln during Wake's episcopate. At his first visitation in 1706 the bishop demanded the exhibition of Letters of Orders, and upon Bannester's failure to present any credentials justifying his incumbency at Upton, called for further explanation. On 15 May 1707 the culprit replied that he had lost his Letters, but contended that the exercise of ministerial functions for fourteen years past was proof presumptive and sufficient of the regularity of his ordination. During the prolonged correspondence which ensued he was driven from one prevarication to another in his attempts to conceal the fact that he had never been admitted to Holy Orders. On 22 May 1709 he simulated great indignation that his veracity and the validity of his ordination should be called in question, affirming that he had been ordained by Archbishop Marsh of Dublin "about fourteen years ago", and that he had served four years in Ireland, and six in England before receiving the broad seal for Upton some four years ago, without having been challenged at any time. Notwithstanding this assurance he betrayed his sense of insecurity by repeated requests that Wake would ordain him at his ensuing ordination to set all doubts at rest, to which the bishop replied by a demand for the production of copies of his Orders from Dublin and the threat to suspend him from officiating at Upton until such documentary proof was forthcoming. Against the enforcement of these conditions Bannester raised a variety of objections; the poverty of his living, only £30 per annum, the number of his family (as if "six pretty children" were adequate substitute for Orders), and the difficulty of discovering his contemporaries at Trinity College, Dublin, to corroborate his testimony. Always he concluded his letters with the request that "as ordination is not a sacrament and his lordship believed he was not ordained", he might be admitted to Orders at the bishop's pleasure.[1] Further he alleged a series of ingenious excuses, urging that even "registers were not infallible", but failed to move his diocesan beyond a respite, prolonged finally until Michaelmas 1709, after which time

[1] W. Bannester to Bp. Wake. A series of letters in Arch. W. Epist. 17, items ccciii–cccxxviii, ff. 393–423.

action was threatened. Meanwhile Wake, having prosecuted enquiries on his own behalf in Ireland, found no confirmation but rather refutal of Bannester's allegations. In April 1707 the archbishop of Dublin reported that the registers of his see contained no record of the ordination of Bannester;[1] whilst two years later, in May 1709, Dr Edward Synge, a friend of Wake resident in Dublin, presented a more detailed account; that in 1693, the year in which Bannester dated his ordination, his age was only twenty, that "the registrary of the diocese...had searched the book for that year and could not find that archbishop Marsh did in that year ordain any one person", that appeals had been made without response at public visitations for the testimony of any contemporary of Bannester who could affirm him to be in Orders, and finally that Dr Lloyd, his tutor at Trinity College, had declared that "he was an ill man and never took any degree".[2] In face of this cumulative evidence Wake pronounced sentence of deprivation upon Bannester at Michaelmas 1709, whereupon the pretender withdrew to the profession of schoolmaster at Ealing, from which he made a series of unsuccessful efforts to induce the bishop to admit him to Orders upon the title of his school or a promise of the dowager countess of Suffolk to appoint him as her chaplain.

The significance of the episode was wider than its individual relevance, since it indicated not only the motive prompting such deception but the means by which its fraud was so long accepted. Bannester confessed that "when he did it 'twas because he knew not how to get bread for his family", and "after he had unhappily made the first false step he knew not how to get right again". More important was the admission by Dr Synge of the irregularity of records in Dublin, where

the custom in that diocese for registering those that were ordained, (and as far as he had found, it was the same throughout Ireland), was thus; everyman before he was ordained, made his subscription before the bishop in a book or roll provided for that purpose. But his ordination was never...entered into the public register until he took out his letters of orders, which some having neglected to do, had after the death of the bishop that ordained them, been put under some difficulty to make authentic proof of their having been ordained.

From such laxity there ensued many possibilities whereby unscrupulous men might contrive a plausible fraud, as was emphasised by a further Irish case during Wake's episcopate at Lincoln. In December

---

[1] Abp. Dublin to Bp. Wake, 17 April 1707. Arch. W. Epist. 17, item cxliv, f. 171.
[2] Dr E. Synge to Bp. Wake, 4 May 1709. *Ibid.* item clxxxiii, f. 218.

1715 the bishop directed Archdeacon Frank of Bedford to find a suitable clerk for presenting to the vicarage of Warden, whereupon Mr Frank sought out Mr Jonas Elwood, curate of Newport Pagnell, whose reputation there was that of "a discreet, sober, able, and painful minister of God's Word". Upon enquiry his career was suspected of irregularity. "He was only in deacons' orders, to which he was admitted in June 1710 by the bishop of Meath; after which he said that he lived about two years in Trinity College, Dublin, then assisted his father, a clergyman in Ireland, and about two and a half years since came into England to solicit some temporal concerns and lived in London till he came to Newport Pagnell".[1] After the manner of his kind Elwood, upon investigation of his record, migrated to another part of the country, and was found in 1719 by Bishop Chandler of Lichfield and Coventry in his diocese.

"I have lately driven one Elwood out of my diocese", reported his lordship to Archbishop Wake. "He pretended deacons' orders from the last bishop of Meath in Ireland, and came last from Newport Pagnell where he was curate whilst your grace was at Lincoln. He was only deacon, and his orders bore great marks of forgery. I therefore consulted the present bishop of Meath about him, and having no satisfaction from him that he was ever ordained, (his name not being in the register, which yet was deficient about the time he said he was ordained), and certain proofs that he was a very ill man in Ireland, I inhibited him; and he is now gone Londonwards to herd, as he gives out, with the Dissenters."[2]

These cases of Irish clergy, though more difficult of disproof, were paralleled within the English provinces, and the existence of the class of strolling clergy, into which imposters found easy admittance, constituted one of the insoluble problems of episcopal administration. Most bishops from their experiences in this regard could echo the protest of Secker to the clergy of his archdiocese of Canterbury in 1758 that "they could not think it right that he should be left in ignorance who served a church under his care, till he learnt it by accident or by private enquiry, perhaps many months after; through which omission men of bad characters, men not in Orders, might intrude, as there had been lately a flagrant instance in his diocese".[3]

Apart from the residence of bishops in London for the greater part of the year, with the consequent infrequent contact with their dioceses, intercourse with their clergy was hindered further by the magnificent

[1] T. Frank to Bp. Wake, Arch. W. Epist. 20, Lincoln I, item xxxii, f. 51.
[2] Bp. Chandler to Abp. Wake, 27 June 1719. Arch. W. Epist. 8, Canterbury III.
[3] Secker, Charge VI, *Works*, v, 433.

state associated with episcopal households which severed them by a deep gulf from the poverty of the inferior beneficed clerks and curates. The biographer of Archbishop Sharp counted it a particular mark of his grace's condescension that

to his clergy he ever expressed the utmost civility and respect. The meanest man in his diocese who wore a gown, (provided he were not obnoxious to his censure) was welcome at his table as often as he pleased; and he was received with as much affability and kindness as if Providence had set them both upon the level.... His house was always open and his table public to the clergy; that is, there was no time when they might not have ready access to him and entertainment too if they pleased.[1]

Upon occasion similar graciousness was observed in Bishop Warburton, as when, before preaching an anniversary sermon for the London Hospital at St Lawrence's Church, in the vestry and in the presence of the Lord Mayor, his behaviour was "beyond measure condescending and courteous, and he even graciously handed some biscuits and wine on a salver to the curate who was to read prayers".[2] The consciousness of the dignity and pomp of the episcopal state contributed to the tone of abasement and servility with which the inferior clergy addressed their bishops in frequent request for preferment. But if the necessities of the unprovided required them to omit no opportunity of laying their condition before their superiors, the paternal solicitude of the episcopate led to the despatch of answers characterised by kindly encouragement and appreciation even when unaccompanied by promise of practical alleviation. The editor of *The Diary and Letter Book of Thomas Brockbank* observes of its author that "his chief characteristic (and I know not why he should be blamed for it) appears to have been his determination to get on; he had an eye on every vacant chapel or parish, on every chance of preferment";[3] though his ambition was not realised until in 1706 after many obstacles he secured the vicarage of Cartmel. In the meantime his diary recorded the receipt of not a few generous letters from Bishop Stratford of Chester assuring him that "he was sorry he was no better provided for, and would be glad of an opportunity of putting him into more easy circumstances", or, upon information of another change of curacy, expressing regret "that he was forced to take up a curacy and wishing it were in his power to make better provision for him".[4] Archdeacon Paley counselled the inferior clergy to combine

[1] *Life of Sharp*, ii, 51.
[2] A. W. Evans, *Warburton and the Warburtonians*, p. 137.
[3] *Brockbank*, p. viii.   [4] *Ibid.* pp. 140, 160.

a proper proportion of humility and dignity in their solicitation of preferment. "Carry the same reserve into your correspondence with your superiors. Pursue preferment, if any prospects of it present themselves, not only by honourable means, but with moderate anxiety."

The contrast between the wealth of the fortunate pluralist clergy and the indigence of their poorer brethren possessed of small benefices or curacies was generally accepted by the conscience of the age. Boswell ventured in 1777 to discuss with Johnson

"a common subject of complaint, the very small salaries which many curates had, and maintained that no man should be invested with the character of a clergyman, unless he had a security for such an income as would enable him to appear respectable; that therefore a clergyman should not be allowed to have a curate unless he gave him £100 a year". To which the Doctor replied: "To be sure, sir, it is very wrong that any clergyman should be without a reasonable income; but as the church revenues were sadly diminished at the Reformation, the clergy who have livings cannot afford, in many instances, to give good salaries to curates without leaving themselves too little; and if no curate were to be permitted unless he had £100 per year, their number would be very small, which would be a disadvantage, as then there would not be such choice in the nursery for the church, curates being candidates for the higher ecclesiastical offices according to their merit and good behaviour".[1]

Even Archbishop Secker defended the existence of opulent benefices as the only practical means of attracting to the profession of Orders a sufficiency of candidates both of quality and quantity.

The few endowments that may appear larger than was necessary, are in truth, but needful encouragements to the breeding up of youth for holy orders. And were they lessened, either an insufficient number would be destined to that service, or too many of them would be of the lowest rank, unable to bear the expense of acquiring due knowledge, and unlikely to be treated with due regard.[2]

Such a standpoint naturally caused lukewarmness in supporting the equalisation of revenues demanded by Bishop Watson. Nor did the operations of Queen Anne's Bounty encourage further projects for the augmentation of poor benefices, since, apart from the distribution of a portion of their funds in sums of £200 to poor livings to which private donors would add an equal sum, they proceeded to disburse the

---

[1] Boswell, *Life of Johnson*, 15 Sept. 1777.
[2] Secker, Charge III, *Works*, v, 356.

remainder in like amounts upon benefices selected by the hazard of the lot. This procedure did not produce any immediate improvement in the general standard of poor livings, for though by 1815 it was computed that 7323 augmentations of £200 had been made, there were cases in which the same parishes had received five or six additions by the uncertain fortune of the lot, in which no regard could be paid to considerations of population or other conditions of particular cases.

The differences which separated the several grades of clergy were too wide and deep to admit of easy generalisation concerning the social position of their order in Hanoverian England. To the fortunate minority, possessed of prebends and other cathedral dignities, both wealth and position were accorded in good measure. In the churches also of the cities of London and Westminster, to which the best abilities of the Church were attracted, learning, piety, and pastoral zeal were recognised and respected. In the middle grade were settled the parochial clergy of the calibre of James Woodforde, who remained entirely contented with the £300 per year of Weston and the company of his Norfolk neighbours. Socially indeed he received and gave hospitable entertainment with the Custances, whose relations with the parsonage were ideally friendly; but when upon occasion he was drawn into the higher social circles of the Townshends in which his friend DuQuesne moved with natural ease, or was invited to dine in the company of the bishop of Norwich, he returned with the sentiment "that being with our equals is much more agreeable".[1] Far beneath the comfortable establishment of Weston stood the category of depressed clergy, rewarded by the small livings or by stipendiary curacies, whose circumstances were characterised by poverty and neglect. Their condition afforded a congenial theme for the satire of anti-clerical writers, who concentrated attention upon the indigent curate, threadbare in cassock and burdened with domestic responsibilities, upon whose shoulders they affected to place the entire parochial administration of rural England.

> Though lazy, the proud prelate's fed;
> This curate eats no idle bread.
> The wife at washing, 'tis his lot
> To pare the turnips, watch the pot.
> He reads, and hears his son read out,
> And rocks the cradle with his foot.[2]

[1] *The Diary of a Country Parson*, ii, 104.
[2] H. H. Jebb, *Life of Bishop Samuel Horsley*, p. 68: quoting a print of 1775.

From this class Swift drew his picture of the career of the neglected curate of talent, Eugenio, who having served many years in a London curacy, at length

wearied with weak hopes and weaker pursuits, accepted a curacy in Derbyshire of £30 a year, and when he was five and forty, had the great felicity to be preferred by a friend of his father's to a vicarage worth annually £60, in the most desert parts of Lincolnshire; where, his spirit sunk with those reflections that disappointment bring, he married a farmer's daughter and is still alive, utterly undistinguished and forgotten.[1]

The contrast between the success of the dunce Corusodes and the degradation of the able Eugenio afforded a proper topic for the mordant decanal wit; but allowing for the exaggeration native to Swift's genius in the account of feminine gallantry as an avenue to eminence, the diverse fortunes of such virtuous clergy as the Dentons and Robsons of Cumberland supported his invective against the fortuituous circumstances which determined the prosperity or adversity of clerical careers. When the diarist William Jones at Broxbourne had escaped from the unbeneficed to the beneficed state, he uttered many thanksgivings for his good fortune, and lamented the condition of his less happy brethren.

As to those who court this genteel profession with no other prospect but of being journeymen—"soles" not "upper-leathers", which is, being interpreted poor curates—they are truly to be pitied. If they regard present circumstances, without having respect unto the future recompense of reward, they would, I am sure, do better for themselves and their families by making interest for upper servants' places in a genteel family than by being mere soles or understrappers in the church. A journeyman in almost any trade· or business, even a bricklayer's labourer, or the turner of a razor-grinder's wheel, all circumstances considered, is generally better paid than a stipendiary curate.[2]

Yet even to the clergy who drew at best but a small prize from the ecclesiastical lottery, there were compensations for their hardship and penury. Thomas Brockbank in his north-country parishes retained the scholastic instincts which had inspired his desire to live an university life; and to clerks of such inclination the 78th canon afforded encouragement and protection against competition by its decree that

In what parish or chapel soever there is a curate which is master of arts, or bachelor of arts, or is otherwise well able to teach youth, and will willingly do so, for the better increase of his living, and training up of children in

[1] Swift, "An Essay on the Fates of Clergymen", *Works*, iii, 291–8.
[2] *Diary of William Jones* (ed. O. F. Christie), pp. 148–9.

principles of true religion; we will and ordain that a licence to teach the youth of the parish where he serveth be granted to none by the ordinary of that place, but only to the said curate.

In accordance therewith Bishop Stratford, being informed by Brockbank of his desire to teach at Garstang, assured him cordially that "if he could submit to the trouble and fatigue of teaching in a school, he doubted not but he would do good service to the public; and in undertaking that, he should have not only his approbation, but thanks for it".[1] Robert Robson on the other hand preferred a more homely participation in the outdoor sports of the countryside. "I'm glad to hear your parish is so well stocked with game, and of the finer sort", wrote his brother James of the Sussex parish where Robert served as curate; "and I hope you'll exercise yourself well amongst them." Further injunctions followed this exhortation to a proper enjoyment of the recreations of the country. "Pray write soon and tell me what rural amusements engage your time", commanded the bookseller in the succeeding summer. "Do you ever go a fishing? Or does gardening take up your leisure hours? In either of which employments I dare venture to proclaim you happy." With the change of seasons, and especially the coming of spring, the townsman envied the fortunes of his rustic clerical brother. "How happy are you, who as the seasons change, are ever presented with new scenes of delight. The gun is now laid up, and angling wholly engages your attention."[2] To the majority of country clergy the pleasures of these sports appealed more closely than the pursuit of letters, and afforded both consolation and contentment for the isolation of their situation. Thus settled the parson was identified with the life of the countryside to which he ministered.

> His talk was now of tithes and dues;
> He smoked his pipe and read the news;
> Knew how to preach old sermons next
> Vamp'd in the preface and the text.
> At Christ'nings well could act his part,
> And had the service all by heart. . . .
> Found his head filled with many a system,
> But classick authors—he ne'er miss'd 'em.

Towards his reconciliation to these conditions the philosophy of the age proferred its counsels, instinct with a realistic acceptance of the

[1] *Brockbank*, p. 190.
[2] James Robson to Robert Robson, 23 Oct. 1753, 18 June 1754, 7 April 1757. *Op. cit.* pp. 79, 80, 82.

existing order of society as entirely consonant with the decrees of Providence.

"In the first place", observed Paley in an ordination sermon preached at Carlisle in 1781, to the humble curacy, "the stations which you are likely for some time at least to occupy in the church, although not capable of all the means of rendering service and challenging respect which fall within the powers of your superiors, are free from many prejudices that attend upon higher preferments....Another and still more favourable circumstance in your situation is this: being upon a level with the greatest part of your parishioners, you gain access to their conversation and confidence, which is rarely granted to the superior clergy without extraordinary address and the most insinuating advances on their parts. And this is a valuable privilege; for it enables you to inform yourselves of the moral and religious state of your flocks, of their wants and weaknesses, their habits and opinions, of the vices which prevail and the principles from which they proceed; in a word it enables you to study the distemper before you apply the remedy...I put you in mind of this advantage because the right use of it constitutes one of the most respectable employments not only of our order, but of human nature; and leaves you, believe me, little to envy in the condition of your superiors, or to regret in your own."

The archdeacon was nothing if not practical; and accordingly he recommended to his auditors the cultivation of two virtues as essential to their estate, frugality and retirement. The one would enable them to live upon a provision "adequate in most cases to the wants and decencies of their situation but to nothing more"; and the other would school them to the difficult yet indispensable discipline of living alone, since "in situations like theirs, to be able to pass their time with satisfaction alone and at home was not only a preservative of character but the very secret of happiness".[1]

[1] Paley, *Works*, Sermons, v, 18.

CHAPTER VI

THE WHOLE DUTY OF MAN

"I am always very well pleased with a country Sunday", declared Addison in *The Spectator* of Monday, 9 July 1711; "and think if keeping the seventh day holy were only a human institution, it would be the best method that could have been thought of for the polishing and civilising of mankind. It is certain the country people would soon degenerate into a kind of savages and barbarians, were there not such frequent returns of a stated time in which the whole village meet together with their best faces and in their cleanliest habits, to converse with one another upon different subjects, hear their duties explained to them, and join together in adoration of the Supreme Being. Sunday clears away the rust of the whole week, not only as it refreshes in their minds the notions of religion, but as it puts both the sexes upon appearing in their most agreeable forms and exerting such qualities as are apt to give them a figure in the village. A country fellow distinguishes himself as much in the churchyard as a citizen does upon the 'Change, the whole parish politics being generally discussed in that place either after sermon or before the bell rings."

The social and religious significance of church attendance in the Hanoverian age could hardly secure more faithful delineation and interpretation than from the pen of the essayist who, though writing during the high church *régime* of Anne, discerned the features of rural religion which persisted throughout the greater part of the century. Both the strength and shortcomings of contemporary churchmanship were adumbrated in his picture; the association of social graces with attendance upon divine service on Sunday, as a means also of refreshing the notions of religion banished by implication from the weekday avocations: the characteristic conviction of the eighteenth century that the essential content of Christianity consisted in the recognition of a Supreme and Beneficent Creator and the inculcation of precepts of morality for the conduct of men in society: and the harmonious blend of mundane and other-worldly motives which inspired the village community to assemble weekly in church and churchyard. Nor without such understanding of the religious observance of the countryside is it possible to appreciate the religious standard and achievement of the Church of Georgian England. The numerous catalogue of adminis-trative anomalies which are alleged as the peculiar vice of the century—the residence of bishops in London for the greater part of the year, the extent of pluralism with the consequence of widespread non-residence, and the poverty of the majority of the parish clergy beneficed and un-beneficed—were in fact survivals of medieval abuses which had hindered the effective operation of the ecclesiastical system through many centuries and in particular had militated against the fulfilment of the pastoral ideal of the parochial ministry. The Georgian age was differentiated less by its quiet acceptance of such secular abuses than by the new religious temper which informed its belief and practice as a result of the popularity of the Latitudinarian school of churchmanship.

In external appearance the parish churches of Addison's England maintained the traditions bequeathed by the Protestant reforms of Tudor times. The Hanoverian age was not a period of church-building, and by consequence has left little expression of its spiritual ideas in architecture. Apart from the minority of churches actually built of the fifty new London churches approved by parliament in the reign of Anne, and the proprietary chapels which represented sporadic efforts of the end of the century, either to meet the new expansion of popula-tion, or to provide evangelical services for select congregations, hardly any church building stood to the credit of the epoch. At the outset, indeed, little general need for further construction existed, for the middle ages had endowed their successors liberally in provision of churches, and the revolutionary changes in the size and distribution of population created by industrial development presented a challenge beyond the capacity of the unreformed Church to meet in the last quarter of a dying century. The age was satisfied generally if it could keep in decent repair the sacred fabrics inherited from the piety of the past. The disparity between the increasing wealth of a prosperous commercial epoch and the poverty of endowments bestowed upon specifically religious objects such as church-building, was indeed the subject of comment in episcopal charges. Butler in his primary visitation at Durham in 1751 affirmed that

in the present turn of the age, one might observe a wonderful frugality in everything which has respect to religion, and extravagance in everything else. But amidst the appearances of opulence and improvement in all common things, which were then seen in most places, it would be hard to find a reason why those monuments of ancient piety should not be preserved in their original beauty and magnificence. But in the least opulent places they must be preserved in becoming repair.

In which connection he quoted the words of Fleetwood's charge at St Asaph in 1710 that "unless the good public spirit of building, repairing, and adorning churches prevailed a great deal more, and be more encouraged, an hundred years would bring to the ground an huge number of our churches".[1] In 1753 Secker exhorted the clergy of his diocese of Oxford to urge upon persons of rank and figure in their parishes their responsibility in regard to the keeping in repair of churches; reminding them

that sacred fabrics are appropriated to the noblest of uses, the worship of the great God; and to preserve them and put them in a condition suitable to it, is one very proper method of expressing and cherishing a sense of piety in their own minds, and spreading it through their families, neighbours and dependents; whereas by suffering His house to be an object of contempt and scorn, while perhaps they spare nothing to beautify their own, they will be understood and will tempt all around them, to despise the service performed there and Him to whom it is paid; and that repairing and embellishing their churches will employ the poor full as beneficially as adorning their seats and gardens, and procure them a much better grounded and more general esteem.

The bishop expressed indeed his surprise

that noblemen and gentlemen will squander vast sums in the gratification of private luxury and vanity, for which more condemn them than applaud them, and not consider that much smaller sums bestowed upon public works, especially in honour of religion, would gain them the admiration of a whole country.[2]

For the interior adornment of churches the century had one sovereign agent, the whitewash, which in addition to its cheapness and appearance of cleanliness, possessed for that age a symbolic value as typifying the dispersal of mysticism and obscurity by the penetration of the pure light of reason. Not only cathedrals of the English Church but that of Nôtre Dame de Paris suffered whitewashing from the laudable desire to inculcate in the minds of worshippers the doctrine that God is light, and in Him is no darkness at all. To an epoch persuaded of the falsity of mystery and reacting from its cultivation by the dim religious light, Gothic architecture seemed an abomination, the dark corners of whose buildings should be brought into the clear white light of day. In parish churches the liberal disposition of whitewash obliterated all except mural memorial tablets, commemorating the virtues of clergy and people in homely if untheological terms, and the panels of the east end containing scriptural texts. Upon the adornment of the sanctuary tradition laid

[1] Butler, Durham Charge (1751), i, 294. Butler's *Works* (ed. J. H. Bernard, 2 vols. 1900).
[2] Secker, Charge v, *Works*, v, 408–9.

much stress. The 82nd canon of the Canons of 1604 had required "that the Ten Commandments be set upon the east end of every church and chapel, where the people may best see and read the same, and other chosen sentences written upon the walls of the said churches and chapels in places convenient". Articles of visitation, both episcopal and archidiaconal, enquired particularly if this injunction were observed, and Sir Roger de Coverley, "being a good churchman had beautified the inside of his church with several texts of his own choosing". Current tradition attached much importance to these testimonies of the Protestant character of the Church.

"I have already said in speaking of chancels", observed Secker to his clergy in 1753, "that the ornaments of sacred places ought not to be light and gaudy, but modest and grave. Amongst these a very proper one, of the cheaper kind, is writing on the walls chosen sentences of Scripture. This was done as early as the fourth century; but in process of time, ceased to be done, at least in the vulgar tongue; and being restored at the Reformation, was forbidden as promoting that cause by bishop Bonner in Queen Mary's reign. It not only diversifies the walls very agreeably and decently, but affords useful matter for meditation for the people before the service begins; and may afford them useful admonition when their eyes and thoughts are wandering in the course of it. For these reasons, I presume, the 82nd Canon directs that such sentences be written in convenient places; and likewise that the Ten Commandments be set upon the east end of every church and chapel; to which undoubtedly the Creed and Lord's Prayer, though not mentioned in the canon, are very fit companions."[1]

Above these scriptural texts there stood generally the royal arms; their position, in the words of a contemporary writer, being chosen "to satisfy all those who tread the courts of the Lord's House and are diligent in the performance of their duty agreeably to the contents of these grand rules of the Christian religion, (viz. the Ten Commandments, the Lord's Prayer, and the Creed) that they shall meet with encouragement and protection from the state".[2]

Beneath the sanctuary walls, thus austerely adorned, there stood usually the Holy Table in correspondent simplicity of vesture, bearing a carpet of silk or other decent stuff in the time of divine service, and upon the celebration of the Sacrament covered further by a fair linen cloth. Other ornament it had usually none, save two candles, generally unlighted. The superimposition of a cross was infrequent, and Bishop Butler earned much notoriety by this innovation in the chapel of his

[1] Secker, Charge v, *Works*, v, 410.
[2] John Lucas, *History of Warton Parish* (ed. J. R. Ford and J. A. F. Maitland), p. 16.

palace at Bristol. The Marquis de la Rochefoucauld, visiting England in 1784, observed of the parish churches of East Anglia that even at the celebration of the Eucharist, the altar, "always placed at the end of the chancel, is entirely without ornament".[1] But upon occasion the Table might not stand in the sanctuary nor be railed, especially in the early years of the century when the race of Church Puritans was not yet extinct. Among the private acts of piety performed by Sir Roger de Coverley to his parish church was his giving "a handsome pulpit cloth and railing in the Communion Table at his own expense". The prescription of the 82nd canon was that the Holy Table at the time of administration "shall be placed in so good sort within the church or chancel as thereby the minister may be more conveniently heard of the communicants in his prayer and ministration, and the communicants also more conveniently and in more number, may communicate with the said minister". Mr Arthur Onslow, speaker of the house of commons from 1728 to 1761, recalled of Mr Edward Warner, rector of Merrow, near Guildford, with whom he had lodged during his schooldays, and who maintained the principles of the Church Puritans, that "during all his time the Communion Table stood in the middle of the chancel, and he administered the Sacrament always in that particular place and not at the east end". Onslow believed this custom to be not only "a matter of some curiosity" but also "the only instance of it remaining then in England";[2] but more than half a century later, under the date 1767, *The Blecheley Diary of William Cole* revealed that antiquary and high churchman of Georgian England, in preparation for the Christmas Communion at Waterbeche, ordering "the Table to be set under the middle east window, it being before in the middle of the chancel".[3] Typical of the history of many parish churches was the account of Warton Church compiled by John Lucas in the early eighteenth century, with its story of the vicissitudes of the Holy Table.

In the time of our happy Reformation, King Edward VI appointed that one decent Table should be provided for every parish to be set in the body of the church, where they remained until archbishop Laud's time, when it was removed to the east end of the choir and enclosed with rails; but the factious party soon after prevailing, they broke the rails down and levelled the place with the rest of the church; at the Restoration, 1660, the Altar Table was set in its place again, and the rails set up...about the year 1699.[4]

---

[1] *A Frenchman in England* (tr. S. C. Roberts), p. 85.
[2] Onslow MSS. p. 498. Hist. MSS. Comm. 14th Report, Appendix, Pt. IX.
[3] *The Blecheley Diary of William Cole*, 1765–7 (ed. H. Waddell), p. 304.
[4] John Lucas, *op. cit.*, p. 13.

Bishop Nicolson in his visitation of the diocese of Carlisle in 1703 found many instances correspondent to this record, and some churches in which the Holy Table on weekdays served as a desk on which the scholars of the parish wrote their exercises and rested their books; whilst Archdeacon Frank of Bedford reported to Bishop Wake in 1706 that within his jurisdiction "the Communion Tables were generally mean and used by the glaziers for the working of their glass, and by school-boys for writing". Where ornaments were found above the Holy Table, they took the form generally of painted altar-pieces, of which unhappily the two most famous were those of St Clement Danes, where a representation of St Cecilia was believed to be a portrait of the wife of the Old Pretender, and therefore a focus of Jacobite intrigue; and of Whitechapel, where the rector, Dr Welton, set up a painting of the Last Supper in which the features of Judas Iscariot were an exact copy of those of Bishop White Kennett. The general sentiment of the age disapproved of mural paintings in sacred edifices, as Bishop Newton found in his capacity of Dean of St Paul's when the project of Sir Joshua Reynolds for adorning the dome of his cathedral with divers pictures was vetoed by Bishop Terrick of London.

In the body of the parish churches the three-decker pulpit of the Georgian age has achieved the distinction of remembrance when all other features have been forgotten, save perhaps the pretentious pews, characteristic likewise of the period, which afforded opportunities for social intercourse and sleep during the progress of divine service. To the mind of one foreign visitor de la Rochefoucauld, the spectacle of the three-decker pulpit conveyed the erroneous persuasion that at divine service, "there are always two ministers, one in a pulpit and the other below him, who read alternately".[1] But the provision of pews was the chief feature of the Hanoverian century, ministering to the pride and ostentation of individuals rather than contributing to the decorum of public worship. In the satire of Swift, *Baucis and Philemon*, the article of domestic furniture most suitable for conversion into a pew was the bed.

> A bedstead of the antique mode,
> Compact of timber many a load,
> Such as our ancestors did use,
> Was metamorphosed into pews:
> Which still their ancient nature keep,
> By lodging folks disposed to sleep.

[1] *A Frenchman in England* (tr. S. C. Roberts), p. 85.

Even Sir Roger de Coverley was found upon occasion to have passed from the state of meditation to that of slumber, and the size and character of the private pews contributed undoubtedly to the prevalence of a standard of behaviour during divine service reminiscent of the irreverencies of the middle ages. For the poorer people whose places in church were encroached upon by this intrusion of pews, and who were relegated to seats with little prospect of the Holy Table or even of the pulpit, few accessories of worship were provided. Sir Roger de Coverley found further expression for his charity in an attempt to remedy this neglect. "He has often told me", recollected Addison, "that at his coming to his estate, he found his parishioners very irregular, and that in order to make them kneel and join in the responses, he gave every one of them a hassock and a common prayer book." Archdeacon Frank had noted in his visitations a similar reluctance on the part of the congregation to kneel during the prayers, for the remedy of which he adopted the method of Sir Roger by "the provision of mats for kneeling at the parish charge, the which he had secured in some parishes and hoped to effect in others", according to his report to his diocesan in 1706.

The prominence of the pulpit in Georgian churches and the weekly gathering of the parishioners to hear the sermon indicated the principal feature of public worship, namely the performance of the divine service of Morning or Evening Prayer accompanied by a discourse. In the preceding century George Herbert's account of the Sunday duties of the parson had emphasised the greater popularity of the sermon over sacramental worship; for according to his standard the parish priest,

having read divine service twice fully, and preached in the morning and catechised in the afternoon, thinks he hath in some measure, according to poor and fragile man, discharged the public duties of the congregation. The rest of the day he spends either in reconciling neighbours that are at variance, or in exhortations to some of his flock by themselves, whom his sermons cannot reach....At night he thinks it a fit time, both suitable to the joy of the day and without hindrance to public duties, either to entertain some of his neighbours or to be entertained of them.[1]

Further testimony to the importance of preaching is accorded by his rule that "the parson exceeds not an hour in preaching, because all ages have thought that a competency".[2] More than a century later the

[1] G. Herbert, *A Priest to the Temple*, ch. VIII, "The Parson on Sundays".
[2] *Ibid*. ch. VII, "The Parson Preaching".

Marquis de la Rochefoucauld was impressed by these characteristics of the English services to which he was taken by his East Anglian hosts.

I went to service on two occasions. It lasts an hour and a half, and consists of a prayer in which the people make their responses to the minister, followed by a reading from the Bible, and a sermon. . . . The sermon is based on a text, which is either some point of morals, or a passage from Scripture, or something calculated to enjoin observance of the laws. The evening service is shorter. Everything that is read, or spoken, or preached is in English so that it may be within the reach of everybody.[1]

Practical obstacles indeed prevented the realisation of this standard of Sunday duty in a majority of parishes, since the effect of pluralism and non-residence was to deprive them of one of the two services of the day on Sunday. The returns to Archbishop Herring's Visitation Articles at York in 1743 revealed that of 836 churches making replies, 453 "failed to have both Matins and Evensong on Sunday all the year round", whilst 383 attained to this standard.[2] Similar conditions were indicated in the diocese of London (excepting the cities of London and Westminster) during the episcopate of Gibson in 1742, when of 466 churches represented in the returns to visitation queries, 236 maintained divine service twice every Sunday, and 210 once, whilst twenty parishes fell below the minimum of one weekly service. The number of small benefices which compelled their incumbents to serve two churches each Sunday necessarily deprived many parishes of the full complement of Sunday services, and bishops generally accepted the compromise of one service with sermon in each of two churches, whilst discouraging as far as lay within their power the performance by the same person of divine service in three different churches each Lord's day.

The combination of interests, political and religious, which brought the country worshippers to church as depicted by Addison was not wholly conducive to the decorum of public worship. Archbishop Secker suggested indeed the suspicion that the discussion of parish politics in the churchyard before service began led to disturbance of its course by the frequent entry of late-comers who had given statecraft a preference over divinity.

Another thing, and no small one, which I believe many of your parishioners often want to be admonished of, is to come before the service begins. Undoubtedly allowance is to be made for necessary, especially unforeseen,

---

[1] *A Frenchman in England* (tr. S. C. Roberts), pp. 84–5.
[2] *Archbishop Herring's Visitation Returns* (ed. S. L. Ollard and P. C. Walker), i, p. xv.

business, and some allowance for not knowing the time exactly; but I hope you will obviate both these pleas as far as you can, by consulting their convenience in the hour you fix, and then keeping punctually to it. And at the same time you will remind them, that a due degree of zeal in religion would incline them to be rather a great deal too early at the house of God than a little too late; that no part of the service can be more needful for them than that which comes first, the confession of their sins; that instruction in their duty is better learnt from the psalms and lessons, which are the word of God, than from sermons, which are only our explanation of it; and that by coming so irregularly, they not only are great losers themselves, but disturb and offend others.[1]

Once safely ushered within the sacred edifice, the type of service at which they assisted has been made often the butt of satire and ridicule. The most unfavourable account may be taken from the testimony of an opponent, the edge of whose criticism was sharpened by the rancour of religious rivalry. John Wesley in 1757, writing to a correspondent in Truro in defence of the public worship of the Methodist societies, contrasted it to its own great advantage with the divine office of the Established Church, both in regard to the official performance of the minister and the behaviour and devotion of the congregation.

The longer I am absent from London, and the more I attend the service of the Church in other places, the more I am convinced of the unspeakable advantage which the people called Methodists enjoy; I mean even with regard to public worship, particularly on the Lord's Day. The church where they assemble is not gay or splendid, which might be an hindrance on the one hand; nor sordid or dirty which might give distaste on the other; but plain as well as clean. The persons who assemble there are not a gay, giddy crowd, who come chiefly to see and be seen; nor a company of goodly, formal, outside Christians, whose religion lies in a dull round of duties; but a people most of whom do, and the rest earnestly seek to, worship God in spirit and in truth. Accordingly they do not spend their time there in bowing and courtesying, or in staring about them, but in looking upward and looking inward, in hearkening to the voice of God, and pouring out their hearts before Him.

It is also no small advantage that the person who reads prayers, though not always the same, yet is always one who may be supposed to speak from his heart, one whose life is no reproach to his profession, and one who performs that solemn part of divine service, not in a careless, hurrying, slovenly manner, but seriously and slowly, as becomes him who is transacting so high an affair between God and man.

[1] Secker, Charge II, *Works*, v, 346.

Nor are their solemn addresses to God interrupted either by the formal drawl of a parish clerk, the screaming of boys who bawl out what they neither feel nor understand, or the unseasonable and unmeaning impertinence of a voluntary on the organ. When it is seasonable to sing praise to God they do it with the spirit and with the understanding also; not in the miserable, scandalous doggerel of Hopkins and Sternhold, but in psalms and hymns which are both sense and poetry, such as would sooner provoke a critic to turn Christian than a Christian to turn critic. What they sing is therefore a proper continuation of the spiritual and reasonable service; being selected for that end, not by a poor humdrum wretch who can scarce read what he drones out with such an air of importance, but by one who knows what he is about and how to connect the preceding with the following part of the service. Nor does he take just "two staves", but more or less, as may best raise the soul to God; especially when sung in well-composed and well-adapted tunes, not by an handful of unawakened striplings, but by an whole serious congregation; and these not lolling at ease, or in the indecent posture of sitting, drawling out one word after another, but all standing before God and praising Him lustily and with a good courage.[1]

The indictment loses in force what it gains in comprehensiveness, for it omits no item of the public service of the church susceptible to disparagement, however innocent or laudable in itself. The discerning may select the points upon which criticism found its proper target; the indecorous behaviour of many worshippers, nestled securely within their pews designed more for slumber than devotion, or of the poorer sort whose places encouraged ill-attendance upon the sacred service, concerning which many episcopal charges offered warning and admonition; the uncleanly state of many fabrics despite frequent episcopal exhortation and archidiaconal remonstrance; the easy target for contempt furnished by the parish clerk upon whose shoulders fell the responsibility for the selection of psalms and the leading of the singing by his introductory "two staves" to the congregation (even Parson Woodforde recorded on one occasion that "his clerk made a shocking hand of it in singing that afternoon at church—much laughed at");[2] and the debatable virtues of Hopkins and Sternhold's metrical version of the psalter. Yet allowance being made for fair comment, there remains much in Wesley's philippic which caricatured rather than represented the divine service of the country Sunday which had delighted the heart of the essayist of *The Spectator*. In particular the problem of

[1] John Wesley to a Correspondent, 20 Sept. 1757. *Letters of John Wesley*, iii, pp. 226–8, Standard edition.
[2] *The Diary of a Country Parson*, iii, 292 (14 Aug. 1791).

congregational singing was one of real difficulty to the parish clergy. Amongst the good works performed by Sir Roger de Coverley to his parishioners was the generosity with which "he employed an itinerant singing master who went about the country for that purpose, to instruct them rightly in the tunes of the psalms, upon which they now very much value themselves and indeed outdo most of the country churches". A frequent theme in episcopal charges was the duty of providing aids and helps towards a congregational rendering of psalmody, together with the distribution of selected courses of singing psalms whereby the eccentricities of parish clerks might be avoided. Typical of such injunctions and valuable as a corrective of Wesley's denunciation was the counsel of Secker to his clergy in 1741.

Another part of divine worship concerning which I think it needful to speak, is psalmody; a part clearly appointed in Scripture, both expressive and productive of devout affections, extremely well fitted to diversify long services, and peculiarly to distinguish the several parts of our own, which were originally separate....You will always endeavour that your parish clerks be persons of discretion as well as skill and seriousness. But however, you will be much surer of no impropriety happening in this part of the worship if you either direct them every Sunday to suitable psalms, or assign them a course of such to go orderly through. And unless the generality of your parish are provided with books, and able to make use of them, ordering each line to be read will both secure a greater number of singers, and be very instructive to many who cannot sing. All persons indeed who are by nature qualified, ought to learn, and constantly join to glorify Him that made them, in psalms and spiritual songs....For the improvements made by a few in church music, were they real improvements, will seldom equal the harmony of a general chorus, in which any lesser dissonances are quite lost; and it is something inexpressibly elevating, to hear the voice of a great multitude, as the voice of many waters and of mighty thunders, to speak in the words of Scripture, making a joyful noise to the God of their salvation, and singing His praises with understanding. Persons of a ludicrous turn may represent everything in a wrong light; but those of any seriousness, if they will lay aside false delicacy, and that preposterous shame of religious performances with which the present age is so fatally tainted, will find themselves very piously affected only by hearing this melody, much more by bearing a part in it; and therefore I beg you will encourage all your parishioners, especially the youth, to learn psalmody, and excite them, if there be need, with some little reward; for you will thus make the service of God abundantly more agreeable and their attendance on it more constant.[1]

[1] Secker, Charge II, *Works*, v, 343-4.

The translation of such precept into practice was not easy. Parson Woodforde in his curacy at Castle Cary had difficulties with the Cary singers.

"I sent my clerk some time back to the Cary singers, to desire that they would not sing the Responses in the Communion Service," runs an entry in his diary of 12 November 1769; "which they complied with for several Sundays, but this morning after the first Commandment, they had the impudence to sing the Response; and therefore I spoke to them out of my desk, to say and not sing the Responses, which they did after, and at other places they sang as usual."[1]

At Weston, his relations with the singers and appreciation of their endeavours were exceedingly cordial. On 15 April 1792 he recorded that "the Elsing singers sang at Weston Church that afternoon and tolerably well indeed", so that he "gave them by way of encouragement 2s. 6d."; and on 26 August following he noted with pride that "the Weston singers sung at church for the first time", his pleasure in the performance being such that on 9 September he gave them a guinea towards books, and on Christmas Day again observed that they "sang the Christmas anthem at church and very well indeed".[2] Accordingly, when on 21 April 1793 divine service was unaccompanied by singing, he was offended. "The Weston singers talk of giving it up", recorded his diary: "which I think is behaving towards me very shabby, as I gave them a guinea to purchase books, and likewise gave them 5 shillings at Christmas".[3] Happily they returned on the first Sunday of the following month, and further pleasant tributes to their performance found due record in the diarist's pages; as when on Christmas Day 1793 "the singers sang the Christmas anthem very well, between the Litany and Communion".[4] Instrumental music further diversified the performance when "the Mattishall singers were at church and sung exceedingly well, attended with a bass-viol and a hautboy" in the following February.[5] During the last years of Parson Woodforde's life he was much incapacitated by illness, and when in July 1800 the Mattishall singers again visited Weston Church, the curate Mr Dade forbade them to sing; but the final note of the diary is an extract from a letter of 1803 announcing that under Woodforde's successor the church was to enjoy singing again.

[1] *The Diary of a Country Parson*, i, 92. It will be noted that Woodforde read the Ante Communion from his desk, not at the Holy Table.
[2] *Ibid.* iii, 345, 370, 372, 400.　　　　[3] *Ibid.* iv, 21.
[4] *Ibid.* iv, 87.　　　　[5] *Ibid.* iv, 97.

The popular demand for a sermon as the condition of attendance at church was emphasised further, in churches which had the good fortune of divine service twice each Sunday, by the difficulties surrounding the afternoon reading of prayers without preaching. The 59th canon required "every parson, vicar, or curate upon every Sunday and holy-day before Evening Prayer" for the space of half an hour or more, to "examine and instruct the youth and ignorant persons of his parish in the Ten Commandments, Articles of Belief, and in the Lord's Prayer", and to "hear, instruct, and teach them the catechism as set forth in the Book of Common Prayer". Endeavours were made accordingly to persuade adult parishioners to consider the exposition of the catechism at the afternoon prayers as equivalent in interest and edification to the sermon. In 1700 Thomas Brockbank reported to the bishop of Chester the result of conversations with the inhabitants of Cartmel concerning the condition of their church. "They complain that their pulpit is always empty in the afternoon; and when I would have persuaded them that the latter part of the Lord's Day might be as well, or better, employed in catechising, reading of Homilies, expounding the doctrine of the Church &c., as in preaching, they assented to what I said, but told me that none of these things were done."[1] Archbishop Secker attempted to turn the flank of the ubiquitous argument that people would rather walk to a more distant church where an afternoon sermon was being preached than attend their parish church only for the reading of prayers by urging the development of the catechising into similar form.

If the number of people be small, the service is not less enjoined, and is more easily performed. If they had rather have a sermon at another church, than merely prayers at their own, they ought to have more than prayers, an exposition of the catechism, which they will account equivalent to a sermon; or you may reduce it with ease into the form of a sermon, and then many of them will come to their own church who now go to no other but prophane the rest of the day.[2]

In like manner Wake upon his elevation to the see of Lincoln exhorted his clergy both publicly and in private to pay particular diligence to the catechism of the young. "I am glad to hear", he wrote to Dr Charlett, Master of University College, Oxford, and rector of Hambleden, "that your curate is so constant and canonical in his catechising. It is my

---

[1] *The Diary and Letter Book of the Rev. Thomas Brockbank* (ed. R. Trappes-Lomax), p. 187.
[2] Secker, Charge VI, *Works*, v, 429.

earnest desire to revive the credit and practice of it in the diocese of Lincoln, for by experience I found that I did more good to my parish and got more and better notions of divinity myself by my catechising than by all my preaching."[1] Accordingly in 1711 he issued a formal letter to his archdeacons, in which he lamented "the neglect of catechising, which though both the canon expressly required all ministers to perform every Sunday and holy-day without distinction, and the rubric ordered it to be performed diligently by them at the same times, yet it was but too notorious that this useful exercise was omitted in many places, not only upon holy-days, but even upon Sundays and reserved to the short time of Lent". This he declared to be "a neglect which ought by all means to be reformed".

Such aspirations were doomed to disappointment, for exhortations to greater frequency of catechising became mere counsels of perfection, and the practice tended generally to be confined to the season of Lent, supplemented by additional instruction when notice was received of an impending visitation and Confirmation by the bishop. No feature of Parson Woodforde's diary is more curious and striking than the absence from its voluminous pages of reference to his catechising of the youth of Weston. It may be doubted whether any impression could be formed from his record of the traditional place of the catechism in the ecclesiastical discipline. Even his sermon preached "on the benefits and use of Confirmation" upon receipt of the bishop's appointment of a Confirmation day in his neighbourhood, followed by the visit of "thirteen young people come to be examined" preparatory to the administration of the rite (to whom he kindly gave "cake and a glass of wine"), do not suggest any particularly detailed or strict form of instruction.[2] The evidence of *The Blecheley Diary* makes clear the practice of the high churchman, William Cole, whose catechising was confined to Vespers on the Sundays during Lent; though, like Woodforde, on receipt of notice of the approach of a Confirmation he preached two sermons on that subject and examined the several candidates from his parish, giving to each a ticket to certify his approbation after examination.[3] Further testimony to this end is furnished by the returns to Archbishop Herring's Visitation Returns, which reveal the clergy's endeavours to fulfil this duty either during the Lenten season or upon Sundays in summer when daylight and other conditions favoured the enterprise; a condition of

[1] Wake to Charlett, 26 July 1707. Ballard MSS. iii, f. 42.
[2] *The Diary of a Country Parson*, iv, 135–40.
[3] *The Blecheley Diary of William Cole*, pp. 19, 96, 98–9. "I catechised the children, as usual, in the afternoon, all Lent."

affairs prevalent also in the diocese of Exeter according to the Visitation Returns of Bishop Claggett in 1744.[1] In general the episcopate had to be content with such observation of this responsibility as they could secure, accepting approximation to the canonical rule in lieu of literal performance. Secker, despite his theoretical injunctions, realised the necessity of compromise. Commenting on the canonical standard of catechism every Sunday, he observed,

Not that a strict observation of this rule was probably expected during the winter season in the generality of country parishes, or where the children, being few, were more easily taught. But plainly it was intended that how much time soever was needful to do this work well, should be faithfully employed in it. I thank God there are few places in this diocese, and I hope there will soon be none, where catechising is omitted. But I observe that in many it is practised only in Lent. Now I should apprehend that the summer season would in general be much more convenient both for the minister and the congregation. But at least the space of a few weeks is by no means sufficient to fix the knowledge of their Christian duty so firmly in the minds of young people, but that in the many months which pass from the end of one Lent to the beginning of another, a great part of it will be to learn again. Therefore whenever this exercise is begun, it should be continued much longer; and whenever the constant repetition of it is left off, it should be occasionally resumed for a Sunday or two, at proper distances of time.... I am sensible that some clergymen are unhappily obliged to serve two churches the same afternoon: who may therefore plead that they have scarce ever time to hear the children repeat their catechism, much less explain it to them. And God forbid that any needless addition should ever be made to their burden. But as I am sure they will be desirous of doing what they are able, in a matter of this importance, so I should hope that in the longer days, at each of their churches alternately, they might hear the catechism repeated one Sunday and expound part of another, or hear only part of it repeated and expound that, or find some way to prevent the entire omission of so necessary a duty.[2]

More than three-quarters of a century after this exhortation of Secker, John Skinner, the rector of Camerton, Somerset, informed the children of his parish in 1826 that "he would hear their catechism that ensuing Lent in church";[3] and the reality of his teaching was testified by his action in 1823 when in preparation for Confirmation he "heard the

[1] "An Eighteenth-Century Visitation", by H. R. Gamble, Dean of Exeter, in *The Church Times*, 4 November 1921.
[2] Secker, Charge II (Oxford, 1741), *Works*, v, 333–6.
[3] *The Journal of a Somerset Rector* (ed. H. Coombes and H. N. Box), p. 107.

children at their catechism and explained the several Articles", refusing to give the ticket of admission for confirmation to fourteen collier boys who would not say their catechism.[1] Mr Skinner, a Latitudinarian surviving out of due time into the stormy days of the first Reform Bill, was indeed particularly exacting in his preparation for confirmation, as his delivery in August and September 1824 of a course of sermons on that rite indicated; wherein he purposed to explain "the promises made for them at the time of their baptism, which promises, now they were come of age, they were themselves bound to perform", and also to "enlarge upon the ceremony of Confirmation, established in the early ages of the church, and continued to the present time".[2] At his first coming to Camerton he had established a Sunday School, whilst he was a staunch champion of the foundation of National Schools, and his parish possessed six day schools, which sufficed for the education of girls and young boys, though further provision was needed for the older boys. Despite these improvements in the means of education, he had to struggle hard to secure the religious instruction of the youth and found the task of catechising little easier than his predecessors of the mid-century, who complained that the majority of the children of their parishes too often needed to be taught reading before they could understand the catechism.

The neglect of catechising was paralleled by the decline in the observance of holy days, and of weekday public prayers. In this respect indeed the beginning of disuse was noted in the first decade of the century by Bishop Beveridge, who observed that "daily prayers were shamefully neglected all the kingdom over, there being very few places where they had public prayers upon the week-days, except perhaps on Wednesdays and Fridays".[3] Similar testimony was borne by Wake at Lincoln in 1711, who, after reciting the several obligations upon the clergy—of performing divine service upon all Sundays, holy days, and the eves of both, of reading the Litany on Wednesday and Friday of every week, and of saying Morning and Evening Prayers daily either privately or openly—declared that "whatever might be pretended against such a constant usage of the daily service in the church, certain it was that no allowance was made for the omission of it upon Litany days, holydays, Sundays and their eves". With the advance of the century country churches slipped into increasing neglect. William Cole

[1] *The Journal of a Somerset Rector*, p. 56.
[2] *Ibid.* p. 85.
[3] W. Beveridge, "Necessity and Advantages of Public Prayer", quoted in Abbey and Overton, ii, 443.

at Blecheley indeed read Matins on saints' days and daily during Holy
Week, but the absence from the pages of Woodforde's diary of mention
of these festivals suggests a lack of observance of their incidence by
public prayers at Weston; though at Castle Cary he had read divine
service on St John Baptist's Day, New Year's Day and the Epiphany,
and on Ash Wednesday, whilst on St Luke's Day 1766 he had noted
that he "entirely forgot that this was St Luke's Day and therefore did
not read prayers at Castle Cary, which he would have done otherwise",
adding that "as it was not done wilfully, he hoped God would forgive
it".[1] Nor when the clergy fulfilled their part by offering services, did
the laity always accompany them. When Parson Adams read the service
on a holy day, his congregation consisted usually of his wife, his clerk,
and an occasional visitor, the paucity of whose number testified to the
disinclination of country parishioners to attend weekday prayers. The
same difficulty presented itself to William Cole, whose diary recorded
the scanty attendance upon saints' days and upon occasion his abandonment of the intention to read service since no parishioners appeared.
The general disesteem in which saints' days were held is illustrated by
the comment of Archbishop Herring to Lord Hardwicke in 1750 that
"he wanted to form a right judgment as to the reform of the calendar
and how many of the old saints policy and the business of the world
would require should be kept in, for religion had nothing to do with it".[2]
With regard to weekday prayers on ferial days, the observance of
Wednesdays and Fridays during Lent proved generally the maximum
attainable in rural parishes, as at Blecheley during the ministrations of
Cole, albeit a high churchman. Archbishop Sharp had desired that his
clergy should "more particularly oblige themselves to the reading of
prayers on Wednesdays and Fridays and holydays, or in populous
towns every day, unless they were hindered by some urgent business";[3]
but the diocese of York in 1743, according to Herring's Visitation
Returns, had only twenty-four churches with daily prayers, representing
the chief towns of Yorkshire and Nottinghamshire, eighty with services
on Wednesdays, Fridays and holy days, and of the total of 836 parishes
only "253 had some kind of weekday service more or less frequently".[4]
Bishop Butler lamented the disappearance of religious observance from
the weekday life of the community, despite the provision of the Prayer
Book for public service. "A great part of this", he observed to his

[1] *The Diary of a Country Parson*, i, 48, 61, 70.
[2] Herring to Hardwicke. 28 July, 1750. Add MSS. 35599, f. 13.
[3] *Life of Archbishop John Sharp*, i, 188.
[4] *Archbishop Herring's Visitation Returns*, i, pp. xv–xvi.

clergy at Durham in 1751, "is neglected by the generality amongst us; for instance, the service of the Church, not only upon common days, but also upon saints' days. Thus they have no customary admonition, no public call to recollect the thoughts of God and religion from one Sunday to another." So convinced was he of the popular antipathy to public service on weekdays that he cast about for alternative means of preserving the sense of the religious significance of common days.

Since the body of the people, especially in country places, cannot be brought to attend it oftener than one day in a week, and since this is in no sort enough to keep up in them a due sense of religion, it were greatly to be wished they could be persuaded to anything which might, in some measure, supply the want of more frequent public devotions or serve the like purpose. Family prayers, regularly kept up in every house, would have a great and good effect.[1]

Even more despairing was Secker's review of the decay of weekday religious observance.

"It is appointed that all ministers of parishes read prayers on holydays, on Wednesdays and Fridays," he reminded the clergy of the diocese of Oxford in 1741; "and undoubtedly your endeavours to procure a congregation at such times ought not to be wanting. . . . Where you can get a competent number to attend at these times, you will act a very pious and useful as well as regular part; your own houses will sometimes furnish a small congregation, and what success you may have with others, nothing but trials, repeated from time to time, can inform you. But they whose parishioners are the fewest and the busiest of all, I hope do not fail of bringing them to church at the least on Good Friday and Christmas Day, besides Sundays. For though in some of your answers to my enquiries, these are not mentioned as prayer days, yet I presume that this arose from your taking it for granted I should understand they were. But if in any place they be not, I earnestly intreat they may; for at such times there can be no difficulty of getting a congregation. I hope likewise that you are not wanting in due regard to those which are usually called state holydays."[2]

In great part the indifference to weekday prayers resulted from the omission of a sermon, since even on Good Fridays Parson Woodforde, though diligent in the reading of divine service, never essayed the preaching of a sermon as a means of attracting more of his parishioners to the public remembrance of that solemn day. It was counted an act of particular piety in Dr Johnson that "he went more frequently to

---

[1] Butler, Durham Charge (1751), *op. cit.* i, 294–5.
[2] Secker, Charge II, *Works*, v, 350–1.

church when there were prayers only, than when there was also a sermon, as the people required more an example for the one than the other, it being much easier for them to hear a sermon than to fix their minds on prayer".[1] Lacking equally in the provision of a sermon, the state holy days held the advantage over ecclesiastical saints' days of their relation to immediate and contemporary events, which, especially during the Jacobite fears of the beginning and the revolutionary wars of the end of the century, pressed with urgent crisis upon the attention. The attack of insanity indeed which afflicted George III in 1788 moved Woodforde to the unusual utterance of extempore prayer, when on Sunday 16 November he offered suffrages for his majesty "out of his own head, no prayer [having] yet arrived" from ecclesiastical authority.[2]

In their administration of the sacraments the clergy maintained such a standard of regularity as the prevailing conditions of pluralism and non-residence permitted. James Woodforde showed great diligence in baptising the children of his parish, whether the numerous scions of the Custance household whose presentation was accompanied by the generous gift of a five guinea note, or the sons and daughters of the poorer amongst his flock to whose parents in turn he generously remitted the fee for churching because of their necessity. Characteristic likewise of his age was the frequency with which he administered the rite privately outside the church, a custom dictated often by practical necessity in view of the high rate of infant mortality, but lending itself in the hands of careless clergy to accompaniments more suggestive of a mundane feast than a religious ordinance. Mr Cole of Blecheley was induced to baptise an infant in the parlour of his house, where also he churched its mother, immediately after having married its parents in church; which irregularity he attempted to justify by pleading that "as the discipline of our church, through the practices of dissenters, is now so relaxed as to come to nothing, there is no parleying with one's parishioners on any point of doctrine or discipline".[3] Such practices occasioned the admonition of Secker to his clergy that they must "go through every office of religion with dignity", especially that of baptism;

which, when administered in private houses without necessity is too often treated, even during the administration, rather as an idle ceremony, than a Christian sacrament; or however that may be, is commonly close followed

---

[1] Boswell, *Life of Johnson*, 5 April 1772.
[2] *The Diary of a Country Parson*, iii, 65–6.
[3] *The Blecheley Diary of William Cole*, p. 8.

by very unsuitable, if not otherwise also indecent levity and jollity. In these circumstances it is highly requisite that the minister should, by a due mixture of gravity and judgment, support the solemnity of the ordinance; and either prevent improprieties in the sequel, or if it be doubtful whether he can, excuse himself, with a civil intimation of the unfitness of them, from being present.[1]

It is however with regard to the infrequency of its administration of the Holy Communion that the Georgian Church has drawn upon itself more criticism and disfavour than in relation to any other aspect of its religious tradition. The customary divine service in the morning on Sundays was that of Morning Prayer with the Ante Communion, an ordering of public worship which commended itself to the generality of country clergy as conformable to the practice of their fathers and which they performed without prescience of the singular exegesis by which their usage would be brought by their successors within the ambit of catholic tradition by its interpretation as the Missa Catechumenorum. Controversy indeed arose concerning the proper place from which the minister should say the Ante Communion, whether at the Holy Table or at his reading desk; and it is not without interest therefore to note that Parson Woodforde in his curacy at Castle Cary, when rebuking the singers because they sang the Responses to the Commandments, "spoke to them out of my desk".[2] Secker argued from the constant reading of the Ante Communion that the congregation should be moved to proceed to communicate more frequently, since "part of the Office is read every Lord's day in every church for an admonition of what it were to be wished the people could be brought to".[3] The tradition of infrequent Communion was the legacy of the past. George Herbert, writing in the early seventeenth century, had observed "touching the frequency of the Communion, the parson celebrates it, if not duly once a month, yet at least five or six times in the year: as at Easter, Christmas, Whitsuntide, afore and after harvest, and the beginning of Lent".[4] During the Hanoverian age the general standard in country parishes was established at four Sacrament Sundays each year, on the three great festivals of the Church, and in the autumn after the ingathering of the harvest. This quarterly celebration of the Holy Communion was observed throughout the years of Woodforde's incumbency at Weston, and satisfied no less the principles of the high churchman Cole at Blecheley. More frequent celebrations were main-

---

[1] Secker, Charge VII, *Works*, v, 452.   [2] *The Diary of a Country Parson*, i, 92.
[3] Secker, Charge II, *op. cit.* v, 432.
[4] *A Priest to the Temple*, ch. XXII, "The Parson in Sacraments".

tained by churches in the larger provincial towns, but the rule of Weston and Blecheley applied widely to the country churches of which they were typical. Of the 836 churches represented in the Returns to Herring's Visitation Articles at York in 1743, only seventy-two attained the standard of monthly celebrations, 363 had quarterly Sacraments, and 208 fell below this standard, whilst 193 varied between four and six Sacrament days each year.[1] The general acceptance of the quarterly Communion was testified by Secker's exhortation to his clergy to persuade their parishioners to more frequent Communion.

"One thing might be done at present in all your parishes," he observed, "as, God be thanked, it is in most of them; a Sacrament might easily be interposed in that long interval between Whitsuntide and Christmas; and the usual season for it, about the feast of St Michael (when your people having gathered in the fruits of the earth have some rest from their labours, and must surely feel some gratitude to the Giver of all good) is a very proper time. And if afterwards you can advance from a quarterly communion to a monthly one, I make no doubt but you will."[2]

The infrequent celebration of the Holy Communion by no means implied paucity of communicants. Indeed a striking feature of the century generally was the large proportion of adult parishioners who communicated at Easter. Typical instances of the numbers attending the Easter Sacrament might be quoted from country parishes in all dioceses. In the extensive diocese of York in the middle of the century, at Bolton upon Dearn, Doncaster, there were about eighty communicants, of which "near one half usually received, and above 70 received the last Easter";[3] at Brompton, Rydall of "about 237 communicants, 200 usually received";[4] at Linton in Craven, which embraced 160 families, there were fifty communicants at the quarterly Sacrament and about 300 at Easter;[5] at Mansfield, Nottingham, of near 500 communicants, about fifty received at the monthly celebrations and about 200 at Easter;[6] at Aston, and Arksey, near Doncaster each parish had about 200 communicants of whom about 160 communicated at each church at Easter;[7] and at Almondbury, where the total number of communicants was estimated at about 5000, at Easter 1343 received, whereof the vicar

[1] *Archbishop Herring's Visitation Returns*, i, pp. xvi–xvii. Cf. "An Eighteenth Century Visitation", "An Early Nineteenth Century Visitation", by H. R. Gamble, Dean of Exeter, in *The Church Times*, 4 Nov. 1921 and 29 Aug. 1924.
[2] Secker, Charge II, *Works*, v, 342.
[3] *Archbishop Herring's Visitation Returns*, i, 73.
[4] *Ibid.* i, 91.   [5] *Ibid.* ii, 146.
[6] *Ibid.* iv, 178.   [7] *Ibid.* i, 21–3.

related that "he had nobody to assist him and was frequently in the church from 10 o'clock to near 2 before he had finished the Communion service", adding that "the truth was, he had work upon his hands sufficient to employ a dozen clergymen, and when a case happened thus, a man must be content (let his intentions be never so upright) with a very imperfect discharge of his duty".[1] Similar testimony may be gathered from the diary of Mr Bulkeley of Brynddu in the parish of Llanfechell of the county of Anglesey, which covered the period from 1734 to 1760 and embraced various items of ecclesiastical interest. In this parish of ninety families, the number of Easter communicants in 1734 was 230, whilst in the last year of the diary, 1760, the figure stood at 217.[2] The Registrar of the diocese of Bangor indeed has produced evidence from the most unpromising quarter (for the see of Bangor has borne more than its proper share of the opprobrium cast upon the contemporary Church) of the vigour of church life in north Wales in the middle of the eighteenth century. His summary of the Returns made to the Visitation Articles of Bishop Zachary Pearce in 1749 indicates that "the Holy Communion was administered on the great festivals at least, and in most parishes monthly, and the children were catechised as a rule every Sunday in Lent....The number of communicants at Easter is very remarkable when we consider the population of the parishes, and seems to show that, after making allowance for the young, the old, and the infirm, the main body of adults were communicants".[3]

Canon Ollard was likewise much impressed by the evidence accorded by Archbishop Herring's Returns of widespread popular fidelity to the Easter Eucharist.

The figures of "communicants" in the parishes are often startling in their size. Examination of the point has made it clear that the term "communicant" is used in the sense of "potential communicant", that is, they are of age to become communicants and might be communicants if they wished. Further, in comparing the number of Easter communicants with the figures of to-day, it must be remembered that the Test and other acts were still in force, and that not to be a communicant argued a disagreement with the state in the matter of religion.[4]

In view of the relative infrequency of episcopal confirmation tours and particularly of the difficulties of journeying through so large a diocese

[1] *Archbishop Herring's Visitation Returns*, i, 17–18.
[2] A. I. Pryce, *The Diocese of Bangor during Three Centuries*, p. lvii.
[3] *Ibid.* p. lxii.
[4] *Archbishop Herring's Visitation Returns*, i, pp. xx–xxi.

as that of York, it was essential to adopt the permissive admission to the Communion, according to the rubric prefaced to the Order of Confirmation, of persons desirous to be confirmed when opportunity was afforded. It is uncertain how much weight should be allowed to the contention concerning the political attendance of the dissenters; for whereas on the one hand such communions were relatively small in numbers, on the other hand, according to the practice of many dissenters since 1662, the privilege of occasional communion with the Church as a symbol of charity and religious concord continued to be used and valued, and contributed undoubtedly to the impressive totals of Easter communicants. Canon Ollard is on safer ground in drawing attention to the fact that in the mid-eighteenth century there was in most country parishes "no real rival to the Church", until the influence of the Methodist movement was felt in the revivification of the principles of dissent. At the outset indeed the effect of the Methodist revival was to increase the numbers of communicants, since John Wesley exhorted his followers to "keep close to the Church and Sacrament", that is, to maintain membership of the National Church and as a particular sign thereof to communicate regularly at their parish churches. But the impossibility of securing permanent obedience to this counsel became evident as early as 1755, when incidents occurred of some Methodist preachers administering the Communion to some adherents of their societies; and the majority of Wesley's converts were themselves indifferent whether the Communion which they received were that of the episcopal church or not. The extension of the movement, especially in the new centres of industrial population, increased the proportion of adherents unattached by any bond to the Church; and the demand for Communion administered within the Methodist societies withdrew their members from attendance upon the parish churches, until the logic of development drove Wesley himself into acts of formal schism. The clergy of the last decades of the eighteenth and the early period of the nineteenth centuries, harassed by the aggressive organisation of the Methodist churches which had recreated the principles of dissent on an unprecedented scale, lamented, like John Skinner at Camerton, the decline in the number of their communicants and the desertion of parishioners running after strange traditions. But these changes belonged to the last generation of the age, and the Church of the early and middle Georgian epoch appeared secure in the affections of the people as testified by their fidelity to the Paschal Eucharist. Parson Woodforde found the pleasant backwater of his country parish at Weston little disturbed by Methodist incursions, and the pages of his diary are singularly free from echoes of the controversies between churchmen and dissenters, and the rancour following therefrom. In 1783 he noted with more curiosity than spleen that at the Christmas Communion, "amongst the rest was his thatcher Harrison, and received the Holy Sacrament from his hands: he was reputed to be a rank Methodist"; and in 1801, the year before his course was finished, he made the placid entry under the date 27 April that "a Methodist meeting we heard is held at Whisson's house on Sundays—very near us".[1]

The religious observances of the churches of the cities of London and Westminster require separate mention, for the different standards of public service prevalent in them and in the country churches were as striking as the disparity in the temporal condition of the clergy who served them. The parishes of the capital attracted to their incumbency the most eminent divines of the age. Many were held *in commendam* by bishops or in plurality by cathedral dignitaries, who found in them useful pulpits for their exercise of the ministry of the word during their residence in London. The London churches accordingly set forth the best divinity and oratory of the times, and even into their inferior pastoral offices clergy of talent and ability were recruited in the hope of commending themselves to the notice of influential patrons. The brightest young divines from the universities accepted curacies or lectureships in the capital as a recognised vantage point for future preferment. The position of Lecturer was particularly coveted, and the list of prelates who had adorned this office testified to its importance as a first stage on the ladder of promotion. The biographer of Archbishop Sharp considered that in the early years of his career "that which most tended to advance his character in the pulpit was his taking the Friday lecture at St Lawrence Jewry . . . where there was not so much a concourse of people as a convention of divines, especially those of the city who had customarily attended those lectures from the time that Dr Tillotson, who was the Tuesday lecturer, had so successfully led the way in reforming the method and style of composures for the pulpit".[2] Divines of all political and ecclesiastical complexions, whigs of the calibre of Hoadly and Gibson, and tories such as Blackhall and Atterbury, rejoiced to possess such a platform for their eloquence. Thomas Newton on leaving Cambridge came up to London with twenty sermons of his own composition as his theological stock in trade (observing that "having some stock in hand he was not under the necessity of making sermons in a hurry"), which he preached as curate

[1] *The Diary of a Country Parson*, ii, 112; v, 312.
[2] *Life of Sharp*, i, 30–1.

of St George, Hanover Square, transferring thence to be reader and afternoon preacher at Grosvenor Chapel, South Audley Street, and thence being appointed morning preacher at the chapel in Spring Gardens. There he had "a full and polite congregation, consisting principally of a few noble families from Whitehall, and of those of the lords of the Admiralty and other good families in the neighbourhood".[1] The London lectureships held their popularity until the migration of population to the suburbs led to the foundation there of chapels of ease; to which wealthy patrons attracted able young divines, exactly in the manner of the chapel served by Newton, which had been built by "Mr Southwell for the convenience of his tenants in Spring Gardens, and he very generously gave all the profits arising from the rents of the pews to be divided in certain proportions between the officiating ministers". The office of Lecturer was recognised as impermanent in character, designed only to set the occupant's feet upon the road to promotion, for Newton, though admitting that he received "better than £200 a year", affirmed that "lectureships in general were precarious and disagreeable preferments, being subject to so many various humours and depending altogether upon the goodwill and pleasure of so many different persons", especially such as were in the gift of "the parish at large, which of all elections of lecturers and ministers was the worst".[2]

The fashionable churches of London and Westminster provided not only sermons but a full complement of services for their worshippers. Mr Wickham Legg's studies in *English Church Life from the Restoration to the Tractarian Movement* have assembled details of the divine offices performed in the capital. In most churches the Eucharist was celebrated at least monthly, and in some weekly, eleven churches being noted as attaining the standard of weekly communion in 1728. Amongst high churchmen it was customary to receive the Sacrament monthly, as Queen Anne made her practice, and in certain cases weekly. It was observed of Archbishop Sharp that during his residence in London on each Sunday he "constantly attended the early Sacraments, for the most part at Whitehall, that he might be at liberty afterwards to preach in the parish church or attend the Queen's chapel, whither he generally resorted for the morning service".[3] Further, in 1714 there were in London and Westminster seventy-two churches and chapels inviting worshippers to divine service twice daily, and towards the middle of the century in 1746 this standard was still maintained by fifty-eight

---

[1] *Life of Dr Thomas Newton*, in *op. cit.*, ii, 43.
[2] *Ibid.* ii, 117.
[3] *Life of Sharp*, ii, 76.

churches within the Bills of Mortality, whilst an outer fringe had prayers on Wednesdays, Fridays, and holy days.[1] Contemporary references support the inference that this provision of services was not lacking in response from the laity. Steele contributed to *The Guardian* of 26 May 1713 an account of his attendance at Morning Prayers; when

the other morning he happened to rise earlier than ordinary and thought he could not pass his time better than to go upon the admonition of the morning bell to church prayers at six of the clock. He was first there of any in the congregation;...there was none at the Confession but a poor set of scrubs, who could sin only in their wills, whose persons could be no temptation to one another;...when these poor souls had presented themselves with a contrition suitable to their worthlessness, some pretty young ladies in mobs popped in here and there about the church, clattering the pew door after them, and squatting into whispers behind their fans.[2]

The suggestion that some of the congregation gathered less for devotional than for social exercises is supported by Fielding's tilt at "those pure and sanctified virgins who, after a life innocently spent in the gaities of the town, begin about fifty to attend twice per diem at the polite churches and chapels".[3] The association of weekday attendance at public prayers with the accepted routine of polite society was emphasised by the faithful performance of divine service daily in such fashionable watering-places and spas as Bath and Tunbridge Wells, with its chapel dedicated to the Royal Martyr, whereas the *parvenu* character of the pretensions of Harrogate was illustrated by its stigma in lacking such provision until subscriptions were collected in 1743 for the building of a chapel of ease and the chapel completed in 1749.[4]

In one respect town and country were alike, in the desire of the generality of churchmen to hear a sermon upon their assistance at divine worship. The eighteenth-century palate for sermons however differed both as to the form and content of pulpit discourses from that of its predecessor. The contemporary biographer of Tillotson regarded the Caroline divines as the chief corrupters of the tradition of English pulpit oratory.

The whole form of the discourses there was oppressed with an unnecessary mixture of various languages, affected wit, and puerile rhetoric; and the general sense of the text was totally neglected, while every single word of it

---

[1] J. Wickham Legg, *English Church Life from the Restoration to the Tractarian Movement*, chs. II, IV *passim*.
[2] *The Guardian*, No. 65, Tuesday, 26 May 1713.
[3] Fielding, *Joseph Andrewes*, bk. I, ch. XVIII.
[4] *Englishmen at Rest and Play* (ed. R. V. Lennard), p. 56.

was separately considered under all its possible meanings. The history of preaching in our own country and language...would shew that from the beginning of the seventeenth century as false a taste had affected the pulpit as had prevailed after the corruption of the Roman eloquence from the time of Seneca to the lower empire.[1]

The principal culpability was ascribed by Dr Birch unequivocally to Bishop Andrewes, whose sermons, he contended, illustrated "the great corruption of the oratory of the pulpit". Nor was this reaction from seventeenth-century style confined to low churchmen. John Sharp, during his residence as tutor in the household of Sir Heneage Finch, being dispensed from the making of sermons and required to read printed discourses, at the age of twenty-five resolved to wean his patron from a liking for Andrewes' sermons.

Mr Sharp, who ever disliked playing upon words in discourses on religion, took occasion on a Christmas Day, when he was directed to read Bishop Andrewes' sermon upon this text: "Thou shalt call his name Emmanuel", (where there is a whimsical jingle upon the most solemn word in the sentence), to lay his emphasis in such a manner on that passage which was most offensive to him, that Sir Heneage perceived he intended to put him out of conceit with that way of writing, which that good bishop sometimes affected. And the design was answered; for Sir Heneage never ordered those sermons to be read again in his family.[2]

The model of the new age was found in the style of Tillotson himself, even amongst divines remote from the Latitudinarian theology which he represented; and the merits of his style were admitted by Warburton as "simple, elegant, candid, clear, and rational", despite that prelate's avowed preference for the oratory of Barrow and Taylor.[3]

Correspondent with this clarity and simplicity of diction was the theology of the Latitudinarian movement which stamped its peculiar character upon the religious belief and practice of the Georgian Church. Its doctrines were marked by plainness and directness; and the essential content of the Christian evangel was epitomised in the proclamation of the Fatherhood of God and the duty of benevolence in Man. Persuaded of the centrality of this cardinal tenet of the beneficence of the Creator towards his creatures, the men of Latitude deduced the obligation on the part of mankind to imitate the divine charity by the performance of good works towards each other. Public worship was designed, as

[1] T. Birch, *Life of John Tillotson*, p. 24.　　[2] *Life of Sharp*, i, 20.
[3] *Letters from a late Eminent Prelate to one of his friends*, Letter L, p. 127. The transition in the style of pulpit eloquence is fully illustrated in *English Pulpit Oratory from Andrewes to Tillotson*, by W. F. Mitchell (London, 1932).

Addison observed, for the adoration of the Supreme Being and the inculcation of the duties of men living in society. Thus conceived, religion was in no wise divorced from the affairs of this world. Its profession did not involve abstention from the innocent relationships of social life, but rather supplied the best motive for the conduct of citizens whose membership of an earthly kingdom was the preparation for that of an heavenly city. Inevitably this conception tended to decline in popular estimate into the idea of religion as supplying an additional bonus to a course of moderation and virtue rather than as sounding a call to renunciation and asceticism. This sentiment found typical expression in Addison's poem on the manifold mercies of God throughout the stages of human life.

> Thy bounteous hand with worldly bliss
> Has made my cup run o'er,
> And in a kind and faithful Friend
> Has doubled all my store.

Christianity thus afforded a prudential assurance of the wisdom in this world of the practice of sobriety and piety, buttressed by the proleptic rewards promised in the future state to practitioners of its precepts. The eminently practical character of this presentation of religion was well suited to the temper of an age which, in reaction from the furies of theological strife of the seventeenth century and the extremes of Independency and Popery, desired to expend its energies in the profitable task of advancing the national wealth by the pursuit of trade and commerce and in the enjoyment of domestic peace. Archbishop Tillotson declared that the injunction "to depart from evil" was very fit "to express the whole duty of man", and in his sermons on the advantages of religion to societies, and to particular persons, laboured to demonstrate that obedience to its moral precepts constituted the surest guarantee of individual happiness and of peace in society, no less than eternal felicity. Further, the demands of Christianity upon men were not burdensome nor too heavy to be borne.

This theme was developed in Tillotson's sermon on the text, "His commandments are not grievous"; in which he undertook to show "that the laws of God are reasonable, that is suited to our nature and advantageous to our interest; that we are not destitute of sufficient power and ability for the performance of them; and that we have the greatest encouragements to this purpose". Upon the first head he affirmed that God "hath commanded us nothing in the gospel that is either unsuitable to our reason or prejudicial to our interest; nay, nothing that is severe and against the grain of our nature, but when either the apparent necessity of our interest does require it, or an extraordinary reward is promised our obedience". He deemed it self-evident that the practice of temperance and chastity was suitable to the nature and condition of men, since "some virtues plainly tend to the preservation of our health, others to the improvement and security of our estates, all to the peace and quiet of our minds, and, what is somewhat more strange, to the advancement of our esteem and reputation". In cases, indeed, of men whose previous course of life had been attended by excess and indulgence, the struggle to attain moderation might be difficult at first, but for these individuals, even more than for ordinary Christians, there remained the incentive to be drawn from the manifest encouragements accorded by God.

Two things make any course of life easy; present pleasure and the assurance of a future reward. Religion gives part of its reward in hand, the present comfort and satisfaction of having done our duty; and for the rest it offers us the best security that heaven can give. Now these two must needs make our duty very easy; a considerable reward in hand, and not only the hopes but the assurance of a far greater recompense hereafter.

In the accomplishment of this task, the means of attaining to the standard required by Christianity were afforded by the efforts of the individual and the assistance of the Spirit of God. Tillotson was aware of the objections which might be pressed against his thesis from the numerous passages of the New Testament in which the Christian life is represented as attended by persecution and tribulation and by the necessity for constant wrestling and striving. To these he replied that the references to actual persecution related to the conditions of the Church before the kingdoms of this world adopted the official profession of Christianity, and were therefore no longer relevant to contemporary circumstances. He allowed the need for "a very vigorous prosecution and great earnestness of endeavour" in the business of religion, but denied that the standards exacted by God were beyond the compass of ordinary human achievement.

If men would but go to church with as good a will as men ordinarily do to their markets and fairs, and be in as good earnest at their devotions as men commonly are in driving a bargain; if they would but endure troubles and inconveniences in the way of religion with the same patience and constancy as they can do storms, and foul ways and mischances when they are travelling about their worldly occasions....I am confident that such a one could not fail of heaven.

Indeed this effort was within the capacity of every man, for God would not ask what was beyond the means of common men to perform.

All that I have said signifies no more but that men should use their sincere endeavours, and this surely every man can do. For to use our sincere endeavours is nothing else but to do as much as we can, and it is nonsense for any man to deny that he can do as much as he can. And if we would do thus much we are sure of God's grace and assistance, which is never wanting to the sincere endeavours of men.[1]

Such precepts of belief and practice, urged *viva voce* upon the auditors in the churches of the capital, found their echo in the pulpits of the country churches of the kingdom. Tillotson's sermons indeed were amongst the most favoured purchases of rural divines. Thomas Brockbank's bookseller in Oxford reported in 1697 that "all Dr Tillotson's works that he published himself were lately printed in folio, and would cost 20*s.*, and there were three volumes in octavo since his death, and there would be a fourth out soon after Easter, and they are 5*s.* each volume".[2] Among the works of piety performed by Sir Roger de Coverley was a benefaction to his chaplain, to whom "at his first settling with him he made a present of all the good sermons which had been printed in English, and only begged of him that every Sunday he would pronounce one of them in the pulpit". Accordingly Tillotson had his place together with Fleetwood, South, Sanderson, Barrow, the dissenter Calamy, and other living divines, in the yearly round of discourses delivered to the knight and his parishioners.[3] But where the *ipsissima verba* of his utterances were not read from the pulpit, the sentiments of Tillotson and of the school which he represented permeated the conservative traditions of parish exhortations. Canon Watson has brought to notice recently the teaching of Anthony Hastwell, incumbent of the two small and adjacent parishes of Kildale and Great Ayton in the north riding of Yorkshire from 1758 to 1793, four of whose manuscript sermons have survived as a faithful testimony to the influence of the movement of Latitude in a remote country cure.[4] The basis of his theology lay in the doctrine of the beneficence of God.

We love Him because He is our Father, and our great Benefactor, whose power gave us being, whose providence preserves us, whose goodness presents us with blessings, whose long-suffering bears with us, whose mercy

---

[1] *Tillotson's Sermons*, 2 vols., Sermon VI, i, 152–73 (London, 1742).
[2] *Brockbank*, p. 115. [3] *The Spectator*, No. 106, Monday, 2 July 1711.
[4] E. W. Watson, "An Eighteenth-Century Clergyman", *Church Quarterly Review*, No. 210, vol. cv, January 1928, pp. 255–71, from which the references to Hastwell are taken.

forgives us; and the love is by no means faulty in its motives, since 'tis founded upon gratitude and a due sense of the favours which we have received from the Author of all happiness.

From this premiss it was an easy step to deduce the obligation of men to be imitators of God, since contemplation of the divine perfections "should lay us under the strongest obligations to be, in some proportion, kind, merciful, and charitable towards our brethren, as God has been infinitely good and merciful to us".

One of Hastwell's sermons was preached from the text "His commandments are not grievous", and between his discourse on this subject and that of Tillotson there exist evident parallels. Hastwell was concerned to emphasise the same truth of the agreeableness of virtue to the constitution of human nature and its consequent superiority over vice even from the standpoint of worldly prosperity. "When all things are considered, it will be found that as the way of God and virtue is much plainer and easier than that of vice and wickedness, so a man may take less pains to be very good than very bad; and will more consult his own ease, pleasure, and satisfaction by living a religious than an irreligious life." In support of this contention he pointed to the circumstance that the practice of virtue

puts us to little bodily pain, brings no great weariness or consumption of spirits on us, is not contrary to, but exceedingly well agrees with the constitution and frame of our nature; and is besides such a design that whosoever undertakes it may assuredly promise himself success.... It will quicken our diligence and industry, even as to the prosecution of our secular affairs. It will employ our love and desires after that which is good, and make us daily more active and vigorous in the prosecution of it, till at last we shall be translated into a state of everlasting and never-ceasing activity.

Having demonstrated thus the profit of religion to human interest, the preacher, following the pattern of the archbishop, proceeded to bring its observance within the compass of every man by the assurance that God would demand no unreasonable standard of goodness from his children.

God almighty, in the laws He gave us by Christ, never intended to require an exact and unsinning obedience to them; but in the Gospel sense we are said to obey God's laws when we use our sincere endeavours to obey them; when in the main of our lives we live up to them; when we do not indulge ourselves in any known wilful course of sin; but, as far as the weakness of our nature and the circumstances of our lives will permit, we do as much as we can to mortify our corrupt affections, and live holy and virtuous lives.

From this argument the conclusion followed naturally that "every considerate man, from the evidence of truth, must be forced to acknowledge that, all things considered, 'tis more easy, safe, and desirable, and delightful to be good, to serve God, to live in obedience to His laws and discharge a good conscience than to enjoy all the pleasures of sin, which are but for a short season". It was plain that every means had been adopted to temper the demands of Christianity to the infirmities of unregenerate human nature, and to promise the consolations of religion to the weakest of its professors. The tenor of such preaching has been described by Canon Watson as tending to degrade the Divine benevolence into mere good nature and to minimise the achievement required by God of His creatures. "Let them be kind, and honest, let them be sober on market days, and then they will certainly go to heaven, and will probably reap a good harvest." Certainly parish ministers of the school of Hastwell were exceedingly solicitous not to quench the smoking flax nor to bend the bruised reed. But, if their doctrine lacked fire and other-worldly urgency, it should not be forgotten that its exposition of the whole duty of man laid stress upon the two great commandments, as interpreted by the twin offices of "loving God, admiring and being delighted with all His wise and wonderful works, continually singing praises to our gracious Creator and Redeemer; and doing all kind and good-natured offices to our fellow creatures, and this with perpetual alacrity, pleasure, and joy, without weariness and decay of spirits".

As of the sermons preached by Anthony Hastwell in north Yorkshire, so of those spoken by James Woodforde at Weston Longville, four only have been preserved to posterity. Those of Woodforde are dated 20 and 27 January and 3 and 24 February 1793, and the manuscripts are written in his neat, regular hand.[1] It is a matter for regret that these sermons should belong to four almost consecutive Sundays, and more particularly to those of January 1793, for, as the evidence of the diaries indicates, the news of tragic contemporary events in France had reached England and cast a gloom over the spirits of the diarist in his remote country parish of Norfolk. On 17 December previous, rumour had reported the murder of Louis XVI and his consort,[2] and, though this report proved incorrect, on 19 January following, the day before the

---

[1] The Four Sermons of Parson James Woodforde, 278, 279, 280, 281, are the property of Canon F. J. Meyrick of the Vicarage, Hove, Sussex, to whom I am greatly indebted for the privilege of reading, and the permission to reproduce quotations from them.

[2] *The Diary of a Country Parson*, iii, 396.

first of the surviving sermons was preached, Woodforde noted in his diary that "by the public papers this day, there appears but very small hopes at present of the King of France long remaining here upon earth, his blood-thirsty enemies being so wicked and inveterate against him. Pray God, however he may escape; if not, may his earthly crown be changed into an heavenly one".[1] The anticipated act of regicide occurred on 21 January and on the 26th, the day before the delivery of the second sermon, the event was recorded in the diarist's pages.

The king of France, Louis XVI, inhumanly and unjustly beheaded on Monday last by his cruel, blood-thirsty subjects. Dreadful times I am afraid are approaching to all Europe. France the foundation of all of it. The poor king of France bore his horrid fate with manly fortitude and resignation. Pray God he may be eternally happy in Thy heavenly kingdom. And have mercy upon his queen, two children, and their aunt princess Elizabeth, all of whom by the papers are very ill indeed in their confinement. Their lives are in great danger now of being taken away by the French assassins or ruffians.[2]

In the sermon preached by Woodforde on 20 January from the text "When I am in heaviness, I will think upon God; when my heart is vexed, I will complain",[3] there was no mention of the regicide anticipated in France, but the evils of the times affected the theme of the preacher, who discoursed of the uncertainty and fluctuation of all human happiness apart from the assurance of religion. At the outset he painted a dark picture of human disappointments. Life was "one incessant struggle, one scene of toil, of suffering, of cruel fate"; and "its instability will never bear the weight of the most slender dependence; our expectations are infinitely larger than our enjoyments, and our supposed happiness seldom within our reach and seldom a single minute assured to us". The influence of the prevalent gloom was seen more clearly in his pessimistic view of the corruptness of human nature. The boundless optimism of the early Deists, and the shallow diagnosis of Rousseau concerning the essential goodness of Man, had largely broken down under the pressure of events. To Woodforde how "guileful and detestable are the ways of Man, formed in the image of God but transformed into that of Satan"! "Without thee, O Religion, what were unenlightened Man? A savage, rude, void of every moral excellence, every social bliss, every tenderness, and every virtue that can refine the drossy corruption of life and render us more like the God we

---

[1] *The Diary of a Country Parson*, iv, 2, 3.
[2] *Ibid.* iv, 4.   [3] Psalm lxxvii. 3.

ought to worship." In times of calamity he remarked that even corrupt man would remember God. "We pay Him the compliment of giving attendance to our last necessitous shifts and presume to think that He will be ready to relieve us; but only let us consider that this mercy is not at our but at His discretion". Therefore the moral of his discourse was the need of continual attendance upon the ordinances of religion, which would inspire both charity towards men and resignation under the will of God. In the former regard "the soul inspiring virtues [of religion] should warm the conscious heart of charity, should dilate wide the wish of benevolence, should raise the social sigh and even the social tear, and improve the passions to their original and refined excellence". In relation to God, and in the face of "the silent oblivion of the grave", it must be remembered that "to render ourselves the more worthy we must be devout towards God, without any hypocrisy or ill-worship; sincere towards mankind without the leaven of malice; and just and rational in the regulation of our own lives".

On the following Sunday afternoon, Woodforde preached from the text, "Behold, happy is the man whom God correcteth; therefore despise not thou the chastening of the Almighty";[1] and his endeavour was to justify the incidence of suffering and sorrow as part of the penitential discipline of God. The sermon was a conventional exposition of the necessity of pain in a life which was "not a place of reward but of trial", with a great wealth of Biblical reference, especially to the examples of Job and of Christ, and with an iterated insistence that God permitted affliction "not to gratify any sullen humour of His own, any ill-natured delight He takes in grieving or afflicting the children of men, but for our sakes; not for His own pleasure but for our profit, that we may be made thereby partakers of His holiness". Its conclusion was a practical exhortation to self-examination to discover the lesson designed to be taught by suffering; whether the loss of temporal estate did not indicate that it was "more than probable that our estate has been raised by injustice, increased by covetousness, or wasted by luxury and dissipation"; and with particular warning against "the folly of those who make their afflictions the excuse for their intemperance, and (to use their own expression) drink to drown their sorrows".

Before the next Sunday the village of Weston had been bereaved by the death of a young man who had barely attained his majority, who "was beloved of all that knew him, it was said, as being a very good-natured, inoffensive man", and whose body was interred on Sunday afternoon attended by a great number of people and by the Weston

[1] Job v. 17.

singers who sang on the occasion.[1] At Morning Prayer Woodforde delivered a discourse upon the text "It is the Lord, let him do what seemeth him good",[2] in which, although without reference to the actual domestic calamity, he urged the duty of resignation before the will of God in contrast to infidel railings against Providence. "Such a noble resignation as this [of Eli] should not only fill the mouth, but influence the heart of every believer, every pretender to Christianity; such a confidence in the Deity as this, such language as the text, bespeaks the rational creature and the man." The commendation of this Christian attitude furnished occasion for a severe condemnation of "the features of our modern depravity, the attendants upon corruption, the ideas that our freethinkers, or, which is much the same, irreligious Christians, would conceive on the same dismal occasion". Reflection on this miserable company led Woodforde to enunciate again his despair of humanity apart from the influence of religion.

What is man without this civilising principle? A proud, headstrong, ungovernable brute. What is he without the influence of this refiner? Nothing but an heap of rubbish and a bundle of corruption. What is he without this soother of the passions, this mistress of our spiritual childhood? A man without, but a beast within. But what is he when polished by religion? An honour to his Maker, an ornament of the creation, and the being of the two worlds.

Truly this was a far declension from the original and continuing righteousness with which Thomas Paine believed man to be endowed! But if the rustic congregation of Weston received this dark doctrine with acceptance, it may be wondered with what ears they heard a strange digression to denounce the practices of foreign travel on the part of young Englishmen and the social gaieties of their sisters! After a further lament concerning the principles of an age "which gives charters to infidels and franks the character of the deist", Woodforde turned aside to belabour

"the leading principle of our very refined age, in which the sound dictates of old fashioned common sense are frittered into nothingness of affectation, vanity, and singular nonsense. No wonder", he observed, "that this gross perversion of things should obtain, since the young people of these times, of either sex, are so erroneously educated and falsely instructed. The male part, before they can properly read their mother tongue, have ascertained the laws and customs of their own country, or have formed any settled notions of religion, are indulged with the name of taking a foreign tour; whilst the

---

[1] *The Diary of a Country Parson*, iv, 5.   [2] I Samuel iii. 18.

females, instead of cultivating those useful virtues which would adorn the state for which they are early candidates and for which God and nature have designed them, are taught to consider dress as their idol, novels as their Bibles, and cards as their Prayer-Books".

Peradventure the youth amongst the preacher's audience had given way to slumber, in which state alone the majority of their number might hope to enjoy the delights of foreign travel or a round of social entertainments, before they were recalled to the prosaic conditions of actual life by the concluding warning of the imminence of death; for although "no particular decree of death hath been revealed against us, yet our provocations every day are so heinous, our offences so great, and our rebellion so obstinate, that we every moment deserve to be cut off and doomed to eternal death".

The last sermon, delivered in the afternoon of 24 February to "a large congregation", was based upon the text, "So likewise shall my heavenly Father do also unto you, if ye from your hearts forgive not everyone his brother their trespasses",[1] and expounded the duty of human forgiveness in accordance with the example of divine mercy revealed in Christ Jesus. Woodforde presented first a summary of the parable from which his text was drawn, and urged his auditors to apply its lesson to their own condition.

It is astonishing we can so soon forget the benefits we receive from our superiors, as the next moment to deny them to those that are dependent upon us. It is unnatural so to act; our innate feelings forbid and condemn it. The love of virtue is naturally inherent in the human breast, and approved even by wicked men.... Nature has given us an upright face and commanded us to look up to heaven...to reflect upon our wonderful creation, and Thy more watchful preservation; to meditate upon the numberless sins which by thought, word, and deed we daily commit against Thy divine majesty.... To ponder all this goodness should humble the pride of our revenge, blunt the edge of our cruelty, and soften us into an imitation of that kindness which we cannot but see and never sufficiently admire.

This modified optimism concerning the goodness of man, who is by nature attracted to imitation of the divine perfection, relieved somewhat the preacher's gloomy picture of human degradation; and his discourse proceeded to enforce the duty of applying the forgiveness of Christ to social relationships.

How then can we reflect on that amazing instance of tenderness and pardon without blushing at every principle which looks like persecution and hardness

[1] St Matthew xviii. 35.

of heart. . . . Our brother stands upon a level with us, enjoys the same rights of creation and redemption, all subject to the same obligations, nor can any the best of us plead anything of superiority but what Providence has vested us with.

With a view to contemporary political circumstances the moral was brought home in regard to the value of religion to the state, and the necessity of forgiveness of injuries to avoid reprisal and civil disturbance.

The true cultivation of this principle is of such consequences to the peace, order, and happiness of the community, that without it the laws of the land lend but feeble aid to prevent and restrain personal injuries. Religion is the strongest bulwark to any nation, and the best security to the legislature. The most religious man, from inward conviction, without the fear of penal sanctions of the law, will always prove the most peaceable subject.

It is not possible to ascertain whether these four sermons of the first two months of 1793 were representative of the preaching of Woodforde's long incumbency at Weston, the more particularly in view of the political events of the French Revolution at that time. Their tenor would suggest that the vogue of humanistic optimism had spent its force, as it was shortly to be discredited by the excesses of the revolutionaries across the narrow seas. Only in the last sermon did Woodforde assert even a qualified belief in the inherent love of virtue in men, and affirm the typical Latitudinarian doctrines of the divine Fatherhood and human brotherhood, whereby the Christian "whilst he strives to love God will most certainly demonstrate, as an example to the other, that he loves his brother also, and that these two duties, thus naturally united, we may never put asunder". Hastwell was certainly more representative of his age than the Woodforde of these discourses. Both however give the impression of men of understanding and education, able to express their thoughts with clarity and force, and judged by their standard the sermons preached in country churches were worthy of respectful attention. Dr Johnson indeed allowed the objection against them that they were above the understanding of rustic auditors, in contrast to the effusions of the Methodists.

"Sir," he declared to Boswell of the latter's success, "it is owing to their expressing themselves in a plain and familiar manner, which is the only way to do good to the common people, and which clergymen of genius and learning ought to do from a principle of duty, when it is suited to their congregations; a practice for which they will be praised by men of sense. To insist against drunkenness as a crime, because it debases reason, the noblest faculty of man, would be of no service to the common people; but to tell them that they may die in a fit of drunkenness, and shew them how dreadful that would be, cannot fail to make a deep impression."[1]

Upon another occasion he observed in the same strain

that the established clergy in general did not preach plain enough; and that polished periods and glittering sentences flew over the heads of the common people without any impression on their hearts. Something might be necessary, he observed, to excite the affections of the common people, who were sunk in languor and lethargy, and therefore he supposed that the new concomitants of methodism might probably produce so desirable an effect.[2]

The lesson of the need to abandon formal discourses and rational exposition in order to reach the understanding of the people was not easily learned by disciples of the school of Latitude. A full generation after the death of Woodforde, John Skinner at Camerton, despite the increase of methodism and its proselytism from his flock, refused to depart from the tradition of written and unemotional sermons, deeming it his duty "to shew what was the meaning of the sacred writings and to do so in a rational manner", and to insist that "belief in Christ consisted in practice, not in words, and that it was to be shewn by active duties towards our fellow-creatures, not by mere expression of feeling".[3] Accordingly he delivered courses of apologetic sermons on the evidences of Christianity, the Apostles' Creed, and the Lord's Prayer; and under the date of 5 August 1832 recorded in his diary this defiant resolution. "If I were to commence a new system as an evangelical teacher, the methodists would attend; but I cannot prevail upon myself to do evil to work no good, unless it be good to gratify one's vanity by procuring full benches at the expense of one's principles".[4]

The dominance of the Latitudinarian tradition in the Hanoverian Church did not deprive of their portion churchmen of other schools, who found means in the performance of their pastoral duties to express the peculiar emphasis of the high or low church principles of their profession. At Blecheley William Cole observed the Nativity of our Lady as the dedication feast of his church, and at Matins a sermon was preached "exhortatory to the parishioners in what manner to celebrate the wake or feast"; and on the Sunday following music adorned the continuation of the festival in addition to its being the only day on which two sermons were delivered.[5] After his removal to Waterbeche,

[1] Boswell, *Life of Johnson*, 30 July 1763.   [2] *Ibid. Collectanea*, 1770.
[3] *The Journal of a Somerset Rector*, pp. 161–2.   [4] *Ibid.* p. 287.
[5] *The Blecheley Diary of William Cole*, pp. 116, 119, 260–1.

Cole noted on Christmas Day 1767 that certain of his parishioners "had the Elements carried to them" from the Christmas Communion.[1] In contrast to this practice of Cole was the injunction of Thomas Brockbank to a parishioner, to whom he had been unable to administer the Holy Sacrament privately, concerning the efficiency of spiritual communion.

Robert, let [not] my not coming to you this morning at all discourage you, for 'tis not through any thoughts of your unfitness to receive the Holy Sacrament that I came not to administer it, but for other reasons, which I think sufficient. However know this, that if you truly repent you of your sins, and firmly believe that Jesus Christ hath suffered death for you, and that His blood was spilt for your Redemption, earnestly remembering the benefits thereof, and giving Him thanks therefore, then you do eat and drink the body and blood of Christ profitably for your Soul's health. Your earnest desire in this case will be accepted (I assure you) as if you did receive the bread and wine. But this do you remember, that what good purposes and resolutions you now have to amend your life, when it shall please God to restore you to health again, you then put them into practise, especially for the more meet and convenient communicating at Easter, which I hope you will live to see. I am not now at leisure to give you any other directions, only this that you would desire some of your fellow servants to read to you out of some good book, to raise your devotion, and to confirm you in your good resolutions.[2]

At Blecheley also the custom of Rogation processions was maintained in which the people went the rounds of the parish.[3] These perambulations were commended and approved indeed by authority, though for the characteristic reason that, being stripped of superstitious ceremonies, they served the useful purpose of ascertaining parish boundaries. Archbishop Wake urging their continuance upon Dr Charlett at Hambleden, observed that

the perambulations of the Rogation week have been old establishments by the Canon Law; and in times of Popery were accompanied with many superstitions. Queen Elizabeth by her Injunctions... took away the former, but reserved the latter. They now stand upon the Common-Law Ecclesiastical; and ought to be kept up as the only way to prevent disputes about the bounds of parishes, and in that to prevent also many other controversies which may depend thereupon.[4]

---

[1] *The Blecheley Diary of William Cole*, p. 304.
[2] *Brockbank*, p. 153.   [3] *The Blecheley Diary of William Cole*, p. 46.
[4] Wake to Charlett, 10 May 1716. Ballard MSS. iii, f. 61.

Secker in 1750 grounded his approval of the custom on similar advantages, advising his clergy of the diocese of Oxford to recall that
"amongst several other uses to which it extends, it might be very
serviceable to ascertain the rights of livings". For, having

been long freed from superstition, and if preserved also from intemperance
and tumultuous contests, (the last of which evils may be prevented by
friendly discourse beforehand with the chief inhabitants of their own and
neighbouring parishes), the thanksgivings, prayers, and sentences of Scripture,
with which the injunctions of Queen Elizabeth direct it to be accompanied,
will render it a very pious ceremony; and the civil benefits of it may be
considerable.[1]

In the visitation of sick parishioners, the diaries of Cole, Woodforde
and Skinner testify to the conscientious discharge of this branch of the
pastoral office. All three clergy were diligent in ministering both to
the material and spiritual wants of the poor, reading prayers and
carrying foods, whilst upon one occasion, Cole, being a high churchman, pronounced a formal Absolution over a parishioner.[2] From the
beginning of the century there were suggestions that the clergy felt the
office for the visitation of the sick ill-suited to their needs. Archdeacon
Frank informed Bishop Wake in 1706 that in his jurisdiction that office
"was generally complained of as imperfect, and the clergy used a greater
liberty than the office directed"; whilst Wake himself two years later
admitted it to be "certainly some defect...in our Establishment that
we have not some offices published by authority for the visitation of
the sick", adding that as a parish priest he had himself collected from
Jeremy Taylor and other private manuals "many excellent devotions,
till public authority should supersede the need of them".[3] In the
peculiar intimacy of ministration to the sick and dying the clergy
claimed and were allowed the latitude of adapting official forms to the
circumstances of individual cases.

The widespread vogue of the five volumes of *The Diary of a Country
Parson* has established James Woodforde in popular estimation as
representative of the country clergy of Georgian England, and the
Church of his age need not hesitate to be judged by his standards.
Superficially indeed his frank pleasure in the material things of life, in
meats and drinks, and in the common affairs of mundane existence, may
appear to imply an insensitiveness to the commerce of the spirit.

[1] Secker, Charge IV, *Works*, v, 388–9.
[2] *The Blecheley Diary of William Cole* p. 239.
[3] Wake to Charlett, 2 Sept. 1718. Ballard MSS. iii, f. 45.

Further, the ecclesiastical framework of his religious practice was undeniably simple, consisting of the performance of divine service with sermon once per Sunday at Weston alternately in the morning and afternoon, together with the quarterly Sacrament, the observance of Good Friday, and the ministration of the occasional offices of baptism, burial, and visitation of the sick. Nor was the outward tenor of his course marked by asceticism, the only lingering traces of which were found in the tradition of his father to abstain from playing cards in Passion Week (which custom "he thought not amiss though there might be no harm"), and his own practice of fasting from all flesh, meat, and from cards on Good Friday.[1] Yet behind this inelaborate façade there existed a definite religious tradition, of which Woodforde was a faithful, if partly unconscious, exponent. His diaries illustrate the translation into practice of the theology of divine benevolence preached in Hastwell's sermons. The frequent and spontaneous ejaculations of piety which mark in his record the incidence of events, domestic and parochial, whether birthdays and occasions of rejoicing, or news of illness, misfortune and tidings of sadness, testify clearly to a background of religion and to the measuring of eternity. James Woodforde was plainly unfamiliar with formal systems of theology, but his aspirations for the rest and refreshment of the souls of his dying parishioners were the utterances of a pious and pastoral heart; of which perhaps one example may suffice, under the date 9 December 1790, concerning the burial of two parishioners: "Pray God they may both be happy in heaven. May almighty God everlastingly reward poor Henry Nobbes for his very, very great sufferings here. His poor aged mother attended at the funeral and came to see me after with tears in her eyes to thank me for what I had done for him. But O Lord, not unto me but unto thy divine Goodness be ascribed all the praise".[2] No reader of the diaries could doubt the writer's faithful discharge of the pastoral office in relation to the sick and dying, his concern for their recovery or for their eternal felicity, and the sincerity of his prayers for them both privately and in the formal services in Weston Church.

The most outstanding feature of Woodforde's ministry was his practice of the doctrine of the divine beneficence. The ubiquitous works of charity, of gifts of food and drink, and of provision for the poor, sick, and infirm, with which his diary abounds, were the parochial representation of the humanitarian impulse which led to the foundation of hospitals as a means of exercising that benevolence

[1] *The Diary of a Country Parson*, i, 73; *passim* for Good Friday, e.g. iii, 267.
[2] *Ibid.* iii, 367.

towards mankind which was deduced from the goodness of the Creator to His creatures. The eighteenth century was the epoch of hospital foundations; in London of the Foundling Hospital in 1742, of the Westminster Hospital in 1719, Guy's in 1723, St George's in 1734, the London in 1740, the Middlesex in 1745, the Lock Hospital in 1746, the Lying-in-Hospital for married women in 1749, and in 1750 the City of London Lying-in-Hospital, Queen Charlotte's Hospital in 1752, the Royal Maternity Hospital in 1757, and the Westminster Lying-in-Hospital in 1765; and in the country at large the foundations in the university towns of Addenbrooke and Radcliffe and of the county hospitals testified to the inspiration of the belief in the Fatherhood of God. James Woodforde was familiar with the vogue of sermons in behalf of hospitals and charity schools, as when on 2 August 1792 he went to Norwich Cathedral to the musical meeting for the benefit of the public hospital. At the entrance to the cathedral he gave one guinea for the charity, "which was reckoned handsome"; after prayers the bishop, Dr Manners Sutton, "gave a very good discourse on Charity, more particularly that for which they were assembled", from the text "I was a stranger and ye took me in, naked and ye clothed me; I was sick and ye visited me"; and his sermon was followed by selections from Handel's compositions. The occasion was truly edifying, as the diarist recorded. "All together it was not only delightful but seemed heavenly, and gave us ideas of heavenly music".[1] Equal evidence of pastoral care for the sick could be gathered from the diaries of Cole and Skinner, who were alike in their anxiety to relieve suffering and to console the afflicted. Country clergy of the type of Woodforde, though they might not conceive themselves as ordained to a priestly office for the offering of gifts and sacrifices for sins, strove to make themselves acceptable ministers of One who went about doing good.

Apart from the performance of their ecclesiastical duties, the parochial clergy, where resident, exercised an important influence on the social life of their communities. Dr Johnson indeed reaffirmed the dictum of Dean Percy of Carlisle "that it might be discerned whether or no there was a clergyman resident in a parish by the civil or savage manner of the people".[2] James Woodforde's relations with all estates and conditions of men in his parish were cordial and friendly. It may be conjectured that amongst the most enjoyable days at Weston parsonage were the tithe frolics when the rector made merry with the farmers who came to pay their dues. With the persons of quality in his parish, the household

[1] *The Diary of a Country Parson*, iii, 367.
[2] Boswell, *Life of Johnson*, "Letter to a Young Clergyman", Letter 385, 1780.

of Mr Custance, he maintained relations not only of social propriety but of real affection and esteem, of which the frequent and diverse gifts of Mr Custance to Weston Church and its rector were repeated testimony. Their friendship was reminiscent of that between Sir Roger de Coverley and his chaplain, commended by Addison; and the value of such cordiality to the good estate of a parish is emphasised by the contrary spectacle of the continual quarrels between John Skinner and the family of the manor house at Camerton. Further, Woodforde sought no preferment or repute outside his parish. Indeed he described as "disagreeable" the invitation received on 12 October 1783 to preach in Norwich Cathedral, and resolved to beg the bishop to release him. He deemed it an occasion of complaint that he should be named "on the combination list to preach at the cathedral the 8th of February next, when his name had been inserted but a few years back; to which his lordship replied that as he did not then preach in propria persona was one reason, and the second was that his lordship was willing that the pulpit at the cathedral should be filled properly by able and beneficed clergy, and that it was a compliment conferred by him on those appointed".[1] Despite this persuasion Woodforde would have preferred to be excused, and felt it some indignity when on the morning of his preaching, he found "neither bishop, dean, or mayor at the cathedral".[2] Similarly in December 1785, when he received an episcopal summons to preach in Norwich in the following spring on behalf of the Charity Schools, he "did not relish it"; but went instead to the bishop, and "acquainted him that he had preached a sermon at St Stephen's in the year 1780 for the benefit of the Charity Schools. His lordship said he did not know that he had, and therefore told him that he would appoint another clergyman instead of him".[3] His age had few occasions also when clergy congregated for conference on ecclesiastical matters; and apart from his social meetings with his brethren of the immediate neighbourhood, attendance at archidiaconal visitations were the chief times of his association with them, and even these formal sessions were valued as much for their dinners as for the charges solemnly delivered in church.

Notwithstanding the hard things said of the clergy of the eighteenth century, the personal records of Brockbank, Woodforde, Cole, and Skinner present a not unpleasing picture of fidelity to duty according to the standards of an epoch which embraced ministers of the devotion of Dr Johnson's ideal parish priest, Prebendary Zachariah Mudge, vicar

[1] *The Diary of a Country Parson*, ii, 98, 100.
[2] *Ibid.* pp. 117–18.   [3] *Ibid.* pp. 219, 221.

of St Andrew's, Plymouth, and prebendary in Exeter Cathedral, and the typical characters of fiction, Parson Adams, and the vicar of Wakefield. In support of this testimony the evidence gathered from visitation records has led to welcome signs of a sounder appreciation in recent years of the achievement of the Hanoverian clergy. The verdict of Canon Ollard on the Visitation Returns of Archbishop Herring at York in 1743 is that

on the whole the strong impression left by the returns is that of a body of conscientious and dutiful men, trying to do their work according to the standard of their day. Over the grave of one of them, the rector of Bainton, William Territ, was written when he died in 1783, this tribute... "a very learned and sound divine, chearful and peaceable, constantly resident and attentive to the duties of a minister". With the possible exception of the words "very learned"... close examination of these returns suggests that a like description would apply to many others of those who made them.[1]

The editor of *The Diary and Letter Book of Thomas Brockbank* likewise summarises his estimate of the work of the inferior clergy in the statement that "as regards the clergy, the outstanding features are the prevalence of non-residence and plurality on the part of the superior ecclesiastics; but in no small degree this is counterbalanced by the earnest and hard-working lives, but hidden lives of many (if not most) of the local ministers".[2] The Registrar of the diocese of Bangor has produced evidence of regularity on the part of the clergy of that remote see; whilst contemporary witness testified to the good condition of the diocese of St Asaph in the middle and later parts of the century. Bishop Drummond reported after his primary visitation in 1753 that he found its state "in general much better than was imagined by strangers. The provision for the clergy was not so small but that they might live with credit and comfort; and the body of the clergy, though not learned, were good and able parish priests".[3] In 1802 Bishop Horsley confirmed this impression during his first visitation which gave him "reason to think well upon the whole of the state of the diocese with regard to its parochial duties. It afforded but few instances... of culpable non-residence, and with respect to the public services of the Church, he was willing to flatter himself that it was less in that than in many other parts, neglected and curtailed".[4]

[1] *Archbishop Herring's Visitation Returns*, i, p. xviii.
[2] *Brockbank*, p. vii.
[3] Bp. Drummond to the Duke of Newcastle, 27 July 1753. Add. MSS. 32732, f. 371.
[4] H. H. Jebb, *Life of Bishop Samuel Horsley*, p. 174.

The reproach of impiety attaching to the eighteenth century must admit of notable exceptions in regard also to the laity of the Church, amongst whom Dr Johnson has been accorded an admitted pre-eminence. His observance of the public prayers of the English Church, his appreciation of holy days as being "of great use in religion", and his perusal of devotional works, testified to the merits of the religious tradition in which he had been reared. Nor was his churchmanship unrepresentative of the best lay religion of his age. His veneration for the Holy Communion was profound, and entirely consistent with infrequent reception of the Sacrament and with approach to the Holy Table after partaking of normal food. Mr Wickham Legg has observed that Johnson tells us expressly that he did not keep the fast before communion, since on Easter Day 1779, "by neglecting to count time, he sat too long at breakfast, so that he came to church at the First Lesson"; and the same writer has drawn attention to the fact that there is "no evidence of his communicating oftener than once a year, at Easter".[1] Yet Johnson's careful preparation for the Easter Eucharist was noteworthy, as in 1773 when he went to church on Good Friday twice with Boswell, his behaviour being "solemnly devout", read the Greek Testament and fasted, and on Easter Day, attended Matins and the Litany, read his special prayer and chosen collects for meditation, "communicated with calmness", and afterwards at home repeated his private devotions and perused the Greek New Testament.[2] Boswell observed on Good Friday 1775 that Johnson "fasted so very strictly that he did not even taste bread, and took no milk with his tea", whilst after the departure of his friend, the doctor performed further religious duties, "giving Francis, his servant, some directions for preparing to communicate, reviewing his life, and resolving on better conduct". During the course of Easter Eve he continued his preparatory devotions, with fasting, prayer, and devout reading, whereof his faithful biographer related that "the humility and piety which he discovered on such occasions was truly edifying".[3] Further details of his religious exercises are recorded at the Easter season of 1777, which illustrate the observation of Boswell in the previous year that "there was always something particularly mild and placid in his manner upon that holy festival, the commemoration of the most joyful event in the history of the world, the resurrection of our Lord and Saviour, who, having triumphed over death and the grave, proclaimed immortality to mankind".[4] Equally

[1] J. Wickham Legg, *English Church Life*, pp. 36, 55.
[2] Boswell, *Life of Johnson*, 9 and 11 April 1773.
[3] *Ibid.* 14 and 16 April 1775.   [4] *Ibid.* 7 April 1776.

significant of Johnson's careful preparation for the reception of the Sacrament was his unwillingness to communicate without preconsideration, as when on Sunday 3 June 1781 he went with Boswell to Southill Church where, the Sacrament being administered, Boswell stayed to partake but Johnson withdrew. Upon which the doctor commented afterwards, "You did right to stay and receive the communion; I had not thought of it"; implying, as his friend understood, "that he did not choose to approach the altar without a previous preparation".[1]

Other evidence of lay piety may be quoted from the practice of men of affairs and statesmen. For although the profession of politics in eighteenth-century England embraced eminent libertines, amongst whom Bolingbroke, the high tory and leader of the church party, would take prior place to his rival, the whig Walpole, yet churchmen of sincere religion were numbered also with its adherents. Viscount Percival, first earl of Egmont, was a busy politician of the times of Walpole, who devoted himself further to many good works in connection with the religious and moral welfare of the inhabitants of the new colony of Georgia, and at the board of the Society for the Propagation of the Gospel. His diary reveals him as a regular and frequent communicant not only upon the great festivals but upon ferial Sundays, attending divine service twice generally on Sundays, either in the privacy of his family or at public worship, and training his household to make special commemoration of Good Friday, as the entry for 7 April 1732 illustrates. "This being Good Friday, my wife and I and children kept the fast, and went morning and evening to St James' Church."[2] Bishop Newton related likewise of George Grenville that he was "a religious, good man, and regularly attended the service of the church every Sunday morning even while he was in the highest office";[3] whilst Bishop Pearce testified of his friend William Pulteney, earl of Bath, that "he constantly attended the public worship of God and all the offices of it in his parish church, while his health permitted it, and when his great age and infirmities prevented him from so doing, he supplied that defect by daily reading over the Morning service of the church before he came out of his bedchamber".[4]

Not the least representative of the laity of Georgian England was the duke of Newcastle, whose affection for the Church which owed to him

[1] Boswell, *Life of Johnson*, 3 June 1781.
[2] *Diary of Viscount Percival, earl of Egmont*, i, 255. Hist. MSS. Comm.
[3] *Life of Dr Thomas Newton*, in *op. cit.* ii, 157.
[4] *Life of Zachary Pearce*, in *op. cit.* i, 408.

so many ornaments of its episcopal bench was sincere and profound. An obituary notice in the *Annual Register* of 17 November 1768 described him as "affable and religious, having divine service constantly performed twice a day in his family, both in town and country, and at stated times the Sacrament was administered, at which he constantly communicated". At Claremont his episcopal friends were always welcome, and his invitations to them to spend a week-end in his house were accompanied not infrequently by an injunction to pack a sermon in their bag, whilst in the absence of such distinguished divines his faithful chaplain, Thomas Hurdis, was an acceptable preacher to his patron. But the duke's attitude towards the solemn duty of receiving the Sacrament was most characteristic of his own disposition and illustrative of the religious temper of his age. Hanoverian churchmen approached the Holy Communion with a sense of awe, and upon occasion with a haunting fear lest unworthy participation should provoke not a blessing but a curse upon them. Their especial desire was that reception should be attended by feelings of inward peace and assurance. On Easter Day 1777 Dr Johnson recorded his sentiments upon attendance at church. "I was for some time much distressed, but at last obtained, I hope, from the God of peace, more quiet than I have enjoyed for a long time. I had made no resolution, but as my heart grew lighter, my hopes revived and my courage increased; ...I... passed the afternoon with such calm gladness of mind as it is very long since I felt before."[1] Boswell in like manner, after receiving the Communion on 3 June 1781, expressed himself "with unrestrained fervour to his guide, philosopher, and friend. 'My dear Sir, I would fain be a good man; and I am very good now. I fear God, and honour the king; I wish to do no ill, and to be benevolent to all mankind'".[2] The wish to experience this sense of consolation and elevation led to a great emphasis upon the approach to the Sacrament with due preparation; as to which Boswell noted that

good men entertained different opinions, some holding that it was irreverent to partake of that ordinance without considerable premeditation; others, that whoever is a sincere Christian and in a proper frame of mind to discharge any other ritual duty of our religion may without scruple discharge this most solemn one. A middle notion I believe to be the just one, which is, that communicants need not think a long train of preparatory forms indispensably necessary; but neither should they rashly and lightly venture upon so awful and mysterious an institution. Christians must judge, each for himself, what degree of retirement and self-examination is necessary upon each occasion.

[1] Boswell, *Life of Johnson, ad loc.*   [2] *Ibid.* 3 June 1781.

The Whole Duty of Man

If the spacious leisure of Dr Johnson did not induce a readiness to receive the Sacrament without premeditation, the busy official career of the duke of Newcastle might excuse a considerable perturbation on his part concerning the propriety of his proceeding from the council chamber to the Lord's Table to partake of the Holy Communion. In this perplexity of mind he turned naturally to his especial episcopal *protégé*, Bishop Hume of Oxford and Sarum, who exercised the office of spiritual director to his grace, and whose counsel in this high matter of conscience is revealed in a series of private letters during the years 1765–6. These letters are indeed of so intimate a nature that intrusion upon their confidences might be unpardonable, save for the obligation to portray the indubitable piety of that minister of state whose political probity has been universally besmirched. In December 1764 the duke wrote to his friend to the effect that "he had read over the Communion service, where there were some expressions which, he might say, gave him some uneasiness, or created some doubt of what he proposed to do", though he omitted to specify them in detail.[1] The bishop in reply could only conjecture that the scruples related to the fear of receiving unworthily, which he explained by expounding the particular scandals of the Corinthian church by which St Paul's warnings had been provoked. This assurance did not allay his grace's fears; whereupon Hume wrote more particularly on the matter.

"The passion of fear", he urged, "may get the better of reason and often does; but still reason cannot cease to be reason, though it may cease to have its proper influence upon our minds. But after all, what is *your* fear in particular? Is it not a fear of offending God? Is it not a fear of your unworthiness? Consider then. Does not this fear of offending imply a desire of doing what is acceptable? Does not this fear of unworthiness imply a humble desire of rendering yourself more worthy? In this view the fear itself is the strongest proof of worthiness; it never springs up in a worthless, presumptuous, or profligate mind. In you it can be no more than a just sense of your own unworthiness, which we all ought to carry with us in all our addresses to God. This is a sense which, if we repent of the past and intend to obey Him for the future, so far from deterring us to come to Him, is the strongest motive that ought to induce us, because it is the only means of pardon for the past, the surest means of obtaining grace for the future, and we have His express promise that whoever comes to Him with this humble frame of mind He will in no ways cast out....I firmly believe that, instead of alarming yourself, after performing this act of devotion you will find a

---

[1] Bp. Hume to Duke of Newcastle, 19 and 20 Dec. 1764. Add. MSS. 33068, ff. 265, 267.

serenity and composure of mind from a consciousness of having endeavoured to pay a debt of humiliation and gratitude to the beneficent Author of all happiness both in this world and the next."[1]

Unfortunately the duke was prevented by infirmity from making his Christmas Communion, but Hume bade him not to be uneasy in mind on that account.

"Religion lays us under no such severe obligations as to expose our health to such manifest hasard", he insisted. "We are in the hands of a most gracious Creator who knows whereof we are made, who judges of our actions by the intentions of our hearts, who makes allowances for every circumstance, every infirmity, and is always more ready to extend His mercy to us than we are to ask it. Your grace's purposes of endeavouring to render yourself still more acceptable against another season will, I doubt not, derive a blessing on them, while the consciousness of those prayers and endeavours will satisfy your own heart and strengthen it with more confidence in the mercies of God through Christ."[2]

The vacillation and timorousness which characterised Newcastle's political conduct penetrated unhappily into his devotions, and he was harassed repeatedly by fears of his unworthiness to communicate as the great festivals of the Church recurred in their season. On St Thomas' Day 1765, the bishop of Oxford counselled him again to cast out such unreal fancies.

"You have done it so lately and so properly", he observed, "that I wonder you should not think yourself in a proper state of mind (for business is no objection); but as you have some doubt about it, determine at once to defer it to another season when your mind is more disengaged from worldly concerns. As your doubt arises from your opinion of the high importance of the duty, your absenting yourself cannot spring either from neglect or wanting to avoid it; but only that you cannot at this particular juncture satisfy yourself or answer your own ideas of what you ought to be."[3]

The duke however could be content neither to receive nor to abstain, for uncertainty vexed him even when he had resolved to wait for a more distant occasion. On Christmas Day he wrote to the bishop to explain, in his customarily voluminous manner, the reasons which had prompted his abstention.

The additional circumstances of having been hurried up to town yesterday by the ministers, returned to dinner at six o'clock last night, and I am to go

---

[1] Bp. Hume to Duke of Newcastle, 22 Dec. 1764. *Ibid.* f. 275.
[2] Same to Same, 25 Dec. 1764. *Ibid.* f. 283.
[3] Same to Same, 21 Dec. 1765. Add. MSS. 33069, f. 357.

to town to attend a chapter of the Garter tomorrow, to have a private conference with my lord Rockingham in the evening: these things have so filled my mind that I really have not had time enough seriously upon subjects of greater importance, or to make any preparation to satisfy myself; and therefore I determined to lay aside the thought of it this day. And as I did so, I thought it more decent to have church at home than come away after sermon.... With regard to any other part of the service of the day, I can assure you I had no loss. For Mr Hurdis made one of his best and most edifying sermons upon the day that I ever heard or read. You may be surprised. I am sure I have got a great deal by it. It was to prove the truth of Christianity from the prophecies in the Old Testament.... Notwithstanding I can't say I am quite easy in having absented myself this day. I doubt my reasons were not quite sufficient. The appearance as well as the reality of having distinguished and separated myself from the others who did their duty better, gives me some uneasiness. But however I shall endeavour to comfort myself by knowing the real truth of my motives and from your kind letter.[1]

With the near approach of Easter hesitation and disquietude resumed possession of his mind, and after the receipt of episcopal advice justifying either reception or the reverse, his grace resolved finally to partake of the Communion. Despite this happy action he was perplexed once more upon the advent of Whitsun, when Hume despatched a further exhortation to tranquillity of mind.

For the approaching festival itself was instituted to put us in mind that without the grace of God we can do nothing, but to comfort us at the same time with promises of divine aid to supply our defects, and to render our imperfect services acceptable to our Creator.... While we continue in this world, we have a part to act in it, which cannot be carried on without engaging our thoughts and attention, but while these thoughts exclude not the thoughts and attention to another world, they are innocent and very consistent both with reason and religion, nor need we think ourselves bad Christians for being good citizens.[2]

The episode of his Whitsun Communion illustrated moreover the duke's concern for careful preparation for the Sacrament. He left London for Claremont on the Thursday, and "having by that means on Friday and Saturday some leisure, he employed it in the best manner he could", and accordingly "considering that no other opportunity would offer till Michaelmas, he did resolve to do that which he thought was his duty, and hoped would be acceptably received by his Creator and

[1] Newcastle to Hume, 25 Dec. 1765. Add. MSS. 32972, f. 339.
[2] Hume to Newcastle, 10 May 1766. Add. MSS. 33069, f. 469.

Redeemer, and best tend to remove his former difficulties".[1] Even more thorough was his preparatory exercise for the Christmas Eucharist of 1766, concerning which he consulted the bishop of Sarum on 4 December, adding the invitation to his lordship to come to Claremont on the Sunday before the Nativity, "and by his conversation in that week prepare him for it". In his own regard he had been reading Addison, and Tillotson's sermons. "So far as I have read", he averred of the archbishop's discourses, "they relate to the great mysteries of Christianity, the existence of our Saviour before the creation of the world, His not being created but the Creator of all things, our Saviour's Incarnation, etc. These points are very necessary and material to know, and I intend to go on with reading them".[2] But Archbishop Drummond of York had hinted to Newcastle that his theological studies should "not go too deep"; whereupon the duke appealed to Hume for the recommendation of less exhaustive books. The bishop in reply argued that the archbishop's advice "did not relate to any particular writers on religious subjects, but to himself in reading them"; so that he should

"rest satisfied on the great leading Facts on which the truth of religion is founded, without seeking for an explanation of mysteries which are in their own nature inexplicable. As to particular works," continued his lordship, "I know of none more proper than those your grace has been reading, or are now reading; such as Tillotson, Sherlock, Addison. Dr Clark's sermons are also very clear and instructive. But my lord, I really think you read as much as is necessary for you. Religion does not consist in reading; it is one of the means by which we come to religion and by which religion is kept up, and preserved in the soul; but if we find our hearts truly devoted to the will of God as revealed to us through Christ, we have all the essential benefit that reading can give and are always prepared for the most solemn acts of homage we can pay to our Creator. What else would become of the religion of those who cannot read? I say this because I am really afraid of your grace's introducing confusion into your ideas instead of light by reading too many authors on the same subject; for they are apt to differ in their reasonings though all agree in the main point on which they reason".[3]

The sincere piety which underlay the scruples and unworthy fears of Newcastle in his recourse to the most comfortable Sacrament of the Body and Blood of Christ was testified by his custom of reading "the lessons of the day, or if he omitted it one day, making it up afterwards", and by his requests to Hume to prepare occasional special prayers for

[1] Newcastle to Hume, 20 May 1766. Add. MSS. 32975, f. 225.
[2] Same to Same, 4 Dec. 1766. Add. MSS. 33071, f. 71.
[3] Hume to Newcastle, 9 Dec. 1766. Add. MSS. 33071, f. 83.

his private devotion. In August 1765 the bishop drew up a series of meditations for the Communion, embracing one suffrage of his own composition, two prayers from the Book of Common Prayer (the collect for the Fourth Sunday after Easter and the penultimate prayer at the end of the Communion Office), together with a short suffrage for daily use, morning and evening. In addition to these he recommended the recitation of the Lord's Prayer, "which is, and ought to be, used of course, since that indeed, if understood in its full extent and duly attended to, would almost render every other prayer superfluous", and in conclusion of the General Thanksgiving.[1] Accordingly the duke drew up in his own hand, and caused Hurdis to make fair copies of, a short form of devotion for the Holy Communion, including ejaculatory prayers before the service, before and after the reception of each of the elements, and two prayers to be said respectively after the conclusion of the action and in private thanksgiving subsequently.[2] During the last year of his life and upon recovery from an illness in the early winter which presaged the fatal attack, he asked his friend to compose a prayer of thanksgiving.

"The many serious conversations that I have had with your lordship," he wrote on 31 January 1768, "and the wise and convincing letters which I have had from you upon religious subjects, have made the most serious impressions upon my mind, and have prepared me for that happy state in which I hope by the blessing of God, it is now. And the blessing which I have lately received and which it has pleased God to grant me, by my recovery from the severe and dangerous fever I have had, has fixed in me a just sense of duty and gratitude for this mark of divine Providence, and a most lively and unfeigned belief of the truth of the holy gospel, and that our Saviour laid down His life to save sinners by faith and repentance. I must beg your lordship to prepare me a prayer of thanksgiving for His great mercy to me and for my recovery from this dangerous illness, accompanied by such marks of duty and gratitude as you may think proper."[3]

The response to this request was one of the last services which the bishop was able to render to his patron, for in the November following his grace deceased. The revelation of the traditional master of political corruption in the privity and intimacy of his religious devotion is not the least unexpected or edifying feature of a century, the quiet pieties of which have been overlooked in much noisy denunciation of its infidelity.

[1] Hume to Newcastle, 8 Aug. 1765. Add. MSS. 33069, ff. 157, 159.
[2] Paper of Devotion in Newcastle's hand. *Ibid.* f. 163. Extended copies in Hurdis' hand, ff. 164, 165. See Appendix B for these Private Devotions of Newcastle.
[3] Newcastle to Hume, 31 Jan. 1768. Add. MSS. 33072, f. 93.

The religious tradition of eighteenth-century churchmanship was admittedly homespun and practical. Between the standards of clergy and laity there was no gulf fixed, but their conception of the duties of religion was homogeneous no less than moderate. The Church was conceived less as the august custodian of the keys of heaven and hell, than as the religious counterpart of civil society, wherein churchmanship was complementary to citizenship. The predominant tone of sermons was that of moderation, and their content was rational and ethical rather than emotional, dogmatic, or mystical. The absence indeed from the texture of representative Georgian divinity of a mystical element was an outstanding characteristic of the theology of an age, whose temper was hostile and alien to the notion of a *mysterium tremendum fascinans*. The villagers of the country and the citizens of the towns who paid their attendance upon Sundays at their parish churches did not conceive their approach as unto mount Sion, unto the heavenly Jerusalem, and to an innumerable company of angels. Rather they came to a concourse of their neighbours and acquaintance, "to converse with one another, to hear their duties explained, and to join in adoration of the Supreme Being". When in the last exercise their thoughts turned from the visible society there assembled to the communion of the spirits of just men made perfect, they numbered in that host of ghostly witnesses the brethren of their parishes whose virtues were recorded in homely phrase upon mural tablets before their eyes, and who were of the humble succession of those who sit not high in the congregation, but whose work will maintain the fabric of the world and in the handywork of whose craft is their prayer.

CHAPTER VII

THE ALLIANCE OF CHURCH AND STATE IN ENGLAND

"In England alone", wrote William Warburton in 1736, "the original terms of this convention [between the religious and civil societies] are kept up so exactly that this account of *The Alliance between Church and State* seems rather a copy of the church and state in England, than a theory as indeed it was, formed solely on the contemplation of nature and the unvariable reason of things; and had no further regard to our particular establishment than as some parts of it tended to illustrate these abstract reasonings."

This confident optimism concerning the correspondence between the establishment of England and the eternal order of the universe was congenial to Warburton's contemporaries of the middle of the eighteenth century, who accepted readily his demonstration that the Revolution settlement of the position of the established church and of the toleration act had fixed the relations of church and state upon an unassailable basis.

"Nothing in the world is more contrary to my judgment of things", affirmed Archbishop Herring to Lord Hardwicke in 1748, "than to make alterations in our establishment, of which in some sense the toleration act is a part; and what I am determined to stick to, is the support of these two in conjunction. I think philosophy, Christianity, and policy are all against changes."[1]

The sentiment of abhorrence of innovation was intensified during the later generations of the century by the eruption of Methodist "enthusiasm" at home and of atheistic tendencies abroad during the revolutionary upheaval in France. By comparison with such extremes the *Ecclesia Anglicana* appeared as a providential city of refuge both from fanaticism and infidelity, preserving religion from the contamination of superstition and statecraft from degeneracy into regicide. But the assurance of the excellence of the English model in church and state which characterised the latter half of the Georgian era had not been attained without endurance of much controversy and dispute in the early years of the century, which had opened with the dynastic revolution of 1689. That revolution, though relatively peaceful in execution, was not

---

[1] Herring to Hardwicke, 13 Sept. 1748. Add. MSS. 35598, f. 342.

the less thoroughgoing in essentials, since it effected a root and branch extirpation of the monarchy ruling by divine hereditary right and substituted therefor a parliamentary elective kingship. The gravity of the breach with tradition effected thereby was emphasised by the non-juror secession, in which the primate Sancroft, with five of his suffragans, and followed by about four hundred of the inferior clergy, suffered deprivation rather than commit the sin of perjury involved in swearing allegiance to the new monarchy. Nor was their departure concealed by circumstances of secrecy and privity. Instead it gave occasion to a pro-tracted literary controversy, the protagonists of which challenged the validity of the position of the established church as a true branch of Christ's Catholic and Apostolic Church, by asserting its schismatic character against the faithful remnant of non-juring congregations who had preserved the integrity of their profession. The ensuing dispute covered the entire ground of political and ecclesiastical issues raised by the Revolution settlement, upon the determination of which depended the stability of the new *régime*. The consideration of the alliance between church and state in eighteenth-century England must commence there-fore with an examination of the significance of the events of 1689 and of the rival theories deduced therefrom, upon the basis of which its further development rested.

The esteem and reputation of the non-jurors have risen greatly since Macaulay's opprobrious aspersion of their tenets as sacrificing "both liberty and order to a superstition as stupid and degrading as the Egyptian worship of cats and onions".[1] Instead of this contemptuous dismissal of their polemic, it is not unusual in the present age to read justifications of their secession as an assertion of the spiritual inde-pendence of the church, and by implication of all voluntary associations of men, against the overwhelming authority of the modern state. A recent commentator has affirmed the bold opinion that

in challenging the assumption of the lay power to control ecclesiastical affairs and in their unflinching insistence on the spiritual autonomy of the church, the Non-Jurors were not the conservative defenders of a forsaken belief, but were pioneering in the attempt to save the church from Erastianism. Not only so, they were unwittingly, but none the less surely, asserting the rights of individuals and minorities against the omnicompetence of the Hobbesian state, for to admit man's essential freedom in spiritual matters was to open the door for his claim to freedom in other directions also. They were helping to win freedom of conscience for the individual no less than that freedom

---

[1] Macaulay, *History of England* (ed. C. H. Firth), vol. IV, ch. xiv, p. 1711.

which is so vitally necessary to the existence of associations within the state. If on the "state point" time has proved them to have been on the losing side, on the "church point" it has no less certainly been in their favour.[1]

It may be doubted however whether the non-jurors would have recognised the divorce between the state and church points necessary to establish this conclusion, and it is perhaps scarcely open to doubt that the advocacy of the spiritual freedom of the church contained in some writings of their members would have been as incompatible with the rule of the lawful sovereigns, Charles and James II, as with that of the intruders William of Orange and George of Hanover. Mr Laski has averred more truly that "the real interest of the non-juring schism was political rather than religious, and its roots go out to vital events of the past",[2] bearing only an accidental parentage to the principles of the future.

The non-juror protest against the deprivation of prelates unable to accept the oath of allegiance to the new monarchy was based less upon a persuasion of the incompetence of the lay power to exact such oaths than upon the incapacity of the parliamentary rulers set up by the Convention Parliament to require any loyalty from their subjects save that of involuntary acquiescence in conquest by force of arms. James II's suspension of Bishop Compton of London from the exercise of the functions of his office and the appointment of three bishops to discharge his episcopal duties was no less a violation of the spiritual independence of the church than the nomination by William III of Tillotson to the see of Canterbury vacant by the deprivation of Sancroft. But the former act provoked no disavowal of communion with the church thus oppressed by the Stuart king, and no charge of Erastianism, albeit Sancroft had refused to serve on the Court of High Commission created by that sovereign to exercise his jurisdiction as Supreme Ordinary. The essential difference lay in the circumstances that James II was the king *divino jure*, whose tyrannies must be suffered with no more protest than passive resistance, whilst William III was an usurper and no lawful king, whose deprivations involved his ecclesiastical supporters in the sin of schism and compelled resistance to the extent of the setting up of separate congregations claiming to be the true Church of England. The same action performed successively by the Lord's Anointed and by the creature-king of a self-styled parliament assumed a different character

---

[1] L. M. Hawkins, *Allegiance in Church and State: The Problem of the Non-Jurors in the English Revolution*, pp. 167–8 (London, 1928).

[2] H. J. Laski, *Political Thought in England from Locke to Bentham*, p. 66.

in each case and evoked a different reply from believers in the divine right of kings. Nor may the later demands of the non-juring leaders, developed under the stress of controversy, for the complete freedom of the church from control by the civil power admit of reconciliation with the historic policy of the later Stuart kings. If the contention of Leslie in his *Case of the Regale and the Pontificate* be sound—namely that "the right to meet, to consult, to make rules or canons for the regulation of the society is essential to every society as such, and consequently to the Church as she is a society"—then not only was the Act of Submission of 1534 (whereby the convocations could not be summoned without the royal writ directing the archbishop thereto, nor proceed to the framing of canons without royal licence) an improper usurpation by the crown under which the Reformed Church had suffered from the moment of its disavowal of papal obedience; but further, Charles and James II had inflicted an additional violation of its rights by their deliberate omission to issue such licence to the convocation from 1664 to 1689, thereby condemning that body to merely formal assembly for the space of a quarter of a century. No other name than Erastian could surely be applied to an oppression which had deprived the church thus of the opportunity of deliberation upon the things concerning its peace. But the prerogatives of the Lord's Anointed were unlimited, even though painfully exercised. The non-juror protest was therefore political in principle, looking backwards to the obsolescent doctrine of divine indefeasible hereditary right. Notwithstanding, it had ecclesiastical implications of vital importance alike for seceders and conformists, the exploration of which bears evident relevance to the problem of the alliance of church and state in the century following the revolution settlement.

To the personal probity, sincerity, and conscience of the non-juring churchmen ample tribute has been paid by contemporary and succeeding generations. To their fellows indeed they presented a moving, and occasionally accusatory, spectacle of leaders who esteemed the reproach of the doctrine of the Cross greater riches than the treasures of the establishment, and chose rather to suffer affliction with the remnant of true believers than to enjoy the pleasures of sin for a season by perjury. Nor was any other course of action open to them upon their own premiss of the inviolability of oaths taken to the lawful sovereign. Recognition of William and Mary was impossible, since their enthronisation symbolised the victory of *force majeure* over the principles of divine right. Equally inconceivable was the continuance of non-jurors in the offices of a church which prayed for the new monarchs in its public services to the exclusion of the proper sovereign of the realm. Secession and refusal of conformity were therefore inevitable, and from such steps the formation of separatist congregations was a necessary consequence. Bishops and priests could not cease so to be by virtue of deprivation of benefices and emoluments; and their ministrations must be transferred from the perjured congregations to the faithful gatherings of Jacobite dissentients. Neither formal theory nor the exigency of practical consistency was lacking to support this procedure. But the act of separation once made, endeavours towards a theoretical justification followed naturally; and in the literary controversy which ensued, the seceders adopted a bold offensive, stigmatising the established church as schismatic and apostate, and asserting that the true succession of catholic and apostolic principles of churchmanship had devolved upon their own societies. From their standpoint the established church was no longer the true episcopal church of the realm, any more than William and Mary were its rightful sovereigns. A fatal breach had been effected in the polity of both church and state, whereby the monarchy *divino jure* was resident in the exiles' court at St Germain, and the catholic tradition in religion amongst the separated non-juror assemblies.

The gravamen of the charge against the conformist establishment lay in the deprivation of the non-juring prelates and priests by the crown and its nomination of other divines to the offices thereby vacated. Upon this point the controversy centred. It has been argued by a recent champion of the non-jurors that

these deprivations were carried out without the semblance of ecclesiastical authority, and, emanating from the purely secular court of parliament as they did, they were in the eyes of the high church party absolutely illegal and void. When, in course of time, the sees of the deprived bishops were filled (again by the secular authority), the new holders by accepting office not legally vacant, came to be regarded as anti-bishops, and therefore as the creators of a schism in the church.[1]

It may be granted that the church which acquiesced in the Revolution settlement must justify its acceptance of the deprivation of the non-juring clergy, though the fundamental issue at stake is industriously obscured by allegations of lack of ecclesiastical authority and of purely secular procedure, since it was precisely upon the truth of such contentions that the dispute was concentrated.

"If it be unlawful to succeed a deprived bishop," observed Stillingfleet in his *Vindication of their Majesties' Authority to fill the sees of the Deprived*

[1] L. M. Hawkins, *op. cit.* pp. 47–8.

Bishops, "then he is bishop of the diocese still; and then the law that deprives him, is no law, and consequently the king and parliament that made that law, no king and parliament; and how can this be reconciled with the oath of allegiance, unless the doctor can swear allegiance to him who is no king and hath no authority to govern?"

The question of the rectitude of the deprivations turned therefore upon the authority of the king and parliament which had imposed the oath of allegiance. If their authority were unreal and usurped, as the non-jurors contended, all their actions were unlawful; but if the practical necessity for the deposition of James II were accepted as justification for the Revolution, then the imposition of oaths of allegiance to the new rulers was proper and necessary. Once again to the non-juring seceders the state point and the church point were indissolubly connected; and their objection was not to the exercise of the right of deprivation by the sovereign, but to its exercise by one who was no rightful king but an usurper.

This point was specifically admitted by Kettlewell.

In Christian kingdoms the church is incorporated into the state, and by the benefit of this incorporation bishops and pastors have their spiritual ministrations backed with secular effects and censures. All these secular fortifications, jurisdictions, and encouragements in their ministrations, conferred on bishops and pastors of an incorporate church, are the gifts of the state, and are secular additions to what spiritual powers they received from Jesus Christ. And what the state gives, the state when it sees cause may deprive them of.[1]

His conclusion therefrom was clear, that "although the state has no power either to give or to deprive the ministers of Christ of their mere spiritual powers, yet it has a direct authority to grant and deprive them of their temporal additions". The nomination of the non-juror bishops themselves to the sees to which they were consecrated had been the act of the king, and the royal mandate for consecration had been read as part of the office for their setting-apart to that function. Further, they had taken the oath of allegiance to the sovereign, and done homage for the temporalties of their sees. In their deprivation therefore the civil power had taken away merely what it had bestowed, namely the right to enjoy the temporalties attaching to the episcopal dignity, and to exercise the office and work of a bishop within the territorial jurisdiction

[1] J. Kettlewell, *Of Christian Communion to be kept in the Unity of Christ's Church*, Pt. II, ch. I.

to which they had been nominated by the crown. No attempt had been made to degrade them from the ecclesiastical order to which they had been ordained or consecrated, nor to impugn the spiritual validity of the sacraments and rites which they continued to administer. The problem as to whether their deprivations were "carried out without the semblance of ecclesiastical authority", and therefore their sees were "not legally vacant", depended upon the view taken of the validity of the change of monarchy from James II to William III, since the only ground for aspersing the latter's actions as lacking semblance of ecclesiastical authority and legal force lay in the conviction that no human resolution could alter the divine appointment of an hereditary monarchy in the kingdom. The suspension by James II of Bishop Compton from exercising the spiritual functions of his episcopate, though allowing his retention of the revenues of his see, had been equally a violation of the spiritual independence of the church as the deprivations of William III. The same logic indeed which justified the non-juror secession could be employed to establish the position of their opponents, granted the initial point of the lawfulness of breaking the hereditary succession to the throne. Herein again it was not to Erastianism that the non-jurors objected, but to the apostasy involved in the expulsion of the king *divino jure* and the substitution of an elective monarchy. Persuasion of the inviolability of the divine decree of hereditary monarchy inevitably led them to secession; and a conviction of the lawfulness of the Revolution settlement as logically led divines supporting William III to accept at his hands nominations to the sees vacated by the refusal of their occupants to take the oath of allegiance. Accordingly the sees were filled, not merely "by the secular authority", but by virtue also of the co-operation of the ecclesiastical power in capitular election and consecration of the bishops-elect by three of their brethren, according to the same procedure and rite as their non-juring predecessors.

There were individuals indeed amongst the clerical associates of the victorious whigs who were not afraid of the accusation, nor the fact, of Erastianism. The posthumous publication in 1716 of the papers of Dean Hickes provoked from the pen of Hoadly *A Preservative against the Principles and Practices of the Non-Jurors both in Church and State*, in which the axe was laid to the root of their principles. Hoadly was nothing if not thorough, for he undertook to answer the triple contention of Hickes by asserting the justification of the Revolution as a civil transaction, the power of the state to deprive any ecclesiastics who aspersed the legality of the consequent settlement, and the erroneous character of all notions of the church as a *societas perfecta* as being subversive of the true nature of the Christian religion. In the first two categories he stated current opinions. The deposition of James II was justified on the ground of incapacity to rule, which incapacity in the circumstances of a Protestant nation consisted evidently in the profession of Popery; and accordingly the Revolution was restrained to the setting aside of popish branches of the royal family, "the very first Protestant branches in the same family being declared heirs and the succession from them declared and confirmed". In the matter of deprivations Hoadly swept aside equivocations and half-measures, such as were advanced by persons who "acknowledged deprivation by the lay power to be invalid, and only pleaded against carrying the matter to a separation upon that account". He enunciated the general doctrine of "the right which the supreme power hath to all things necessary to its own defence and preservation", and which embraced the "right inherent in it and inseparable from it, to guard the society from being undone by ecclesiastical officers as well as by laymen".[1] In the particular case of the deprived non-jurors he insisted that whatever the character imparted by consecration, "the right of exercising this authority in their particular dioceses ariseth originally from the nomination of the king", and therefore deprivation meant simply the inhibition of these bishops "from the right to execute the episcopal office" within any diocese of the established church.[2] Not indeed that he denied to the state the power to take away what it had not conferred if that were necessary to its preservation, such as the freedom of individuals to public expression of their religious opinions where such opinions, as in the case of the non-jurors, impinged upon matters of civil nature. Since therefore "public praying and preaching against a civil government is to that government entirely of a civil nature", it followed that "deprivation by the civil power is a point of a civil nature, and ariseth not from any mixing of two incoherent powers, but from the one undoubted and undeniable principle of self-defence".[3]

It would have been well for the peace of the establishment if Hoadly had rested content with this demonstration that the non-juring prelates "having been rightfully deposed, their successors were the regular bishops and the church of their successors the true church"; for the consensus of national opinion, both clerical and lay, supported the jurors against their dissentient brethren. But the attempt of the non-jurors to justify their secession had led them into profounder specula-

---

[1] Hoadly, "A Preservative against the Principles and Practices of the Non-Jurors" (*Works*, i, 574).

[2] *Ibid.* pp. 570, 572.   [3] *Ibid.* p. 582.

tions concerning the inherent spiritual rights of the church, wherein they adumbrated theories subversive certainly of the traditional conditions of the establishment in England. In their isolated circumstances the enunciation of such doctrines had little practical import; but whereas their theories of the church as a *societas perfecta* and of its inherent spiritual independence might have provoked little notice and produced less practical effect apart from the retort of Hoadly, the opportunity presented by his extreme affirmations of the power of the state in relation to the church was not missed by non-juring combatants to besmirch the revolution settlement with the opprobrium of Byzantine Erastianism.

In the last section of his polemic against non-juror principles Hoadly denied in set terms that God could possibly require as a condition of salvation that all men should belong to one external communion, and that He could commit the power of absolution to any society of fallible mortals. Only the papal church by its claim to infallibility could pretend to such a divine delegation of authority. In contradiction to which authoritarian doctrine he declared his own principle of unfettered private judgment as the essence of Christianity. "Every one may find it in his own conduct to be true, that his title to God's favour cannot depend upon his actual being or continuing in any particular method, but upon his real sincerity in the conduct of his conscience and of his own actions under it." From which premiss he concluded that "the favour of God follows sincerity considered as such; and consequently equally follows every equal degree of sincerity".[1] The implications of this evangel of unrestrained individualism were made explicit in the famous sermon preached on 31 March 1717 from the text, "My kingdom is not of this world", and originating the furious Bangorian controversy. The purpose of the discourse was to rescue the word "church" from erroneous and confused ideas which had become associated with it; and this was to be achieved by identifying the church with the kingdom of Christ and deducing the character of the former from the meaning attached by Christ to the word "kingdom". From this standpoint Hoadly laid down two basic principles: first, that in the kingdom of Christ "He is Himself sole lawgiver to His subjects; and Himself the sole judge of their behaviour in the affairs of conscience and eternal salvation"; and secondly, that the *differentia* between His kingdom and the kingdoms of this world lay in the circumstance that "He had in those points left behind Him no visible human authority, no vicegerents who

---

[1] Hoadly, "A Preservative against the Principles and Practices of the Non-Jurors" (*Works*, i, 593).

can be said properly to supply His place, no interpreters upon whom His subjects are absolutely to depend; no judges over the consciences or religion of His people".[1] Accordingly the Christian Church was declared to bear subjection only to an absentee ruler, Christ Himself, who neither intervened personally to interpret His laws nor commissioned any person to act in His stead.

For if this were so, that any such absolute vicegerent authority, either for the making of new laws or interpreting old ones, or judging his subjects in religious matters, were lodged in any men upon earth; the consequence would be, that what still retains the name of the Church of Christ would not be the kingdom of Christ, but the kingdom of these men, vested with such authority. For whoever hath such an authority of making laws is so far a king; and whoever can add new laws to those of Christ, equally obligatory, is as truly king as Christ Himself; nay, whoever hath an absolute power to interpret any written or spoken laws; it is he who is truly the lawgiver to all intents and purposes, and not the Person who first wrote or spoke them.

The practical consequences of these principles were alarming, at any rate when professed by a bishop of the established church. For if Christ were sole ruler of the church, "all His subjects in what station whatsoever they be, are equally subjects to Him; and no one of them more than another hath authority, either to make new laws for Christ's subjects, or to impose a sense upon the old ones; or to judge, censure, or punish the servants of another Master in matters relating purely to conscience or salvation". In effect the church was an invisible society, consisting of "the number of men, whether small or great, who truly and sincerely are subjects to Jesus Christ alone as their lawgiver and judge in matters relating to the favour of God and their eternal salvation".[2] Profession of Christianity should not be associated with temporal rewards, nor should the church invoke the secular arm to support its authority; and in matters of belief Christians should have recourse solely to the private reading of the New Testament, seeking there "all these particulars in those plain and short declarations of their king and lawgiver" contained in the evangelic record. It was evident from the tenor of this sermon that Hoadly had reduced the visible church to ruins, and enthroned in its place the principle of unlimited private judgment.

Before passing to a consideration of the Bangorian controversy which ensued, it may be not impertinent to observe that this theorising con-

---

[1] Hoadly, "The Nature of the Kingdom or Church of Christ" (*Works*, ii, 404).
[2] *Ibid.* p. 406.

cerning the abstract authority and rights of the Christian Church was as irrelevant to the points at issue between juror and non-juring churchmen as the doctrines of Leslie in their turn. The problems of the political and ecclesiastical issues of the Revolution settlement, especially the lawfulness of oaths of allegiance to William III and the deprivations of non-juror prelates, had been discussed and determined by Hoadly antecedent to his excursus on the Nature of the Kingdom or Church of Christ. In point of fact the great majority of churchmen who supported the new *régime*, including the most eminent whig divines, repudiated the extreme theories of Hoadly concerning ecclesiastical authority as heartily as they did the notions of Leslie. The practical choice lay, not between a society divested of all authority in accordance with the Bangorian sermon and a *societas perfecta* demanding entire freedom of action in spiritual matters from the state, but between the establishment as menaced by the actual policy of James II and as safeguarded by the provision of the Revolution settlement that the ruling monarch must always be in communion with it. It was no essential part of the new order to deny to the church a proper authority within its own sphere; for though the sentiments of the notorious sermon received the imprimatur of royal approval, the volume and vehemence of denunciation which descended upon the author afforded convincing proof, if such were needed, to the whig administration that their ecclesiastical policy could not be allied with such a veritable kingdom of fairies.

Notwithstanding, the doctrines enunciated with such uncompromising thoroughness plunged the church and realm into an orgy of controversy. Into its details it is happily unnecessary to penetrate even so far as to enumerate the number and various quality of pamphlets pouring from the press. Nor need attention be diverted to the minor incidents upon which overmuch ink was spilt, such as the difficult question whether the adjective "absolute", wherewith the preacher had qualified his references to church authority, had been originally spoken from the pulpit or had been added before printing upon the advice of a friend, together with a host of trivial circumstances. For, although the insertion of such an epithet might enable Hoadly to escape the evident deductions from his doctrine, there can be little doubt that his argument was interpreted correctly by William Law as designed "to dissolve the church as a society". It was from the pen of this distinguished writer that the most direct counter-attack upon Hoadly's position proceeded, and from a perusal of his *Three Letters to the Bishop of Bangor* the inadequacy of the notions expounded in the sermon may be realised. At the outset Law ridiculed the theory that sincerity alone should be the test of religious profession, since though it might testify plainly to moral integrity, it would in no wise discriminate between true and false beliefs.

If the favour of God equally follows every equal degree of sincerity, then it is impossible there should be any difference, either as to merit or happiness, between a sincere martyr and a sincere persecutor; and he that burns the Christian, if he be but in earnest, has the same title to reward for it, as he that is burnt for believing in Christ. . . . It will be allowed that sincerity is a necessary principle of true religion, and that without it all the most specious appearances of virtue are nothing worth: but still neither common-sense, nor plain Scripture, will suffer me to think that when our Saviour was on earth, they were as much in the favour of God who sincerely refused to be His disciples, and sincerely called for His crucifixion, as those who sincerely left all and followed Him.[1]

If private judgment were the sole constituent of religious allegiance, it would be impossible, not only to justify the continuance of the establishment, but to defend the creation of any visible Christian society. Hoadly had dissolved, whether deliberately or unwittingly, the entire fabric of organised corporate religion.

"Your lordship", retorted Law, "is ours, as you fill a bishopric; but we are at a loss to discover from this discourse what other interest we have in your lordship: for you openly expose our communion, and give up all the advantages of it, by telling all sorts of people, if they are but sincere in their own way, they are as much in God's favour as anybody else. Is this supporting our interest, my lord?"[2]

Upon the basis of private judgment also no bishop ought properly to examine candidates for ordination as to whether their individual persuasion agreed with the official confessions of the church, if indeed the office of bishop embraced any authority whatsoever over fellow-Christians and equal subjects of the sole Lawgiver and King of Christ's kingdom.

Can these be called ministers of Christ or received as His ambassadors? Can they be thought to act in His name, who have no authority from Him? If so, your lordship's servant might ordain and baptise to as much purpose as your lordship: for it could only be objected to such actions, that they had no authority from Christ.[3]

[1] W. Law, *Three Letters to the Bishop of Bangor* (ed. J. O. Nash and C. Gore), pp. 52-3 (London, 1893).
[2] *Ibid.* p. 52.   [3] *Ibid.* p. 57.

In a passage of mordant irony Law counselled the bishop of Bangor in performing the rites of confirmation and ordination to caution the recipients against belief in their efficacy, and

to make them this declaration. "My friends, for the sake of decency and order, I have taken upon me the episcopal character; and, according to custom, which has long prevailed against common-sense, am now to lay my hands upon you; but I beseech you, as you have any regard to the truth of the Gospel or the honour of God, not to imagine there is anything in this action, more than an useless empty ceremony; for if you expect to have any spiritual advantage from human benedictions, or to receive grace from the imposition of a bishop's hands, you affront God and in effect renounce Christianity".[1]

Against Hoadly's insistence only upon sincerity, as "that which will help us to the communion of saints hereafter, though we are in communion with anybody or nobody here", Law proceeded to build up a constructive apologetic for orthodox Christianity conceived as a corporate society exercising authority over its members in matters of faith and practice. He had little difficulty in establishing his case from the evidence of apostolic times—wherein he observed that Hoadly must be compelled "to give up the apostles as furious high-church prelates, who aspired to presumptuous claims and talked of conferring the graces of God by their own hands"[2]—from the writings of the Fathers, and from the official formularies of the Reformed Church of England. Upon the basis of a consistent and impressive consensus of evidence, he contended for the authority of the traditions of historic Christianity, and concluded that his episcopal adversary had "by his doctrines, condemned the scriptures, the apostles, their martyred successors, the Church of England and his own conduct; and had thereby given some reason . . . to suspect whether his lordship, who allowed of no other church but what was founded in sincerity, were really himself a member of any church".[3] The refutation of the tenets of the Bangorian sermon was complete, but the validity of Hoadly's defence of the Revolution settlement in church and state was unaffected by the reverse which he sustained in this further controversy. The statement of the extreme Erastian position had demonstrated chiefly the isolation of its author among his clerical brethren, for in ecclesiastical polity as in its other eccentricities *Christianity secundum usum Winton*, as Secker aptly termed Hoadleian doctrine, was an individual heresy.

[1] W. Law, *Three Letters to the Bishop of Bangor* (ed. J. O. Nash and C. Gore), p. 83 (London, 1893).

[2] *Ibid.* p. 86.   [3] *Ibid.* p. 88.

By an accidental circumstance however the Bangorian controversy brought its originator into notoriety in another connection, by virtue of the fact that the intention of the lower house of Canterbury Convocation to draw the attention of the upper house to the strange tenets professed by one of its members, provoked a hasty prorogation of its session in May 1717 on the part of the administration of the day. Thus Hoadly became the immediate cause of that protracted suspension of convocation which continued until the middle of the nineteenth century. The history of the convocation controversy, which had raged almost continuously for twenty years previous and was the real cause of the silencing of its tumultuous assembly, presents a problem of difficulty by reason of its complexity. In the first place there were two convocation controversies, the one designed to secure the concession from the crown of a sitting convocation, and the other to emancipate the lower clergy when in session from the authority of the archbishop as president of the convocation. The latter dispute reflected also the delight of the inferior clergy to harass the Latitudinarian prelates who had been appointed by William III to bear rule over them, as was illustrated in the endeavour to procure a synodical censure of Burnet's *Exposition of the Thirty-Nine Articles*. With this purpose was connected the rivalry of whig and tory parties in the state, so that the fortunes of the convocation battle varied with the rise and fall of the influence of the political leaders with Queen Anne. So long as her majesty remained under whig counsel she intervened on the side of the bishops; as when in 1706 she declared her resolve "to maintain her supremacy and the due subordination of presbyters and bishops as fundamental parts thereof", and again in the following year she denounced a petition of the lower house as "a plain invasion of her royal supremacy" with the threat "to use such means for punishing offences of this nature as are allowed by law". When in 1710 the general elections returned a fervent tory house of commons and enabled Anne to confide the business of state to a purely tory administration, a studied slight was inflicted upon Archbishop Tenison for his whiggism, by the intrusion of the primate Sharp of York into preliminary discussions with the ministry concerning business to be laid before the convocation of Canterbury, from which his grace of Canterbury was excluded although the assembly related to his province; and by the issue of a royal licence of business specifying the subjects to be discussed but without nominating the primate as president. Amid such a medley of apparently unrelated elements, it is difficult to pursue a clear thread through the long dispute centring round the powers of the convocation; but beneath the accidental and transient rivalries of the moment real problems of the practical operation of the relations between church and state were latent, and it was upon these that the importance of the controversies rested.

When Francis Atterbury published in 1697 his *Letter to a Convocation Man* to sound the trumpet of danger to the clerical order, his insight had convinced him aright of the precarious situation of the historic assembly of the church. It is a commonplace to observe that William III had allowed no sitting convocation since 1689, when the lower clergy had exhibited so hostile a temper towards his favoured project for a comprehension. Less often is attention directed to the fact that in so doing he was but following the precedent set by Charles and James II, who had similarly made an end of sitting convocations during the quarter of a century between 1664 and the Revolution. But although the year 1664 is a vital landmark in the history of the convocations, the origins of the languor which afflicted their proceedings must be sought still farther back in the record of the seventeenth century. In fact the dream of a parity betwixt the convocation and the parliament, which was the inspiration and evangel of the forlorn campaign of Atterbury, had become impossible of realisation from the outbreak of the great Civil War. Previous to that watershed of constitutional development, the possibility had lingered that the convocation might transact ecclesiastical business by virtue of a royal licence to frame, and the royal assent to completed drafts of, canons which would possess the same legal authority as acts of parliament, but without the intermeddling of the parliament in affairs of an ecclesiastical character. If the clerical assembly could assert its exclusive right to deliberate upon matters concerning the church, under the protection and direction of the crown as supreme governor, then the coveted equality with the parliament would be established.

Behind this claim to parity there lay a respectable intellectual heritage. So learned a canonist as Dr Gibson, himself a chief opponent of the demands put forward by Attèrbury on behalf of the lower house of convocation, gave the weight of his name to that interpretation of the preamble to the Act of Appeals of 1533 which elevated the status of the convocations in relation to parliament. Commenting in the Introductory Discourse of his *Codex Juris Ecclesiastici Anglicani* upon the declaration in that preamble that the English Church

always hath been reputed, and also found of that sort, that both for knowledge, integrity, and sufficiency of number, it hath been always thought, and is also at this hour, sufficient and meet of itself without the intermeddling of any exterior person or persons, to declare and determine all such doubts, and to administer all such offices and duties, as to their rooms spiritual doth appertain,

he averred

that England is governed by two distinct Administrations: one Spiritual, for matters of a Spiritual nature; and the other Temporal, for matters of a Temporal nature. And for the same ends, hath it two Legislatures, the one consisting of persons Spiritual, and the other of persons Temporal; whose business it is, to frame the Laws for the government of Church and State; and these Laws being enacted and confirmed by the Prince, as Sovereign and Supreme Head, become obligatory to the people, and rules for the administration of justice in spiritual and temporal matters.[1]

This impeccable constitutional theory had been fulfilled in practice only partially by the Tudor monarchs themselves, as the melancholy "abstract of several things relating to the church, which have been done since the 25 Henry VIII by private commission or otherwise, out of convocation", collected by Wake in his *Authority of Christian Princes over their Ecclesiastical Synods asserted*, plainly testified. For into that category there fell both the Prayer Books of Edward VI, the Ordinal, and the Prayer Book revision of Elizabeth in 1559. Under the early Stuart kings a more consistent endeavour was made to observe the strict theory of church and state, and in 1604 the convocation and crown co-operated in the enactment of the Canons of 1604 without reference to parliament. Charles I espoused this method of procedure resolutely, and in a royal declaration issued in November 1628 and prefixed to the Articles, affirmed

that out of our princely care that the churchmen may do the work which is proper unto them, the bishops and clergy from time to time in convocation, upon their humble desire, shall have licence under our broad seal to deliberate of, and to do all such things as, being made plain by them, and assented unto by us, shall concern the settled continuance of the doctrine and discipline of the Church of England now established; from which we will not endure any varying or departing in the least degree.

In accordance with this policy the convocation of 1640 revised the Canons of 1604, presenting to the crown for assent the Canons of 1640, which became a symbol of the dispute between crown and parliament in ecclesiastical matters. For, although the validity of the canons has been called in question upon the legal ground of the continuation of the sessions of convocation beyond the dissolution of the Short Parliament,

---

[1] E. Gibson, *Introductory Discourse*, p. xxix.

it would appear that since "the parliament and convocation are separate bodies, independent of one another and called together by different writs, therefore the dissolution of the parliament doth not necessarily, or in any respect, dissolve the convocation, so that they may continue to sit longer than the parliament, if the king pleases".[1] Upon the assembly of the Long Parliament, the house of commons, not content with the passing of a resolution declaring the new canons invalid, proceeded further to resolve "that the clergy of England convented in any convocation or synod or otherwise, have no power to make any constitutions, canons, or acts whatsoever in matter of doctrine, discipline, or otherwise to bind the clergy or laity of this land without common consent of parliament". The commitment of the differences between the king and parliament to the arbitrament of the sword led to the abolition of the entire ecclesiastical administration of the church during the Commonwealth, and suspended the resolution of the rival claims of convocation and parliament to control ecclesiastical legislation.

With the Restoration of 1660, the convocations appeared to have come into their own again. Even granting the careful disqualification of the Canons of 1640 by an act of 13 Charles II, cap. 12, which denied to any "archbishop, bishop, or any other ecclesiastical judge or officer" the power "to confirm the canons made in the year 1640, or any of them, or any other ecclesiastical laws or canons not formerly confirmed, allowed, or enacted by parliament, or by the established laws of the land as they stood in the year of our Lord 1639", the task of Prayer Book revision was committed by royal letters of business to a joint committee of the convocations of Canterbury and York, which thus exercised a direct influence for the first time upon the liturgical standards of the church. But the faithful commons of the Cavalier parliament, though accepting by ninety-six votes to ninety, on 16 April 1662 the proposed changes without discussion, were careful to record and reserve the right to debate them, lest the omission so to do should prejudice their claim against the convocation. The final blow to the prestige of the convocations came in 1664 when

by a private agreement between the archbishop [Sheldon] and the lord chancellor Clarendon, and other the king's ministers, it was concluded that the clergy should silently waive the privilege of taxing their own body, and permit themselves to be included in the money bills prepared by the commons. And this hath made convocations unnecessary to the crown and inconsiderable in themselves.[2]

[1] R. Burn, *Ecclesiastical Law*, Article: "Convocation", i, 407 (2 vols. London, 1763).   [2] *Ibid.* p. 407.

The importance of this surrender indeed can hardly be exaggerated. Henceforth the crown had no need of their regular summons, and the intrinsic weight of the business commonly laid before them was insufficient of itself to ensure their regular session. The immediate consequence was the suspension of sitting convocations during the twenty-five years which divided the surrender of 1664 from the Revolution of 1689, in which space they were for the most part "only called and very rarely did so much as meet together in a full body and with the usual solemnity".

By 1697 therefore, when Atterbury launched his campaign for the revival of sitting convocations, the experience of a generation had emphasised the full meaning of the defeat which they had sustained at the hands of both the parliament and the sovereign. To outward appearance their very continuance seemed nigh unto vanishing away and their authority declined with each year of continued quiescence. The boldness of argument contained in the *Letter to a Convocation Man* was therefore noteworthy, inasmuch as it revived the strongest traditional claims for the parity of convocation and parliament. In his effort to raise the clergy from lethargy and indifference, Atterbury was resolved plainly to be content with no half-measures. His contention rested upon the perpetuation in the writs summoning the bishops to parliament of the Praemunientes clause first introduced by Edward I, from which he deduced that "the premonition or warning, being to those who are members of and constitute the lower house of convocation, is an argument of invincible strength to establish the necessity of convocations meeting as often as parliaments".[1] Further, when summoned the convocation enjoyed, according to his interpretation, the same rights and powers of deliberation and debate as the parliament, since the fact of its summons in obedience to royal writ "did not import a power of licensing them in their debates any more than it did in the case of a parliament". The chief objection to his theory lay in the terms of the famous Act of the Submission of the Clergy of 25 Henry VIII, cap. 19, by which the convocations promised

that they will never from henceforth presume to attempt, allege, claim, or put in ure, enact, promulge, or execute any new canons, constitutions, ordinances provincial, or other by whatsoever name they shall be called, in the convocation, unless the king's most royal assent and licence may to them be had, to make, promulge, and execute the same, and that his majesty do give his most royal assent and authority in that behalf.

[1] *A Letter to a Convocation Man*, 1697, p. 38.

To circumvent this restriction Atterbury adopted an ingenious hypothesis.

"To what purpose", he asked, "is a licence beforehand to make canons, since the king's assent must be had to them afterwards before they can be promulged? Does the Act say there shall be a double licence from the king? A leave in general to make canons is given them by their very writ of summons, and a leave in particular to make this or that canon is given them when the king assents to this or that particular canon; and what other leave, besides these, can be imagined or desired?"[1]

If this interpretation were accepted, the convocation would enjoy the same degree of liberty in debate and deliberation as the parliament, possessing freedom to initiate discussion of any particular topic, and to frame the draft of canons thereon subject to their ratification by the king. If therefore their right to meet with every parliament could be established and the corollary of their power to enter upon deliberation without further licence be allowed, the convocations might aspire again to play an important part in ecclesiastical matters. At least Atterbury had not shrunk from declaring the whole counsel of the inferior clergy, and he had further clothed his plea with the specious theory of "the great resemblance there is between a parliament and a convocation", which became the chief plank in his platform in the ensuing controversy.

The implications of his argument were not lost upon the majority of readers of his pamphlet, and from the pen of William Wake there appeared shortly a volume asserting *The Authority of Christian Princes over their Ecclesiastical Synods* in no uncertain tones. At the outset the gulf which divided Wake from Atterbury was evident in the former's studied depreciation of the value of frequent assemblies of convocation. Wake confessed frankly that "hitherto he did not see what need there was of a convocation, or what it could do to make things better than they were"; rather he "must needs say that should a convocation be allowed to meet so regularly, and to act so freely, as some men desired, he feared it would soon appear that the remedy was worse than the disease".[2] In his judgment therefore,

as in a well-established church it could hardly be supposed that there should be such frequent need of convocations; so to oblige the clergy frequently to come together, when there was no manner of reason for their so doing, would be in truth to injure the church and oppress its ministers; inasmuch as it

---

[1] *A Letter to a Convocation Man,* 1697, p. 56.
[2] Wake, *The Authority of Christian Princes over their Ecclesiastical Synods asserted,* 1697, pp. 324, 325.

would require them to leave their cures and be at the trouble and charge of attending the convocation, without doing any manner of good either to the church or realm by such their meeting.[1]

From a historical survey of the rights and authority exercised by Christian princes over their ecclesiastical synods from the days of the Christian Roman Empire, Wake passed to a more particular study of the case in England, which he summarised as contrary to the contention of his opponent in every point. He allowed only that "the church had a right to have its convocation called as often as the parliament was assembled";[2] but in differentiating sharply between the mere summons and sitting for the discussion of business, he insisted "that the king never ought to require the convocation to meet (more than out of form in parliament time) but when he has some business for it to do".[3] In the determination of the need for a sitting convocation Wake "knew no law besides the absolute and free power of the prince".[4] Since the king could determine the expediency of allowing the convocation to sit, so also he alone could decree the subjects of discussion when assembled. Without royal licence the convocations could not embark upon the consideration of even the slightest topic. "And as their sitting, so I affirm that their acting too does depend upon the will of the prince." Accordingly Wake concluded that "they cannot enter upon any business without his special commission for it; and whether he will grant them such a commission or no, depends entirely upon his own will".[5] Even when canons were presented for the royal assent, the king could "not only confirm, or disallow, but might sometimes even alter and correct what was done, according to his own liking".[6] The basis of this staunch defence of the royal authority rested upon a clear perception of the falsity of Atterbury's inference that the convocations met in response to the Praemunientes clause of the episcopal writs; which theory he dismissed with the irrefutable observation that

this is a convocation that for many years past has had no existence; and the convocation of which we are now disputing, is quite another thing, is summoned by another kind of writ, and consisted of another sort of persons; ...so that this invincible argument has one terrible defect in it; that, whether it could otherwise be answered or not, yet 'tis evidently nothing at all to the purpose.[7]

To high churchmen such doctrine was naturally anathema; and Atterbury lost no time in entering the lists again to show "the ab-

[1] Wake, *The Authority of Christian Princes*, p. 268.
[2] *Ibid.* p. 268.   [3] *Ibid.* p. 271.   [4] *Ibid.* p. 141.
[5] *Ibid.* pp. 142–3.   [6] *Ibid.* p. 136.   [7] *Ibid.* p. [284].

horrence he had of the unworthy treatment, which the reputation and rights of the Order had found from Dr Wake, and of the slavish tendency of his principles, in respect both to church and state".[1] Nor did he disdain the assistance rendered to his polemic by robustness of style and vigour of expression, as in his dismissal of the offending volume as "a shallow, empty performance, written without any knowledge of our constitution, any skill in the particular subject of debate", and again as "nothing more than a series of long, flat, impertinent accounts, attended with suitable reflections, but without one wise word spoken or true stroke struck in behalf of his point from the beginning of the book to the end of it".[2] He paid Wake the compliment however of embarking upon a historical survey of the development of ecclesiastical synods in England in order to base his conclusions upon sound foundations, but refused to move from his essential principles. Despite an admission of the ineffectiveness of the Praemunientes clause to secure Edward I's purpose of incorporating the inferior clergy in a national parliament, he maintained still that the provincial convocations had assumed thereby a parliamentary character.

These provincial assemblies, though held apart from the parliament, yet belonged to it; met by the parliamentary, no less than the provincial writ; and were state-meetings, as well as church synods; in them parliamentary matters were transacted, and parliamentary forms and methods observed; the members of them were entitled to parliamentary wages and enjoyed parliamentary privileges.[3]

Even more remarkable was the ingenious interpretation of the Act of Submission to which further reflection had led him, for whilst reiterating his previous contention that the convocations had been restrained thereby only from the final enactment of canons without royal assent, he announced that its general effect had been to curtail the powers of the metropolitan whilst leaving those of the remaining members intact.

The 25 of Henry VIII then has not in the least altered the law of convocations, in relation to any of the powers or privileges of the inferior clergy. They can still freely consult and debate, petition or represent, propose the matter or form of new canons, and consider about the enforcing or abrogating old ones; in a word, act in all instances and to all degrees as they could before the passing of that statute. Indeed my lord archbishop's hands are tied by it; for he cannot now call a convocation without the king's writ, which before

---

[1] F. Atterbury, *The Rights, Powers and Privileges of an English Convocation*, 2nd edn. 1701, p. xviii.

[2] *Ibid.* pp. i, xxiv.   [3] *Ibid.* p. 74.

this act he might, and in elder times frequently did; he cannot now enact and constitute anything by his own authority as, in imitation of the papal power in councils, and of the royal power in parliaments, it was usual for him to do; he must, before he passes any act of the two houses, have the king's assent to it; and, after it is passed, the royal power must come in also to promulge and execute it. In these several respects the metropolitan's authority is considerably lessened by this act; the exercise of which is now chiefly seen in moderating the debates of the synod, and giving his vote last upon any question proposed there.... But the powers and privileges of all other members of convocation continue whole and entire to them, notwithstanding this statute.[1]

Herein lay the final strategy of the champion of the presbyterate against the authority of their episcopal governors. For, with the convocations now enabled to deliberate and debate upon any subjects they pleased in accordance with his exposition of the Act of Submission, subject only to the final ratification by the crown of any proposed canon, and with the archbishop as president (notwithstanding the compliment paid to his office as correspondent in medieval times with that of the pope in councils and the sovereign in parliaments) now reduced to the status of chairman with a casting vote, the way was open for the assertion of the independence of the lower clergy of all authority save that of the crown; to whom the majority of their projects would not be submitted since they would proceed to the formal passing of canons infrequently. To this end were directed the iterated references to the clergy as "still an estate of the realm, necessarily attendant on the parliament",[2] and to the fact "that the parliamentary interests and privileges of the commons spiritual and temporal ran always even, or at least were never far asunder, and they do therefore, when made out, mutually prove each other".[3] The authority of Christian princes over ecclesiastical synods in England had been winnowed considerably in the interest of the freedom of the convocations, and therein the inferior clergy had been emancipated from the restraining authority of the upper house of bishops. In reaction against the abhorred Erastianism of Wake, Atterbury had gone far to subvert the principles of catholic order by the studied depression of the metropolitan's power over his provincial synod; but at least the valiant author had retracted none of his original affirmations.

The controversy had mingled historical precedent with contemporary design; and the task of Wake in his final rejoinder, *The State of the*

---

[1] F. Atterbury, *The Rights, Powers and Privileges of an English Convocation*, p. [131].

[2] *Ibid.* p. 306.   [3] *Ibid.* p. 343.

Church and Clergy of England in their Convocations, published in 1703, was to defeat the present assault by a refutal of the pseudo-historical foundation alleged by his antagonist. In the eight and a half hundred pages of his massive folio volume the duty was well and truly discharged. Beginning with a historical survey of the development of the parliamentary conventions and provincial councils of the clergy, he proved conclusively the differences between the two bodies; demonstrating that, whereas the clergy assembled in obedience to the Praemunientes clause were drawn from both provinces, the archiepiscopal mandate had reference to one province only; that the parliament was summoned by the king's writ alone, the provincial convocation meeting in response to the metropolitan's summons; that the decrees of the former obliged the entire realm, the canons of the latter affecting only their own province; and that whereas the time and place of meeting of the parliament were specified in the royal writ, both were left in the case of provincial convocations to the discretion of the archbishop. He concluded therefore:

> That the assembly which consists of the clergy of one province only; whose constitutions bind only that province for which they act; which admits only of ecclesiastical persons, and can determine only of ecclesiastical affairs; in which the archbishop of the province had anciently the ultimate power, and by virtue thereof, presided, ordered, and governed in it; must be altogether of a different nature and constitution from such an assembly, in which all these were quite otherwise; in which the clergy of both provinces met together; whose acts bound the whole realm; which consisted chiefly of the laity; and had authority in all kind of matters, without confinement or limitation; in which lastly the king had the last concluding power; and did finally order, rule, and govern all; summoned it by his writ, and dissolved it at his will.[1]

By a similar *catena* of historical precedents he demolished the contention of Atterbury concerning the necessity for the summons of a convocation together with the meeting of every parliament.

> The modern pretence of attendance in this case is not only a new invention, but such as the practice of above two hundred years after the settlement of our Great Councils upon their present establishment does apparently contradict; in all which time not one parliament in ten had either of the convocations called together with it, nor one in twenty or thirty had both.[2]

---

[1] Wake, *The State of the Church and Clergy of England*, 1703, p. 21.
[2] *Ibid.* p. 430.

The custom alleged by his adversary indeed dated from the Reformation, since which period the sovereigns "having taken up the method of confirming the grants of their clergy by the authority of parliament, had generally ordered the one to be assembled as often as the other". Yet even in this regard Wake proved by tabulated instances that on many occasions the dates of the sessions of the two bodies had differed very considerably, and justified his conclusion that the convocations had no

right by the rules of our constitution to sit always in time of parliament; but may upon good and just grounds be either not summoned, or be prorogued from time to time without entering on any business; nay, or even be dissolved (as now they are) and the parliament nevertheless lawfully continue to meet and act without them.[1]

Upon the further question of the restraining force of the 25 Henry VIII, cap. 19, in relation to the authority of the convocation when assembled to proceed to business, Wake adduced a wealth of historical precedent to illustrate his standpoint. Observing that so long as the inferior clergy

"continued to grant their own money, they had no need of any licence, either to debate of, or to come to a final resolution upon, any subsidies for the government," he argued that "if they had any addresses to make, or any petitions to present to the bishops, the parliament, or the prince, they had, and still have, a full liberty to make and to offer them. And, as before, if they saw it needful to proceed to any proper synodical debates, in order to the regulating of anything that might be wanting in the doctrine, or discipline of the church, they had an undoubted right to draw up their requests to their archbishops and bishops for leave or directions to proceed upon it; so I do humbly conceive, they may do the same now; only with this difference, that their petitions must now run, not for their leave and consent (who are no longer able to grant them any), but that they would obtain the Prince's licence and assent, who alone since this act, can authorise them in this particular. And here,...the power of the convocation as such determines. If they mean to proceed any further, and to confer, not in order to a petition for a licence, but...to constitute canons, they must first qualify themselves for such conference by the king's licence; or they will come within the penalty of that statute which prohibits any such attempt".[2]

In regard to the royal licence, he was willing to allow that an oral permission from the king to the metropolitan might be sufficient authority, provided that "the convocation be satisfied itself and can

---

[1] Wake, *The State of the Church and Clergy of England*, p. 534.
[2] *Ibid.* pp. 536–7.

upon occasion make a legal proof to others that the prince did give his royal assent to their proceedings"; but he insisted that tradition had established the custom of a formal licence under the great seal. The final authority therefore remained with the sovereign, alike to decide whether the convocations should be allowed to sit for deliberation, and to determine what topics of business, if any, should be submitted for their discussion. Upon these points Wake established his case clearly against his opponent, as he had done triumphantly upon the previous matters of the alleged correspondence between the convocation and the parliament. It is possible perhaps to observe a slight nuance and difference of emphasis in relation to the restraining influence of custom upon the entire liberty of the prince in his allowance of sitting convocations, between the two books of Wake, though in no case does this affect the substantial soundness of his main position nor the overwhelming weight of historical precedents amassed in favour of his argument.

"I make no doubt," he affirmed of the ecclesiastical affairs of the realm, "but that it is the duty as well as wisdom of a Christian king, to consult of all these matters with those who have the government of it committed to them by God; and by their direction and assistance to manage himself in the exercise of this great branch of his royal supremacy; and neither obstinately to refuse the clergy liberty to assemble when they think it would be for the service of the church and the benefit of religion to come together; nor yet unreasonably require their attendance, when there is nothing at all, or nothing of any consequence to be done by them. But should it so fall out... that the prince should neglect his duty in this particular and so not give his clergy the opportunity of meeting and acting, when it would be of a real benefit to the church that they should assemble and provide for the estate of it. In that case I conceive it would be the duty of those who are the fathers and governors of it, to apply to him for his permission to come together; to remonstrate with humility, but yet with a Christian freedom too, the necessities of the church, the evils that are to be remedied, and the reason they have to hope that by their assembling, they may provide some remedy for them; and to press him in the name of God and in pursuance of that trust which the public has reposed in him, to give a favourable answer to their requests."[1]

To this exhaustive survey of the historical development of all the ecclesiastical assemblies of the English church and realm, Atterbury ventured no reply, but allowed the volume to remain alike as a monument to the scholarship and diligence of the author, and as a complete

---

[1] Wake, *The State of the Church and Clergy of England*, pp. 85–6.

refutal of his own theories concerning the rights, powers, and privileges of an English convocation. In spite also of the conciliatory spirit of Wake's second tome, the bounds of the controversy thus initiated were enlarged steadily by Atterbury. By the time Wake's thorough examination of the question of the power of the sovereign in relation to the convocations was published, the dispute had changed in character and had moved to the contesting of other points. In the apt phrase of Gibson, "the controversy produced a sitting convocation, and the sitting convocation produced a new controversy". With the advent of a new ministry of William III in 1700 the experiment of allowing the convocation to sit and debate was again essayed; and after this victory for his cause Atterbury's interest in his dispute with Wake evaporated. No further need existed to argue concerning the tyrannous refusal of the king to allow the clergy synodical rights of deliberation, and the enemy became now the archbishop, whose rights as president of the convocation were an insuperable barrier to the ambition of Atterbury to emancipate the lower house from the control of the upper. Atterbury accordingly devoted his ingenuity to the elaboration of that depreciation of the metropolitan's authority in the convocation, which he had adumbrated in his interpretation of the act of submission of the clergy. Into the details of this further controversy it is happily unnecessary to enter, for it concerned not the relations of church and state, but the internal organisation of the church itself. Against the penetrating analysis of his arguments by Gibson, Atterbury fared even worse than he had done in his dispute with Wake. His contention for the independence of the lower clergy in convocation from the authority of the episcopal house was manifestly fallacious in relation to an assembly wherein the metropolitan had power to pronounce sentence of contumacy against clergy who did not obey his writ of summons, and especially in view of the contemporary circumstance of the convocation of York which consisted still of a single house over which the northern primate presided personally. Notwithstanding, Atterbury refurbished his old arguments concerning the parliamentary original and correspondence of the two houses of convocation, the powers necessarily inherent in an "house" as such, and the supersession of the authority of the archbishop's writ of summons by the royal writ precedent thereto. But defeat on the battle ground of literary controversy did not moderate the passions of the leaders of the rebel clergy in the actual convocations, and the history of synodical proceedings from 1700 to 1717 was a tale full of sound and fury, the fury of spiritual tempers. The protracted disputes, characterised upon occasion by unseemly altercations between individual members of the two houses, provoked a heavy weight of censure upon the lower clergy, alike for the contradiction between their professions of veneration for the divinely instituted episcopal order and their contempt of its authority in practice, and by reason of the scandal of continuous recrimination. But the rebel presbyters could not be restrained, until in 1717 they rode boldly to their own destruction by the attack upon Hoadly's sermon which drew upon them the prorogation of 17 May, which became the first of a long series of prorogations destined to effect an end of sitting convocations for a century and a half.

The association of the suspension of 1717 with the Bangorian sermon has brought an undeserved notoriety upon the whig authors of the prorogation and upon the incident of prorogation itself. The real cause of the silencing of the convocation was the open scandal of its own internal dissensions. For a period at least most churchmen welcomed an enforced cessation of the protracted controversy between bishops and presbyters. If such were the result of sitting convocations, then Wake had prophesied truly that the remedy would be worse than the disease. But beneath the temporary and transient incidents of current disputes lay the more serious causes of the languor of the convocations. Viewed from this standpoint the surrender of 1664 was the real cause alike of the immediate suspension of a quarter of a century which followed, and of the further suppression of 1717. The historical researches of Wake had demonstrated conclusively that the chief interest of kings in the sessions of convocation had lain in the relief of their financial necessities by the vote of clerical subsidies, which satisfaction having been made, the assemblies had been prorogued generally without further debate. With the surrender of this monetary privilege, the reason for regular sessions disappeared, for the administrative problems of the church were capable of solution by the issue of royal injunctions to the archbishops. The convocations themselves lacked sufficiency of strength and prestige to maintain their sessions upon grounds of intrinsic importance.

The fundamental weakness of the convocations was illustrated throughout the period of the controversies by the quiescence of the York Convocation. Atterbury was confronted continually by the afflicting spectacle of the entire passivity of the northern assembly, which supplied the refutal in practice necessary to complete the discomfiture of an advocate already driven off the field in argument. His most favoured theory, of the meeting of the convocation in response to the Praemunientes clause, suffered total shipwreck when brought to the test of applicability to the convocation of York. "'Tis hard for one of the province of York to comprehend it", wrote Bishop Nicolson of Carlisle to Wake. "The parliamentary writ calls us to Westminster, and the provincial, at the same time, to St Peter's in York. Can both these be meant of the same numerical bodies of men? Angels themselves would not be able to obey both the summons."[1] Equally discouraging was the complete indifference of the northern convocation-men to their duty in relation to the synodical prerogatives which seemed to their southern brethren worthy of such bitter dispute. The tradition crystallised in the seventeenth century by Thomas Fuller's dictum that the York Convocation was like the face of a clock, the works of which were at Canterbury, became the subject of good-natured jest in the succeeding epoch.

"Now that you are weary of rolling your convocation stone, or rock of offence, in the southern province," observed Nicholson humorously to Wake in 1711, "you are mightily kind indeed in recommending the diversion to us. No, no, continue your own labours, and take the whole credit of bringing them to perfection. We are fully resolved to persevere in our primitive course of passively submitting to such laws, statutes, and ordinances as you judge proper for us. And therefore, when a circular letter comes from on high, we hand about transcripts of the royal paper, but give not one syllable of directions how to have it obeyed. Should we, in the days of our dotage, pretend to open our eyes, and say, 'We see,' how would our masters in Henry VII's chapel take it? Would they not look on us as endeavouring traitorously to alter the state and scene of the war by a North-British invasion? In short 'tis not our business to set precedents, but to follow them; though I trust we shall not be so entirely slavish as to imitate you in your last ten years' squabble. 'Twould be a difficult matter for a well-disposed presbytery to maintain a claim of parliamentary rights in this province, where no man living can pretend to have seen so much as the face of two distinct houses."[2]

In a similar vein, a generation later, Archbishop Herring of York, in requesting Lord Hardwicke in 1744 to take care

"to order the writs for the prorogation of the northern convocation regularly to issue with those that concerned that of Canterbury", added the comment. "We think of ourselves with modesty and in due subordination to that venerable synod, but yet we are somebody, and were thought so at the passing of the Bartholomew Act, when old Lamplugh spoke of the whole as lost, if the convocation of York did not instantly concur with Canterbury, and they did it with precipitation enough, in all conscience. That concurrence and

---

[1] Nicolson to Wake, 19 Nov. 1709. Arch. W. Epist. 17, item ccx, f. 251.
[2] Same to Same, 17 Sept. 1711. *Ibid.* item clii, f. 323.

thanking Queen Anne for her gift in the first-fruits, is the only business done here in the convocation way since the Restoration".[1]

The venerable synod of Canterbury, despite its superior strength, could not escape the influence of the surrender of 1664 in the diminution of its own prestige and importance during the half century which divided that incident from the suspension of 1717. In truth little business could be found for sitting convocations to transact, else perhaps the long disputes between the two houses might have been sooner appeased. The outspoken opinion of Wake concerning the paucity of occasions for a convocation represented a fair statement of the circumstances militating against its importance in the ecclesiastical constitution.

When a national church is once thoroughly established, and neither needs any further laws to be made for the enforcing of its discipline; or any new confessions to be framed for the security of its doctrine; when its liturgy and other offices are fixed and stated; and there is so far from being any need of altering or improving any of these, that it is thought a crime but even to suppose that it is possible to improve them, or to make any alterations in them but for the worse; then I cannot imagine, until something arises to unsettle such a constitution, what a convocation could have to meet about.[2]

In view of the additional testimony to this conclusion borne by the dissipation of so much time and energy in the controversy between the inferior clergy and their bishops, little censure could attach to the administration responsible for the prorogation of May 1717. At first the prorogation was only until the following November, but was then renewed. It is difficult to affix the exact responsibility for the act, since a contemporary newsletter affirmed that "the earl of Sunderland and lord Stanhope declare that they had no hand in proroguing the convocation; the archbishop of Canterbury says he was neither consulted with nor consenting to it, and said further that lord Cadogan governed both church and state".[3] The person to whom the suppression is traditionally ascribed, Walpole, was certainly wholly inculpable, since he had resigned from the administration in the previous April. Of the expediency of a temporary suppression the judgment of Gibson may be quoted, that the disputes had produced "a jealousy and coldness between the bishops and their clergy, a handle to the enemies of both to represent them as men of turbulent spirits, not fit to be trusted together in a public assembly, . . . and a general disgrace upon convocations themselves".

[1] Herring to Hardwicke, 1 June 1744. Add. MSS. 35598, f. 27.
[2] Wake, *The Authority of Christian Princes*, pp. 277–8.
[3] Portland MSS. v, 536.

Notwithstanding, it might be thought too severe a penalty for these indiscretions that the suspension should continue throughout the rest of the eighteenth century and the first half of the nineteenth, thus depriving the church of the means of synodical correspondence and deliberation between the episcopate and the lower clergy. Upon several occasions during the Hanoverian period the question of venturing again upon the experiment of sitting convocations was discussed; and in 1741, in consequence of the strong representations of Archbishop Potter and Bishop Gibson, the convocations were allowed to meet for business, only to provoke a hasty prorogation when the lower house re-asserted its independence of the upper. In face of this misfortune, further risks could scarcely be taken; and the pious opinion debated by the duke of Newcastle upon the assembly of the first parliament of George III— "the convocation to meet to do business or not"—was decided by a prudent negative.[1]

It is worthy of note that contemporary laments uttered over the defunct sitting convocations did not emphasise the neglect of business as an ill-consequence of the suspension. Gibson himself placed first among "the very good effects which sitting convocations had, the training up of those clergy who were chiefly concerned in the debates there, to a facility and readiness of speaking in the debates of a higher assembly"; adding as a second point, the "turning the minds of the whole body to a much closer attention to the public concerns of the church than had been observed among the clergy since the disuse of sitting convocations".[2] The former argument was advanced by Bishop Newton in excuse for his silence in the debates of the house of lords; namely that

he, as well as most other bishops, entered into the house at a time of life too late to begin such exercises. Some previous practice was requisite, which rendered lawyers so much readier and abler speakers than the generality of divines. While the convocation was allowed to sit, it was a kind of school of oratory for the clergy, and hence Atterbury and others became such able speakers in the house of lords.[3]

Despite the suspension of deliberative sessions and the denial of matters of business for their debate, the clergy of the Canterbury Convocation continued at the assembly of a new parliament to hold formal meetings in order to transact the legal preliminaries necessary to their

[1] Memorandum, 8 Oct. 1761. Add. MSS. 32929, f. 111.

[2] N. Sykes, *Edmund Gibson*, p. 50.

[3] *Life of Dr Thomas Newton*, in *Lives of E. Pocock, Z. Pearce, T. Newton, and P. Skelton*, ii, 186.

constitution as an house, and election to the office of prolocutor remained a coveted distinction. In 1754 Archbishop Herring held a lengthy and anxious correspondence with Lord Hardwicke upon the matter of ensuring the appointment of a staunch whig to that position; and it was recorded of Dr Zachary Pearce, as a sign of his care to preserve the dignity of the office, that

all the while he was prolocutor, he attended the house in Henry VII's chapel every day to which it stood prorogued; he always gave notice of the day of meeting in the Daily Advertiser, and engaged some of his acquaintance among the members who lived in or near Town to be present there; he read the Latin litany as soon as they were met; and while he waited with them in the chapel till the archbishop's schedule came down for the prorogation of the convocation to another day, he invited all who were present, with the two actuaries, to dine with him at his house in St Martin's churchyard, which they generally did.[1]

Posterity may not be ungrateful for such efforts to preserve even the face of convocation proceedings, since so many constitutional agents have fallen into irreparable desuetude from neglect to maintain their external forms. But little surprise may be occasioned that few prolocutors attached such a precise importance to a formality which appeared to the eyes of the majority, as to Dr Pyle, "an insignificant pre-eminence". On three occasions Pyle himself was present when "the principal divines of the Church of England met together at St Paul's, at Westminster Abbey, and at court, for the forming and perfecting of that poor, harmless creature (of man's invention) called the Convocation".[2] With the reduction of convocation to this condition it had become harmless indeed. Only traditional reverence for an ancient institution could have inspired the readiness of Dr Johnson to "stand before a battery of cannon to restore the convocation to its full powers".[3] Such restoration was beyond the power of human resolution, for the dream of a parity betwixt convocation and parliament had passed beyond the possibility of realisation. If "the explosion of high-church zeal" which moved Atterbury to embark upon his furious convocation controversy may be extenuated by its professed aim to renew the authority of that assembly, its result was certainly to emphasise the impracticability of achievement. Even since its revival in 1855 the record of convocation has not been impressive, and since the enactment

[1] *Life of Zachary Pearce*, in *op. cit.* i, 394.
[2] E. Pyle, *Memoirs of a Royal Chaplain*, p. 224.
[3] Boswell, *Life of Johnson*, ch. VIII, 3 Aug. 1763.

of the Enabling Act of 1919 its practical operation has suffered evidently from the superior deliberative authority of the Church Assembly, which embraces a house of laity in addition to the complete personnel of the two clerical houses of convocation.

The problem of the relations of the convocation and the parliament was not the only difficulty, nor perhaps the most serious, bequeathed to the church by the Revolution settlement of 1689. The primary purpose of the substitution of William and Mary for James II had been the protection of the established church from the machinations of a popish sovereign, which had been secured by the legal requirement that all future kings should join in communion with that church. But the Protestant Succession and the maintenance of the established church were but two portions of a tripartite compact. The Protestant dissenters demanded some security and reward for their refusal of the toleration extended by the dispensing power of James II. Their claim could not be ignored, and with the failure of the attempt to heal the divisions between episcopalian and presbyterian by a scheme of Comprehension, their relief took the form of a Toleration Act. Grudging and partial though the provisions of that statute were when viewed from the standpoint of the dissenters, they were revolutionary in the eyes of high churchmen, who witnessed with alarm the rapid increase in the number of dissenting chapels erected under the protection of the law. The precarious character of the concession thus made was emphasised immediately upon the accession of Anne by the appearance of occasional conformity bills, designed to prevent such dissenters from participating in the administration of the country except at the cost of religious apostasy. The campaign of violence which accompanied the Sacheverell agitation and found expression in the destruction of conventicles, secured a parliamentary victory in the passing of the Occasional Conformity and Schism Acts, which testified to the fate of dissenters at the hands of a zealous and unrestrained tory party. Even the Hanoverian succession brought no immediate relief, though in the rebellion of 1715 no section of the community was more loyal than the Protestant nonconformists; and the difficulties encountered by the administration of Stanhope, in piloting through the parliament his measure for the repeal of these two acts, illustrated further the reluctance of the church party to meet the demands of their religious rivals. From the dissenting standpoint the maintenance of the Test and Corporation Acts was a badge of inferiority, for the removal of which they were bound to contend. Accordingly, after an abortive canvassing of the question of "the repeals" in 1732, when Walpole employed Hoadly to persuade the dissenting deputies of the political inexpediency of a parliamentary debate at that juncture, the matter was revived in 1735 with a determination to challenge a division in the ensuing session.

In such circumstances apprehension naturally possessed the mind of many churchmen. The temper of the newly elected commons of 1734 was perceived to be no less unfriendly towards ecclesiastical matters than that of their predecessors, and in addition to the frontal attack offered by the agitation for the repeal of the Test Act, other occasions of friction might arise upon the least mention of the questions of church rates and tithes. The church-whigs indeed were finding great difficulties in maintaining intact the alliance with the whig politicians, upon which they had rested the security of the establishment since the Hanoverian succession. From their predecessors of the reign of Anne they had inherited an anomaly, that of the establishment in North Britain of a presbyterian church and in England of an episcopal, the goad of which their tory rivals did not cease to press upon them. Further, in South Britain the traditional whig profession of support for the Protestant Succession, the Church Establishment and the Toleration Act, as the triple basis of the Revolution settlement, seemed of uncertain continuance at the present juncture. Nor, since the virtue of that settlement had lain in its delicate balance of conflicting forces, could the removal of one safeguard fail to provoke demands for the revocation of the rest. In the eyes of their opponents the church-whigs were discredited also by their inability to defend the maintenance of the restrictive acts against dissenters save upon the ground of expediency and compromise, upon which the church establishment in like manner rested. In this situation and amid such straits, the appearance in 1736 of a treatise, from the pen of a young divine, which professed the audacious aim of justifying the existing relations of church and state upon the ground of their exact correspondence with the eternal order of Providence, offered a welcome relief. The aim of William Warburton's first considerable essay in statecraft was declared by its title: *The Alliance between Church and State: or, The Necessity and Equity of an Established Religion and a Test Law, demonstrated from the essence and end of Civil Society, upon the fundamental principles of the Law of Nature and Nations.* The combination of ingenuity of argument with fecundity of invention assembled in support of this bold affirmation attracted immediate attention, and the author had the gratification of a widespread acceptance of his position. Professor Laski indeed has confessed his persuasion that "in the hundred and twenty years which passed between the Bangorian controversy and the Oxford Movement, there is only one volume upon the problem of church and state which deserves more than passing notice",[1] an eulogy which might have brought upon his head the retort courteous from the irascible Warburton.

In addition to the exposition of the major points of his theme, Warburton adorned his tractate with divers reflections upon other problems of the day. His genius indeed was fashioned after the manner of the beasts of the Apocalypse, "with eyes before and behind", whereby he was enabled to perceive (and therefore to fall upon) a host of antagonists lurking in his path on every side. His talent suited exactly the phrase applied by Paine to Burke, of "a genius without a constitution, a genius at random and not a genius constituted". As catholic in his adversaries as insatiable in controversies, he turned aside to break a lance with non-jurors, Hoadleians, Quakers, and scribblers in the convocation disputes; and in each case his animadversions lacked neither point nor directness. His observation upon the non-juror contention penetrated to the heart of that discussion by his insistence that, although "no ecclesiastic of the established church could exercise his function without the magistrate's approbation and allowance", yet this did not imply "that the magistrate, by virtue of this branch of the supremacy, can make or confer the character of priest or minister; for this could not be given him by the convention" between church and state.[2] *Per contra* he cut the ground from the feet of Hoadly by an affirmation of the necessity of a visible church to the profession of Christianity and by challenging that bishop's interpretation of the text of his Bangorian sermon. The convocation found in Warburton an unexpected ally. For, whilst defending the restrictions imposed upon that body by the Act of Submission as consistent with the nature of an establishment, he argued that

still there is reason that propositions for such laws [concerning ecclesiastical matters] should sometime come from the church; which we must suppose well skilled (as in her proper business) in forming and digesting such new regulations, before they come before the consideration of the legislature.... For to have laws framed and modelled solely by the state, and (without previous communication) imposed upon the church, is making of it the meanest and most abject of all the state's creatures. For every little company and corporation hath the honour to be consulted with, before any law is enacted that may affect its constitution.[3]

[1] H. J. Laski, *op. cit.* pp. 92–3.
[2] W. Warburton, *The Alliance between Church and State* (1736), Pt. II, Sect. III, p. 84.
[3] *Ibid.* p. 87.

These sentiments he iterated to Hurd many years afterwards.

"I know", he observed, "how widely theory and practice differ: *fit* and *right* in politics are two things, though in morals but one. I am convinced of the *rights* of convocations; but the expediency of their frequent sitting is another matter. I believe all you say of the mischiefs they would produce. But I think we have avoided one extreme only by falling into another."

His indignation was aroused particularly because "for the sake of screening a writer, who was for destroying the very being of a religious society, the convocation had been kept gagged for about forty years together"; whilst in the literary disputes between Atterbury and his opponents, he championed the former, not merely because his adversaries were "two of the dullest fellows in the world", but because "he went upon *principles*, and all they could possibly oppose were *precedents*, and these were nothing when they opposed the genius of a constitution".[1] Against the quaker refusal to pay tithes for the support of the established church in England, Warburton turned the two-edged sword of their payment of taxes designed for the prosecution of military operations, and the practice of William Penn himself in setting up in the colony bearing his name an established church with a protective test law.

These were but the bypaths into which Warburton's combative zeal ever tempted him to stray. His main theme was the justification of an established church and a test law as necessary to the constitution of every state, which he modestly proposed to accomplish in a discourse of such compass "as that the whole may be commodiously read at once". His starting-point in discussing the origin and purpose of civil society was the contemporary doctrine of a social compact, designed to provide "security to the temporal liberty and property of man". His adoption of this position had the dual advantage that his theory was based upon the current whig political creed, and that it delivered him from the objection that his own abstract scheme of the relations of religious and civil societies was a mere figment of his imagination. For when challenged to produce the original charter of this alleged universal convention between church and state, he replied that

it may be found in the same archive where the famous original compact between magistrate and people, so much insisted on in vindication of the rights of mankind, is reposited. Now when a sight of this compact is required of defenders of civil liberty, they hold it sufficient to say that it is enough to all the purposes of fact and right, that the original compact is the only

---

[1] *Letters from a Late Eminent Prelate* (2nd ed. 1809), Letter cxiv, pp. 313–14.

legitimate foundation of civil society; that if there was no such thing formally executed, there was intentionally; that all differences therefore between magistrate and people ought to be regulated on the supposition of such a compact, and all government reduced to the principles therein established, for that all the happiness of which civil society is productive, can only be attained by it when formed on those principles. Now something like this, we say of our Charter of Convention.[1]

Little difficulty attended his endeavour to demonstrate, upon the accepted whig principles, that civil magistrates had no concern with the religious opinions of their subjects, since the end of civil society embraced, not the eternal salvation, but the temporal happiness of men. Accordingly it behoved not the magistrate to interfere in religious matters, save in so far as the belief in the existence of God, His Providence, and the essential difference between moral good and evil, was an essential basis for the conduct of men in society. Yet, forasmuch as the foundations of civil society were uncertain without some inner constraint operating within the hearts of its citizens, compelling them to the discharge of social duties, the security of an oath was necessary, and the obligation of an oath rested plainly upon a religious sanction.

The need and function of religion as ancillary to the stability of civil society being manifest, Warburton proceeded to delineate the proper purpose and end of religious profession. In this connection one of the most important and noteworthy of his contributions to the understanding of the problem of the relation of religion and civil affairs was made by his firm insistence on the necessity of a visible church to the exercise and profession of Christianity. He allowed the essentially individual nature of religion, as a commerce between each man and his Maker, wherein no man could deliver his brother nor make agreement unto God for him; and from this standpoint it appeared a plausible deduction that religion was "but a kind of divine philosophy in the mind, which composes only a spiritual and mystic body of its followers". But the need of a visible church was asserted from the circumstance that man is no immaterial spirit, capable of satisfaction by this mental religion and invisible communion in things divine.

Such a religion as is suitable to the nature of man here, must have the meditation on the divine nature drawn out into articles of faith, and the meditation on our several relations to Him into suitable and correspondent acts of religious worship; and both of them to be professed and performed in common.[2]

[1] Warburton, *The Alliance between Church and State*, Pt. II, Sect. III, pp. 90–1.
[2] *Ibid.* Pt. I, Sect. V, p. 38.

This emphatic insistence upon the corporate character of religious profession and upon the conception of the church, not as an intangible communion of the spirits of just men made perfect, but as a true society of persons, living in the world and associated for the realisation of the twin ends of religion—"first to procure the favour of God and secondly to advance and improve our own intellectual nature"—delivered Warburton from the fruitless controversies into which Hoadly's sermon had drawn many writers. It enabled him further to educe alike with clarity and consistency the implications of his standpoint by examination of the rights and functions of a church. As a society it must of necessity possess independence of all other societies in matters proper to its end, and assert its own inherent sovereignty within the sphere of its operation. It followed therefrom that a church must have authority of excommunication, that is of excluding from its fellowship members who transgressed its terms of association. But since its aim was the cultivation of religion, and since in principle religion implied the unimpeded commerce between each individual and God, excommunication must be devoid of civil penalties, and ecclesiastical authority must be divorced from coercive power. Warburton thus made plain both the rightful authority of a church over its members in matters spiritual, and the inalienable right of every man to complete freedom of conscience and religious persuasion.

From these premises it was evident that the formation of any alliance between church and state partook of the nature of a compact between two sovereign and independent powers, each ordained for its own proper function, and by consequence that such an alliance must be based upon a sense of the mutual support which each society was able to afford to the other.

Having found that each society is sovereign and independent of the other, it as necessarily follows that such union can be produced only by free convention and mutual compact. But nothing can give birth to a free convention but a sense of mutual wants, that may be thereby supplied; or a view of mutual advantages to be thereby gained. Such then is the nature of that famous union which produces a Church Established, and which is indeed no other than a political league and alliance for mutual support and defence.[1]

From this alliance the state gained the employment of the influence of religion in support both of the institutions and personnel of its administration, and removed the possibility of the church's hostility to ordered government. In return for its acceptance of the church into

[1] Warburton, *op. cit.* II, Sect. I, p. 53.

partnership, the state required the surrender of the independence possessed by the spiritual society in its former condition of absolute sovereignty. But the church secured from the compact evident advantages; a public endowment for its clergy, the presence of its prelates in the legislative assembly of the realm, and the bestowal of coercive power upon ecclesiastical courts, all which privileges must determine with the dissolution of the alliance between the civil and religious societies. Within the framework of this compact Warburton would allow no independent action on the part of the church. Its officers could not exercise their spiritual ministry without the allowance of the civil magistrate, the chief magistrate of the state became supreme head of the church, the convocations were restrained from deliberation and legislation without the royal licence, and excommunication could not be imposed without the concurrence of the civil authority. But if the church surrendered thus the means of self-defence and the power of independent action, it must receive in recompense full protection from the state; which implied, in a country where diversity of religious profession prevailed, the enactment of a test law to exclude members of other religious societies from entry into the legislature, lest thereby they should inflict harm upon the established church. This partial restriction imposed upon citizens who were not members of the established church did not impinge upon the universal right of freedom of religious persuasion which was the prerogative of all men, for its operation was confined to political matters, and in this regard there could be no doubt of the authority of the civil society to impose such restrictions upon the civil rights of its members as were necessary for public tranquillity and peace.

By this argument Warburton constructed a theory of the alliance of church and state applicable to any civil and religious societies throughout the world. The ingenuity of his contention was indisputable, as was his evident pleasure in demonstrating to critics of the English system

how unreasonable and even impolitic they are, when, in their ill-humour with establishments they choose to pick a quarrel with their own; where the national religion is on a footing exactly agreeable to the nature of a free convention between church and state, on the principles of the laws of nature and nations; a felicity, they should have known, that scarce any other people on the face of the earth can boast of.[1]

Much ridicule has been poured upon the author for the pretentious appearance of his theorising from an artificial pattern of the relations

[1] Warburton, *The Alliance between Church and State*, Pt. II, Sect. IV, p. 91.

of church and state laid up in the heavens to the prosaic compromise of the revolution settlement in England. But, as Dr Figgis pertinently observed,

the ancient and modern political theorists have shared the same criticism. Nearly every system which professes to be deduced from general philosophical principles will be found on investigation to bear a very close relation to the facts of some existing government. Hegel was accused of using his whole philosophy to discover the Idea incarnate in the Prussian despotism.[1]

The legal and unhistorical character of Warburton's universal convention between church and state was shared exactly by the famous original compact for the creation of civil society upon which contemporary whig political philosophy rested, as he pointed out with penetration and acumen. Within the framework sketched for himself, he enunciated not a few principles of real importance to the proper understanding of the relations between church and state. He perceived clearly that the state in its alliance with the church was not concerned at all with the question of the truth of the doctrines professed by the religious society, but with the practical advantages secured to itself by the addition of religious sanctions to its own inherent authority. No power was committed to the civil magistrate to become a judge and divider between the claims of differing churches to possess an exclusive divine authorisation for their belief and polity. The state could therefore make alliance in every country with whatever church proved able to accord the greatest measure of support by virtue of holding the allegiance of the majority of its citizens.

If there be more than one [church] at the time of convention, the alliance is made by the state with the largest of the religious societies. It is fit it should be so, because the larger the religious society is (where the difference is not in essentials) the more enabled it will be to answer the ends of the alliance, as having the greatest number under its influence.... Hence we may see the reason and equity of the episcopal church being the established church in England, the presbyterian the established church in Scotland, an absurdity in point of right which our adversaries imagined the friends of an establishment could never get clear of. From hence we may discover the duration of this alliance. It is perpetual, but not irrevocable, i.e. it subsists so long as the church thereby established maintains its superiority of extent; which when it loses to any considerable degree, the union is dissolved. For the united church being then no longer able to perform its part of the convention, which

[1] J. N. Figgis, "William Warburton", in *Typical English Churchmen from Parker to Maurice* (ed. W. E. Collins), p. 232.

is formed on reciprocal conditions, the state by that failure becomes disengaged. And a new alliance is of necessity entered into with the now
prevailing church.[1]

As a corollary from this theory it followed that the established church
would make its terms of communion as wide as was consistent with its
proper character as a religious society, in order to ensure the fulfilment
of its part of the compact and its continuance as the established church.
"The more general the terms of communion are, and the wider the
bottom is made (consistent with the well-being of a society) the wiser
and juster is that institution."[2]

The insistence upon the essentially social nature of religion, which
saved Warburton from the perils of the dissolution of the idea of a
church in the interest of religious individualism, enabled him to
adumbrate also the notion, unfamiliar to his age, of the personality
and will of social groups. Anticipating the objection to his argument
for the alliance of church and state that "it is a convention of those
individuals with themselves under different capacities, and all such
convention is as groundless and ineffectual as that which one individual
would make with himself", he rejoined that he intended to prove that
the two societies, civil and religious, had two distinct wills and
personalities.

When any number of men form themselves into a political society, whether
civil or religious, that society becomes a body, different from what the
number of individuals made before the society was formed. Otherwise the
society is nothing, or in other words no society is formed. Here then is a body
distinct from what the number of individuals make; and is called *factitious*
to difference it from the natural body, because it is the creature of human will.
But a body must have its proper personality and will, which without those
is a name, a shadow, and no more. This personality and will is neither the
personality and will of one individual, nor of all together.... We conclude
then that the will and personality of a community is as different and distinct
from the will and personality of the individuals of which it is composed,
as the body itself is; and that, as in the erection of a community, a factitious
body was created, so were a factitious personality and will.[3]

The enunciation of the theory of corporate personality and will by
which, as Warburton perceived, the creation of an inexhaustible series
of social groups within the state, each with its independent and sovereign
authority, was justified, gave great satisfaction to Dr Figgis. "It is

[1] Warburton, *The Alliance between Church and State*, Pt. III, Sect. I, p. 111.
[2] *Ibid.* Pt. I, Sect. V, p. 38.
[3] *Ibid.*, Pt. II, Sect. V, p. 102.

strange indeed", he commented, "that Dr Gierke and Professor Maitland should have their counterpart in a latitudinarian ecclesiastic, writing at a time when political and theological thought was essentially atomistic; yet it can hardly be denied that Warburton was what they would have called a "realist", even if the realism be imperfect."[1]

Upon many grounds indeed Warburton's exposition of the relations of church and state possesses a closer correspondence with the modern situation of their alliance than most rival theories. His recognition of the fundamental circumstance that the interest of the state lay in practical utility, not in the abstract truth of religion, adumbrated the development of the modern state, neutral and indifferent in matters religious, if not professedly secular in outlook. Yet at the same time he preserved the authority of the church as an independent society, sovereign within its own proper sphere, and therefore neither destroying the basis of its own existence nor receiving additional authority in the proper province of religion, from an alliance with the state. It could not be expected of Warburton that he should foresee the progressive removal of all restrictions of religious disqualification from membership of the civil legislature, which ensued in the nineteenth century, though his position rested upon the official maintenance of a test law. Herein lay its weakest joint. For there were already signs of the practical breakdown of the restrictions of the Test and Corporation Acts, despite the failure of all attempts to secure their formal repeal. Stanhope himself had carried in 1718 an Act for Quieting and Establishing Corporations,

the first of a series of Indemnity Acts which facilitated the presence of Protestant Dissenters on corporations for over a century till the repeal of the Test act in 1828. By this act all such members of corporations as had not complied with the law but whose tenure of office was not questioned for six months were confirmed in their offices; thereby no Nonconformists then holding office could be displaced for the remainder of their lives—for in those days corporation offices were normally held for life—while for the future the limited period for objections proved in effect a considerable safeguard to Nonconformists elected to corporations. A further concession was made by the series of annual Indemnity Acts inaugurated by Walpole himself in 1727, whereby the qualifying Sacrament could be taken after, instead of before, election as a bar to possible objections.[2]

It may not be denied that such acts assaulted the principle of the test law insisted upon by Warburton. Yet it is not too great an exercise of the imagination to suppose that he would have allowed the con-

[1] J. N. Figgis, "William Warburton", in *op. cit.* p. 231.
[2] B. Williams, *Stanhope*, pp. 394–5.

tinuance of the church establishment upon the conditions of the Enabling Act of this present century. For the reservation to parliament of the right of final veto upon ecclesiastical measures would have seemed to his eye essential to the nature of the convention between church and state; whilst the delegation by parliament to the church assembly or the task of preparing draft legislation for parliamentary approval, and the restriction of the authority of the legislature to the right of final veto without the power of amendment, would have realised his desire for the possession by the church of a deliberative assembly functioning in its proper sphere. Peradventure his unusual genius might even have found some basis of correspondence in the law of nations and nature for the contemporary anomalies in the relations between the church assembly and parliament, which since the rejection of the Prayer Book revision of 1927–8 have sorely perplexed the minds of ecclesiastical statesmen.

In no respect did Warburton's theories register the distance which severed the Hanoverian church from the non-juror principles more emphatically than in his insistence upon utility rather than divine right as the measure of statecraft. The non-jurors represented the dying tradition which rested the authority of all government, secular and religious, upon conformity to an alleged divine prescription.

"So much safer are we in the hands of God than of men", observed Leslie, "in that government which He has established for the good of the people, than in all their own contrivances of electing and deposing their own kings and framing new schemes of government to themselves."[1]

Inevitably this theory involved the search for the true pattern of government only in the pages of Holy Scripture, as the same author affirmed in his contention that "it would be an affront to human understanding to follow the arguments of 'heathen authors' in political affairs in preference to the adoption of doctrine laid down in the Scriptures". The Revolution of 1689 had crossed the Rubicon which divided such theological politics from the utilitarian theories of the eighteenth century. Warburton relied little upon precedents drawn from Jewish history, since his purpose was to justify the English establishment both upon grounds of conformity with the law of nature and upon the practical basis of utility. In the non-juror position he detected the fundamental error which had vitiated all previous speculation upon the relations of church and state.

The defenders of an established religion have all along gone on to maintain it on the motives of truth and not of utility. That is, that religion was to be

[1] C. Leslie, *The New Association*, Pt. II, Supplement.

established and protected, as it was the true religion, not for the sake of its public utility; which is the great principle whereby we erect an established religion and a test law.[1]

The basis of his contention rested upon the recognition, which he emphasised in the conclusion of his tractate, "that the true end for which religion is established, is not to provide for the true faith, but for civil utility"; albeit in his opinion since "public utility and truth coincide, then to provide for that utility, truth must be provided for".[2]

The success of Warburton's defence of the conditions of the establishment in England upon so bold a ground as their reflection of the universal principles of the law of nature, reassured his contemporaries as to the excellence of their religious settlement, and there remained to William Paley the humbler and more restricted task of delineating the perfect correspondence between the constitution of the established church and the political administration of the kingdom. Paley's importance indeed lay in the exactitude with which he represented the *zeitgeist*, unembarrassed by the eccentric genius of a Warburton. The opening sentence of his chapter *Of Religious Establishments and of Toleration* enunciated the cardinal principle of public utility. "A religious establishment is no part of Christianity, it is only the means of inculcating it"; and therefore "the authority of a church establishment is founded in its utility."[3] Regard to this point of public utility had caused the Founder of Christianity, according to Paley's understanding, to advance

no pretensions which by disturbing the arrangements of human polity, might present an obstacle to the reception of His faith. We may ascribe it to this design, that He left the laws of His church so open and indeterminate, that whilst the ends of religious communion were sufficiently declared, the form of the society might be assimilated to the civil constitution of each country, to which it should always communicate strength and support in return for the protection it received. If there be any truth in these observations, they lead to this temperate and charitable conclusion, "that Christianity may be professed under any form of church government".[4]

Upon this premiss all that needed to be said of the English episcopal church establishment was that it accorded with "principles which all

[1] Warburton, *The Alliance between Church and State*, Pt. ii, Sect. v, pp. 148–9.
[2] *Ibid.* p. 154.
[3] W. Paley, *Moral and Political Philosophy*, ch. x, "Of Religious Establishments and of Toleration", *Works* (ed. A. Chalmers, 5 vols. 1819), ii, 28–9.
[4] Paley, Sermon iii, *ibid.* v, 37–8.

parties acknowledge—considerations of public utility". It may be allowed that some of Paley's deductions therefrom were a little surprising even from his sober and prosaic pen. In his sermon preached at an episcopal consecration upon the theme of *A Distinction of Orders in the Church defended upon principles of Public Utility*, he elaborated a justification of the threefold order of the ministry upon the ground that

the distinctions of the clergy ought, in some measure, to correspond with the distinctions of lay society, in order to supply each class of the people with a clergy of their own level and description, with whom they may live and associate upon terms of equality. This reason is not imaginary nor insignificant.

The chief office of the episcopal order therefore was "to provide friends and companions for the superior as well as for the middle orders of the community", since it was evident "that the manners and society of higher life would suffer some depravations from the loss of so many men of liberal habits and education, as at present by occupying elevated stations in the church are entitled to be received into its number".[1]

A characteristic mark of Paley's defence of the establishment was its homespun common sense. He realised that he was dealing with a society whereof not all members be governed with the spirit and word of God, and with ministers subject to human frailties and infirmities. In all human establishments the creation of a separate order of clergy was essential upon the ground of the necessity of the application of study and learning to the profession of religion. He demonstrated the particular relevance of this maxim to Christianity, which, by virtue of its historical character, involved the understanding of ancient tongues and the investigation of problems of testimony and history, upon which the soundness of belief in its precepts depended. The primary advantage of an establishment was that it secured a ministry whereof all should be educated, and some individuals scholars of distinction.

In order to produce a few capable of improving and continuing the stock of Christian erudition, leisure and opportunity must be afforded to great numbers. Original knowledge of this kind can never be universal; but it is of the utmost importance, and it is enough, that there be at all times found some qualified for such enquiries, and in whose concurring and independent conclusions upon each subject, the rest of the Christian community may safely confide.[2]

[1] Paley, Sermon III, *ibid.* v, 40–1.
[2] Paley, "Of Religious Establishments", *Works*, ii, 32.

This end predicated the provision of an adequate emolument to the clergy, which could not be attained in Paley's view without their payment from public revenues instead of by the voluntary contributions of their auditors. For, apart from the weakness of human nature which would result in the paucity alike in number and extent of voluntary donations, such a means of support would degrade the ministerial calling, since "preaching in time would become a mode of begging", and "a ministry so degraded, would soon fall into the lowest hands, for it would be found impossible to engage men of worth and ability in so precarious and humiliating a profession".[1] In order further to attract men of ability into the ministry, the credal formulae and articles of subscription should be as few and as comprehensive as possible. Paley recognised indeed the need of tests of belief, but lamented their abuse.

> For though some purposes of order and tranquillity may be answered by the establishment of creeds and confessions, yet they are at all times attended with serious inconveniences; they check enquiry, they violate liberty, they ensnare the consciences of the clergy, by holding out temptations to prevarication; however they may express the persuasion, or be accommodated to the controversies or to the fears of the age in which they are composed, in process of time and by reason of the changes which are wont to take place in the judgment of mankind upon religious subjects, they come at length to contradict the actual opinions of the church, whose doctrines they profess to contain.[2]

To remedy this defect, he suggested that articles of subscription "ought to be made as simple and as easy as possible", that they should be subject to periodic revision, and that "confessions of faith ought to be converted into articles of peace". By such means the established church might fulfil the end designed by Warburton of comprehending the greatest number of the laity in its communion, and attracting talented and able ministers to the public office of its clergy.

In approaching the more political aspects of the alliance between church and state, Paley's genius was of too mundane a character to follow the imaginative flights of Warburton into the region of original compacts and of the personality and will of corporate societies. Nor would he allow that the civil magistrate had no proper concern with, or authority in, matters of religion.

> We, who have rejected this theory, because we cannot discover any actual contract between the state and the people, and because we cannot allow any

---

[1] Paley, "Of Religious Establishments", *Works*, ii, p. 36.
[2] *Ibid.* pp. 41–2.

arbitrary fiction to be made the foundation of real rights and of real obligations, find ourselves precluded from this distinction. The reasoning which deduces the authority of civil government from the will of God, and which collects that will from public expediency alone, binds us to the unreserved conclusion that the jurisdiction of the magistrate is limited by no consideration but that of general utility; in plainer terms, that whatever the subject to be regulated, it is lawful for him to interfere whenever his interference in its general tendency appears to be conducive to the common interest. There is nothing in the nature of religion as such, which exempts it from the authority of the legislator, when the safety or welfare of the community requires his inter-position.[1]

To prevent this authority from degeneracy into religious persecution and tyranny Paley fell back on the right and duty of each individual in matters of religion to obey God rather than men, and upon the notion of "general utility", which should operate to hinder acts of oppression which, though productive of an immediate end, would entail harmful effects in the long run. In his religious policy the civil magistrate should be guided by the maxims "that any form of Christianity is better than no religion at all, and that of different systems of faith, that is the best which is the truest".[2] Evidently this principle established the right of the magistrate to determine which is the true religion, a difficulty from which Paley sought escape by asserting "the duty of the magistrate in the choice of the religion which he established, to consult the faith of the nation, rather than his own", a guarantee against the appearance of tyranny, but scarcely an assurance of discernment of the true faith. In regard to dissenters from the established religion, Paley perceived that toleration was essential in the interest of truth itself. For to his mind

truth resulted from discussion and from controversy, [and] was investigated by the labours and researches of private persons. Whatever, therefore, prohibited these, obstructed that industry and that liberty, which it was the common interest of mankind to promote. In religion, as in other subjects, truth, if left to itself, will almost always obtain the ascendancy.[3]

But if toleration were admittedly essential in the religious sphere, what could be said of a test law excluding dissenters from the civil adminis-tration? Herein Paley marked a distinct advance upon Warburton in his design to extend the liberty of religion to equality of civil status.

[1] Paley, "Of Religious Establishments", *Works*, ii, p. 44.
[2] *Ibid.* p. 49.   [3] *Ibid.* p. 52.

With the doubtful exception of the Quakers (whose refusal to bear arms made difficult their full service of the state) he could

perceive no reason why men of different religious persuasions might not sit upon the same bench, deliberate in the same council, or fight in the same ranks, as well as men of various or opposite opinions upon any controverted topic of natural philosophy, history or ethics.[1]

Only two possible exceptions to this rule seemed justifiable; the one, if the king endeavoured to subvert the established religion of the people (a last echo of the whig recollection of James II), and the other in the case of papists, whose religious dissent was connected with political disaffection. In the former case Paley approved of a test law requiring the sovereign to hold communion with the established church, and in the latter he desired that exclusive legislation should be of temporary duration and be repealed so soon as public tranquillity permitted. With this approval of the admission of dissenters from the established church to offices of state and the desire to abolish all restrictions upon religious opinion, Paley not only registered a stage in advance of Warburton, but allowed in principle the attitude of the modern state in its tolerance of all religious profession, and neutrality towards all organised churches.

Contemporary conditions retarded the logical translation of Paley's theories into practice. "We may say", observed Leslie Stephen of Warburton's tractate, "that he really asserts that the existing compromise was very convenient. Most people agreed with him, and therefore did not trouble themselves about its theoretical basis."[2] The Georgian church corresponded well indeed with the unreformed parliament and with the *régime* of privilege and patronage in the civil administration. Nor did the temper of the eighteenth century seek innovations in any established institution. When to its natural conservatism and dislike of change there was added the sinister example of revolution, alike in religion and politics, in the neighbouring kingdom of France, suspicion of reform hardened into abhorrence and repudiation. Few members of the Hanoverian parliaments possessed the genius or eloquence of Burke to elevate their prejudices into the dignity of philosophical systems, but the majority of his fellow-commons agreed cordially with his impassioned defence of traditional institutions.

"Here I assume", he affirmed in his speech upon the petition of the Unitarians in 1792, "that by far the greater number of those who compose

[1] Paley, "Of Religious Establishments", *Works*, ii, p. 55.
[2] L. Stephen, *History of English Thought in the Eighteenth Century*, vol. ii, ch. x, Sect. 41, p. 169.

this house, are of opinion that this national establishment is a great national benefit, a great public blessing, and that its existence or non-existence is of course a thing by no means indifferent to the public welfare."[1]

In his *Reflections on the Revolution in France*, he avowed still more emphatically the virtues of the church establishment, "the first of our prejudices, not a prejudice destitute of reason, but involving in it profound and extensive wisdom", and being an institution "first, and last, and midst in our minds". To him, equally with Warburton, the religious establishment was correspondent with the eternal principles of nature and providence. Of his fellow-countrymen he declared that

they do not consider their church establishment as convenient, but as essential to their state; not as a thing heterogenous and separable; something added for accommodation; what they may either keep up or lay aside according to their temporary ideas of convenience. They consider it as the foundation of their whole constitution, with which, and with every part of which, it holds an indissoluble union. Church and State are ideas inseparable in their minds, and scarcely is the one ever mentioned without mentioning the other.[2]

---

[1] E. Burke, "Speech on the Petition of the Unitarians", 11 May 1792.
[2] Burke, *Reflections on the Revolution in France* (1790), pp. 147–8.

CHAPTER VIII

"LATITUDINARIAN TRADITOURS": BISHOPS HOADLY AND WATSON

Among the divines of Hanoverian England who attained to the order of prelacy Benjamin Hoadly and Richard Watson have achieved a peculiar primacy of infamy. Their names are remembered where all else of the history of the Georgian Church is forgotten; and that remembrance is associated by accepted tradition with the accusation of singular episcopal infidelity, inasmuch as Hoadly is represented never to have visited his first spouse of Bangor, and Watson to have been guilty of protracted indifference to his only see of Llandaff. Even their virtues are an object of suspicion. Bishop Ken denounced the leaders of the theological movement which displaced the tradition of Caroline high churchman-ship as "Latitudinarian Traditours, who would betray the baptismal faith"; and although Gibbon "dare not boast the making Watson a bishop", his commendation of him, as "a prelate of large mind and liberal spirit", seemed to the orthodox sufficient testimony of his unfitness for episcopal office, since praise from the arch-infidel was its own condemnation. The dark shadow of this reproach and neglect has fallen heavily upon the Church of which Hoadly and Watson were bishops, and the student who would essay the bold venture of presenting a less censorious picture of its condition must confront the spectre of their ill-repute. Nor is the combination of their names in popular legend lacking contemporary justification in the admission of Watson that he "had satisfaction in finding that his thoughts on many points, both religious and civil, were in perfect coincidence with those of Hoadly; and he gloried in this notwithstanding the abuse that eminent prelate experienced in his own time".[1] In some respects they were indeed representative of their age, being whigs in politics and Lati-tudinarian in religion, and ascending to the dangerous eminence of the episcopate by virtue of fidelity to this dual tradition.

To the University of Cambridge fell the distinction of indoctrinating both divines with the principles of civil and religious liberty which they ever professed, Hoadly being student, tutor, and fellow of Catharine Hall, and Watson sizar, scholar, and fellow of Trinity College. Hoadly

[1] R. Watson, *Anecdotes of the Life of Richard Watson, Bishop of Llandaff*, i, 70 (2 vols. London, 1818).

indeed found relatively little scope for his talents in collegiate society, and left Cambridge for London in 1701, resigning his fellowship on marriage and settling as lecturer of St Mildred, Poultry, in the city. During the ten years of his tenure of this important office, "he preached it down to £30 per year (as he pleasantly observed), and then he thought it high time to quit it". Before this unhappy termination, however, he was appointed in 1704 by the dean and chapter of St Paul's to the rectory of St Peter Poor, Broad Street, and his incumbency there covering the greater part of the reign of Anne, when party strife ran its fullest course in politics, his reputation was enhanced by a series of sermons in defence of whig principles, which merited the jaunty description of "the old cocks that fought the battles of liberty in good Queen Anne's days".[1] His zeal attracted the notice of the whig house of commons in 1710, which recommended him to her majesty with the request "that she would be graciously pleased to bestow some dignity in the Church upon Mr Hoadly for his eminent services both to Church and State". The provenance of this testimonial ensured its non-fulfilment during the years of tory predominance which followed the Sacheverell prosecution, and Hoadly, accepting the office of chaplain to the duke of Bedford and qualifying thereby to receive from his patron the rectory of Streatham to hold in plurality with his city living, retired to that country benefice until the tyranny of Harley and St John should be overpast. Notwithstanding the temporary setback to his fortunes, his reputation as an avid political controversialist had marked him out for high preferment whenever his whig patrons enjoyed the prizes of office again.

In addition to the fundamental similarity of the profession of whig politics, the rise of Watson to fame was accompanied by greater eminence in scholarly pursuits, and based upon the establishment of his reputation in the learned society of this college and university. His academic career was typical of the class,of poor student whose temporal prospects depended upon the most profitable exploitation of their natural talents. "Knowing that his future fortune was to be wholly of his own fabrication", he resided in college for two and a half years from his matriculation "without having gone out of it for a single day", until his ability converted his sizarship into a scholarship; whereupon, after a brief visit to his native county, he resolved "to make his Alma Mater the mother of his fortunes". In Cambridge he was noted for his

---

[1] For a fuller survey of Hoadly, see N. Sykes, "Benjamin Hoadly", in *The Social and Political Ideas of Some English Thinkers of the Augustan Age* (ed. F. J. C. Hearnshaw), Harrap, 1928.

provincial dialect and remembered long (like his fellow northcountry-men of Queen's College, Oxford) "for the modest plainness of his habits and demeanour, his dress being constantly a coarse mottled Westmorland coat, and stockings of blue yarn".[1] Further, since the study of mathematics was native to Trinity College, he resolved to become a mathematician in order to gain the favour of his society. The diligence of his studies was rewarded by his graduation as bachelor in January 1759 and his election to a fellowship of this college in the following September. Already the independence of judgment which was so marked a feature of his character was observed, particularly in his decision not to entertain the offer of the curacy of Clermont, made by the vice-chancellor with the advice "to accept it, as it would give him an opportunity of recommending himself to the duke of Newcastle, then chancellor of the university". It may be conjectured that very few young men at the outset of their career, the more especially if their fortunes depended upon the attraction of some influence lacking by their own circumstances, would have refused the opportunity of present favour, and the virtual certainty of future preferment thus presented. But Watson, "then and always prizing his independence above all prospects, declined accepting the offer".[2] At the same time he refused an invitation to go to India as chaplain to the factory at Bencoolen, on the ground of his lacking priests' orders, a circumstance which after-wards gave him pleasure to have been "disappointed of an opportunity of becoming an Asiatic plunderer".

The refusal of the curacy implied no hostility to the personal character or political principles of the duke of Newcastle, with whom, as chancellor of the university, Watson was careful to maintain cordial relations. Accordingly, when the professorship of Chemistry was vacant in 1764 and names of candidates were canvassed, William Talbot, fellow of the duke's college, Clare Hall, and one of his grace's chaplains, reported to his patron on 15 November that "Mr Watson of Trinity, a zealous friend of his grace, had been with him that morning; he offers himself a candidate for the professorship of Chemistry". To which item there was added the significant comment: "As there is no stipend annexed, I believe he will meet with no opposition. He is a man of reputation, and purposes reading lectures".[3] On 19 November the election was duly made, and since Watson's reputation was unconnected with the study of chemistry, of which by his own confession "he knew nothing

[1] *Life of B. Porteus*, by a Lay Member of Merton College, p. 72.
[2] R. Watson, *Anecdotes*, i, 34.
[3] W. Talbot to Duke of Newcastle, 15 Nov. 1764. Add. MSS. 32963, f. 409.

at all, had never read a syllable on the subject, nor seen a single experiment in it", his purpose to deliver lectures instead of treating the
office as nominal involved "very extraordinary exertions" which issued
at the end of fourteen months in his production of an inaugural series
of discourses.[1] It was not unnatural that such signs of activity and
determination in the office should evoke a corresponding desire for
emolument; and through the good offices of Mr Luther, knight of the
shire for Essex, who was reputed to have "spent above £20,000 in
establishing the whig interest" in that county, Watson preferred to the
duke of Newcastle his request that a salary might be attached to the
chair. Accordingly the duke's list of memoranda for the marquis of
Rockingham of the 17 April 1766 contained the item: "Mr Luther of
Essex: A salary for Mr Watson, Fellow of Trinity College and Professor
of [Chemistry]: recommended by the vice-chancellor, and the Cambridge bishops etc.";[2] whilst on 22 April his grace wrote to his colleague
that "Mr Luther has been again with me about his friend, Mr Watson,
the professor of Cambridge, to get an allowance to his professorship.
It is certainly a very proper benefaction to the university, and will be
of great service to that seat of learning. And as chancellor of the
university I humbly recommend it, through your lordship, to his
majesty's favour".[3] Unfortunately public business was not despatched
with haste, and four more ineffectual memoranda passed from Newcastle
to Rockingham on 21 May, 18 June and 15 and 16 July, urging the
presentation of the petition to George III.[4] During the last month
Watson, in waiting upon the duke, observed with more directness than
tact that the delay was occasioned by a matter of court etiquette;
"because lord Rockingham says your grace ought to speak to the king,
as chancellor of the university; and your grace says that lord
Rockingham ought to speak to the king as minister". Newcastle,
unused to such bluntness of speech, "stared at him with astonishment",
but sent him straightway to Rockingham with a letter missive, which
proved effective; for although the administration was on the point of
dismissal, the minister offered a stipend of £100 to be settled on Watson
for life, which the professor converted into an endowment of his office
not of himself.[5] Henceforth, since Watson's principles allowed gratitude
for favours rendered, whilst forbidding sycophancy in the expectation

---

[1] R. Watson, *Anecdotes*, i, 46.
[2] Memorandum for Lord Rockingham, 17 April 1766. Add. MSS. 32974, f. 398.
[3] Newcastle to Rockingham, 22 April 1766. Add. MSS. 32975, f. 1.
[4] Memorandums. Add. MSS. 32975, ff. 232, 436; 32976, ff. 138, 155.
[5] R. Watson, *Anecdotes*, i, 49–52.

of favours to come, he maintained friendly relations with the chancellor, now out of office and therefore unable further to reward his clients. Upon his grace's recovery from a severe illness in January 1768 Watson together with other members of the university presented his felicitations; to which the duke replied on 26 January,

sending his best compliments to Mr Professor Watson, with his very sincere thanks for Mr Watson's kind congratulations upon his recovery....The duke of Newcastle was very happy if he had had an opportunity of shewing his sense of Mr Watson's merit, and had at all times great pleasure in distinguishing persons who bore so good a character in his university as Mr Watson had always done.[1]

Before the next prize of academic striving, the professorship of Divinity, was the subject of contest in 1771, the great whig chancellor was no more. Since Watson had become the object of clerical criticism on account of his devotion to the study of chemistry, he resolved now to become the formal divine, and upon this office his ambitions centred. Although it was only "by hard travelling and some adroitness" that he secured the statutory qualification of a doctorate of divinity, obtained by royal mandate, his candidature was successful despite his comparative youth. To the chair of Divinity he brought the same qualifications as hitherto to that of Chemistry: a total ignorance of the subject of his profession, an unwearied zeal for the acquisition of knowledge, and a financial genius which raised the emoluments of the office from £330 to £1000 per annum. Thus established in one of the most arduous and honourable situations in the university, Watson's opinions on matters of statecraft were of almost equal importance with his pronouncements in divinity. His stout avowal of whig principles in politics, his opposition to the policy of George III and his ministers in their prosecution of the war against the American colonists, and his denunciation of the growing influence of the crown in the management of parliament, earned him enemies as well as friends. Until the advent of an administration determined to end the war with America, his ecclesiastical promotion was naturally retarded. During that period he added to his academic offices a sinecure rectory in North Wales procured from the bishop of St Asaph by his friend the duke of Grafton, which he resigned in 1774 upon his preferment to the prebend of the second stall at Ely, the archdeaconry of Ely in 1779, and in 1781 the rectory of Knaptoft in the gift of the duke of Rutland, whose brother's election as knight of shire for Cambridge in 1780 had been due largely to his exertions. The

[1] Newcastle to Watson, 26 Jan. 1768. Add. MSS. 33072, f. 67.

combined influence of Grafton and Rutland with the Shelburne administration procured the expected first step of a little bishopric for Watson in 1782, when he was nominated on 27 August to the see of Llandaff. His own frank confession of the reason for his elevation testified to the value placed upon his political services; for he believed that he owed the promotion, not "to the zeal and industry with which he had for many years discharged the functions and fulfilled the duties of an academic life", but to the opinion entertained that "he was a warm and might become an useful partisan. Lord Shelburne indeed had expressed to the duke of Grafton his expectation that he would occasionally write a pamphlet for their administration".[1]

The whiggery which had brought Hoadly to the see of Bangor in 1716 and Watson to that of Llandaff in 1782 forms an interesting comparative study in the application of the same fundamental principles of political action to the differing circumstances of the reigns of the first two Georges and of the third monarch of the Hanoverian line. Both Hoadly and Watson were Revolution whigs; and though charged with affection for republican principles, they were both zealous for the maintenance of the careful balance of constitutional forces achieved by the settlement of 1689. In a speech in the house of lords on 22 January 1789 in the debate on the Regency Bill, Watson enunciated clearly the position of the Revolution whigs against the new democratic movement in politics.

I am no friend to republican principles, none to prerogative principles, none to aristocratic principles, but a warm, zealous and determined friend to that equilibrium of the three powers, on the preservation of which depends the conservation of the finest constitution (not perfect perhaps either with respect to its civil or ecclesiastical part, for what human thing is perfect?), but yet the finest civil constitution that ever blessed mankind on the face of the globe. For the preservation of that constitution I would lay down my life.[2]

In accordance with this sentiment he opposed the measure introduced by Pitt's administration as an unwarranted attempt to limit the royal prerogative, and contended in favour of Fox's opinion of the inherent right of the heir apparent to assume the functions of Regent.

This episode indeed illustrated and interpreted the changed conditions under which the two whig prelates at the distance of three-quarters of a century contended for the rectitude of the Revolution establishment. Hoadly was occupied with the defence of the men of 1689 against the Caroline doctrines of divine hereditary right and passive obedience, and

[1] R. Watson, *Anecdotes*, i, 150–4. [2] *Ibid.* i, 353.

against non-juror attempts to assert the usurpatory character of the Hanoverian dynasty and the legality of a Jacobite restoration. His political sermons emphasised the superiority of the legislature to the executive, the contractual basis of civil society, and the justification of rebellion against a prince whose policy tended evidently to the ruin of the people. In conformity with the traditional method of appealing to scriptural precedents as the basis of political theories, he invoked the precept and practice of St Paul, interpreting the apostolic injunctions to obedience to the powers that be in his Epistles by the resolute assertion of his Roman citizenship in protest against arbitrary arrest and stripes in the Acts, and deducing therefrom the sanction of the apostle of the Gentiles for the Revolution principles. Pursuing his opponents further into the recondite fastness of the patriarchal authority of Adam whence was derived the absolute power of kings, Hoadly seized with mordant wit upon the relation in the first Book of Samuel[1] of the episode of the Hebrews' request for the appointment of a king to rule over them instead of reliance upon the direct theocracy, to demonstrate that in this, the only authentic occasion "given to Almighty God by mankind to declare His mind plainly concerning the institution of absolute monarchy", the resultant verdict was a picture of the despotism of the ruler and the slavery of the people. Nor did he omit to point out, for the greater discomfiture of his opponents, that in the divinely directed monarchy of Israel the election of David, the youngest of many brethren, overthrew the law of primogeniture. In his *Preservative against the Principles and Practices of the Non-Jurors both in Church and State*, he insisted that in a Protestant nation the profession of popery was the greatest incapacity in a ruler, which justified his deposition and the exclusion of all members of the royal house of the like persuasion, so that the succession should devolve upon the nearest Protestant branch of the family; which was the exact procedure of the Revolution of 1689. Further, he justified the claim of the new monarch to the allegiance of all his subjects, clergy and laity, and therefore the right of the civil government to deprive of their sees any bishops who refused to take the oath of allegiance to William and Mary in 1689. Upon this basis he argued to establish the constitutional rectitude of the Protestant succession in the house of Hanover, and the schismatic character, not of the Established Church which had accepted this solution, but of the non-juror congregations who had refused recognition of its authority.

By the time of the accession of George III the main principles of these controversies had become long obsolete. No longer were the tories

[1] I Samuel viii. 9–18.

hampered by the Nessus-shirt of Jacobite and Stuart loyalties, for the new sovereign's heart was as entirely English as that of Anne. The whigs of the age of Watson were concerned with other problems, of which the solution was by no means so direct as that of their predecessors. The influence of the crown in determining the policy of its ministers, in commanding the votes of members of parliament in both houses, and in continuing a policy of suppression of the American colonists of which the inspiration lay in the personal determination of the king, presented questions of the utmost gravity to the school of old whigs. From the outset Watson "made no scruple of everywhere declaring that he looked upon the American war as unjust in its commencement, and that its conclusion would be unfavourable to this kingdom"; but his mind was exercised more deeply with the domestic repercussions of the royal conduct of public affairs. His master in political philosophy was Locke, and he insisted that "let the pensioners and place-men say what they will, whig and tory are as opposite to each other, as Mr Locke and Sir Robert Filmer, as the soundest sense and the profoundest non-sense".[1] Throughout he was a consistent opponent of the influence of the crown in parliament, and upon the affirmation by the commons of the famous resolutions of Dunning, he burst into rhapsodic ecstasy.

Glorious resolutions these! fit to be inscribed on tablets of gold, and hung up in both houses of parliament, to inform succeeding ages that the principles of the Revolution stimulated, in 1780, a majority of the house of commons to struggle against the danger impending over the constitution from the increased and increasing influence of the Crown!![2]

The foundation of Watson's political conduct lay in his convinced adherence to the doctrine of Locke that the ultimate source of authority in civil societies lay with the people, which he insisted to be the basic principle of the Revolution of 1689 and therefore of the creed of all whigs. "We contend", he urged in reply to a tory pamphlet, "that in all *just* governments, the people have delegated to their governors the particular degree of trust with which they are invested, [and] have limited the extent of the control to which they are to be subjected." In like manner, he adopted also the traditional whig attitude in restricting the occasions on which the people might justly exercise their abstract right of resuming the government to themselves and appointing new governors.

As to the practicability of exercising it, that is quite another question, in the decision of which a great many circumstances may arise which cannot be

---

[1] R. Watson, *Anecdotes*, i, 93.   [2] *Ibid.* i, 130.

foreseen in speculation or generally estimated. It was exercised at the Revolution: and we trust that there will never, in this country, be occasion to exercise it again; for we hope, and are persuaded that the wisdom of the house of Hanover will keep at an awful distance from the throne men professing principles which have levelled with the dust the house of Stuart.[1]

Upon these premises it was not surprising that Watson, whilst admitting in theory that "the clear and decided voice of the people was superior not only to the house of commons but to the whole legislature", was uncertain whether parliamentary reform would remove the existing possibilities of influence exercised by the crown upon members of both houses. In a paper which he drew up for the freeholders of the county of Cambridge in 1780 he expressed the uncertainty "whether that reform may be best accomplished by recurring to triennial parliaments, by disfranchising the lesser boroughs, by increasing the number of the knights of the shires, by regulating the expenditure of public money, or by other means".[2] Four years later he confessed to a correspondent anxious to promote the reform of parliament that

the general question of parliamentary reform had his warmest wishes for a favourable issue to its discussion; but he was not sanguine in his hopes of seeing much good resulting to the constitution from any mode of representation which he had yet heard of; nor was he able, though he had often speculated on the subject, to devise any plan which he himself durst propose, as likely to advance the end in view.[3]

His diagnosis of the evil found no hope of remedy save in removing the means of influence at the disposal of the crown, which to him, in contradistinction to the earlier whigs of Hoadly's times, was the great problem of public administration.

The mode of corruption may be changed, but corruption itself will remain, as long as there is so much public wealth to be distributed, and so many public honours to be disposed of, among members of the house of commons and their connexions. The manner of electing members of the house of commons, and the time for which they are to be elected, are subjects on which men's minds are much divided; I consider them as matters of importance only so far as they contribute to the introduction of honest and independent members into the house, and to the keeping them so whilst they sit there. And hence I am not one of those who stickle for the abstract right of every individual having a vote in the election, nor for the ancient practice of having

[1] "An Answer to The Disquisition on Government and Civil Liberty" (1782), in R. Watson's *Miscellaneous Tracts*, ii, 344, 346 (2 vols. London, 1815).
[2] R. Watson, *Anecdotes*, i, 134–5.   [3] *Ibid.* i, 219.

a new parliament elected every year, provided the integrity of parliament could be obtained by other means. I freely own to you that I fear this end will never be obtained to any salutary extent by any means. Other means, however, of doing all that is possible, may perhaps be thought of, less obnoxious to cavil and misconstruction, than the extension of the right of voting to every individual, or the restriction of the duration of parliament to a single year.[1]

Accordingly, it was little remarkable that Watson, though approving in general of the political experiments of the American colonists and of the French republic in its early stages, regarded them with some suspicion as novelties. In a speech in the house of lords in January 1795, whilst advocating the opening of peace negotiations with France irrespective of its political constitution, he declared in relation to the republics of France and the United States that

it was enough for his argument, it was enough for the people of England to know, that they were new; their novelty rendered them suspicious; when those machines should have gone on for a century as well as their most sanguine admirers could expect, it might be soon enough then for our posterity to examine whether the people enjoyed under them more solid blessings than they themselves, he trusted, would then enjoy under the present constitution of Great Britain.[2]

In one regard both Hoadly and Watson preserved an unspotted whig record, by their unwavering championship of the claim of Protestant dissenters to enjoy the full rights of citizenship and the full opportunities of public service. Throughout his career Hoadly supported the demands of the dissenters for the repeal of the Test and Corporation Acts, after he had added his own efforts to secure the repeal in 1718 of the Occasional Conformity and Schism Acts, and even when in 1732 he accepted the commission of Walpole to represent to the dissenters the minister's opinion of the inopportuneness of pressing at that juncture for further concessions, he did not disguise his own approval of the principle of their cause as distinct from the particular point of political expediency. A like liberality of sentiment characterised the public conduct of Watson. In 1787 at a meeting of bishops summoned to advise Pitt concerning the repeal of the Test and Corporation Acts, Watson and Shipley of St Asaph were the only prelates in favour of the proposal, and motions for repeal were lost in the commons in 1787, 1789, and 1790.[3] Before the last attempt was made, fears of the spread

---

[1] R. Watson, *Anecdotes*, i, 220–1.   [2] *Ibid.* ii, 14.   [3] *Ibid.* i, 262–3.

of revolutionary ideas and the vulgar accusation against dissenters of republican politics had removed the possibility of an impartial examination of the question; notwithstanding which prejudices Watson adhered to his opinion of the expediency no less than the justice of reconciling them to the established order by measures of toleration and liberty. Towards papists he entertained the universal suspicion of his age, excepting them from his schemes of liberal protection, as Hoadly had done, on the ground of their owing allegiance to a foreign power and being in effect an *imperium in imperio* rather than a body of religious dissenters.[1] With the progress of the war against France, however, instead of advocating measures of repression against them, his opinion was given increasingly on behalf of conciliation. In 1798 he championed a comprehensive project, embracing the co-establishment of the Roman Catholic Church in Ireland together with the Reformed Episcopal Church by the payment of the salaries of the popish clergy from the public funds, the grant of Catholic Emancipation, and the enactment of the legislative union of the Irish and English parliaments.[2] To the Irish papists he was prepared to extend similar measures of toleration as to other dissenting bodies provided securities could be taken for their political loyalty, and this he conceived might be done by the parliamentary union, which would become itself, as he hoped, the parent of sentiments of reconciliation and peace between the peoples of the two islands. The proposal of such a project, and the retention of so large a degree of whig principles after the outbreak of the war with France, were indeed the truest testimony to the sincerity and conviction of his political profession. His further publication in November 1803 in the form of a pamphlet of a speech which he had intended to deliver in the house of lords, in which he advocated both Catholic Emancipation and the repeal of the Test and Corporation acts, evoked the comment of George III to Bishop Hurd that "what he said of the Roman Catholic clergy of Ireland and our great safeguards the Test and Corporation acts was most improper, and in his [majesty's] mind criminal in a member of the Church of England and still more coming from a bishop. Eminent talents and discretion were not always allied and no stronger instance could be given than himself of the truth of that position".[3] The reply of Hurd that "parts and prudence do not always go together", was abundantly true of Watson; but it might be rejoined that courage

---

[1] R. Watson, *Anecdotes*, i, 215, 251–4, 397–8.

[2] *Ibid.* ii, 61–4.

[3] George III to Bishop R. Hurd, Windsor, 30 Nov. 1803. *Hurd Papers*, vol. i, No. 44, Hartlebury Castle.

and sincerity were uncommon virtues, and that few whigs maintained such consistency of opinion as to declare, as he did again in 1812, that "a cordial reception of Catholics and Dissenters into the bosom of the constitution, by the extinction of all disqualifications, was become necessary to secure the independence of the empire and the safety of the country".[1]

Together with the espousal of unpopular principles in politics, Watson was a resolute and vehement professor of Latitudinarian doctrines in religion. The identification of Latitudinarianism with whiggery errs on the side of narrowness, for the influence of the new theological temper overpassed differences of political persuasion. The eighteenth century is not accorded usually a high place in the catalogue of the ages of faith. Indeed the general verdict upon its character ascribes to it the unpleasing title of an epoch of unbelief. In point of fact, though infidel by comparison with contemporary standards of orthodoxy, it was penetrated by a widespread if diffuse faith in certain elementary articles of theistic religion. The occasion and the origins of the movement of Latitude may be found partly in reaction against the religious disputations of the preceding age and in part as a consequence of the scientific spirit of enquiry which was inspiring new discoveries concerning the created universe. The seventeenth century had been fecund in theological controversy no less than in wars of religion, the effect of which had been not unity but dissension, and a natural weariness caused men to turn from such fruitless logomachies to seek a formula of reconciliation between the warring Christian sects. Further, the generation which witnessed the discovery or popularisation of the telescope, the microscope, the barometer, and the thermometer, began to interpret theological dogmas concerning the nature of God in accordance with new standards. Against the unseemly wrangles of Calvinist and Arminian upon dark matters of election and reprobation, there stood the new conception of the Deity deducible from the harmony and order of the created universe. Creation testified with a convincing authority to the wisdom, majesty, and universality of its Creator. The realisation of the rule of law in the visible universe evoked a welcome appreciation of the nature of God as rational and reliable, not arbitrary and capricious. This sense of relief was intensified by the conviction that the Creator was not only wise, but beneficent. For a brief space under the inspiration of this benign creed of optimism, men became literally as little children, hailing each fresh evidence of the

[1] R. Watson, *Anecdotes*, ii, 433.

benevolence of the Deity with rejoicing in the novelty and variety of creation, and engaged

> in tireless play
> attentivly occupied with a world of wonders,
> so rich in toys and playthings that naked Nature
> wer enough without the marvelous inventary of man.

The inescapable evidence of this attitude was seen in the unvarying description of the Deity as the Supreme Being and the universal Father of mankind. The new theology of divine beneficence penetrated even the language of religious poetry and hymns, and Addison expressed exactly the prevalent content of piety in its speculative no less than its practical aspects.

> The Spacious Firmament on high,
> With all the blue etherial sky,
> And spangled heav'ns, a shining Frame,
> Their great Original proclaim:
> Th' unwearied Sun, from day to day,
> Does his Creator's power display,
> And publishes to every land
> The work of an Almighty Hand.
>
> Soon as the evening shades prevail,
> The Moon takes up the wondrous tale,
> And nightly to the listning Earth
> Repeats the story of her birth:
> Whilst all the stars that round her burn,
> And all the planets in their turn,
> Confirm the Tidings as they rowl,
> And spread the Truth from pole to pole.
>
> What though, in solemn silence, all
> Move round the dark terrestrial Ball?
> What tho' nor real voice nor sound
> Amid their radiant orbs be found?
> In Reason's ear they all rejoice,
> And utter forth a glorious voice,
> For ever singing, as they shine,
> "The Hand that made us is Divine".

In such an universe man was oppressed by no fears of his own insignificance, but inspired rather by a consciousness of his dignity, for whose instruction so splendid a galaxy of spheres had been contrived.

Accordingly, men became absorbed in the exploration of the mysteries of their own nature. Hobbes indeed had set the fashion in the preceding century by his endeavour to explain all human conduct, whether political or religious, by an examination of the psychology of the individual. But the programme which had been identified hitherto with the sceptical philosopher of Malmesbury was championed now by the papist poet, Pope, whose lines

> Know then thyself, presume not God to scan,
> The proper study of mankind is Man,

became the shibboleth of the new anthropocentric movement. In speculation concerning the nature and destiny of humanity, psychology and morality, to be worked out by observation and reasoning, displaced arguments based upon texts of Scripture and theological doctrines of the essential depravity of fallen human nature.

From such tendencies there ensued evidently the vogue of natural religion. The interpretation of the Divine Nature in terms of scientific concepts led inevitably to the disparagement of the notion of revelation. The Deity whose attributes were deducible from the study of creation was evidently the Father impartially of all races and peoples. Inasmuch also as the witness of the universe to His wisdom, regularity, and beneficence was set forth so plainly that he who runs may read, irrespective of diversity of tongues, all mankind might find its essential unity in religion by the profession of such tenets as were provable from the visible creation. Into this potential harmony of religious creed the pretence to a particular revelation, vouchsafed to the primitive Hebrew people and continued in the dispensation of the New Covenant, seemed an intrusion and impertinence, unworthy of the Deity who made the worlds. The limitations necessarily involved in the notion of an historical revelation, both in regard to the extreme slowness with which it could be communicated by the preaching of its disciples to all the races of mankind, and in relation especially to the accidental concomitants of its communication in a particular language and through the medium of the history of an obscure people, presented formidable difficulties, in respect of which it compared unfavourably with the direct and universal religion of nature. Hence arose the school of Deists, the core of whose creed was the superiority of the universal natural religion to the parochial traditions of revelation, and whose chief appeal was to the general religious consciousness of mankind as furnishing the few essential doctrines necessary for the conduct of man in society and the education of his soul for the future state of rewards and punishments. Ancillary to this attack upon the fundamental premises of revealed religion was the ridicule poured upon the different theological creeds formulated by the several Christian sects, who were unable to agree even in the exegesis of their inspired Biblical oracles. How could the Deity, whose law was written in the language of nature and in the innate principles of religion and morality of the human mind, be the Author of a revelation embarrassed by such doubtful points of divinity as to provoke the disputes of Calvinist and Arminian concerning the proper interpretation of the Divine purposes? Even amongst theologians who essayed the defence of revelation against the champions of natural religion, the tendency was strong to ignore diversities of confession and church polity as things indifferent; and to concentrate on the proof of the claims of Christianity as enforcing and re-affirming the tenets of natural religion, with additional sanctions and with the testimony of the prophecies and miracles relating to the mission of Jesus Christ. The extent of the revolt against creeds and forms of church order found convincing illustration in a quarter naturally most unfavourable to levelling tendencies in religion, the poetry of the professed papist, Alexander Pope, who enunciated the principles of indifferentism without equivocation.

> For Forms of Government let fools contest:
> Whate'er is best administered, is best;
> For Modes of Faith let graceless zealots fight:
> He can't be wrong, whose life is in the right:
> In Faith and Hope the world will disagree,
> But all Mankind's concern is Charity;
> All must be false that thwart this one great End:
> And all of God, that bless Mankind, or mend.

In the battle thus joined between the champions of natural and revealed religion, the defenders of Christianity essayed the dual strategy of demonstrating that natural religion was neither so clear, so perfect, nor so universal as the Deists professed, and that the evidence of the divine commission to Moses and Christ, the authors of the Old and New Covenants of the Jews, was sufficient for belief in the doctrines of their proclamation. In this argument Bishop Butler's *Analogy of Religion Natural and Revealed to the Constitution and Course of Nature* not only achieved a rapid pre-eminence in the contemporary contest, but established its claim as a classic of orthodox apologetic. The victory over Deism thereby won for orthodox Christianity was of astonishing completeness. In the first part of his work Butler turned against natural religion all the objections which its supporters alleged against revelation, and directed its virtues to the service of revealed religion. In the second part he examined the conditions and evidences of Christianity, affirming them to be adequate for credence, since probability is the very guide of life. Around the massive defensive works thus constructed a host of lesser writers contributed ancillary buttresses, generally in the form of detailed examinations of the authenticity and credibility of the Gospels and other books of the New Testament. The study of evidences, in order to prove the apostles to have been neither forgers nor liars but sincere and well-informed narrators, became the chief occupation of divines, resulting in the compilation of "that Old Bailey theology, in which, to use Johnson's expression, the apostles are being tried once a week for the capital crime of forgery".[1] In this university the benefaction of John Hulse was typical of the spirit of his age alike in its prescriptions and prohibitions. For by the provisions of his will of 21 July 1777 his Christian Advocate was "to prepare some proper and judicious answers to all such new and popular or other cavils and objections against the Christian or Revealed Religion or against the Religion of Nature"; and his Preacher was "to show the evidence for Revealed Religion and to demonstrate in the most convincing and persuasive manner the Truth and Excellence of Christianity"; whilst both were enjoined to direct their assaults "only against notorious infidels, whether atheists or deists, not descending to any particular sects or controversies (so much to be lamented) amongst Christians themselves, except some new and dangerous error either of superstition or enthusiasm, as of Popery or Methodism, either in opinion or practice, should prevail".[2] In like manner John Norris bequeathed money by his will of 26 June 1770 for the foundation of "a Professorship of Revealed Religion".[3] In the University of Oxford the defence of orthodoxy was set forward by the foundation of the Bampton Lectures (the first of which were delivered in 1780), by the will of John Bampton, canon of Salisbury (1689–1751), which provided for the endowment of eight divinity lecture sermons to be delivered yearly "to confirm and establish the Christian Faith and to confute all heretics and schismatics".

The results of this intensive and critical investigation of the New Testament, gratifying as a refutal of the Deist assertions, bore the

[1] Mark Pattison, "Tendencies of Religious Thought in England, 1688–1750", p. 260, in *Essays and Reviews*, pp. 254–329 (8th ed. 1861).
[2] J. W. Clark, *Endowments of the University of Cambridge*, pp. 117 *seq.*
[3] *Ibid.* pp. 104 *seq.*

properties of a two-edged sword in relation to the orthodox attitude towards the Scriptures and the theological confessions deduced by the several churches therefrom. If the Deists could be defeated by recourse to the Bible, it seemed reasonable that the orthodox should be content to frame their confessions of faith in terms directly drawn from the Sacred Writings. Belief in the Creator and Father of mankind being common to natural and revealed religion, the essence of Christian faith was defined by John Locke to consist in acceptance of the claim of Jesus of Nazareth to be the Messiah, whose advent was foretold by the prophecies of the Old Testament, and whose mission was authenticated by the miracles of the New. But the gulf between this simple creed, or that of the primitive converts baptised by the apostles into the belief that Jesus was the Son of God, and the elaborate statement of the Christian doctrine of the Godhead contained in the so-called Athanasian creed was wide; and the rationalistic method of approach to the Scriptures popularised by the intellectual movement of the age led to a widespread rejection of the Athanasian symbol, and therewith also of the authentic Athanasian interpretation of the Trinity. The doctrines of Arius received a new vogue and acceptance; not as the private speculations of individual divines, but as the true doctrine of Scripture. The appearance of Arian theories in orthodox circles had been emphasised during the reign of Anne by the publication in 1712 of Dr Samuel Clarke's *Scripture Doctrine of the Trinity*, and despite the weighty defence of the traditional doctrine by Waterland, the tendencies represented by Clarke continued. The temper of the eighteenth century was averse from the appeal to antiquity and inclined rather to trust to the enlightenment of its own age; so that, although the desire of ardent spirits for the reformation of the doctrines and liturgy of the Church in accordance with the principles of the *aufklärung* was frustrated, a middle way was advocated widely of the formulation of articles of subscription only in terms used in the Scriptures. Even among circles of professed orthodoxy in this regard a readiness to avoid burdening the conscience of persons less zealous for the Athanasian doctrine was observed. Thus the influence of Deism upon orthodox churchmanship was of considerable importance, despite the formal defeat of its assault by the apology of Butler. In many minor skirmishes, and in the general tone of defences of revealed religion, much ground was gained by the principles, if not the conclusions, of its champions.

Of this movement of Latitude in its widest significance Hoadly and Watson were representative, though in differing degree. Hoadly indeed was an inconsiderable theologian, whilst Watson by virtue of his chair was officially professed of the study of theology, albeit his divinity, like his political creed, was *sui generis*. The fame of Hoadly rests not upon his theological writings but upon his essays in political statecraft; and the Latitudinarian tradition in its earlier stages was represented with greater distinction by his friend Dr Samuel Clarke, whose unorthodox opinions were supported by solid learning. Hoadly's sermons and incidental pronouncements on matters of theology were characterised rather by repetition of the opinions current in the entourage of Clarke than by the proposition of original theories. But he was not the less representative of the general temper of his age because of his lack of originality. In one respect the fidelity of his reflection of current tendencies was especially noteworthy, namely in his refusal, when engaged in controversy with the non-jurors, to descend to detailed consideration of the arguments drawn by his opponents from specific Biblical texts, the apparent meaning of which supported their position. Thus when confronted in his disputes concerning the authority of the Church by passages from the Gospels purporting to convey to the apostles a divine commission to forgive and retain sins, Hoadly, instead of contesting the traditional exegesis of such texts, appealed to another court. "Whatsoever contradicts the natural notions of God and the design and tenor of the Gospel cannot be the true meaning of any passage in the Gospel." The contention that dark and difficult Scriptural references should be interpreted in accordance with the concept of the Deity derived from natural religion, or the innate religious ideas of mankind, was particularly characteristic of the age. By its useful means the Pauline arguments concerning divine election were expounded, and therefore annulled, in accordance with the belief in the Divine Benevolence as the chief attribute of God, involving the rejection of contradictory qualities. In complete accordance with this conception Hoadly, in an incidental phrase of the famous Bangorian sermon, defined true religion as the practice of "virtue and charity under the belief of a Supreme Governor and Judge". Further, in applying his principles of criticism to the elucidation of the doctrine of the Eucharist, in his *Plain Account of the Nature and End of the Sacrament of the Lord's Supper*, he proclaimed its meaning as "a Rite to be seriously performed in remembrance of an Absent Saviour, and taking the bread and wine as memorials of His body broken and blood shed, and not as the Things themselves in remembrance of which they were ordained to be received".[1] Of equal interest with his conclusions were his methods of approach to the problem. At the outset he insisted that "it is of small

[1] Hoadly, *Works*, iii, 846.

importance to Christians to know what the many writers upon this subject since the times of the evangelists and apostles have affirmed", since "it cannot be doubted that Christ Himself sufficiently declared to His first and immediate followers the whole of what He designed should be understood by it or implied in it". Notwithstanding, Hoadly found nothing inconsistent in his own endeavour to interpret their meaning by the enlightened divinity of his own day! Such incursions into the sphere of theology were occasional, and his chief contribution to ecclesiastical theory lay in the argument of his sermon *On the Nature of the Kingdom or Church of Christ.* From this polemic the visible church emerged, stript not only of distinctions of polity, episcopalian and presbyterian, but of all corporate existence and authority over its members. It was reduced virtually to a voluntary association of seekers after truth, united by the sincerity of their quest despite their diversity of religious profession. Herein lay Hoadly's original speculation, apart from which extreme assertion of individualism in religion, he reflected at second hand current Latitudinarian ideas in theology.

From Watson, as regius professor of Divinity in this university, a more solid and academic statement of his theological position might be expected; and it would be difficult to discover a bolder and more comprehensive profession of the Latitudinarian faith than that entered by him in his *Anecdotes* in relation to his election to that office.

"I reduced the study of divinity", he observed, "into as narrow a compass as I could, for I determined to study nothing but my Bible, being much unconcerned about the opinions of councils, fathers, churches, bishops, and other men as little inspired as myself. This mode of proceeding being opposite to the general one, and especially to that of the Master of Peterhouse [Edmund Law] who was a great reader, he used to call me αὐτοδίδακτος, the self-taught divine! The professor of divinity had been nick-named *malleus haereticorum;* it was thought to be his duty to demolish every opinion which militated against what is called the orthodoxy of the Church of England. Now my mind was wholly unbiassed; I had no prejudice against, no predilection for the Church of England; but a sincere regard for the Church of Christ, and an insuperable objection to every degree of dogmatical intolerance. I never troubled myself with answering any arguments which the opponents in the divinity-schools brought against the articles of the church, nor ever admitted their authority as decisive of a difficulty; but I used on such occasions to say to them, holding the New Testament in my hand, *En sacrum codicem!* Here is the fountain of truth, why do you follow the streams derived from it by the sophistry, or polluted by the passions of man? If you can bring proofs against anything delivered in this book, I shall think it my duty to reply to you; articles of churches are not of divine authority; have done with them; for they may be true, they may be false; and appeal to the book itself. This mode of disputing gained me no credit with the hierarchy, but I thought it an honest one, and it produced a liberal spirit in the university."[1]

From such a robust application of the principles of scientific enquiry to the doctrines of Christianity, and from such a contumelious disregard for tradition as representing but the speculations of the dark ages, Watson evolved an individual creed, strikingly different from the official articles of subscription of the Established Church and strongly influenced by the intellectual temper of his age. He dismissed as unimportant all dogmas derived from abstract speculation concerning the nature and attributes of God, and valued Christianity chiefly as a religion of evidence.

Believing as I do in the truth of the Christian religion, which teaches that men are accountable for their actions, I trouble not myself with dark disquisitions concerning necessity and liberty, matter and spirit; hoping as I do for eternal life through Jesus Christ, I am not disturbed at my inability clearly to convince myself that the soul is, or is not, a substance distinct from the body. The truth of the Christian religion depends upon testimony; now man is competent to judge of the weight of testimony, though he is not able, I think, fully to investigate the nature of the soul; and I consider the testimony concerning the resurrection of Jesus (and that fact is the corner-stone of the Christian church) to be worthy of entire credit.[2]

In accordance with this criterion, he accepted the miracles attendant upon the mission of Christ as Messiah on the ground of historical evidence, but refused to pronounce any definite opinion upon such theoretic questions as the pre-existence of Christ before His Incarnation.

"Whoever professes to believe the canonical books of the New Testament", he wrote, "virtually professes to believe that Jesus Christ did not come into this world according to the ordinary course of nature; that He voluntarily sealed His mission with His blood; that He did not, like the rest of mankind, continue subject to death, but became the first-fruits of the resurrection. These and other fundamental principles of Christianity are so fully and explicitly revealed, that he who admits the truth and genuineness of the books of the New Testament, cannot with any colour or reason be supposed to doubt of them. But concerning the mode of union of the divine and human natures in Jesus Christ; concerning the satisfaction made to

---

[1] R. Watson, *Anecdotes*, i, 62–4.   [2] *Ibid.* i, 24.

vindicate justice by His death; concerning the nature of that original sin which He came to do away; concerning the eternal decrees of God respecting the election or reprobation of particular persons or nations; concerning these and other recondite doctrines of Christianity, whatever uniformity there may be of outward profession, there can be none of inward belief."[1]

When Watson approached the controverted problems of the nature of the Godhead, and the Sonship of Christ, his influence was cast always in favour of the widest practicable latitude of subscription to confessional statements, and his pen was unwearied in urging the propriety of framing such confessions only in the express words and terms of Scripture. His close personal friendship with the duke of Grafton, who became a member of the Unitarian congregation of Mr Lindsey in Essex Street, Strand, prevented him from speaking of persons of that persuasion as non-Christian, in contrast to the majority of orthodox divines of his day.

"I never attempted", he wrote of his relations with the duke, "either to encourage or to discourage his profession of Unitarian principles; for I was happy to see a person of his rank, professing with intelligence and with sincerity Christian principles. If any one thinks that an Unitarian is not a Christian, I plainly say, without being myself an Unitarian, that I think otherwise."[2]

Throughout the public discussions concerning Arian, Socinian, and Athanasian interpretations of the doctrine of the Trinity, Watson supported consistently the demand for the abolition of the requirement of subscription to the Thirty-Nine Articles.

"Systems of theology", in his judgment, "had as much obstructed the progress of revealed truth as systems in philosophy had done that of natural truth; and it would require as much application of genius, industry, and learning to free the Christian world from the dominion of corrupted doctrine, as it did to free the philosophic world from the dominion of Aristotle."[3]

In a charge to his diocese in 1791 he declared his conviction that

nothing had been of more disservice to Christianity than that religious bigotry with which different sects had, in all ages and countries, persecuted

---

[1] "A Letter to the Members of the House of Commons: respecting the Petition for Relief in the Matter of Subscription: By a Christian Whig", 1772, in R. Watson's *Miscellaneous Tracts*, ii, 13.

[2] R. Watson, *Anecdotes*, i, 75–6.

[3] "Considerations on the Expediency of Revising the Liturgy and Articles", 1790, in R. Watson's *Miscellaneous Tracts*, ii, 102–3.

each other—dum hic dicit Ego sum Athanasii, ille vero Ego sum Socini; dum hic dicit Ego sum Lutheri, ille vero Ego sum Calvini, may it not be rightly said σαρκικοί ἐστε πάντες.[1]

In his plea for a revision of the Liturgy and Articles, he asserted indeed that the desire for such change did not imply necessarily the unorthodoxy of the supplicant.

Let no one rashly and injuriously conclude that he who dislikes the Athanasian creed, and wishes to see it expunged from our Liturgy, does thereby shew his disbelief of the doctrine of a Trinity; he may admit the doctrine of a Trinity, without admitting the doctrine of the Athanasian Trinity; nay, he may even admit the doctrine of the Athanasian Trinity, and yet reject the Creed for its uncharitableness.... We do not object to the doctrine of the Trinity because it is above our reason, and we cannot comprehend it; but we object to it because we cannot find that it is either literally contained in any passage of Holy Writ, or can by sound criticism be deduced from it.[2]

Such were amongst the more complimentary of Watson's references to the Athanasian symbol, for in the same plea for revision of the official standards of doctrine and worship, he wrote:

Who will say that our posterity may not be as much astonished at our having believed the Athanasian doctrine of the Trinity, as we are astonished at our ancestors having believed the doctrine of Transubstantiation, which the Romanists maintain to be as credible and as firmly supported by Scripture as *that* doctrine of the Trinity is.[3]

Animated further by a double portion of the confidence of his age in its superior intellectual enlightenment to past times, he ventured to affirm of this creed that

the Church of Christ ought never to have received it. There may be inveteracy of error as well as antiquity of truth; and he who can say nothing for his own opinions but that they are old; or against those of his opponents but that they are new, seems to me to say nothing to the point on either side. I will speak freely. Was I compelled to receive a creed of *human* composition, I would more willingly in these enlightened times receive one from such men as Locke, Clarke, or Tillotson, than from either Athanasius or Arius, or even from hundreds of contentious or political bishops, assembled in solemn council at Nice, Antioch, or Ariminum.[4]

[1] "Charge to the Clergy of the Diocese of Llandaff", 1791, in R. Watson's *Miscellaneous Tracts*, i, 291.
[2] "The Expediency of Revising the Liturgy and Articles", in *Ibid.* ii, 104, 108.
[3] *Ibid.* p. 127. [4] *Ibid.* p. 115.

In like manner he advocated without fear the revision of the Liturgy by contemporary divines.

I profess I cannot listen to the opinion which would compel Protestants of future ages to submit their understandings to the decisions of Cranmer and Ridley, of Parker and Grindal, and other reformers of religion and compilers of liturgies, without astonishment and concern. These men, it is readily allowed, did much; but have Locke, and Clarke, and Hoadly, and Taylor done nothing?[1]

Accordingly he testified his readiness to submit the problem both of forms of subscription and of liturgies to the determination of the parliament; asserting

that were the question concerning the propriety of substituting Dr Clarke's amended Liturgy, or one on that plan, in the place of our present Liturgy, *now* proposed, in order to have the decision of the legislature upon it a twelvemonth hence, so that all serious men might have time to consider the subject, his opinion was, that it would be decided for Dr Clarke's amended Liturgy or one on that plan.[2]

Respect for antiquity was notoriously slight in the age of reason, and in the diocese of Llandaff during Watson's long episcopate the Vincentian canon had no currency, at least in the official pronouncements of the bishop, for elevation to the episcopate in no wise altered his sentiments nor muzzled their expression. In his Charge of 1784 he defended at great length the legality of either Arian or Athanasian views of the Trinity, affirming solemnly that "he could never bring himself to deny the name of Christians to all those who on the one hand could not agree with Athanasius, or on the other with Arius, or with Socinus on that point".[3] Nor did he lack the courage to express his convictions in high places, since in 1790 he agreed with the duke of Grafton to bring into the house of lords a bill for expunging the Athanasian creed from the English Liturgy, assuring his grace that "no distance or business should hinder him from appearing in his place in the house on the day the point should be debated, and standing up with his best ability in support of the motion".[4] The postponement of the project was occasioned by political repercussions in England of current events of the French Revolution which removed the possibility of impartial consideration of any innovations in church or state.

[1] "The Expediency of Revising the Liturgy and Articles," in R. Watson's *Miscellaneous Tracts*, ii, p. 101.   [2] *Ibid.* p. 132.
[3] Charge, 1784, in *Ibid.* i, 321, 325–7.
[4] R. Watson, *Anecdotes*, i, 392–4.

With the enunciation of such views concerning the authority of creeds and articles, it was little surprising that Watson laid no emphasis upon the value of the episcopate as a badge of continuity. In his constant advocacy of the repeal of restrictive legislation against Protestant dissenters, he ridiculed objections based upon the fear of an attack of nonconformists upon the Established Church.

Suppose however even that improbable circumstance to take place, and that a majority of the house of Commons has ceased to be churchmen—what then?...Let it be admitted that, at some distant period of which no man can form a reasonable conjecture, the house of Lords would, by compulsion or choice, agree with the house of Commons, and that the King would agree with them both in establishing Presbytery in the room of Episcopacy—what then? Why then the present form of the Church of England would be changed into another! And is this all?—this the catastrophe of so many tragical forebodings—this the issue of so many improbable contingencies—this the result of so much unchristian contention....A great Protestant nation does not return to Popery—a great Christian nation does not apostatise to Paganism or Mahometanism; it simply adopts an ecclesiastical constitution different from what it had before.[1]

His reprobation of the zeal of many churchmen for episcopacy found curious expression in a refusal to support by his presence and donations the Society for the Propagation of the Gospel in Foreign Parts, on the ground of his suspicion, avowed to a correspondent in 1777, "that its missionaries were more zealous in proselytising dissenters to episcopacy than in converting heathens to Christianity". Despite the fact that "this conduct of his had been considered as exceeding strange and had given great offence", he preferred to affront "all the dignitaries of the church for ever, rather than act contrary to his decided judgment for an hour".[2] Eleven years later, in 1788, and after his elevation to the episcopate, he reiterated these sentiments. His singularity of opinion was testified further by his declaration that "he did not expect much success in propagating Christianity by missionaries from any part of Christendom, but he expected much from the extension of science and commerce".[3] Notwithstanding the circumstance of his entering the lists in defence of revelation against the attack of Thomas Paine, there was much community of spirit between Watson and the Norfolk stay-maker in their naïve confidence in the *aufklärung* of the age and their preference of scientific novelty to traditional conclusions. In the *Address*

[1] R. Watson, *Anecdotes*, i, 425–6.
[2] *Ibid.* i, 105.   [3] *Ibid.* i, 321.

which Watson delivered to the candidates for confirmation in his
diocese, he observed that

if their understanding had been enlarged by a liberal education and they had
been instructed in the principles of true philosophy, especially of astronomy,
they could not fail of having their mind occupied by the most sublime and
devout conceptions of the power and wisdom of that adorable Being who
formed the universe.[1]

Indeed, if the political independence of the bishop of Llandaff had not
precluded the possibility of his promotion to the primacy, for which
he accounted himself a proper candidate on the grounds of ability and
zeal, the *Ecclesia Anglicana* might have suffered a strange meta-
morphosis at the instance of a prelate who, before he had been six
months on the bench, endeavoured

to make a beginning of that reform in the Church, which he sincerely thought
would be for the good of mankind, the stability of the church establishment,
and the advancement of genuine Christianity. For a review of the doctrine
and of the discipline of our Church, and a complete purgation of it from the
dregs of Popery and the impiety of Calvinism, would have properly followed
a wise distribution of its revenue.[2]

The chief charge against Hoadly and Watson however has proceeded
from their attainment of the eminence of the episcopate, without which
added significance of dignity their profession of whiggism and
Latitudinarianism might have passed uncensured. Dr Samuel Clarke,
though sharing the heterodoxy of Arian tenets, is little remembered
by comparison with them, since his aspirations to the bench, albeit
supported by the favour of Queen Caroline, were quenched by the
resolute opposition of Bishop Gibson to the hint of his nomination in
1727 to the see of Bangor. Upon Hoadly and Watson the dangerous
preferment fell; and both were consecrated to Welsh bishoprics, Hoadly
to the notorious see of Bangor and Watson to the impecunious diocese
of Llandaff. The Welsh sees indeed were particularly unfortunate during
the Hanoverian century in the brevity of the episcopates of their
occupants, being regarded generally as merely the first stepping-stone
to higher office, and the memory of their bishops passing away as the
remembrance of a guest that tarrieth but for a day. During the century
which followed the Revolution of 1689, St Asaph was held by fifteen

---

[1] "An Address to Young Persons after Confirmation", in R. Watson's *Miscellaneous Tracts*, ii, 283.

[2] R. Watson, *Anecdotes*, i, 168.

bishops, of whom nine were translated, Bangor by fourteen, of whom eleven were translated, St David's by sixteen, twelve of whom received the reward of translation, and Llandaff by eleven, of whom seven were translated; though in the episcopates of Beaw from 1679 to 1706, and of Watson from 1782 to 1816, this last see achieved an easy record for longevity.

The evident deduction from such statistics was the expectation of Welsh bishops for speedy and lucrative removal to England, of which the correspondence of several individuals afforded piquant illustration. So little regard was entertained for the dioceses of the principality that upon occasion divines ventured to prefer a request for translation before the formalities of their appointment to a Welsh see were completed. In November 1743 Dr John Thomas, dean of Peterborough, the favourite chaplain of George II, was rewarded by nomination to the see of St Asaph, to which he was elected by the chapter, but delayed to proceed to consecration until the bishopric of Lincoln fell vacant in the following January by the death of Bishop Reynolds. Thereupon he employed the good offices of Sherlock of Sarum to approach on his behalf the duke of Newcastle on 16 January, the day after Reynolds' decease, "to intercede with his grace to recommend him to the king" for the English diocese. In support of his request Thomas alleged that, though the value of the sees "was nearly the same", Lincoln was much more accessible, "it being two easy days from London to Bugden", a circumstance of importance to one who found "long journeys more inconvenient";[1] and accordingly he was nominated to Lincoln on 20 January, forsaking his first spouse without passing beyond the preliminaries of betrothal. His successor at St Asaph, Dr Samuel Lisle, made application in due course for translation to Norwich in 1748, to which he was duly nominated by the king. Amongst the competitors for that see was his brother of Bangor, Zachary Pearce, who had solicited the interest of Lord Hardwicke in his own cause, but on hearing of the candidature of Lisle assured his patron that "he thought it so reasonable both on account of his more advanced age, and of his having been four years a traveller in north Wales, that he was very well pleased with the appointment".[2]

Bishop Pearce indeed would fain have left Bangor as precipitously as Thomas had done St Asaph. He was nominated to Bangor on 19 December 1747, and elected on 14 January following, but before the confirmation, the see of Ely was vacated by the death of Bishop Butts

[1] Bp. Sherlock to Duke of Newcastle, 16 Jan. 1743/4. Add. MSS. 32702, f. 13.
[2] Bp. Pearce to Lord Hardwicke, 29 Jan. 1747/8. Add. MSS. 35590, f. 7.

on 26 January. Pearce thereupon wrote to the duke of Newcastle, expressing his supposition that

"there would become a vacancy in one of the English bishoprics now held by a bishop educated at Cambridge. In that case", he added, "I beg your grace's recommendation of me to his majesty that, instead of having my election at Bangor confirmed, I may be appointed to such English bishopric as shall become vacant; which I am the more encouraged to hope for, as your grace was pleased to tell me that Bangor is a fortunate see; and I shall think it so if I can be so happy as to avoid such a long journey".[1]

Evidently the fortunate character attaching to Bangor in the eyes of Pearce lay in the escape therefrom of his two predecessors, Herring and Hutton, to the archiepiscopal thrones of York and Canterbury, though both prelates had served their first see faithfully for a few years before translation, as indeed he was destined himself to do for nine years, in which he endeavoured diligently to fulfil the duties of diocesan administration. Notwithstanding, his instant applications to Newcastle and Hardwicke in 1748 for removal to Norwich, in succession to Sir Thomas Gooch who was translated to Ely, indicated his reluctance to undertake the difficult and arduous journey into the fastness of North Wales. The English aversion to Wales was emphasised in the description by Bishop Moore of his residence at Bangor as employed "by looking round his diocese and endeavouring to civilize it a little".[2]

Nor were the other Welsh bishoprics the object of greater covetousness. The relative neglect of the remote diocese of St David's even by the most conscientious prelates of the age was illustrated by the arguments of Archbishop Herring for the elevation of his friend Dr Anthony Ellis to that see in 1752 in succession to Trevor translated to Durham. Despite the distance of the see-city from London the primate wished to plant there the prelate who was to be the chief sharer of his confidences.

"I know your grace", he wrote to Newcastle, "will not think me unreasonable to wish for a sort of coadjutor-bishop. I know how much I want one. Two of my best predecessors since the Revolution, Tenison and Wake, were indulged in this sort of advantage, though they less wanted it, having great abilities as well as integrity. I claim a title only to the last quality."[3]

[1] Bp. Pearce to Newcastle, 26 Jan. 1747/8: quoted by M. Bateson in *E.H.R.* vol. vii, 1892; cf. Pearce to Hardwicke, Add. MSS. 35590, f. 7.
[2] Moore to Eden, 6 Sept. 1782. Add. MSS. 34413, f. 26.
[3] Abp. Herring to Newcastle, 16 July 1752. Add. MSS. 32728, f. 278.

The request was granted, Ellis became bishop of St David's, and as co-adjutor to Herring divided his time unequally between South Wales and the capital. The extreme rusticity of St David's itself was a not inconsiderable obstacle to the persuasion of clerics of figure to accept promotion to so distant a dignity. In 1761 Lord Hardwicke canvassed the chances of his friend Dr John Green, dean of Lincoln, in relation to the see, expressing to Newcastle his doubts whether so small a prize would be worth his acceptance.

"The archbishop of York told me last night", he observed, "that St David's was no more than £900 per annum. That is low, and without some tolerable commendam would scarce tempt to so long a journey; and yet considering the dean has no family and is single, it would be worth his while to get upon the bench."[1]

Better fortune attended Green in the shape of nomination to the see of Lincoln in the same year, and St David's was the consolation awarded to a faithful chaplain and secretary of the duke of Newcastle, Dr Samuel Squire, dean of Bristol. Upon his death in 1766, Dr Robert Lowth had great difficulty in accepting the bishopric, even though allowed to retain his prebend of Durham and a parochial benefice in that diocese *in commendam*;[2] and the degree of his affection for South Wales may be judged from the circumstance that within three months of his consecration he accepted translation to Oxford. In like manner Dr John Moore in 1774 declared that "if he succeeded to the next vacancy, it was a mercy to have escaped St David's",[3] albeit the next opportunity proved to be another Welsh see, that of Bangor, to which he was consecrated in February 1775. Even the exemplary Bishop Samuel Horsley, having discharged the episcopal office at St David's since 1788, and having successfully solicited from William Pitt in 1793 translation to Rochester, confessed that "he would soon bid adieu but not reluctantly, to those romantic scenes".[4] Indeed, "the circumstances of having a house in Town, and saving himself the annual expense and fatigue of the long journey, made the change very agreeable to him".[5] The problem of emolument played an important part in the filling of all bishoprics, and to some Welsh dioceses the difficulty of poverty was

---

[1] Hardwicke to Newcastle, 19 Jan. 1761. Add. MSS. 32917, f. 396.

[2] Newcastle to Charles Townshend, 15 May 1766. Add. MSS. 32975, f. 191.

[3] Moore to Eden, n.d. Add. MSS. 34412, f. 280.

[4] Horsley to J. Robson, 1 Sept. 1793. G. Smith and F. Benger, *The Oldest London Bookshop*, p. 139.

[5] Horsley to Bp. Hurd, 27 Sept. 1793. *Hurd Papers*, vol. iii, Bp. Horsley's Letters, No. 6.

added to that of distance. St David's was reckoned in 1762 to be of the value of £900, St Asaph to be worth £1400, and Bangor likewise, whilst Llandaff scored an easy primacy of dishonour with a mere pittance of £500 per year.

Little surprise may be occasioned therefore by the discovery that Llandaff was the least coveted of all bishoprics, the majority of its occupants receiving it only as an earnest of further favours to come. When Bishop John Gilbert secured translation to Sarum in 1748 after eight years' episcopate at Llandaff, he expressed most grateful thanks to his grace of Newcastle, assuring him that "'twas a matter of great comfort to himself to be so happily delivered from his present most disagreeable situation".[1] His successor in the see was Dr Edward Cresset, dean of Hereford, whose peculiarity it was to evince a delight in the promotion as profound as Gilbert's in his escape.

"Although the revenues of the see may not be very considerable," wrote Cresset to Newcastle, "I think my private fortune cannot be better employed than in his majesty's service, by enabling me to attend parliament and on all occasions to shew myself a steady and hearty friend to our happy establishment in church and state."

To this expression of appreciation was appended an even more effusive postscript. "The situation of Llandaff is so convenient to me that I shall never desire to leave that neighbourhood."[2] Such sentiments were indeed unusual in bishops of Llandaff, even when newly nominated to the diocese, the more especially since Cresset resigned his deanery of Hereford and fulfilled his promise of contentment by remaining in that see until his death in 1755. Happy was the political minister whose client showed so great gratitude for a little bishopric! And blessed indeed would Newcastle have been if his office books had been filled with such names; but Cresset was the exception, not the rule, as the history of subsequent prelates of Llandaff indicated. In 1761, when the see was vacant by the translation of Bishop Newcome to St Asaph, the royal favour fell upon Dr John Ewer, who showed no zeal to proceed further with the formalities of nomination. Archbishop Secker complained to Newcastle on 9 August that "he presumed Ewer was aiming at something better, because he did not find that in three weeks' time or more he had taken one step towards Llandaff, which yet...he apprehended, might well suffice him for the present".[3] Other more

[1] Bp. Gilbert to Newcastle, 26 Oct. 1748. Add. MSS. 32717, f. 210.
[2] Bp. Cresset to Newcastle, 23 Dec. 1748. *Ibid.* f. 528.
[3] Abp. Secker to Newcastle, 9 Aug. 1761. Add. MSS. 32926, f. 328.

valuable prizes were indeed in the market, and Lord Hardwicke echoed the primate's sentiments to his colleague, Newcastle.

As to the new-intended bishop of Llandaff, I own I think that after he has neglected the king's nomination of him for two months, without taking any one step upon it, his majesty should not submit to give him a better bishopric at present. I may be mistaken, but to me it does not seem decent; and if from any such arrangement, Llandaff should be left for Green, I shall advise him humbly to decline it.[1]

Ultimately Ewer's strategy did not avail him anything, for he had to proceed with his election and consecration to Llandaff, from which he only escaped to Bangor in 1769, being followed in South Wales by Dr Jonathan Shipley who, being consecrated on 12 February to Llandaff, secured nomination to St Asaph on 17 July following.

It is evident therefore that Hoadly and Watson differed from the majority of their contemporaries who accepted Welsh bishoprics rather in degree than in kind in their lack of zeal to execute the office and work of a bishop in the Principality. That Hoadly should never have been raised to the episcopate is manifest from a consideration, not of his opinions, but of his physical lameness, which compelled him even to preach in a kneeling posture and prevented his riding save in a chaise. At the time of his nomination to Bangor, Gibson observed that "his friends thought a good deanery or residentiaryship of St Paul's more proper for him, but it seems he preferred a bishopric; and since it is so, I hope he will be able to attend at Westminster, though at first crutches will look a little ungainly there".[2] If crutches would be awkward in the house of lords how could they be expected to carry their possessor round the vast dioceses of eighteenth-century England (for Hoadly had been covetous even of the huge bishopric of Lincoln to which Gibson himself succeeded) to visit and confirm? Of all sees, that of Bangor was the most unfitting for a cripple, since only an intrepid rider on horseback could traverse its winding ways and mountain passes. The ineffectiveness of Hoadly as bishop of any see was therefore predestined; and in this case the appointment was clearly made without the slightest regard for the discharge of episcopal duties. The authors of his promotion cannot escape censure, nor the partial friends who supported his ambitions; but upon Hoadly himself must fall the chief

[1] Hardwicke to Newcastle, *Ibid.* f. 368.
[2] Gibson to Nicolson, 20 Dec. 1715. Add. MSS. A. 269, f. 52, Bodley.

responsibility for the acceptance of the administration of the episcopate, with the knowledge of his abiding inability to perform its duties. His elevation to the bench is the gravest offence against ecclesiastical propriety of the century, for in his regard the promotion was the mere reward for political services. Even as a political pamphleteer he would have been equally effective in a deanery, for he spoke rarely in the house of lords, and his pen was his chief recommendation to preferment. The lack of suffragan bishops in the Church, upon whose assistance he might otherwise have relied, resulted in his enforced supplication to other diocesan bishops to perform in all his dioceses the office of the confirmation of the laity.[1] Neither to himself, nor to his political allies, the lay whigs, was his appointment to and rapid translations in the episcopate other than discreditable; but the major responsibility for the scandal must rest with himself.

Tradition has repaid his unworthy acceptance of a bishopric by pillorying his unfaithfulness to his spouse of Bangor. Of that diocese, as has been observed, nature compelled him to be an inactive overseer; but in justice to Hoadly mention should be made of a report forwarded to Archbishop Wake in July 1719 by his correspondent Dr William Wootton, on the authority of the precentor of St David's, John Davies. "The Chanter told me a piece of news which made me smile, that the bishop of Bangor is gone into his diocese by sea from Bristow. That *is* going the back way".[2] Despite this laudable attempt to visit his see during the summer calm on sea and land, his lordship was necessarily an absentee from North Wales; and in 1721 he was glad to escape to the border diocese of Hereford, en route for the lucrative dignities of Sarum and Winchester. Bangor indeed suffered similar misfortunes in the brevity of other episcopates during the century. Bishop Reynolds, who was appointed to succeed Hoadly, forsook it for Lincoln after only two years in Wales, being followed by Baker, in reward for his disappointment in not going to Hanover with George I, who was translated to Norwich after four years' incumbency. The result of such rapid changes was that the registers of the see contained no record of any ordinations from 1714 to 1721, a presumptive proof of episcopal negligence though the argument from silence is notoriously weak. It was fortunate for the diocese that amongst its prelates were numbered Herring and Pearce, who fulfilled conscientiously the spiritual oversight committed to them. Herring held formal visitations, supplemented by more informal tours within restricted areas at other times; and Pearce,

[1] See ch. vi, pp. 135–6 *ante.*
[2] Wootton to Wake, 23 July 1719. Arch. W. Epist. 21, item cxxiv, f. 187.

despite his initial reluctance to embrace the banishment of North Wales, settled happily to explore its parishes and valleys.

When he was advanced to the honours of episcopacy, he did not consider himself placed in a state that allowed him any remission from the labours of his ministry. He was not hindered by the distance of Bangor from annually resorting to that diocese (one year only excepted), and discharging his episcopal duties there, to 1753; after which, having suffered greatly from the fatigue of his last journey, he was advised by his physician and friend, Dr Heberden, and prevailed upon not to attempt another.[1]

The record of Bangor was not one of unrelieved neglect, nor may Herring and Pearce be accused of indifference to their duty.

More justice may be found in the complaint, that whilst

the clergy of the diocese, as shown in the registers, were almost entirely Welsh in name,...not a single Welsh name appears in the list of bishops, while the fact that the see was continually used as a stepping stone to more important bishoprics, a policy productive of frequent change in the personnel of the episcopate, aggravated the evil.[2]

The propriety of advancing Welshmen to the sees of the Principality was canvassed by contemporaries, notably in 1721 and 1723. On the nomination of Reynolds to Bangor, White Kennett of Peterborough observed to Archbishop Wake it would have been "very just and generous to the good estate of that country to have given them a man of their own mother tongue, and he hoped upon another avoidance his grace would prevail in the good motion of it".[3] But two years later, when Reynolds was translated to Lincoln, Baker succeeded him, upon which Hough of Worcester remarked that "a Welshman to Bangor, as his grace was pleased to observe, would have been much more welcome to the people and undoubtedly more useful".[4] In the appointment of Englishmen to Welsh dioceses the Hanoverian century was but following the tradition of its predecessors, as Beaw of Llandaff affirmed when in 1692 his claims to the see of St Asaph were set aside on the ground of Welsh sentiment. "It seems", he commented bitterly, "that it had been buzzed into the queen's ears that a Welsh bishop ought to be a Welshman; which was in truth the casting a reproach upon all our late king's primates, who had indifferently imposed Englishmen for

[1] *Life of Zachary Pearce*, in *Lives of E. Pocock, Z. Pearce, T. Newton, and P. Skelton* (2 vols.), i, 420.

[2] A. I. Pryce, *The Diocese of Bangor during Three Centuries*, p. lxvi.

[3] White Kennett to Wake, 30 Sept. 1721. Arch. W. Epist. 9, Canterbury IV.

[4] Bp. Hough to Wake, 24 April 1723. Arch. W. Epist. 22, item cxcii, f. 291.

bishops upon the Welsh people", particularly in the nomination by Charles II of Glenham and Barrow successively to St Asaph. Beaw asserted further that "it was a groundless surmise; there not being a market town in all Wales where they speak not English, and a sermon in Welsh with the most would not be understood".[1] Whatever the justice of the contention concerning the preference and utility of Welsh divines for Welsh sees, it may be granted that the chief obstacle to the good administration of their dioceses lay in the rapidity of translation secured by the bishops of the Principality; and if, as Watson advocated, the practice of translation had been abolished, it is probable that English presbyters would have left the Welsh bishoprics to natives of that country, since the distance from London of such sees as Bangor and St David's constituted their chief disadvantage to divines whose ambition was not satisfied by exile and obscurity.

Llandaff however was the Cinderella of all brides. To the disadvantages of remoteness and uncongeniality common to all Welsh dioceses, it added peculiar deficiencies characteristic of its own state, which made its prelates ready to seek translation even to other sees of the Principality. The extreme poverty of the dowry which it brought to its chief pastors was a source of lament to the majority of their number and to the ministers of state who endeavoured to persuade divines to accept its responsibilities. Further, during the episcopate of Beaw the bishop's residence at Maherne fell into dilapidation owing to that prelate's inability to sustain the cost of repairs, so that henceforth there was no episcopal house within the borders of the diocese; and bishops being compelled to look for some habitat elsewhere, in consequence passed as little time as possible in its inhospitable territory. Correspondent to the lack of provision for the bishop was the dilapidated condition of the cathedral and its capitular houses, the scandal of which aroused the antiquary Browne Willis to a frequent denunciation of the prelates and dignitaries responsible for such neglect. His correspondence with Archbishop Wake was filled with threats and objurgations, for which indeed adequate justification existed in fact. The cathedral had no decanal office, and by an act of parliament of 1713 the treasurership with the prebend thereto belonging were annexed to the bishopric. The prebendaries were denounced by Browne Willis as "a parcel of nonresidents" and as "mercenary remote English clergymen", who appeared at Llandaff for the annual audit, and having divided the spoils, departed again without any thought for the dilapidated state of the

[1] Bp. Beaw to Abp. Tenison, 21 Aug. 1699. *Gibson Papers*, Lambeth MSS. 930, f. 49.

cathedral itself.[1] The ill-repair of the sacred edifice increased with neglect, the roof of the south tower and of the north aisle being open to the sky, the west entrance being closed, the choir service removed to the lady chapel, and the western half of the nave becoming an open ruin during the greater part of the century. In 1721 a brief was secured in order to repair the ravages; but the task of restoring the entire fabric being impracticable, a project for arresting the ruin of the presbytery, choir, and part of the nave, was adopted in accordance with a design in the Italian style drawn up by Mr Wood of Bath. By the time of Watson's episcopate this restoration had been completed; but the rest of the cathedral remained in a semi-ruinous condition until the middle of the nineteenth century; and Llandaff presented a forlorn appearance, forsaken alike by the bishops and its capitular dignitaries. In 1722 Browne Willis had complained that on a personal visit he found that "in short everything about the church was in disorder.... All the furniture of the Communion Table, pulpit, Common Prayer Books, etc., as he saw himself... were not worth forty shillings; and indeed he knew no parish church in that country or England so meanly furnished".[2] So long ago as 1691 Dr George Bull, then archdeacon of Llandaff, had suppressed the choral service of the cathedral, in order to devote the small revenues to the repair of the fabric. The ill condition of the church was such that the idea had been mooted of removing the see-city to Cardiff, a project arousing the utmost indignation of Willis. Bishop Tyler, however, in 1721 declared frankly to Archbishop Wake his opinion of the unsuitable situation of the see "in a small village, not very commodious for consistory courts, audits, and visitations. A parochial church would be big enough for the congregations usually assembled there on Sundays or holydays".[3] When in 1739 Bishop Mawson was appointed to the bishopric, Bishop Herring lamented that it should be found "in so naked a way";—"when there is no sort of house for the bishop to live in, and the cathedral begun but left quite unfinished".[4]

Accordingly, when Watson accepted nomination to Llandaff in 1782 he came to a diocese labouring under severe disadvantages, and with a tradition of neglect. The episcopal revenues remained scanty and insufficient, the cathedral had been saved from total ruin rather than brought back to its pristine condition, and the chapter was distinguished

[1] Browne Willis to Wake, 22 June 1721. Arch. W. Epist. 22, item xxx, f. 42.
[2] Same to Same, 22 Nov. 1722. *Ibid.* item clviii, f. 240.
[3] Bp. Tyler to Wake, 5 June 1721. *Ibid.* item xxv, f. 35.
[4] Bp. Herring to Lord Hardwicke, 19 Dec. 1738. Add. MSS. 35598, f. 8.

by non-residence. Notwithstanding the poverty of the see, its occupant had to maintain the same hospitality within the diocese, and the same residence in London as his wealthier brethren, for which the provision of ample *commendams* was essential. This temporary expedient was evidently a makeshift, designed to afford an interim solution until a lucrative translation could be secured; but in case such translation were unduly delayed, or never materialised, the temporal condition of the bishop of Llandaff became yearly more precarious, his appetite for compensations more avid, and his neglect of the diocese more pronounced. Of such progressive decline the only long episcopates of the century, those of Beaw from 1679 to 1706, and of Watson from 1782 to 1816, provided melancholy illustration. The two cases afforded indeed an instructive parallel. Both divines accepted a small bishopric "in expectation of a sudden remove"; both were anxious to make proper provision for their families; and both sought translation as the years of their rustication and disfavour increased. Beaw expected preferment to Hereford in 1691, to Lichfield in 1692, and to St Asaph in the same year; whilst Watson, though his independence prevented his making application, would have welcomed a remove to Carlisle in 1787, and more particularly to St Asaph in 1806. Beaw in 1699, having endured obscurity for twice the space of a decade, resolved to set before Archbishop Tenison the true state of

the dignity, or indignity rather, which he held, or rather was held as in bonds with, whereby he was rendered unable to perform the offices of his calling; either in his private capacity as a father of many children, for whom as such he was bound to provide, or in his public, as a Father in God, who as such was to be a lover of hospitality, and consequently ought to be endowed with so much of the Church's goods as might fit him for the exercise of that duty.

According to his computation the value of the see at the commencement of the century was but £230 per annum, "and not one farthing more"; whilst the demands of taxation, together "with the expenses of a coach, coachman, and horses, (which he was necessitated to keep for any the least journey, because by the unskilfulness of a Welsh surgeon, he was disenabled to ride, and to go on foot unless on very even and smooth ground)", and of annual repairs, resulted in "his little bishopric's revenues being wholly swallowed up, nothing more appearing of them than what would defray the charges of the quantity of vinegar, pepper, salt, and fire spent in his house". Under such straitness of circumstances he had endeavoured to live "not according to his revenue but answerable to his dignity". In his diocese, he added picturesquely and truly,

I was free in all my housekeeping. I observed no days of fasting or retiring, but all days were equally designed for others (though I fasted myself) for entertainment, come whoso would. The meanest vicar or curate never went hungry away, if he came before or at mealtime. Bread and beer were freely distributed at my doors every day. My gates stood open to all comers, and they were not a few that came for provision of that kind; nor is bread and beer a cheap commodity in the place of my residence but the dearest of any place in the kingdom; yet this was the manner of my living in expectation of a remove, which I could but think would be sudden.

The sum of his condition he described to the primate under the figure of "a consumption of no less than twenty-one years' standing; a disease which none of his predecessors were suffered to labour under so long, but in far less time were, either by God or the king, either by a remove thence to their graves or to a wholesomer air upon earth, perfectly cured".[1]

Bishop Watson's affliction was less pitiful, for he was supplied with liberal *commendams*. In 1787, when ill-health made him desirous to resign his professorship, he demanded some equivalent, since "without it he would have a church-income of only £1200 a year"; and in 1808 he enumerated the several pieces of preferment in his possession, amounting to £2000 per annum, and embracing "the tithes of two churches in Shropshire, of two in Leicestershire, of two in his diocese, of three in Huntingdonshire (on all of which he had resident curates), of five more as appropriations to the bishopric, and of two more in the Isle of Ely as appropriations to the archdeaconry of Ely".[2] In return for this he exercised the functions of a bishop in South Wales from the distant residence of Calgarth Park on the banks of Windermere, whither he withdrew into retirement in 1789. In fairness to Watson notice should be directed to the extent of his personal discharge of the spiritual oversight of his diocese. During his episcopate of thirty-four years at Llandaff, he delivered in person nine visitation charges, whereof the first was read in 1784 and the last in 1813, after which his health declined seriously. Upon two of these occasions his own testimony establishes the fact of his confirming also; in 1788 when "he gave away to above a thousand persons whom he then confirmed a small tract entitled, 'An Address to young persons after Confirmation', written by himself";[3]

---

[1] Beaw to Tenison, 21 Aug. 1699. *Gibson Papers*, Lambeth MSS. 930, f. 49.
[2] R. Watson, *Anecdotes*, i, 258; ii, 349.   [3] *Ibid.* i, 323.

and, more noteworthy, in 1809 when at the age of over seventy, "in the extensive visitation of his diocese which he made that year, he went over the mountains from Neath to a place where no bishop had ever held a confirmation before, Merthyr Tidvil". This town having grown from a village to a place of more than ten thousand people, he "thought it his duty not only to go to confirm the young people there, but to preach to those who were grown up, that he might, if possible, leave among the inhabitants a good impression in favour of the teachers in the Established Church when compared with those of many of the sectarian congregations into which the people were divided".[1] It is to be presumed that the bishop joined confirmation to the task of visitation on all the other occasions when he made his triennial visit to his diocese. At least the argument from silence is unconvincing in this regard. More than this cannot be predicated of him. He was content with the fulfilment of the minimum requirement of triennial visitation and confirmation, after which he resumed his agricultural labours on the banks of Windermere.

In the discharge of the duty of ordination Watson attained a higher standard of regularity. The surviving evidence of his episcopate embraces three Subscription Books, and a few scattered papers preserved at Llandaff, which, though imperfectly kept, enable some conclusions to be reached concerning his fidelity to this branch of the episcopal office.[2] From the Subscription Books it is clear that he ordained in person in his cathedral church during the summer months (almost invariably June) of the years 1784, 1785, 1787, 1788, 1790, 1791, 1795, 1804, 1805, 1809, 1811, and 1813. For the intervening years there are records of subscriptions, but not of ordinations, save that ordinations are recorded without specification of place for the years 1791, 1792, 1793, and 1802. From the supplementary evidence of papers preserved at Llandaff the fact of the bishop's holding ordinations at Llandaff in 1802, 1807, 1808, 1810, and 1812 is established, again always during the month of June. It should be remembered further that in 1804 Watson was sixty-seven years of age, and since he continued during the years from 1807 to 1812 to make the annual journey to confer Holy Orders in his cathedral, it is probable that he had maintained the custom during the period from 1791 to 1802 concerning which the Subscription Books are silent. From the papers at Llandaff it is proved also that the

---

[1] R. Watson, *Anecdotes*, ii, 367–8.
[2] The Subscription Books Nos. 8, 9 and 10 are preserved in the Diocesan Registry at Cardiff; and the several papers relating to Watson's episcopate in the Cathedral Library at Llandaff.

bishop held ordinations at the place of his residence at Windermere in 1803, 1804, 1805, 1806, 1808, 1809, 1810, 1812, and 1813, though never during the month of June. Although it is not possible to affirm with certainty, owing to the lack of conclusive evidence, it would appear probable that Watson paid an annual visit to his see-city to ordain in his cathedral on Trinity Sunday, and contented himself with issuing Letters Dimissory or summoning candidates to attend upon him at Calgarth Park at other seasons of the year. Such a standard of duty, though by no means unexceptionable, is at least far in advance of that allowed to him by most of his critics, who interpret his residence at Windermere as evidence of his never having visited his diocese to perform the episcopal offices of ordination, confirmation, and visitation.

Occasionally in his visitation charges he made passing reference to his exile from the flock over which he was appointed overseer. In his primary charge he admitted to the clergy "the uneasiness which he felt in not being able to reside amongst them", affirming that the duty "not merely to superintend their labours, but to co-operate with them in every matter tending to the edification of the flock of Christ", could not be discharged sufficiently by appearance only at formal visitations. But whilst allowing that visitations were "very inadequate to the great purposes which a bishop ought always to have in view", he "forbore enlarging upon an evil which it was not in his power to remedy"; and concluded his address with an exhortation to his brethren "every one of them to consider their diocesan, though absent in person, as present in affection with them, as willing and desirous to become their servant for the sake of Jesus Christ".[1] More than a decade afterwards, in 1798, he introduced his address with an intimation that he "had once determined to put off the visitation to another year, but, on second thoughts, it appeared to him not wholly to be consistent with the duty he owed to his clergy and diocese, to desert them both in that time of general apprehension and impending danger" from the effects of the French Revolution. Whereupon, after delivering his sentiments upon the political state of England and exhorting his clergy to loyalty, he uttered the pious aspiration that God might "help both them and him so to perform the duties of their several stations, that at the last day they might not have cause to lament their negligence in any particular".[2] At his next visitation in 1802, he redistributed copies of the Confirmation address first printed in 1784, with the assurance that he had composed it "with the express design of co-operating with the clergy of his

[1] Charge, 1784, in R. Watson's *Miscellaneous Tracts*, i, 311–12, 338.
[2] Charge, 1798, *ibid.* pp. 125, 150.

diocese in saving the souls of men; he knew it was his duty, who was taken from them in presence, not in heart, to endeavour to sow the good seed, and to pray God to give the increase".[1] The fullest defence of his absence however was vouchsafed at the visitation of 1809, when he dealt at great length with his attitude towards a projected parliamentary bill in 1808 to enforce the residence of the clergy on their benefices, in regard to which he had insisted upon the prior provision of a sufficient income.

"It is not unnatural, reverend brethren," he observed, "for a bishop to wish for the esteem of the clergy of his diocese; and I own an ambition to possess yours has been a principal motive for making the detail with which I have now troubled you. I am aware that Episcopum τὰ περὶ ἑαυτοῦ balbutientem atticae fastidiunt aures; yet I could not repress my anxiety to shew you, that though I have no place of residence amongst you, nor a church income sufficient to enable me to attend every year my parliamentary duty, yet I have never slept on my post, or neglected any fair opportunity of promoting that change in the church establishment, which I had not recommended many years ago without due consideration, and which the legislature, I hope, will now finally accomplish."[2]

It may be presumed that the peculiar manner of address adopted by his lordship in his final charge in 1813—"it is not unknown, I presume, to many amongst you that I have been your bishop for above thirty years"[3]—represented a modest disavowal of any harsh episcopal rule, rather than an apology for non-residence, since it is evident that his conscience acquitted him of any blame in this matter and that he laid the responsibility for absence upon circumstances beyond his control or power of remedy.

Apart from the fundamental fact of non-residence, which vitiated in practice the most exalted theories of his addresses concerning the importance of the pastoral office in his clergy, his charges were not devoid of sound practical counsel and direction. Amongst other topics, he dealt with the discharge of the parochial ministry in preaching, study of the Bible, teaching in schools, and the necessity of a resident clergy. Upon occasion he introduced matters of public moment, such as the pernicious results of the French Revolution, the virtues of the British Constitution, the position of Roman Catholics both in England and Ireland; and he discoursed freely of the controverted theological questions of the age concerning clerical subscription, Arian views of

---

[1] Charge, 1802, in R. Watson's *Miscellaneous Tracts*, i, 268.
[2] Charge, 1809, *ibid.* p. 231. [3] Charge, 1813, *ibid.* p. 157.

the Trinity, and Christological disputes, always with a fervent defence of latitude of interpretation and a plea for charity and tolerance of diversity of opinion. His Confirmation address contained much wise advice concerning the practice of prayer, the reading of the Bible, attendance at the Holy Communion, and the careful avoidance of occasions of evil and of disreputable society. Not infrequently in his public visitations he dwelt upon his desire for the friendliest possible correspondence with his clergy and his belief that such an ideal was realised in their relations. Particularly in 1802, after reminding them that "a bishop and his clergy having but one and the same end in view, the spiritual welfare of the people committed to their care, ought on all occasions to be guided by a common will", he congratulated them upon the circumstance that they had lived together "on friendly terms for twenty years"; for the perpetuation of which he besought them quaintly "never to make improper applications for licences for non-residence, since he was certain it would become him, whatever uneasiness he might feel in the refusal, not to grant them if made".[1]

Since the entire record of Watson's life refutes at once any whisper of insincerity of speech or innate lethargy of disposition, the reason for his complacent acquiescence in his own protracted non-residence in his diocese and preoccupation with the agricultural pursuits of his home at Windermere must be sought elsewhere than in suggestions of deliberate infidelity to duty or hypocrisy in undertaking the office and work of a bishop. The explanation is to be found in the circumstances of the poverty of his see and its lack of episcopal residence on the one part, and in the disappointment engendered by his long neglect at the hands of ministers of state on the other part, as testified by their failure to offer the expected translation. To the importance of both conditions his autobiographical narrative bears the fullest testimony. He prided himself indeed that, although driven into retirement by ministerial neglect, he had employed his strength at Calgarth Park in fruitful efforts for the support of his family and the good of the country.

"I have now spent above twenty years in this delightful country," he wrote of the Lake District, "but my time has not been spent in field-diversions, in idle visitings, in county bickerings, in indolence or in intemperance; no, it has been spent partly in supporting the religion and constitution of the country by seasonable publications; and principally in building farm-houses, blasting rocks, enclosing wastes, in making bad land good, in planting larches and in planting in the hearts of my children prin-

[1] Charge, 1802, in R. Watson's *Miscellaneous Tracts*, i, 266–7.

ciples of piety, benevolence, and of self-government. By such occupations I have much recovered my health, entirely preserved my independence, set an example of spirited husbandry to the county, and honourably provided for my family."[1]

To this *apologia* he returned constantly.

"It is not my fault", he assured a correspondent in 1797, "that some of the best years of my life have been thus employed; had I met with the encouragement in my profession, which would have enabled me to make a moderate provision for eight children, I never should have commenced agriculturist".[2]

Again, to a friend who in 1803 reproached him for neglect of his parliamentary attendance, he replied that

his church preferment would not afford a journey to London every year; and he did not feel himself bound by any principle of prudence, of honour, or of duty, to waste his little private fortune, which by incessant exertion of his own and the kindness of his friends, he had provided for his children, in the public service. For eighteen years he had attended parliament; his children during that period wanted education; that want being over, he gave up three years ago his house in Town, with a determination that till he was better provided for, he would not go to London, excepting every other year.[3]

Three years later he reiterated this defence, insisting that agriculture was an occupation

"which he would probably never have thought of, had he not been compelled by the duty of making a moderate provision for a large family. If the world has lost anything", he added, "by a long intermission of the means of improving my faculties, and by a now absolute dereliction of all learned labour, the government is in fault; their neglect obliged me to raise myself to exertions, useful no doubt and necessary to my family, but not agreeable to myself".[4]

Nor may it be doubted that the iron of this neglect in ecclesiastical translations had eaten into his soul. Despite his efforts to rise superior to the petty vices of envy and repining, he could not avoid the stigma of being passed over, with the consequent "anxiety for his reputation, lest the disfavour of a court should by some be considered as an indication of general disesteem or a proof of professional demerit".[5]

---

[1] R. Watson, *Anecdotes*, i, 389.   [2] *Ibid.* ii, 118.
[3] *Ibid.* ii, 165–6.   [4] *Ibid.* ii, 266–7.   [5] *Ibid.* ii, 116.

Upon the disappointment of his hopes of a removal to St Asaph in 1806 he confided his sentiments to his diary.

I cannot truly say that I was wholly insensible to these and to many similar arrangements by which I had been for so many years neglected, and exhibited to the world as a marked man fallen under royal displeasure; but I can say, that neither was the tranquillity of my mind disturbed, nor my adherence to the principles of the Revolution shaken, nor my attachment to the House of Brunswick acting on these principles, lessened thereby. I knew that I possessed not the talents of adulation, intrigue, and versatility of principle, by which laymen as well as churchmen usually in courts ascend the ladder of ambition. I knew this, and I remained without repining at the bottom of it.[1]

It is worthy of note that William Wilberforce shared Watson's sentiments of the unseemliness of his neglect, assuring him that "a change in situation" ought "in public justice" to have been offered to him, and declaring that "it was a subject of painful reflection to him" that no such preferment had been bestowed.[2] Even within his remote and forsaken diocese of Llandaff, a certain Mr Crawshay, an iron-master of Merthyr Tidvil, "expressed his astonishment at the manner in which his lordship had been neglected by the court", accompanying his words by the practical proof of confidence in the offer at any time of £5000 or £10,000.[3] It was evident that the cloud which Watson believed to overshadow his public activities was no figment of his imagination, but rather the inevitable consequence of neglect in a century which considered the little bishoprics of Wales only as stepping-stones to a lucrative English diocese.

It was the more creditable therefore to Watson that his ill-success proceeded directly from the sturdy virtues of his northern extraction, namely his individual independence, his sincerity of opinion, and his political incorruptibility. From the moment when as a young man he refused the offer of the curacy of Clermont lest propinquity to his grace of Newcastle should sully the integrity of his political profession, to his advocacy during the perilous years of the French Revolutionary and Napoleonic Wars of the cause of Roman Catholic emancipation in Ireland, he maintained a consistency of independence and conviction in political utterances which could scarcely be expected to commend him to party leaders. It was impossible for him to remain in alliance with either the administration of the day or the opposition. Thus as a

---

[1] R. Watson, *Anecdotes*, ii, 278–9.
[2] *Ibid.* ii, 114–15.   [3] *Ibid.* ii, 368, 371.

critic of the policy of the crown in the American Independence War and of its influence on the parliament, he was reckoned a supporter of the opposition, and, as such, summoned on 4 November 1783, when the tide of fortune had turned, to come up to Town to vote for Fox's famous India Bill. In reply he severed all connection with the official policy of that ministry by insisting that "it was impossible for him who had on all occasions opposed the corrupting influence of the crown, to support the measure which was pregnant with more seeds of corruption than any one which had taken place since the Revolution". The only concession which he offered was that, instead of speaking against it, as he had intended, he would absent himself from the debates.[1] In like manner during the long administration of the younger Pitt, Watson found himself alternately in support of and opposition to the projects of the administration, opposing the proposed commercial treaty with France and declaring in favour of that with Ireland. He was indeed fully conscious that this extreme independence of attitude made impossible his close association with any administration of whatever complexion, and admitted the ill-effect thereof upon his ecclesiastical fortunes. "I had not the usual prudence, shall I call it, or selfish caution, of my profession at any time of life", he observed in 1780, before his elevation to the episcopate. "*Ortus a quercu non a salice*, I knew not how to bend my principles to the circumstances of the times."[2] Or again:

My temper could never brook submission to the ordinary means of ingratiating myself with great men; and hence Dr Hallifax, afterwards Bishop of St Asaph, whose temper was different, called me one of the βιασταὶ and he was right enough in the denomination. I was determined to be advanced in my profession by force of desert or not at all.[3]

Equally to Watson's credit was his refusal to abandon this principle of conduct when elevation to the bench increased the opportunities and emphasised the need of political compromise. His own shrewd prediction upon his nomination to Llandaff was fulfilled. "I have hitherto followed, and shall continue to follow, my own judgment in all public transactions; all parties now understand this, and it is probable that I may continue to be Bishop of Llandaff as long as I live."[4] Even to Lord Shelburne, by whose agency he had been raised to the episcopate,

[1] R. Watson, *Anecdotes*, i, 203–5.
[2] *Ibid.* i, 112.
[3] *Ibid.* i, 115. The reference is to St Matthew xi. 12.
[4] *Ibid.* i, 154.

he enunciated the doctrine that private friendship should not sway political judgment on matters of public import.

"As to my public conduct," he declared, "I would ever assert to myself the right of private judgment, independent of all parties. This doctrine, I could perceive, was quite new to Lord Shelburne, and, in truth, few great men can relish it; they want adherents, and they esteem no man who will not be their instrument. This plain dealing with men in power made many persons say that I knew not the world; they were mistaken; I knew well enough that it was not the way to procure preferment; I remembered what I had learned as a boy, the different effects of obsequiousness and of truth: *obsequium amicos, veritas odium parit*; and I preferred, as a man, the latter."[1]

To this outspoken assertion of the right of individual freedom Watson added a complete inability to compromise in matters of public policy, which effectively relegated him to the obscurity of a minor bishopric. He desired to see his private opinions translated into official action, without regard to the difficulties attendant upon the attempt to carry a reforming programme in church or state. Of the thorough-going nature of his projected reforms no doubt could be entertained. In 1782, upon his acceptance of the see of Llandaff, Shelburne "expressed a desire that they might become well acquainted; and said, that as he had Dunning to assist him in law points, and Barry in army concerns, he should be happy to consult Watson in church matters".[2] In response to this invitation to share the ministerial confidence the new bishop produced a comprehensive scheme of ecclesiastical reconstruction as the price of his alliance. Although eager to embrace both doctrine and discipline within the ambit of reform, he limited his first suggestions to administration and revenue. The main points he proposed were:

first, a bill to render the bishoprics more equal to each other both with respect to income and patronage; by annexing, as the richer bishoprics become vacant, a part of their revenues and a part of their patronage, to the poorer. By a bill of this kind, the bishops would be freed from the necessity of holding ecclesiastical preferments *in commendam*—a practice which bears hard on the rights of the inferior clergy. Another probable consequence of such a bill would be a longer residence of the bishops in their several dioceses; from which the best consequences both to religion, the morality of the people, and to the true credit of the church might be expected; for the two great inducements to wish for translations, and consequently to reside in London, namely superiority of income and excellency of patronage, would in a great measure be removed. Secondly, a bill for appropriating, as they became

[1] R. Watson, *Anecdotes*, i, 207–8.   [2] *Ibid.* i, 155.

vacant, a half, or a third part of the income of every deanery, prebend, or canonry, of the churches of Westminster, Windsor, Canterbury, Christ Church, Worcester, Durham, Ely, Norwich, etc. to the same purposes, mutatis mutandis, as the first fruits and tenths were appropriated by Queen Anne. By a bill of this kind, a decent provision would be made for the inferior clergy in a third or fourth part of the time which Queen Anne's bounty alone would require to effect. A decent provision being once made for every officiating minister in the church, the residence of the clergy on their cures might more reasonably be required than it could be at present, and the licence of holding more livings than one be restricted.[1]

It was only natural that Shelburne, affrighted by the boldness of such a project, should "earnestly dissuade any immediate publication" on the author's part, though Watson wished to submit it to public debate, affirming that "he had the business so much at heart that in order to effect it, he would readily abandon the great prospects which his time of life, connexions, and situation opened to him in as probable a manner as they were opened to most bishops on the bench".[2]

The first step of the bishop of Llandaff as ecclesiastical counsellor thus extinguished his reputation as a practical man of affairs. Notwithstanding, he remained unswervingly faithful to his favourite scheme, convinced that "by becoming a bishop he ought [not] to change the principles which he had imbibed from the works of Mr Locke".[3] Accordingly, he published his plan in the form of a letter to the primate, to whom and to all members of the bench he despatched a copy, though only Porteus of Chester made acknowledgment of so dangerous a present. In 1800, when proposals were being canvassed for the enforcement of clerical residence, he reverted to his original design for augmenting the revenues of parochial benefices as the essential prerequisite to the compulsion of residence. His own consistency of opinion was testified by a letter to Archbishop Manners Sutton in 1808 in which he asserted with truth that

long before he was a bishop, he entertained a deliberate opinion that some things respecting the discipline, some respecting the doctrine, and some respecting the distribution of the revenues of the church, might be innovated with great advantage to religion, and with perfect safety to the establishment. He gave to the public his sentiments on the last of these points in a letter to the then archbishop of Canterbury; and he had not during the twenty-six years that he had been bishop of Llandaff seen any reason to alter his opinion.[4]

---

[1] R. Watson, *Anecdotes*, i, 156–8. [2] *Ibid.* i, 164.
[3] *Ibid.* i, 156. [4] *Ibid.* ii, 346.

Little surprise may be occasioned by the circumstance that a reformer of such zeal, whose avowed resolve was to purge the Church also from the dregs of Popery and Calvinism, awakened alarm rather than enthusiasm amongst both ministers of state and prelates of the Church, and sealed his own fate as an impracticable man, unversed in the pliancy essential to the smooth execution of public business. Against the *vis inertiae* of the age his entire career was indeed a continuous but unavailing protest, for the efforts of an individual iconoclast could not prevail against so widespread a tendency.

There remained therefore as the scene of the fulfilment of the pilgrimage of so staunch an ecclesiastical and political Ishmael as Watson only the wilderness of the diocese of Llandaff, whose singular misfortune it was to provide the solitariness necessary for the enterprise. The long episcopate which he discharged in that see affords an apt illustration of the evils latent in the contemporary Church system; since in the Hanoverian age, as in all epochs in which the episcopal office has been nearly connected with affairs of state, the intimate commerce of prelates with statecraft must be judged in part at least by consideration of its effect upon the proper execution of their ecclesiastical administration. It may not be doubted that Watson accepted nomination to the see of Llandaff with the resolve to be a zealous and faithful pastor of the Church in accordance with the standards of the age. The intrinsic disadvantages of that bishopric, its poverty of revenue and the lack of an episcopal residence, might be endured for a season; but when there was added the delay of the expected translation and finally the conviction that further ministerial favours were never to be anticipated, he ceased to attempt more than the minimum obligations required by the canons. Herein lay the especial evil of the association of political allegiance with ecclesiastical preferment. Such long neglect as Watson suffered was interpreted as a stigma alike upon his political and professional character, and by consequence destroyed his ability to fulfil even the responsibilities of his ecclesiastical station. Of the thirty-four years of his tenure of the see of Llandaff, full twenty-five were spent in residence on the shores of Lake Windermere. Yet Watson never felt the least degree of culpability for this withdrawal from Wales, the necessity of which he lamented in his transient appearance at triennial visitations. He had indeed set forward at the very outset of his episcopate a scheme of ecclesiastical reform which, by enabling the occupants of little bishoprics to live of their own and removing thereby the most urgent temptation to solicit translation, would have remedied the conditions under which he laboured. But the impossibility of carrying any effective reforms, combined with his own neglect when suitable translations were available, justified to his mind the pleasant retirement of Calgarth Park. The most significant feature of his episcopate (and by implication the sternest verdict upon the ecclesiastical system of his age) was its very inadequate appreciation of the responsibility of the office and work of a bishop as an obligation demanding personal discharge irrespective of political circumstances. Instead of seeking consolation for the neglect of the world by devotion to the spiritual estate of his bishopric, by purchasing peradventure a house in South Wales and mingling agricultural pursuits with the pastoral oversight of his flock, Watson interpreted the growing length of his episcopate at Llandaff as sufficient excuse for an equally long withdrawal to the Lakes. He would have repudiated indignantly the suggestion of censure for non-residence which posterity has passed upon him by general tradition, as indeed he would have insisted that it was a very small thing to him that he should be judged of man's judgment. The epitaph upon his life inscribed by his son at the end of his *Anecdotes*, and affirmed to have been "his favourite rule of conduct", was the psalmist's injunction: "Keep innocency and take heed unto the thing that is right; for that shall bring a man peace at the last". To this should be added the apostolic counsel to those seeking the responsibility of episcopal office that, in desiring such a good work, they should have especial care to "feed the flock of God, taking the oversight thereof, not by constraint, but willingly; not for filthy lucre, but of a ready mind; neither as being lords over God's heritage, but being ensamples to the flock".

CHAPTER IX

YEARS OF PLENTY

"An alliance between church and state in a Christian Commonwealth", observed Burke in his speech on the petition of the Unitarians, "is in my opinion an idle and fanciful speculation. An alliance is between two things that are in their nature distinct and independent, as between two sovereign states. But in a Christian Commonwealth the church and the state are one and the same thing, being different integral parts of the same whole. For the church has been always divided into two parts, the clergy and the laity; of which the laity is as much an essential, integral part, and has as much its duties and privileges, as the clerical member; and in the rule, order, and government of the church has its share. Religion is so far in my opinion from being out of the province or the duty of a Christian magistrate, that it is, and it ought to be, not only his care, but the principal thing in his care; because it is one of the great bonds of human society, and its object the supreme good, the ultimate end and object of man himself."[1]

Between the emphatic insistence of Burke upon the proper province and function of the laity in the Christian Church and the contention of Atterbury in his *Letter to a Convocation Man*—that "'tis a little too much to suppose country gentlemen, merchants, or lawyers to be nicely skilled in the languages of the Bible, masters of all the learning of the Fathers, or the history of the Primitive Church"—whereby he sought to depress the position of the laity, there is a great gulf fixed. The measure of its width indeed is the record of the difference in temper between the Caroline age and its high church tradition, of which Atterbury was a survivor, and the Georgian epoch with its Latitudinarian leanings. The eighteenth century witnessed a steady and progressive laicisation of religion, which is the keynote of its ecclesiastical development. Hostile critics have preferred to describe the process as the secularisation of the Church; but it may be contended that the laicisation of religion is a more accurate phrase; for albeit the clerical order generally was characterised by a markedly unprofessional temper, the laity not only deemed themselves a proper and necessary part of the organisation of the Christian Church, but acted upon that persuasion with vigour and conviction.

[1] E. Burke, "Speech on the Petition of the Unitarians", 11 May 1792.

The basic principle of their action was enunciated in formal language in the judgment of Lord Hardwicke in 1737 in the case of Middleton *v.* Crofts.

Now the constant practice ever since the Reformation (for there is no occasion to go further back) has been, that when any material ordinances or regulations have been made to bind the laity as well as clergy in matters ecclesiastical, they have been either enacted or confirmed by parliament; of this proposition the several acts of uniformity are so many proofs; for by these the whole doctrine and worship, the very rites and ceremonies of the church, and the literal form of public prayers are prescribed and established.[1]

In accordance with this doctrine the faithful commons did not in the leastwise consider their ignorance of oriental languages, nor their imperfect acquaintance with patristic and historical studies, a barrier to their deliberation of ecclesiastical and theological questions, of which the debate in their house upon the Feathers' Tavern petition afforded illustration. In this judgment they were supported by the more liberal amongst the clergy, who were anxious to encourage the co-operation of the laity in the most intimate concerns of faith and liturgy. Richard Watson, in his plea for a revision of the Articles and Liturgy of the Church, asserted boldly his belief in this regard; and, referring to the project of revision produced by the commission appointed by William III in 1689, observed that

"the particulars then thought necessary to be changed and others since thought necessary, might, it was presumed, when properly prepared, be submitted to the deliberation and decision of parliament at that time, with a good prospect of success. I say", he continued, "of parliament; for laymen are as much interested in the truth of Christianity as churchmen are; and in this enlightened age are as capable of seeing what is revealed in their Bible".[2]

This singular divine was prepared to go still further in recognition of the authority of parliament to determine controversies of faith, being ready to submit to its deliberation the dispute between Athanasian and Arian interpretations of the doctrine of the Trinity. He affirmed his persuasion

that the Trinitarian worship should be continued in the church at present; not upon the ground of its being most conformable to Scripture, (for who shall judge of that?), but on the ground of its being *now* believed to be so by the legislature of the kingdom; and that those who believe otherwise should

[1] L. T. Dibdin, *Establishment in England*, pp. 56–7.
[2] R. Watson, "Considerations on the Expediency of Revising the Liturgy and Articles", in *Miscellaneous Tracts*, ii, 88.

have the most absolute liberty to worship God in their way and to publish whatever interpretations of Scripture they should judge proper in support of their doctrines. If, in the vicissitudes incident to all human opinions, the legislature of this country, which represents (really or not, is not now the question) the majority of the people, should be persuaded that the Unitarian form of worship was more conformable than the Trinitarian to the Word of God, then it would be proper that the Unitarian worship should be the worship of the national church, and that the Trinitarians should be allowed the same absolute liberty of worshipping in their way and of publishing in support of their opinions, which he thought was due and ought now to be granted to the Unitarians.[1]

The episode of the Feathers' Tavern petition was of particular importance, alike in its intrinsic quality as the occasion of a serious debate in the lower house of parliament concerning the question of clerical subscription, and in its wider significance as the defeat of the first measure designed towards the enactment of a comprehensive scheme of liturgical revision in accordance with the theological tenets of the age. The petition itself was the natural outcome of the religious unsettlement and of the tendencies towards Unitarian or Arian conceptions of the Godhead and of the Person of Christ characteristic of the age. The desire of the petitioners was for a form of subscription to the Bible only as the source of divine truth and without affixing any definition of the sense in which it was to be interpreted, instead of the customary clerical subscription to the Thirty-Nine Articles. Its supporters comprised divines who were undoubtedly Trinitarian in belief, though scarcely Athanasian, and others whose inclination was definitely towards an Unitarian position. Though the signatories were not impressive numerically, amounting to only two and a half hundred, they were influential especially from an academic standpoint. Indeed the petition was largely a Cambridge movement, and was signed by the Master and all the Resident Fellows of one College of this University, Peterhouse, whilst the presence of other names of academic distinction amongst its supporters testified to the strong intellectual character of its championship. Amongst beneficed clergy its foremost sponsors were Archdeacon Francis Blackburne of Cleveland, who had published anonymously in 1766 *The Confessional*, setting forth the case for relaxation of the terms of subscription, and Theophilus Lindsey, vicar of Cleveland, who after the defeat of the venture resigned his preferments and joined the formal

---

[1] R. Watson, "Considerations on the Expediency of Revising the Liturgy and Articles," in *Miscellaneous Tracts*, pp. 130–1.

Unitarian profession, whilst the archdeacon remained within the communion of the Established Church.

Accordingly, the petition was presented by Sir William Meredith to the house of commons and by that assembly debated on 6 February 1772, being rejected upon a division by 217 votes to 71. The adverse verdict was influenced largely by the speech of Burke, who, although careful not to deny the right of the Church to effect alterations and changes in its theological confessions or in its public liturgy, nor to asperse the sincerity of the petitioners, enunciated the vital principle that such reforms should be enacted not in response to the demand of a minority but in reply only to the clear and unequivocal desire of a majority of churchmen, clerical and lay.

"The ground for a legislative alteration of a legal Establishment is this", he observed, "that you find the inclinations of a majority of the people, concurring with your own sense of the intolerable nature of the abuse, are in favour of a change. If this be the case in the present instance, certainly you ought to make the alteration that is proposed, to satisfy your own consciences and to give content to your people. But if you have no evidence of this nature, it ill becomes your gravity, on the petition of a few gentlemen, to listen to anything that tends to shake one of the capital pillars of the state, and alarm the body of your people upon that one ground, in which every hope and fear, every interest, passion, prejudice, everything which can affect the human breast, are all involved together. If you make this a season for religious alterations, depend upon it you will soon find it a season of religious tumults and religious wars."

In reply to the argument concerning scrupulous consciences, he urged that clergy unable to subscribe the formularies of the Church should withdraw from its communion until they had persuaded a majority of their fellow-churchmen to become of their opinion. But his steady refusal to enter into discussion of the abstract justice of the case indicated the basis of his contention in expediency rather than in truth. "I will not enter into the question, how much Truth is preferable to Peace. Perhaps Truth may be far better. But as we have scarcely ever the same certainty in the one that we have in the other, I would, unless Truth were evident indeed, hold fast to Peace, which has in her company Charity, the highest of the virtues."[1]

It is probable that the eloquence of Burke reflected the general sense of the members of the commons' house. Dr Johnson defended the requirement of subscription to creeds and confessions, as being no im-

[1] E. Burke, "Speech on the Act of Uniformity".

position, but "only a voluntary declaration of agreement in certain articles of faith, which a church has a right to require, just as any other society can insist on certain rules being observed by its members. Nobody is compelled to be of the church, as nobody is compelled to enter into a society". Therefore he denominated the advocates of change "bigots to laxness".[1] The question was not however so simple as this summary treatment would indicate, as indeed the doctor himself admitted upon another occasion when, in reply to Boswell's enquiry as to "whether it is necessary to believe all the Thirty-Nine Articles", he declared: "Why, Sir, that is a question which has been much agitated. Some have held it necessary that they should all be believed; others have considered them to be only articles of peace, that is to say, you are not to preach against them".[2] If the latter view be entertained, then agitation for relaxation of subscription was justified, and almost inevitable; for not only to the Latitudinarians of the eighteenth century, but to the Oxford divines of its successor, the need of a wider latitude of interpretation than contemporary standards approved was vitally necessary to a continuing sincerity of churchmanship. Certainly the cynical sarcasm with which Gibbon summarised the debate in the house of commons was wholly inadequate to the gravity of the occasion. To his correspondent Holroyd, he wrote on 8 February 1772

congratulating him on the late victory of our dear mamma the Church of England. She had last Thursday seventy-one rebellious sons, who pretended to set aside her will on account of insanity; but two-hundred-and-seventeen worthy champions, headed by lord North, Burke, Hans Stanley, Charles Fox, Godfrey Clarke, etc, though they allowed the thirty-nine clauses of her testament were absurd and unreasonable, supported the validity of it with infinite humour.[3]

Despite the rejection of the petition, discussion of the propriety of some measure of revision did not cease; and no better proof of the urgency of the matter, nor of the widespread desire for some relaxation, could be adduced than the endeavours to set forward this cause by so discreet and cautious a divine as Beilby Porteus.

"At the close of the year 1772", ran his own account, "and the beginning of the next, an attempt was made by myself and a few other clergymen, among whom were Mr Francis Wollaston, Dr Percy now Bishop of Dromore,

---

[1] Boswell, *Life of Johnson*, 27 Aug. 1773.
[2] *Ibid.* 26 Oct. 1769.
[3] Gibbon to Holroyd, 8 Feb. 1772, Letter xvii, p. 335, *Memoirs of Gibbon and a Selection from His Letters* (ed. H. Morley).

and Dr Yorke, now Bishop of Ely, to induce the bishops to promote a review of the Liturgy and Articles, in order to amend in both, but particularly in the latter, those parts which stood in need of amendment. This plan was not in the smallest degree connected with the Petition at the Feathers' Tavern, but on the contrary, was meant to counteract that and all similar extravagant projects; to strengthen and confirm our ecclesiastical establishment; to repel the attacks which were at that time continually made upon it by its avowed enemies; to render the 17th Article of Predestination and Election more clear and perspicuous, and less liable to be wrested by our adversaries to a Calvinistic sense, which has been so unjustly affixed to it; to improve true Christian piety amongst those of our own communion, and to diminish schism and separation by bringing over to the National Church all the moderate and well-disposed of other persuasions. On these grounds we applied in a private and respectful manner to Archbishop Cornwallis, requesting him to signify our wishes (which we conceived to be the wishes of a very large proportion both of the clergy and the laity) to the rest of the bishops, that everything might be done, which could be *prudently* and *safely* done, to promote these important and salutary purposes. The answer given by the archbishop, 11 February 1773, was in these words: 'I have consulted severally my brethren the bishops, and it is the opinion of the bench in general, that nothing can in prudence be done in the matter that has been submitted to our consideration.'"[1]

With this response the agitation, public and private, being deprived of any reasonable hopes of success, diminished; and to the credit of the house of commons there stood the decision by which a determined attempt towards the further revision of the standards of worship and belief of the Church had been defeated. The part played by Porteus was noted with approbation by George III, who praised "the very proper conduct held by him on the attempts to alter the Liturgy", and urged this in 1776 as a ground for his being the next Cambridge divine to be elevated to the bench.[2]

The incidents of the Feathers' Tavern petition lose much of their significance if viewed in isolation and apart from other manifestations of the quasi-Unitarian movement sporadic throughout the century. So early as 1727 Gibson had placed his veto upon a proposal of Queen Caroline to nominate to the see of Bangor the protagonist of the Trinitarian controversy, Dr Samuel Clarke, judging rightly that his promotion would entail public consequences of the utmost importance to the Church. Clarke indeed desired the eminence of the episcopate,

---

[1] R. Hodgson, *Life of B. Porteus*, pp. 38–40 (London, 1811).
[2] *Correspondence of George III* (ed. J. Fortescue), iii, 409, No. 1943 (19 Dec. 1776).

if at all, only as a situation of greater influence for the forwarding of his favourite scheme for the reformation of things intolerable to his position in the Prayer Book and Articles.[1] Two decades later Archbishop Herring, upon being pressed to accept the primatial see of Canterbury (which Gibson and Sherlock had refused), confessed his deep-seated apprehensions of a renewal of the demand for reform, in face of which he felt himself wholly inadequate to the situation of archbishop. He assured Newcastle that he had "very particular and...alarming evidence that some business on the scheme of a reformation of our establishment in its doctrines, discipline, and liturgy, was then on foot and ready for publication (having been long digesting)"; and although he knew the project to be "very serious and explained with decency", yet he feared it would be presented with determination and even peremptoriness "as the united sense of some of the best of the clergy and laity in the kingdom".[2] Throughout his primacy Herring was at pains to avoid such a tempest, especially in the form of suggested petitions to the convocations, and his policy was clearly avowed to Hardwicke in 1754 that "these were no times for stirs in the church, and he owned our present establishment and liturgy good enough for him".[3] His successor at Canterbury, Secker, was equally averse to any proposal of reform, and because of his opposition the public agitation of the question did not become acute until the primacy of Cornwallis, who was believed to be not unsympathetic towards the principles of the movement. His cautious discouragement of reform, announced in his reply to the private deputation of Porteus and others, quenched the hopes of official sanction, and likewise diminished the practical prospects of success. Notwithstanding, the continued discussion of the question in pamphlets testified to the gravity and importance of the problem, and but for the paralysing influence of the French Revolution, the zeal of Richard Watson might have secured some modification of the situation in favour of relaxation. In 1756 Bishop Clayton had moved formally in the Irish house of lords for the omission of the Athanasian and Nicene creeds from the Prayer Book of the Irish Church, but the matter had terminated with his death shortly afterwards. In 1790 Bishop Watson, always a cordial advocate of reform, agreed with the duke of Grafton to move in the English upper house for the omission of the Athanasian symbol, a design frustrated by the political alarms raised in Great Britain by the French Revolution. Nor

[1] N. Sykes, *Edmund Gibson*, pp. 134–5.
[2] Herring to Newcastle, 12 Sept. 1748. Add. MSS. 32716, f. 213.
[3] Herring to Hardwicke, 10 Oct. 1754. Add. MSS. 35599, f. 217.

was the temper of change confined to the British Isles; for in the constitution of the Protestant Episcopal Church of the United States of America framed after the successful issue of the colonists' rebellion, it was proposed to omit from the Apostles' creed the clause concerning the descent of Christ into Hell, and to excise entirely the Athanasian and Nicene creeds. The final compromise by which the Apostles' and Nicene creeds were retained in their entirety at the price of omitting the Athanasian symbol was only secured after much pressure by Archbishop Moore and other members of the Anglican episcopate, who scrupled to confer the episcopal character upon a church shorn of such considerable portions of its catholic heritage.

The academic character of the Feathers' Tavern petition itself did not reflect adequately the widespread sympathy for its aims existing amongst the generality of churchmen. In the Hanoverian as in other ages of the church the close connection between the *lex credendi* and the *lex orandi* was fully recognised; and it was natural and germane to the theological temper of the epoch that schemes of liturgical revision should be set forth in the hope of bringing the forms of public worship into greater consonance with its standards of belief. Such projects were defended indeed upon the familiar ground of the necessity of adapting traditional definitions alike of faith and practice to the new discoveries of the century in order to enable educated laymen to join in communion with the church and clergy honestly to retain their preferments. The pattern for such revision was adumbrated by Dr Samuel Clarke himself, who bequeathed to posterity a carefully interleaved copy of the Book of Common Prayer with suggested alterations written in his own hand.[1] Into the great number of its details it is as impossible as unnecessary to enter, for his industry had worked carefully through the entire compass of the book and made many alterations of varying degrees of importance and felicity. The general tendency of the revision was indicated sufficiently by certain salient reforms; chief of which perhaps were the entire omission of the Athanasian and Nicene creeds (the place of the latter in the Communion Office being taken by a psalm), and the retention of the Apostles' creed with the addition of a comma after the first mention of God, so as to read "I believe in God, the Father almighty". In like manner all specifically Trinitarian formulae throughout the Book of Common Prayer were rephrased; so that instead of the *Gloria Patri* was to be said: "Glory be to God by Jesus Christ through

---

[1] Two copies of Dr Samuel Clarke's Prayer Book are preserved respectively in the British Museum and in Dr Williams's Library (the former in his own handwriting, the latter an exact copy) from which the details quoted have been taken.

the heavenly assistance of the Holy Ghost", or alternatively in the words of St Paul, "Unto God be glory in the church and in Christ Jesus unto all generations for ever and ever" (Ephesians iii. 21). The *Te Deum* was remodelled to avoid all direct address to Christ and to substitute an indirect address through the Father; and the Trinitarian suffrages of the Litany were modified so as to run: "O God who by the precious blood of Thy only begotten Son hast purchased to Thyself Thy Church for a peculiar people, have mercy upon us, miserable sinners": and "O God who by the guidance of Thy Holy Spirit dost govern, direct, and sanctify the hearts of Thy faithful people, have mercy upon us". Several of the Collects were rewritten, most particularly that for Trinity Sunday, which was to read:

Almighty and everlasting God, who by Thy Son Jesus Christ hast commanded all those who believe in Him to be baptised in the Name of the Father, and of the Son, and of the Holy Ghost; grant that we, having ever before our eyes our baptismal covenant, may in all things constantly obey the rules of that most holy Gospel, which Thou our almighty Father hast revealed to us by Thy Son and confirmed by the manifold testimony of Thy Holy Spirit. Grant this, O heavenly Father, for Thy Son Jesus Christ's sake, our only mediator and advocate. Amen.

In his revision of the Communion Office Dr Clarke was conservative, retaining by far the greatest part of its traditional structure. Save for the removal of the Nicene creed, he made no changes in the form of service until the end of the Prayer for the Church Militant, after which he rephrased the several exhortations, but retained the Invitation, Confession, Absolution, Comfortable Words, *Sursum Corda*, and *Sanctus* unaltered. Of the Proper Prefaces, that for Trinity Sunday was excised, and verbal alterations made in that for Christmas Day. The Prayer of Humble Access was unchanged, and in the Prayer of Consecration for "satisfaction" there was substituted "atonement", whilst the words of administration of the elements were likewise unaltered. Verbal changes were made in the Prayer of Oblation, but the *Gloria in Excelsis* was remodelled in a thoroughgoing manner; and instead of the Trinitarian blessing, the office was concluded with the form of grace at the conclusion of St Paul's Second Epistle to the Corinthians ("The grace of the Lord Jesus Christ, and the love of God, and the fellowship of the Holy Ghost, be with you all"). The doctrinal standard of Dr Clarke in respect of the Eucharist was indicated by his substitution for the response in the Catechism, in reply to the question concerning the inward part or thing signified by that Sacrament,—"The

Body and Blood of Christ which are verily and indeed taken and received by the faithful in the Lord's Supper"—of this answer: "The union of Christians with Christ their Head and with each other by their Communion in the memorials of His Body and Blood". Several changes were made in the Baptismal and Confirmation offices; whilst in the Ordinal, the *Veni Creator* was omitted from the Office for the Ordaining of Priests, and the Bishop's prayer at the imposition of hands was revised so as to read:

Grant, O Lord, that this person may receive the Holy Ghost for the office and work of a priest in the Church of God now committed unto him by the imposition of our hands; that under the direction of the Spirit of truth and holiness, whosesoever sins he forgives may be forgiven, and whosesoever sins he retains may be retained; and that he may be a faithful dispenser of the Word of God and of His Holy Sacraments in the church where he shall be appointed to minister. Amen.

After the same principles the prayer at the imposition of hands upon the person to be consecrated to the episcopal dignity was so rephrased as to run:

Grant, O Lord, that this Thy servant may receive the Holy Ghost for the office and work of a Bishop in the Church of God now committed unto him by the imposition of our hands; and that he may continually remember to stir up Thy gifts which are in him, to Thy glory and to the good governance of Thy Church, and the salvation of the souls of men. Amen.

It was entirely in accordance with these changes that the direct form of absolution in the Office for the Visitation of the Sick should be replaced by the form used in the Communion Office for the absolution of the congregation after their corporate confession of sin.

Compared with the Caroline revision of 1662, or even with that projected by the royal commissioners of 1689 for the reconcilement of moderate dissenters, this scheme of Samuel Clarke may well seem to have laid the axe to the root of the tree of catholicity and orthodoxy in the Church of England. But the progress of anti-Trinitarian opinions was so rapid during the latter part of the century that by comparison with later proposals published during the controversies of the Feathers' Tavern petition, his initial step towards reform seemed moderate and sober. Several projects based upon his original suggestions were set forth; of which that published anonymously in 1774 with the title *The Book of Common Prayer Reformed according to the Plan of the late Dr Samuel Clarke* may be regarded as characteristic. The title indeed was scarcely veracious; for though the editor professed to have added only "such further alterations as were judged necessary to render it unexceptionable with respect to the object of religious worship", he had departed as widely from the copy of his model as Clarke himself had originally done from the Revision of 1662. In this drastic purgation little indeed was left of the traditional ordering of public worship. The Apostles' creed appeared shorn not only of the clause declaring the descent of Christ into Hell, but also of those relating to the Holy Catholic Church and the Communion of Saints. In the Choir Offices of Morning and Evening Prayer even the declaratory form of absolution was expunged, and the *Te Deum, Magnificat*, and *Nunc Dimittis* were replaced by psalms. In the Sacramental Offices scarcely a trace was left of notions treasured alike by high churchmen and evangelical Calvinists. The Baptismal Office was a brief and simple act of dedication, from which all references to original sin and baptismal regeneration had been excised. The Holy Communion was to be preceded always by a revised form of Morning Prayer and commenced therefore with the Invitation, having lost its traditional form of preparation. In place thereof was prefixed the Litany, two Lessons taken from the Old and New Testaments respectively and each followed by a psalm, the Lord's Prayer and the prayer immediately following in the Communion Office of 1662, the General Thanksgiving, the Prayer of Chrysostom, and the Grace. In the Communion Office proper the Confession was retained (omitting only the affirmation concerning the people's sins that "the burden of them is intolerable"), and the Absolution, Comfortable Words, *Sursum Corda*, and *Sanctus* were likewise unchanged. Of the Proper Prefaces, those for Trinity Sunday and Ascension Day were expunged, and those for Christmas and Easter Days rewritten, whilst the Prayer of Humble Access was also omitted. In the Prayer of Consecration all reference to the sacrifice of Christ upon the cross ("Who made there, by His one oblation of Himself once offered, a full, perfect and sufficient sacrifice, oblation, and satisfaction for the sins of the whole world") was omitted; and the aspiration was expressed "that we may receive this bread and wine in grateful remembrance of His death and sufferings". The delivery of the elements to the communicants was to be accompanied by the commemorative sentences: "Take and eat (or drink) this in remembrance of Christ". In the Post-Communion, the Prayer of Oblation suffered verbal alterations, and the *Gloria* was rewritten. In view of such extreme schemes of liturgical revision, the warning of Burke to his fellow-commoners in the debate on the Feathers' Tavern petition, that "if they made that a season for religious alterations, they would soon find it a season of religious tumults and religious wars", bears an appearance of greater probability than might be conjectured from the modest request of the petitioners upon the issue of subscription. For it may not be forgotten that divines of the ability and eminence of Richard Watson were eager and zealous in their desire to press upon the legislature the consideration of "the propriety of substituting Dr Clarke's amended Liturgy or one on that plan in the place of our present Liturgy" as a means of effecting the desired reform of the Church from the dregs of Popery and Calvinism. Against such measures it may be accounted fortunate that the eloquence of Burke, the conservatism of the faithful laity of the house of commons, and the prevalent persuasion of the wisdom of the principle *quieta non movere* offered a barrier for the defence of the established order in church no less than in state.

For the space of a full generation indeed before the presentation of the Feathers' Tavern petition, the waters of religious life in Great Britain had been stirred by the Methodist movement which had spread from its origins in the secluded academic society of Oxford to the unlettered populations of towns and villages throughout the British Isles and beyond the Atlantic ocean. The two Evangelical revivals, led respectively by John Wesley and George Whitefield, although differing sharply and deeply from each other on the theological points which separated Arminian from Calvinist, had arisen definitely in reaction and protest against the dominant rationalistic and Latitudinarian tradition in the church. John Wesley himself, as was natural, was in many respects a child of the century of his birth; but he broke away with astonishing rapidity and completeness from its prevalent intellectual fashions in religion. For although in a letter to his mother of 29 July 1725 he proclaimed in the typical phraseology of his time that "faith is a species of belief; and belief is defined as 'an assent to a proposition upon rational grounds'; without rational grounds there is therefore no belief, and consequently no faith; faith must necessarily at length be resolved into reason";[1] yet before the end of that same year he had abandoned this standpoint in favour of the conclusion that "saving faith (including practice) is an assent to what God has revealed because He has revealed it, and not because the truth of it may be evinced by reason".[2] By this affirmation, written on 22 November 1725, five years before his return to Oxford to stimulate the religious society founded by his brother Charles, and twelve years before his own

[1] John Wesley, *Letters*, i, 22 (Standard edition, ed. J. Telford, 8 vols. 1931).
[2] *Ibid.* i, 25.

famous experience of conversion, he had crossed the Rubicon which divided the new Evangelical revival from the Latitudinarian tradition then dominant. Henceforth the Methodist movement became a conscious and deliberate challenge to the rationalistic attitude towards religion characteristic of the churchmanship of the age. Naturally also John Wesley found himself unable to pursue to the end his attempted reading of the controversial writings of Atterbury and Hoadly, for "he could not conceive that the dignity of the end was at all proportioned to the difficulty of attaining it; and he thought the labour of twenty or thirty hours, if he were sure of succeeding, which he was not, would be but ill rewarded by that important piece of knowledge, whether Bishop Hoadly had misunderstood Bishop Atterbury or not".[1] Instead of such arid endeavours, his career became an increasing fulfilment of his promise to his brother Samuel that "leisure and he had taken leave of one another, and he proposed to be busy as long as he lived, if his health were so long indulged to him"; and his business was that of his Father in heaven.[2] Into the personal details of his evangelistic work it is foreign to this survey to enter; nor indeed is it necessary to retell the thrice-told tale of the expansion of the Holy Club into the agency for the conversion of the people of England. Of the effect of the revival which he inspired upon the condition and situation of the Established Church some account must be taken; but regarded from this standpoint and allowing fully the importance of the vast popular religious movement which he directed, attention must be concentrated chiefly upon the personal religious development of Wesley and his unparalleled powers of organisation and systematisation.

His own spiritual history was woven of many strands, for both his grandparents had been ejected as Puritans in 1662, his father was of the Caroline high church tradition, and his mother before marriage had been a benevolentist with tendencies towards the fashionable Unitarianism. Accordingly it is little surprising that his own development was marked by violent changes from the exclusive high church sacramentarian views of his early years to the presbyterian and evangelical doctrines of his maturer age. Beneath a variety of outward metamorphoses, which caused him to part company with a number of teachers and colleagues in turn, William Law, Peter Böhler, and George Whitefield, not always without some sharpness of judgment upon their shortcomings, he retained a constant Arminian conviction that Christ died for all and that the Father willed all men to come to a knowledge of His saving truth, and an abiding sympathy with all true religion of

[1] John Wesley, *Letters*, i, 40.   [2] *Ibid.* i, 34.

the heart; which led him to a steady avoidance of controversy for its own sake and to a generous tendency to accept good works as of greater importance than correctness of theological opinion. "Of Calvinism, Mysticism, and Antinomianism have a care", he wrote to a disciple in 1783, "for they are the bane of true religion; and one or other of them has been the grand hindrance of the work of God wherever it has broke out."[1] This sentiment was characteristic of all his teaching. Even greater than his gifts as a preacher however was his genius as an organiser; and it was to the careful edifice of organisation which he created, from the small social unit of the class meeting to the Conference of Preachers, combined with the enthusiasm aroused in his converts for the new church system, that the permanent influence of his religious preaching was due. The establishment of a new and extensive Christian denomination within the compass of a single lifetime, albeit that life embraced the span of more than half a century after the famous conversion and the particular individual was endowed with the indefatigable energy of mind and body possessed by John Wesley, was indeed an astonishing fact. But the success and coherence of the Methodist organisation created inevitable difficulties with the Established Church, from which formal severance became eventually necessary.

To that end of separation many factors were contributory. Wesley himself was a determined critic of the parochial system which lay at the basis of the Anglican administration, since he could not believe that the protracted ministrations of one clergyman to the same congregation could be for the spiritual profit either of pastor or people. Not only was he convinced of the ubiquitous field of his own pastoral ministry, but to Samuel Walker of Truro, who urged him in 1756 to secure the ordination in the English Church of such of his lay preachers as were fitted therefor and the settlement of others as readers in certain societies, he repudiated the very idea and principle of a fixed ministry.

> Be their talents ever so good, they will ere long grow dead themselves, and so will most of them that hear them. I know, were I myself to preach one whole year in one place, I should preach both myself and most of my congregation asleep. Nor can I believe it was ever the will of our Lord that any congregation should have one teacher only. We have found by a long and constant experience that a frequent change of teacher is best. This preacher has one talent, that another. No one whom I ever yet knew has all the talents which are needful for beginning, continuing and perfecting the work of grace in one whole congregation.[2]

---

[1] John Wesley, *Letters*, vii, 169.   [2] *Ibid.* iii, 195.

The employment of lay preachers was essential to the effective propagation of the Methodist revival, for throughout its course the number of ordained clergy attracted to its service was small, at first because of the unpopularity aroused by Wesley's preaching and later by reason of the strongly Calvinistic convictions of the leading Evangelical clergy within the Church of England. But if the work of lay preachers was indispensable to Wesley, their activity created a series of difficulties, the effects of which might be restrained for a season by his personal authority, but could not be avoided permanently. So early as 1755 he was driven to admit that "if he could not stop a separation without stopping lay preachers, the case was clear—he could not stop it at all"; and he added the more damaging confession that "his conclusion (which he could not yet give up), that it was lawful to continue in the church, stood, he knew not how, almost without any premises that were able to bear its weight".[1]

To the majority of his converts, in whom indifference towards the rules and ordinances of the Established Church took the place of his sentimental attraction to the society of his upbringing and ordination, the sense of obligation thereto was naturally weak. The very circumstance which contributed so largely to the success of the Methodist movement, its appeal to large sections of the population which had lain outside the Anglican parochial ministration, accentuated the difficulty of retaining these disciples in friendly correspondence with the clergy and congregations of the Church. The rule of Methodist societies prescribed attendance upon their parish churches for the monthly reception of the Sacrament, and this precept Wesley reiterated to the close of his life; as when in 1788 he "advised all their people in his name to keep close to the Church and Sacrament",[2] and again in 1790 he insisted earnestly "on their going to church every fourth Sunday", declaring to Bishop Tomline of Lincoln that "the Methodists in general are members of the Church of England, they hold all her doctrines, attend her service, and partake of her Sacraments".[3] Despite the evident desire of Wesley to preserve this connection, circumstances and the precipitate action of his followers, who lacked his personal attachment to the Church, created the inevitable precedents to schism. In 1755 authority to administer the Sacrament to such of their converts as were unable or unwilling to attend their parish churches was assumed by certain lay preachers, amongst whom were the two Perronets, sons of the vicar of Shoreham, Joseph Cownley, and Thomas Walsh. The issue thus

---

[1] John Wesley, *Letters*, iii, 144–6.
[2] *Ibid.* viii, 80.   [3] *Ibid.* viii, 223–4.

raised was of the utmost gravity and importance; but it was evaded for the moment by Wesley's opposition, the decision of the Leeds Conference after three days' deliberation against the expediency of separation, and the promise of the culprits not to repeat their offence. The significance of the episode caused profound disquiet to Charles Wesley; and even his brother confessed that Walsh's undertaking "not to administer even amongst themselves", though "an huge point given up", was "perhaps more than they could give up with a clear conscience".[1] His judgment was indeed sound; for beneath the action and the prohibition there lay a clear conflict of principle. John Wesley on the one hand believed that lay administration of the Sacrament was wrong; whilst certain of his preachers on the other deemed it their duty to administer. In consequence it was little surprising that at Norwich in 1760 the irregularity should be repeated, when Paul Greenwood and his colleagues celebrated the Holy Communion for the benefit of their adherents. The conflict between the rebels who transgressed the rule of Wesley and their leader who disapproved and endeavoured to prevent the spread of the practice, continued until the end of the latter's life; for even after his ordination of Taylor and Hanby for Scotland, Wesley attempted to prohibit them from administering the Sacrament to those who for scruples of conscience could not go to the Church. The cumulative effect of a series of such incidents was evident; and although respect for the personal authority of Wesley restrained the Methodist societies from formal separation until after his death, that action was ultimately inevitable. Nor was it surprising that the majority of the Methodist converts, drawn from the ranks of dissenters or the classes neglected by the ministrations of the Church, should sit loose to the relics of Anglican religious practice retained by their leaders. Their interest lay in the new church organisation evolved by John Wesley, not in the old system in which he had been reared; and not even his powerful personality nor his great authority could indoctrinate them with the few elements of churchmanship which were superimposed upon the more important tenets of his preaching.

More spectacular was the barrier to continuance in communion with the episcopal church built by John Wesley's own exercise of the authority to ordain presbyters, which he believed to be inherent in his office as a priest. In this regard he was in harmony with the prevalent tradition of his age, both within the Established Church and without, which laid little stress upon particular types of Church Order and regarded the difference between presbyterian and episcopal ordination

[1] John Wesley, *Letters*, iii, 129.

as a relatively unimportant element in the profession of Christianity. It was indeed from Stillingfleet's *Irenicon* and from the *Enquiry into the Constitution, Discipline, Unity and Worship of the Primitive Church* of Lord Chancellor King that he imbibed the persuasion of the identity in the apostolic age of the presbyterate and episcopate, and of the consequent validity of presbyterian ordination, and of his own authority to ordain equally as to administer the Sacrament. He had reached this conclusion so early as 1746, but refrained from acting upon it for the sake of expediency and the preservation of union with the Church, for the space of a generation. In 1747 he commissioned Joseph Cownley as a preacher by placing the New Testament in the hands of the kneeling postulant with the injunction, "Take thou authority to preach the Gospel". But not until 1780 did he act formally upon his mature conviction, and even then he ordained only for the American colonies, not for the home country. Later he was driven by the logic of his action to ordain also for Scotland and finally for England, though he admitted to the presbyterate only three men for service in England. Despite the evident gravity of these steps, John Wesley continued to profess his inviolable attachment to the Church and his strong personal resolve not to allow the Methodists to secede from it. "The alteration which has been made in America and Scotland", he wrote in 1784, "has nothing to do with our kingdom. I believe I shall not separate from the Church of England till my soul separates from my body."[1] Four years later in 1788 he admitted that separation would follow his own death, though still believing that a majority would remain of his persuasion in the matter. "Whenever I am removed, there can be no doubt but some of the Methodists will separate from it and set up independent meetings: some will accept of livings: the rest (who I trust will be the largest third) will continue together on the itinerant plan."[2] In accordance with this spirit successive Conferences continued to discountenance formal severance, in 1786, and in 1792 by the drawing of lots which fell against schism; whilst even in 1795 the Conference decided to leave to the several congregations the decision whether they desired to receive the Sacrament at their parish churches or from the hands of their own ministers. But the logic of events proved stronger than the ties of sentiment, and the Methodist societies drifted steadily into a position of secession.

If sentiment had been able to rescue the situation there were not lacking evidences of an increasing sympathy towards John Wesley on the part of many Anglican clergy during the later years of his life.

---

[1] John Wesley, *Letters*, vii, 321.   [2] *Ibid.* viii, 71.

"I still think", he observed in 1787, "that when the Methodists leave the Church, God will leave them. Every year more and more of the clergy are convinced of the truth and grow well-affected towards us. It would be contrary to all common sense as well as to good conscience to make a separation now."[1] The only feature which marred this sense of *rapprochement* was the circumstance that the great majority of those clergy of the Established Church who had been affected by the Evangelical revival had adopted its Calvinist, not its Arminian form. Methodists who were ready to follow their founder's advice to attend the parish churches found difficulty when the preacher uttered stout Calvinist doctrine; and accordingly the Conference of 1782 decided "that it was highly expedient [that] all the Methodists who had been bred therein should attend the service of the church as often as possible; but that, if the minister began either to preach the Absolute Decrees or to rail at and ridicule Christian Perfection, they should quietly and silently go out of church, yet attend it again the next opportunity".[2] Four years later Wesley admitted that, though the Conference might refuse to support corporate separation from the Church, "it was not unlikely many would be driven out where there were Calvinist ministers".[3] Thus was the possibility of a renewed understanding frustrated, and the Methodist revival in its Arminian guise hardly touched at all the Established Church.

Into the dark history of the bitter controversies waged by Calvinists against Arminians it is happily unnecessary at this distance of time to enter. Whitefield was the champion of Calvinist teaching, as Wesley was of its antithesis; and disagreement on this vital matter prevented co-operation and finally dissolved their partnership in evangelism. The two preachers were reconciled personally and maintained a spirit of charity despite theological differences; but between their followers every accompaniment of obloquy and abuse sharpened the edge of religious controversy, and in the pages of the *Arminian Magazine* and of its rival the *Gospel Magazine*, the extremes of invective may be found. The separation of Wesley and Whitefield had important consequences for the Evangelical revival in the Established Church; for though Whitefield was incomparably the greater orator, he lacked entirely the organising genius of his colleague, and apart from the influence of the Countess of Huntingdon in providing a centre and nucleus round which the Calvinist tradition might group its adherents, it remained by comparison with Wesley's societies inchoate and amorphous. The band of chaplains professing Calvinistic opinions gathered round her

[1] John Wesley, *Letters*, vii, 377.   [2] *Ibid.* vii, 99.   [3] *Ibid.* vii, 326.

household by the Countess Selina exercised a wider influence than their numbers warranted, and their work was characterised by a close association with the dissenters. The college established in 1768 at Trevecca trained ministers indifferently for the episcopal and non-episcopal churches in England and Wales; and the tradition of co-operation was accepted so completely that when Samuel Horsley was consecrated to the see of St David's in 1788 he found the native-born candidates for ordination in his diocese to have been prepared for their ministry at the Carmarthen Academy, supported by the London Congregational and Presbyterian Boards. In 1780, however, several of the chapels built by the Calvinist preachers under the aegis of Lady Huntingdon took out licences for public worship as dissenting chapels, and in 1783 some of her chaplains assumed the authority to ordain. With the definite foundation of Lady Huntingdon's Connexion, the severance between the Anglican and Nonconformist elements became patent; and those of her former chaplains who had accepted benefices in the Established Church broke off relations with the new body, and devoted themselves to the stimulation and propagation of the Evangelical movement within the communion of the Church.

The Anglican Evangelical revival exhibited affinities with both the Methodist movements. From Whitefield it borrowed its stern Calvinistic doctrine, and from both leaders it adopted in the persons of some of its outstanding clergy the itinerant method of preaching the good tidings. Such characteristic figures as Grimshaw and Berridge were peripatetic evangelists; and amongst the results of their labours was the erection of independent chapels in which the purest tenets of Calvinism might be preached in parishes where the incumbent disapproved of the revival and its doctrines. Grimshaw assisted the building of a preaching house at Haworth, and Venn at Huddersfield, when his successor in that benefice was not of the Calvinist persuasion, headed the subscription list for the erection of an independent chapel, employing his influence likewise for the same end at Halifax and Holmfirth. The common profession of Calvinistic beliefs tended to draw together Anglican and Nonconformist evangelicals, especially those of the Congregationalist denomination; but the status of the auxiliary chapels and of their ministers became a problem of delicacy and difficulty in relation to the position of the Anglican leaders in their own episcopal communion. Other evidences of the close co-operation with dissenters were seen in the joint-foundation of religious societies, such as the British and Foreign Bible Society which symbolised their association by its dual secretariat of an Anglican and a dissenting minister.

To the religious influence of the Evangelical revivals, both without and within the Established Church, ample tribute has been paid by historians alike of church and people. They supplied the new leaven to quicken and revivify the religion of the nation, and especially of those unlettered classes which remained untouched by the Latitudinarian theology of the cultivated clergy and laity though not protected from the vices of the age. The monument of John Wesley's apostolate was written in the hearts of his converts, and in the work of his Methodist societies not only in the British Isles but in the New World, before the time of his death. Within the Established Church the revival was represented by such clergy as James Hervey, William Grimshaw, John Berridge, William Romaine, Henry Venn, John Newton, Thomas Scott, Joseph and Isaac Milner, to mention but a selection of its adherents, whose labours were apostolic in zeal and power. Furthermore it attracted to its allegiance laymen and women of social position and influence, who were able to extend its authority not only by the example of personal devotion but by the added prestige of their situation. Such were William Wilberforce, who lent a peculiar dignity to the movement, William Cowper, whose poetry embodied its essential piety and religious spirit, Hannah More, who, like Wilberforce, set forward its cause both by pen and personal social service, and Lords Dartmouth and Teignmouth, who helped to bridge the gulf which had divided the Methodism of Wesley from the educated and polite circles of the court. Nor was the revival unfruitful in the creation of societies for the propagation of its tenets by tract and voice, as in the Religious Tract Society and the British and Foreign Bible Society on the one hand, and in the famous missionary associations on the other, the London Missionary Society and the renowned Church Missionary Society. Of the importance of the Evangelical revival alike in individual and social life, and in devotion to evangelistic effort beyond the British Isles, abundant evidence may be found in the contemporary events and chronicles of the age.

Inevitably its least satisfactory aspect lay in its retrograde intellectual influence. Owing its origin and strength largely to a reaction against the rationalistic and Socinian tendencies which had developed from the Latitudinarian movement in theology, it went to extremes in depreciation of the intellectual study and criticism of the Bible. Even John Wesley, despite his academic training and scholarly attitude, was almost superstitious in his notions of the special interventions of Providence attendant upon the most ordinary details of his life, and in his recourse to the expedient of the *sortes liturgicae* for the determination of his problems. With Whitefield the situation was much worse, for he lacked altogether the education and cultured influence of his colleague; and the Calvinistic doctrine was peculiarly liable to exaggeration in the depreciation of learning and all human aids to salvation. Thus the theological and literary productions of the Evangelical revival were of little importance or permanent value to the tradition of the *ecclesia docens*; and the intellectual glories of the Georgian Church remain with the evidential and philosophical writers of the calibre of Butler, Waterland, Warburton, and Paley.

The religious influence which permeated society as a result of the Methodist and Evangelical movements was of greater value by reason of the unchanged condition of the Established Church in respect of revenues, administration, and temporal situation. The several generations of the eighteenth century were bound together by an evident homogeneity in the external circumstances of ecclesiastical order; and the long reign of George III accentuated the characteristics of his predecessors. The new monarch himself was as truly English and Anglican as Queen Anne had been, and like her majesty valued no branch of his royal prerogative more highly than that which placed in his hands the responsibility of nomination to the episcopal bench. His correspondence with ministers upon ecclesiastical matters abounded in injunctions "to find a man of exemplary conduct to be brought upon the bench", that "a man of learning and of an exemplary life" should be recommended for his consideration, or that he wished to prefer such a "clergyman who for private character, as well as orthodoxy and learning, might seem best qualified to be brought upon the bench".[1] Such requests did not imply in the leastwise that the king lacked preferences of his own; for upon occasion he intervened decisively and with firmness to ensure the promotion of his personal favourites. In December 1776, upon the vacancy of the see of York by the death of Archbishop Drummond, he commanded that Terrick of London should be offered the translation, and upon his refusal on the score of age, that Markham of Chester should be preferred; whilst to the see of Chester he insisted upon the nomination of Dr Beilby Porteus because that divine "would be an ample match in any debate in the house of lords in answering the Bishop of Peterborough", Hinchcliffe, who had opposed the policy of the administration in regard to the American colonists, and also in consideration of "the very proper conduct held by Porteus on the attempts to alter the Liturgy".[2]

[1] *Correspondence of George III* (ed. J. Fortescue), iii, 400, 436; v, 252.
[2] *Ibid.* iii, 400, No. 1923; iii, 407, No. 1939; iii, 409, No. 1943.

Even more noteworthy was the constant friendship shown by George III for Dr Richard Hurd, whose *Moral and Political Dialogues* his majesty greatly admired, and whose talents had been brought to his notice by Lord Mansfield, Bishop Warburton, and Mr Charles Yorke. Accordingly the king declared to Lord North in May 1772, in response to pressure from Lord Hardwicke for the advancement of his brother Dr James Yorke, dean of Lincoln to the bench, that he must accord priority of favour to Hurd, whose elevation "would undoubtedly meet with general approbation".[1] Two years later therefore on 30 December 1774 Hurd was nominated to the see of Lichfield and Coventry, in succession to Brownlow North translated to Worcester.[2] In 1776 a further mark of the royal pleasure was conferred upon him by his appointment to the office of preceptor to the Prince of Wales and the Duke of York. Henceforth Hurd was the favourite prelate of the king, who interchanged correspondence with him upon religious and political subjects and resolved to advance him to higher dignities in the church. In 1781, upon the death of Bishop John Thomas of Winchester on 1 May, Brownlow North was translated to that see from Worcester, and the king gave orders to Lord North that Hurd should be appointed clerk of the closet "the moment he shall find that the present possessor is no more",[3] and should also be advanced to Worcester. To Hurd himself his majesty wrote

I trust that any opportunity that brings you nearer to my person cannot be unpleasing to you....I have also directed Lord North to acquaint you that I propose to translate you to the see of Worcester. I should hope you will allow Hartlebury to be a better summer residence than Eccleshall; and I flatter myself that hereafter you will not object to a situation that may not require so long a journey as either of these places every year.[4]

The contingency hinted in the concluding sentence was realised only two years later when the see of Canterbury itself was vacated by the death of Cornwallis on 19 March; whereupon, despite the solicitation of Lord Shelburne on behalf of his friend Bishop Shipley of St Asaph,[5] George III instantly made the offer to Hurd.

"Had the offer of the archbishopric from his majesty", ran the entry in Hurd's *Dates of Some Occurrences in my own Life*, "with many gracious

[1] *Correspondence of George III*, ii, 515, No. 1059 A.
[2] *Ibid.* ii, 151, No. 1550; ii, 155, No. 1560.
[3] *Ibid.* v, 223, No. 3313.
[4] Hurd MSS. vol. i, No. 3 (2 May 1781).
[5] *Correspondence of George III*, vi, 291, No. 4216.

expressions, and pressed to accept it; but humbly begged leave to decline it, as a charge not suited to his temper and talents, and much too heavy for him to sustain, especially in these times. The king was pleased not to take offence at this freedom, and then to enter with him into some confidential conversation on the subject. It was offered to the Bishop of London, Dr Lowth, and refused by him, as was foreseen, on account of his ill-health. It was then given to Dr Moore, Bishop of Bangor."[1]

The close friendship between king and prelate was entirely unaffected by this refusal of the primacy, and his majesty continued to write to Hurd concerning religious topics such as the confirmation of members of the royal family, and their reception of the Sacrament, and upon political affairs, such as the grave crisis which occasioned the resignation of the younger Pitt in 1801, when George III sent to his episcopal counsellor a full account and justification of his own attitude towards the question of Catholic Emancipation.[2] So late as 1805 the king enquired anxiously of the aged Hurd as to his impressions of the new archbishop, Manners Sutton, in whose elevation his majesty had played so notable a part, and expressed the hope that "his choice would meet with approbation" in so valued a quarter.[3]

In other circumstances also where no personal friend was involved, George III showed the utmost solicitude in episcopal preferment, as upon the death of Terrick of London in 1777, when he commanded Lord North to consult Archbishop Cornwallis concerning the prelate most proper for translation to a see requiring "abilities, temper, and dignity in its possessor".[4] The primate having recommended Lowth of Oxford, his majesty concurred that his talents "pointed him out as the most fit on the bench for the vacant see of London", and agreed that North should propose the bishopric of Oxford in that event to Dr John Butler in return for his meritorious political service by his defence of the American policy of the administration.[5] In like manner upon the vacancy of Ely by the death of Bishop Keene in July 1781, Yorke of Gloucester was translated thither, and by the advice of Hurd and North George III resolved to appoint to Gloucester Dr Thomas Balguy, archdeacon of Winchester, whom he was convinced to be "the first man in point of reputation in the republic of letters in either university, besides it was he put an end to the meeting some years ago

[1] Hurd MSS. *Dates of Some Occurrences in my own Life.*
[2] Hurd MSS. No. 37 (13 Feb. 1801).
[3] *Ibid.* No. 50 (5 Sept. 1805).
[4] *Correspondence of George III*, iii, 436, No. 1981.
[5] *Ibid.* iii, 437–8, Nos. 1983–5.

at the Feathers' by the charge he published as archdeacon".[1] To the disappointment of the king, Balguy declined the honour, though his majesty observed that "his conduct did him great credit, and had he accepted the bishopric the motive of acting right would have alone decided him"; so that the offer was creditable, and no man could object to being invited second to him, which was itself "an honourable distinction".[2]

The *cause célèbre* of George III's reign in relation to ecclesiastical preferment occurred with respect to the vacancy of the see of Canterbury in 1805 upon the death of Moore. Already Pitt the younger had resolved upon seizing this opportunity, when it should happen, to place the coping stone upon the rewards bestowed by his influence on Bishop Pretyman Tomline of Lincoln. His majesty however had other intentions and had fixed his eye on Manners Sutton of Norwich. Accordingly the minister, setting forth both in conversation and writing before the death of Moore the distinguished merits and qualifications of his friend, perceived that his advances met with no cordial response; whereupon at the actual vacancy of the primacy he penned a weighty remonstrance. He protested

how deeply his feelings were wounded, and his hopes of contributing to his majesty's service impaired, by his majesty's apparent disregard of his recommendation of the bishop of Lincoln to succeed the archbishop of Canterbury. He entreated his majesty humbly to reflect that such a recommendation appeared uniformly to have been graciously accepted for a long course of time in every instance but that of the nomination of the last archbishop, which, he said, took place in the interval between the resignation of one administration and the appointment of another. The king's refusal to comply with his request could hardly be understood by himself, and would certainly not be understood by the public, in any other light than as a decisive mark of his majesty's not honouring him with that degree of confidence which his predecessors had enjoyed.

Notwithstanding this solemn declaration, the king remained firm, replying on 23 January 1805 that, though he "was ever hurt when he could not bring himself to concur with Mr Pitt in any matter which Mr Pitt seemed to have at heart", yet he "by no means could view the archbishopric in the light of a common bishopric. It was the person", he concluded, "upon whom he must most depend, and of whose dignity

---

[1] *Correspondence of George III*, v, 254, No. 3371. The reference is to Balguy's Charge *On Subscription to Articles of Religion*, published in 1772.
[2] *Ibid.* v, 260, No. 3383.

of behaviour, good temper, as well as talents and learning, he felt best satisfied; the archbishop as well as the king are for life".[1] In making so firm a stand, and insisting upon carrying Manners Sutton to Lambeth, George III was but following in the tradition of Queen Anne; and his success testified to the reality of the personal authority of the sovereign in determining ecclesiastical promotions even against the wishes of so powerful a minister as the younger Pitt.

Few clerical careers illustrated with more fidelity the continuity of the later and earlier parts of the eighteenth century than that of Sir George Pretyman, who later assumed the name of Tomline. The foundation of his fortunes was laid, as had been that of Francis Hare, bishop of Chichester, in his pedagogical relationship to a future prime minister, for Pitt the younger retained an abiding affection for his university tutor. This relationship was converted from 1783 to 1787 into that of unofficial private secretary, in which capacity Pretyman was rewarded by presentation to the sinecure rectory of Corwen in Merionethshire in 1782, by a prebend of Westminster in 1784, and by the crown rectory of Sudbourn cum Offord in 1785. Though Pitt did not recompense the financial and mathematical abilities of his ally, as Walpole had done the talents of Hare, by the offer of the ushership of the exchequer, he found such capacities very useful, and in February 1787 Pretyman was elevated to the bench as bishop of Lincoln, to which valuable see was added *in commendam* in the following month the deanery of St Paul's. "Mr Pitt", commented a disappointed contemporary, Dr John Douglas, "seemed willing to shew the extent of his power by loading his favourite with an uncommon share of preferment." Thus advanced in wealth and dignity, Pretyman was able to find consolation for his disappointment in regard to the primacy in 1805, and in 1820 was translated to the rich see of Winchester, resigning his deanery. Nor were other instances lacking during the reign of George III to demonstrate the continued influence of the temporal nobility in determining the succession to bishoprics and deaneries in behalf of their relatives and dependents. Thomas Thurlow, brother of Lord Chancellor Thurlow, secured the valuable rectory of Stanhope in 1771, and in the year following was appointed Master of the Temple, but his brother, then attorney-general, did not deem this sufficient recognition of his merits. In 1775 therefore the deanery of Rochester, although designed for another candidate, was bestowed upon him; since Lord North represented to the king his fear "that some

[1] Pitt to George III; George III to Pitt, 22 and 23 Jan. 1805: quoted in A. W. Rowden, *The Primates of the Four Georges*, pp. 386–9.

discontent and ill-humour which had lately appeared in the conduct of the attorney-general might proceed from his disappointment of obtaining an additional piece of preferment for his brother". North observed indeed that, though "it was of great consequence that the attorney-general should cordially co-operate with them in the arduous affairs in which they were engaged", it was doubtful whether "the buying off discontent by favours" was the best way of promoting good humour amongst all the servants of the crown.[1] Four years later, in 1779, Thurlow was raised to the bench as bishop of Lincoln, to which was added the deanery of St Paul's *in commendam* in 1782, which he resigned upon translation to the see of Durham in 1787. Reminiscent also of the expedients of the duke of Newcastle was the influence of the local and territorial position of Lord Gower in securing the deanery of Lichfield in 1776 for his nominee, Dr Baptist Proby, and that of Lord Wentworth in compassing the promotion of his uncle Dr Rowney Noel to the deanery of Salisbury in 1780.[2]

No contest for promotion could have borne a closer relationship to the days of the great whig duke and dispenser of patronage than that for the see of Carlisle upon its vacancy by the death of Bishop Edmund Law on 14 August 1787. Bishop Watson of Llandaff would have welcomed translation to his native county, but he was not sufficiently *persona grata* with the administration.[3] The local influence of Lord Lonsdale was exerted actively to secure the nomination of some divine of his own recommendation. At first he joined with Sir James Lowther in supporting the latter's kinsman Dr Lowther, whom Bishop Watson believed to be wholly unfitted for such a dignity, and who declined the offer when made to him. His lordship then put forward the name of Dr B. Grisdale, a minor canon of the cathedral and schoolmaster in the city, which recommendation was mentioned to the primate by Pitt. Archbishop Moore replied in such terms that an answer was sent to Lonsdale

that no encouragement could be given to such a project; that a man of much more respectable pretensions must be thought of, if his lordship was anxious to recommend to the vacant see with success. This was taken at first angrily, but Mr Pitt was firm; and Dr Grisdale was withdrawn. Some other fancies from the same quarter occasioned further delay; till it was signified that it was high time to fill up the vacancy forthwith. This brought from his lordship a full recommendation of Dr Douglas, which was acceded to.[4]

[1] *Correspondence of George III*, iii, 261, No. 1715.
[2] *Ibid.* iii, 343, No. 1830; v, 39, No. 2984.
[3] R. Watson, *Anecdotes*, i, 304–7.
[4] Abp. Moore to Bp. Hurd, 22 Sept. 1787. Hurd MSS. vol. iii, Sect. 4, No. 1.

By such means was Dr John Douglas, residentiary of St Paul's, whose long political service and numerous writings had been hitherto inadequately recompensed, raised to the episcopate, and the mind of the primate "relieved from no small anxiety". The consummation of the negotiation lay aptly in the manner of its announcement to the beneficiary; for Lord Lonsdale was so eager not to miss the opportunity of exercising a voice in the nomination that he rode himself to Southampton where Douglas was staying.

"I was sent for", related the canon, "to the George Inn on Wednesday night, 19 September, to a gentleman who had just arrived; and I found his lordship. He soon opened his business with me and after a pretty long conversation, in no part of which he hinted any expectation of return but such as gratitude must require, I accepted; and he set out again the next morning for London to effectuate his proposal. On Friday my name was given by him to Mr Pitt, and the king that very day readily consented."[1]

By such evident affinities of the influence of local connections on episcopal promotions and by such feats of ministerial diplomacy was the generation of George III and the younger Pitt linked to that of Walpole, Newcastle, and their master George II in a convincing continuity of spirit and practice.

But whilst the Georgian Church continued its placid official course, wherein all its ways were pleasantness and all its paths were peace, the face of the kingdom to which it was appointed to minister was changing rapidly by reason of the shifting of population consequent upon the rise of industrial towns. The far-reaching religious and social problems created by this migration of industrial workers and their aggregation in the mushroom cities which replaced former villages constituted the chief task of the Church of the last quarter of the eighteenth century, and one moreover towards the solution of which its genius was entirely unable to address itself. The paucity of church building which had been lamented by Butler and other prelates of the mid-century became now a scandal and a reproach of grave magnitude, for the spectacle of an immobile parochial system in the face of a mobile population afforded a ready object for the criticism of infidels and the shame of churchmen. Not the least of the services of the Methodist movement to the nation lay in its ministration to the industrial workers of the towns, and its erection of preaching houses for their exercise of public worship. In part the paralysis of the Established Church in prospect of the emergence of social problems of such importance lay in the circumstance that for the

[1] *Autobiography of Bishop Douglas*, pp. 54–5. B.M. Eg. 2181.

creation of each new parish a private act of parliament was requisite, a cumbrous method of procedure which effectively prevented the task of parochial subdivision, in part in the lack of missionary and evangelistic enterprise characteristic of the churchmanship of the century, and in part in the fear of financial readjustment and the disturbance of vested interests which a thoroughgoing reform of its administration might involve. Apart from the independent chapels built by the Anglican Evangelicals such as Grimshaw and Venn, and the sporadic erection of proprietary chapels by enterprising individuals, the national church made little endeavour to meet the needs of the rapidly changing social organisation. Even these chapels were the product generally either of the Calvinistic zeal of particular congregations or of the speculative genius of preachers who, like Thackeray's Mr Honeywood, hoped by their eloquence and oratorical gifts to repay from the revenues of their pew-rents the capital borrowed for their ventures in church building. Such occasional and incidental action was indeed all that could be expected, unless the cry for reform in revenues and administration were taken up and translated into practice by the leading prelates and laity of the age. With the elevation of Richard Watson to the bench in 1782 the possibility of such a campaign seemed to have dawned; for he was not slow in affording evidence that promotion had not cooled his zeal for remedial measures. Nor was he lacking in boldness to lay the axe to the root of the tree; since, perceiving that no reform could be effective which did not first enable the parochial clergy to residence by providing them with a sufficiency of income, he proposed a bold redistribution of episcopal and capitular revenues to attain this end. The aversion of Lord Shelburne and of the episcopate from such radical pillage frustrated his desires; and the opportunity was lost. On the issue of the sanctity of private property and of vested interests whig and tory alike in the eighteenth century held common ground; and the general verdict upon Watson's schemes was expressed by the biographer of Beilby Porteus, who, whilst professing the utmost sympathy with the poor clergy, denounced as outrageous the proposal to relieve their necessities from the abundance of others.

It is impossible for any one who has a due feeling and regard for the religious and even for the civil interest of the state, to see the pitiable condition of the inferior clergy without a mixed emotion of indignation and compassion. Let any one consider what the state owes to the labours of these industrious working husbandmen in the Christian vineyard.... It would certainly not be too much to say that the whole morals of a people are formed by the officiating clergy, in other words by the curacy of the kingdom.

But when reviewing the scheme to compensate them "from the funds of the richer clergy" the writer could only pronounce it "certainly an outrage against the rights of property", and refer particularly to Watson's notions as "a violation of the rights of property, and in the proposed method of application contrary to all received ideas of political economy".[1]

The slight hope entertained by the bishop of Llandaff that continuous advocacy of the cause of reform, supported by growing practical evidences of its urgent necessity, might prevail to effect some measure of his plans was extinguished finally by the outbreak of the French Revolution. The unhappy generation from 1793 to 1826 contributed more than any of its predecessors to the ill-repute of the eighteenth century by its policy of repression and reaction, which, though resolute in opposing all who laid even the mildest hands upon the established order in church and state, allowed the accumulation of anomalies and abuses in such magnitude as to provoke the radical reform epoch which succeeded. "Since the miserable event of the French Revolution", observed Watson sadly, "it may be said to every man in England and in Europe who attempts to reform abuses either in church or state—*desine, jam conclamatum est*."[2]

In their influence upon the Established Church the fear of revolutionary movements and the abhorrence of events in France operated in a diversity of ways. In face of the formal abolition of orthodox Christianity in the French republic and the worship of the goddess of Reason, attachment to the Established Church in England became more widespread and cordial. The reception in this country of the exiled clergy of the French Church awakened not only a personal sympathy for their individual sufferings, but a sense of the value of the religious establishment in England as a bulwark against enthusiasm and levelling tendencies. The status of the clergy rose perceptibly with their assumption of the new dignity of officers in the army against atheism, infidelity, and regicide; and parochial ministers of the type faithfully and ubiquitously portrayed in the novels of Jane Austen became more common, as the younger sons of the nobility and gentry adopted the profession of Orders in still greater numbers. Amongst the prelacy the sermons and vigour of Bishop Samuel Horsley testified to the patriotism and zeal of their order. Even the worst abuses and anomalies of ecclesiastical administration became sacrosanct as symbols of tradition and continuity, and congenial moreover with the *régime* of inequality and privilege in

[1] *Life of B. Porteus*, by a Lay Member of Merton College, Oxford, pp. 93–5.
[2] R. Watson, *Anecdotes*, i, 222.

parliament and at the court. To the imaginative mind of Burke such things, far from being an occasion of shame or apology, constituted a title to praise and congratulation.

The people of England know how little influence the teachers of religion are likely to have with the wealthy and powerful of long standing, and how much less with the newly fortunate, if they appear in a manner no way assorted to those with whom they must associate, and over whom they must exercise, in some cases, something like an authority. What must they think of that body of teachers, if they see it in no part above the establishment of their domestic servants? If the poverty were voluntary, there might be some difference.... But as the mass of any description of men are but men and their poverty cannot be voluntary, that disrespect which attends upon all lay poverty will not depart from the ecclesiastical.... For these reasons, whilst we provide first for the poor, and with a parental solicitude, we have not relegated religion (like something we were ashamed to shew) to obscure municipalities or rustic villages. No! We will have her to exalt her mitred front in courts and parliaments. We will have her mixed throughout the whole mass of life and blended with all the classes of society. The people of England will shew to the haughty potentates of the world and to their talking sophisters, that a free, a generous, an informed nation, honours the high magistrates of its church; that it will not suffer the insolence of wealth and titles, or any other species of proud pretension, to look down with scorn upon what they look up to with reverence; nor presume to trample upon that acquired personal nobility, which they intend always to be, and which often is, the fruit, not the reward, (for what can be the reward?) of learning, piety, and virtue. They can see, without pain or grudging, an Archbishop precede a Duke. They can see a Bishop of Durham, or a Bishop of Winchester, in possession of ten thousand pounds a year, and cannot conceive why it is in worse hands than estates to the like amount in the hands of this Earl or that Squire.[1]

Stripped of the adornment of such glittering rhetoric, the prosaic facts of the ecclesiastical revenues and administration were less comfortable to the conscience of churchmen of the succeeding generation. Apart from the adventitious wealth accruing to the chapters of such cathedrals as Durham and St Paul's through the mining of coal and the profits of land let to lease for building respectively, the spectacle of episcopal opulence and nepotism contrasting with the immobility of the parish system, its inability to cope with the new civic populations, and the relative poverty of the majority of the inferior clergy, seemed an

---

[1] E. Burke, *Reflections on the Revolution in France* (1790), pp. 153–4.

argument for reform rather than thanksgiving. Many gross exaggerations of the extent of episcopal wealth were circulated and believed; but the sober commentary furnished by the report of the Ecclesiastical Commissioners appointed to enquire into the ecclesiastical revenues of England and Wales, issued in 1835, testified to the ill-consequences of delay and complacency. The net income, based upon an average of three years ending in 1831, of the see of Canterbury was estimated to be £19,182, that of York £12,629, of London £13,929, of Durham, £19,066, of Winchester £11,151, whilst among the middle-bishoprics Ely enjoyed £11,105, St Asaph £6301, Bath and Wells £5946, Lincoln £4542, and Worcester £6569, and at the bottom of the list came Llandaff with £924, accompanied by Rochester with £1459 and St David's with £1897. Of the total number of 10,478 benefices of which returns were made to the commissioners (exclusive of sinecure rectories and benefices annexed to other preferments), 3528 were still under the value of £150 per annum, 4882 under £200, and 6861 under £300 per annum; whilst of the total aggregate of 5230 curates scheduled in the report, of whom 1006 were employed by resident incumbents and 4224 by non-resident, the average salary was no higher than £81. Such a legacy of anomaly and injustice might well provoke the criticism of enemies (less partial than the conservative Burke to the defence of traditional institutions), that "though the Church of England is ostentatiously styled the *Reformed* Church, it is in truth the most unreformed of all the churches". In contemplation of these inequalities, and of the pastoral problems presented by the huge undivided parishes of such cities as Manchester and Leeds, the heirs of the eighteenth century might well lament the artificial protraction of its course and the prohibition of change by the long continuance of the Revolutionary and Napoleonic Wars in Europe. Richard Watson died in 1816 without seeing any of the reforms for which he had pressed so eagerly carried into effect; and the measure of the restraint exercised upon England by the foreign wars may be found in the chronological circumstance that a half-century divided his elevation to the episcopate and proclamation of the need of change from the enactment of the first Reform Bill which set in operation the series of reconstructive laws in church and state. Nothing indeed could restore to the history and reputation of the Georgian Church and state the unhappy years which the locust and the caterpillar had eaten during the generation from the outbreak of revolution in France to the death of George III, which had added to the span of that monarch's reign twice the respite of years granted to the piety of Hezekiah.

In essaying a summary appreciation of the character and achievement of the English Church during the eighteenth century, the chief difficulty lies in the circumstance of the sweeping away of so much of its outward fashion by the reforming legislation of the third decade of the succeeding epoch. So many of the exterior lineaments of the Hanoverian Church were destined shortly to disappear in the whig removal of things that were shaken by the tempest of reform agitation, that it is easier to realise the kinship of the unreformed Church of Georgian times with its medieval predecessor of the fifteenth century than to acknowledge its paternity of the *Ecclesia Anglicana* of the Victorian age. The introduction by Anthony Trollope of the new bishop of Barchester, Dr Proudie, was attended by the melancholy reflection that the revenues of the see were shrunken, in accordance with the provision of reform acts, from the £9000 enjoyed by his predecessor Dr Grantly to a modest £5000, upon which an aspiring prelate might find it difficult to maintain the traditional hospitality of his palace at Barchester and also to retain the residence in London necessary to his hopes of a translation in due season. In consequence of the legislation following upon the report of the Ecclesiastical Commissioners in 1835, the Church of England suffered a second reformation, more thoroughgoing in its financial and administrative purgation than that guided by the hand of the Tudor monarchs. The deprivation of the opulent sees of Canterbury, York, London, Durham, and Winchester of their excessive wealth for the benefit of poorer brethren, the abolition of the vast host of simple prebends in the cathedral and collegiate churches, and the creation of the Ecclesiastical Commissioners as a corporate body for the administration of the revenues thus placed at the disposal of the Church, involved the disappearance of the outstanding features of the pre-reform ecclesiastical society of Hanoverian England. Further changes of equal importance ensued in the division of unwieldy dioceses, the revival of the suffragan bishoprics, the creation of new ecclesiastical parishes by the simpler expedient of an Order in Council and without altering the boundaries of the civil parishes, and the augmentation of parochial revenues upon a more scientific and rational basis than the hazard of the lot employed by the commissioners of Queen Anne's Bounty. The vexed problem of the pluralism of benefices *cum cura animarum*, which had militated against the proper operation of the parochial system from pre-Reformation times, virtually ceased to exist, and the parallel evil of non-residence was reduced within narrow limits. Thus the abuses and anomalies of the unreformed order in England, in which church sinecures had been first cousins to rotten boroughs, places, and pensions in the state, were abolished root and branch by the zeal of whigs who were resolved to usher in an era wherein old things were passed away and all things had become new.

In retrospect of the eighteenth century, however, it is possible to survey its character from a less partial standpoint than that of radical and utilitarian reformers, and to delineate the fundamental features of the Church in faith and practice. In regard to the episcopate little doubt may be entertained that the particular contribution of that age to its history lay in the importance attained by the bench as a political influence in parliament and the country, and in the alliance of prelates with the whig and tory parties. The peculiar prominence of the episcopate in the house of lords coincided almost with the limits of the eighteenth century itself; for whereas the custom of annual parliamentary sessions lasting for five or six months of each year was a result of the development of the Revolution settlement of 1689, so the expansion of the number of temporal peers, begun by the creations of the younger Pitt, and the restriction of the spiritual peers to the quota established at the Reformation, which was agreed upon when new dioceses were formed in the nineteenth century, led to the gradual but steady diminution thereafter of the influence of the episcopal element. The Victorian epoch was graced indeed by many bishops who were active and eminent party men; but viewing the position of the bench as an unit, the Georgian age represented the acme of its political importance in the upper house of parliament. From this circumstance has proceeded the chief criticism of its personnel, as composed of time-serving divines, elevated by the intrigue of corrupt ministers for political services rather than for piety and learning, and ambitious always for further advancement by translation. Of the reality of the personal influence of the sovereign in controlling ministerial recommendations to the bench, the history of the century affords abundant example; for rulers of such different character as Anne, George II, and George III intervened upon occasion with decisive effect to assert their wishes, though the extent of the exercise of their prerogative in ecclesiastical matters was veiled generally by their cordial agreement with their ministers and their own party predilections. It was inevitable also that, in an epoch of fierce party strife, beneath which serious issues of the succession to the throne and the security of the Revolution settlement in its ecclesiastical no less than civil provisions were at stake, the episcopate should assume a political and party character, and that divines should be raised to the bench from motives of political allegiance. But granting the occurrence of a few scandals, such as the elevation of Hoadly, and the presence of sundry episcopal mediocrities (from which few ages are even predominantly free), it would not appear that a general charge against the kings or their ministers of trafficking in spiritual dignities for unworthy ends can be sustained. Second to the career of Hoadly, the evils of the close association of ecclesiastical advancement with party profession in politics were emphasised chiefly in the case of Richard Watson, though in his circumstances other influences, such as his individual independence and reforming convictions, assisted to encompass his neglect; and neither of these examples was typical of the age.

The particular misfortune of the eighteenth-century episcopate indeed has lain in the public and ubiquitous parading of the names of Hoadly and Watson and the representation of their careers as normal and characteristic of the bench. It may be contended with justice that such a judgment is unfair; and that it would be as equitable to asperse the Caroline episcopate by the unworthy examples of Barlow, Smith, Crewe, and Beaw, as to pillory that of the succeeding epoch by the constant mention of these two bishops. Even numerically they did not constitute a majority of the bench, and their negligence was not copied by the generality of their brethren. The severest critics have allowed the presence of at least a minority of divines of worth, though their specification of individuals has differed widely according to information and predilection.

> The royal letters are a thing of course,
> A king that would, might recommend his horse!
> And deans, no doubt, and chapters, with one voice,
> As bound in duty, would confirm the choice.
> Behold your bishop! well he plays his part,
> Christian in name, and infidel in heart,
> Ghostly in office, earthly in his plan,
> A slave at court, elsewhere a lady's man....
> [But] Providence, that seems concerned t' exempt
> The hallow'd bench from absolute contempt,
> In spite of all the wrigglers into place,
> Still keeps a seat or two for worth and grace,
> And therefore 'tis, that though the sight be rare,
> We sometimes see a Lowth or Bagot there.[1]

The poet's exceptions are unduly exiguous; for a century which embraced amongst the English episcopate alone such names as Tillotson, Burnet, Hough, Tenison, Nicolson, Wake, Potter, Gibson, White

[1] W. Cowper, *Tirocinium: or A Review of Schools.*

Kennett, Tanner, Benson, Secker, Herring, Butler, Pearce, Hume, Warburton, Hurd, Porteus, and Hallifax, together with the avowed high churchmen Sharp, Dawes, Atterbury, Sherlock, and Horsley, may not be accounted deficient either in learning or piety. Against a bench adorned by such talents it would seem eccentric indeed to frame an indictment of infidelity and secularity.

Nor does a general survey of the episcopal administration of the age afford surer grounds for a censorious verdict, apart from the few cases of individual negligence. It is singular, for example, that few historians of the nineteenth century in praising the high standard of episcopal duty set by Bishop Samuel Wilberforce of Oxford and Winchester offer the obvious comparison with Gilbert Burnet of Sarum during the reigns of William III and Anne. Yet that indefatigable pastor anticipated in his own person and diocese most of the reforms of Wilberforce more than a full century later, in regard to confirmation tours, regular and frequent preaching in the parish churches of his jurisdiction, the solemn observance of ordination embertides, the personal examination of candidates and the emphasis upon the pastoral office, and even the attempted establishment of a theological college to remedy the evident defects of a system which brought young men direct from graduation at the universities to the charge of a cure of souls without preparation or apprenticeship. Burnet was a staunch whig and Latitudinarian divine, and as a bishop outstanding amongst the prelacy of his generation. But the survey presented of the office and work of a bishop, as interpreted and discharged in typical ordinations and confirmation tours of other eighteenth-century bishops, would seem to justify the conclusion that they endeavoured faithfully and diligently to grapple with the formidable problems attending their ecclesiastical administration and pastoral oversight, in accordance both with the standards of their day and the difficulties of their situation. In neither of these two respects were their customs or obstacles of their own creation. The tradition which retained them in the capital for the greater part of each year, though emphasised in that century by the increased importance of parliamentary attendance, was by no means peculiar to their generation, but rather an inheritance from medieval times, reinforced by the Stuart precedent of attending on the counsel and service of the sovereign at his court. In like manner the practical problems of the extent of many dioceses, the remoteness of others, the impossibility of travel into country districts during the season of ill-weather, the restriction of the means of conveyance to the horse or coach, and the necessity to consult the avocations of the laity, were such as to impose severe restrictions upon episcopal itineraries.

The improvement of roads and especially the invention of railways, combined with the subdivision of dioceses and the restoration of bishops suffragan, in the nineteenth century made possible different standards of pastoral oversight on the part of the episcopate. No verdict upon the bishops of eighteenth-century England which regards them in isolation from their predecessors of Stuart days, or ignores the vast changes wrought in the times of their successors in means of transport, can claim historical justice or proper impartiality.

More vulnerable was the practice of the Georgian age to regard some sees as the providentially appointed portion of younger sons of the temporal nobility. Yet even in this respect it should not be forgotten that the tradition of the nobility to accord their patronage to divines of parts and ability, albeit of humble birth and narrow circumstances, opened a real, if restricted, career to talents and an avenue to preferment in the Church. The episcopate which numbered amongst its personnel Potter, Gibson, Warburton, and Hurd, to name but a few, did not deny even the highest stations to the poor scholar of talent. The invasion of the dignities of the Church by scions of the noble houses was a characteristic trait of the eighteenth century, reflecting alike the settled condition of society and the assured place allowed in its traditions to the Established Church. Without doubt some of the aristocratic prelates were not of outstanding merit either in erudition or devotion; but it should not be forgotten that nobility of birth was in itself no disqualification for piety. Bishop Keppel, who rose to the episcopal dignity by the influence of his brother Lord Albemarle, combined with his own ambition, proved a not unworthy bishop in Devon and Cornwall. Shute Barrington's rise was even more rapid and noteworthy; yet his episcopate was characterised by a fervent piety and pastoral zeal. Upon his translation to Durham in 1791 he assured Bishop Hurd that he considered "fortune and patronage as trusts for which he must be responsible", and expressed the aspiration that the idea might "never be absent from his mind".[1] In his administration of that see he achieved a reputation "for the exemplary discharge of his duties, for piety and well-regulated benevolence"; and during his residence there for more than a generation until his death in 1826 "he was venerated for his blameless character, his well-regulated life, his unostentatious hospitality, his attention to every petition, his unaffected humility, and his unbounded liberality".[2] The tributes of a chaplain may err indeed on the

[1] Bp. Barrington to Hurd, 23 June 1791. Hurd MSS. vol. iii, Sect. 4, No. 2.
[2] *Theological Works of the first Viscount Barrington: with a brief Memoir of his son, the Bishop of Durham* (ed. G. Townsend), i, pp. xlvi, xlix (3 vols. 1828).

side of charity; but the organisation of the bishop's daily course testified to his piety and deep religious convictions. Being called at 7 o'clock each morning, after completion of his toilet he devoted the time until breakfast to devotional reading and private prayer, concluding his exercises with family prayers at 9.15 a.m., after which the repast was served. The middle portions of the day were usually occupied in the necessary ecclesiastical and social business of his office; but in the evening at 8 p.m. "the bishop ended the day as he had begun it, by the perusal of devotional books or by private meditation and prayer" until the corporate evening prayers of the household at 9.45 p.m.[1] Such an apportionment of time belonged to the spacious leisure of a byegone age, when bishops deemed it sufficient evidence of industry to write from two to nine letters daily. But though it is evident that the aristocratic tradition of the eighteenth century tended overmuch to regard the episcopate as in some sort its private property, the occurrence of such pastoral and pious examples as Barrington must be reckoned in weighing praise and censure.

The episcopate escaped indeed the worst influences of the contemporary practice to determine promotion to the dignities of the Church by relationship to or dependence upon some nobleman or by political services done to a minister of state. The full weight of this evil custom fell upon the cathedrals, and especially upon the simple prebends, which afforded ample ground for the exercise of the rival pretensions of the temporal nobility and the servants of the crown. In the nomination to the dignities and prebends of the cathedral and collegiate churches the complaint could certainly be substantiated that preferment waited upon social connection rather than upon merit or piety.

> Church ladders are not always mounted best
> By learned clerks, and Latinists professed.
> The exalted prize demands an upward look,
> Not to be found by poring on a book.
> Small skill in Latin, and still less in Greek,
> Is more than adequate to all I seek.
> Let erudition grace him, or not grace,
> I give the bauble but the second place.
> His wealth, fame, honours, all that I intend,
> Subsist and centre in one point—a friend.
> A friend, whate'er he studies or neglects,
> Shall give him consequence, heal all defects.

[1] *Theological Works of the first Viscount Barrington, with a brief Memoir of his son, the Bishop of Durham* (ed. G. Townsend), i, pp. lii–lv.

> His intercourse with peers and sons of peers—
> There dawns the splendour of his future years.
> In that bright quarter his propitious skies
> Shall blush betimes, and there his glory rise.[1]

The results of the haphazard method of appointment prevailing in relation to cathedral offices were unfortunate alike from the standpoint of the ecclesiastical administration of those churches and from that of the hungry host of chaplains avid for prebendal stalls. In no sphere was the need of reform more evident and urgent than in the related fields of prebends and the spiritual retainers of the nobility. In an age when the education of the sons of the aristocracy was conducted by a domestic tutor and chaplain, the need for such clerks was manifest, and the possibilities of a conscientious discharge of their pedagogic duties were worthy. But for the army of titular chaplains, whose appointment to such office was purely nominal, no defence could be urged. Even in regard to the individuals concerned, their situation was productive less of virtue and piety than of worldliness and intrigue. "Preferments when conferred by the great on their dependents are not so properly favours as debts," observed Hurd; "a course of years spent in servitude is the price they pay for such things; and when promotion comes at last, it comes in the way of recompense, not of obligation. Would not any one laugh to hear of a slave's gratitude to his master?"[2] Nor was the character of a reward entailing few real duties proper in its turn to evoke the cultivation of those finer attributes of temper which a long period of solicitation and servitude had suppressed.

Beneath the fortunate clergy who possessed a pluralism of prebends and benefices with cure of souls stood the numerical majority of the priesthood whose office was the fulfilment of the parochial and pastoral ministry of the Church. Some of their company, like James Woodforde at Weston, presented to rectories or vicarages of considerable revenues, lived in contentment and peace, aspiring

> not to higher name
> Than sober clerks of moderate talents claim,
> Gravely to pray and reverendly to preach.[3]

But for the less fortunate of their brethren, the incumbents of benefices of an annual income of £50 or less, or even from £50 to £100, few consolations sweetened the obscurity and relative poverty of their lot.

---

[1] W. Cowper, *Tirocinium: or A Review of Schools*.

[2] F. Kilvert, *Life of Hurd*, pp. 82–3.

[3] G. Crabbe, *The Squire and the Priest*.

More depressed still, the unnumbered host of the curacy of the realm, eking out a scanty subsistence by serving the cures of two or three non-resident incumbents, sustained a precarious and uncertain living without hope of reward or advancement. Between the affluent minority of pluralist clergy and the majority of clerks passing rich on £50 a year, and counting £80 wealth abounding, there was a deep gulf fixed. Nor did the conscience of the century find the spectacle of such inequalities afflicting. During the last quarter of the epoch indeed the revenues of most benefices and also the salaries of curates showed a considerable and comforting appreciation, though it should be remembered that even so late as 1835 the average of curates' stipends was only £81, and that 3528 livings were still of the value of less than £150 per annum. The existence of a residuum of degraded and outcast clergy was an inevitable consequence of a system, described truly as a lottery, which allowed an unregulated host of poor scholars from the universities to enter each year into Holy Orders without regard to the number of benefices available for their preferment. To the ill-favoured, whose pristine, albeit uncertain, hope of securing a small prize waned into the hard reality of drawing a perpetual series of blanks, the philosophy of the age offered the sparse consolation that the poverty of their original circumstances fitted them for that of their profession, and that if their standard of living approximated to that of the rustic peasants, so most probably did the *angusta domi* of their birth. To the vast majority of parochial clergy whose lack of influence denied them the coveted pluralities, solitude and isolation were the common conditions of their estate. "Were I required to comprise my advice to young clergymen in one sentence", declared Archdeacon Paley, "it should be in this, Learn to live alone"; a lesson which, if not learnt in youth, would be enforced by the discipline of years.

With the progressive spread of pluralism and non-residence throughout the century, from above in the accumulation of preferments by the privileged minority and from below by the pressure to combine two or more benefices productive of small annual revenues, little surprise may be evoked by the comparatively low standards of parochial duty. The customary round of public worship, embracing the performance of Divine Service with sermon once per Sunday, or as a maximum twice (though the second service would lack the attraction of a sermon), the quarterly Sacrament, and the administration of the Occasional Offices as needed, may be deemed indeed severely inadequate from the standpoint of a later epoch, but was accepted as sufficient and satisfactory according to the traditions of that age. Within its framework the faithful laity of Georgian England sought and found sustenance for their souls, and consolation in prospect of their eternal destiny. To foreign visitors, bred in the warmer churchmanship of Popish countries, the Anglican interpretation of Christianity and the religious obligations required of its adherents seemed frigid and unexacting by comparison. In the diary of *A Frenchman in England* the Marquis de la Rochefoucauld recorded pertinent and interesting reflections upon the clergy and laity of the country which he visited in 1784.

In the matter of belief they differ very little from us. They do not believe either in the transubstantiation of the Body and Blood of Jesus Christ in the Sacrament of the Eucharist, or in the authority which God has given to the pope as the visible head of the Church, or in the intercession of Saints, or in the power of the priest to remit sins. Such are the main points in our religion which they do not accept. The rest is common to both. Their religion enjoins upon them the practice of the virtues, as does ours; and so a virtuous man anywhere will be a man of good and sound religion. As to the way in which the English practise their religion, it is much more easy-going than ours. They do not go to confession, they go to the Holy Table very rarely. When they do so, they go in a different spirit; they do not believe (as I have already said) that they receive the Body of Jesus Christ, but they approach the Holy Table as an act of commemoration. They are not under an obligation to go to church every Sunday through rain or fog or heat—a very slight excuse will keep them away; but they are under an obligation to read the Bible as often as they can. It is in this book that children learn and grown-up people perfect their reading.[1]

The impressions formed by a stranger and based upon a short visit may not be regarded as an authoritative index to the religious customs of the Church of England in the Hanoverian age, for it would be evidently impossible for the distinguished French nobleman to perceive for example such items as the devout preparation of Dr Johnson for the reception of the Holy Eucharist. But many of the features outlined in the marquis' diary reflect faithfully the dominant characteristics of contemporary churchmanship. He remarked the voluntary nature of confession, noting that since it was not enforced as a compulsory discipline its practice was rare, and hazarding the guess that "not more than one Englishman in ten thousand will make his confession".[2] By reason of the infrequent administration of the Communion and the rarity of

---

[1] *A Frenchman in England* (tr. S. C. Roberts), pp. 83–4.
[2] *Ibid.* p. 86.

private confession, he drew a sharp contrast between the exercise of the priestly vocation in the churches of France and England.

> The ministers of this religion are not occupied in the same way as ours, whose most laborious tasks are hearing confessions, carrying the Blessed Sacrament into the country by day or night, and so on. The parishes too are much larger than in France, and the duties are performed by a rector, who corresponds to the French *curé*. He is paid by means of tithe and has a house, a garden, and several acres of land. . . . Generally speaking the position of a rector is well worth having and the rectors themselves are men of some merit.[1]

The sombre fear of death which characterised English religion in the eighteenth century (being notable even in a man of so serious a piety as Dr Johnson) struck the observant mind of the visitor, as reflected especially in the mournful aspect of funerals. But his conclusion remained firm in its persuasion of the facility with which an Anglican churchman might discharge the duties of his faith. "From this short review, it may be clearly seen how easy it is for the English to fulfil the obligations of their religion. Nothing could be simpler—they have no fasts, no fish-days, no Lent; even their Sunday service is not obligatory."[2]

In good measure the justice of this criticism of contemporary standards must be admitted. It would be vain to pretend that churchmanship in the Hanoverian age was of a mystical or other-worldly character; or even that within the sphere of earthly citizenship it exalted the heroic virtues and called for asceticism and self-denial. Like the epoch of which it was born, it was prosaic and calculating, conceived as a prudent investment promising assured blessings both temporal and celestial. The doctrine of moderation showed to least advantage when applied to religion, and the virtues upon which it laid chief emphasis were those of self-control, temperance, and rational conduct, such indeed as were native and necessary to a century of commercial prosperity and the acquisition of wealth. Yet beneath the apparently superficial exercises of religious duty, in addition to the deep devotion of Dr Johnson there should not be forgotten the restrained piety of Viscount Percival, nor the sincere churchmanship of the duke of Newcastle, whose private prayers indicate the unrecognised possibility that even a whig may be devout. Despite the undue simplification of theology by the eighteenth-century temper, the popular doctrine of the Fatherhood of God enabled many to lay hold upon the assurance of the trustworthiness of the Divine character and action, from which they drew strength and con-

---

[1] *A Frenchman in England*, pp. 92–3.   [2] *Ibid.* p. 91.

fidence amidst the circumstances of this world. Archbishop Herring testified, in relation to the ephemeral religious emotion stirred amongst the careless and worldly-minded of his day by the catastrophe of the Lisbon earthquake, that "he was a great friend to the wisdom of taking hold of these awakening instances of Divine Power, but were he to choose his good man, it would be he who is steadily so upon contemplation of the regular course of nature, the rising and setting of the sun, the return of the seasons, and the stability, not the shaking of the earth". At its best the Latitudinarian teaching delivered its adherents from unworthy and superstitious notions of God by its emphasis upon the witness borne to His nature by the order of the created universe and by the doctrine of His Fatherhood proclaimed in the Gospel, so that its evangel prepared men with fortitude to resign their souls into the hands of a Maker whose mercy is even as His majesty.

To one aspect of the achievement of the Hanoverian Church full justice has been done by historians, namely to its intellectual services in the debate with deism and the assault of infidelity. The fulfilment of this task was perhaps the abiding contribution of the church of that age to the fullness of the history of the Christian Society. For the attack made upon the foundations of revelation was of a character hitherto not experienced by the defenders of orthodox theology. To their apology neither the patristic erudition of Bull nor the Biblical strength of Chillingworth availed anything; since the new vogue of natural religion reckoned little of the authority of either Church or Scriptures. Its insistence upon the sufficiency of natural religion without the supplementary aid of revelation, and its confidence in the superiority of the common religious beliefs of Man to the particular doctrines of Christianity, constituted a novel challenge to all Christian believers, and demanded new canons of defence. Amongst the divines of the eighteenth century therefore the names of Butler, Conyers Middleton, Warburton, and Paley, followed by the lesser writers such as Sherlock, Waterland, and Chandler, have received chief recognition and praise for their several parts in the battle against deists and freethinkers. From a general depreciation of revelation, the critics advanced to a specific denial of the prophecies of the Old Testament concerning the advent of the Messiah and of the miracles wrought by Jesus of Nazareth in proof of His Christhood. This criticism took the form alike of objections to the primitive moral standards of the Deity of the Jewish Covenant and of attacks upon the honesty and integrity of the Evangelists of the New Testament. In reply to these contentions Butler demonstrated conclusively the liability of the deist position to the same assaults to which its champions had subjected Christianity, and proceeded then upon the basis of his maxim that probability is the very guide of life to indicate the sufficiency of the evidences for revelation. In an age which preferred certainty and assurance to probability and moderation the works of Warburton were perhaps more appetising, for he delighted in confident assertion and paradox. His purpose was to turn the flank of the deists' attack by proving that the very circumstance which they hailed as conclusive in their favour, the absence of a doctrine of individual immortality from the early religion of the Hebrews, was itself the sign of its divine origin since no system of human invention could have subsisted under such a defect.

Humbler tasks attended the pens of Waterland and Chandler, who essayed defences of the orthodox interpretation of the prophecies, and even of Sherlock, whose contribution to evidential literature, the *Trial of the Witnesses*, became a model of contemporary apologetic in behalf of the honesty and credibility of the evangelical records of the Resurrection. Both critics and defenders of orthodoxy were hampered by their bondage to a literal theory of Biblical inspiration, which allowed no possibility of error of detail in the Sacred Writings and by consequence reduced deists to attacking the moral probity of their authors and churchmen into defences of their integrity. From this impasse Conyers Middleton endeavoured to rescue the debate, professedly in the interest of revelation, though with doubtful success. He challenged indeed the notion of the literal inspiration and complete accuracy of the Bible, and investigated also the grounds of differentiation between true and false miracles; but his feet were set upon slippery paths in both adventures. To an age lacking the magic key of an evolutionary conception of the development of religious dogma the idea that a *tertium quid* might be established between the absolute inerrancy of the Scriptures and deliberate forgery on the part of their authors was as uncongenial as revolutionary; whilst the zeal of Protestants to accept the miracles of Christ and His apostles though rejecting those claimed for ecclesiastical saints by papists found a doubtful ally in Middleton's arguments. His writings achieved indeed the distinction of facilitating the conversion of the youthful Gibbon to Roman Catholicism, by impressing him with a persuasion of the continuance of miraculous powers in the Church during the first four or five centuries of Christianity; but it may be perceived that the real influence of Middleton's principles found a logical extension in Gibbon's later survey of the history of the Christian Church in *The Decline and Fall of the Roman Empire*. Towards the end of the century its series of controversies were summarised by

Archdeacon Paley, who surveyed the ground covered by the disputes and collected the theological systems of the age, basing his structure upon natural religion, and erecting thereupon the fabric of revelation, supported by proofs of the miracles of the New Testament and of the authenticity of its component writings. Paley represented the consummation of the apologetic and evidential studies of the epoch with singular clarity and force.

The acknowledgment accorded to the intellectual defence of revelation by the divines of the Hanoverian Church has been attended by much censure upon those of their number who declined into heterodox opinions in the course of attempted justifications of orthodoxy. The indifference of Richard Watson to the issues involved in the Athanasian and Arian controversies concerning the doctrine of the Trinity, and his proposals for a thorough reformation of the Liturgy and Articles, were however no mere eccentricities of a self-taught professor. They proceeded rather from a genuine and intelligible desire to retain the adherence of the educated laity of the nation to the communion of the Established Church by removing all occasions of intellectual offence. For the deist movement was no tradition of the academy and of the schools. In the person of its characteristic apostle, Thomas Paine, the stay-maker of Norfolk and the constitution-framer of the United States of America, it was presented as the new religion of democracy, needing neither church nor priesthood, but making every man his own divine and casuist, and basing its appeal upon a rationalistic criticism of the Bible. In the face of such widespread assault, the gravity of the situation appeared to dictate to the orthodox the necessity of a strategy of concentration; of which the fundamental principles were the abandonment of such credal statements as the Athanasian symbol, which were beyond the comprehension of Paine's common man, and the expression of confessional articles in the *ipsissima verba* of the Scriptures. It is manifestly unreasonable and unscientific to allege the surprising parallels between the guesses of Paine concerning the literary and historical problems of the Bible and the accepted conclusions of modern Biblical scholarship as evidence of the insight and ability of the deists; nor is it more equitable and just to censure Samuel Clarke and Watson for their inability to conceive that theological dogmas fashioned in post-apostolic ages might be more accurately framed and expressed than definitions couched only in terms of the Biblical writers. The attitude of the school of Clarke and Watson made shipwreck indeed of the proportion of catholic faith; but they lacked Newman's doctrine of development, and combined therewith a disdain of patristic theology.

This contempt of theologians for patristic studies was typical of the general temper of their age towards the heritage of the past. Few centuries have been possessed of so high a degree of self-confidence, of assurance of their own superior wisdom, and of profound neglect of the accumulated experience of humanity as the age of common sense. The children of the *aufklärung* rejoiced in the day and generation of their birth. For historic monuments they had often a scorn and ridicule, which they were at little pains to conceal in act or speech. Gilbert Burnet, beholding the glories of the cathedral of Milan, pronounced it to have "nothing to commend it of architecture, being built in the rude Gothic manner". Towards the history and achievement of the ages of faith even less compliment was paid. Thomas Paine believed that "the Christian system laid all waste; and if we take our stand about the middle of the sixteenth century, we look back through that long chasm to the times of the ancients as over a vast sandy desert, in which not a shrub appears to intercept the vision of the fertile hills beyond". Nor were these sentiments the effusion of plebeian ignorance. The historian Hume led his contemporaries into an estimate of the middle ages which had little of commendation or appreciation. "In a striking passage of his *History* Hume pictures the interval between Augustus and the Renaissance as a great trough or depression, in which humanity wallowed for more than a thousand years, a prey to ignorance, barbarism, and superstition."[1] In his verdict upon Thomas Becket he lamented the irrational tributes of praise bestowed "on the memory of pretended saints, whose whole conduct was probably to the last degree odious and contemptible, and whose industry was entirely directed to the pursuit of objects pernicious to mankind".[2] The utmost concession made to the middle ages was his grudging allowance that the administrative talents and worldly ambitions of churchmen mitigated somewhat the chaos and rude manners of a barbarous epoch. "Though the religion of that age can merit no better name than that of superstition, it served to unite together a body of men who had great sway over the people, and who kept the community from falling to pieces by the factions and independent power of the nobles."[3] Consequently the chief profit of the study of medieval history was to enhance the repute of the age of enlightenment; for "if the aspect of some periods seems horrid and deformed, we may learn thence to cherish with the greater anxiety that science and civility which have so close a connection with virtue and

---

[1] J. B. Black, *The Art of History*, p. 87.
[2] Hume, *History of England*, i, 421–2 (8 vols. 1782).
[3] *Ibid.* ii, 157.

humanity, and which, as it is a sovereign remedy against superstition, is also the most effective remedy against vice and disorder of every kind".[1]

In full consonance with this temper, Warburton described "church sanctity", as practised by monks and hermits, as none other than a fruitful parent of "all the follies of superstition or fanaticism"; and Herring echoed the prejudices of the age in his offer to consent freely to the translation of the remains of Anselm of Canterbury to Aosta, with the observation that "he had no great scruples on this head; but if he had, he would get rid of them all, if the parting with the rotten remains of a rebel to his king, a slave to the popedom, and an enemy to the married clergy (all this Anselm was), would purchase ease and indulgence to one living Protestant".[2] The kindness of the primate's heart in his genuine zeal to save fellow Christians from persecution, (since he "believed a condescension in this business might facilitate the way of doing it to thousands"), did him more credit than the judgment of his head upon the services of one of the greatest of his predecessors in the chair of Augustine; though it may be noted in palliation of his attitude that he so scorned the superstition of the king of Sardinia, who coveted the relics, as to be quite willing "to make no conscience of palming on the simpletons any other old bishop with the name of Anselm". From the standpoint of such an epoch the rehabilitation of the middle ages in the novels of Scott seemed distant and chimerical indeed.

The dawn of the Romantic Revival lay yet below the horizon of the eighteenth century; and had the signs of its advent been perceived, they would have suffered contemptuous dismissal as another manifestation and expression of that "enthusiasm" which was the bugbear of its course. To the sympathetic feeling for nature and the appreciation of the place of the emotions in the economy of human personality, instinct in the poetry of Wordsworth, the age of common sense was wholly insensible. Neither admiration nor understanding of the beauties of mountain scenery characterised its temperament, a circumstance adding to the unpopularity of the dioceses of North Wales, where even Zachary Pearce, as he rode amidst the grandeur of Snowdonia, reflected upon its correspondence with the habitat of the fallen angels in *Paradise Lost*. More alien still from the rationalism of the Georgian epoch was the revival of supernaturalism in the poetry of Coleridge, or the romantic reconstruction of medieval life in the prose writings of Scott.

[1] Hume, *History of England*, iii, 297.
[2] Herring to Dean Lynch, 23 Dec. 1752. H.M.C. Various Collections, i, 226.

Towards the entire complex of feelings enumerated by Newman as "especially called catholic", of which he found evidence in the literary works of all these writers and of which he believed the Church of Rome to be the providential conservator, the temper of the age of enlightenment exhibited repugnance and hostility. In consequence it found that church an incomprehensible phenomenon, save as an oppressive and corrupt political system. "I have always regarded Popery", declared Warburton to the earl of Chatham, "rather as an impious and impudent combination against the sense and rights of mankind than as a species of religion."[1] In which sentiment, as in many other respects, he but gave expression, in pointed phrase peculiar to his genius, to the general opinion of his generation.

The eighteenth century was not wholly unresponsive to the nobler impulses of the spirit nor neglectful of the cultivation of the arts. It was an era fecund in musical composition, especially in church music, and in the practice of campanology. In addition to the manifold fruit of the genius of Handel which may be said to have been naturalised in England, the epoch embraced the full careers of such composers as William Boyce, Maurice Greene, William Croft, John Blow, and Thomas Norris, whilst it may claim some share in Samuel Wesley, Thomas Attwood, and William Crotch who belonged to its later years; all of whom still find representation in quires and places where the Anglican musical tradition is treasured. Nor may the impressive testimony to the humanitarian spirit of the Hanoverian times expressed in the foundations of twelve new hospitals in London, of the hospitals of the university towns, and of the ubiquitous county hospitals throughout the extent of the realm, be forgotten, since they remain as an abiding monument to the power of that belief in the Divine Benevolence to which the entire Christian doctrine of God had been reduced in popular estimate.

Of the typical Latitudinarian churchmanship dominant in the century it may be affirmed, in contemporary phrase, that "practical Christianity was its talent and delight". Its faith was testified in conduct and works; and in its regard for practical religion it attached little weight to membership of any particular visible church, deeming "that if we should be shut out of heaven for our sins, it will be no great comfort to us what church we were members of on earth". The chief contrast indeed between the eighteenth century and the Oxford Movement which succeeded it lay in their respective valuations of the corporate Christian society. In part the indifference of the former age to organised church-

[1] *Chatham Correspondence*, ii, 189 (14 Nov. 1762).

manship was a reaction against the theological squabbles of the seventeenth century, from which Archbishop Tenison himself drew the conclusion and warning "that at home and abroad we were in danger of losing Christianity in the name of the Church". The injunction of Tillotson that "charity is above rubrics" became a maxim congenial to the times; and the slight esteem of points of church order and polity found expression in a variety of ways. In Hoadly's notorious sermon the authority of the visible society was wholly dissolved into an unrestrained liberty of individual judgment; and Paley defended the threefold ministry of the church as consonant with the divisions of contemporary society. No better measure of the gulf severing the Latitudinarian from the Tractarian positions can be found than the comparison of Paley's consecration sermon, *A Distinction of Orders in the Church defended upon the Ground of Public Utility* delivered in 1782, with that of Liddon at the consecration of King and Bickersteth in 1885 declaring the apostolic succession and the necessity of episcopacy to a true branch of the Church. In exterior ceremonies the eighteenth century was similarly unchurchly; for in addition to the comment provoked by Butler's superimposition of a cross upon the Holy Table of his chapel at Bristol, even Tenison was accounted to have suspicious high-church leanings because within his household at Lambeth "he bowed at going into chapel and at the name of Jesus, obliged his family to a great strictness in prayers, let his chaplains say grace, and seemed to mind little in his family more than that they strictly conformed to the church services and ceremonies".[1] With such indifference as to principles of church order and liturgy it was natural that the opinion of the age should adopt a prosaic conception of the nature of the Kingdom or Church of Christ. Thus it came to pass that Warburton found no incongruity in comparing the Church, not to that Jerusalem from above which is free, nor to the bride of Christ without spot or wrinkle, but to the society, predominantly unclean, of the Ark of Noah. "The Church," he observed to Hurd with characteristic pungency and indelicacy of phrase, "like the Ark of Noah, is worth saving; not for the sake of the unclean beasts and vermin that almost filled it, and probably made most noise and clamour in it; but for the little corner of rationality that was as much distressed by the stink within as by the tempest without."[2]

Such sentiments were in no wise inconsistent in the judgment of eighteenth-century divines with a sincere devotion to and laudation of

[1] Wake to Charlett, 15 Aug. 1695. Ballard MSS. iii, f. 14.
[2] *Letters of a Late Eminent Prelate*, Letter xlvi, p. 114.

the contemporary Church of England. Warburton himself insisted emphatically that the Christian Church was a society sovereign and independent by its own nature, and lacking nothing to the completeness of its existence as such; and at the same time he exulted in the condition of the English Church, "where the national religion is on a footing exactly agreeable to the nature of a free convention between church and state on the principles of the laws of nature and nations, a felicity that scarce any other people on the face of the earth can boast of".[1] The *Ecclesia Anglicana* of the eighteenth century indeed was the heir by affiliation of the Caroline epoch which preceded it, though its chief virtues were differently conceived and appraised. It retained its continuity of tradition with the Church of which Sancroft affirmed that

if there be now in the world a church to whom that eulogium, that she is a lily among thorns, is due and proper, it is this church of which we are members, as it stands reformed now and established amongst us; the purest certainly upon earth, as being purified from those corruptions and abuses which the lapse of times, the malice of the devil, and the wickedness of men had introduced insensibly into the doctrine and worship and government of it.[2]

In like manner could John Sharp testify his affection and faith in it as

undoubtedly both as to doctrine and worship, the purest church that is at this day in the world; the most orthodox in faith, and the freest on the one hand from idolatry and superstition; and on the other hand from freakishness and enthusiasm of any now extant. Nay, he would further say, with great seriousness and as one that expected to be called to account at the dreadful tribunal of God, for what he now said, if he did not speak in sincerity, that he did in his conscience believe, that if the religion of Jesus Christ, as it is delivered in the New Testament, be the true religion, then the communion of the Church of England is a safe way of salvation, and the safest way of any he knew in the world.[3]

To the principles of these testimonies of high-church prelates concerning the orthodoxy and apostolicity of the English Church its confessors of the eighteenth century would have assented fully, though their phraseology would have differed and their emphasis lain upon other aspects of its character. Peradventure their appreciation of its genius may find its best expression in the words of one of its laity, Edmund Burke; who, in his speech on the petition of the Unitarians, set before

---

[1] Warburton, *The Alliance between Church and State*, p. 91.
[2] G. D'Oyly, *Life of Sancroft*, i, 166–7.
[3] T. Sharp, *Life of Archbishop John Sharp*, i, 354.

churchmen an ideal of the Church no less than a defence of its establishment; and by loyalty to which ideal the *Ecclesia Anglicana* of his age may consent not unworthily to be judged in the operation of its endeavours to work out its own salvation and that of its generation.

If you think it to be an invaluable blessing, a way fully sufficient to nourish a manly, rational, solid, and at the same time humble piety; if you find it well fitted to the frame and pattern of your civil constitution; if you find it a barrier against fanaticism, infidelity, and atheism; if you find that it furnishes support to the human mind in the afflictions and distresses of the world, consolation in sickness, pain, poverty, and death; if it dignifies our nature with the hope of immortality, leaves enquiry free, whilst it preserves an authority to teach, where authority only can teach, *communia altaria, aeque ac patriam, diligite, colite, fovete.*[1]

[1] E. Burke, "Speech on the Petition of the Unitarians", 11 May 1792.

APPENDIX A

I. CONFIRMATION TOURS OF BISHOP WAKE AT LINCOLN

Date	Place	Number confirmed	
	Leicestershire		
1709. 31 May	Harborough	800	
2 June	Loughborough	600	
4	Leicester, St Margaret's	500	3100
5	Leicester, St Martin's	400	
6	Melton Mowbray	800	
	Lincolnshire		
7 June	Grantham	1200	
16, 18, 19	Lincoln Cathedral	800	
21	Caister	600	
23	Louth	500	5200
25, 26	Horncastle	600	
28	Boston	1000	
30	Stamford	500	
	Huntingdonshire		
5, 6 July	Huntingdon, All Saints'	250	750
31	Stilton and Glatton	500	
	Bedfordshire		
7 August	Blonham	550	
30	Bedford	200	900
31	Ampthill	150	
	Buckinghamshire		
2 Sept.	Bletchley	550	
2	Buckingham	400	1250
5	Aylesbury	200	
7	Beaconsfield	100	
	Oxfordshire		
4 Sept.	Banbury	800	
	Hertfordshire		
9 Sept.	Welwyn	150	350
11	Hitchin	200	
	Huntingdonshire		
18 Sept.	Kimbolton	450	

Total: 12,800

	Date		Place	Number confirmed		
1712.	22 May		Hertford	*circ.*	500	
	23		Baldock	*circ.*	450	
	25		Wheathamstead	*circ.*	150	1600
	26		Welwyn	*circ.*	100	
	27		Hemel Hemstead	*pl.*	400	
	28		Agmondesham	*circ.*	530	
	29		*Idem*	*circ.*	110	
	30		Aylesbury	*circ.*	300	2280
	31		Stoke Hammond	*circ.*	340	
	1 June		Leighton Beau-Desert	*circ.*	500	
	2		Stony Stratford	*circ.*	500	
	4		Ampthill	*circ.*	250	750
	6		Bedford	*circ.*	500	
	17		Huntingdon	*circ.*	130	210
	19		*Idem*	*circ.*	80	
	25		Lutterworth	*pl.*	600	
	26		Colesbach		23	
	27		Leicester	*circ.*	160	2283
	28		Swepston	*pl.*	700	
	29		Leicester	*pl.*	500	
	30		*Idem*	*circ.*	300	
	2 July		Folkingham	*circ.*	500	
	4		Sleaford		765	
	6		Lincoln	*circ.*	332	
	9		*Idem*		507	
	11		*Idem*		273	
	13		*Idem*	*circ.*	800	6707
	14		Gainsborough	*circ.*	830	
	15		Epworth	*pl.*	800	
	16		Barton	*pl.*	600	
	17		Caister	*pl.*	1000	
	19		Louth	*pl.*	300	
	20		*Idem*	*pl.*	900	
	21		Alford	*pl.*	850	4500
	22		Horncastle	*pl.*	750	
	24		Spalding	*Fere*	2000	

Total: 18,330

II. CONFIRMATION TOURS OF BISHOP HURD
AT WORCESTER

	Date	Place	Number confirmed
1782.	20 July	Shipston	2000
	21 (Sunday)	Warwick (town only)	240
	22	*Idem*	300
	23	Aulcester	1200
	24	Kidderminster	550
	26	Pershore	600
	27	Upton	480
	28 (Sunday)	Worcester Cathedral	270
	29	*Idem*	320
	2 August	Dudley	290
	4 (Sunday)	Hartlebury	240

Total: 6490

1785.	21 August (Sunday)	Stratford (town)	200
	22	*Idem*	600
	23	Henley	400
	24	Bromsgrove	1000
	26	Pershore	400
	28 (Sunday)	Worcester Cathedral	250
	29	*Idem*	400
	30	Evesham	300
	1 Sept.	Droitwich	250
	13	Old Swinford	1200
	18	Hartlebury	260

Total: 5260

1788.	10 June	Shipston	900
	11	Kineton	1000
	12	Warwick	1100
	13	Alcester	1200
	14	Pershore	600
	16	Upton	700
	17	Worcester Cathedral	1000
	20	Kidderminster	500
	22 (Sunday)	Hartlebury	300
	27	Hales Owen	900

Total: 8200

Date		Place	Number confirmed
1792.	31 May	Worcester, St Helen's Church	988
	2 June	Upton	440
	4	Pershore	720
	5	Evesham	592
	7	Shipston	700
	8	Stratford	1022
	9	Henley	692
	11	Bromsgrove	1850
	12	Kidderminster	286
	14	Old Swinford	1248
	17	Hartlebury	407

Total: 8945

1795.	27 May	Worcester Cathedral	713
	28	Upton	650
	1 June	Pershore	609
	3	Shipston	512
	4	Warwick	608
	5	Stratford	300
	6	Alcester	602
	8	Bromsgrove	883
	10	Old Swinford	513
	14 (Sunday)	Hartlebury	404

Total: 5794

1799.	26 May (Sunday)	Hartlebury	393
	28	Hales Owen	426
	31	Kidderminster	305
	3 June	Bromsgrove	1069
	4	Alcester	827
	5	Stratford	653
	6	Warwick	697
	7	Shipston	751
	10	Worcester Cathedral	1152
	11	Upton	512
	13	Pershore	679

Total: 7464

1805.	First Part by the Bishop of Chester		
	27 March	Stratford	1283
	28	Bromsgrove	1785
	29	Hales Owen	826
	Second Part by Bishop of Hereford		
	14 June	Worcester	1441
	15	Pershore	830
	17	Kidderminster	1019

Total: 7184

III. CONFIRMATIONS IN THE DIOCESE OF EXETER

Date	Place	Number confirmed

A. Bishop Keppel 1764

Date	Place	Number confirmed	
Thursday 17 May	Honiton	399	1785
Friday 18	*Idem*	1386	
Wednesday 23 May	Tiverton (forenoon)	644	
	(afternoon)	528	1762
Thursday 24	*Idem*	590	
Saturday 26	South Molton		1414[1]
Sunday 27	Barnstaple	252	
Monday 28	*Idem*	919	
Tuesday 29	*Idem* (forenoon)	1293	2496
	(afternoon)	32	
Wednesday 30	Bideford		1314
Thursday 31	Torrington	783	
Saturday 2 June	*Idem*	1030	2079
Sunday 3	*Idem*	266	
Tuesday 5	Okehampton	496	1362
Wednesday 6	*Idem*	866	
Thursday 7	Tavistock (forenoon)	507	544
	(afternoon)	37	
Friday 8	Plymouth	950	1482
Saturday 9	*Idem*	532	
Tuesday 12	Totnes	1509	
Wednesday 13	*Idem*	889	4396
Thursday 14	*Idem*	1998	
Friday 15	Newton Bushel		720
Tuesday 26	Exeter	337	
Thursday 28	*Idem*	343	
Monday 2 July	*Idem*	620	
Tuesday 3	*Idem*	656	
Tuesday 10	*Idem*	380	3616
Thursday 12	*Idem*	452	
Monday 23	*Idem*	173	
Tuesday 24	*Idem*	283	
Thursday 26	*Idem*	372	
Thursday 5 July	Morchard Bishop		531
Friday 6	Shobrooke		445

Total number confirmed upon the Episcopal Visitation 1764: 23,946

[1] One by a forged ticket.

Date		Place	Number confirmed	
B. Bishop Ross 1779				
Wednesday	9 June	Exeter	514	⎫
Thursday	10	Idem	351[1]	⎬
Saturday	12	Idem	808[2]	⎭
		+ 17 tickets found since in the third day's confirmation	1690	
Saturday	19	Shobrooke	352	
Sunday	20	Morchard	71	⎫ 550
Monday	21	Idem	479	⎭
Wednesday	23	South Molton	626	
Friday	25	Barnstaple	4016[3]	
Saturday	26	Bideford	935	
Sunday	27	Torrington	539	⎫ 1640
Monday	28	Idem	1101	⎭
Wednesday	30	Okehampton	438	⎫ 1354
Thursday	1 July	Idem	916	⎭
Saturday	3	Launceston	804	⎫ 1048
Sunday	4	Idem	244	⎭
Monday	5	Camelford	454	
Tuesday	6	St Columbe	955	
Wednesday	7	Truro	248	⎫ 901
Thursday	8	Idem	653	⎭
Friday	9	Penryn	484	
Saturday	10	Helston	497	⎫ 928
Sunday	11	Idem	431	⎭
Tuesday	13	Penzance	618	
Wednesday	14	St Earth	399	
Thursday	15	Redruth	947	
Friday	16	St Austell	745	
Saturday	17	Lostwithiel	276	
Tuesday	20	Bodmin	654	
Thursday	22	Liskeard	1399	
Sunday	25	Plymouth	1479	⎫ 2024[4]
Monday	26	Idem	545	⎭
Tuesday	27	Kingsbridge	706[5]	
Thursday	29	Totnes	1464	
Friday	30	Newton Abbot	383	
Monday	27 Sept.	Tiverton	579	
1780				
Tuesday	30 May	Honiton	546	

Totals in Devon and Cornwall: 25,548 + 579 + 546 = 26,673

[1] 10 without tickets.   [2] 38 without tickets.

[3] 400 supposed to be without tickets.

[4] Without tickets supposed at least 400.

[5] Besides the number that must have been confirmed by means of the Chancellor's altering the scheme of confirming at Kingsbridge to Lodderswell after the church at Kingsbridge was filled with candidates and tickets delivered in.

Devon and Cornwall

Date		Place	Number confirmed	
1782.	19 June	Exeter	867	
	20	*Idem*	632	1499
	22	Crediton	781	
	24	Ottery St Mary	514	
	27	Tiverton	444	
	29	South Molton	492	
	2 July	Barnstaple	883	
	4	Torrington	796	
	6	Okehampton	544	
	8	Tavistock	459	
	10	Launceston	908	
	11	Camelford	240	
	12	Padstowe	324	
	15	Truro	842	
	16	Falmouth	444	
	18	Helston	530	
	20	Penzance	559	
	22	Redruth	376	
	23	St Austell	296	
	24	Lostwithiel	245	
	26	Bodmin	260	
	29	Liskeard	620	
	2 August	Plymouth	711	
	5	Totnes	1334	
	6	Newton	838	

Total: 14,939

Devon

Date		Place	Number confirmed	
1785.	31 May	Tiverton	830	
	13 July	Exeter	1147	
	14	*Idem*	647	1794
	18	Honiton	760	
	23	Crediton	552	
	24	Morchard	198	
	25	Chumleigh	578	
	27	South Molton	587	
	29	Barnstaple	1101	
	30	Bideford	732	
	2 August	Torrington	669	
	4	Okehampton	885	
	5	Tavistock	578	
	8	Plymouth	1700	
	10	Totnes	1380	
	11	Newton Bushell	812	

Total: 13,156

Cornwall

Date		Place	Number confirmed	Females	Males
1786.	5 July	Launceston	1012	518	494
	6	Camelford	315	168	147
	7	Padstowe	238	125	113
	8	St Columbe	515	251	264
	11	Truro	1051	529	522
	12	Penryn	559	331	228
	14	Helston	863	500	363
	17	Penzance	985	605	380
	18	Redruth	816	494	322
	19	St Austell	609	352	257
	20	Lostwithiel	383	206	177
	22	Bodmin	454	247	207
	25	Liskeard	1333	668	665

Total: Females: 4994

Males: 4139

9133

APPENDIX B

I. PRAYERS DRAWN UP BY BISHOP HUME FOR THE DUKE OF NEWCASTLE

O Almighty God, the Author and Preserver of my Being, to whom I owe every blessing that I have enjoyed, and on whom I depend for all my future happiness, accept the humble homage of Thy creature that lifts up his soul to Thee, not confiding in his own merit, but in Thy gracious goodness and great mercy. Thou knowest, Lord, the secrets of my heart, the weakness of my understanding and the instability of my best resolutions. O touch my heart that I may love Thee, and my understanding that I may worship Thee as I ought! Teach me to do the thing that pleaseth Thee; confirm and strengthen my weak endeavours and guide me in the way to everlasting life which Thou hast revealed and promised us through our Lord and Saviour, Jesus Christ. Amen.

A short prayer to be used Night and Morning:

Unto Thy grace and protection O Lord we commend our souls and bodies this day (or this night) and for evermore, through Jesus Christ our Lord. Amen.

(Add. MSS. 33069, f. 159.)

A Prayer of Thanksgiving

O God the Author and Preserver of my being, in whose hands are the issues of life and death, to Thee I bow down my soul in humble adoration of Thy Supreme Goodness. Thou hast raised me up from the bed of sickness; Thou hast touched my heart that I should feel Thy mercy; Thou hast restored me to health that I should live to praise Thee. But how, O Lord, can Thy poor and dependent creature adore and thank Thee as he ought. Thy mercies surpass the utmost stretch of my powers to praise Thee. O preserve me in that sense of them which Thou hast now given me, and perfect the good work which Thou hast begun in me. Confirm and strengthen every good resolution I have formed when I was in trouble, and help me to act up to them with firmness, consistency and devotion. O suffer me no longer to fluctuate through life under the divided influence of Thee and the world. But let Thy kingdom in my heart be absolute. Let Thy will be my guide to lead me and comfort me; that I may go on from strength to strength, from loving, obeying and praising Thee on earth to that everlasting state of bliss in heaven, which Thou hast promised to all that love and seek Thee. Through the merits and mediation of Thy Son, Jesus Christ our Lord. Amen.

(*Ibid.* f. 161.)

II. PAPER OF DEVOTIONS FOR THE HOLY
COMMUNION

Before the minister begins the service.

I lift up my soul to Thee, O God, humbly imploring Thy blessing upon me, and gracious assistance of me, for the holy action I am now about. Forgive my want of due preparation, and accept of my sincere desire to perform an acceptable service to Thee. Through Jesus Christ our Lord.

Before receiving of the Bread.

I am not worthy of the crumbs that fall from Thy Table.

After the receiving of it.

Greater love than this hath no man, that a man lay down his life for his friends.

Before receiving the Cup.

What shall I render to the Lord for all His blessings? I will receive the cup of salvation: I will bless the name of the Lord.

After the receiving of it.

Blessed be God for this unspeakable gift, His dearly beloved Son, Jesus Christ; in whom we have redemption through His blood, even the forgiveness of sins.

After the conclusion of the whole action.

Bless the Lord, O my soul, and all that is within me, bless His holy name. Bless the Lord, O my soul, and forget not all His benefits, who forgiveth all thine iniquities and healeth all thy diseases. Who redeemeth thy life from destruction and crowneth thee with loving kindness and tender mercies; who satisfieth thy mouth with good things. Bless the Lord, O my soul.

A prayer to be used in private afterwards

I praise and magnify Thy great and glorious name, O Lord my God, for the blessed opportunity afforded to me this day of commemorating Thy infinite goodness and mercy to me and all mankind, in sending Thy only Son into the world, to take our nature upon Him, to submit to the infirmities and miseries of it, to live among us and to die for us; and to preserve the memory of this great love and goodness of Thine to us for ever in our hearts, that Thou hast been pleased to appoint the blessed Sacrament for a solemn remembrance of it. Grant O Lord that I may faithfully keep and perform that Holy Covenant which I have this day so solemnly renewed and confirmed in Thy

Presence and at Thy Table. Let it be an eternal obligation upon me of perpetual love and obedience to Thee. Let nothing seem hard for me to do or grievous for me to suffer for Thy sake, who, whilst I was a sinner and an enemy to Thee, loved me at such a rate as never any man did his friend. Grant that by this Sacrament, there may be conveyed to my soul new spiritual life and strength and such a measure of Thy grace and assistance as may enable me to a greater care of my duty for the future. That I may henceforth live as becomes the redeemed of the Lord; even to Him who died for my sins and rose again for my justification and is now sat down on the right hand of the throne of God to make intercession for me; in His holy Name and words I conclude my imperfect prayers; Our Father, which art in heaven, hallowed be Thy Name; Thy kingdom come, Thy will be done on earth as it is in heaven. Give us this day our daily bread, and forgive us our trespasses as we forgive them that trespass against us. And lead us not into temptation, but deliver us from evil, for Thine is the kingdom, and the power, and the glory, for ever and ever. Amen.

(Ibid. f. 165.)

BIBLIOGRAPHY

MANUSCRIPT AUTHORITIES

Wake MSS. Christ Church, Oxford.

Ballard MSS. Bodleian Library, Oxford.

Letters from Gibson to Nicolson. MSS. Add. A 269, Bodleian Library, Oxford.

Correspondence of the Duke of Newcastle. Add. MSS. British Museum.

Hardwicke Papers (Correspondence of Herring and Hardwicke). Add. MSS. British Museum.

Autobiography of Bishop John Douglas. Eg. 2181, British Museum.

Auckland MSS. (Letters of Moore to Eden), Add. MSS. British Museum.

Tenison and Gibson MSS. Lambeth Library.

Hurd Papers. Hartlebury Castle.

Episcopal Registers: Canterbury, Chichester, Exeter, Gloucester, Lincoln, Llandaff, Worcester.

HISTORICAL MANUSCRIPTS COMMISSION

Portland MSS. Vols. iv, v, and vii (Harley Papers ii, iii). 1897, 1899, 1901.

Egmont MSS. Diary of Viscount Percival, 1st Earl of Egmont. 3 vols. 1920–4.

15th Report on MSS. in Various Collections. Part I. 1901.

14th Report. Appendix, Part IX. 1895.

PRINTED BOOKS

ABBEY, C. J. *The English Church and its Bishops* (1700–1800). 2 vols. London, 1887.

ABBEY, C. J. and OVERTON, J. H. *The English Church in the Eighteenth Century.* 2 vols. London, 1878.

ATTERBURY, F. *A Letter to a Convocation Man.* London, 1697.

—— *The Rights, Powers, and Privileges of an English Convocation.* 2nd ed. London, 1701.

Atterbury, F., Life of. By H. C. Beeching. London, 1909.

Barrington, J. S., Viscount, Theological Works of, with a brief memoir of his brother *Shute Barrington.* London, 1828.

BATESON, M. "Clerical Preferment under the Duke of Newcastle." *English Historical Review,* 1892, vii, 685–96.

BAXTER, RICHARD. *The English Nonconformity under Charles II and James II truly stated and argued.* London, 1689.

BIRCH, T. *Life of J. Tillotson.* London, 1753.

BLACK, J. B. *The Art of History.* London, 1926.

Black Book, The Extraordinary, of Church, State, Law, and Representation. London, 1831.

BLACKBURNE, F. *The Confessional.* London, 1766.

BOGGIS, R. J. E. *A History of the Diocese of Exeter.* Exeter, 1922.

BROCKBANK, T. *Diary and Letter Book,* 1671–1709. Edited by R. Trappes-Lomax. Printed for the Chetham Society. 1930.

Bull, G., Life of. By R. Nelson. London, 1713.

BURKE, EDMUND. *Reflections on the Revolution in France*. London, 1790.

Burke, Edmund, The Works of. 10 vols. London, 1818.

BURN, R. *Ecclesiastical Law*. 2 vols. London, 1763.

BURNET, GILBERT. *History of his own Time*. 6 vols. (Notes by Dartmouth.) Oxford, 1833.

 Supplement to Burnet's History of his own Time. By H. C. Foxcroft. Oxford, 1902.

Burnet, Gilbert, Life of. By T. E. S. Clarke and H. C. Foxcroft. Cambridge, 1907.

Butler, Joseph, Works of. Edited by J. H. Bernard. 2 vols. London, 1900.

CALAMY, EDMUND. *An Historical account of my own life, 1671–1731*. Edited by J. T. Rutt. 2 vols. London, 1829.

CARDWELL, E. *Synodalia*. 2 vols. Oxford, 1842.

—— *Documentary Annals of the Reformed Church of England*. 2 vols. Oxford, 1844.

Cartright, T., Diary of. Camden Society. London, 1843.

CASSAN, S. H. *Lives of the bishops of Bath and Wells, from the earliest to the present period*. London, 1829.

Chatham Correspondence. 4 vols. London, 1858.

CLARK, J. W. *Endowments of the University of Cambridge*. Cambridge, 1904.

CLARKE, SAMUEL. Dr Clarke's Book of Common Prayer, with MS. alterations in his own hand. 1724. In the British Museum, C. 24, b. 21, F. 29127.

 Another copy, not in Clarke's own hand. In Dr Williams's Library, Gordon Square.

 The Book of Common Prayer, reformed according to the plan of the late Dr Samuel Clarke: together with the Psalms of David. Anonymous. London, 1774.

COBBETT, WILLIAM. *Parliamentary History*.

Cole, William, The Blecheley Diary of, 1765–7. Edited by F. G. Stokes. Introduction by Helen Waddell. London, 1931.

Commission, Ecclesiastical. The Report of the Ecclesiastical Commission of 1835.

CROSS, A. L. *The Anglical Episcopate and the American Colonies*. Vol. ix in Harvard Historical Studies. New York, 1902.

CROSS, F. L. *The Oxford Movement and the Seventeenth Century*. S.P.C.K. 1933.

DuQuesne, Mr, and Other Essays. By John Beresford. Oxford, 1932.

FEILING, K. G. *A History of the Tory Party, 1640–1714*. Oxford, 1924.

FIRTH, C. H. "Dean Swift and Ecclesiastical Preferment." *Review of English Studies*, vol. ii, No. 5, Jan. 1926.

Fothergills of Ravenstonedale, The; their Lives and their Letters. Transcribed by C. Thornton and F. McLaughlin. London, 1905.

GAMBLE, H. R. "An Eighteenth Century Visitation." In *The Church Times* of 4 November 1921.

—— "An early Nineteenth Century Visitation." In *The Church Times* of 29 August 1924.

GARNETT, R. "Correspondence of Archbishop Herring and Lord Hardwicke during the Rebellion of 1745." *English Historical Review*, 1904, xix, 528–50, 719–42.

GEORGE, M. D. *London Life in the Eighteenth Century*. London, 1925.

George III, Correspondence of, 1760–83. Edited by J. Fortescue. 6 vols. London, 1927–8.

Gibbon Edward, Memoirs of, written by himself, and selections from his Letters. Edited by H. Morley. London, 1891.

GIBSON, EDMUND. *Codex Juris Ecclesiastici Anglicani.* 2 vols. London, 1713.
—— *Synodus Anglicana.* London, 1702.
GODLEY, A. D. *Oxford in the Eighteenth Century.* London, 1908.
Grenville Correspondence, The. Edited by W. J. Smith. 4 vols. London, 1852–3.
GWATKIN, H. M. *Church and State in England to the death of Queen Anne.* London, 1917.
HAWKINS, L. M. *Allegiance in Church and State: The problem of the Non-Jurors in the English Revolution.* London, 1928.
HOADLY, BENJAMIN. *Works.* 3 vols. London, 1773.
Horsley, Samuel, Life of. By H. H. Jebb. London, 1909.
Hurd, Richard, Life and Writings of. By F. Kilvert. London, 1860.
   The Correspondence of Richard Hurd and William Mason. Edited by E. H. Pearce and L. Whibley. Cambridge, 1932.
Johnson, Samuel, Boswell's Life of. 10 vols. London, 1835.
Jones, the Rev. William, The Diary of, 1777–1821. Edited by O. F. Christie. London, 1929.
Kennett, White, Life of. London, 1730.
   Monitions and Advices to the Clergy of Peterborough, at his Primary Visitation, 1720. London, 1720.
KETTLEWELL, J. *Of Christian Communion to be kept in the Unity of Christ's Church.* 3 parts. London, 1693.
Kidder, R., Life of, by himself. Edited by Mrs A. E. Robinson. Printed for the Somerset Record Society. Vol. XXXVII. 1924.
LASKI, H. J. *Political Thought in England from Locke to Bentham.* London, 1919.
LAW, WILLIAM. *Three Letters to the Bishop of Bangor.* Edited by J. O. Nash and C. Gore. London, 1893.
LEGG, J. WICKHAM. *English Church Life from the Restoration to the Tractarian Movement.* London, 1914.
LE NEVE. *Fasti Ecclesiae Anglicanae.* Edited by T. Duffus Hardy. 3 vols. Oxford, 1854.
LENNARD, R. V. *Englishmen at Rest and Play.* London, 1931.
LESLIE, C. *The New Association.* Part II. London, 1703.
LUCAS, JOHN. *History of Warton Parish.* Compiled 1710–40. Edited by J. Rawlinson Ford and J. A. Fuller-Maitland. Kendal, 1931.
MACAULAY, T. B. *History of England.* Edited by C. H. Firth. 6 vols. London, 1913.
Marlborough, Duke of, Memoirs of. Edited by W. Cox. 3 vols. Bohn's Library, 1905.
Marlborough, Sarah, Duchess of, Memoirs of. Edited by W. King. London, 1930.
MATHIESON, W. L. *English Church Reform,* 1815–40. London, 1923.
MITCHELL, W. FRASER. *English Pulpit Oratory from Andrewes to Tillotson.* London, 1932.
NAMIER, L. B. *The Structure of Politics at the Accession of George III.* 2 vols. London, 1929.
—— *England in the Age of the American Revolution.* London, 1930.
NEWTON, T. *Some Account of the Life of Dr Thomas Newton, late Lord Bishop of Bristol:* written by himself. In *The Lives of Dr Edward Pocock, Dr Zachary Pearce, Dr Thomas Newton, and the Rev. Philip Skelton.* 2 vols. London, 1816

NICOLSON, W. *Miscellany Accounts of the diocese of Carlisle,* 1703. Edited by R. E. Ferguson. London, 1877.

NOBLE, M. *A biographical History of England, from the Revolution to the end of the reign of George I; being a continuation of the Rev. J. Granger's Work.* 3 vols. London, 1806.

OLLARD, S. L. "Confirmation in the Anglican Communion." Essay III in vol. i of *Confirmation or the Laying on of hands.* S.P.C.K. 1926.

OLLARD, S. L. and WALKER, P. C. *Archbishop Herring's Visitation Returns,* 1743. 5 vols. Yorkshire Archaeological Society. 1928–31.

OVERTON, J. H. *Life in the English Church,* 1660–1714. London, 1885.

—— *The Evangelical Revival in the Eighteenth Century.* London, 1886.

Paley, William, The Works of, and a Life of. By Alexander Chalmers. 5 vols. London, 1819.

PATTISON, MARK. "Tendencies of Religious Thought in England, 1688–1750." In *Essays and Reviews.* 8th ed. London, 1861.

PEARCE, E. H. *Hartlebury Castle.* S.P.C.K. 1926.

Pearce, Zachary, Life of. In *The Lives of Dr Edward Pocock, Dr Zachary Pearce, Dr Thomas Newton, and the Rev. Philip Skelton.* 2 vols. London, 1816.

PETRIE, C. A. *The Jacobite Movement.* London, 1932.

PLUMPTRE, E. H. *Life of Ken.* 2 vols. London, 1888.

Porteus, Beilby, Life of. By R. Hodgson. London, 1811.

Porteus Beilby, Life of. By a Lay Member of Merton College. London, 1810.

POWICKE, F. J. *The Cambridge Platonists.* London, 1926.

PRYCE, A. I. *The Diocese of Bangor during three centuries—Seventeenth to Nineteenth.* Cardiff, 1929.

PYLE, E. *Memoirs of a Royal Chaplain,* 1729–63. Annotated and edited by A. Hartshorne. London, 1905.

ROCHEFOUCAULD, F. DE LA. *A Frenchman in England,* 1784. Edited by Jean Marchand; Translated by S. C. Roberts. Cambridge, 1933.

ROWDEN, A. W. *The Primates of the Four Georges.* London, 1916.

Sancroft, William, Life of. By G. D'Oyly. 2 vols. London, 1821.

Secker, Thomas, The Works of, with Life. By B. Porteus. 6 vols. London, 1811.

SCHUYLER, R. L. *Josiah Tucker. A Selection from his economic and political writings.* New York, 1931.

Sharp, J., Life of. By T. Sharp. 2 vols. London, 1825.

SKINNER, JOHN. *Journal of a Somerset Rector* (1772–1839). Edited by H. Coombes and H. N. Box. London, 1930.

SMITH, G. and BENGER, F. *The Oldest London Bookshop,* Appendix, "The Robson Family Correspondence". London, 1928.

STEPHEN, LESLIE. *History of English Thought in the Eighteenth Century.* 2 vols. London, 1902.

STOUGHTON, J. *History of Religion in England.* Vols. iii–vi. 8 vols. London, 1901.

SWIFT, JONATHAN. *Writings on Religion and on the Church.* 2 vols. In his *Works* edited by Temple Scott. London, 1898.

SYKES, N. *Edmund Gibson, Bishop of London,* 1669–1748. Oxford, 1926.

—— "Episcopal Administration in England in the Eighteenth Century." *English Historical Review,* July 1932, xlvii, No. 187, 414–46.

—— "Benjamin Hoadly." In *Social and Political Ideas of Some English Thinkers of the Augustan Age.* Edited by F. J. C. Hearnshaw. London, 1928.

SYKES, N. "The Church." In *Johnson's England*. Edited by A. S. Turberville. 2 vols. Oxford, 1933.

Thoresby, Ralph, Diary and Correspondence of, 1677–1724. Edited by J. Hunter. 4 vols. London, 1832.

Tillotson, Archbishop, Life and Works of. Edited by T. Birch. 10 vols. London, 1820.

TURBERVILLE, A. S. *The House of Lords in the Eighteenth Century*. Oxford, 1927.

—— *The House of Lords in the reign of William III*. Oxford, 1913.

WAKE, WILLIAM. *The Authority of Christian Princes over their Ecclesiastical Synod asserted*. London, 1697.

—— *The State of the Church and Clergy of England*. London, 1703.

WALPOLE, HORACE. *Memoirs of the reign of George II*. Edited by Lord Holland. 2nd ed. revised. 3 vols. London, 1847.

—— *Memoirs of the reign of George III*. Edited by Denis le Marchant. 4 vols. London, 1845.

WARBURTON, WILLIAM. *Letters from a late Eminent Prelate*. 2nd ed. London, 1809.

—— *The Alliance between Church and State*. London, 1736.

Works. *Life* by Bp. Hurd. 7 vols. London, 1788.

Warburton and the Warburtonians. By A. W. Evans. Oxford, 1932.

Essay on Warburton. In *Typical English Churchmen, from Parker to Maurice*. By J. N. Figgis. S.P.C.K. 1902.

WATSON, E. W. "An Eighteenth Century Clergyman." *Church Quarterly Review*, January 1928, No. 210, cv, 255–71.

WATSON, R. *Miscellaneous Tracts on Religious, Political, and Agricultural subjects*. 2 vols. Vol. i, *Charges and Sermons*. Vol. ii, *Political and Agricultural subjects*. London, 1815.

Watson, R., Anecdotes of the life of. Edited by his son, R. Watson. 2 vols. London, 1818.

Wesley, John, The Letters of. Standard edition, 1721–91. Edited by J. Telford. London, 1931.

Wesley, John, Journal of. Standard edition. Edited by N. Curnock. London, 1909–16.

WILLIAMS, BASIL. *Life of William Pitt, Earl of Chatham*. 2 vols. London, 1913.

—— *Stanhope. A study in Eighteenth Century War and Diplomacy*. Oxford, 1932.

—— "The Duke of Newcastle and the Election of 1734." *English Historical Review*, 1897, xv, 448–523.

WILSON, F. W. *The Importance of the reign of Queen Anne in English Church History*. Oxford, 1911.

WINSTANLEY, D. A. *The University of Cambridge in the Eighteenth Century*. Cambridge, 1922.

INDEX

Addison, Joseph, 147, 190, 231, 237, 238, 258, 273, 281, 344

Albemarle, 3rd earl of (George Keppel), 147, 158

Alston, Sir Thomas, 106

Andrewes, Bishop Lancelot, 46, 144; his pluralism, 187; 257

Anne, Queen, and episcopal nominations, 34–5, 37–9, 40, 46–7, 59, 136, 399, 403, 411; Queen Anne's Bounty, governors of, 212, 226–7, 255

Anson, George, 1st baron, 172–5

Appia, Cyprian and Paul, ordination of, 101

Arian movement, and opposition to Athanasian creed, 348, 352–4, 381–2, 384–6

Arnald, William, 100

Ashburnham, Sir William, bishop, 98, 155, 157, 177

Atkinson, James, 207

Atterbury, Francis, bishop, 39, 44, 254, 318, 379, 413; *A Letter to a Convocation Man*, 298, 301–2; *The Rights, Powers and Privileges of an English Convocation*, 304–5; controversy with Gibson concerning the convocation, 309; and Hoadly, 391

Austen, Jane, 407

Avery, C., 201

Bagot, Lewis, bishop, 139–40, 412

Baker, William, bishop, 152, 362–3

Balguy, Thomas, archdeacon, 401–2

Ball, David, 209

Ball, Thomas, dean, 82

Ballard, Reeve, 181

Bampton, John, 347

Bangorian Controversy, 292–6

Bannester, William, and pretended Orders, 222–3

Baptism, administration of, 22, 249–50

Barker, James, archdeacon, 82

Barlow, Thomas, bishop, neglect of his diocese, 15, 144, 412

Barrington, Shute, bishop, 158; his rapid promotion, 159; his piety, 414–15

Bateman, John, 2nd viscount Bateman, 172–5.

Baxter, Richard, 9, criticism of Anglican confirmation services, 131

Beauclerk, Lord James, bishop, 157

Beaw, William, bishop, circumstances of his preferment and early career, 15–17; as bishop of Llandaff, 64, 363–4; complaint of the poverty of his see, 366–7, 412

Benefices, smaller, value of, 212

Benson, Martin, bishop, political conduct, 64; ordinations, 101, 105; confirmations, 124, 135; 213, 413

Beveridge, William, bishop, and neglect of ferial prayers, 246

Bishop, Sir C., 82, 84

Bishoprics, revenues of, 61

Bishops, suffragan, need of, 9, 14, 96; attempts to revive, 141–2

Black Book, The Extraordinary, 5, 149

Blackburne, Francis, archdeacon, *The Confessional*, 381

Blackburne, Lancelot, archbishop, and the election of 1705, 78; ordinations at York, 99, 100, 103; confirmations, 124; desire for a prebend of Westminster, 150; Hanover chaplain and bishop of Exeter, 151–2

Blackhall, Offspring, bishop, 38, 254

Bossuet, J. B., bishop, 18, 22, 37

Bostock, John, 182

Bowchier, Richard, archdeacon, 128

Bower, W., 202

Bradford, Samuel, bishop, 98, his confirmations, 122

Brockbank, John, 191, 193, 195, 197–8, 199–200

Brockbank, Thomas, *Diary and Letter Book*, 6, 191; batteler at Queen's College, Oxford, 193–4; studies, 195; poverty, 194, 196; choice of profession, 197–8; difficulty of securing a title, 199–200, 203; salary as curate, 207–8, 209–11; offer of vice-principalship of St Mary Hall, Oxford, 211; ambition for preferment, 225; schoolmaster, 228–9; catechising, 243, 260; and visitation of the sick, 269; and standards of pastoral duty, 274